AMERICAN
DRIVE

AMERICAN DRIVE

HOW MANUFACTURING WILL SAVE OUR COUNTRY

RICHARD E. DAUCH
with **HANK H. COX**

ST. MARTIN'S PRESS 🙢 NEW YORK

www.stmartins.com

Book design by Steven Seighman

ISBN 978-1-250-01082-7 (hardcover)
ISBN 978-1-250-01083-4 (e-book)

First Edition: September 2012

10 9 8 7 6 5 4 3 2 1

I dedicate this book to the CEO of our family,
my loving wife of fifty-two years, Sandy Dauch.

CONTENTS

FOREWORD

Dick Dauch can seem like a force of nature—irresistible, bringing dramatic change as he sweeps through the land.

Yet Dick's impact on the world comes not just from the power of his personality. In my years of knowing Dick from the intersecting worlds of manufacturing and government, he has proved himself to be a man with a plan. He knows what he wants to accomplish and he knows how to do it.

Dick Dauch's purposeful approach stands as a model for American business, and not just the auto industry where he made his reputation. In *American Drive*, Dauch draws on his experience at the highest levels of corporate America, automaking, and the auto supply parts industry to illustrate how business can surmount high-stakes global competition, rapid technological change and, at times, tension between labor and management. These are lessons that should be studied by not just United States business leaders, but our national leaders as well.

His most-renowned accomplishment is, of course, American Axle & Manufacturing (AAM). Dauch purchased General Motors' deteriorating and unprofitable axle-production facilities in the troubled areas of Detroit and Hamtramck. Co-founding American Axle, he built and led a team that first refurbished and upgraded five plants in Michigan and New York, and went on to create a global industry leader.

The physical transformation he brought to the Detroit plants and the bleak urban neighborhoods that surrounded them continues to amaze, and Dick tells the story with vigor and insight. It seems logical enough to start by fixing the equipment, replacing the broken windows, and creating a workplace that invited effort and a focus on quality, but Dick and his team went further—buying up abandoned buildings, ridding the neighborhood of drug houses and blight to construct a company campus as green and attractive as you can find anywhere in industrial America.

As a state legislator and three-term governor of Michigan, I had the opportunity to witness this corporate and urban transformation firsthand. Michigan officials lent state support when appropriate, primarily in the form of helping build a road to the Detroit/Hamtramck factory. Government's contributions were modest, the kind available to many qualifying projects, and I have no doubt Dick and his team would have accomplished the same goals without the infrastructure support. In any case, the payoffs have been enormous for the cities, the state, and the people of Michigan.

I stress that word "team," even though the term's promiscuous use in the management world has rendered it close to a cliché: Who these days doesn't claim to be a team player, working with a team to achieve team goals?

In Dick's case, the term means something. He is, after all, a hard-charging former fullback and linebacker who played Division I football for his beloved Purdue Boilermakers. In his 1993 book, *Passion for Manufacturing*, he even described his principles as "Gridiron Fundamentals," where leadership and teamwork are indivisible. He observed, "On the football field, leadership comes from the coach, team captains, and quarterback, and occasionally a wild-eyed linebacker."

I never had a chance to see Dick play football, but I had many opportunities to see his leadership in action in the boardroom and on the factory floor at American Axle. His team was no abstraction; it consisted of men and women he recognized, appreciated, and constantly pressed to do better. The appreciation—and the demands—starts with wife Sandy and his children, who played key roles in the growth of American Axle, and Dick's other ventures.

I always admired Dick's ability to walk through the factory, greeting employees by name and asking detailed questions about their work, fitting their efforts into the bigger picture of the plant's operations, and indeed, the company's goals. In the same way, Dick applies the individual experiences of American Axle and his other business accomplishments to the challenges the U.S. economy now faces.

Dick's achievements prove that to succeed in global competition, you have to be willing to do more than make a few fixes on the margins. If the market requires you to invest more in equipment, improve your workers' skills through training, and constantly upgrade quality and productivity to stay ahead of the game, well, that's what you do, even if your original business plan did not anticipate the need. Your policies adjust.

The same holds true for American manufacturing. Dick Dauch has always been a champion of industry, but a clear-eyed one who has witnessed the harm that results from extolling the past while failing to prepare for the future. Let us not mistake Detroit's rise as the only model to follow, and its decline as an inevitability for which protection and subsidy are the only solution.

Our nation's policymakers too often fall into this trap, repeating history instead of learning from it. Dick's approach is far better: If the global marketplace requires policies to encourage investment in infrastructure and research, to refocus education and training on needed skills, or to promote productivity through increased domestic energy production and restrained regulation, well, that's what you do. Your policies adjust.

Never forget that the world has changed. The United States remains the largest, most productive manufacturing country in the world, but we no longer live during the nineteenth century's Industrial Revolution or the postwar era of the 1950s, when U.S. industrial might was rarely challenged. To build his bottom line and serve his customers worldwide, Dick has expanded far beyond the U.S. borders, bringing his attention to quality and productivity to such varied lands as Brazil, Thailand, India, Poland, Scotland, Mexico, and China.

Yet the willingness to manufacture abroad does not mean letting other governments off the hook for unfair competition. Throughout his career, including his leadership as a member of the board and, in 2003–4, as chairman of the National Association of Manufacturers, Dick fought hard to make sure the terms on which U.S. companies compete internationally are equitable. United States policymakers cannot allow foreign competitors to win on the basis of government-imposed advantages. This is a man who knows his playing fields, and he insists they be level.

Above all, I think of Dick as a leader. As his life story, corporate successes, and the recollections of this book so ably demonstrate, leadership matters. Yes, this is the man whose expertise comes from America's automotive industry, who in the '80s and early '90s, at Chrysler, helped revive the company's reputation for quality and implemented the just-in-time materials management system and the three-shift manufacturing vehicle assembly process. He does more than preach quality and lean manufacturing, he puts them into effect, and the U.S. auto industry and its supply chain are stronger as a result.

You could put Dick Dauch in charge of a failing manufacturer of paper towels, yogurt, or the proverbial widget, and he would turn the company around. He is a competitor and a winner—an American winner.

America was built by people like Dick Dauch who stepped up, took risks, and took charge. When Michigan was becoming the "Arsenal of Democracy" in the 1940s, it was because we had people like Dick Dauch leading the way. In the twenty-first century, if U.S. manufacturing is going to continue to compete in the tougher-than-ever global environment, it will be because America still produces leaders like Dick Dauch. Our success depends on policymakers creating an environment that enables America's businessmen and women to transform their vision, leadership, and risk-taking into successful ventures.

I'm proud to say I knew Dick Dauch while he was just starting out on his American Axle journey. In the early days, what I heard from Dick was his vision of what a successful American Axle auto parts supplier would look like: It would be a company with a skilled workforce, working hard in a safe environment, creating a high-quality product sold to meet demand in the competitive world marketplace.

Dick's vision became reality. Failing plants became profitable, a blighted area of urban Detroit became an oasis, and American Axle produced products that succeeded globally. In *American Drive*, Dick Dauch shows us how that vision can be replicated nationally and internationally, applying the lessons of Detroit and American Axle, leadership and team-building, quality and innovation, to U.S. manufacturing and our nation's economy. These are lessons for us all, but most importantly, ones that America's national leaders must take to heart.

—JOHN ENGLER

President, Business Roundtable (former three-term governor of Michigan)

AMERICAN
DRIVE

Introduction

Leaders are made, they are not born. They are made by hard effort, which is the price which all of us must pay to achieve any goal that is worthwhile.

—*Vince Lombardi*
Coach, Green Bay Packers

My name is Richard E. "Dick" Dauch. Over nearly a half century in the auto business, it has been my privilege to lead teams on the cutting edge of many things—new products, new processes, new management techniques, new plants, new workforces, new companies—that have had lasting impact on the auto industry and the people who work in it. In most of these ventures into unfamiliar ground, my teams have enjoyed conspicuous success, and I am not the least bit shy about claiming credit for the things we have achieved. As Muhammad Ali said, it ain't bragging if you can do it. Those who take the risks, also enjoy the rewards.

At the same time, I recognize that breaking new ground is disruptive. My willingness to strike out in new directions has alienated a few people. That is a very human trait that goes along with the territory. It is the reason so many people are reluctant to stick their necks out, take risks, and express contrary opinions. When you're out there all alone, you can feel very vulnerable. You know if you fall on your face, the critics will be quick to say they told you so. If you are successful, they will push you aside and claim credit for your achievement. I have heard it said that the world is divided between those who do the work and those who take the credit, and I have often found that to be the case.

So be it. In fairness, some of the slings and arrows launched in my direction over the years can fairly be described as self-inflicted wounds. I can be outspoken, aggressive, and impatient. *Can be?* Hell, I am! A corporate bureaucracy will squeeze the life out of you if you let it. When you are trying to get things done in that environment—and I am without question hotwired to get things done—you have to be direct, determined, demanding, and tough. From the first day I walked on the floor of a General Motors factory, I have been rocking the boat. I set high standards for myself and those who report to me. I have no tolerance for mediocrity. Mistakes, yes, mediocrity, no. Anyone who takes on tough challenges will make mistakes, but mediocrity is intolerable. If you are having trouble doing your job, I will ask what you need to get it right. New equipment? New resources? More training? Better maintenance? But if I determine your attitude is the problem, you will soon be gone. Attitude begets attitude.

At the same time, I have managed to acquire the loyalty of a cadre of extremely able business executives who have joined with me to take on many challenges across a span of decades. Every time I called on them, they knew it would be tough, and that I would demand a lot from them. Yet they also knew I would return their loyalty with interest and support. I have left many millionaires in my wake, which is a matter of pride to me. Even more precious to me are the many lasting friendships I have acquired over the years. I would not swap them for all the U.S. treasury bonds in China. It is highly fulfilling.

One of those friendships is with the legendary Lee Iacocca, who earned lasting fame for rescuing the Chrysler Corporation from oblivion back in the early 1980s. At Chrysler, Lee inherited an ineffective organization that was hemorrhaging hundreds of millions of dollars a year. Lee knew finance, marketing, engineering, and sales. He also had a deft hand for working with dealers, communicating with the public, working with banking institutions, and handling politicians. He managed to persuade the Federal Government to guarantee loans to Chrysler, buying him time to turn the company around. Back in those days, government bailouts of private companies did not come easily. But Iacocca won loan guarantees which then became akin to a running soap opera for several years, a staple of the nightly news, until Chrysler paid them back seven years early, with 17 percent interest.

What Iacocca could not handle on his own was manufacturing, quality and labor relations. That was a problem because in the final analysis, the fatal flaw of Chrysler in those days was poorly built products that did not hold up well. Before Iacocca could revive car sales, he needed cars that people wanted to buy. For that you need quality manufacturing, and back in those days quality was still an unfamiliar concept in many parts of Detroit. At Chrysler, especially at that time, quality was lacking at least partially because of confrontations between labor and management. A critical institution that had to be dealt with to correct this problem was the United Auto Workers (UAW).

So Iacocca went to see his friend Roger Penske, one of the biggest names in Detroit and the auto industry, a celebrated former race car driver who also is a renowned corporate entrepreneur. Penske gave Iacocca a list of people who could help him turn Chrysler's manufacturing and quality problem around. There was one name on that list—mine.

Roger's advice resulted in a pivotal moment in my career, and one I will always remember fondly. It would present me with an extraordinary opportunity to show what I could do in a campaign—to help save Chrysler—that the whole nation was watching with interest. I was ready for such a challenge and endowed with an immense reservoir of energy, confidence, and experience. I would need all of those qualities when I sat down to cut a deal with Iacocca. To salvage Chrysler's manufacturing and quality problems, I needed the authority and a free hand. Anyone who knows Lee Iacocca knows he holds authority close to his chest. That was a tough and protracted negotiation. Yet I knew if I did not carve out my territory and authority going in, I would never get it later on. I hung tough, knowing I wanted the job but that I needed running room to get it done.

I cannot say with certainty why, but since my earliest days of self-awareness I have believed I was capable of being a leader. It could not have been a birthright, because I was born to humble circumstances. My family operated dairy farms near Norwalk, Clarksfield, and Ashland, Ohio. There is very little about tending bovines to inspire notions of grandeur, or commend a young boy to the volatile and demanding auto industry.

Nor was I the anointed son. I was the youngest of seven children, and five of my six older siblings were brothers. In the manner of country farm boys, we were all rough and ready characters eager for a dare or a challenge. Fighting was frequent, and as the youngest and smallest, I usually caught the worst of it. It wasn't that my brothers did not love me, but in today's terminology, that affection would be described as "tough love."

My parents were disciplinarians, loving but stern. They expected a lot of us, beginning with the farm responsibilities. Cows have to be milked twice a day. They don't take off weekends or holidays. It gets mighty cold at 5:00 A.M. on an Ohio dairy farm in deep winter, but that's just too bad. When Dad sent us out to do a job, we learned early not to come back complaining that it was too cold or there was three feet of snow on the ground. Dad did not want a weather report; he wanted to know if the work got done. He expected production, performance, and accountability. Come to think of it, I feel the same way about the people who report to me. I can get the weather from the newspaper or TV.

I knew early in that time and place that I wanted to do something with my life, and I had a hunch what it would be. Since the age of nine, I can remember being fascinated by cars and trucks. I watched them, listened to them, and learned about them. My brothers were impressed by the way I could lie in bed at night listening to trucks and cars running up and down the highway near our house, identifying their make and power by the sound. It was second nature to me. It was the 1950s. The Interstate Highway System was being built. The great American motor vehicle adventure was in its heyday, and I wanted to be part of it.

I still could have been caught up in the agricultural cycle, farming like my parents did, were it not for sports. I grew up big and fast, and my brothers made me tough. To build my strength and contend with "brotherly love," I got some weights and worked out on them religiously. Not surprisingly, I savored sports, especially football, where my speed, size, and toughness served me well. As early as the fifth grade, I saw sports as my ticket off the farm and into something more interesting.

By the time I was a senior in high school, I was one of the best high school football players in Ohio, a state rabid about football. My senior year I rushed for nearly 1000 yards and scored 20 touchdowns. I was wooed by more than forty colleges and universities, including Purdue, Kansas, Iowa State, Cornell, the Naval Academy, and Cincinnati. Woody Hayes tried to recruit me to play at Ohio State. I chose Purdue for a variety of reasons, but mainly the opportunity to study industrial management, science, and technology.

The day I graduated from high school led into one exciting summer—I graduated in June, got married to my high school sweetheart Sandy in July, played in the Ohio North-South All-Star Football Game in August, and then reported to Purdue. Those were 120 exciting days for a young fellow still in his teens. It was only the beginning.

At Purdue, I played for the legendary Hall of Fame football coach Kenneth W. "Jack" Mollenkopf. In those days, Purdue was one of five Big Ten teams ranked among the top ten in the nation on a regular basis. Mollenkopf was tough as nails. When recruiting, he could have been a Methodist minister—all smiles and gentleness—but when you got out on the field, he could be the most demanding man you ever met. He was very much in your face and very stern, but he had a big heart and you knew he cared about you. He and his coaches kept tabs on all of us. If you were having trouble in class, they knew about it and helped you through it. If you acted irresponsibly, you were gone. They were there to mold men, not just football players.

Mollenkopf had little patience with injuries. If you could walk, you were expected to play—and man, did we play. There was no liberal substitution in those days of college football. You went out on the field and you stayed there until intermission. I played fullback on offense, linebacker on defense, and whatever they needed on special teams, including kicker. On Sunday, we reviewed films of the previous day's game. If you did something really spectacular, they showed it once or twice. If you screwed up, they showed it over and over. You wanted to find a place to hide.

We had some great games and were nationally ranked. We always came up a bit short in the final standings, but we had our moments. We beat Michigan State, Notre Dame, Michigan, and the Washington Huskies. We played a heartbreaker against the Miami Hurricanes in the Orange Bowl stadium. We were inside the 10-yard line twice and did not score, ended up losing 3–0. That hurt big time, but you learn in defeat. In my last game, we beat Indiana 21–15. All in all, I was privileged to be part of a top Division I football team, and to learn from Mollenkopf about teamwork, determination, self-sacrifice, and discipline—qualities that have served me well over a lifetime. I believe Jack was proud of me then, and would be proud of me now. I know I was proud of him and his able staff.

I had legitimate pro opportunities. I was invited to the Green Bay Packers training camp. Those were the days before professional football players raked in the really big money. I thought about it long and hard, but I had a family by then and there are no guarantees in professional football. One blindside tackle can end your career forever. I took a job at General Motors—I had always aspired to a career in the automotive industry—and I never looked back.

When I started working at GM, I was on the production line supervising tough guys—hard-bitten factory workers who had moved to Detroit from all over the south and Midwest looking for economic opportunity. The plant floors were loud, dirty, and often dangerous. If those guys did not come with an attitude toward management, they quickly absorbed one from the UAW, which was born in violence and steeped in hostility toward management. Those guys were totally unimpressed by a young football player from a Big Ten university. No one at GM, management or hourly labor, cut me any slack. I had to earn respect. The factory floor became my testing laboratory.

The management techniques I had learned from my father and a series of sports coaches—including Mollenkopf—served me well on the factory floor. I got to know the people who reported to me and established personal relationships with them. I asked about their families, their problems, and their aspirations. I knew where they went on vacation and which sports teams they followed. I set high standards for them and made it clear I expected excellence—but I also made it clear I was always ready to help them achieve excellence. If they needed a new machine, I went to bat to get one. If they needed more training, I helped them get it. I was there when they came to work and when they left. I did not tolerate mediocrity in anything. We kept a clean and orderly shop, and observed safety precautions up and down the line. I made them my team, or strived to. We always gave the highest priority to making quality products for GM customers.

Of course, within the context of a UAW workplace, there were restrictions on my authority. I understood that and learned to work within the contract. I became familiar with the rules and went out of my way to deal effectively with the shop stewards. I made it a point never to blindside them. When I had a problem with an employee's performance or attitude, which were usually the same thing, I worked to correct it within the existing guidelines. I have found that most of the time in the industrial setting, it comes down to a simple matter of caring and respect. When you show people respect, they are inclined to cooperate with you. I am a great believer in people. A supervisor's job is to bring the best out in them.

On the negative side, I quickly became disgusted with the rank and file attitude toward absenteeism—it was about 20 percent daily back then, as it still is today in Detroit—but I was in no position to do much about that. It was part of the Detroit industrial landscape, and remains a debilitating affliction of a segment of the UAW workforce, at least in Detroit. It goes back to an attitude, culture and behavior problem. I learned to live with it, juggling work assignments as best I could to compensate for missing hands.

I did well at GM. I got results and my ability to obtain positive performance from a UAW workforce impressed my superiors. I earned a series of promotions and was eventually promoted to plant manager. That was a first—at the age of thirty I was the youngest plant manager in the history of GM's Chevrolet Motor Division. It was quite an achievement and I proved I could handle the additional responsibility. In fact, I thrived in that environment. It was tough on my family because I was gone much of the time—often working from before sunrise to well after sunset—but Sandy is loving and resourceful, and did a wonderful job of covering for me when I could not be there. I did make it a point to be there for important things, like ball games and school events. I always advise everyone who works for me that they must have *balance* in their lives. But there is no question this kind of life demands a lot of people like me, and our families. It isn't for everyone.

I was on the fast track—and some were predicting I would eventually make it to the fourteenth floor of GM, which is the executive level. I was never certain of that, however. I knew how to make cars, trucks, and axles. I was well ahead of the trends in lean manufacturing and quality, anticipating the influence of Japanese carmakers that was just then beginning to be felt in Detroit. But to get the results I wanted, I often stepped on toes, some of them in highly polished corporate shoes. My aggressive style and approach to senior office protocol did not endear me to everyone.

So I was receptive when Jim McLernon, a former senior GM executive, invited me to join him moving over to Volkswagen of America (VWoA) in 1976. Here was another first for me—a chance to launch a high volume auto assembly plant in the United States for a foreign automaker—Volkswagen Group (VWAG). That had never been done before.* Back in those days, all the Toyotas and Nissans being sold in the United States were made in Japan. None of the foreign automakers had been willing to set up shop here to make their products until Volkswagen took the lead. In fact, Volkswagen took the lead setting up manufacturing facilities all over the world. Volkswagen recognized the potential backlash that could occur if they displaced too much of a domestic industry, and knew that creating jobs in host countries was an excellent way to reduce any such resentment. They were a global company before true globalization occurred.

We finished building the VWoA plant in New Stanton, Pennsylvania, in Westmoreland County. It became known simply as the Westmoreland Plant. We got it started six months ahead of schedule, and by 1979 were cranking out nearly 200,000 VW Rabbits and pickup trucks a year.

I had been attracted to the VWoA deal because of Volkswagen's legendary focus on quality, service, and advanced technology. It also got me into the front office as an officer of a major enterprise and a world-respected company. In military terms, I had jumped four ranks moving from GM to VWoA. Further, I had been led to believe that the Westmoreland plant was the first of many

---

* Rolls-Royce built cars in Springfield, Massachusetts, 1921–31, but not very many. The Volkswagen plant in Pennsylvania was the first foreign automaker plant in the U.S. in the modern era to produce automobiles in high volume.

VWoA investments to come, and that I would have a great chance to play a key part in it. Events back in Germany, though, undermined that commitment. The German labor unions had representatives on the VW board of supervisors, the Aufsichtsrat, and they were annoyed that the company was creating jobs in the United States instead of Germany. For the time being, VWoA's ambitions for expansion in the United States were put on hold, as were my career ambitions.

That's when Iacocca came calling. I had signed a contract to work for VWoA for four years, 1976–80. By the time that contract was winding down, and it appeared VWoA would be building no more plants in the U.S. in the immediate future, I was looking around for another professional opportunity. After Penske played matchmaker, Iacocca and I began discussions in earnest. We were both working at our day jobs, so we met in the evenings and on weekends. This was not especially difficult because we lived near each other. I would go by his house and we would chat for hours, often into the early morning.

The gist of our meetings was my insistence on having a free hand at Chrysler in terms of spending capital money, integrating manufacturing into an advanced design process, establishing a new in-line sequence for production, buying new equipment, and investing more in worker training. It wasn't just a matter of Iacocca being reluctant to cede authority to a junior officer (though that was surely a factor), but also a matter of dollars and cents. At the time Chrysler was losing $7 million a day. *A day!* I knew if I went in there without a clear mandate to invest millions in quality and manufacturing processes, the financial people would have me for lunch. In meeting after meeting, I pounded it into Iacocca— Chrysler could not come back without a tremendous turnaround in product quality, that I was the only guy who knew how to do it and who was prepared to make the commitment to make it happen. I would need money and time to do it.

We went back and forth for eleven months. As in most tough negotiations, we would seem to make progress on some days and lose ground on others. We would break off communications for a while and then get back together, back and forth, back and forth. Finally, we reached an agreement giving me what I needed. On April 1, 1980, I went to work for Chrysler. I could have used a few days off by that time, but there was no time to lose. Chrysler was in crisis. It was time to dive in and go to work!

The rest, as the old saying goes, is history. I pulled together a team of veteran managers, most of whom had worked with me at GM and/or VWoA. Among these was a smart, tough manager named George Dellas who years later would figure prominently in the story I tell in this book. "There were some odd ducks at Chrysler," Dellas said. "The place was basically bankrupt; they just refused to admit it. We were working long hours like the Dauch team always did, but the old-time Chrysler guys were just Cadillacing along, drifting in about nine thirty, taking long lunches, leaving early. The company is basically dying and we are the only ones working. That always mystified me."

To salvage Chrysler, I had to get labor on board with us. I established a positive working relationship with Marc Stepp, the UAW vice president for Chrysler. Marc was a forward-looking union leader who understood the need for change if Chrysler were to survive. Most importantly, we needed more flexibility with the workforce, which meant less restrictive work rules and fewer job classifications. We needed a full commitment to produce quality products at Chrysler. We called it the Product Quality Improvement Partnership (PQIP). "The union had to make concessions, not so much in money but in labor practices," Stepp said. "In Chrysler's Jefferson Avenue plant, located on the East Side of Detroit, we had 107 job classifications. We reduced that down to eleven."

The radicals in the union fought Stepp every step of the way, but he held firm and worked around them. It was gratifying to me to see a senior UAW leader stand up before thousands of his members and tell them they had to start coming to work every day. That was a very big deal and got a lot of attention in Detroit. With his determination and leadership, we persuaded the great majority of hourly workers to buy into a new work ethic. For a while, absenteeism actually dropped. Chrysler was a major league challenge but we hit the ground running. Within a short period of time, most everyone at Chrysler was committed to quality—and we were producing quality vehicles. It was very fulfilling to see the teamwork in action.

Of course, much of the credit for the Chrysler turnaround belongs to Iacocca and the lead product planner/engineer, Hal Sperlich. Both Iacocca and Sperlich had worked many years at Ford Motor Company, and both had been fired by Henry Ford II. We will never know what provoked Ford to dump Iacocca, one of the most dynamic auto executives in history, who had brought Ford the Mustang among other triumphs, but Sperlich's offense apparently was his vigorous advocacy of a new type of vehicle, sort of a crossover between a pickup truck and a car. The new vehicle would seat as many as seven people and could be used to haul a lot of stuff. Working together, Iacocca, Sperlich, Gerry Greenwald, Jack Withrow Jr., Steve Sharf, myself, and others came up with a revolutionary innovation: the minivan—which has proven to be one of Detroit's most successful vehicles ever. It created a whole new segment in the automotive industry. It was a great example of innovation.

Here was another first in my career. It was my responsibility to actually produce the minivans. That was no small chore given that it was a totally new design. We had to start from the ground up.

There was no way of gauging whether the public would respond positively to such a vehicle. Producing it—especially for a company that was hemorrhaging cash like Chrysler was at the time—and risking the massive investment that any new vehicle requires, was an act of great courage and leadership. We were betting the farm on this product. Sperlich had the idea and I made certain it was well built at our plant in Windsor, Ontario, Canada, but Iacocca was the leader who took the risk and put his neck, and Chrysler's future, on the line. Had it failed, his reputation would have been tarnished and his career probably over. I doubt Chrysler would have survived.

Fortunately, the Chrysler minivan took off like a rocket. In 1983, the year we launched it, the company turned a $923 million profit! In July of that year, we paid off the loans that the government had guaranteed for us, with 17 percent interest. The following year, Chrysler earned $2.4 billion, an all-time record. We started racking up more than $2 billion net profit every year. The minivans continued to fly out the door and soon our major competitors, including our Japanese friends, were developing imitative products. It would take them many, many years to catch up, and Chrysler is still making the best minivans today.

The creativity required in launching a totally new product like the minivan gave us a certain amount of freedom to adopt revolutionary new processes. Some of the most notable were in-line sequencing, which had never been used in the United States; the rolling model change (RMC) that eliminated the need to shut down assembly lines for two weeks to accommodate a new product model; applied statistical process control (SPC) that denoted a quantum jump forward in product quality; and the concept of common locating points (CLPs) for different products that greatly improved flexibility and productivity. All of these were firsts that are today standard throughout the U.S. auto industry. We also maxed out on the use of robots and automation.

The minivan was so hot we could not make them fast enough. Iacocca called me in and recommended we go to three shifts. He asked me to do it in three to four months. I told him it would more likely take three to four years. The logistics of running a factory twenty-four hours a day are highly complex and demanding. Just getting thousands of workers in and out three times a day is a challenge. Then you have to factor in delivery of materials and parts, plus maintenance which is always a major ticket item in an auto plant. But we were the first in North America to do it successfully. Today, everyone does it—when they have enough volume to justify three shifts.

I can't resist adding what may have been our most significant first because this was born of our extraordinary achievements in quality improvement at Chrysler. In 1985, Chrysler began offering a "Five Years or 50,000 Miles" warranty for its products. We had improved our quality dramatically. No other carmaker had done that before. Today, competitive warranties are standard throughout the industry.

One of my more interesting responsibilities at Chrysler was the manufacturing of the XM1 Abrams tank for the U.S. Army. As soon as I was given responsibility, I learned we had problems. I flew to Washington to meet with the four-star general in charge of the tank's development. I told him there were two key problems—one was the tracks provided by a supplier that were not validated and which were coming off the tank in routine exercises. The other was the 1,500-horsepower turbine engine that was not reliable after a few hours of use. I recommended we stop production for thirty days to give us time to correct the problems. I promised we would to make up lost production in the first year. The general accepted my plan, we did as we promised, and when Desert Storm erupted ten years later, those tanks performed flawlessly and played a key role in helping the United States win the war.

Another one of our achievements at Chrysler—and another definite first for the auto industry—was developing a new technique for handling sludge. Every auto plant back in those days produced mountains of oily sludge that were hauled away to landfills, taking up space and creating potential environmental problems for the future. At Chrysler, I called in our engineers, environmental people, and key suppliers and challenged them to find a better way. They put their thinking caps on and with support from the front office—which means both encouragement and money—came up with a process for recycling all of that material. In 1986, Chrysler's Warren Truck Assembly Plant in Warren, Michigan, became the first truly "green" auto facility in the United States, recycling all of the sludge it produced internally. Today, most if not all U.S. auto and truck plants recycle the sludge they produce, but we were first and showed the others how to do it. Leadership is vital to progress of this nature.

I was very proud of my work at Chrysler, and my team's contributions to what was one of our country's great corporate success stories. Achieving such success required a tough, take-no-prisoners approach to make the changes that were required. There were some within the organization who felt threatened and intimidated by such aggressive efforts—my team and I had not endeared ourselves to everyone. When Iacocca announced he would retire in 1993, I was not chosen to succeed him. There were many people who thought that was a mistake, I among them, but such is life. There were some low achievers in the organization who probably had nightmares about the prospect of reporting to me, and with good reason. I would have introduced them to the Dauch work ethic—and demanded results.

"After Dick left, the fun went out of Chrysler," said one of my best lieutenants, Bill Smith. "Some people at Chrysler were greatly relieved. Senior managers had been running to Bob Lutz,* complaining that Dick spoke harshly to them."

Indeed I did, and with reason, but that is all water under the bridge. I was led to understand that my position with the company would be uncertain after Lee stepped down, and I had no doubt of it. I understand how the world works and took my leave without complaint. I had a good run at Chrysler, enjoyed success, and was well compensated. Many of the senior managers I had brought with me also chose that time to retire or find new employment because they were known as "Dauch guys." We achieved great things at Chrysler, but it was time to move on.

After retiring from Chrysler, I spent about a year working on my first book, *Passion for Manufacturing,* which I authored with the able assistance of Dr. Jack Troyanovich. It would be published in 1993 by the Society of Manufacturing Engineers. By late 1992, I was done with the book and getting restless. I was still a young man, only fifty years old, in good health. I needed a fresh challenge.

As fate would have it, in December 1992 GM announced that it intended to sell eighteen of its facilities, including six axle, driveline, and forging plants. I saw a report about it in *The Wall Street Journal,* probably in early 1993, and began a discreet investigation of what was at stake. One of my first inquiries was directed toward Jim McLernon, the former GM executive who had taken me with him to VWoA in 1976. By then, Jim was retired. He had also noticed the GM announcement with interest. We were in fact both looking at the assets of GM's Saginaw Division that made axles and driveline systems. Jim was well known and respected by the senior management of GM and he was familiar with the operations that were on the block.

---

* Bob Lutz would serve as Chrysler president and vice chairman before he, too, moved on to other things.

As it turned out, the senior GM people not only held McLernon in esteem, but they remembered me favorably also, and had high regard for my management ability. I was exactly what they needed to revive the business. Nine other companies were bidding to buy the GM facilities, but we had the inside track.

I had served in senior posts with GM, VWoA, and Chrysler, but I was always reporting to someone higher in the pecking order. For once, I wanted to be the guy walking the bridge. I had it in my head to prove to a disbelieving world that it was still possible to create a world-class, sustainable, multibillion-dollar global automotive company in Detroit, Michigan.

This would not technically be another first. Others had done this—but many generations before, when the auto industry was in its infancy. No one had done it in recent history. There was a consensus out there that it was no longer possible, that Detroit had lost its competitive edge. I was determined to prove that consensus wrong.

1

The Wheels Come Off

*Adversity has the same effect on a man that severe training
has on a pugilist: it reduces him to his fighting weight.*
—Josh Billings

It was late summer 2009 when I reached the rock bottom of my professional
career in a highly visible and dramatic crisis that threatened economic doom for
my company, American Axle & Manufacturing (AAM), along with the trusty
crew that had helped me create the company and steer it for sixteen years
through the choppy waters that always beset the auto industry.* I stood at my
office window on the seventh floor of our headquarters on Holbrook Avenue in
Detroit, overlooking our lineup of clean, modern factories—now mostly empty
and inactive—that we had worked so hard to rebuild. I recalled the grotesque
array of rust-bucket manufacturing plants surrounded by drug dens, vacant
boarded up houses, and rubbish-strewn parking lots that greeted us when we
took over from GM on March 1, 1994. I swelled with pride to think of the countless hours of hard work, thoughtful planning, and creative innovation we
brought to bear to transform that industrial wasteland into a world-class, competitive, global company. We had made a name for ourselves of which we were
all justly proud. Now, because of forces beyond our control, it was all teetering
on the brink of destruction.

In *The Perfect Storm* by Sebastian Junger, a fishing boat named the *Andrea*

---

* AAM is a Tier One auto supplier, which means we are one of the larger companies pro-
    viding parts to the major automakers—in our case axles, gears, differentials, drive-
    shafts, and other components.

Gail is caught up in violent weather when a hurricane coming up from the south encounters two powerful weather fronts coming from the northwest and the northeast, producing gale winds and massive seas that spell doom for that boat and everyone on it. The *Andrea Gail*'s crew was composed of veteran seamen who knew what they were doing. They brought many years of experience and knowledge to their work. They were tough and resourceful. But sometimes knowledge and experience and toughness are not enough. Sometimes the impersonal forces of nature will overwhelm the most resilient people. That storm was like nothing those fellows had ever seen, and it swallowed them.

I and my team, like the crew on that fishing boat, were seasoned veterans, in our case with four decades in the auto industry. We knew we were in a difficult business and took nothing for granted. We foresaw every known contingency based on our years of experience dealing with all manner of challenges and crises that attend our industry—changing product lines, labor disruptions, economic downturns, intensifying and sometimes unfair foreign competition. We had seen it all, or thought we had. We knew what we were doing, and we were tough, but nothing in our experience prepared us adequately for what we were facing this time. We were caught up in a perfect storm of converging economic forces that threw the entire U.S. auto industry into its worst tailspin since the Great Depression and left many once-great companies in bankruptcy. The question was, would American Axle & Manufacturing be one of them?

We had the first hints of trouble to come in 2005 when our profits fell for the first time ever. Our net income in the fourth quarter fell to $4.5 million, down from $31.3 million in the same period the year before. Our full year income for 2005 dropped to $56 million from $159.5 million in 2004. Times were hard, but we were still making profits, which is more than I could say for the competition. In fact, by early 2006, several Tier One auto suppliers, many of them our major competitors, had already gone into bankruptcy—among them Delphi, Dana, Collins & Aikman, Federal-Mogul, Meridian, and Tower Automotive.

We were better prepared for lean times than the competition. Robert Sherefkin, writing in *Crain's Detroit Business* in March 2006, attributed the plight of Dana to competition from us, quoting a Dana manager who said we put a lot of pressure on their margins. "AAM is still vulnerable," he wrote, "profits fell last year, but it has weathered the storm better than most, and certainly better than Dana."

The storm was only beginning. General Motors, our biggest customer, was reporting declining sales and planning severe employee cutbacks. Of course, this was nothing new. For as long as I had been in the auto industry—including tours at GM, VWoA and Chrysler—we had endured boom and bust cycles. The major auto companies and their suppliers would lose money during a recession, then recover when the economy bounced back. But this time the bounce back was to be a long time coming. The overall economy was beginning a nose dive that we now realize was the leading edge of the longest and deepest recession since the Great Depression—but we did not realize it at the time.

The proximate cause was the housing bubble that finally burst, as bubbles always do eventually. Over a period of several years, housing prices had risen at a dizzying pace, making consumers feel much wealthier than they actually were. All of that paper wealth had helped boost sales of cars, trucks and SUVs— our bread and butter vehicles—but that wealth, and the consumer confidence it generated, disappeared almost overnight. Within a couple years, housing fell through the floor. Home foreclosures became commonplace. Millions of home owners found themselves "under water," meaning they owed more on their homes than they were worth. People in that situation are unlikely to buy a new car, pickup truck, or SUV. Vehicle sales were beginning a slide that would only get steeper with each passing month and year.

The handwriting was on the wall, but few of us could read it. I was quoted in the *Detroit Free Press* on March 26, 2006, predicting that, "Everybody will start coming out of this thing in the second half of 2007." I was basing that on past experience with previous recessions. I had no way of knowing that this recession would be in another class altogether.

Any recession by itself is bad enough, but even worse was the timing of this one—when the Big Three auto companies were more vulnerable than ever before because they had lost their competitive edge. Tier One auto suppliers like American Axle & Manufacturing were equally vulnerable because we were very dependent on the Big Three—in our case on GM and Chrysler—to purchase our products. That is a basic law of life in Detroit: When the Big Three catch a cold, Tier One suppliers like AAM get pneumonia.

A fundamental problem for GM and most Tier One suppliers like us, which left us acutely vulnerable to a steep economic downturn, was high labor costs resulting from inflated wage scales and extravagant benefits promoted and defended by the International Union, United Automobile, Aerospace and Agricultural Implement Workers of America (UAW). This situation had evolved over a period of several decades when the Big Three claimed the lion's share of the U.S. market, and fell into a habit of caving to the UAW every time contracts came up for renegotiation. The companies figured they could just pass along the increased labor costs to consumers, and for a long time they were able to do just that. But foreign competition was undermining their market dominance and exposing the danger of uncompetitive wages and benefits. In a world of intense global competition, no industry can afford to price itself out of the market the way the U.S. auto industry had done. Our chickens were at last coming home to roost.

At the time, a typical employee of the Big Three enjoyed a fully loaded wage and benefit package equal to about $75 per hour. I know that because most of our AAM associates enjoyed the same level of compensation as employees of Chrysler, Ford, and General Motors. Granted, we were not saddled with the same level of "legacy" costs as the Big Three—mainly pensions and medical care for legions of retirees—because we had launched relatively recently in 1994. Yet by the time our major Tier One competitors emerged from bankruptcy with dramatically reduced labor cost burdens, our competitive position was adversely affected. They were competing against Japanese automakers operating in the nonunion southern states that paid less in wages and benefits and carried fewer legacy costs. We were competing with other Tier One suppliers whose workers earned less than half what we were still paying. It is hard to compete and make a profit in that situation. Impossible, in fact.

Another major bone of contention, and one I spoke out about often, was the so-called "jobs bank," a program in which laid-off hourly UAW workers were paid nearly full wages and benefits while their employers tried to find them new jobs. At the time, we had 1,100 workers in the jobs bank—receiving full pay for sitting around doing nothing. *The Detroit News* summed it up in an editorial on May 23, 2006: "Anyone with a lick of common sense knows that paying people not to work is bad for business. So called jobs banks at the Big Three and their suppliers with United Auto Workers contracts cost hundreds of millions of dollars a year to maintain with zero return for the companies." The editorial said correctly that the auto companies were spending between $100,000 and $130,000 a year for wages and benefits for each employee sitting idly in a jobs bank, up to $2 billion in 2006 for employees, "many of whom have been reporting to the job to read, watch movies and do crossword puzzles for years."

It was that kind of economic insanity that had been pushing the U.S. auto industry toward the brink for years, and when the big recession set in, it was to prove the straw that helped break the camel's back.

But hindsight is always perfect. At the time, we assumed we were in for another typical economic downturn such as we had endured often before. We laid off workers in response to declining demand and we implemented a round of severe cost cutting. (I should stress here that cutting costs did not include research and development, which at AAM enjoys general immunity from the vagaries of market fluctuations. One of the biggest mistakes many companies make in times of stress is to consume their seed corn. Not in our darkest days did I ever lose faith in the future of our company, and we did not shortchange R&D.)

By late 2006, we were facing a difficult decision regarding our gear, axle, and likage plant in Buffalo, New York. In the early years of AAM, we recognized the Buffalo workforce as first rate and pumped substantial resources into that plant, even building a new multimillion-dollar paint facility there. But that workforce and its union were resistant to labor cost reductions, which meant that despite their efficiency, by 2006 we were losing money every day that plant operated. By then, five hundred of the plant's associates were on layoff and seven hundred were still on the job. GM was in the process of canceling the Buffalo plant's main product line, which had included axles for the Chevrolet Colorado, GMC Canyon, Chevrolet Trailblazer, and GMC Envoy. Sales of all of them were declining. The question on the table was whether AAM would make the substantial investments necessary to gear up the Buffalo plant to make products for GM's revamped Chevrolet Camaro, a contract we had in hand.

Because of the uncompetitive wage and benefit structure in Buffalo, it came down to a question of whether we wanted to make money or lose money. When the Buffalo UAW local union refused to agree to cost reduction changes, we decided to send the new business to our plant in Guanajuato, Mexico, and shut down the Buffalo facility. It was a tough decision we did not make lightly, but it was a matter of survival. Life presents us with difficult choices.

As if to underscore the point, we reported a $62.9 million loss for the third quarter of 2006, the first quarterly loss in the history of the company. We ended up spending about $250 million in compensation to the associates in Buffalo and other AAM plants who lost their jobs because of the downturn and shifts in production. At the time, we were spending about $75 million a year to pay 1,400 idled workers in the jobs bank, a cost which we were determined to reduce, but to do it we had to transition many of them out of the company. We used buyouts that ranged up to $100,000 per for associates with ten years or more of service. After twelve years of uninterrupted success, all of a sudden we were hemorrhaging cash. Not surprisingly, we began to see warnings in the business media that AAM was living on borrowed time. One New York analyst said we were an "ax-cident waiting to happen." We chief executives hate to read that kind of thing about our companies.

I should add yet another aspect of the economic storm that engulfed us in that dark time: soaring energy prices. Our country has suffered for a long time from lack of a sensible energy policy and in 2006 the price of gas at the pump began to rise rapidly, eventually cresting above $4 a gallon for most grades. At that price, people who depend on their vehicles for transportation begin to feel serious pain. The types of vehicles that we supported were mostly pickup trucks and SUVs, noted for power and versatility, not gas economy. GM had enjoyed a long, profitable run producing those types of vehicles but the bloom was off the rose. Overall, North American sales of pickup trucks fell 30 percent in 2006. This was a train wreck in the making.

We limped into 2007 hoping against hope that the worst was behind us and good times were just around the bend. On February 2, we reported a net loss of $188.6 million for the fourth quarter, compared with net income of $4.5 million for that period the year before. Overall we lost $222.5 million in 2006, our first annual loss. Our stock price suffered accordingly.

I remained upbeat, however, telling business reporters we would return to profitability in 2007. I had reason to be optimistic. We were expanding our product portfolio and new business backlog to support the growing all-wheel-drive passenger car and crossover segment of the market. We also launched new products for GM, Chrysler, Ssangyong Motors, Hino, Jatco, Koyo, and Harley-Davidson while expanding our footprint in Europe and Asia. Even though sales of light trucks were still weak and expected to remain so, I projected we would increase total revenues $100 million in 2007 to $3.3 billion.

At the same time, I made it clear to everyone that we had work to do before we would get back on our feet. "We expect 2007 to be a transition year," I told *Crain's Detroit Business*. "This is a year in which we restructure, resize and re-cover." We trimmed three hundred salaried jobs, about 15 percent of the total, to reduce costs. Overall our employment fell from more than eleven thousand to less than ten thousand. We helped a lot of good people move into early retirement or find opportunities elsewhere. I had to bid farewell to many dedicated professionals who had contributed substantially to building the company, but there was no alternative. Both the salaried and hourly associates received generous buyout packages. It was painful for all concerned, but that is the world of manufacturing.

It seemed the worst was behind us; best of all, our reputation for efficiency, innovation, and quality remained undiminished. Mike Weinberg, writing in the May 2007 issue of *Transmission Digest*, noted that AAM was one of the few Tier One suppliers that was fiscally healthy and not in bankruptcy. "I have been in auto manufacturing plants around the globe for the past 45 years," he wrote. "The AAM plants are state-of-the-art and very efficient." In June, the American Society for Quality gave me its Quality Leader of the Year Award, the only time they had so honored a corporate executive who was not a quality professional. AAM's income in the second quarter rose to $34 million compared to $20.4 million in the same period the year before. Things were looking up.

But consumer demand remained weak and we still had that worrisome cloud on the horizon—the UAW. For years I had warned the UAW leadership that its inflated wage and benefit levels were compromising our ability to compete. Several times the leadership promised me that they would address that issue in a future contract, but every time negotiations came around, they turned a deaf ear to our concerns. And every time we prepared to dig in our heels, GM leaned on us to settle and promised to help us meet the added costs. It was a deadly cycle that in effect just kicked the can down the road each time, creating an even worse situation for the next round of negotiations.

Our contract with the UAW was due to expire in February 2008. The rough ride of 2006–2007 had convinced me the time had come at last to stand tough and do whatever it took to get our wages and benefits back to a U.S. market–competitive level. We simply could not keep doing what we had been doing, and I hoped the UAW leadership would finally come to grips with that reality.

Unfortunately, we were marginally back in the black in 2007, a fact that emboldened the UAW. While it was true we logged net earnings of $37 million on $3.25 billion of sales, that was a skimpy profit margin that spoke volumes about the vulnerability of our position. The fact that we were losing money on our U.S.-based, UAW-represented operations escaped the UAW leadership's notice, or at least their understanding. All of our profits were coming from our foreign facilities. We made it clear to the UAW that we meant business this time, that we had to get our labor costs under control, but they were not listening. They were used to dictating terms.

AAM's UAW members walked off the job on February 26, 2008. Back in 2004, they had walked out in a strike that lasted a day and a half. I believe most of them probably thought this would be another cakewalk. GM would lean on us to settle, as it had in times past, and we would capitulate again. They thought wrong. The day of reckoning had arrived.

They misread the situation badly. The auto market remained weak. GM's car lots were overflowing with unsold vehicles—a 150-day supply of pickup trucks and more than 100 days' worth of SUVs. The prospect of an interruption of production was just what the company needed at that juncture to reduce the backlog. "Frankly," said GM chairman Rick Wagoner, "our inventories are fairly high." Even more importantly, the AAM plant in Mexico was ramping up production to meet GM's reduced needs even as our U.S. salaried associates began manning the production lines in place of the striking hourly associates.

The strike was bitter, as they usually are. UAW president Ron Gettelfinger accused us of demanding "extreme sacrifices" from his members. It no doubt appeared that way to the associates on strike because they had become accustomed to inflated wages and overly generous benefits. They quite naturally assumed their situation was normal. This is what can happen when you keep putting off tough decisions for another day.

In reality, AAM was simply insisting on the same provisions the UAW had already granted to our primary competitors in the U.S. We were stuck with a fully loaded labor cost of $73.48 per hour in wages and benefits, nearly three times the rate of our competitors. If we had agreed to the union demands, we would have been on schedule to reach $106 per hour within the span of the new contract! As Sean McAlinden, chief economist at the Center for Automotive Research in Ann Arbor said, AAM was left as the highest cost supplier in North America. The five AAM plants being struck had not been profitable in years. Why the UAW singled us out for this confrontation I do not know, but it was to prove a major miscalculation on their part that did us and them lasting damage.

About 3,650 AAM associates were to remain on the picket lines for eighty-seven days—the eighth longest strike in the history of the UAW. During that time, GM was required to cut back production or shutter as many as eighteen plants, but gradually most of them quietly resumed production again—to the UAW's consternation. The union leaders expressed dismay at that, wondering where the parts were coming from. For example, the GM assembly plant in Fort Wayne, Indiana, resumed building trucks in April. A spokeswoman for the plant declined to say where the parts were coming from. The fact that AAM had a major operation in Mexico was hardly news, but apparently the UAW brass missed the memo.

The UAW began calling wildcat strikes at GM plants here and there in an effort to prod GM into leaning on AAM to settle, as it had done several times in the past. But GM vice chairman Bob Lutz told a reporter the strike had not hurt GM because of its bloated inventory of full-size pickup trucks and SUVs for which AAM produced axles. "If the market is red hot for pickups and SUVs, and with every day of the strike you are missing production volumes, then it becomes painful," he said. "But when you have lots of retail inventory for the dealers to sell down, then it puts you in a strategically better position to withstand a strike."

All the while, our main customer GM continued to bleed cash because of declining sales. It reported a first quarter loss of $3.3 billion, attributing about $800 million of the loss to the AAM strike, but most of it to plummeting sales of pickup trucks and SUVs.

The end of the strike, when it finally came, was painful for everyone. It consisted largely of buyouts, in which we basically paid hourly associates to take early retirement if they were eligible, or to simply leave, and buy-downs, in which we provided associates with cash settlements to cushion the transition to a lower wage scale. All 3,650 hourly workers were offered buyouts that averaged about $140,000 each. This was even more expensive than buyouts for employees of original equipment manufacturers (OEMs) like GM and Chrysler.

The UAW appeared determined to hurt AAM financially. It was literally squeezing the blood out of AAM. Overall, we reduced our U.S. hourly workforce by about 2,100, while 1,600 associates took the buy-downs. The strike cost AAM about $130 million in lost profits and $370 million in sales. That did not include the $400–$450 million we paid out to associates as part of the settlement. At the last moment, GM stepped in and provided $213 million to help pay the associates to leave or accept lower wages, a move that assisted us to reach a settlement with the UAW. All three institutions had been severely injured by this unnecessary strike.

Obviously, all of this took a toll on the company. AAM posted a loss of $644 million in the second quarter, far and away our biggest loss up until then. I told a reporter from the *Detroit Free Press* it was "the most challenging and difficult quarter" in the company's history. We had to borrow a lot of money to cover all of these charges, but we figured we had to do it to get rid of the labor legacy costs that were making us uncompetitive. Once we had the labor costs under control, and were able to take advantage of reduced operating costs, I foresaw a steady comeback.

Still, our worst days lay ahead. I have heard it said that the Good Lord never puts more on our shoulders than we can carry, but I am here to tell you sometimes He apparently wants to see just how much you can bear. While we were going toe-to-toe with the UAW, laying off associates and borrowing huge sums of money to get free of the inflated UAW labor costs, the economy continued to deteriorate. The seasonally adjusted annual rate (SAAR) of sales for passenger vehicles went into free fall from 16.5 million in 2006 to 16.1 million in 2007 and to 13.1 million in 2008. It is probably just as well we did not know then what the 2009 total would be—only 10 million. It was to be a precipitous and rapid fall.

By autumn, the bad news was echoing throughout the auto industry. AAM had long since cut away the fat and we were now gnawing at the bone. Word was out that we were cutting back production at our Cheektowaga machining plant and planning to close our Tonawanda forge, both in New York. In September, Congress approved a $25 billion low-interest loan package for the automotive industry, and the industry was asking for another $25 billion that would bring the total to $50 billion. I told the *Detroit Free Press* that Congress would probably come through with the loans, but that the auto industry needed to offer realistic plans to change the way it operates. "I cannot fathom, in my lifetime, America letting its proud auto industry that put the world on wheels go the way of the horse and buggy," I said.

On November 30, we shut down our Detroit forge, reducing use of our facilities on Holbrook Avenue by one million square feet. "We have taken what I call the hard, necessary decisions that give us structural, transformational changes," I said. "I think that is what Washington is looking for, strong, balanced, transforming changes and reformation." At the same time, we were expanding operations and adding associates at our facility in Three Rivers, Michigan, where the UAW local members had chosen to go their own way from the international union, agreeing to a competitive wage and benefit package. In reality, all we needed at that point in the story was a rebound in sales of motor vehicles.

To no one's surprise, AAM stock was on a steady downward trajectory. In November, I bought 430,000 shares to demonstrate my confidence in the company. It did not stem the decline. By December 29, AAM shares were down to $2.18, reflecting a decline of 88 percent during the year. And that was three days after our two main customers, GM and Chrysler, got $17.4 billion from Uncle Sam, funded from the $787 billion approved by Congress to save the financial industry. A year before, at the end of 2007, AAM shares had been selling for $18.62.

I was quoted in the *Detroit Free Press*, calling 2008 "the year from hell," which it surely was. We lost about $1 billion in special charges, paying for attrition plans and plant closures. All told, we shed about three thousand associates through buyouts and buy-downs. We suspended our quarterly dividend of 2¢ per share. Our senior executives agreed to take a 10 percent wage cut and waive annual bonuses for 2008 and 2009. Even the board of directors accepted reduced compensation.

The bad news just kept coming. In March, we were informed by the New York Stock Exchange that we had fallen below the continued listing standard based on market capitalization and stockholders' equity, which cannot be less than $75 million over a thirty-day period. Stock analysts said AAM was "on the bubble." On March 10, AAM stock closed at 29¢ per share, which was both embarrassing and devastating. The price popped back up within a few days, but remained depressed compared to historical levels.

On May 1, 2009, Chrysler declared bankruptcy. One month later, General Motors followed suit. For many of us, that came as a shock even though we were expecting it. Over 101 years, GM had built 450 million cars and trucks. It had 463 subsidiaries and employed 235,000 people worldwide, 91,000 in the United States, to whom it paid $476 million in salaries and benefits each month. GM spent $50 billion a year buying parts and services. Now it was kaput. All those stockholders were left holding worthless pieces of paper. For many Americans, perhaps most of us, GM had always been seen as a rock-solid pillar of the nation's economy. For GM to go bankrupt was simply unimaginable, but there it was lying on the road like a dead skunk. The news took my breath away.

We thought we had adequate financing and contingency plans to get us through the downturn, but when GM and Chrysler announced they would stop producing vehicles, it threw all of our plans out the window. GM and Chrysler are our two biggest customers. Together they were responsible for most of our cash flow. Together they owed us more than $300 million for parts we had already made and delivered, money that we desperately needed to stay in business. We went from $500 million revenues in the first quarter to $246 million in the second quarter. We could not survive that situation for long without assistance. We needed the money owed to us, not IOUs.

All eyes were on Washington, D.C. Would it intervene on behalf of GM and Chrysler? The answer had implications far beyond those companies. "Unless the industry gets help, hundreds of suppliers will disappear in the next four months," said Neil De Koker, chief executive of the Original Equipment Suppliers Association (OESA), quoted in *Barrons*. "Some firms will fail within 60 days, and at least 500 more are at risk of failure later this year."

One of those suppliers deemed most at risk was AAM. Republic Steel stopped shipping steel to us because of concern about our financial viability. We cannot make axles and drive trains without steel. The bad news just kept roaring through my office door. One of my key management axioms is TMT, TME— tell me the truth and tell me early. I have always figured that good news can wait, but I need to know where the problems are right now. But I was reaching the point I really longed to hear some good news.

"Only three Michigan companies on my nostalgic chart remain unscathed, for now, by bankruptcy or predation," wrote Daniel Howes in *The Detroit*

News, "Ford Motor Company, Compuware Corporation and American Axle & Manufacturing, the most likely of the survivors to take its own turn in the ditch depending on the outcome of GM's blast through bankruptcy."

We had bills coming due, payments and interest on the loans we had taken out to pay former associates, and there was a serious question as to whether we would be able to make them. In early August, we reported a net loss of $289 million in the second quarter. The business media were filled with predictions of our imminent demise. Not if I could help it. I made it clear to everyone who asked that we were determined to avoid bankruptcy. "It is AAM's primary objective to complete our restructuring outside of a bankruptcy process," I said. "Bankruptcy is far too extreme and disruptive for AAM and our shareholders."

By midsummer, Congress had enacted a major bailout package for GM and Chrysler, but the legislation did not include direct assistance to auto suppliers like AAM. We obtained first one waiver and then another from lenders on our loan covenants, but by September we were running out of time. Our only real hope was that GM, now out of bankruptcy, would make a major payment on the money it owed us. By law, GM did not have to pay us. Going through bankruptcy had essentially freed it from debt obligations. On the other hand, if GM wanted to resume production and become profitable again, it needed axles and drivetrains. At that point, GM would have had an extraordinarily difficult time finding any other company to provide the validated parts it had to have to resume operations.

Everything I understood about the situation—everything I had been led to believe—told me that GM would come up with the money. I had gone to Washington, D.C., with the GM senior staff to negotiate with the government for assistance. I knew the players and I was in the loop, but I also knew GM was now owned mainly by the government, which is more responsive to politics than real world economic forces. I also knew that 17 percent of GM, through courtesy of the government, was now owned by our nemesis, the UAW, which would not be sympathetic to our plight.

Our chief financial officer, Michael Simonte, came to see me and closed the door. Mike is a financial wizard. He helped me steer AAM through many difficult times over the years. He knows the ropes and is unflinchingly loyal to the company. He is also direct and to the point. He told me that we were five days away from bankruptcy.

Dr. Samuel Johnson famously said that the prospect of a hangman's noose in a fortnight will concentrate a man's mind wonderfully. A fortnight is two weeks. We were down to five days.

2

Making the Deal

Once more unto the breach, dear friends, once more.
—William Shakespeare, Henry V

"Far and away the best prize that life offers," said President Theodore Roosevelt, "is the chance to work hard at work worth doing." I do not know if my parents were familiar with that quote, but they did convey to me and my siblings the joy and satisfaction that comes from hard work—and also the success. I really would not know what to do with my time if I did not have fresh challenges in front of me every day.

That was a problem I encountered after I left Chrysler and finished writing my first book, *Passion for Manufacturing*. When GM announced in December 1992 that it intended to sell eighteen operations, I contacted Jim McLernon, the former GM executive who was now retired and living in Florida. Jim, like me, was interested in the assets of GM's Saginaw Division. I knew he could be of inestimable assistance to help us to close a deal with GM, if we chose to pursue one. Eventually, we decided to pursue the deal directly with GM executive vice president J. T. Battenberg and GM CEO Jack Smith.

Another guy on the top of my list was Bob Mathis, who had worked for me at Chrysler, and helped me with my first book. Bob is a man of diverse talents—an MBA, an attorney and a gifted manager with a flair for negotiating contracts and writing. He had retired from Chrysler and was enjoying life on the golf courses of South Carolina. I said, "Bob, you've been retired five years, how much golf can you play? This is not a normal project. Let's do something great, get back in the game." Bob was to be a key player in the creation and launch of AAM—rock steady, unflappable, attentive to details, and always there. In fact, most days he turned on the office lights in the morning and turned them off at night. I don't mind telling you he had to bend the clock around to get in more hours than the rest of us did.

Other inspired car guys I called on were George Dellas, Tom Delanoy, Rick Rossmann, and Marion Cumo. Dellas had worked for me way back when I was a plant manager for Chevrolet. Delanoy's father had actually helped hire me at GM long before that, and I had shot basketball with Tom when he was a teenager. They said they were ready, willing, and able.

I called Rossmann and Cumo "Fire and Ice" for the way they complemented each other, Rossmann with his fiery intensity and Cumo with his icy, imperturbable glare that made people squirm. Anyone who dropped the ball and got caught between those two guys was in for a long day. After leaving Chrysler, they both launched their own businesses. Rossmann was salvaging distressed properties and Cumo was managing a Chrysler dealership in Cincinnati. They are the kind of people who are always successful at whatever they put their minds to. It took a bit of cajolery but they both agreed to abandon their new careers and rejoin me if I could put a deal together.

McLernon, Dellas, Mathis, Cumo, Rossmann, Delanoy—our new organization was coming together. They were all former colleagues that I had worked with at GM, VWoA, and Chrysler. This team of guys knew the auto industry and were reliable, smart, and competitive. There are not that many people who know how to wrest world-class quality from an ancient industrial workplace or have the fortitude to manage hardened union workers in the auto industry. I had a list of such people and I knew I would need them. I felt like Yul Brynner calling on old friends for a big adventure in the 1960 movie *The Magnificent Seven*, one of the better westerns I have seen. Come to think of it, we would all end up in Mexico just like Yul Brynner's gang did, but I am getting ahead of the story. Those guys were the nucleus with which we began. By March 1994, I would have many more former colleagues at my side for the launch of AAM.

We came up with a strategy to earn the status of "earnest buyer" in the eyes of GM, which had several suitors interested in purchasing the assets that were on the block. In fact, GM already had nine earnest buyers, including some prominent names like Dana, Rockwell, A. O. Smith, TRW, MascoTech, and Eaton. American Axle, of course, had no track record, but we as individuals all had proven track records and reputations for effective management. That counts for a lot in Detroit.

In this case, GM had a real problem. Their axle and drivetrain factories had been allowed to deteriorate to the point that they were not only losing money, but were missing shipments and supplying poor-quality products that both undermined GM sales and created excessive warranty costs. GM needed someone who could turn it around and I knew we were the only guys in town who could do that. There were obviously people at GM who agreed with that assessment because they took us seriously from the beginning.

One of them was Guy Briggs, a senior GM executive who would eventually rise to group vice president for Manufacturing and Labor Relations for North America. "Dick was the deal," he said. "Those facilities had been let go, not invested in. It was not a focal point for the company. We had a lot of issues—*supply* and *quality* problems. We had a lot of axle outages before AAM. Dick and his team fixed it."

Through much of 1993 we were conducting due diligence* on the GM facilities and business we aspired to purchase—checking out the structures, the machinery and equipment, the condition it was in, and to the extent possible the quality and morale of the workforce. One day I took Dellas and Cumo on a walk around the Detroit facilities for three or four hours just so they could see up close and personal what I was getting them into. On the one hand, the facilities were in deplorable condition. On the other hand, it was a juicy challenge much like the one we had taken on at Chrysler more than ten years before. We had been there, done that.

"Dick, George and I are walking through the Detroit plants," said Cumo. "I'm keeping my mouth shut, trying to see what's going on. We get to the forge plant. Everyone knows Dick. This big, muscular guy is on a gangway up above us. I think he was a UAW shop steward. He yells down, 'Hey Dauch, whatcha doin,' you gonna buy this place?' Dick shows no emotion, just walks up the steps alone, meets with his old acquaintance for a few minutes. The guy told Dick they would work with us. Dick cemented that relationship then and there. He came back down and said that was probably the best five minutes we were going to have here today."

"We knew right off that a lot of consolidation had to be done," continued Cumo. "Buildings had to be torn down or refurbished. We said, why not, we can do this. We went through due diligence for months in Detroit, Buffalo, Tonawanda, Parma [Ohio], Saginaw, St. Catherines [Ontario] and Three Rivers."

"We toured the factories," said Rossmann. "I looked them over. Half the

---

* George Dellas was at a loss when instructed to perform due diligence. He went to a law library looking for a definition of the term and was unable to find one. He finally concluded it simply meant being diligent, and he was.

lights were out, scrap everywhere, machines down, half stripped, cannibalized. I thought, what in the hell are we going to do with this? We walked through plant #3. Dick said, what could you get out of this plant if I gave you some money to fix it up? I said if I had some money and time to put in discipline, we could do fifteen hundred axles a day."

That was exactly what I wanted to hear. At the time, it was producing eight hundred a day.

All of this had a purpose. I wanted to see for myself what we were getting into and I wanted my top guys to fully appreciate the scope of the challenge. If we made the deal, I wanted a team that was fully aware of the real situation, sleeves rolled up and ready to take it on.

Somewhere along the line, McLernon introduced me to a GM veteran named Joe Richards who had recently retired. Joe knew the facilities and the products we were looking at backward and forward. I took an instant liking to Joe, who is a veteran car guy through and through. He had worked his way up from the floor to plant manager and chief engineer. He helped us immeasurably in assessing the quality of the plants and acquiring the properties in the neighborhood that we wanted to clean up and make presentable, and he later helped us build our new Technical Center in Rochester Hills. Thank you, Joe.

To make the deal, we had to bring a lot of pieces together, and one of them was someone with money—and I mean serious money. I had always done well in terms of earning a living and providing for my family, but there was nothing in my bank account to cover this kind of investment. We needed a big-time investor.

Fortunately, McLernon knew a couple of guys who fit that description, Ray Park and Mort Harris. Ray in particular was to prove the pivotal figure in making the venture possible. I had worked with Ray when I was with VWoA. Like me, Ray was born to humble circumstances, but he was born with a gift for alchemy—in medieval terms, that was the power to transform base metals into gold. In the modern era, it meant that Ray had built up a substantial business by purchasing old machinery from shuttered factories around the country and packaging it for resale, either to another company that needed the machinery or as scrap for recycling. He saw value where other people saw junk. Given the transformation that our nation's economy has gone through, this was to prove a valuable ability. Ray, based in Cleveland, would not only put up a substantial amount of cash to close the deal, but take an active hand in the negotiations with GM to make sure we struck an advantageous deal.

In the early stages of negotiations, Park and his people were leery of us and

I did not blame them for a minute. We were talking about a major investment and there were many reasons to question its chances of success. But Park looked at the assets on the block and saw what I saw, and he must have acquired some confidence in me as the talks continued. We had our tough moments. At one point, he told me I would be the only officer of the company. I told him no, I would start with five officers, not counting myself, because I had to have a team working with me that I could trust and rely on. "If you know how to run a company in this business, then you go ahead and do it," I told him. "If you want me to do it, I need my team with me." I won that one.

By midyear, our negotiations with GM were intensifying. There were literally hundreds of difficult issues to be worked out, one at a time. I and my staff had countless meetings that often ran into the wee hours of the morning. At first, we were meeting at my house over the kitchen table. After a while, when it became increasingly clear we had the inside track, GM gave us some space at an old office building in Pontiac, Michigan, on South Boulevard, about an hour north of Detroit.

We were all meeting with GM people together and as individuals to address issues and build relationships. I already knew many senior GM executives well including CEO Jack Smith; Executive Vice President J. T. Battenberg; Chief Financial Officer Rick Wagoner (who would later become GM CEO); North American Group Vice President for Truck Operations C. J. "Cliff" Vaughn; Group Vice President for Manufacturing and Labor Relations for North America Guy Briggs; and others. They knew me from when I worked there, and were aware of what I had accomplished at VWoA and Chrysler. But they had to satisfy their board of directors that I and my team were up to the challenge. The future of GM depended on a steady supply of quality axles and drivetrains for their pickup trucks, SUVs, and passenger cars.

"We would meet day after day with the GM people to go over all the various issues," said Mathis. "Someone would say this isn't looking so good; then the next day they would be more optimistic. They were long, drawn-out negotiations. Will this work? How will that work? We had an initial understanding by September, but it was a huge process to get everything ready for closing. We hoped to close by the end of the year, but we didn't make it."

"It was an emotional roller-coaster ride for me," said Dellas. "We would be down there to two or three in the morning thinking we had a deal, and then next morning the deal would fall apart again. Things would be stagnant for a week or two, and then the parties started talking again."

As at Chrysler, a major challenge was labor. The UAW had more than

6,500 members at the plants GM had on the block and was determined to keep them in the fold. It was essential to get the UAW on board with our plan because they had enough power to bog down the deal, if not kill it outright. GM has never had the gumption to stand up to the UAW, which is another story I will get to later on. By the autumn of 1993, I was spending a lot of time at Solidarity House, the UAW headquarters in Detroit, often taking Mathis and Rossmann with me. In dealing with the union, personal relationships are critical. We told the union officers we would accept their contract as it stood, with all of its inflated wages and benefits, but we would need major changes in the work rules, and would need to transform the labor cost structure within ten years from that of an OEM, like GM or Chrysler, to that of a parts supplier. The whole point of our effort was to transform the old plants into models of efficiency producing quality products, and for that we had to have flexibility.

"We told them they had to accept the rules changes if they wanted to work with us," said Rossmann. "If you don't sign up with us, someone else will get the properties, like Dana, for example, and they will parcel it off and there will be nothing left for you. We had some hard meetings. They did not trust us at first. But I told them Dick is not kidding about this. We are offering to save your jobs with the agreement you have, but you have to work with us. Gradually, they came around." They knew I did not bluff. I would be very straight with them.

We all knew that sooner or later we would have to stand up to the UAW. The wage and benefit scales they demanded even back then were economically unrealistic and clearly unsustainable to anyone with an ounce of understanding of what was going on in the world. But at that time, we had to bite our lips and make a deal. "The nature of the purchase was such that the deal would probably never have taken place without the UAW's approval," said Mathis. "Their contract carried over for three years. That was all part of the deal. The UAW had already cut a deal with GM and we were not in a position to challenge it."

I would like to believe that my old friend Marc Stepp was somewhere in the background during this period, telling his colleagues at the UAW that Dick Dauch was someone they could work with, who could be trusted. Stepp was always ahead of the curve in his understanding that global pressures were changing the dynamics of Detroit, and that the UAW had to change, too. The radicals had accused him of "selling out" when he dealt with me at Chrysler, but when the contract came to a vote, the overwhelming majority of UAW members voted with Stepp, and with progress. In any event, by late 1993 or early 1994, the senior UAW leadership decided to work with us and the union challenge was resolved, at least for the time being.

We were working with GM management to hammer out a deal, we had an investor willing to put up some serious money, and we had a constructive conversation going with the UAW. At that point, I needed to go to the GM front office and talk to the head honcho, Jack Smith, who served as chief executive officer of GM from 1992 to 2000, and as chairman of the board of GM from 1996 to 2003.

As CEO of GM, Jack undertook one of its most sweeping reorganizations, overturning a cumbersome and inefficient structure created in the 1920s by Alfred Sloan and left virtually unchanged since then. Starting with purchasing in 1992 and ending with engineering in 2003, he brought together separate overlapping functions related to the various divisions that formed the company, while also expanding operations into Asia. In this transformation, which subsequently included terminating the Oldsmobile brand, many core management positions were eliminated, corporate decision-making became faster and easier, production efficiencies and quality improved, and, above all, the bottom line went from near-bankruptcy losses to decent profits.

Jack was the driving force behind GM's decision to turn over the "troubled plants" to someone who could restore them to health. To survive, GM had to have a steady supply of quality axles and drivetrains for its pickup trucks and SUVs, which were its strongest line of products, and getting stronger. Jack and I knew each other, but not intimately. I assume he knew of my reputation or GM would not be considering us for the buyout and Jack would not have met with me in person to talk about it. I laid it all on the line for him. I told him the world was watching and he would be the one held accountable if GM went bankrupt. GM could not fix itself without fixing its axles and driveline production. I told him he should disregard the other nine companies bidding for the purchase and go with me and my team because we knew what we were doing and they did not. I told him, I know GM, I know Detroit, I know axles, I know the union, I know the customers, and I will commit to it. I said the other bidders are just winking at it. TRW wants to buy it just for the steering linkage business. MascoTech wants to buy it just for the forging business. Dana wants it just for the axles. And none of them want the Detroit plants while I will take it "where is, as is" and transform it into a first rate, competitive company that GM can depend upon.

I believe I made an impression on Jack that lived up to my reputation. After that meeting our negotiations seemed to pick up momentum, though there were still many hills to climb. By September, we had a signed GM letter of intent that the company would negotiate only with us for these properties. We hoped to get the deal wrapped up by Christmas.

It was not to be. We had an agreement, or thought we had, in December 1993, but the GM board of directors voted it down. I really have no idea why they rejected that first agreement, but we went back to the drawing board for another sixty days of wheeling and dealing. By February 1994 we had resolved the outstanding issues. In this business, you must have persistence and the patience of Job.

It would be impossible to summarize all of the agreements that were part of the overall package, most of them about obscure matters that would seem irrelevant in retrospect, but which carried weight at the time. The deal was complex. Questions kept popping up. Who would cut checks for the employees—soon to be AAM associates—right out of the gate? I wanted those first checks to be on AAM letterhead. Who would pay the suppliers? Who would pay for the utilities? Who had legal liability for the products? What about the products made before we took over? How would warranty be handled? And on and on.

We did secure some important provisions that would go a long way toward helping us become profitable. Perhaps the biggest was GM's agreement to pay us every day for our deliveries. This was unheard of in the auto industry, but it assured us an all-important cash flow from day one. When we launched, within two or three days, we had $20 million in the bank. We did not have to pay our suppliers until mid-April, so we had a nice cash cushion. GM also agreed to hold us harmless for materials—to continue providing purchasing services for buying the steel, aluminum, bearings, and other productive materials we needed for the time being. GM was confident that with its buying power, it could keep a lid on the price of steel. GM was wrong about that, and this provision saved us a lot of money. "GM took the materials risk to hold us harmless for price increases," said Gary Witosky, a skilled financial executive working for Ray Park who later came to work for AAM. "If they had not done that, I don't think the deal would have been done."

GM also agreed to give us the right of first refusal on new products that fell within our scope of work—primarily axles and drivetrains for pickup trucks and SUVs. That essentially meant we did not have to compete for upcoming jobs—a great advantage. "AAM had a sweet deal that put them in the driver's seat," said Guy Briggs. "But for the guy receiving the stuff and putting the trucks together, GM, it was a good deal."

Ray Park was deeply involved in all this, especially on the financial issues. He wanted the ability to increase the prices of products, mainly to cover the loans we would need to make the deal. But GM was adamant it would not pay higher prices for the products.

Another thorny issue was the real estate titles for the properties that had been in GM's pocket for almost a century. Conveying all that property to the new company was a complex legal challenge in its own right. Thank God Bob Mathis is a lawyer and I am not. We got the job done.

I had told Jack Smith I thought it would take five to ten years to transform the old GM purchased plants into a world class operation. He took me at my word and insisted that I commit to the project for ten years as part of the deal. I had originally committed to five years, but after conferring with my CEO— Sandy Dauch—I agreed to ten years. Jack was right to demand that. Thank you, Sandy, for your support.

GM also insisted on another provision that I did not care for, an "access and security" agreement that enabled GM to resume control of the facilities and business being sold if we did not meet our product delivery and quality commitments. I understood their reasoning. GM absolutely had to have our products in a timely fashion. If for any reason we failed, GM was up the creek. Still, it stuck in my craw and I was relieved when we finally put that nuclear option away.

At one point, as we got near to closing the deal, Ray Park threw a wrench into the works by insisting he did not want to accept the GM plant in Three Rivers as part of the arrangement. I had sent Rick Rossmann over there—it is about three hours west of Detroit—and he came back with an upbeat assessment of the possibilities. "I said it has its problems, but we can fix it," Rossmann said. "I had spent a good bit of time there. Ray finally dropped his objections."

We were negotiating for a major league loan to cover most of the cost, but in the end we did not need it. GM essentially loaned us most of the money by putting up $220 million in preferred stock and taking a five-year note for $90 million in inventory we would acquire on day one. I put up $500,000 and Mort Harris put up $1 million. Ray Park came up with the "serious" money—more than $20 million. So the whole deal came in for about $340 million. We would pay GM back by 1997. It was time to sit down and sign the papers.

The GM people asked if they could put three people on our board of directors. I said no. Not long after, Smith called me about it. He said if GM could put up all that money to help us buy the facilities and the business, the least we could do was give them board representation. I explained that we needed to expand and diversify our customer base. If I sent someone to Japan to meet with Mr. Toyoda about doing business with them, and he found out we had GM representatives on the board, it would kill the deal immediately. Jack said I was right. We had no GM people on our board.

"They had these big tables, long and wide," said Dellas. "The entire circumference of the table, including a row inside, was filled with closing documents. We stood in line and signed this stack and then went on to the next and signed that. There were stacks upon stacks of paper. After everyone was done signing—this was late on February 28—it was like, wow, we can go home to bed now."

As of March 1, 1994, American Axle & Manufacturing, Inc. owned assets, including the patents, designs, engineering, licenses, technology, and intellectual property of the Final Drive and Forge Business Unit of the Saginaw Division of General Motors, and assumed 100 percent of operating control. This was a big deal!

It was, as I recall, two in the morning on February 28, technically March 1. I told my guys to go home and grab a couple hours of sleep, but to be at the plants at 5:00 A.M. the next morning to greet the "associates" of AAM, and introduce them to their new employer. Joe Richards had done his job making sure each plant entrance was crowned with red, white, and blue American Axle & Manufacturing signs.

It is said that after the Constitutional Convention had concluded its work, a woman stopped Ben Franklin on his way out of the building and asked, "What kind of a government have you given us?"

"A republic, madam," he said, "if you can keep it."

A new company was ours, but to keep it we had to make it competitive and profitable—and do it quickly.

3

Launching a New Corporation

Dick had an aggressive business plan. He's an extremely focused and willful guy buying all this new equipment, modernizing everything, buying up property in this crime-infested Detroit neighborhood, taking it from a crack den—a place where murders happened—almost to a corporate park, a truly remarkable transformation.

—Stephen Schwarzman,
Chairman and co-founder, Blackstone Group

Someone asked Sir Edmund Hillary why he climbed Mount Everest. "Because it is there," he replied. Many people have asked me, then and later, why I took on the challenge of resuscitating GM's antiquated axle, driveshaft, steering linkage, and forge plants. Anyone driving by those rusting hulks of ancient factories could see I was taking on a major league challenge. The smart money was against me. So why do it? I had nothing to prove. I had already recorded a sterling record of achievement in the auto industry at GM, Volkswagen of America, and Chrysler. What we did at Chrysler, bringing it back from the brink of bankruptcy under the inspired leadership of the legendary Lee Iacocca, had earned me considerable renown and reward. Sandy and I had more than enough resources to meet our needs—we have never been into conspicuous consumption. Thus, I was under no pressure to prove myself or earn more money. So why do it?

Part of the reason was a sense of mission. I am a manufacturing missionary. I could see that Detroit was losing its competitive edge and needed an infusion of creative energy. The industry had grown complacent and business as usual was leading it to disaster. It needed someone to rock the boat. I knew I was just the guy to do that. I have been rocking the boat for a long time.

Part of it also was my desire to finally walk the bridge, to be the chief executive officer. I had held high positions in some great auto companies, but I was always reporting to someone higher in the pecking order. I had no doubt of my ability to handle the top job and, having been passed over at Chrysler when Iacocca prepared for retirement, was determined to make it happen on my own. I have always believed I was ready to lead and wanted to prove it. This time I put my destiny in my own hands—not some bureaucracy.

Maybe the main thing was, I was simply hungry for a fresh challenge. I was fifty years old, in great shape mentally and physically, and full of energy. Plus I like to work. I could not see myself sitting around the house collecting cobwebs. I needed to get back in the game and the auto industry was where I belonged. Thus, the opportunity to buy the GM facilities and business assets appealed to me on several different levels. I have always said that if you are coasting, you're going downhill. I am not built for coasting. I need to wake up every morning with a mountain to climb. Dynamic tension has always enabled me to focus like a laser beam on challenges.

With American Axle, I got all the challenge I had bargained for and then some. We had performed due diligence on the GM assets we were buying, and we were well aware the plants were in sad shape, but we did not know the half of it. The neighborhood surrounding the Detroit facilities was one of the worst in Detroit. There were vacant lots covered with litter, abandoned houses (some inhabited by squatters), crack houses serving the drug trade, and houses of prostitution. On one corner where our headquarters is today was a gasoline station alleged to have been fronting for a prostitution ring. Not far away was a "party store" that we had been led to believe fronted for an illegal drug operation. The area was a magnet for crime. It was a Detroit ghetto.

The factory buildings dated back to before World War I, and it showed. The plant area looked like a war zone. The exterior walls were moldy, rusty, and covered with graffiti. Windows were broken and doors missing. The parking lots around the plants were strewn with discarded bags, rusting cans, worn out tires, broken booze bottles, used drug paraphernalia, and grocery carts that, outside a grocery store area, you could assume were being used to transport stolen merchandise. Most of the exterior lighting was out, creating an inviting environment of which local criminals were not slow to take advantage. At least one car a day was being stolen. One weekend, not long after we took over, sixteen vehicles disappeared while their owners were at work!

Car theft was by no means the worst of it. A deliveryman driving a juice truck was shot in the middle of the day as he drove down Holbrook Avenue through our plant complex, right outside our executive offices. His truck careened down the street, banging into parked cars until it finally came to a halt. The driver was dead at the wheel. Witnesses said the shooter tossed his gun into some bushes nearby and casually walked back down Holbrook to the other side of Interstate 75, in no apparent hurry. To our knowledge, no suspect was ever apprehended for that crime.

On another occasion a would-be car thief was caught in the act by our security personnel when the car's owner, a feisty woman who worked for us, saw him trying to hotwire the ignition and demanded that he desist. He fled into our offices and hid in a bathroom. The police finally came to get him. He was a local character well known to the officers. He had, in fact, jumped bail and was being sought, but even so the officers would not arrest him until we promised to prosecute. Apparently, most people in that area at that time were reluctant to pursue criminals in the court system. We were not.

Then there were the mounds of discarded parts and machinery strewn about the grounds, rusting in the rain and snow. I had never seen so much junk in one place before. "The whole perimeter of each of the buildings was surrounded with old stuff—junk all around," said Dellas. "The first year, we just started loading this stuff up and selling it for scrap, four hundred and seventy truckloads the first year at just the Detroit plant!"

The infrastructure was in a similar state of disrepair. The roads were deeply rutted and riddled with potholes, totally inadequate to handle the huge amounts of freight we produced daily. The railroad junction created a traffic bottleneck and required upgrade. The sewer that served our factory dated from 1898 and was made of wood, if you can imagine that. The entire neighborhood conveyed a message of terminal blight.

The interior of the plants was, if anything, even worse. The ceilings and walls had not been painted in many years. The floors were covered with dirt, oil and grease. Some of the walls were stained with urine where the men relieved themselves because they did not want to use the foul restrooms. The lunch areas were so vile they would stifle anyone's appetite. The air was full of dirt and oil particles emitted from the archaic gear-cutting machinery we inherited, which was also inefficient, excessively loud, and prone to breakdown. The conditions were such that you could not see from one side of the plant to the other. My old and trusted friend Steve Sharf said to me, on a visit through the plants, that he thought I had bought part of the Smithsonian Institute.

"When I came here twenty-nine years ago, and it rained, the roof leaked," said the UAW's Jim Edwards. "When it was raining, GM said they couldn't fix the roof when it was raining. And when it wasn't raining, they said the roof didn't need fixing."

We had a problem with vermin, especially in plant #3, which was overrun with mice and rats. There are several ways to deal with mice and rats, but I always liked the solution we had on our farm where I grew up. So I enlisted Delanoy, who had grown up like me on a farm, and the two of us made a few calls on some farmers we knew. We collected altogether about two dozen big old farm cats and turned them loose in the plant. These were not your household tabbies. They were really big cats, twenty pounds or more, the kind that, when they can't find rats, go looking for groundhogs. We gave them milk but they had to find their entrées on their own. They soon took care of the vermin.

With broken windows, missing doors, and holes in the roof, it goes without saying that our associates were exposed to the elements—in a town where the weather is frequently nasty. In Detroit, it is often raining, blowing or snowing. In sum, the plant environment was dark, dirty, decrepit and dangerous—not an inviting place to work. It looked to me like a replay of the plants I had inherited when I went with Chrysler back in 1980, only worse.

Worst of all was the demoralization of the workforce—the most important variable in our quest to create a competitive business. The workplace environment was reflected in the dysfunctional attitudes of the people employed there. With notable exceptions, they were generally apathetic, resentful, and disinclined to work hard—or, in some cases, at all. "In the early days, when I first walked in here, it was like they had an attitude," said Delanoy, who I put in charge of manufacturing at the Detroit axle plant. "It didn't matter who you were. Management wasn't even recognized. The associates are going back to their hole, take a nap, maybe later build a few parts. If they made axles, fine. If not, fine. There was no reason to work, no measurement, no communication between hourly workers and management. No sense of urgency. None of that, 'hey, we have to get it done' attitude."

There was a small pump house structure on the top of one of the plants. Bob Mathis and I went up to check it out. The walls were adorned with *Playboy* pinups. There were cardboard mattresses in every nook and cranny, empty booze bottles and litter all over the place. It was not a place where quality automotive products were being made. We realized we had to change the entire environment and culture.

The general work ethic that prevailed was dismal. There was rampant *featherbedding*—people getting paid to do jobs that were no longer in existence. In some cases, we had ten people doing one person's job. The UAW defended every position to the death, and I presume the previous management just did not have the will to fight it out. Even worse, many if not most associates worked to what they called "pegs," which were minimum amounts of production that had been deemed acceptable by the previous management. Where these pegs came from, God only knows, but they had an absolute death grip on productivity. A machine might be capable of producing a hundred quality parts an hour, but if the peg was fifty, that was what the operator produced. Then he went on break for the remainder of the shift, had a smoke, read the paper, played cards, talked to friends, whatever. This was actually not an unusual practice in the auto industry at the time—*but not in my house*. We immediately clamped down on featherbedding and made it clear there would be no more pegs.

"There was cheating and lying on the production reports," said Rossmann. "Safety guarding was missing and electrical switches were bypassed. We would come in at one or two in the morning and find people involved in unacceptable activities. They were soon gone."

Of course, I knew change would not come easily. The auto industry has always been a tough environment for both management and labor. "The union guys had almost taken over the place in terms of the day-to-day operations," said Mathis. "I would not have wanted to be a supervisor in there. The practices had been allowed to deteriorate. It was a tough place."

There was widespread theft, people walking out with tools and diamond bits in their pockets. Ray Park asked me why we had so much inventory shrinkage. I said because many of the associates were thieves. Today we have systems to keep track of inventory and a culture that discourages dishonesty. But it did not happen overnight. Some of the people that we fired sued me. When the facts came out, though, they ran for cover. I made the case that they were thieves, and I won.

For some of the associates, both salaried and hourly, the workday was a continuous party. "Some of them were leaving two hours after punching in," said Delanoy, "or out at a bar getting drunk. There were vans that would pick up my people and take them to the bar where they would get drunk in the middle of the day. One day I followed the van to the Hamtramck Bar and Grill, a few blocks from the plant. The next day I went to the bar at lunchtime. I walked in and took everyone's names. There were management people there drinking with hourly people at lunch time for an hour, an hour and a half, just having a leisurely lunch."

Delanoy did not put up with that kind of behavior. He fired a few of the worst offenders, which sent a message to the others. Naturally, that did not go down well with some and he was threatened. Tom wore an armored vest for a few weeks and had security for his wife and children, but there was never any thought of backing off. We supported Tom, knowing full well we would all be on the firing line sooner or later, and we were. You don't take on that kind of entrenched corruption and culture without getting pushback. As it happened, that was actually a pretty good place for us to put the hammer down and send a message to the associates and the union. Drinking on the job is both an efficiency issue and a safety issue. AAM associates work with heavy machinery that must be respected and handled carefully. No drunks allowed. There were shop rules in place prohibiting that sort of thing so we did not need to cut any deals with the UAW, just enforce the rules. We eventually imposed a rule that associates could not leave the premises during working hours, and that solved the drinking on the job problem.*

Drinking during work hours, however, was by no means the worst of it. We discovered that some of our associates were operating prostitution rings, selling drugs, and running numbers from the plants. It is difficult to believe that things could have degenerated to that point, but they had. We worked with the Detroit City Police and the Federal Bureau of Investigation to conduct in-depth investigations. When you are talking about potential criminal indictments, it is absolutely imperative that you make certain you get the facts right and proceed according to the law. By year's end, the authorities were frog-marching some of the perpetrators out of the workplace in handcuffs and ankle shackles. Our associates saw a real change occurring before their eyes. Discipline started to return to this old and once proud plant.

We assisted the investigations every way we could. It was good we did because we discovered that some of our own security team were heavily involved in the drug trade. The following December, just before Christmas, we fired fifty-eight people! We were up against an ingrained, corrupt, "anything goes" culture among all too many members of the team. I knew it would be a long, tough slog to clean it up.

Some of the most troublesome activities we had to deal with were not illegal in the strictest sense of the word, but possibly even more troublesome in

---

* It came to a halt at AAM, but not necessarily everywhere. More recently, on September 27, 2010, WJBK TV in Detroit aired a report of autoworkers at the Chrysler Jefferson North Plant in Detroit drinking beer and using illegal drugs during their lunch break.

terms of our quest to become productive and competitive. In those days, the associates were more than happy to see the production lines interrupted because that meant they could come in on weekends to make double-time pay or on holidays to make triple time. Supervisors worked out deals with the workers—give me your time card, I will swipe it on Sunday to show you were here, and we split the extra money. Well, why not? If your employer is giving away free money, why not take it? We had janitors in those plants making more than $100,000 a year! And GM wondered why it was losing money. We are first and foremost in the people business. We had to get the organization straightened out.

"Many of these people were used to making all that money," said Rossmann. "They would say to me, how am I going to live without it? We fell back on our basic story line. If you don't work with us, this factory will not be here, your job will not be here. We cannot afford to bleed cash like GM did. And we only have so much time to get this turned around."

From the beginning, absenteeism was one of our biggest headaches, typically ranging from 18–22 percent on any given day, with the worst days being Mondays and Fridays. Associates would get their checks on Friday and just not come to work on Monday. If there was a big event of some kind like the Super Bowl on a weekend, we could expect 30 percent absenteeism on Monday morning. That meant if we had three thousand people on the payroll at the Detroit plant, nine hundred didn't show up for work that day! It is difficult to maintain a productive work schedule when people are not on the job. Often those associates who did come to work would drift in an hour or two late and goof around a while before they finally made their way to the work area. There were doctors in the neighborhood who for a small fee would write notes certifying that one of our associates was ill on a given day. It was all part of the corrupt mentality that prevailed in the greater Detroit area.

It pains me to say that is one area in which we were never able to make much progress. Absenteeism, for better or worse, was not a unique AAM phenomenon, but rather an endemic disease of the Detroit-based auto industry. Fourteen years later, when we finally went to the mat with the UAW, the absenteeism rate had not changed significantly. I do not think you will find this phenomenon anywhere else in America, at least not on this scale. In Detroit, there is a pervasive entitlement mentality that says you are entitled to your job with good pay and generous benefits regardless of whether you actually show up for work or contribute when you get there. I have spent my professional life struggling against it. It has been passed along from one generation to the next. Many take a certain dysfunctional pride in beating the system, but in the end they have driven job opportunities away from the city of Detroit.

AAM's second president, Joel Robinson, who had worked for me at Chrysler, was another hands-on manager who did not hole up in his office. "It was funny, but the hourly workers were not used to seeing anyone from senior management come out of their offices onto the production floor," he said. "One day we had a major breakdown in plant #2 that had to do with shim dispensers, which call out a shim that needs to go into an axle to set the pattern. The system was down and there was no work going on. The dispenser was up overhead. So I climbed up in my shirt and tie to see what the problem was. It was a total mess up there, shims all over the floor, all mixed up. I blew my top. I made them pull everything and restock the system right. I made it clear that if it happened again, someone would pay dearly. The next day, this one old-timer said to me, 'Man, we never saw anyone come out of the front office before, never mind up to the platform.'"

Not surprisingly, the quality of the axles coming out of the Detroit facilities was abysmal. There was an overall defect average of 13,441 parts per million (ppm)! That's an F minus; you just cannot get much worse than that. At the same time, sales of GM pickup trucks and SUVs were beginning to take off. GM needed quality parts and we were having trouble getting them out the door. The plants were not only falling short of GM's production needs, but also compounding the problem by sending them marginal products.

All in all, it was not an auspicious beginning. On the last day of February 1994, we signed the final papers taking control of five former GM plants and their 7,500 employees—henceforth known as associates. The next morning when the associates showed up for work, the buildings were adorned with freshly painted American Axle & Manufacturing signs. At every entrance stood one or more of my senior staff—including me—introducing ourselves, shaking hands, and welcoming our associates to the new company.

We knew we had to hit the ground running. Thousands of axles and driveshafts had to be made and delivered to GM that very day. We had no bureaucracy to perform routine corporate functions, only a few leftover GM staffers of uncertain ability and loyalty. In those days, I and my senior staff routinely put in sixteen-hour days, usually seven days a week. That was an exhausting schedule but there was no other way.

One of my first priorities was to clean up the facilities and provide good quality, affordable food in a clean lunchroom. I really do believe the environment of a factory is a key ingredient of company morale and culture. No one feels good about reporting to work at a run-down, filthy, rust-bucket factory. If you are going to have a world-class quality workplace, it must look the part. Right out of the gate, I had crews applying fresh paint to the buildings in AAM's new red, white, and blue color motif. Broken windows and doors were repaired or replaced. We quickly arranged for a crew to repair the leaky roof. You can't have water pouring on people working heavy machinery making axles.

From day one, we made it clear that safety was a top priority and a responsibility of both management and hourly associates. I wanted them to see these changes taking place so they would know we were serious about bringing positive change into their work lives.

I had the parking lots cleaned up and lighting and fencing upgraded. Hundreds of external light fixtures were dark. We put new bulbs in, lit up the area. I was cautioned that installing new lights would cost money. I knew that already, but criminals thrive in the dark. Simply putting the lights back on helped us reduce the incidence of illegal activities. Criminals hate light.

Still, the neighborhoods surrounding the plants were a problem. I controlled the plants, but not the other structures in the surrounding area—the prostitution houses, drug dens, beer joints, and gambling parlors. Fortunately, our chief investor and Vice Chairman of the Board Ray Park gave me able assistance on this challenge for which I will be eternally grateful. Using $10 million approved by Ray and other members of the board, we quietly began buying up the properties in and around the plants. Ray had a fellow in his employ named Paul Chamberlain do this in a way that did not announce to the world that AAM was on a buying spree. Had that news hit the streets, the prices of the houses—many of them derelict and deserted—would have skyrocketed. We got many of the derelict houses for about $5,000 apiece or less. There were a few businesses here and there that cost more. We paid $340,000 for the previously mentioned gas station. We immediately demolished these properties. I told Ray we were "thinning the firing zone."

On his own initiative, Ray Park strolled into the party store one day and told the proprietor he had always wanted to own a party store. He bought it for $320,000.

Where occupied residences were involved, we bent over backward to treat people fairly. A few of the homes were inhabited by poor people who lived there simply because they had no alternatives. We could have bought them out for $5,000 or less, but there was no place they could move to for that amount. We sweetened the pot for them to enable them to move to another neighborhood, and I hope to a better living situation. Any place would have been better.

A key man in the acquisition process was Richards, who had worked for GM for thirty-five years. "When you vacate a building, squatters move in," he said. "You can't do anything about a squatter. If he pays the bills, you're out of luck. But the minute our guy would call and say we had the deed to a property and it was vacant, we sent in the heavy equipment. A bulldozer would knock the walls down. A backhoe would scoop up the debris and dump it in the trucks that took it away. That's one way to clean up a ratty neighborhood."

Some of the properties were assembled for us to purchase by the city, which was glad to get rid of them. Pricing was not a big issue. Some had been abandoned and the owners were anxious to unload them. "Most of them were vacant anyway," Richards said. "The people who had lived there were already gone or eager to leave. The neighborhood was about as bad as you can imagine. You wouldn't want to walk down the street there."

Richards supervised the demolition of the infamous party store that Ray Park had purchased. "There was a desk near the back where the proprietor did his business," Richards said. "We found it was lined all the way around with heavy steel. When the bullets started flying, he could crouch down behind it for protection."

One homeowner held out a long time. He wasn't necessarily trying to squeeze us for money—we suspected he had a thriving drug trade going. Yogen Rahangdale, a soft-spoken gentleman who would play a key role in helping me forge AAM into a global enterprise, had that fellow's number. He arranged to have that house bathed in bright lights from early morning until late at night. Soon the owner contacted us to make a deal. To us, this confirmed our suspicions that it would be hard to run a thriving trade in illegal drugs when you are in a spotlight. Thank you, Yogen.

Crain's Detroit Business reported:

> *American business spends millions on substance abuse prevention, but Dauch uses a bulldozer. The throng of bars, party stores and crack houses that once surrounded his American Axle & Manufacturing Inc., complex in Detroit has disappeared quietly since Dauch and a group of investors bought the giant automotive-parts supplier.*
>
> *The latest to succumb to his bulldozer was Happy's Bar on Lumpkin Avenue near Hamtramck. Like the liquor-selling establishments before it, Happy's passing last week was marked only with a finely graded dirt parking lot.*
>
> *American Axle has offered to buy up a half-dozen nearby bars and party stores—in one case $500,000—to eliminate the impact of alcohol and drugs*

in the workplace, according to a dozen interviews with United Auto Workers officials and home and bar owners in the area.

An unknown number of drug houses and hideouts for stolen cars, which also populated the turn-of-the-century industrial neighborhood surrounding the former General Motors Corp. complex, also have been acquired and bull-dozed, according to Detroit police.

"It used to be a terrible area," said Donald Chalmers, patrol inspector for the city's 13th precinct, but "it is definitely a safer place now."

"I wish we had more companies in Detroit that cleaned up their area like that," he said.

Larry King, president of UAW local 235, which represented UAW workers at the Detroit plants, said at the time that the rank and file were not complaining.

Also not complaining were the minister and parishioners of the Russell Street Missionary Baptist Church that serves the local community. I believe the churches in Detroit are positive forces in a city woefully short of positive forces. My wife Sandy and I reached out to the local church. We visited there several times, getting to know the minister and offering assurance that AAM would respect and support the church. Several of my senior staff accompanied us on these visits.

We kept our word to Rev. Anthony Campbell and the church. It sits there still amid a green landscape of grass and trees that surround AAM's gleaming, well-kept factories. The new minister is Dr. DeeDee Coleman. We continue to work closely with her and her congregation. We were proud to have Dr. Coleman participate in the ceremony dedicating our new world headquarters on July 23, 2004.

Altogether, we bought and dismantled structures on 162 lots. It took a lot of money, about $8.3 million, but it enabled us to create a green oasis of manicured grass and gardens around our Detroit plants, right in the middle of one of the most depressed sections of the city.

Inside the plants, the transformation was even more dramatic. We went to work immediately to bring in more modern machinery and adopt more efficient work processes. It was a traumatic transition for all of us, management and hourly associates. There was a crisis every fifteen minutes as we began the wrenching process of cleaning up the mess we had purchased and persuading the workers to trust us and embrace our new system.

I never knew where the next crisis would come from. In the first few days, Dellas came to me to report that The Timken Company was refusing to ship ball bearings to us. You cannot make axles without bearings. I told George to get me the name of the Timken president and I would show him how to handle problems like this. It happened to be Joe Toot Jr. I called Mr. Toot and employed forceful language to impress upon him the necessity of keeping the bearing shipments on schedule. In fairness, I assume someone in the Timken organization had failed to recognize the name of our company and was concerned about our ability to pay. I explained the situation to Mr. Toot and the bearings came on schedule. Thank you, Joe.

One of our first orders of business was to decide which members of senior management, in particular plant managers and supervisors, would stay and which would go. In some cases, this took a few hours; in others a few months. Some of the older hands were so tied into the old GM way of doing things they just could not embrace a new management philosophy. In all honesty, I believe that GM, knowing it was going to sell the plants, had shifted some low performing salaried personnel there. In any event, they learned rapidly that they had to be 100 percent with us or 100 percent gone. Several of them would seize the opportunity and prove to be stars at AAM.

The UAW hourly associates had a choice. Under terms of the GM deal, the hourly associates could "flow back" to GM if they preferred. Since no one had ever heard of AAM, and GM was one of the world's premier companies, more than 3,500 opted to transfer back.

"The average age of those associates back in 1994 was fifty," said Delanoy. "They all had twenty-seven years of seniority or more, so we were dealing with older people set in their ways. Now here comes AAM saying you can't do it that way anymore, you have to do it differently. That is why many of them went back to GM." The ones most obstinately opposed to change were the so-called skilled-trades personnel, who had enjoyed a relatively pampered life at GM.

I was walking the plant floor one day with my eldest son Rick when a worker stepped in my path, spat at my feet, and said, "You may have bought the company, but we don't work for you." I thanked him politely for his service and walked on.* Out of earshot, I told Rick that was the mentality we were dealing with, and that was clearly one associate destined to either experience a 100 percent transformation or he would be gone.

---

* All of this discussion centers on the Detroit plants. We had similar issues going on at the plants in Buffalo and Tonawanda, New York, and in Three Rivers, Michigan, but the Detroit plants were the flagship of the company, employed the most people, and exhibited the most extreme pathologies.

Overall, more than half of the 6,500 UAW hourly workers we received from GM eventually flowed back. In Detroit, it was more like 70 percent. Some of my senior people were alarmed by this. I said not to worry, let them go. Those were the people we wanted to leave. We could then hire new people to replace them who could embrace the AAM culture. It was a difficult process. We endured a massive churning of our associates for about three years.

Fortunately, under the terms of our deal with GM, the transition was orderly. We could not have all of our experienced associates leaving at once and still produce the axles GM had to have. Thus, there were three criteria for a transfer to occur. First, the associate had to formally apply to return to GM. Second, GM had to have an opening for that associate. And third, AAM could control when the associate would be released. This enabled us to keep control of our personnel situation.

In the meantime, my team had to make certain the axles were made and delivered, the bills were paid, materials delivered, workers managed, paychecks cut—all the basic corporate duties for five widely separated plants employing 7,500 workers. My team was putting in long days, often seven days a week. It was a grueling schedule, but there was no other way. The amount of work to be done was simply astronomical. I had gone to great pains to assemble a crackerjack team of highly skilled and capable veterans to help me climb this mountain, and they fully earned their pay. I could not have done it without them. They were and are an extraordinary team.

It comes down to *leadership*. We were visible on the floor every day. We shook people's hands, looked them in the eyes, got to know their names. The next day we came back again and the day after that. We took note of what needed to get fixed. You cannot make change happen writing memos at a desk; you have to be out on the shop floor correcting problems and putting systems in place. That was what was missing. There were no charts in manufacturing areas saying whether we were running 90 percent OEE or 20 percent OEE (operating equipment effectiveness). We had to make union leadership understand that every day we would be on the floor making sure everyone came to work and that the machines were running to full capacity. We pounded it home that it was important to come to work every day and be on time. That was to be a never-ending battle, but the associates needed to understand we were shipping to sixteen assembly plants all over North America. They did not know this. No one had ever told them before. We spent a lot of time explaining why we needed to change, and the benefits that would accrue to them from change, the main one being the company would survive and they could secure their jobs. You cannot negotiate job security; in a market system like ours you have to earn it. For the next several years, the amounts on their W-2s went up and they also earned profit sharing bonuses. Those who stayed were happy.

Of course, we also found a lot of low-hanging fruit, some of it easy to fix quickly. We would pick out a department, the worst, grungiest department we could find, and invite hourly associates to stop their work for a few moments and talk to us. We asked, what are your issues today? How's your equipment running? A typical example—an associate said he had a hose leaking oil for three months. Did he call maintenance? Yes, but those guys said they would get back to me but never did. So he just kept using more oil. That was a typical situation. The associate is pouring oil into the machine and within a short period of time, it was out on the floor. Because of that, the equipment was running maybe 15–20 percent of capacity. If it was supposed to make one hundred pieces a day, it was making maybe fifteen or twenty, and of those perhaps 20 percent were acceptable quality. So we spent a lot of time getting machines to run up to specs like they were supposed to.

One of the first things Mathis noted was that the skilled-trades people who set the machines and make sure they keep working properly were housed far off to the side, some in another building, about as far away from the plant operations as they could be. These highly skilled people are essential to the operations. We relocated them to where they were needed. There was caterwauling enough to make you lie awake at night, but then that is the way life is. People hate change, even when it is in their best interest. The older they were, the more set in their ways. We had to be very firm in our direction and decisions.

We were dealing with older people who had done things the same way for twenty to thirty years, and here comes AAM saying you cannot do this the same way anymore, you have to do it differently. We needed to explain why over and over again, that the factories and workers had to change to survive, and even then could not get through to everyone. That is probably the most important reason so many of them went back to GM. In their eyes, GM provided security and an easier lifestyle.

We would focus on one area of a plant at a time, put in a new machining line, redo the entire area, including lights, floor, and paint. Meanwhile, the plants had to keep running, supplying GM with quality axles, linkages, driveshafts, and forgings.

All the while we were enduring frequent beatings from GM about the quantity and quality of our production. This, of course, is why they sold us the properties in the first place, and we understood we had to get them into shape, but we

Welcome
Lee Iacocca

September 12-16, 2005

...lity time with Lee. 2005 at AAM—WHQ.

On the Detroit shop floor with two old warhorses, Lee Iacocca and Marion Cumo, 2005.

Developing my sons with ultimate leadership roles, 2005.

Launching Chrysler's first minivan. Windsor-Ontario, Canada, 1983. Lee Iacocca, Dick Dauch, Plant Manager George Hohendorf.

My siblings—1946. Jack Dauch, Nancy Dauch, Dick Dauch, Bill Dauch, David Dauch, Gale Dauch.

Dick Dauch—gassing up Dad's 1951 Studebaker pickup.

Our little family—1961. Dick, Sandy, and Rick Dauch, Purdue University married student courts.

eiving a trophy at Purdue Award Ceremony. Hall of Fame head coach Jack Mollenkopf, student athlete
ck Dauch, head freshman football coach Al Parker, 1960.

nning for daylight, #32 Purdue fullback Dick Dauch at Camp Randall Stadium. Madison, Wisconsin, 1963.

Detroit Manufacturing Complex (DMC) 1994—Original Facility and Equipment Conditions.

Detroit Manufacturing Complex (DMC) 2011—Current Facility and Equipment Conditions.

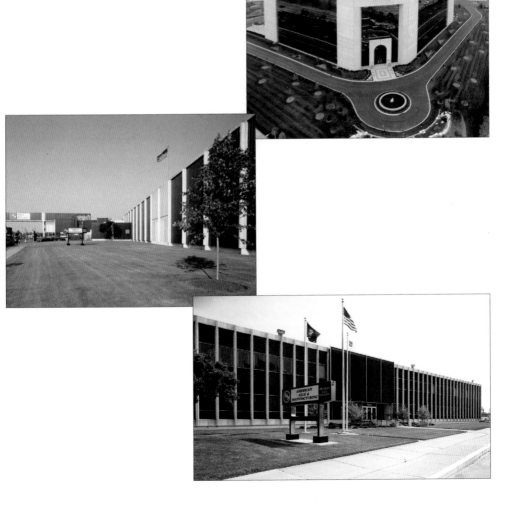

Original AAM Board of Directors—1994. Front row: Mort Harris, Jim McLernon, Ray Park, Dick Dauch. Back row: Matt Kent, Kelley Park, Dan Park.

"Ringing the Bell" at NYSE Listing, January 29, 1999. Bob Mathis, Rick Dauch, George Dellas, David Dauch, NYSE Chairman Dick Grasso, AXL-CEO Dick Dauch, Sandy Dauch, Marion Cumo, Bob Krause, Gary Witosky, Joel Robinson.

March 24, 1997. Celebrating the production of American Axle & Manufacturing's ten millionth axle are (from left to right): James A. Kline, Plant Three Area Manager; Richard H. Rossman, Vice President, Manufacturing; Richard F. Dauch, Detroit Gear & Axle Plant Manager; Tom Jones, Plant Three District Committee Man, UAW Local 235; and Richard E. Dauch, President & CEO.

August 26, 2010. Richard E. Dauch with Admiral Michael Mullen, Joint Chiefs of Staff, Detroit Marriott, Renaissance Center, discussing industry hiring of military personnel. Bill Ford, Executive Chairman, Ford Motor Company, shown at left.

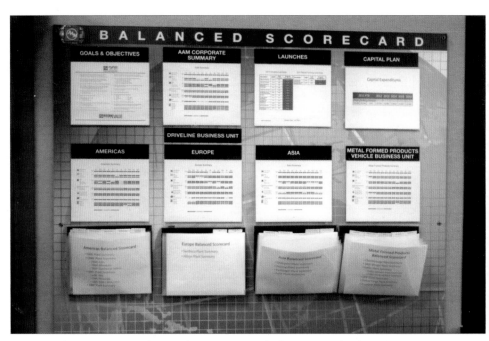

Lean manufacturing starts at the top of any company. The lean principal Balanced Scorecard, David C. Dauch, President and COO's office. This is a global operations scorecard for Safety, Quality, Delivery, and Cost. The scorecard is updated each month in his office using Green, Yellow, Red categories.

The company's Vision, Strategy, Priorities, Goals, and Objectives are all aligned. Then are cascaded to the next-level executives—Vice Presidents, Directors, and Plant Managers. They are standardized to the plant floor for associates to review daily.

could not do it overnight. We understood GM had been getting stuck with huge bills for warranties. These were the same people who for whatever reason had been unable to manage these properties effectively before we took over, but this information was of no interest to them and no use to us. We had to get better products flowing more rapidly, and until we did we would be regularly and frequently criticized. There is precious little sympathy and courtesy in manufacturing. If you need sympathy, you should look for it at home or in your church, not on the factory floor where the only thing that matters is results. You have to get the work done quickly and get it done right with consistent repetition. Manufacturing is not for the faint of heart. It requires total dedication.

At the same time, we also took on a daunting public relations challenge, convincing political leaders that the new company is a viable concern here to stay. Mathis and I made the rounds in Michigan and New York meeting with mayors, city councils, legislators, various government representatives, and Michigan governor John Engler to sell our vision of a rejuvenated AAM and to seek investments in roads and infrastructure to support a growing corporation that would soon be creating jobs in their locales. Politicians, at least state and local politicians, love manufacturing. They understand we not only create jobs in our factories, but that those factory jobs support lots of jobs in other sectors of the economy—and generate huge tax revenues.

I asked the States of Michigan and New York to chip in $10 million each to help rebuild infrastructure in the neighborhoods where our plants were located. We eventually got that funding in both states, improving our ability to produce products competitively.

At the end of March, after only thirty days of operation under new management, AAM turned a profit. This was made possible by a variety of factors. For one, the market for pickup trucks and SUVs was taking off, creating strong demand for our products. Had we launched into a market downturn, the AAM story might have turned out differently. Also we benefited from some advantageous provisions we managed to have included in the GM contract, such as the daily payments to AAM, an unheard of practice in the auto industry. So we had cash flow to draw on right off the bat. In addition, we had some favorable associate benefit payment provisions for the first two years.

The main factor, however, was elimination or significant revision of the pegs. Suddenly our machines were producing at the levels they were designed for. Our OEE shot up overnight, as did our cash flow. By the end of March, we had increased axle production from 9,500 per day to more than 12,000 per day!

At the end of that first month, Ray Park directed a full audit of the books.

He could not believe the company had become profitable so quickly. Ray was ever and always a realist and knew full well how easily some people can "cook the books" to make a business seem more successful than it is. But our results were real. That first year, AAM recorded a profit of $66 million. Performance drives profits. We were building value for the enterprise.

I took a deep breath on March 31. I had wanted to be CEO of an American-owned, Detroit-based automotive company. My vision was to create an entirely new automotive Tier One global supply company to compete with the big boys throughout the world such as Dana, Meritor, TRW, GKN, ZF, and Eaton. But before we could go global, we had to succeed and prosper in Detroit. I wanted our headquarters to be based in Detroit and to profitably grow in Detroit. My intentions were to buy it, fix it, and make it world class. The fledgling company was off and running, but the future was anything but certain. I knew we were into a classic two-chinstrap game.

4

Forging a New Culture

You change the culture of a company by changing the culture of its leaders.

—*Larry Bossidy,*
Retired chairman and CEO of Allied
Signal, later chairman of Honeywell

"To be good is noble," said Mark Twain, "but to teach others to be good is nobler, and a lot less trouble."

With all due respect to Mark Twain, when you aspire to get people to change their attitudes and behavior, you have to lead by example. The first and most overriding challenge we faced when we created American Axle & Manufacturing was to create a new *culture*—a positive one based on *integrity* of purpose and commitment to quality work. Of all the obstacles we had to surmount—raising investment capital, negotiating the asset purchase sale with GM, reaching an accord with the UAW, grasping the reins of a far-flung empire, cleaning up the facilities, adopting advanced technology and processes, upgrading quality, positioning to go global—perhaps none was more complex and daunting than that of remolding a defeatist culture that prevailed among the associates working at the facilities we purchased. The key to any manufacturing operation is people, and the people working at the operations purchased from the GM Saginaw Division had been caught up in a dysfunctional situation for so long, they accepted it as normal.

We inherited a dispirited workforce, apprehensive about potentially losing their jobs and their futures. It was not that they did not want to do good work. I am sure most of them did, but given the situation they were in, good work was not always doable. And they were skeptical about us, to put it mildly. No one had ever heard of American Axle; we were a new company. Many people outside the company did not expect us to survive the first year. We also had GM's "access and security"* agreement hanging over our heads. The workers were quite naturally anxious about their futures.

We were determined to change that situation, to allay their anxieties and forge a new culture based on teamwork, open communication, and commitment, to bring in modern technology and advanced work processes, to create a work environment where people would thrive, grow, and be productive—not only to make their jobs doable, but to make them enjoyable and productive. We had also a core message to deliver—that the world was changing all around us and that, like it or not, *global competition,* more brutal and relentless than anything we had seen before, was here to stay. If we wanted to survive, and if they wanted to keep their jobs, we had to develop a new positive attitude. The old ways of doing business would have to go.

However, you cannot change a corporate culture by issuing memos from the executive suite. You have to go to the shop floor, get to know your associates one on one, speak to them in person, let them see you and question you, listen to their suggestions and sell them on a new vision. The CEO is first and foremost a salesman, and never more so than to his own people. When you say you are going to do something, you must do it, even when it is not convenient. *Culture is a mind-set and changing it is a process.* You cannot do it overnight.

Make no mistake, when you speak to associates about embracing a new set of values about their work and their relationship to the new company—a new culture—you will not get far if it is only words. Like Mark Twain said, anyone can give advice. Talk is cheap. Your people will listen respectfully to what you say, but they will watch what you do and make up their own minds if your words are for real. They are looking for actions. When there is a noticeable gap between your words and your deeds, you will be dismissed as a fraud, and rightly so. When I speak to the importance of ethics and values, whether to my associates or my family or a college graduating class, it is understood that those ethics and values begin with me. To be effective, it's not enough to talk the talk, you have to walk the walk.

The old GM plants we bought were dark, dirty, decrepit, and dangerous. The machinery was loud and obsolete, prone to breakdowns. The air was dark-

---

* The "access and security" agreement basically provided that if we failed to deliver the goods, GM could reassume control of our plants and equipment.

ened by oily mist. Safety guarding was off and switches were routinely by-passed. Injuries were commonplace, some of them fatal. There was deception and cheating on production reports. There was drinking, drug abuse, and prostitution going on in and around the plants. The parking lots around the plants were littered with trash; graffiti was everywhere. You cannot expect people in that kind of environment to have a positive attitude toward their work or to be productive. Also, they knew the factories they worked in were inefficient and in danger of being shuttered.

The mayor of Buffalo, New York, Anthony Masiello, had toured our Buffalo plant a couple of years before we took over, and recalled seeing despair and uncertainty on the face of the workers. By the end of 1994, he said the workers were smiling and hopeful. "It's a new era and a new time," he said.

That observation reflected a change in culture taking place. The fundamental key to forging a new, positive, and responsible culture is unyielding integrity, up and down the line, and the first and clearest definition of integrity is simple honesty and candor. This is not baseball; nobody around here is allowed to do any stealing. I do not care if it's an operator filching a tool from the shop floor or an office associate sending out personal mail through the company postage meter, it is not tolerated. The first time you make a mistake of that nature, you are out of here. There will be no second instance—zero tolerance!

First and foremost, integrity is the foundation of our relationship with our own people. If we expect them to exhibit integrity in their work and with our customers, we have to treat them with integrity. We were committed from the beginning to convey our commitment to creating a positive workplace environment where everyone has a chance to grow and succeed, without regard to any external issues. We inherited a racially diverse workforce from General Motors, but only 7 percent of our associates were female when we launched in 1994. Because of computerization and advances in technology, there are very few jobs in the modern industrial workplace that require substantial physical strength, and no reason women could not play a more active role. Within four years we had the female component up to 20 percent of our workforce. American Axle was and remains totally committed to equal opportunity.

For people to take advantage of that opportunity, they must expand their skill sets and have a healthy attitude toward continued learning. The first year, we budgeted $10 million for worker training. We have made it a basic guideline that every associate gets approximately fifty hours of training every year. Multiply that by ten thousand or however many associates we have had at a given moment and you are talking real money, but it is part and parcel of our commitment to our people. In turn, we expect them to be willing and eager to learn and we provide support, including aid to associates who want to pursue studies at local colleges or universities. In some cases, we even bring the college course work right to our factory locations.

Integrity obviously means honesty in financials. In recent years, we have seen more than one great business run aground on the rocks of financial deceit. There is obvious incentive for any company to manipulate the numbers—to please stockholders, secure good credit ratings, and attract new investors—but once you start down that slippery slope, it gets mighty hard to get back on solid ground. I have made it abundantly clear since day one at American Axle that our financial reports are to be totally up front about our situation, regardless of how those reports may affect our agenda, bottom line and stock price.

This is not as simple as it may sound. Corporate financial reports are extremely complex, and the nation's tax laws are even more intricate. Getting it right takes a lot of time and effort. When I took over this operation there were two certified public accountants (CPAs) on board. Today we have more than forty.

I have spent a lifetime acquiring a reputation for character and integrity. I could lose that reputation in a millisecond with one devious financial report. We go over every number time and again until we are absolutely certain it is correct.

When you see a financial report from American Axle, you can take it to the bank—or to the brokerage, as the case may be. We have integrity—of people, product, and financials. And we share the financial information with the people on the shop floor, including the UAW, which represents a significant component of our workforce. "They've shared financial information with us that we'd never see from General Motors," said William P. Webster, who served as bargaining chairman of UAW Local 2093, representing our plant in Three Rivers, Michigan. We always played fair and square with Webster, one of the UAW's real forward-thinking officers. He was always square with us, an honest and team-oriented leader. Largely because of him, Three Rivers survived the downturn and continues to prosper years after Webster retired. He had integrity and leadership skill.

Integrity means quality products. We strive with every fiber of our intelligence and energy to produce world-class products in a never-ending quest for perfection. If we see a better technology that produces a finer quality than what we have, we acquire that technology, whatever its cost and wherever we have to go to get it. If we find a process that helps us advance the quality frontier, we embrace it and put it to work. We are always investing in research and development of products, processes, and systems in a never-ending quest to raise the bar. As *Automotive Engineering* magazine noted in 2000, "In its first year, American Axle made 9000 axles a day and they were not of the best quality. Six years and $1 billion later, volume has doubled and quality as measured in discrepancies at parts per million (ppm) [*has improved 99 percent,*] (italics mine) with more than 95 percent of the company's products at 0 ppm." Today we are achieving 0 ppm at several of our plants! We are not at that level everywhere, not yet, but we will continue working on it until we are, and then will find ways to raise the bar higher. American Axle products must and do have integrity.

Integrity also means elbow grease. We are all here to work. If you are accepting a paycheck and not working, you are stealing. Like I said, this is not baseball. I acquired my values early on as the youngest son of a solid dairy-farm family in Ohio. Like all dairy farms, it was a sunup to sundown operation. Dad always said, "I only want half your time." So in a twenty-four-hour day, we only had to work twelve hours. After that we could go to school, eat dinner, do our lessons, play sports, and sometimes grab a little sleep.

I report this not to complain, but to explain. I work long hours but I don't believe I have ever worked harder than my father did, and he lived to the age of ninety-five. Work is a tonic for what ails you. I bring *energy* with me to the work and I expect the people who report to me to do the same. There is nothing in this world quite as beneficial to our economy, our society, and our people as hard work, discipline, and teamwork. I am known as a demanding boss, but that is the price of success. We all want to succeed and hard work is the key. The only place I know where success comes before work is in the dictionary. In any comprehensive definition of integrity, I would include a person's work ethic.

Integrity also means doing what's right with the people you deal with in business, the people you supply, and the people who supply you. You always have to do what is right, not what is popular. All around me I see people in business trying to gain advantage through one-sided deal making. Given the intense competition we are contending with, I suppose that is only natural. We all want to cut a good deal, but in the long term it is self-defeating. You cannot have a win for one party and a gouge for the other; there is no trust in that relationship. That's one reason why we're seeing so many companies in the auto sector go belly up. That is one big reason American Axle survived—we have always played it straight with our suppliers, our customers and our workforce.

Integrity means not being trampled by events. Manufacturing is a very competitive business, not for the faint of heart. The realities of life intrude at the most inopportune moments. The important thing is to go into it with a positive attitude, open-minded and business oriented, and then work at it as a team from open, objective analysis, not emotion. I tell my people, never let yourself get frustrated. Get remotivated. Working together, we always find a way through the minefields. There is a fulfillment in overcoming difficult situations that you cannot find anywhere else.

If you put in forty years in an average career, you are going to have to endure and adapt to at least three wars, at least one depression, at least five recessions, and probably two or three catastrophic events. Nobody is going to feel sorry for us, so I don't give many sympathy calls around here. I tell them to suck it up, adjust, life is real but not necessarily fair. Let's focus on what we can do better than the competition. Get on with the game.

We knew forging a new culture at the new American Axle & Manufacturing would be a long-term project, actually an endless project. Nothing scares adults more than change in their lives. I knew the transformation of going from GM to American Axle would cause great anxiety for the workforce. They were being asked to leave one of the great pillars of our country, one of the greatest companies in history, indeed at one time the biggest company in the world, for a new enterprise of uncertain promise. I knew that going from an adversarial work environment that prevailed with GM and the UAW to a situation where the company and union worked together would be a shock. They must have all felt like strangers in a strange land, at least at first.

Yet the crew of auto industry veterans I assembled to help me manage this undertaking knew me and what I stood for, and what I aimed to achieve. They knew we would sink our teeth into the challenge and turn it every which way but loose. Indeed, I believe that is probably what drew them into the job, which for many was the second or third time around with me. Many of them had worked with me at GM, Chrysler, or Volkswagen of America, some at all three places. They were retired or doing other things. They did not need the money— but they needed a challenge, and to be part of something bigger than themselves. I believe we all do. As we would soon find out, creating American Axle was all the challenge we imagined, and then some.

If you do not know where you're going, any road is as good as another. From the beginning, we knew exactly where we were going. We wanted American

Axle to be a truthful company, a company with integrity, a company based on open, honest communication among our men and women with a clear understanding of what we were there for—to create precision, world-class, high-technology products and to make money for our shareholders.

Like any business, we have to make a profit or perish. That is the ultimate determinant of whether our venture or any private sector venture will succeed. One of our first important achievements was to deal with the mechanical and process issues that caused frequent interruptions of the work flow, leading to expensive overtime work on weekends to make up for lost production. Obviously this was an inefficient and costly way to operate, and it really did not take a lot of effort to curtail it. The main problem was that the production and maintenance personnel resisted our changes because they had come to depend on the extra pay they got from overtime work. They saw it as part of their expected compensation package. This was one of our first direct confrontations with the old corrupt culture that we were determined to change. There was a lot of grumbling, but we were able to sharply reduce the overtime while increasing production, efficiency and quality.

The key to our success was and remains our commitment to creating and maintaining a new culture based on integrity, teamwork, and great products.

Culture is the fabric of who and what you are, what you stand for, your sense of self, your core values. You contribute to the culture you are in and you draw strength from it. When you are operating in a healthy culture, you make tough decisions even when they create difficulties because they are right, and you know your colleagues and superiors will back you up because they are part of the same culture. It is one for all, and all for one.

THE FIVE C'S

I focus on what I call the five C's in this company, and they are key elements of American Axle culture:

Number one is Character by which I mean the ability to know the difference between the right thing and the wrong thing, and a solid inclination to do the right thing. Many people gain adulthood with serious character flaws of one kind or another. Perhaps it is a debilitating vice or maybe just a propensity for deceitful behavior. In business management, we sometimes encounter people who try to manipulate their way up the ladder instead of earning it, by exaggerating their contributions and denigrating those of their colleagues. That kind of behavior sticks out like a sore thumb around here, and we do not tolerate it. Character flaws are all too common, and if allowed to fester can poison a company culture. Reluctance to take aggressive personnel actions to remove such people is one of the most common managerial failings in many companies, but not at AAM.

Second, we look for Competency. All of the character in the world will not get you by if you don't know what you are doing. We are a business, not a government agency, and we have to turn a profit. Profits become elusive when your people are not meeting their responsibilities. When we have people who are not performing, our first reaction is to help them figure out why and address the problem. If it is an operator on the shop floor, maybe there is a problem with a machine or a process. If it is someone in the professional ranks, maybe they need more training or education. We help them get it.

Our core competencies are very simple. We designed them in 1993 and they have not changed. *Engineering* is the left bookend. The right bookend is *validation* of the product, process and system. In between is the manufacturing value added by *forging, machining, welding, heat treatment* and *assembly*. Underpinning it all is a steady stream of innovation reflecting our commitment to research and development. The end result is world-class quality products executed with a precision down to tolerances less than the width of a human hair, products made of top-quality steel, aluminum, and metallics that last a long time and add value and utility to the vehicles in which they are installed. That is it. Easy to say, hard to do, so I demand consistent precision of execution. We always strive for perfection.

We are absolutely fanatical about training and education. We will always go the extra mile to help our people improve their performance, but nobody gets a free pass. Sooner or later, it is up to you.

The third C is Confidentiality because we are routinely dealing with enormously proprietary issues. We invest huge amounts of resources into research and development because we understand the technology curve is constantly bending and if we are to grow and prosper, we must stay ahead of that curve. It is a matter of fierce pride to me that almost 90 percent of our products were developed in the last five years, and it is a key factor in our continuing success. Yet it does us little good to develop innovative products and processes if careless associates are going to share our proprietary information with the competition. *Never feed the enemy.* The same applies to financial information. Our associates understand that what happens at American Axle stays at American Axle.

The fourth C is Chemistry as in among people, not a laboratory. There are quite a few former athletes on the AAM team and there may be a good reason for that. Athletes have a teamwork ethic, at least the good ones do, and they bring it with them to the job. We support and encourage individual effort, but it has been my experience that it's when we put our egos aside and work together as a team that we really make progress. A member of a team is always willing to let someone else take the spotlight if that moves the team closer to the goal. I feel chemistry at work when I see coworkers fully engaged, having fun, encouraging each other and getting results.

The fifth C stands for Class which is what American Axle is and will ever strive to maintain. From the outset, our overriding goal has been to create a class company that produces world-class products, that enjoys a reputation for honesty, reliability, and value in which our associates can take pride. We are a class outfit, from top to bottom, and it is all based upon integrity and commitment to the team.

GETTING THERE

Our people started to transition to our new culture and accept it during the first two years. It helped that our first year, 1994, was successful, in that we were profitable. As I noted earlier, we were lucky in part because it was a good year for the automobile and truck business. But a big part of our luck was the simple fact that we knew what we were doing, we had clearly defined goals, and we were working as a united team to get there.

Our people saw the changes taking place all about them. They not only kept their jobs but saw their take-home pay begin to grow. The plants they worked in rapidly became cleaner, more cheerful, brighter, safer, and more efficient. They were getting new, more advanced machinery with which to work. By 1995, we were seeing a compounded annual growth rate (CAGR), the most meaningful measure of progress, of 8 percent! The people began to see there was a direct link between what we said we were going to do, and what we were actually doing. In 1996, we grew again, this time a bit over 8 percent CAGR, and more of our people were beginning to believe in our vision and to buy into it. The associates were also receiving eye-popping profit-sharing checks, significantly larger than what GM employees were getting.

We were off and running in a new direction with a steady drumbeat of open and timely communication. I majored in management in college, not communications, but the first chance I had to take an elective course, I chose speech. I knew I would need communication skills in manufacturing, and I have put that knowledge to good use over the last forty-eight years.

In the first few months, I and senior members of my team went to every plant and office where we addressed all of our associates personally, all 7,500 of them. We spoke to them in groups and to the extent humanly possible met with them one-on-one. First of all, we wanted to make certain that they knew we wanted them to stay; second, that we were prepared to invest in their future— both new technology on the shop floor and training; and third, that we would allow a process for them to determine their own future over a three-to-four-year cycle, deciding whether they wanted to stay with American Axle or return to General Motors. I believe these sessions reduced a great deal of the anxiety and uncertainty.

We made it clear we wanted everyone involved and that we welcomed input and ideas. For example, early on at our Three Rivers plant we found that suggestions were backlogged and took on average 158 days to be evaluated and acted upon. Granted, we run a complex business and sometimes it takes a lot of time to evaluate the advisability of a suggestion. Still, 158 days is just too long. In 2002, we tried a new approach. Ideas would be prescreened for an hour every Monday by the plant manager's staff, the manufacturing manager, manufacturing area managers, and UAW associates. The response time dropped to no more than ninety-four days, but we were still not satisfied. We moved to prescreening ideas every morning. We got the turnaround time down to fifty-eight days. Of 696 associate ideas received that year, 174 were adopted. That's how you get your people to buy into your program, to feel valued and respect the system.

Plant manager Tom Delanoy was quoted in *The Detroit News*: "The old ways don't work. We have to lift up the rugs and see the dirt and admit it's there and clean it up. Supervisors who have been foremen for 20–25 years are used to kicking ass and taking names. I don't want no ass kicking and name taking around here. We're going to build axles with people."

I couldn't have said it better. Delanoy, a great friend, was one of American Axle's best managers, and it was a sad but proud day for the company when he retired.

I think an even more telling quote in that same newspaper article about American Axle was from one of our lathe operators, a woman named Gwen Turner: "They let us know we are necessary and appreciated," she said. "Dick Dauch is either a genius or magician with a magic wand."

Soon many associates who had opted to return to General Motors were having second thoughts, and were inquiring about returning to American Axle. I was not surprised. Word was getting around that we offered a new vision of the future, and we were soon paying larger profit-sharing payments than GM. However, their return was not allowed by our agreement with GM. GM didn't want associates jumping back and forth, and neither did we. That kind of turmoil causes confusion and disarray on the factory floor. The flow back to GM was a one-way street. They had their chance and passed on it. The American Axle train had left the station. Life is a series of choices. Once you make your decisions, you have to live with the consequences.

In the final analysis, integrity to me means faith: faith in God, faith in our country, faith in our shared values, faith in our families and coworkers, and—perhaps most important of all—faith in the future. In these days of economic turmoil, terrorism, and international tensions, it's easy to despair of what the future holds. I believe that despite whatever troubles beset us and hardships we have to work through, we will as a nation come through them stronger, wiser, and better, like we always have.

When an avalanche hits, as it hit us in 2008–2009 with a withering strike followed by the worst economic downturn in generations, you have to take a deep breath, keep your cool, and rely on your experience, team, and faith. We did not go running around with an ax cutting expenses here, there, and everywhere like some of our competitors did. We had to lay off associates, and we were as generous with them as we could be, but we did not cut back on research and development, nor did we stop funding for our wonderful summer intern program where we bring in bright young people to begin their careers in the automotive business. That is the future we are talking about, and come what may American Axle will never betray the future. A healthy company is always investing in the future, even when it may appear it cannot afford it. In fact, I know of many companies that *have saved their way into bankruptcy.*

The companies that have survived this brutally competitive industry and shakeout of automotive suppliers have adhered to a few basic principles:

- They invest in people
- They invest in new, high-tech product, process equipment and systems technologies
- They continue to invest in R&D, regardless of the economic climate
- They proactively support critical engineering and maintenance functions

- While they respect the past, they focus on the future, meeting the changing needs of their customer base and the marketplace
- And they continue to build their companies with a global presence and competitiveness.

We take our principles seriously, and that is the main reason we have survived and prospered.

5

The Early Years

Obstacles are those frightful things you see when you take
your eyes off your goal.

—Henry Ford

We had lofty goals when we launched American Axle & Manufacturing. We wanted to be a world-class company. We wanted to go global. We wanted to adopt new technologies and create new products. We wanted to earn a reputation for quality and consistency—to be on the cutting edge of innovation. And yes, we wanted to grow and make good profits.

But as the old saying goes, when you are up to your ass in alligators, it is hard to remember you came to drain the swamp.

Our first challenge was to clean up the mess we had acquired—and without question it was a first-class mess. For years, the bean counters at GM had starved the axle and drivetrain plants in the Saginaw Division, foregoing routine maintenance, allowing machines and buildings to deteriorate, and virtually ceding control of the factory floors to the unions. Unfortunately, there was no extra time built into our takeover strategy—we had to start delivering axles to GM the day we took over. We had a lot of work to do before we could even think about our lofty goals, never mind make them a reality.

We rolled up our sleeves and plunged in. It was basically just me and my small team. We had no office bureaucracy to handle routine chores like letters and copying and errands—we had to do everything ourselves. We were working long hours of the kind when you go to work before dark and come home after dark, just taking it on faith that there is such a thing as sunshine. And you hope that just maybe there's a light at the end of the tunnel.

From the beginning, we launched an aggressive communications outreach program to let the associates know who we were, what we aspired to achieve, and the opportunities we would provide for them—the most important one being an opportunity to continue working.

I am comfortable before a crowd. I acquired lots of speaking experience over the years and have put it to good use. My investment partner Ray Park gave me high marks for my oratorical skills. "Dick was talking to a group of people in a restaurant back when we were first putting the deal together," he recalled. "By the time he finished, half the people in the restaurant who were not even in the meeting wanted to come work for him."

On another occasion, not long after we launched the company, we were having a big rally with AAM associates, suppliers, local political leaders, the mayor of Detroit, and Michigan governor John Engler. I gave my standard "charge the barricades" speech. I was pumped up that day, as I am most days, and I got everyone in the room pumped up, too. Everyone was yelling and cheering. Governor Engler, who is no slouch himself in the oratory department, turned to Ray Park and said, "Now what in the hell am I supposed to say after that?"

We were on the floor every day observing the work processes, talking to associates, identifying problems, and whacking away at the more obvious issues that had been allowed to fester for months or years. We had a major quality problem that I knew would take time to fix, so there was no time to waste.

"We were in those plants day and night," said Cumo. "The first year I did not take a vacation. I stayed home Christmas Day, that was it. We were all going flat out wearing different hats. Dick would call in the middle of the day and say, 'Come meet me.' He needed to get away from the paperwork for a little bit, walk the floor, talk to the associates on the line. That was a basic part of Dick Dauch's management style, getting to know everyone who worked there. He loved that and he knew I loved it, too."

"We would all sit down together as a group, discuss our successes and our failures, what we would do differently the next day," said Rossmann. "We were inseparable. We believed in our basic values, and we would not let any one of us fall down. We were in the factory all of the time. Dick said, 'I want you to know everybody's name within a year, and I'm going to test you.' I gave it my best shot. I learned most of them. We just kept at it."

Delanoy was assigned to the Detroit axle plant that really needed aggressive hands-on management. "I was out there every day, walking the floor, waking people up, getting to know everyone," Delanoy said. "They are thinking they will never see me again, but they soon learned different. I was out there every day. I took my staff with me. We're walking the lines, looking for problems. We would pick out the worst section, invite the hourly associates to come off their jobs and talk, discuss their problems.

For some of our associates, this was like manna from heaven. They had been trying to do quality work for years in a situation that simply did not encourage, or in some cases even permit, quality work. They never had any direct contact with senior management. Now they had ready access to me and all of my team.

An excellent example was Al Knight, a twenty-eight-year GM veteran machine operator when we set up shop in 1994. Until we appeared on the scene, no one had ever asked Knight to do anything other than show up and run his machine. But we were communicating with all of our associates, inviting suggestions and looking for talent, and in Knight we found a real gem. For years, Knight had been writing technical manuals about gear cutting on his home computer, three manuals in all. We soon had him training other associates in the finer points of making quality gears. "This is a big change in my life," he said. It was also a big change in the lives of other associates who were able to learn from him, and who also realized AAM had a different way of doing business.

One of my first hires was Joel Robinson, who had worked with me at Chrysler and who would eventually serve as AAM president. "When I walked in, it looked like a hell hole," he said. "We all sat in this one room. Tiles were broken. The furniture didn't match. I went out on the floor in plant #3. I opened a door to go into the factory. Holy smoke, it's not running. I could hear people snoring. Half the lights were burned out. Fuel was running on the floor. It was the worst I had ever seen. I went back into the office, addressed the GM guy who had been held over and demanded to know how he could run a factory like this. He looked embarrassed."

In fact, we would find that quite a few of the GM managers were highly capable and would flourish under AAM's management. Whether hourly associates on the plant floor or managers in the front office, people need to know they are part of a credible organization, that they are valued, that the work they do matters. That requires constant communication and repetition. "Dick, Bob Mathis, and I personally interviewed more than five hundred salaried personnel, deciding who we should keep," said Rossmann. "The first thing we had to do was convince these people we were worth taking a chance on. We told them if you work with us, we can make this company viable. If you don't work with us, it will be broken up, someone else will get it, and you will lose your jobs and benefits."

"We had to win over individual workers," Robinson said. "We had meetings after or during a shift, with one group at each plant at a time. The first meetings were mainly bitch sessions, and that was to be expected. But soon they became less focused on bitching and more focused on business metrics, something the hourly associates had never heard of. We had to build a new culture brick by brick. It takes a long time to change attitudes."

Along with the new culture we had to rebuild the mechanical infrastructure of our axle and drivetrain plants. All of our facilities were saddled with the old, five-cut, wet cut gear technology that had been standard in the industry for many decades. It was inefficient, it produced uneven quality, and it filled the air with oily mist. You literally could not see from one side of the plant to another even though we had air filters working constantly. It was a major reason for the ghastly error rate of almost 14,000 ppm that we inherited. "I had never seen 14,000 ppm before," said Robinson. "I couldn't believe it. It was time to throw the baby out with the bathwater."

I knew it would take time to deal with the quality challenge, but it was horrendous and there was no time to waste. I challenged my guys to cut that 14,000 (actually 13,441) ppm rate in half every year. So the first year we got it down to 6,500—still terrible. The next year we got it down to 3,250 or thereabouts. By year four we were down to 700, still bad but much better. By then we had the defect problem on the run. People were beginning to believe in AAM.

One of the most critical phases of our process is the production of ring gears that are essential to axles and drivetrains. These are heavy-duty steel components that interact with each other. If they are not cut precisely to mesh, the steel will grind loudly and wear out quickly, causing a noisy ride in the vehicle and leading to warranty problems. I was aware of more advanced gear-cutting technologies that were available, one from the Swiss-German company Oerlikon and another from the U.S. firm Gleason, that involved only two cuts and did not fill the air with oil. Which to choose? We had to make the right decision because it entailed a massive infusion of cash and we would have to live with the results for a long time.

Rossmann hatched a plan. He cleared out a large bay area in one of the plants, forty feet by eighty feet, and installed two machines, one Oerlikon and one Gleason, side by side. I have always said that to have a really good horse race, you need at least two horses. We allowed our associates to work with both machines for sixty days. We found advantages to both systems. We ended up buying gear-generating equipment from Oerlikon and blade-sharpening equipment from Gleason. Seventeen years later we are still working with both suppliers. The decision process was effective.

"Going from five-cut, wet cut to two-cut, dry cut was a pure technology transition that helped our efficiency tremendously," said Delanoy. "A lot of our hourly folks didn't like it because it made good pieces too quickly. They wanted to run their old machines at a leisurely pace. We had ten people doing one person's job, and they liked it that way. We were making a mind-boggling change that made a big difference. That was one of the easiest things we did—bringing in new technology. The tough part was the training. The hourly associates did not want to learn how to use the new technology and lose all of that overtime."

We made the transition from five-cut, wet cut to two-cut, dry cut at our Detroit plant first, then Buffalo, New York, and finally in Three Rivers, Michigan. It took a lot of money and a good bit of time to install the new equipment and train the workers for the new system, but it was well worth the investment. We got better quality products for less cost, we got cleaner and safer working facilities, and our associates could readily see we meant business about improving the quality of their environment and work life.

I insisted on more precise heat treatment of our gears. Once the gears are formed, they must be heat treated to make the steel hard enough to take the pounding of constant wear and tear in the vehicle. Our heat-treat ovens were running between 1,700 and 2,200 degrees Fahrenheit, with a 100-degree variance. I insisted they get that variance down to 5 degrees. By creating tight, controllable heat systems, we all but eliminated warpage and scrap. Little things like that can make all the difference in quality—and warranty costs.

On forging, I insisted we move from conventional gear forging to near net shape and ultimately net shape. On welding, we went from puddle welds to slug welds. Each piece was part of the overall puzzle of bringing an outdated facility up to date with the latest technology.

To send a message to everyone, both inside and outside AAM, I ordered the return of the limousines being used by President Bill Clinton and Vice President Al Gore. They were GM products with axles and drivetrains made by the old regime. At our expense, we replaced those with quality AAM parts. I did not want the senior leaders of our country riding around in defective and noisy vehicles.

By October 1994, we announced we would invest $19 million in a new painting facility in our Buffalo plant. This was in large measure a reflection of changing consumer tastes. About 80 percent of the axles made in that plant went on minivans, light trucks, and SUVs where they were in plain view. At the time, about half of the axles from that plant were sent to a subcontractor in Michigan for painting, and the others were not painted. "This is American Axle's entrée into the painting business," said plant manager Al Monich, one of the holdovers from GM who would prove to be one of our most capable, reliable and versatile managers. We made it known we were planning to add four hundred associates at the Buffalo axle plant and the Tonawanda forge not far away. We were off and running.

We knew space, time, and dollars were limited, so we were careful. The new painting system, installed in about nine months, featured nearly 1.5 miles of conveyor, robots, and other automated equipment, enough to paint 6,000 axles a day, all in 67,000 square feet of space. The secret to our success was *concurrent engineering* of the building, conveyors, and process equipment—all put in place as the building was erected. We performed extensive computer simulation to ensure that the new conveyor system and the existing manufacturing system would not logjam each other.

The identification of each type of axle was maintained throughout the painting process to provide part-specific instructions to the painting robots. Radio frequency identification (RFID) permitted axles to be racked with like parts for shipment from the paint facility on just-in-time delivery to customers throughout the Eastern and Midwestern states, as well as Canada.

During the mid-1990s, we made substantial investments in our axle plant in Buffalo and our forge in Tonawanda. The list of capital improvements included a "hot-former" machine to produce gears and wheel spindle hubs, a "cold header" unit and a 700-ton press for tie-rod sockets, a 1,600-ton mechanical shear, a 4,000-ton forging press for ring gears, and four electric discharge machining (EDM) units for die manufacturing. The development of net-shape gears also necessitated the purchase of two 1,000-ton forging presses and a graphite machining center. It was a lot of money, but quality manufacturing demands substantial capital investment. "We are investing in our associates and factories," I told the *Buffalo News*. "Our people must have the best equipment to work with if we are to remain competitive in the global market."

Another aspect of the investment in Buffalo was our continuing campaign to negotiate more flexible working arrangements with the UAW. At that time, we employed about 2,000 associates at the Buffalo plant and 800 more at the Tonawanda forge. The UAW local in Buffalo was tough but receptive to our concerns when they saw we were serious about upgrading the facilities. "We're giving them the flexibility needed to meet global markets," said UAW Local 424 president John Kennedy. "We want job stability. In order to have that, you have to grow the business. In order to grow the business, you have to stay in business." Kennedy was one of a small group of enlightened UAW leaders who grasped the reality of globalization. Regrettably, he was in the minority, but he helped us immensely in the early days.

Meanwhile, back in Detroit, we were installing two new "upsetters" in plant #3 of Detroit Forge. They are big, loud machines that transform iron bars into axle shafts. They cost $5 million. We spent another $5 million renovating the forge tool and die room—the heart and soul of a good forge operation.

We saved money and improved quality by getting better control of inventory. We began using returnable containers, which eliminated messy cardboard packaging. We got rid of the old, oily conveyer systems and installed more advanced computer-numerical-controlled (CNC) tooling. Piece by piece, we were remaking the AAM industrial landscape.

New equipment was a key part of the equation, and so was upgrading worker skills. "Our goal is to breathe new life into these factories and the workforce," I told a reporter from *The Windsor* (Ontario) *Star*. "To that end, we will be spending about $10 million on 360,000 hours of training for our [associates] in the first year of business."

The reporter misquoted me. I did not say "employees," I said "associates." We call them associates because they are much more than just hired hands. They are our partners, vital participants in the conduct of our business.

By December 1994, less than a year after we launched, we announced we would build a new Technical Center in Rochester Hills, about forty minutes north of the Detroit facilities. "Establishment of the Technical Center is part of AAM's commitment to the future and our plan for success in leading the industry in the design, manufacture, and delivery of quality driveline systems," I told a reporter. "The facility will include a state of the art metallurgical laboratory, product test and validation facilities with driveline dynamometers and a noise reduction room. We also will include an advanced manufacturing process development and validation center."

Perhaps the most revolutionary concept we introduced into the plant floors that first year was a simple fax machine. Up until then, customers who had problems with the products had to go through a bureaucratic maze in GM's front office. We had no bureaucracy and no maze. We put in fax machines so the complaints could go directly to the people making the axles. They communicated directly with the customers. What a concept!

As mentioned before, after ten months of operation we had racked up a $66 million profit. In March 1995, we paid our associates profit-sharing checks averaging $1,349. The people who left us to return to GM received $550 each. Predictably, the ex-AAM crowd was unhappy, but as UAW Local 235 president

Ronnie Allen said, "They did it on their own." Among the happy recipients of the profit sharing were 1,300 new AAM associates we had hired to replace the ones who left. The new hires were younger and better educated than the ones who left, a trend that would continue in the years ahead.

One of our longest serving and most respected supervisors, Ben Hogan, who had begun working for GM in 1953, told me many years later of a numbers runner working at the plant at the time. Many associates that day placed bets on that profit-sharing check amount—1349—and as fate would have it, that number came in. The next day, they were all looking forward to a big payoff, but it never arrived. Ben says that fellow disappeared off the face of the earth and was never seen again, at least not in Detroit. Everyone assumed he just took the money and moved to a different town. His wife said she had no idea where he went, but two or three months later she also disappeared, or so Ben says. I am sure there is a moral to this story, but I have no idea what it might be.

After one year, we were ranked nineteenth among Michigan businesses in terms of dollar volume and fifteenth among the top OEM suppliers in North America. When we took over the company, it was making 9,000 axles a day. A year later we were producing 14,000 a day, and this was before the shift from five-cut to two-cut. AAM sales topped $1.3 billion in 1994 and we were on course to generate more than $2 billion in 1995. Not surprisingly, we were starting to generate some good press.

John McElroy, editorial director of *Automotive Industries* in the June issue that featured my face on the cover, wrote:

> Deep in the center of Detroit, in a gritty run down industrial sector of the city, something of a miracle is unfolding . . . A collection of old factories, some dating back to World War I, are changing into a gleaming production site, home to American Axle & Manufacturing, Inc. Fresh paint now shines where a hodgepodge of tasteless industrial hues spattered the landscape only a few months ago. Windows with decades of dirt caked on them have been scrubbed clean. And long neglected machinery is being refurbished to boost both quality and production . . .
>
> Even the neighborhood is undergoing a metamorphosis. The oldest multi-story factories have been demolished. The seedy liquor store which sold a steady supply of booze into the plant is gone. And the corner gas station has been bulldozed out of existence. As a result, crime has dropped 35 percent in one year.

We kept working, gradually transforming an industrial frog into a prince charming. In April 1996, *The Washington Post* sent a reporter named Frank Swoboda to Detroit to see what we were up to. "In the two years since American Axle bought the plant from General Motors Corporation," he wrote, "production has soared from 9,500 to 13,000 axles per day, the business has expanded and the company has added nearly 1,000 new jobs on sales of $2 billion. For the UAW, American Axle is an example of how things should be done.

"I've seen the good, the bad and the ugly, and this is good," said Jim Edwards, an official of UAW Local 235, one of two locals that represented the 3,200 associates at AAM's Detroit plants. Edwards added that grievances had dropped 30 percent since AAM took over.

Perhaps *The Hamtramck Citizen* offered the most fulsome praise of all in an editorial: "From the onset when the company took over the aging and, frankly, decrepit General Motors parts manufacturing plant, this new company has shown an inspiring gung-ho approach as well as an admirable civic-mindedness. . . . It takes a gutsy and conscientious company to make these types of investments. Its President, Richard E. Dauch, appears to be leading a winning team here, and the city should keep this in mind about what a good corporate neighbor we have."

I should mention that part of the AAM deal with GM involved us taking over axle production at GM's plant in St. Catherine's, Ontario. GM wanted us to assume all of those operations, but I declined. For one thing, the axle production was only one part of a much larger facility that produced a variety of automotive products. It would have been difficult if not impossible to treat the axle production operation as a separate unit. Also, that plant was organized by the Canadian Auto Workers Union. We already had the UAW albatross around our neck; we did not need the CAW, too. We worked out a deal in which we assumed control of the axle production but not the facility or the workforce. We worked with them on scheduling, quality, and capital investments, and took a percentage for the axles produced. It actually worked out quite well for us. When, a few years later, GM decided to cancel the products using the axles produced at St. Catherine's, it was not an issue for AAM. It was a unique, proactive, and effective solution to a thorny issue.

At some point, GM's CEO Jack Smith got tired of hearing about the "miracle" taking place on Holbrook Avenue. "He brought a few GM guys with him and met with Dick," said Delanoy. "After the tour, he took me aside and demanded to know how we had done this. So I said, 'I won't tell you, I will show you.' We went walking across the plant floor. My people are coming up to me, saying, 'Tom, look what I did. I made sixty-six good pieces today, I could have made sixty-eight but for this problem. I called maintenance. They came in ten minutes.' I told [Smith], we're visible, we communicate, we trust our people and we hold them accountable."

While working on quality and productivity, we were slowly but surely expanding our product line. We were making rear axles, front four-wheel drive axles, all-wheel drive systems, stabilizer bars, steering linkages, propeller shafts, and forged products for a range of GM vehicles. For Ford, we were making axle shafts for large cars and sports cars, sport utilities, minivans and F-series pickup trucks. We were also producing a variety of products for Chrysler, Toyota, New Venture Gear, and Honda. We were beginning *diversification*.

All the while, we moved quietly but steadily ahead in our quest for better quality. In early 1996, our Three Rivers plant became the first AAM plant to be awarded registration in the ISO 9002 category. That signified compliance with the international standard for quality systems, and the culmination of eighteen months of training associates, management, and UAW officials to review, assess, and adapt the plant's systems to the international standard. It was definitely a group project for which all of our people, associates and management, deserve much credit. By the end of the year, our other facilities had also passed this important quality hurdle.

In March, I issued an ultimatum to all of our salaried and associate staff: "We want to be the low-cost producer of driveline systems. To achieve this goal, we must pick up the pace and achieve 10 percent productivity improvements across the board, year after year."

In the near term, I challenged them to:

- Build and ship 15,000 axles per day
- Achieve a 50 percent improvement in rejected parts per million
- Achieve a 30 percent improvement in customer warranty
- Increase inventory turns by 15 percent
- Improve productivity by 10 percent each year

In December 1996, I told the Hamtramck Rotary Club that one of our first goals—to renovate the plant built eighty years before—was complete, but there was no time for complacency. "If you coast, you have only one way to go—downhill," I said. "To stay in the race you must sustain the pace. We are investing hundreds of millions of dollars into the Detroit-Hamtramck plants because we want to be here."

As the year drew to a close, we were looking forward with some trepidation to negotiations with the UAW. Up until then, we had been operating under the old GM contract in which our associates were compensated the same as GM workers. It was clear to all—or at least it should have been clear—that a Tier One supplier like AAM could not sustain the same wage scales as an OEM like GM. The average GM wage scale at the time was $43 an hour, which seems rather quaint now, but was a major stumbling block for us in 1997. The UAW proposal would have AAM associates making $50 an hour by 1999.

The UAW was always overreaching. Their constant demands were for more money and less work effort. From their perspective, though, I assume we looked like easy pickings. We posted more than $2 billion in revenue in 1996. About 7,700 of our associates would be idled if the UAW struck us, and of course many GM plants would be affected as well. GM had no other source for truck and SUV axles, which made up about 40 percent of GM's sales and 65–75 percent of its vehicle profits. Not for the first or last time, the UAW was holding the best hand and determined to milk us for all we were worth. They liked to call this negotiating, but to us it looked like extortion. The UAW's lead negotiator was Richard "Dick" Shoemaker.

I knew AAM could not afford to pay GM wages and benefits. The other Tier One companies we were competing against were paying much less. *The Detroit News* quoted an unnamed industry source saying that if AAM agreed to the UAW's demands, "American Axle will be dead in four years."

We were determined not to be dead in four years. In fact, we were determined to go public. An onerous labor contract would make it difficult for us to do that and expect a decent price for our stock. But there was an invisible face at the negotiating table—our biggest customer, GM. In what would become a recurring pattern, GM was determined to avoid a strike that would interrupt the flow of critical parts for its popular pickup trucks and SUVs. GM leaned on us to settle and in return agreed to guarantee us new projects and pay a higher price for the parts we delivered. About the only concession of any significance we got from the UAW was a lengthened "grow in" period that would allow us to take more than three years to bring new hires up to full GM wages. Existing UAW associates got a $2,000 payment followed by a 3 percent general wage increase in September 1997 and another in September 1998. The agreement also strengthened their job and income security provisions.

"Obviously, from our side, this is very positive," an unnamed UAW official told *The Flint* (Michigan) *Journal*. That kind of talk gave me a headache. The union leaders were focused on near term gains while they sacrificed the future.

Even then, the UAW membership was already in a free fall from which it has never recovered. They simply did not understand or respect the American market system and the need for business and global competitiveness.

For the time being, business was good. That month, February 1997, we reported that we had delivered 10 million axles in our short lifespan, and cut the defect rate by 72 percent while the rate of returned products fell 91 percent. We were on a roll.

Everyone was making money. AAM was bringing online one of our first major innovative products, the TracRite axle differential. An SUV equipped with a TracRite in both front and rear axles could provide true four-wheel drive. In some four-wheel drive applications, the transfer case could be eliminated or greatly simplified, providing significant advantages in packaging and mass reduction while creating full-time, all-wheel drive. It was a major breakthrough, the first of many to come.

In May 1997, we took out a paid ad in *Auto World Magazine*: "American Axle & Manufacturing, as it begins its fourth year, has developed into a profitable, stand-alone Tier One automotive supplier. We are using those profits to invest in our future and the future of our customers. AAM is providing leadership in the automotive driveline industry. Our product lines are expanding, and we are focused on reducing costs. As a result, our customer base is growing. AAM is positioned to respond quickly and creatively to our customers' ever changing requirements."

That month the Michigan Manufacturers Association honored me as 1997 Manufacturer of the Year. "This year's recipient characterizes that for which the award was created sixteen years ago," said John D. Thodis, MMA president and CEO, and one of the great figures of Michigan business. "Mr. Dauch has been a true leader and visionary in manufacturing for more than three decades. We are honored to have such a dedicated individual whose commitment and integrity to the manufacturing sector has positively impacted the lives of thousands of people."

The early part of the AAM story was drawing to a close. Big changes were in the air. I knew we needed to expand abroad, especially in Mexico, to give the company a more solid base, but my investment partner Ray Park was adamantly opposed. Six times I had my senior people present a proposal for investing in Mexico to the board; six times the board, led by Vice Chairman Ray Park, turned us down. I also knew we were going to have to take on debt to retool for GM's new 800 series of pickup trucks. Ray was opposed to taking on debt.

We had a leadership problem.

At one point during a holiday party, Ray pulled me aside and told me excitedly that we had reached the point we could sell AAM for a handsome profit. I told him that was never part of my plan. I wanted to build a first-class global automotive parts corporation that would become a permanent fixture on the nation's industrial landscape. Ray wanted to turn a big profit and go on to other things. Ray's objective was not my objective. We were reaching an impasse. I realized someone had to go, either me or Ray and the board of directors. It was decision time. This was a big-stakes game.

6

Leadership

The best executive is the one who has sense enough to pick good men to do what he wants done, and self-restraint enough to keep from meddling with them while they do it.
—*Theodore Roosevelt*

One of the greatest leaders of the last century—or probably of any century—was Dwight D. Eisenhower of Kansas who rose to be Supreme Commander of the Allied Forces in World War II and later served two distinguished terms as President of the United States. Among his more notable achievements was the Interstate Highway System, which loomed large in the fortunes of the Detroit auto industry. Eisenhower knew a thing or two about leadership. He used a piece of string lying on a table to demonstrate his understanding of the core leadership challenge. "Pull the string, and it will follow wherever you wish. Push it, and it will go nowhere at all." It's just that way when it comes to leading people.

In my own career, I have employed a balance of pulling and pushing to get the best out of people working for me, but after many years in the trenches I agree with Eisenhower—pulling is by far more effective than pushing. People are more inclined to follow you if you are out front, with your sleeves rolled up, taking the heat and showing the way. To exercise effective leadership, you must first inspire people to follow you, and that can be done only by force of character and personal example.

Since I launched my career in the auto industry, I have earned a reputation as a leader who takes on tough challenges and gets positive results. To the extent I have been successful, I attribute it to my ability to bring out the best of the people who work for and with me. Stated another way, I focus on helping others succeed, and their success enables me to succeed. I have, over the years, developed a few techniques for leading people and almost all of them hinge upon personal relationships. There is a lot that goes into leadership, but first and foremost it is a matter of nourishing positive relationships with people up and down the line in the organization.

One of the most effective and admired leaders I ever knew personally, and one who had tremendous influence on me, was Kenneth W. "Jack" Mollenkopf, head football coach of Purdue University from 1956 to 1969. I attended Purdue on a football scholarship from 1960 through 1964, playing on the varsity team from 1961–63. (Freshmen were not allowed to play on the varsity squad in those days.)

Mollenkopf and his coaches were tough, disciplined, and demanding, but fair, and the regimen could be brutal at times. Could be, hell, it often was. But at the same time there was never any doubt that they were intensely interested in us, that they wanted us to succeed, and that they were willing to go the extra mile to help us succeed. If we came up short in some way, on or off the field, they worked with us to deal with the problem and help us overcome it. Failure was simply not an option.

Today, there is a term for this approach: "tough love." I do not recall if that term was in use then, but that is what it was. It was the same kind of discipline I had received at home growing up on the farm, and it served me as well in college as it did in my youth.

"Mollenkopf and all the coaches made it clear they cared about you," said my teammate Forest Farmer, who had an injury-shortened pro football career before a much longer and more successful one in the auto industry. "Even after you left school, they were always available to you."*

I learned a lot under Mollenkopf that stayed with me. The importance of teamwork was critical. You cannot achieve anything by yourself on a football field. You play your part in a game plan, you compensate your teammates for their weaknesses, and you draw from their strengths. Regardless of whether you win or lose, you go back to work on Monday. There was no time or tolerance for gloating or moping. It is like that in manufacturing. Sometimes you win and sometimes you lose, but there is no crowing or crying in manufacturing. On Monday morning you hitch up your britches and get to work.

---

* Farmer joined the AAM board of directors in 1999.

ON TO GENERAL MOTORS

I brought that experience with me when I was graduated from college and accepted a position at GM. They asked me if I wanted to work on staff or on the assembly line. I said the line—that's where the products are created. I wanted to get my hands dirty and make things, not shuffle papers and write memos. They asked if I wanted cars or trucks, I said trucks. I knew even then that trucks, especially pickup trucks, would emerge as major consumer products in the years ahead. It was just a common sense recognition that for many people, especially people in rural areas, pickup trucks were more useful than cars. To the extent that I am a visionary, as some have labeled me, it hinges at least in part on this insight. Years later, *The Detroiter* magazine labeled me the "quintessential truck guy." I saw what others didn't—trucks and more trucks, it said. "And SUVs on truck frames. All using special axles and drivelines developed by AAM."

I was endowed with a thick hide, and I needed it. The autoworkers, then as now, were a tough bunch, not easily impressed. Like longshoremen, iron workers, deep-sea fishermen, lumberjacks, soldiers, and sand hogs, they performed hard, often dangerous, work and took pride in that fact. By and large, management was just as tough. Making cars and trucks is a demanding calling. All day long you are bending steel. The pace is fast, often frantic. The working conditions, at least back then, were rough—the roofs leaked, the air was dirty, and the plants were noisy. We all worked amid heavy machinery and merciless conveyor systems that never stopped. To work in that environment, and especially to exercise authority in that environment, you had to eat nails for breakfast. At the same time, you had to maintain your composure and concern and compassion for other people. No matter how tough it gets, you always have to remember you are in a people business.

I had two obstacles in the way when I started out. I was young and I was a college graduate. There were other college graduates in the front office, but most GM line supervisors were trained by GM itself, working their way up from the ranks. GM also had its own university, General Motors Institute in Flint, Michigan, which trained people for management and engineering jobs in the auto industry. I knew I had to prove myself. They would all take their licks at me.

I was not intimidated by the challenge; in fact, I embraced it. For reasons hard to explain, I had always felt I was born, bred and developed to be a leader.

The best leaders, said Rich Wellins, a senior vice president at Development Divisions International, have a strong motivation to lead, to influence, to get things done for others. "Many management skills can be learned," he added, "but the disposition and motivation to lead—you either have it or you don't." I have that disposition in abundance. Thank you, Mom and Dad Dauch.

From my childhood days—when I would lie awake at night listening to the trucks roaring down the highway, identifying the models from the sound of the engines to the amusement and amazement of my brothers—I have known the auto industry was exactly where I wanted to work. Within no time, I made myself known to the people who reported to me that I was a boss who knew what was going on and was determined to get it right. I was there when they got to work and I was there when they left. I was on the floor with them, not holed up in an office somewhere. When problems arose, I was never far away or reluctant to deal with them, be they mechanical, process, or people problems. Most important, I was always there to help them and listen to them.

Then as now, it was the people part of the equation that I embraced with the most enthusiasm. I began with the basic attitude that most people truly want to do well, especially in their jobs that they depend on for a living. They are eager to prove themselves, eager to succeed, eager for recognition, and eager to achieve things. The job of the manager is to unleash that positive spirit, and to create an environment for people to apply fresh ideas. The world will always step aside for the fellow who knows where he is going and is determined to get there. I dealt with my subordinates the same way Coach Mollenkopf dealt with his athletes: I got to know them as individuals—not just their names, but where they lived, the names of their wives or husbands and kids, how they were doing, where they went on vacation, what they aspired to be. I made it my business to know when there was an illness in the family, or a wedding or a birth. Mainly I began by making it abundantly clear that I *knew* what they were doing on the job because I was always there paying close attention. When they screwed up, they heard about it; when they did well, they heard about that, too. One of the most productive incentives any employer can offer to the people doing the work is a pat on the back when it is merited. All people appreciate true recognition and a caring attitude, and it doesn't cost a nickel. People yearn for and appreciate sincere recognition and appreciation.

On the other hand, one of my favorite sayings is that the difference between a pat on the back and a kick in the ass is about six inches. But even the kicks in the butt, if administered the right way, convey the same message—that your work is being watched and evaluated, that your work is important, and that your boss wants you to get it right and will help you get it right. One of the worst things that ever happens to people is to be cast adrift in a work vacuum where it seems no one is paying attention to what you do, or cares if you succeed or fail. That reflects an abdication of leadership. I do not permit that to happen on my watch, or in my management system.

That is not to suggest my leadership style is all sweetness and light—far from it. The basic thrust of my approach across the board is that laxness and complacency are not acceptable, especially in an industry like ours where competition is relentless and often ruthless. It is absolutely imperative that everyone up and down the line know that we have to be constantly striving to do it better and more efficiently. We are there to make a profit and that demands productivity, quality, and creativity. Like the knights of old in quest of the Holy Grail, we are seeking zero ppm defects in the products we make. Only the knights had it easier than we do. Finding that Holy Grail would be a cakewalk compared to eliminating defects in automotive products. Zero ppm is one tough nut to crack, but we crack it on a regular basis. We also demand perfect on-time delivery to our customers so they will have no supply interruptions. This requires a steely discipline and full professional commitment.

When I send you to do a job, don't come back to me and say you could not get there because there was three feet of snow on the ground. As my dad used to say to me, I do not want a weather report—I want the work done, and I want it done right and on time. If you cannot deal with that, then we have a problem, but we are not going to have it for very long. I expect positive and consistent results.

I got results and my superiors noticed. I was promoted several times to higher levels of responsibility, and before long—at the ripe old age of thirty—I was made plant manager of Chevrolet's Spring and Bumper Plant in Livonia, Michigan. I was the youngest plant manager in the history of Chevrolet, a brand with a long and illustrious history dating back to 1911. The Livonia plant had more than 3,000 employees and processed 50,000 tons of steel a month. That assignment excited and humbled me. By then, I was already identifying junior managers with grit, determination, and loyalty, many of whom would follow me to other challenges in years to come. I was building a team that was mentally ready and able to respond to tough challenges, and I challenged most everything they did on safety, quality, labor management relationships, financial accountability, and business responsibility. Overall, we had an excellent and responsive workforce. Our products were leaf springs, coil springs, front and rear bumpers, control arms, suspension components, and much more.

Then and throughout my career, it was a major focus of mine to work effectively with union labor. The UAW was founded upon an adversarial relationship with management and it has poisoned the U.S. auto industry for generations, dating back to 1937. I saw it as a fact of life with which I had to deal. I was determined to surmount the adversarial mentality and I enjoyed considerable success, at least up until 2008. I struck up working relationships with UAW leaders and developed a rapport with workers on the line. I earned a reputation for being interested in people, for fair play, and for being a man of my word. When I made a commitment, I kept it. The word spread. You are what you do.

TAKING ON A NEW ADVENTURE

Having the incredible privilege of transforming a moribund manufacturing enterprise at Chrysler over an eleven-to-twelve-year span was a major highlight of my professional career, and I will always be grateful to Lee Iacocca for the opportunity. I had worked at the top of a great enterprise, accomplished many things, earned excellent money, and made a stellar reputation for myself. When I organized the creation of AAM, though, I was stepping out and up as an owner-entrepreneur. That was a totally different ball game—a giant leap from what I had done before. I was putting my money on the table and my reputation on the line. From then on I was responsible for much more than manufacturing; it was the whole enterprise and I had nowhere to pass the buck. It stopped at my desk. I was ready for this leadership challenge. I made a total commitment to this new enterprise, AAM.

For three decades in the auto industry, I had been honing my leadership skills, applying them in the real world, seeing what worked and what did not, but always answering to someone above me, usually someone focused on dollars and cents with little patience for my focus on people, products, and perfection. This has been the root cause of Detroit's troubles over the years—financial people in the front office with far too much power and not nearly enough understanding of the real business. Making quality automotive products requires major league investment in training, capital equipment, and state-of-the-art systems. This time I was the one walking the bridge, setting the tone for the whole organization. I believed I was up to the task; it was time to find out. This was my automotive Super Bowl.

I began by rallying a group of excellent managers who had worked with me at GM, VWoA, and Chrysler. We were teammates who had established our bonds under the white-hot pressure of the factory floor. I knew they were people I could count on when the going got tough, and that they would carry our shared values to the new enterprise. We built a wonderful team.

Within a short period of time, we sorted out the salaried staff we inherited from GM. Some of them had to go back to GM, or somewhere else, but we found quite a few diamonds in the rough, many of whom still work for AAM. In many cases, they found opportunities with AAM that they had never found with GM. That was always a key facet of my leadership—identifying talent and giving the person opportunity to succeed. Among the hourly associates, as I have said earlier, we found a few gems and also inherited a lot of baggage. About half of them flowed back to GM. We lost some key skills here and there, but mainly we divested ourselves of negative attitudes. We ended up hiring thousands of new people who came to us with open minds and positive attitudes. They were not afraid to work and take on demanding challenges. They performed well.

As with my time at GM, I had always made it a point to get to know the people who worked for me, but as I found myself higher up the totem pole, that became more and more difficult because of the sheer numbers involved. At our peak in 2003, AAM had well over 12,000 associates.

The main reason many senior executives elevated to the front office do not succeed is they do not realize their role changes dramatically as they move up. The same interpersonal skills that facilitated my success at lower levels of management were not fully applicable to the top job. There were too many responsibilities and people to permit that one-on-one relationship that I so enjoyed, but that is just the nature of corporate management. You have to delegate most assignments, which means your most important task is selecting the right people for key positions, and giving them enough independence to do their jobs.

I never confused delegation with abrogation. Ultimately, final responsibility resides with the CEO. You have to know what's going on in the trenches so you can ask the right questions of your subordinates and hold them accountable. The minute your senior staff decides you are out of touch, you are in deep trouble. You have to live the job and over the years I have done just that. More than twenty straight years (1993–2012) of being CEO of the same company—in America—is an absolute rarity. I have enjoyed every day of it.

I expect all of our senior executives and supervisors to know the people who report to them, their names and stories. When I tour our facilities, I make it a point to quiz the plant managers about the associates. When I find a plant manager who does not seem to grasp this dynamic, I bring down the hammer. "I will be back by the end of the month," I say, "and by then you had better know the names of these people, and key things about their lives." I come back every time as promised and by then the plant manager has done his or her homework. The next time I come around, they know what is expected of them. The standards are well defined and full compliance is expected.

FINDING TALENT

It is not enough that I provide leadership, but I must make certain the people I place in positions of responsibility also display leadership. This is a tough one because first-class manufacturing supervisors are hard to find. There is no manufacturing equivalent to law school or medical school. An MBA will afford you some useful skills, but does not necessarily equip you for a career in manufacturing. An engineering degree is useful but that is only one piece of the puzzle. There is actually one program at the Massachusetts Institute of Technology (MIT) that trains management people for careers in manufacturing. It is called the Leaders for Manufacturing (LFM) program. I know about it because I helped start it. Beyond that, it's a matter of beating the bushes for people with the right backgrounds, temperaments, and experience they need to get started— and then nurturing them into what is a most demanding calling.

I cannot emphasize that enough. Manufacturing is a challenging field not for the faint hearted or weak of spirit. *Manufacturing is a noble profession.* Supervisors and manufacturing engineers who hold the title of manufacturing manager have the responsibility for making a manufacturing facility work, whether it is one of many plants in a large corporation or a small business with just one site. They must be aware of the big picture. Product is the bedrock of the business, and quality is the key issue and the price of admission. No one who produces high-priced, poor-quality goods will stay in business for long. If there was a time you could get away with that, it is long gone. Today, global competition demands the best from everyone.

Manufacturing managers must know that their decisions and work affect the profitability and, indeed, the viability of the business that puts bread on the table for them and their coworkers. They must realize that they compete not only with the shop on the other side of town, but also with businesses on the other side of the world. They must stay abreast of market trends and, in turn, inform plant management of potential problems and any necessary process and system improvements required.

The corporation relies on them to evaluate and implement the latest technology to maintain manufacturing competitiveness. For this reason, it is important for engineers and supervisors to continue their education, training and skill set expansion. That does not mean everyone has to pursue a PhD, however. You can learn by reading books and manufacturing-related trade journals, attending seminars and conferences, and taking plant tours. Meetings with manufacturing colleagues also can prove useful in exchanging technical and operating information. There is no well-established route to manufacturing management excellence, but if you are bulldog determined, you will find a way.

Besides keeping up with technology, new manufacturing managers must go the extra mile to learn how to deal with people, and to organize, train, and motivate them to use that technology to deliver quality products at competitive prices. Although you can learn much from formal management classes, some lessons must come from experience and understanding human nature. *It is first and foremost a people business.*

New manufacturing managers must also remember that measurable improvements are critical and that one game does not make a season, nor does one season or product cycle make a career. You make improvements within the framework of the organization, and make them continually over a reasonable amount of time. Continual, consistent improvement is healthier and more productive than short, sensational spurts. Everyone needs a minimum of three to five years of measurable improvement to begin developing a track record. You learn as you go along, and a wise CEO with his eye on the future shares his knowledge with subordinates. After forty-eight years in the center ring of auto manufacturing, I share every useful experience I have had, no matter how small or insignificant it may seem, with my senior leaders. It is valuable for them because the greatest teacher of all is, as always, real-world experience and honest counsel.

I advise people I place in management positions to never forget the people who care for their growth and future—or the people who see them as a threat. This is, after all, a very competitive business, not only in terms of company versus company, but in terms of executives seeking to advance their careers. People are always watching and measuring what you do. Image can be as important as reality, so anyone who aspires to succeed must be conscious of how he or she is coming across to others.

Whenever I hire a plant manager, or promote someone to that position, I look for several qualities, character and integrity being the first and most important. A person with serious character flaws can sometimes conceal that weakness in a background position, but a plant manager is always out there, front and center. Plant managers are the corporation's spokespersons in the community and are caretakers of the corporation's image—and are totally responsible for the workforce and assets deployed in his or her facility.

The second set of qualities I look for is competence and high energy. A plant manager must be an on-site CEO with twenty-four-hour, seven-days-a-week, 365-days-a-year accountability. The job requires impeccable credentials and exceptional dedication, determination, and business acumen. It is not for the inexperienced or timid, or for the intellectual lightweight, and you must also be able to balance your emotional involvement and family requirements.

I also ask myself whether candidates would fit in the system and whether they had the energy and enthusiasm to motivate others to positive, focused, results-oriented action. They have to be responsible, positive, and catalytic. I want plant managers who enjoy a good family life as well. In the uphill, long-day battle, people need peace and support at home to be able to give their best on the job. You must be able to *balance* your life.

"One of the true tests of leadership," said the quotable business executive Arnold H. Glasgow, "is the ability to recognize a problem before it becomes an emergency." When you are atop the pyramid, you absolutely must have people telling you the hard truths. This is a recurring challenge to all senior executives because it is a natural human tendency to tell the boss what he wants to hear— and bosses, sometimes subconsciously, are tempted to surround themselves with people who only tell them what they want to hear. That is a surefire prescription for disaster. A manufacturing manager cannot afford a comfort zone. Deal with the facts as they are, and then be decisive and communicate effectively in real time.

I urge my senior staff to give it to me straight, and to actively listen to relevant views from their subordinates. You should require all of your team members to express themselves with *data, facts, trends, and results*. Try to get a consensus and have decisions made at lower levels of the organization, and then be decisive and support them.

In short, success in management requires a lifetime commitment to building one's image and credibility, enhancing your knowledge and skills, and expanding your understanding of the business and the people in it. I tell my people, two-thirds of promotion is motion—so get moving!

It should come as no surprise that a substantial number of our hires are former athletes. Athletes, not necessarily former football players, are a natural fit with any company. They bring discipline, commitment, and a sense of teamwork to the job—all attributes that we appreciate. We do not specifically recruit candidates with sports backgrounds, but I regard it as a positive asset for any job candidate. Athletes know the reality of life will knock you down occasionally. Their athletic training will have taught them to get back up and re-engage themselves to lead their teammates. In the competition to win, former athletes have a distinct advantage.

MILITARY VETERANS

We do actively recruit military veterans. I was in the Reserve Officer Training Corps (ROTC) in college, but by the time I graduated I had a family to support, so I never saw active service. However, during my time at Chrysler I ran the defense division from 1980 through 1982 when we were developing and producing the XM1 Abrams tank, which became and remains the most awesome battlefield weapon ever built. During that period, I was on site at the Pentagon at least once a month for thirty-six months and was mightily impressed with the leadership capabilities of military officers. Their work ethic is exemplary. They are focused on technology, teamwork, education and training, and winning, and are totally committed to safety (an obsession with me).

My first AAM hire, Bob Mathis—with whom I worked at Chrysler—was an ex-marine aviator.* He flew F6 Hellcats and AD Skyraiders from aircraft carriers. I have never flown a plane, but have no doubt landing a plane on an aircraft carrier bobbing up and down in the sea in the middle of the night requires keen knowledge, discipline, and nerves of steel. Bob has all of those characteristics in abundance. He became AAM's executive vice president of Administration.

Another one of our military veterans was John McKinley, a former U.S. Navy captain who joined AAM in our second year. He served on several ships, and toward the end of his career commanded Amphibious Squadron 11, the USS *Belleau Wood* Ready Group, which consisted of four ships and a marine expeditionary

---

* I can hear Bob somewhere right now bellowing, "There is no such thing as an ex-marine!" I know Bob, I know. Once a marine, always a marine.

force. That was heavy-duty responsibility and John, whom I have known since my youth, handled it extremely well. He became AAM's director of Human Resources. John's work especially focused him on helping build our salaried management capability and international salaried leadership group.

"The military is a high-tech business with an emphasis on teamwork," McKinley said. "Training is a priority. When military people are not deployed in combat, they are training for combat. Equipment maintenance is a top priority in the military, as it is in manufacturing. If your systems are not up and operational, you will not be able to serve your customers."

With my eager approval and support, John went frequently to Washington, D.C., where he met with the Retired Officers Association and a private firm called The Lucas Group to identify and recruit military people leaving the service to work at AAM. Many of our first hires in the 1990s were former military people that we actively sought.

Among some of our superb military finds:

GREG BASTIEN: A West Point graduate trained as an engineer, Bastien was a Ranger serving with the 82nd Airborne, our nation's only active airborne division. He mustered out as a captain and, after a series of stateside assignments in Detroit and Three Rivers, became plant manager of our facility in Araucária, Brazil. Under his direction, that plant has produced quality products, found new customers, added associates, and generated profits. Under his leadership, they accomplished zero ppm defects for fourteen months! One quality of military officers that I much admire, and which is a major facet of Bastien's management, is a wholehearted commitment to safety. "At every meeting with my staff, I emphasize safety and quality, which are two things that can always trip you up," he said. "Safety is always first. You can never bypass safety; it is not negotiable. In one meeting, the union rep warned me of a safety issue, said someone might get his hand smashed in this floor washer. On the spot, I shut down lines one and two and summoned maintenance. We fixed the problem in an hour and a half. We solved the problem and, more importantly, conveyed a message that when we talk about safety, we mean what we say." The AAM Brazil plant, at the time of this writing, just surpassed 900 days without an accident. That shows first-class leadership!

JOHN NYQUIST: A pilot in the Air National Guard here in Michigan, John grew up in the Detroit area. A lieutenant colonel, he flew combat missions over Iraq in Operation Desert Storm in 2001 in F-16s. When his unit was required to switch from F-16s to the A10s—the infamous "Warthogs" so beloved of ground troops—he stopped flying and retired, but he is in the Ready Reserve and can be called up if needed. At AAM, John is director of sales for our Metal Formed Products Business Unit, and does a great job. When he was called up for active duty, AAM paid his full salary until he was able to return to us, then immediately put him back to work. We do that for all of our military people in the reserves or National Guard. We support our country—and our military men and women.

Another quality of military training that I admire and put to good use is the ability to take on new assignments and move around to where the organization needs you. I take pride in developing talent and believe strongly that all of us need fresh challenges. "The thing about working for Dick Dauch," said Rossmann, "is that you never know on Friday night what you will be doing on Monday morning."

Dellas observed over many years working with me that I move people to find out where they are most productive and function best, to find their "happy spot." That is, of course, one of my key objectives. To find that spot, people have to be willing to move around. Flexibility in people is as important as flexibility in process. It might be a different job at headquarters, or I may be asking you if your spouse is willing to move with you to Brazil or India, and take the kids along. Anyone and everyone in management ranks at AAM is busy learning foreign languages. We expect all of our middle management to have up to three languages or more. It does not mean they have to be fluent, but you need to know enough to carry on a normal conversation when you get off the plane.

COMMUNICATION

Finding top-notch managers is a critical challenge for a CEO, but that does not mean you give up direct contacts with the rank and file. There is not time enough for me to meet with each individual associate, at least not on a direct one on one basis, but I still get out there to let them know the boss is on the job and interested in them.

I can never stress enough the importance of communication. When we first took over the old GM plants, one of our main messages to the associates was that sixteen GM assembly plants around the country and in Canada and Mexico were depending on us to supply them with axles and drivetrains. As amazing as it may sound, that was news to them. No one had ever told them that before. It is important to let people know why the work many of them do is important, to keep the workforce in the know.

We conduct regularly scheduled Town Hall meetings once a quarter at all AAM facilities where the senior managers, sometimes including me, provide a complete overview of how the company is doing, our successes and challenges, and our strategic plan for the future. That plan is critical. Everyone needs to know what the overall goal of the company is, so they can share the sense of mission. Everyone is free to ask questions and make suggestions. No topic is off limits. If you want your people to feel and act like members of a team, you have to share with them the game plan.

Our senior staff and I conduct frequent operational reviews (ORs) over the course of the year at our various locations. These reviews are with the plant manager and the plant senior staff. It is a thorough business review of that location. We also make some meet with union leadership for their appropriate involvement and contributions.

The ORs begin with a circumference tour of the plant in which we drive completely around the facility to inspect the buildings and the grounds. We take pride in our physical plants. We insist that our associates will come to work in a clean, safe environment that looks good on the outside and the inside. I do not want to see graffiti on the walls, broken windows, or trash on the lawn. It is a simple thing, but may be way down on the plant manager's list. That is my point—if the plant manager does not make appearance a top priority, it will slip. We also expect the parking lots to be clean, safe and well lit. This is our standard worldwide—no exceptions or local compromises.

Once in the plant, I do not permit the plant manager to keep me on a preplanned tour. I quickly take charge and walk into areas where no one expects me to go. I stop and talk to the hourly and salaried associates, including the operators of machines. If I do not know them personally, I introduce myself. I ask about their families, their hobbies, their dreams, and concerns. I invite them to talk about their work environment, what they like about it, what we can do to improve it. I am especially attentive to concerns about safety or the environment. You might be surprised at how free spirited the hourly associates are when given a chance to bend the top guy's ear. When they identify real issues, I make certain they are taken care of promptly. I also make certain they do not get into trouble for communicating negative information to me. By now, actually, I believe that potential problem takes care of itself. Nobody around here gets in trouble for reporting problems to senior staff. As I said, we do not want problems to fester. We want the bad news now, and we certainly want quick and effective solutions.

As we have expanded throughout the world, the logistics have made it impossible for me to perform all ORs. That's all well and good, because as my career draws to a close, I am more conscious of training senior staff to assume all responsibilities, including this one. It is all part of my succession and progression plan. By now, though, all of our senior people have conducted enough ORs with me to know the drill. They each bring their own personal approach to the task, but they are no less demanding and exacting than I am. It is a key part of the AAM management system.

SKIP LEVEL MEETINGS

Among the salaried associates, I created a new program called "Skip Level" meetings, which means what it implies. Associates on the salaried staff come to my office for a personal meeting with me accompanied by his or her immediate supervisor. These are usually people two or more levels down in the organization, so it is a big deal for them, and for me. I really enjoy getting to know these people who are highly opinionated, bright, and full of promise. It gives me confidence that this enterprise to which I have given so much of my life will continue long after I am gone. We want to maintain a sustainable business model.

Actually, sometimes associates get more than one Skip Level session with me, such as Christopher Son, AAM's director of Investor Relations and Corporate Communications, who joined AAM in 2003. "The first Skip Level meeting was less than a year after I started," he said. "I was not intimidated, but then it was not something I would have expected. I made sure I brought my A game when I met with [Dick]. He quizzed me about the company and invited me to ask questions of him, which I did. We talked for maybe an hour and a half. Four years later, when I was promoted into a different position, we had a second Skip Level meeting."

I especially enjoyed getting to know Eric Doyle, our resident patent attorney, who has a degree in electrical engineering in addition to his law degree from the University of Detroit. "It was a matter of him getting to know me and me learning more about him," Doyle said. "I had never heard of a Skip Level meeting. I know of no other CEO who does this. But I believe we have a unique relationship now because he was keen on having an engineer infiltrate the legal staff. He is generally not smitten with attorneys, but he saw me differently."

Maryann Marsolais, a communications specialist in our investor relations group, had been here hardly a month when she came for a Skip Level meeting with me. I was pleased to learn she had started her career as a quality manager. "I was a bit nervous to meet with the CEO," she said. "I thought it was great he would take the time to meet with someone at my level. I was impressed to see someone like him after so many years and so many struggles who still gets pumped up. This business can beat you down, it is a very tough industry. But he is still passionate about what he is doing."

In a typical year, I conduct sixty or more Skip Level meetings that last anywhere from forty-five minutes to an hour and fifteen minutes. My executive assistant Suzanne Lees provides me with complete bios of the people I am to meet. One to three other people to whom this associate reports might also attend the meetings, depending on availability.

Of course, in meetings of this kind—as in random interviews with operators on the shop floor—you never know what you're going to get. I recall in particular one Skip Level session with an associate who reported to Jim Peters, AAM's director of Global Procurement.

"This fellow was very excited about meeting Dick," Peters said. "He even brought Dick a present from his wife. He was a very religious person. Near the end of the interview, when Dick invited him to raise any other issues, the guy said he had an idea that would save AAM $12 million. I just about fell out of my chair. This was the first I heard about it. Dick asked where the idea came from. 'Jesus told me,' the guy said. Dick was taken aback momentarily, but then he said, 'I don't care who told you, $12 million is a lot of money.'"

The idea did not pan out, but the associate is still with us and doing very well.

A variation of the Skip Level meeting is the one-on-one sessions I have with promising executives in key positions—a practice I assume is standard for most CEOs. These are the leaders of the future. I seize every opportunity to call these individuals, regardless of where they may be in the world, to inquire about their families, invite updates on how the work is going, welcome suggestions, and offer instruction or advice. I seldom let a day go by without calling at least one person on the AAM management staff, catching up and offering encouragement and support. I believe these calls are useful to them; I know they are useful to me. It helps me keep up with what is actually happening out there in the real world.

MANAGING

Of course, a major challenge for the CEO of any large corporation is that of steering the enterprise from the executive suite, making certain that senior management is getting all the information it needs, generating creative input, analyzing challenges, making decisions in a timely manner—and ensuring that those decisions are carried out promptly. I do not believe there is any one management organizational structure that is ideal for all situations, but the one we developed has proven versatile and effective up and down the line, at least for AAM.

It begins with the board of directors that is responsible for the overall performance of the enterprise, and also for my performance. We have carefully sought out board members with strong backgrounds in business, especially the auto industry, who are intelligent, diligent and attentive to detail, and very financially focused. The board regularly meets four times a year, as is standard, but I speak with them individually and in small groups more frequently than that. When dramatic events are taking place, such as the strike of 2008 or the market crash of 2009, I am in almost weekly contact with them.

The board has a responsibility to represent the shareholders in providing overall supervision of AAM, and I recognize and respect that role. I am always forthcoming about what we are doing, even when the news is not good. For board meetings, I provide each member with an exhaustive, in-depth report covering every phase of AAM's operations and results. We conduct an ongoing discussion of our long-term strategies and goals. Board members give me and other members of senior management their guidance, drawing on their many years of experience. We accept it gratefully as it enhances our decision making on great and routine matters.

I begin each of our quarterly meetings with an overview of what is going on in the world, especially in the nations where AAM is operating. My purpose is to offer perspective to help them judge AAM's performance in light of the world around us. After all, we do not operate in a vacuum. In the modern world, it is imperative that we all take note of what is going on all over the globe. Like it or not, we are citizens of the world.

I have the highest regard for our board of directors and believe they are a major contributor to our success. During the many crises that beset AAM from 2006 through 2009, the board was solid as a rock and extremely helpful. When we all took cuts in pay, they likewise accepted reduced compensation. They are truly part of the AAM team. I can never adequately express my appreciation for the dedication they bring to this work, and the support they have shown me and all the people of AAM, through good times and bad.

We have an Operating Committee that meets weekly, chaired by our president and chief operating officer, David C. Dauch. If David is not here, and he is often overseas supervising our global operations, the meeting is chaired by John Bellanti, AAM executive vice president of Worldwide Operations. The Operating Committee focuses on five things: people, product, priorities, performance, and profitability. "A number of things hang in that," said David, "but that is the skeleton. All the department heads are represented on the Operating Committee. We cover all the issues at various levels of detail." They meet every Tuesday morning until all agendas and issues are resolved.

David sets the objectives for the company every quarter, and asks all department heads to submit their priorities. They discuss them and establish a priority list based on the importance to the company. "Once a decision is made, everyone must be on board," David said. "We can't have a divided camp." *The final determinant is the key question of what is best for AAM.* As long as everyone stays focused, it will lead them to the right decision.

We have a separate Policy Committee that I chair that meets every other week to set policy and procedures for the company. This is a big-picture meeting in which we go over major points for assessing how the company is doing, whether we are adhering to our basic principles, and which matters require attention. As I have mentioned, safety is a major priority for AAM. An associate injury major enough to require medical attention is brought before the Policy Committee at the next meeting. If we see a problem, we deal with it. When you have thousands of associates bending and cutting steel, there is great potential for mishaps. Avoiding them is everyone's first priority. The Policy Committee makes certain safety retains top-priority status and that everyone up and down the organization is aware of it. Quality and warranty also are exhaustively reviewed, as are financial, legal and personnel matters. We review customer and product activities, and carefully go over all strategic matters for the company.

We have yet another panel, the Plant Loading Committee, composed of our senior staff from all over the world. This group meets twice a year to discuss and make decisions regarding which of our facilities will be producing which products for different customers. These decisions obviously have significant implications for many people at all levels of the organization. It determines which facilities will be getting more investment and possibly more employment, and which will possibly be paring back, or closing. There is a fine line between winning and losing product production assignments.

Once a year, we hold an Executive Leadership Conference and bring in senior staff from our plants for an in-depth review of our progress, the company's fiscal situation, our plans for expansion, new technologies and innovations in the pipeline, and any other business of concern. The chairman opens the meeting and the president concludes it. This is a high-octane session that covers every aspect of AAM's business, in a ten-hour, fully compressed session. No one sleeps through it. It is designed for dynamic tension and forward thinking.

Lurking behind every committee meeting and senior management decision is the Black Book that contains an array of numbers denoting where our investment dollars are going and for which products, now and into the future. Any project that is deemed worthy for funding and planning is duly entered into the Black Book and becomes a part of the overall AAM master plan. Anyone in the organization, including me, may indulge all manner of plans and visions of glory, but until it appears in the Black Book it is but conjecture and possibility. Our CFO Mike Simonte, along with Bellanti, have control of the Black Book, a great and solemn responsibility. I make certain it is never far from my fingertips for review.

THE BALANCED SCORECARD

After all is said and done, the ultimate challenge of management is keeping close tabs on what is happening and holding everyone's feet to the fire. This is a critical area in which you cannot simply accept generalized reports from subordinates assuring you that all is well and that all problems are being dealt with. I hammer it home over and over—give me facts, data, and trends. We will then evaluate the data appropriately within the context of our goals and objectives.

To that end we have developed what we call the Balanced Scorecard—a chart that delineates the most important areas of performance in a color-coded matrix. Green denotes no significant problems; yellow denotes concern; red denotes a failure of some kind. Performance is broken down into seven categories: human resources, safety, quality, supply chain management, productivity, sales, and financials. Each category begins with the target and subsequent lines denote performance. We develop a series of Balanced Scorecard charts: one for the overall company; three for the Americas, Europe and Asia; and then several more for each facility.

We use these charts in both large and small meetings to great effect. All eyes immediately go to the red columns and whoever is responsible is called upon to explain the source of the problem and what we are doing about it—and the time and resources it will take to return it to green. The "action plan" has to be well laid out and fully committed to return the activity from red to green. It forces people's attention, focus, and action.

The Balanced Scorecards are updated on the fifteenth of every month. It is, of course, the responsibility of managers to keep their Balanced Scorecards green as can be. Too much red, and someone will be looking at a new assignment or worse. This is a highly competitive business. Poor performance simply is not acceptable.

Overall, we have a heavy schedule of meetings and conferences scheduled throughout the year in what amounts to a coordinated program to keep everyone informed about what is going on in the company, and to bring all of our intellectual resources to bear on every challenge and opportunity. We have some truly bright people working for AAM, and we are determined to fully utilize all of their creative problem-solving genius and teamwork.

IN CONCLUSION . . .

Let me finish this section by responding to the comment by Maryann Marsolais, who said this is a tough industry that "can beat you down." Yes, it surely is. That is when leadership earns its pay. When the union is blocking the gates, when your main customers are going bankrupt, when your stock is selling for 29¢—*leadership* is called for and it must come with fortitude, ideas, and total commitment to success for AAM and its stakeholders.

There is an old joke that if you can keep your head when all about you are losing theirs, you probably don't understand the seriousness of the situation. Any competent CEO had better understand the seriousness of the situation, better than anyone else in the business, but you cannot show doubt or dismay. Everyone in the organization is watching you closely, looking for any sign of panic. If the CEO shows weakness, even for a moment, it will catch fire and reverberate throughout the organization. Effort will begin to slip. Good people will begin updating and circulating their resumes. I always come cloaked with "Dauch determination," an all-weather uniform that is not Sanforized and does not wash out. This is a two-chin-strap game!

It is when the chips are down and the whole world seems arrayed against you that one's capacity for leadership is tested. I am proud to say that through our darkest days, I kept my chin up and my attitude on an even keel. I spent many hours with the board of directors, our financial institutions, our customers, our suppliers, and our associates, listening to their concerns and reassuring them that the crisis would pass and we would still be here. We never lost faith in the company, or in each other. I do believe that years from now people will say, in Churchill's famous phrase, that this was our finest hour!

7

Changing the Guard

If you don't drive your business, you will be driven out of business.

—*B. C. Forbes*

After weathering the brief standoff with the UAW in February 1997, I had bigger fish to fry. It had become clear to both Ray Park and me that we were not on the same page about the future of AAM. He wanted to cash out while I wanted to move ahead, building a global enterprise. AAM had recently won a huge contract from GM to provide axles, driveshafts, steering linkages, and stabilizer bars for the next generation of full-sized pickup trucks and SUVs. For that, we needed to raise about $500 million to invest in new equipment. Ray was opposed to taking on debt. Also, I remained determined to move forward on our plan to build a plant in Mexico which Ray, along with the board he controlled, continued to veto. We were at an impasse. One of us had to go. There was no personal animosity involved; it was a simple business decision.

So Ray Park and I put our heads together and decided the time had come for me to manage his buyout. For this I needed someone with really deep pockets. We had by then established a serious, respected company that had posted $2.2 billion in revenue the year before. *US Auto Scene* reported that AAM had become one of the world's leading suppliers of driveline systems for light-duty trucks and passenger cars. It noted also that we were expanding our product line, manufacturing a variety of components for the auto industry, including rear axles, front four-wheel-drive axles, all-wheel-drive systems, stabilizer bars, steering linkages, propeller shafts, and TracRite differentials. "AAM's formula for success?" *US Auto Scene* said. "Lean manufacturing plus eternal vigilance in taking costs out of their own system, plus, of course, implementing new technologies."

I do love hard-hitting journalism like that.

Automotive News ranked us seventeenth among top OEM (original equipment manufacturers) suppliers to North America. The *Detroit Free Press* listed us fourth among major development projects in Detroit since Mayor Dennis Archer took office in 1994 because of our investment of $350 million to refurbish the existing buildings in Detroit that we had purchased from GM, and update equipment.

In sum, we had already become a major player in the auto industry, and a key fixture of Detroit. The $20 million or so Ray put up to help me buy the GM properties and business in 1994 was chump change compared to what would be needed to buy the company in 1997.

Ray and I came up with some names of investment companies that had sufficient financial clout to do what we had in mind. We started with a list of twelve or thirteen firms and slowly whittled it down to four or five. We ended up with different names, but I figured as CEO I had the last word—and I knew who I wanted.

During my time working for Lee Iacocca at Chrysler, we had some dealings with the Blackstone Group, a leading investment and financial services company founded by Pete Peterson and Stephen Schwarzman in 1985. Lee allowed me to sit in while he met with Peterson, the former U.S. Secretary of Commerce, and while Lee did most of the talking, I got to know Pete a little bit and had been impressed by his force of character and market savvy. It stuck with me.

So Ray and I went to see Pete Peterson about the AAM project and got a positive reception. Peterson and Schwarzman assigned responsibility for the deal to David Stockman, Blackstone's managing director, who had served as director of the Office of Management and Budget (OMB) during the Reagan Administration. Working with Stockman, we came up with a ballpark figure of about $800 million to $1 billion that was needed to do all the things I wanted to do.

We made the deal with Blackstone because we were looking for a partner that could relate to meeting the requirements of a Tier One automotive supplier, and support AAM's move from a Tier One supplier to becoming a systems integrator for the OEMs. Most suppliers simply produce a component. A systems integrator is involved in all aspects of production—design, engineering, development, tooling, testing, production and delivery, program management, with systems capability. Even then, we were already moving in that direction.

Of course, Peterson and Schwarzman did their homework on me. "I spoke with a top officer at GM, and one or two others in the auto industry, about Dick," Peterson said. "We did our due diligence on him. We determined that he had an outstanding reputation as a manufacturing executive. He did not seem overwhelmed by the problems at all, even though they were very significant. I was greatly reassured by what I heard. It was in the early period of our private equity business, and we wanted to be very careful about our investments."

Peterson recognized there was "a lot of work to be done" and "no shortage of problems," but the fact that there were so many problems in those GM facilities "meant there were also ample opportunities, especially if you had good management."

"We had some involvement previously with a Tier One supplier, Collins and Aikman," Schwarzman said. "They made rugs and other components of cars. They were number one in their businesses, which I later learned was not a good idea, because they could not grow. They had their market share and their customers did not want them to have a bigger market share. They were literally tied to the market."

Schwarzman was impressed by AAM's close relationship with GM. "Because of the company's monopoly position with GM, you basically are in a U.S.-Soviet Union relationship of mutually assured destruction, where GM could not take a strike from American Axle because it would shut down all of their profitable lines and, by the same token, American Axle had fundamentally one customer, so they could not afford to abuse that customer.

"It was a relationship designed for long-term success if you had a sensible person at GM and a sensible person at AAM. We liked that dynamic tension, which was really the need for long-term coexistence because if GM did many bad things to AAM, it could not make the long-term investments it needed to make the quality products that GM needed. We thought AAM's future looked bright. We thought continuing growth of the market for SUVs would be a very good thing because AAM made more money making parts for the bigger vehicles like trucks and SUVs."

"I most admire people who operate well in times of adversity," said Peterson. "I have always thought you really learn about the character of somebody in times of adversity. It is easy to be up and a positive leader in good times, but much harder in bad times. As I recall, the SUV market really fell in one of those years, and he had a combination of problems, partly with the market falling and the union situation, and he handled them more or less simultaneously. I really admired that. I recall from discussions with Dick, that even in the worst of times he had a sense of the future and investing in the future. He made the process work better."

"In my business, when you have a company with a good structural situation and investment premise, and your management is a ten, which Dick is, you're going to have a terrific success," Schwarzman said. "We were quite convinced this was a very low risk investment with a very big upside. Dick was a dream to work with. In truth, I don't know why Ray Park ever sold this thing. You could see it was going to be a great success."

Well, Ray sold it for the reasons he gave me: he got in at the right time, he made a pot of money, and he wanted to cash out. Schwarzman went to see Park at his headquarters in Pittsburgh and got the same explanation from Park that he got from me.

"I believe they [AAM] were talking to others as well as us," Schwarzman said. "You would have to ask him about what our charm was or wasn't. I am not in a position to say, but we believed in [Dick], in the company and his competitive advantages. He had an aggressive business plan. He's an extremely focused and willful guy buying all this new equipment, modernizing everything, buying up property in this crime-infested Detroit neighborhood, taking it from a crack den, a place where murders happened, almost to a corporate park, a truly remarkable transformation."

I told Peterson and Schwarzman that I wanted to constitute a new board of directors with me as chairman. I told them I would want Blackstone to be patient and not lock me into a two- or three-year window. I was aware that most equity firms like Blackstone are very impatient for returns on their investments. I told them I wanted to take the company public, and also that I was determined to invest in Mexico. They said yes, yes, yes, and yes. I have known some people in my life who will not take yes for an answer, but I am not one of them. We made a deal with Blackstone. We also had an understanding, though not in writing, that after a few years Blackstone would start to take its profits and leave AAM as an independent, public corporation. They would prove to be good as their word.

Robert Sherefkin of *Crain's Detroit Business* got wind of this story and wrote about it on June 9, 1997:

> New York investment bankers led by former Reagan Administration budget chief David Stockman are in negotiations on a more than $800 million buyout of American Axle & Manufacturing, Inc. Stockman made an offer on behalf of the New York City-based Blackstone Group, and investment bank-

ers say the deal could reach $1 billion. The buyout package presented by Stockman, Blackstone's managing director, is designed to cash out American Axle's owners, primarily 71-year old Cleveland industrialist Ray Park, the bankers say.

Sherefkin quoted a New York automotive analyst, saying Blackstone could provide the massive capital investment AAM needed to provide parts for an estimated 1.2 million vehicles annually. "American Axle needs money soon because that truck program is the most important program for GM," the unnamed analyst said. Without question, that was a key consideration.

Blackstone waved its magic wand and money appeared. It is truly an amazing thing to watch when the big money boys start doing their thing. In October, we had about one hundred bankers from around the world descending on our Detroit headquarters, eager to compete for an opportunity to make more than $800 million in loans to what *Crain's Detroit Business* called "recapitalization of one of the nation's hottest turnarounds."

In the end, Blackstone raised enough money to buy out Park and our other investor Mort Harris, and also bought GM's 10 percent holding in AAM for $250 million. After the deal was complete, Blackstone owned 63.9 percent of AAM, I and other senior managers owned 29 percent, and Ray Park kept 5.1 percent.

In an interview with *The Wall Street Journal* published September 26, 1997, Schwarzman made clear that I was part of the deal. "One of the key elements of our investment strategy is to back excellent managers, and there is no question Dick Dauch is one of the most outstanding talents in the automotive industry."

Quoted in *Automotive News* in October, in another report by Sherefkin, David Stockman gave me yet another resounding vote of confidence. "We will stay out of Dick Dauch's way," he said. "He's the man who walks on water."

Well, ahem, I don't actually walk on water, but I know where the rocks are. Not long after that, our chairman, Jim McLernon, announced his retirement after forty-eight years in the auto industry. Jim was always a reliable friend and supporter to me, and was invaluable in helping make the deal that became AAM. The new chairman was yours truly, Richard E. Dauch, and at long last I had the freedom of action I needed to take AAM forward. This was the big "L" leadership job that I had worked so hard for. It was also right in the heart of Detroit, which I wanted to help fix.

In essence, Blackstone recapitalized the company, mainly to buy out Ray Park and give me a free hand to profitably grow the company. The Blackstone deal closed on October 28, 1997. Everyone who owned stock, including me, got a payout. I "rolled over" most of my ownership into the newly constituted company.

At the very first meeting of the new AAM board of directors, with me as chairman, the board at long last approved an investment in Mexico. Hallelujah! Also, we immediately began making plans to go public with an initial public offering of AAM stock. We hoped to make this happen by the spring of 1998, but the realities of life would get in the way, as they often do when you make great plans.

The Blackstone restructuring generated a good bit of media attention for AAM and me personally, most of it positive. In January 1998, *Crain's Detroit Business* named me Newsmaker of the Year for 1997. "He has a tremendous passion for what he believes in," said J. T. Battenberg, president of Delphi Automotive Systems, quoted in the article, "whether it is manufacturing or the Boy Scouts [I am an executive board member of the Detroit Area Council of the Boy Scouts of America]. He is part Marine, part preacher, part salesman with a very public personality, all rolled into one."

It's always fun to pick up a newspaper or magazine and read nice things about yourself, but a word of caution is in order. Regardless of what field of endeavor you are in, when the tide turns against you, as it eventually will, those same writers will remove your hide in a New York minute without even passing reference to the earlier praise. It is prudent to keep an even keel through good times and bad. As the old joke goes, "Hearing all this praise makes me feel like the soul on Judgment Day who rose, looked at the words on his tombstone, and said, 'Either I am in the wrong hole, or someone is a terrible liar.'"

Things were picking up speed. In February 1998, we announced we would establish a wholly owned subsidiary in Mexico in the state of Guanajuato to produce driveline systems. We earmarked $120 million for the project, Guanajuato Gear & Axle, where our first product would be an 8.6-inch rear axle for the GM facility in Silao, only six miles away. We were also gearing up to produce an 11.5-inch axle, a new AAM product. Initially, we had 280 associates there, all but a few were Mexican nationals.

I announced also our intent to open business and engineering offices in Europe and Latin America "to extend our global reach and better support our off-shore customers." We already had a regional sales office in Tokyo. We were off and running.

8

Lean Manufacturing

Waste is worse than loss. The time is coming when every
person who lays claim to ability will keep the question of
waste before him constantly. The scope of thrift is limitless.
— *Thomas A. Edison*

Between 1994 when AAM was formed and 2003, a period of ten years, the
amount of labor time we required to produce $1000 in sales declined from
eleven hours to five and a half hours. During that same period, at our plant in
Three Rivers, Michigan, we increased production of pinion flanges, a key part
of the driveshaft system, from 1,500 units a day to more than 3,000 without
adding work shifts. How were we able to do that?

Lean manufacturing.

"I remember a popular song, 'I Was Country When Country Wasn't Cool,' "
said my former boss, retired Chrysler chairman Lee Iacocca. "Dick Dauch was
practicing lean manufacturing and leading the quality revolution years before
those terms became part of the business conversation. He has always been
ahead of the curve."

Lee gives me more credit than I deserve. Lean manufacturing was largely
an innovation of Toyota—the Toyota Production System (TPS)—that has
been studied and imitated around the world for decades. In practice, lean manufacturing means exactly what the term implies—getting rid of the fat and waste
in a work process to achieve maximum efficiency and productivity. As the quote
from Thomas Edison above suggests, however, it is by no means a new notion.

Lean manufacturing sounds simple enough until you get into the details. Indeed, some of the basic precepts of lean manufacturing are counterintuitive. It

requires people up and down the line to adopt a totally new way of thinking and acting. It is, in fact, most challenging and is never quite mastered by anyone, not even the Japanese who made lean famous. Indeed, lean is not a destination, but a journey. It is the relentless quest for lean that makes us more efficient, productive, and profitable, and that is the whole point.

The basic concepts of lean are applicable to any industry but it is generally associated with manufacturing, which is where global competition is most intense. If you are in insurance, medicine, construction, financial services, or food preparation, you are mostly competing with other businesses in your home town or nearby. If you are in manufacturing, you are competing with Asia, Europe, the Americas, and all points in between—and our competitors are serious about what they are doing, especially countries like China, India, Korea, Thailand, and Brazil. They have watched the United States, Europe, and Japan build prosperous societies on the muscular back of manufacturing. They are determined to do the same in their own countries and are willing to employ every possible angle to gain advantage—currency manipulation, piracy of intellectual property, discriminatory tariffs, domestic subsidies, you name it. We may speak wistfully about a level playing field, but there is no such thing. The deck is stacked against us. In manufacturing today, America must be leaner than lean in order to compete and survive.

I had never heard of the Toyota Production System when I began working for General Motors, nor had I heard the phrase "lean manufacturing" (which had not yet been coined), but I could see the waste all around me and knew it was deadly. I set out to do what I could within a tough environment to reduce waste and inefficiency. There was a lot of low-hanging fruit in those days so I did not need any imported philosophy to work from. It is fair to say, as Lee Iacocca did, that I was pursuing lean before the term came into common use.

However, there is a lot more to lean manufacturing than simple waste reduction. Indeed, as it has evolved today, it represents a bold step beyond the mass production techniques that were developed and refined in the United States, probably most effectively and famously on the auto assembly lines of Detroit. We all have some familiarity with the assembly lines where automobiles and trucks in the making are moved along a conveyor system where workers posted at strategic spots install or attach specific components, one after another, all day long. It is not inspiring work, but in its time mass production was revolutionary. It reduced the basic cost of vehicles and other products, making them affordable to a larger segment of the population. The people working the assembly lines, who generally had limited education and skills, earned excellent wages and benefits. It was mass production that made the United States the arsenal of the free world in World War II, and was the basis of our prosperity in the post–WWII era.

As it turned out, mass production, despite its built-in advantages, has some fatal flaws, one being it is easily imitated by other countries. In 1955, the U.S. auto industry hit its peak when GM, Chrysler, and Ford accounted for 95 percent of all vehicle sales in the country. After that, the Big Three began losing market share, slowly at first but eventually with increasing speed in a process that continues. In 2010, Toyota actually surpassed GM in sales to customers in the United States.

Some of this was inevitable as other nations recovered from World War II and began rebuilding their own economies. Yet it is a basic fact of life that we do not learn from success; we learn from failure. It is true in sports, it is true in politics, and it is true in manufacturing. In the immediate post–World War II era, the Big Three were riding high with their dominance of the world's largest consumer market, and the UAW was going along for the ride, like a lamprey hitching a ride on a Great Lakes trout. There is really no compelling reason to unlearn bad habits, or even recognize bad habits, when you are on top and everything is going well.

The Japanese, on the other hand, were desperate for something, anything, that would enable them to rebuild from the ashes of war. In the 1950s and into the 1960s, the products Japan exported to the United States—from transistor radios to cars—were noted for their shoddy workmanship. Certainly, Detroit perceived no threat to its dominance. Rather, the Big Three competed to see who could produce the most exaggerated tail fins and paid little attention to fuel efficiency or quality. Whatever the Big Three produced, American consumers gobbled up.

But the Japanese auto industry was blessed with a genius named Taiichi Ohno, Toyota's chief production engineer. Working with Eiji Toyoda, whose family name had morphed into Toyota, Ohno visited Detroit several times. He concluded that the mass production methods of Detroit were not a good match for Japan, which could not produce the high volumes of auto production comparable to the United States. For one thing, mass auto producers relied on heavy dies for stamping steel into the desired shapes, and would often use the same dies for months or years. Changing dies took hours, sometimes days, a major cost issue for a carmaker dealing in small production runs like Toyota was doing at that time. Ohno undertook to develop a more efficient die-change process in which the production workers themselves made the change, eliminating the disadvantage of making smaller lots of products. By the late 1950s, he had the process down to three minutes and eliminated the need for die specialists. That kind of breakthrough is the very essence of lean.

In making this breakthrough, Ohno made an unexpected and revolutionary discovery. With his new system, it actually cost less to make small batches of parts per unit than large ones that were standard in mass production. Smaller batches meant less carrying costs for excess inventory, and also threw a spotlight on mistakes that showed up almost instantly. In Detroit, it was commonplace to produce large volumes of defective products before the problem was identified. Then the defective products had to be discarded or recycled, a very expensive and time-consuming process. Toyota escaped this deadly cycle.

Another of Ohno's counterintuitive breakthroughs was his insistence that every worker on an assembly line be empowered to stop the conveyor in its tracks to deal with a problem, such as a product defect or an improperly installed product. In Detroit, the accepted process was to permit problems—defective parts or parts improperly installed—to move on to the end of the line where the defective vehicles went into a special area for rework. Ohno reasoned that these problems tended to multiply as the vehicle moved along the assembly line, creating a real mess at the end of the line. When there was an intrinsic problem involved, which was usually the case, such as a defective part or part misfit, it took a long time for it to be recognized and dealt with. Under Ohno's revolutionary system, any assembly line worker who encountered a problem was to pull a cord to stop the line. Immediately, an entire team converged to identify the problem, figure out why it happened, and deal with it. If they ended up tracing a problem back to a flaw in the design, or maybe to an outside supplier, they went right to the source to correct it and make sure it did not happen again. Then and only then did they restart the assembly line.

In the early days of this system, the line was predictably stopping all the time and I can just imagine the financial people in the front office were going nuts. But those very stoppages put pressure on everyone up and down the line in all phases of the production process to make damn sure there were no flaws or mistakes going through. Today, in a Toyota plant or any factory using a credible lean manufacturing system, where everyone has the authority to stop the line, the production lines almost never stop. In fact, in older mass production plants, the lines are stopping much more frequently than in lean manufacturing plants.

Ohno's system virtually eliminated the rework areas that have always been an expensive and time-consuming element of Detroit's mass production. Lean manufacturing simply does not let mistakes go through and pile up at the end of the line. It stops them in their tracks and roots out the cause. That is lean manufacturing at its best.

But perhaps Ohno's most radical innovation was the famous just-in-time delivery system, called *kanban* in Japan, and this one has always been conspicuously counterintuitive, at least to most people. Just-in-time does away with the notion of keeping inventory on hand for when shortages appear. Parts are produced and delivered just as they are needed. The obvious pitfall of this system is, if there is an interruption of supply as when the delivery truck breaks down, assembly grinds to a halt. You have workers sitting around doing nothing, and that runs up costs quickly.

The just-in-time system represented a major efficiency breakthrough, and to understand why it is so effective as a lean concept, you have to consider basic human nature. It is simply normal to have extra inventory on hand, whether you are baking bread in the kitchen, selling goods in a store, or making axles. At some primitive level, we are all squirrels socking away acorns to get us through the winter. But in manufacturing, the urge to accumulate inventory is mother to all manner of inefficiency and waste. You end up with parts stacked in out-of-the-way places that everyone forgets about. It costs money to buy them, it costs money to store them, and it costs even more money to recycle them when they become obsolete without being used, which happens all the time. When we took over the old GM plants to create AAM, we inherited vast amounts of excess inventory that was no longer of any use whatsoever. We had hundreds of truckloads of obsolete parts hauled away to be recycled.

Just-in-time does away with that. When you first adopt it, most people find it very scary. You are suddenly like an acrobat working without a safety net. But once the system is put in place, and everyone is used to it, fewer problems occur. You go from *pushing* parts through the system, and watching them accumulate, to *pulling* parts into the work stations precisely when and where they are needed. Workers up and down the line, and suppliers on the outside, quickly get acclimated to the notion that the parts have to get there at the right time, no sooner, no later.

"In the old days, we would just order material and ended up with inventory lying all around," said Delanoy. "It was very wasteful. But with lean production, we moved to a pull materials system. We began with an ID number that included all the parts that the customer wants for the truck, bar-coded and scanned to make certain the right parts are put on your vehicle. It takes all the guesswork out of ordering parts. We used to have hundreds of people ordering parts. If you order five hundred parts and only make one hundred axles, the result is money lying on the floor. Now we let the system, not the person, order the part. When the part is used, the system sends a pull signal to pull another part to replace it. The system is fully automated."

Just-in-time is even more important now as global competition has intensified over the last decade. It is an effective tool to promote efficiency, improve quality, and reduce waste. It is one way automotive suppliers can eliminate costs while helping customers improve competitiveness. For example, AAM supplies driveline systems and components on a just-in-time basis to GM, Ford, Isuzu, Mercedes Benz, Nissan, Subaru, and CAMI. That's seven sets of standards and requirements from just these seven OEMs. It is demanding, but our ability to master their requirements helps separate us from the competition.

Just-in-time at AAM is now advancing into "Sequential Parts Delivery." Just-in-time normally means that you have a four- to eight-hour window in which to deliver your product to the customer. The window with Sequential Parts Delivery is much narrower since it is measured in one hour or less. It is a more refined and a more demanding process.

Logistics is a differentiator, but not many people talk about that. There are two things you absolutely have to have if you are going to employ just-in-time materials management: *predictability* and *repeatability*. You can then sequentially schedule parts deliveries. The farther away you are from the supplier, the more complications you encounter. When you get multiple time zones away, logistics becomes a much more important differentiator. That is the key reason everyone up and down the supply chain wants their suppliers as close as possible.

PEOPLE POWER

Lean demands that you get rid of positions that do not add value, and expand the role of those that do. If there is one key overriding principle of lean manufacturing, it is transferring the maximum number of jobs and responsibilities to the workers who are actually adding value to the products on the assembly line, and reducing the number of people who are supervising or otherwise standing around adding little value.

To achieve this, you have to have well-trained associates who are empowered to make decisions and committed to getting the work done right. Senior management of the Big Three and most suppliers in Detroit have long been aware of the challenge of lean, but have been slow to come to grips with it, mainly because of the people factor. Confronted with intransigent labor unions and obsolete management theories, the front office "leaders" have historically sought to dance around the people part of the equation. In the 1980s, GM invested billions in robot technology in a futile quest to eliminate the labor equation almost entirely. It did not work.

You cannot eliminate the people part of the manufacturing equation and at AAM we do not want to. To be sure, advanced technology plays a key role in modern manufacturing, of that there is no doubt. AAM's commitment to lean manufacturing was on display early on when we made the massive investment to shift from five-cut to two-cut, wet cut to dry cut. That cost a lot of money and took a lot of time, but it freed up many associates for other jobs and made them much more productive. That is lean manufacturing in practice.

Even after the switchover, we still had associates on the floor. You simply cannot replace everyone with a machine. Most economists define productivity as the dollar amount of work accomplished per employee hour. But while some of our success stems from more productive technology—more expensive machines—a lot of it relates directly to better training of associates and more efficient processes. Advanced machinery is not always the answer. If we replace one associate with a $10 million machine, I do not believe that contributes to productivity. Indeed, it probably lessens productivity. We would have done better to keep the worker on the job and invest the $10 million in R&D.

Eventually, investing in more sophisticated machinery to replace human hands reaches a point of diminishing returns. I have yet to see a machine, no matter how advanced, make a creative contribution to our operations. Our plant in Guanajuato, Mexico, is far and away our most productive, a veritable showcase of lean manufacturing, but it is more reliant on human labor than many comparable plants. The associates there are constantly coming up with ideas and innovations that make AAM stronger and more competitive. A truly lean operation calls on labor for both physical and intellectual contributions, and balances the input of labor and technology to achieve maximum efficiency.

"We went through a phase of trying to automate everything, driving more and more automation," said AAM's executive vice president for Worldwide Operations, John Bellanti. "What I think we have learned is that simple is better, even in some cases if it means more labor. When you are paying $75–80 an hour for labor, you want to reduce it as much as you can. When you are paying $25–30, there is less incentive to reduce labor. In most cases, the OEE will be much higher with a person loading that machine because you have less chance of something breaking down, and need fewer support staff to keep the machinery working."

Regardless of how it is defined, lean manufacturing is an endless quest for improvement at all levels of the operation. As such it demands a lot of all of us, including our associates who are under relentless pressure to streamline the production process and constantly discover more efficient ways of operating.

"Lean manufacturing is not the end in itself, it is a tool," said Inacio Moriguchi, executive director of the AAM Manufacturing System. "In my career, I have seen a lot of companies pretending to do lean. They have nice charts, but they are turning out poor quality and losing money because they are not using the lean tools effectively. Just going through the motions won't do it. Everyone must change the way they think."

This shop-floor attitude is difficult to forge under any circumstances and where labor unions are present, even more so. When unions are deliberately fostering distrust and resentment between management and labor, it becomes even more challenging to forge a cooperative work ethic. I have had some success here and there over the years working with UAW leaders who recognize economic reality and encourage the rank and file to take initiative, but regrettably I have found they are usually the exception to the rule. The UAW leaders who shut down AAM in 2008 were not advocating lean manufacturing; they were advocating more expensive labor costs and restrictive rules that are the antithesis of lean. Today, as a result of an entitlement mentality, thousands more of their members are unemployed.

WASTE AND LOSS

Lean manufacturing is a way of thinking, an endless quest to reduce waste and loss. Waste is defined as anything that increases the cost of production without adding value to the part being produced. On the factory floor, we see seven basic types of waste: overproduction—producing stuff sooner or faster than the customer wants it; wasted motion—movements that do not add value; excess inventory—taking up space, going to waste; excess handling—moving material unnecessarily; overprocessing—unneeded operations; correcting defects—producing defective parts that must be corrected or recycled; and waiting—any breakdown or unevenness that produces idle time.

As for losses, we have identified six major causes:

- Equipment failure—malfunctions demand maintenance intervention. We do everything in our power to make certain the equipment we acquire is of the highest quality and right for the job, and then we insist on rigorous maintenance to avoid breakdowns.

- Setup and adjustment losses—mainly tool and die changes. We invest extensive time and thought into streamlining this process to avoid downtime.
- Idling and minor stoppage losses—interruptions of machine work such as blockages and jams, often the result of operator error.
- Reduced speed losses—the difference between the machines' official rates and the actual cycle times, can be due to a variety of reasons.
- Defects—rework, repair or scrap, none of which make me happy.
- Reduced yield at startup—losses associated with problems that often attend the beginning of a manufacturing process.

THE 5S PROCESS

There are many variations of lean manufacturing, all of which are designed to foster a new way of thinking about the work process. One of my favorites is the 5 S's: sorting, straightening, systematic cleaning, standardizing, and self-discipline. (Or in Japanese, *Seiri, Seiton, Seiso, Seiketsu,* and *Shitsuke.*) Most companies come up with their own versions of the 5 S's, and AAM was no exception. This is our version:

- Sorting (*Seiri*) calls for the elimination of all unnecessary tools, parts and instructions. We go through everything in the plants—the tools, materials, machines, instruction manuals—to eliminate every item that is not essential. We go through every workstation and red tag anything that is potentially unneeded. If it is not needed, we take it away. It is truly amazing how things accumulate. Again, human beings are like squirrels. On AAM plant floors, when an area is not in use because of a change of work or adoption of new machinery, we immediately rope it off and forbid its use. If we did not do this, within a few weeks these "empty" areas would be full of obsolete or unused stuff that we do not need.
- Straightening or setting in order (*Seiton*) decrees that there should be a place for everything and everything should be in its place. Associates tend to finish a job and just drop the tool where they were last using it. To combat that, we assign priority status to tools and parts in terms of their frequency of use. Associates put them in clearly marked storage

bins in terms of their sequence of use. Every item must go into a place expressly labeled for it, and all items should be arranged to encourage smooth, efficient work flow. All tools, parts, and supplies should be kept close to where they will be needed.

- Sweeping or systematic cleaning (*Seiso*) is one lean concept I was born with. I insist that our plants be clean and organized on the inside and the outside. At the end of each work shift, the associates are expected to clean up their work areas and make certain everything is where it belongs. This is done daily. When you walk into a lean manufacturing situation, anyone with a practiced eye can see from a distance whether it is truly lean.

- Standardizing (*Seiketsu*) to make certain all work practices are consistent is another key aspect of lean manufacturing. Within reason, we expect our workstations to be identical. In theory, any employee can walk into a different workstation and begin doing the job, knowing that the tools and supplies will be in the same place. This assures a smooth transition of work performed when people are absent or leave the company.

- Self-discipline (*Shitsuke*) demands that every associate constantly review and maintain standards, as spelled out in the previous four S's. We demand our associates maintain a certain level of attention to the basic requirements, and that they also constantly consider ways to improve the work process. All such suggestions are taken seriously by management, and adopted if they prove viable.

SUPPLIERS

Modern manufacturing is highly integrated with a variety of independent companies occupying different positions in the industrial food chain. AAM is itself a supplier, of course, to OEMs (original equipment manufacturers) making cars, trucks, and SUVs. We work closely with our customers to synchronize delivery of key parts in harmony with their just-in-time needs. We align our computer networks with them to assure we are producing the right products at just the right time to serve their needs—and the needs of their customers.

Similarly, we have a host of suppliers providing us with raw materials and components for the products we make. They, too, must be working to supply our needs on a just-in-time basis. They either are on board with us on this, or they are replaced. All up and down the line, everyone must be singing from the same hymn book.

LEAN ENGINEERING

Lean manufacturing begins long before the product is put together on the plant floor. In my earlier days at GM, VWoA, and Chrysler, I was notorious for taking engineers to the plant floor to make them confront how their best-laid plans encountered hard reality. Your schematic might look beautiful on your computer screen, but still present insurmountable challenges to the assembly line. At that point, it all has to come together.

You have to get the people who are process oriented together with the designers in the studio and with the engineers or else you will end up with a tremendous waste flow that you cannot cut out later. I have always believed that designers and engineers should have a chance to work a minimum of two years in the production manufacturing arena to see where the final product is actually produced, and see the things that they influence but are not ultimately responsible for. It is the basic question of how close your fanny is to the heat; getting really close to the product will motivate you to design it right and engineer the process right.

For example, when we were designing the new AAM painting plant in Buffalo, we knew space, time, and dollars were limited. The new system, installed in about nine months, featured nearly 1.5 miles of conveyor, robots and other automated equipment, enough to paint 6,000 truck axles a day, all in 67,000 square feet of space. The secret to getting that job done right was concurrent engineering of the building, conveyors and process equipment. Conveyors and process equipment were installed at the same time the building was going up, with conveyor installation crews working on site before power and lights were available in the structure. Extensive computer simulation was done to ensure that the new conveyor system and the existing system in manufacturing would not logjam each other. The identification of each type of axle was maintained throughout the process to provide part specific instructions to the painting robots. Radio frequency identification (RFID) also allowed axles to be racked with like parts for shipment from the paint facility on just-in-time delivery contracts to numerous customers throughout the Eastern and Midwestern states and Canada.

I expect our engineers to lead and play an integral role in the campaign for ever leaner manufacturing. Successful manufacturing engineers must bring to the job a range of skills beyond their engineering and management degrees. Because ultimately all decisions are business decisions, manufacturing engineers must be well rounded and business focused, with some formal business and economics education. Cost starts with product, process, and design. They must leave their engineering comfort zone and plunge into the uncharted waters of communications and economics early in their careers. They must possess a working knowledge of metallurgy and materials management. New materials are critical to innovative engineering solutions, opening up opportunities to apply formerly exotic materials such as aluminum and magnesium alloys, metal-matrix composites, and plastics.

A successful manufacturing engineer today must possess a global orientation. He or she must benchmark worldwide for equipment, processes and materials. Technology is a competitive differentiator in the marketplace. We all end up being "passport executives." Air travel to foreign countries is constant.

The constant pressure to shorten product development lead times is driving the need for accurate, efficient product and process simulation. These are vital for today's manufacturing engineer. Manufacturing engineers must be people-focused, with a factory-floor mentality. They must use the creative talents of machine operators, skilled trades personnel, equipment materials suppliers and union leaders to help optimize product, process and systems solutions.

In the final analysis, manufacturing engineers must possess a continuous improvement mentality, and be well versed in lean manufacturing principles. They must be committed to working smarter, harder and more creatively.

As an example of lean engineering, to meet the quality and volume requirements from a customer who hoped to increase the torque and load-bearing capabilities of its full-size pickup trucks and SUVs, AAM engineers developed an innovative process to produce a new rear differential gear carrier. It was the largest the company had ever produced, at 118 pounds. The process initially used a series of large horizontal machining centers (HMCs) to meet the demand for the 11.5-inch carrier. Then, using the same process, fixtures, and tooling, we ramped up using a CNC Flexible System Transfer (FST) line provided by Heller Machine Tools in Troy, Michigan. When volumes went from 35,000 to 240,000 parts annually, the process and equipment permitted the plant to respond quickly and cost effectively to the change in demand while consistently achieving quality goals.

In developing the carrier design, AAM paid special attention to details that would positively affect the part's perceived noise, vibration, or harshness (NVH) characteristics and would thereby provide an advantage to customers in the pickup truck and SUV market.

Once the parts were designed, AAM conducted simultaneous engineering programs with three machine tool companies to evaluate each vendor's approach to its manufacturing challenge. In each case, AAM was interested in flexible manufacturing cells to handle relatively low initial production volumes. We also looked for machine tool vendors that used Hirth couplings on their rotary tables that help meet critical tolerances. This was to prove that the critical dimensions could be consistent on a machining center.

Carrier housings and differential case housings are two important axle components that we supply to our customers. These parts have been produced by a number of different machining processes. For example, carrier housings were machined on single-spindle horizontal machining centers and dedicated transfer lines as well as CNC lift-and-carry transfer lines. System components can be combined to create the system best suited to the application. Because all interfaces between the units are standardized, engineering time is reduced and assembly is accomplished quickly.

The FST was fully assembled and run off on the Heller assembly floor in Troy prior to delivery to AAM. This allowed the FST to be fully operational and on the plant floor in a third-less time than a transfer line usually demands. Because each of the FST stations is computer numerical controlled (CNC), the company can easily accommodate different part geometry as well as change speeds and feed of the machining heads through programming. The FST also used in-line gauging to feedback size compensations (for automatic adjustment) to the finishing tool. This ensures that critical part features are maintained within print tolerance and provides SPC trend data. After initial operations are completed, one part per hour is inspected off line.

The FST control system consists of one central console with identical station controls in an open communication network. This has allowed process engineering to further optimize feeds and speeds to accommodate a change in insert rate from positive to negative, resulting in an increase in tool life from thirty to two hundred pieces. This exercise was lean manufacturing at its best.

THE AAM MANUFACTURING SYSTEM

The AAM Manufacturing System, our unique version of lean manufacturing, was developed to eliminate waste from our operations and improve our competitive position. At the heart of our system is what we call People Focused Practice (PFP) workshops. We realize that to eliminate waste effectively we must leverage the advice and expertise of people who engineer, produce and use our parts on the plant floor. This also includes the associates who are skilled in leading change and applying the principles of lean manufacturing.

PFP workshops include general training in lean manufacturing processes. As a result, we now have a strong team of associates who are skilled in leading change and applying the principles of lean manufacturing. Inventory is better controlled. Use of returnable containers eliminated messy cardboard packaging. Renovation is evident in the removal of old, oily conveyor systems and most important is the installation of more advanced CNC tooling.

We created a Lean Steering Committee charged to assure total workforce involvement in lean. We conduct Quarterly Lean Maintenance and Tooling System Assessments, and Quarterly AAM Manufacturing Systems Conferences. The frequency of meetings focused on lean helps us reinforce the message that lean is a corporate priority and that senior management will not relent on its lean focus for even a second. "I enforce and require these quarterly conferences," said Bellanti. "Everyone knows they must report on their progress to their peer group. It drives action. Otherwise things get put on the back burner and don't get done."

We employ visual systems for constantly reminding everyone of the critical importance of lean and the progress we are making. We employ a system called "Value System Mapping" in which we lay out the process from beginning to end, from the receiving dock to the shipping dock. The value stream map is a tool that displays the flow of materials and information as a product makes its way through the value stream, along with the lead time. Every plant has a "glass wall" that displays the value system mapping for all to see. We identify specific issues and rate them according to our basic color code: green is good, no problem; yellow is an issue that needs work; red denotes a problem that commands attention. Your eyes go straight to the red every time. What is the problem there? What are we doing about it? When will we get it resolved? We want absolutely everyone in that facility focused on the red until it becomes green.

Another reminder is the Hourly Production Analysis Board that shows at a glance the line's pace relative to estimated output, and the reasons why a line or operations system is underperforming or down. These color-coded visual systems are on display throughout every AAM plant floor, living up-to-date scorecards so all of us know how well we are doing. And it should come as no surprise that we have a Plan for Every Part (PFEP) that is also visually depicted on the plant floor.

We focus on time-based management built upon standardized work using the most effective combination of associates, materials and machines to perform an operation using the best current method to meet the customers' demands with as little waste as possible. We focus on what we call Takt time—the time needed to produce one unit of a product to meet the customers' demand. Takt time is calculated as operating time (seconds per working day) divided by daily value (customer demand).

For example, if we have four associates working together on a process to produce a specific product, we measure the number of seconds required to accomplish each step in the process. Maybe you have one associate working 80 percent of the time and another only 40 percent and two others only 20 percent. So maybe we only need three people instead of four. If one associate needs more time than the others to accomplish a particular step, leaving the others working more slowly than necessary, we realign the work responsibilities to achieve a balance. To the extent possible, each associate is fully engaged in the process.

We employ what we call standard work in progress (SWIP) using the minimum amount of work in progress inventory so associates can complete their standardized work smoothly, repeatedly, in the same sequence, and with the same movements. There are four steps to SWIP:

- Develop a process capacity sheet to verify that each operator has the capacity to produce the quality and quantity of parts required per shift (day).
- Develop a work combination table to relate the work sequence and the Takt time to verify that the combination of man and machine movements can meet customer requirements.
- Develop a work chart—a visual description of the critical factors in the correct execution of standard operations.
- Develop a work balance chart to evenly distribute work among all associates while ensuring that each meets the Takt time.

We focus on process stability, striving to produce the same quantity of quality products with the same amount of resources (material, manpower, and machines) over a given period of time. Instability leads to increases in inventory and decreases in customer satisfaction. We work for zero defects, one-piece flow, on demand immediate delivery, and no waste.

In the final analysis, it always comes back to people. A leading portion of the battle for improved productivity takes place right on the plant floor—and that demands active input and participation by associates on the floor. For example, our associates established compact ways to lay out new gear-cutting machinery, freeing up 30,000 square feet of floor space for potential new programs. In doing so, we cut the distance a ring gear travels in the plant by more than 1,700 feet. If you consider that the plant manufactures about 260,000 ring gears a year, we eliminated about 84,000 miles of part travel distance per year.

When I say we engaged all of our associates in lean manufacturing, I do not mean to suggest that we delegate responsibility down the line. To the contrary, responsibility for lean begins with me and is driven by senior management, engaging everyone at every point in the company. "I went to one of our plants and asked the plant manager to review his top initiatives to reduce waste," said Moriguchi. "He said he did not know much about it and referred me to his lean coordinator. That visit was supposed to last an hour; it lasted two minutes. I said I would come back when he had taken ownership of lean. The lean person of each plant should be the leader of that plant."

"Top management must be involved," Bellanti said. "You cannot delegate lean. Senior managers must be at the conferences—not the lean coordinators, the senior managers. You don't put in a pull system for its own sake, but to enhance efficiency. If it doesn't reduce waste and reduce scrap, what is the point? At the end of the day it comes back to profitability. All lean activities must be directly correlated to the business metrics."

We saw our profits drop in 2001 as our customers squeezed suppliers for lower prices. In response, we stepped up reliance on scheduling associates in groups that worked longer hours but fewer days. With one group following another and less overlap, the plant is never idle and no one has to wait to use a piece of equipment. These efficiencies enabled us to win a new contract from Ford. This is the kind of issue the public does not care about, but it is critical if you want to stay effective in manufacturing in this era of globalization.

One result of lean manufacturing is a steady, consistent supply of quality products. *The one thing you never want to have in the automobile industry is a lack of continuity of supply.* Before we took over the old GM plants, for the previous five years, every forty-eight hours GM was out of a part. That meant people were sitting down, drinking coffee, wasting time and money. AAM has never missed a part in eighteen years, with the exception of when the UAW was out on strike. I'm talking 60 million axles and 3 billion forgings, and tens of millions of driveshafts!

I cannot say AAM is totally lean, only that we are working steadily and determinedly to get leaner every day. That, in the final analysis, is what lean manufacturing is all about.

9

Going Public

My introduction to the theory of money and exchange oc-curred when the San Diego Chargers sold me to the Buffalo Bills for $100.

—*Jack Kemp*

When we made the deal with Blackstone to buy out Ray Park, it was with the understanding that we would borrow money to gear up for the new GM project, launch a plant in Mexico, and take the company public. That last point was cru-cial, because going public was key to Blackstone's ability to extricate itself from AAM over time, recapturing its investment and making a profit, by selling its stock to the public.

So it was that within a matter of months after Blackstone bought in, we de-cided to move forward with an initial public offering (IPO). I had never been through an IPO before and, if God is merciful, hope to never go through one again. It was without a doubt the hardest thing I have ever done in business, and that includes helping save Chrysler and creating AAM. It didn't actually take long, but for the time I was obliged to invest in it, the trek was exceptionally arduous.

This was all routine stuff for Blackstone. Those people are masters of the financial world and know all the ins and outs of these things. They arranged for Merrill Lynch to serve as lead banker. We were off and running, but it was an intensely complex process that demanded a lot of us. The process began several months before our initial S-1 filing with the Securities and Exchange Commis-sion (SEC), following a very specific timeline. The SEC reviewed our submis-sion and came back with many suggestions and recommendations, all of which we took seriously and responded to. The SEC is responsible for making certain that new stocks offered to the public are managed responsibly and in accord with the law. The folks in Washington, D.C. just love to issue regulations that are virtually unreadable by normal people. There was a lot of time and effort invested just to get to that point.

On May 26, 1998, we filed with the SEC for an initial public offering of up to $115 million in public stock, saying the net proceeds would go to reduce debt and for general corporate purposes, including capital expenditures. Our filing asserted we were adding offices around the world in our ongoing effort to diversify, strengthen, and globalize our original equipment customer base. At the time, all of our sales of axles, propeller shafts, and other products were in North America; 96 percent of our sales were to GM. That was, of course, a major concern of investors, and an issue of great concern to me. We had a plan to correct this concentricity, but we knew it would take a lot of time to execute.

Actually, we were only putting about 14 percent or less of our stock up for sale initially, but intended to sell more later. There are advantages to going public. A U.S. stock exchange listing and publicly available financial statements allow prospective AAM customers to make a fair assessment of our financial viability and growth potential. I figured being a public company would greatly facilitate our ability to attract new customers and reduce our dependence on GM.

Among the items in our SEC filing:

- AAM's net income fell about 10 percent the year before (1997), partly because of expenses from the sale of a controlling stake to Blackstone in October. The sale left senior AAM management, including me, with a substantial stake.
- Operating income rose 24 percent in 1997 as defect rates plunged and sales outside GM grew. The company generated $88.5 million in non-GM sales in 1997 vs. $38.3 million in the first ten months of our independence from GM. That was a positive.
- Also, AAM was pursuing contacts from Isuzu, Nissan, Mercedes Benz, and CAMI, a joint GM-Suzuki venture. To promote global sales, we were opening sales offices in Mexico and Europe, and already had one in Japan.

Business was going well. We had some debt but we were growing and prospering in tandem with the overall automobile/truck industry. But, but, but— there is always a but. "I have good faith in Dauch," said Don Smith, associate director of manufacturing systems at the University of Michigan's Office for the Study of Automotive Transportation, "but when the market goes down, there's only so much a supplier can do." Truer words were never spoken.

As if to underscore the hard reality behind that remark, the UAW struck GM in June 1998. This brought most of GM's North American production to a standstill. GM was belatedly trying to come to grips with the costly labor costs and restrictive work rules that some at the company realized were driving the company inexorably toward bankruptcy. Since we depended upon GM for 96 percent of our sales, the strike hit us especially hard just when we were preparing to go public. As the *Financial Times* noted, the timing of the strike "could not be worse for American Axle, one of Detroit's biggest car part manufacturers. In late May, just 10 days before the first GM stoppage, the company filed to float its shares on the stock market."

By late June, because of the GM strike, about half of our associates were laid off. The strike continued until the end of July, lasting fifty-four days. It bled more than $100 million right out of AAM. The UAW continued to destroy value and competitiveness for both AAM and GM.

That strike took the air out of our sails. In the six-month period ending June 30, 1998, AAM sales fell by $185 million and profits plummeted 81 percent to $9.9 million, all because of that strike. Long-term debt also increased because of the strike, as we noted in our revised public offering. Two UAW strikes of GM in two years underscored our vulnerability because of our overreliance on GM. "The writing is on the wall that American Axle must diversify beyond GM," one analyst wisely noted. We knew that already, but to reduce our reliance on GM we had to go global and until that very year I had been hamstrung in my efforts to do that.

So we had to put everything on hold for the duration of the GM strike and for several months thereafter as we recouped our losses and got our financial house back in order. By late December 1998, we were forced to revise terms of bank loans because of the strike and the purchase of the Scottish automotive parts manufacturer Albion, which cost us over $90 million.

We were also closely watching a similar process by one of our major competitors, Delphi Corporation, which was also preparing to go public. We were advised there was only so much money out there to invest in auto parts suppliers, so it was important for us to beat Delphi to the punch. In the end, we beat them by a week. I really do not know if our action impacted the outcome of Delphi's IPO, but ours went very well indeed. The timing of the IPO was critical, and we were getting good advice from Blackstone and Merrill Lynch.

One of my first battles, as we were making IPO preparations, was with the underwriters who said they could get us $7–$8 per share. It is in the interests of the underwriters to low ball the offering to ensure a vigorous response, but we wanted to insure the fair value of the stock. As a practical matter, the value of a corporation, like the value of anything else, is a subjective thing. There is no computer program or government agency that can decree accurately what a business is worth. In the final analysis, the value of a corporation, like the value of a house (or a football quarterback), is determined by what someone will pay for it. I performed my own calculations based on our assets and projected revenues. I said to Merrill Lynch, please, any kid in kindergarten could get $7–$8 per share. I insisted on an initial price range of $16–18 per share. I believed I had a good sense of what AAM was worth.

I went on the road with Bob Mathis and Chief Financial Officer Gary Witosky in what proved to be the most grueling fifteen days of my life and it seemed like much longer. We did not go international selling stock, thank God, because it was only a $119 million offering, but this is a big country and you don't need to go overseas to wear yourself out. We went anywhere and everywhere there were major investors who might be interested in buying our stock. We would fly into town, take a limo to wherever the first meeting was, put on our dog-and-pony show, go on to another meeting and another and another, and then hustle back to the airport for the next leg of the trip. It was all a blur to me after a while, but we kept going from town to town like a rock band on tour. We had a well thought out professional presentation complete with PowerPoint and copies of handout reports. At every stop, we were peppered with technical questions from savvy investors who were wise to the tricks of the trade. On the first day of this tour—in just one day—we met with groups of investors in New York, Minnesota, and Missouri. By the time I reached my hotel room, I felt like I had been run hard and put away wet.

"Merrill Lynch set it all up," said Witosky. "The meetings were with people interested in this type of stock. At each meeting, we had fifty minutes to make our presentation. We would go to as many as six places in one day, make the presentation, and then hustle off to the next place. It was all tightly scheduled. Dick did most of the presentation, maybe 80 percent, and I was there to answer technical questions. Some of them asked tough questions and anything was fair game. We got questions about our relationship with the unions and our dependence on GM. As soon as we left one place and got in the car, the people from Merrill Lynch would be briefing us on the next group. It really was exhausting."

Mathis and Witosky performed exceeding well in this IPO process. I suppose I did, too, because it turned out alright, but after a few days of this grueling schedule, I felt I was beginning to lose my edge. It was like I was back at Purdue working out under the watchful eye of Coach Mollenkopf, running and running with no letup in sight.

All the while, the Merrill Lynch people were gauging demand as they felt their way toward what would be our final asking price. And guess what—they settled at $17 per share. On January 29, 1999, just a little over a year since we managed the Blackstone buyout, we went public, offering 7 million shares at $17 per. That first day our stock closed at $16.56, generating $119 million, minus expenses. We were at last a public company listed on the NYSE. That was one of the most memorable days for AAM. We were now running with the "big boys" of the automotive world.

We soon realized, however, that with such a limited amount of our stock on the market, we were limited to trading only 25,000 shares a day. That was not enough *float* to generate the scope of trading we needed to make us a credible corporation, so we soon went back with a secondary and then a tertiary offering to get more of our action into the game. We eventually got up to an 80 percent float, meaning that 80 percent of our stock is on the street, which meant we were at last a true public company. All of a sudden our stock was caught up in the daily brawl between the bulls and the bears on Wall Street. Today it is not uncommon to see 3 million shares of AAM stock change hands in a given day, and up to 20 million if there is some good or bad news out there. The public market is a daily brawl.

In February, we went out and moved $300 million in bonds, raising more resources for capital investment and expansion overseas. Being a publicly traded company made it much easier for us to do that. The access to capital is a critical feature of being a public company.

Also, we were strategically looking for some acquisitions. That same month, we bought Colfor Manufacturing Company in Malvern, Ohio, for about $170 million in cash. Colfor provides forged and machined metal parts to companies like Ford Motor Company, Dana, and Borg-Warner. It had 850 employees at three facilities and generated annual revenues of about $125 million. Unlike AAM, Colfor was not locked into GM as its main customer. This helped reduce our dependence on GM. Also, with the addition of Colfor, we increased our consumption of quality steel bar to between 450,000 and 500,000 tons a year, enabling us to achieve more advantageous volume discounts from our steel suppliers. Colfor remains an important part of the AAM family to this day.

In March, we bought parts maker MSP Industries Corporation of Troy,

Michigan, for about $60 million in cash. MSP brought with it 236 employees at two plants in Oxford, Michigan, and a third in Center Line, Michigan (a suburb of Detroit). MSP makes precision forged powertrain, drivetrain, chassis, and other car components. MSP also remains a vital part of the AAM group.

In April we announced we would buy an abandoned building in Cheektowaga, New York (suburban Buffalo), spending $38 million to transform and equip this facility that would eventually employ more than 100 workers. We got a deal with the UAW to pay the new hires substantially less than what we were paying associates in the Buffalo axle plant and the Tonawanda forge—$12 per hour compared to $21 per hour. The UAW agreed to this, they said, because we would be making a type of gear that we were then buying from outside, non-union companies. I sensed what I thought might have been a small but significant breakthrough in the UAW's tough line. At that time, the UAW was down to 770,000 members, about half what it had been in 1979. I thought perhaps they were reading the handwriting on the wall and might be leaning toward a rendezvous with economic reality. Subsequent events would prove me wrong.

In fact, by September the word was out that the UAW was expecting to make big gains in its next contract to be negotiated in 2000. I thought the UAW attitude was aptly captured by a reporter from the *Buffalo News*, quoting an autoworker at the GM plant in Tonawanda. "We make good money now, I don't have a problem with it," he said. "Whatever they give, I take."

In my opinion, the UAW has long propagated the take, take, take mentality. That attitude has done more to erode the competitive power of Detroit and its all-important auto industry than anything the Japanese have done or the Chinese could ever do.

As for Blackstone, it did quite well from its investment in AAM. By midsummer 2001, its stake was worth, based on the stock price, about $558 million, or five times the $113 million it had invested in 1997. David Stockman was very encouraged by that result and, after giving up his position on AAM's board, went on a buying spree of other auto suppliers. He spent $1.9 billion to buy MascoTech, and then I don't know how much to buy Simpson Industries and Global Metal Technologies, Inc. Unfortunately, those other purchases did not include the AAM management team, and I do not believe Stockman fared as well with them as he did with us.

That same summer, Blackstone began an orderly exit from AAM, selling 7.5 million shares for a handsome profit. This was by mutual agreement between Blackstone and AAM. "Dick wanted an exit strategy and so did we," said Schwarzman. "Having had the experience with Ray Park, Dick did not want to get trapped in the old 'you can veto me' situation. It was a much more intelligent deal, an up-front way of dealing with this, which was great with us."

Blackstone did not want to unload its stock all at once, of course, because that would flood the market and diminish the stock's value. The following year Blackstone sold another 9.5 million shares, reducing its stake in AAM from 42.5 percent to 27 percent. By December 2003, it had sold its last holdings, completing the exit.

Blackstone was happy with the result. "We made six times our money on American Axle," said Schwarzman. "The number of people in the auto business who have made six times their money on anything you can count maybe on one hand."

"I forget the multiple," said Pete Peterson, "but it was a very, very good return.'

Yes, it was. As for me, I was free at last—which is not to suggest that Blackstone constrained me in any way. To the contrary, they were invariably supportive of whatever we wanted to do—be it borrow to invest in capital equipment, make strategic acquisitions, or build a plant in Mexico. With their controlling ownership, Blackstone could have exercised veto power over our decisions, a reality of which I remained acutely aware. Now that the company was purely public, and I was in fact the largest stockholder, I could truly say that AAM was a freestanding company and I had the reins firmly in my hands.

10

Going Global

What is now proved was once only imagined.
—William Blake

From the beginning, I imagined AAM as a competitive global manufacturing enterprise headquartered in Detroit, Michigan. Other people, though, found it difficult to imagine those old Detroit plants ever becoming competitive, much less spreading around the globe. Nothing worth doing comes easy.

MEXICO

Six times, I had my senior staff present to the original AAM board of directors a proposal to launch a factory in Mexico. As always, my staff, led by our highly competent executive Joel Robinson, did its homework and presented a coherent, balanced analysis of why American Axle needed to get a foothold south of the border. Of course, one of the major reasons was and remains that General Motors encourages its suppliers to locate near its key facilities. GM has a major commitment in Mexico and we are GM's main supplier of axles and driveshafts for trucks and SUVs. GM was and remains our largest customer. Beyond that, for any U.S. manufacturing company aspiring to go global, Mexico was the obvious first step.

But each time we put our proposal on the table, the board of directors, led by majority shareholder Ray Park, turned it down. After a while, my guys grew weary of this exercise but I wanted to give Ray every chance to come around. I kept sending them back to try again, and every time we were turned down. As actor Strother Martin said in *Cool Hand Luke,* just after he knocked Paul Newman down a hill, we had a "failure to communicate." On this issue, we simply worshipped at different altars.

Fairness requires that I give Ray Park his due. As I acknowledged earlier, without Ray's substantial financial investment, we could not have bought the old GM operations that were to become American Axle. That required courage and a leap of faith by Ray for which I will always be grateful.

I doubt if we could have created AAM without Ray Park's active support and cooperation, and may not have even launched the attempt. But at the end of the day, he and I were coming to this critical project with conflicting visions. Ray had made his fortune buying distressed properties at fire sale prices, mainly shuttered factories, at a time when the national landscape was littered with them, and reselling them piece by piece for substantial profit. That was how he saw AAM—a chance to turn those old factories around quickly and make a financial killing. There was nothing sinister, deceptive or underhanded about Ray's strategy; that was what he did for a living.

I had a different idea. I wanted to build a world-class, competitive global automotive manufacturing enterprise based in Detroit, one that would profitably grow and prosper over the long haul and (I hope) continue long after I am gone from the scene. To do that, I realized we had to have a global footprint. This is a reality that many of our business and political leaders have been slow to grasp.

Ray did not share this vision. In fact, at a holiday party in December 1995 he took me aside excitedly to inform me we had reached the point we could sell AAM for a handsome profit of several hundred million dollars. I could have sworn I saw dollar signs in his eyes. That was when I first realized we had to go our separate ways and I began looking around for a new partner, which was to be Blackstone.

I should mention we did open a sales office in Tokyo, Japan, in 1996, to begin putting the AAM name before Japanese automakers and building relationships that would eventually generate new business for us. But that was just an office, a small-budget item, and it constituted the full extent of our foreign expansion while Ray Park was majority shareholder of AAM.

In the end, Ray got what he wanted, a phenomenal return on his investment in AAM. I do not know the exact amount, but it had to be his biggest payday, at least up until then.

And I also got what I wanted: a board of directors that respected my vision of going global and was prepared to back me. One of the first actions of the incoming board, of which I was chairman, was to okay the Mexican plan. So we had a double approval. We were off and running—and not a second too soon.

I immediately dispatched four of my top guys—Joel Robinson, Dave Sibley, Bob Fair, and Yogen Rahangdale—to scout the Mexican countryside for a likely site to build a plant. I told them we did not want to be too near Mexico City or the U.S. border cities where crime and corruption were even then serious problems. I said to look toward the center of Mexico, especially the agrarian areas. They focused on the state of Guanajuato in the Mexican highlands northwest of Mexico City, smack-dab in the middle of the country. It is beautiful land nestled below the scenic Cubilete Mountain, cool and dry like the High Sierras.

Under the leadership of Governor Vincente Fox, who would later become President of Mexico, Guanajuato in those days was becoming a Mecca for foreign industrial investment. GM built its main assembly plant there in the city of Silao in the mid-1990s and later expanded it. Numerous other automobile suppliers had set up shop in Guanajuato, including Continental Teves, Delphi, Monroe, ThyssenKrupp, Elay, Hutchinson, CIE Automotive, VCST Industrial Products, Tenneco, and Aventec.

There is no great mystery about Guanajuato's attractiveness to foreign investment. While many Mexican states offer one, two, or three cities with clusters of industries, Guanajuato has fourteen cities with populations of 100,000 or more and each city offers higher education and vocational training facilities. As a result, the state has a highly developed source of educated and trained workers, both in skilled labor and management. Best of all, the people of Mexico are not afflicted with the entitlement mentality that predominates in Detroit. Endowed with a proud and sincere work ethic, they are eager for opportunity and grateful when they find it.

Guanajuato also offers excellent logistics. Two main highways crisscross Guanajuato. Highway 57, the so-called NAFTA Highway, crosses the state on its way to Mexico City, Texas and beyond, while Highway 45 stretches from the port of Veracruz to El Paso, Texas. The state is one day's truck distance from the Pacific ports at Manzanillo and Lázaro Cárdenas, as well as from the Gulf of Mexico ports of Tampico and Altamira. To take fuller advantage of all this, Guanajuato built a 2,470-acre, $100 million inland port that can shift freight between trucks, aircraft, and rail, because it operates next to rail lines and Guanajuato International Airport. It includes an inland customs house, an intermodal cargo terminal, a free trade zone, a private industrial park and an air cargo platform. *In manufacturing, it is very important to have the appropriate infrastructure.*

In sum, Guanajuato was a great place to set up shop. We looked at seven potential sites before settling on one. We really did not know how much land we needed, we simply checked out the GM site nearby and made an estimate based on GM's capacity. With strong encouragement from Governor Fox, we staked out a likely plot of land which at the time was mostly a garlic field. I walked among the garlic leaves and envisioned a large, modern industrial plant where I was standing. But this time the reality was to exceed my vision. When you dream big, you should not be surprised when big things happen.

Property rights presented a challenge. Every piece of land in Mexico is split into parcels with individual names on each. We had to perform thorough searches to identify legal owners of the land we wanted for our facilities. In some cases, we had to track them down. Then the government bought the land from them and resold it to us. We had lawyers from Mexico City helping us in what proved to be a complex process, but we finally acquired legal ownership of the land, as well as the water rights.

Water is a precious commodity in Guanajuato that enjoys a separate status from that of land. Fortunately, we have a good well that has never failed us. Our forging plant in particular needs a lot of water for cooling. We recycle as much water as we can, but still lose a lot to evaporation. There is still at least one farmer with a claim on the water accessible on the plant grounds; when he wants to water his crops, we give it to him. We are good neighbors, and are proud to be guests in Mexico.

When word got around about what we were doing, we had droves of applicants looking for jobs, which enabled us to pick and choose carefully. We would not accept anyone who had not completed high school. We wrote the curriculum for the new AAM associates and trained their instructors, while the government paid their wages for the three months they were in training. Part of the deal was our agreement to keep at least 80 percent of those hires on the job, so we were very careful about the interviews. Almost everyone we hired worked out well.

I put together a crack team of eight AAM managers led by Curt Howell, AAM's director of International Sales, who had worked for me at Chrysler years before. Curt is not only a super manager but also speaks Spanish—one of many versatile people on the AAM staff at that time who were to guide our overseas expansion in the years to come. Curt, in fact, had set up the sales office in Tokyo before taking on the Mexican assignment. He was responsible for setting up the manufacturing while David Sibley and facility savvy, Dick Britten, supervised construction of the plant. Sibley was one of the gems we inherited from GM, and would go on to build AAM plants all over the world.

We had our ground breaking early in 1998, and Governor Fox was among the visiting dignitaries. "Having such important companies in Guanajuato makes us proud because we know that the strategic value of our state is recognized in this context," he said. "We hope that the laying of this cornerstone will be the start of a chain of successes for both the company and the state."

It was not all smooth sailing by any means. In Mexico there is often a propensity for bureaucratic roadblocks and unforeseen delays. Governor Fox assured us we could come to him directly when we had a problem, and he designated a gentleman on his staff, Pepe Mendoza, as our go-to guy. We had occasions to call on Señor Mendoza. For example, at one point we had a big hole in the ground but no roads to get in and out on, which made it difficult to bring in heavy equipment and building materials. We made it clear we could dig a hole somewhere else. Mendoza stepped in and took care of the problem.

We gave Curt and his team eighteen months to get the plant up and going, but GM was prodding us to beat that deadline. We launched in 2000, two months ahead of schedule, producing top quality products.

One advantage to producing in Mexico is the wage scale that is significantly less than in the Detroit auto industry. But then wages just about anywhere in the world are less than in Detroit, which is the major reason so many once-thriving Detroit factories are deserted and decaying. *Detroit as a city, has forty-eight employee unions. They and the UAW in many instances have priced themselves out of the market.*

It must be remembered that labor costs are by no means the main determinant of a factory's competitiveness, at least not in our business. Our biggest cost is materials, mainly the high-quality steel that goes into AAM axles and drivetrains. We gained no advantage in that by setting up shop in Mexico. In fact, Mexico produces very little steel of its own. We have to import about 95 percent of what we use, much of it from the United States. We pay the world price for steel like everyone else does, plus the freight to ship it to Mexico.

The key differentiator in Mexico is not labor costs, raw materials, or infrastructure; it is the extraordinary productivity of Mexican workers. The production workers are all unionized, as required by Mexican law, but the leadership of the Mexican union understands that their primary responsibility is to help their members get and keep good jobs. Of course, the union is concerned about safety and working conditions, as it should be, but it is also concerned about economic opportunity. Our general manager, Greg Tokarz, and his team work extremely well with the union leadership—Señor Dimas Rangel, Señor Bernardo Rangel, Señor Jorge Lopez, and Señor Rogelio Perez. As a result, the AAM associates in Guanajuato have steady work and are among the best compensated industrial workers in Mexico.

The AAM associates in Guanajuato work a six-day, forty-eight-hour work week which is standard in Mexico. We are generally closed on Sunday out of respect for the associates' strong family and religious orientation that characterizes Mexican society, but if there is a crisis—a pressing need for extra production—they will work Sundays and holidays, too. AAM is their company. They very much want their company to prosper and grow, so that they and their colleagues can continue to work and enjoy steady income. What a concept!

Their greatest attribute, at least from my point of view, is flexibility. If there is a balky machine that needs repair, we do not have to follow the intricate, time-consuming practices and procedures prescribed in UAW contracts. In Detroit when you have a mechanical breakdown, the first thing you do is call a sheet metal guy to remove the machine cover, then you call an electrician to shut down the hot wires, then you call someone else to do this and someone else to do that, and on and on, before you eventually get to the problem. If a particular job is not in one employee's specific job description, he simply will not do it. If he did, he would get in trouble with the union. As a result, routine repairs can take hours if not days, resulting in lost production time and higher costs.

"There is no such thing in Guanajuato as an associate saying a specific task is not his or her job," said Dean Samuels, AAM's director of Manufacturing Corporate Engineering, who played a key role in setting up the Guanajuato facilities. "In Mexico, there are few work restrictions among associates, unless specific skills are required. If you tell associates in Guanajuato one day to load components in a bin or truck, they say okay and go do it. They understand they have a job to do, which is whatever they were instructed to do, and they do it consistently and well until told to do something else." (This may not strike most Americans as memorable, but to those of us in the Detroit auto industry, it is refreshing.)

Most of our associates in Guanajuato are cross-trained to do different things and are fully committed to lean manufacturing. There are no transfer lines or high output receiving lines. We do not have to shut down operations for hours or days to change over to a new product; the associates do it in a matter of minutes. Just-in-time delivery is basic. The associates in Guanajuato are also empowered with some of the latest technology that is available for manufacturing auto parts. This is partly because the plants are relatively new. There is no legacy equipment there, just as there are no legacy labor costs—or artificial job restrictions.

There is, however, an intense focus on product quality. Our metallurgy and testing laboratories are among the best in the world. They test steel when it is delivered to the plant to make certain it is of the highest quality. When ring gears and parts are heat treated, samples are tested to make certain they are the right hardness. We have birth certificates for all of our products and traceability when we identify a problem.

We do not economize when buying equipment and machinery; we always go for the best available. From the beginning we demand consistent quality of 2.0 Cpk (Process Capability Index) or better, and our repeatability is extremely high. Our first-time quality (FTQ) is over 99 percent, which means less scrap, fewer problems, and lower costs. Good equipment can last forever if you take good care of it, and we do. We have had precious few quality problems down Mexico way. Thank you, Señor Rangel and team.

We bus most of our Guanajuato associates into the plant facility from outlying districts, a common practice in a country where few people own their own cars. We also subsidize their breakfast and lunch expenses. They must pay a token amount, which I believe is two Mexican pesos, or about 16¢. We have to do that or else the government will declare the meals to be work benefits and tax them accordingly. Wherever you go in this world, government is government.

The experienced managers I have sent to Guanajuato go through a blissful transition stage in which some of them become convinced they have died and gone to manufacturing heaven. What couldn't we do in our own country if the workers came to work with that can-do attitude? Once upon a time they did, but many have lost it. In fairness, the UAW has made some significant concessions on productivity in recent years, including reduction of the number of job classifications, but old attitudes die hard. We are nowhere near where we need to be in the United States, to be fully competitive.

Did I mention that the AAM associates in Guanajuato come to work every day? How about that! The absenteeism rate at our plants in Mexico hovers between 1 and 2 percent. That reflects the normal ebb and flow of human life. You get sick, someone in your family gets sick, you have a car wreck, a water pipe bursts, you have to go to court for something—sometimes people cannot help missing work. Some absenteeism is unavoidable.

We understand that workers will sometimes miss work because they have to, but in our Detroit plants the absenteeism rate hovers around 22 percent! It is just part of the Detroit cultural landscape. If you were out late partying the night before or have a sudden urge to go fishing or hunting, you just do not show up for work. So if one of the key maintenance people is absent, it becomes even more challenging to get that broken machine fixed, and in Detroit on any given day there is at least a one-in-five chance that he or she is not on the job. Our experience in Mexico underscores a critical flaw in our own workforce that must change if America is to reassert its leadership in manufacturing. You begin with the basics—like showing up for work.

UNITED KINGDOM

About the same time we were building in Mexico, we purchased Albion Automotive in Glasgow, Scotland. As part of this deal, we also picked up two other plants, Spurrier Manufacturing Facility—a crankshaft plant in Leyland Preston, England—and a separate component facility in Farrington, England. We ended up folding some of the work from Farrington into the Glasgow facility, and closed down the rest years ago.

Our primary objective in purchasing Albion was to obtain their product line of large axles for commercial vehicles, and pave the way for our expansion into Europe. Previously, we had been stuck at 8,000 pounds axle capacity. Albion extended our reach to 40,000 pounds, enabling us to go after commercial business.

When we took over Albion, it was not doing quality work. Albion's 18,000 ppm defect rate was even worse than what we had found at the Detroit plants, in 1994. But we imposed the AAM systems approach to lean manufacturing and quality, and quickly began to turn that around. By 2010, Albion Automotive was nearly at zero ppm!

Albion made money when business was good, but the commercial vehicle market is very cyclical. In truth, vehicle manufacturing in the United Kingdom has been in decline for many decades. Labor costs are high and the country's currency problem stemming partially from its decision not to adopt the Euro has rendered British products less competitive than they should be. Albion is one of the few automotive manufacturing operations left in Scotland. We had to make some tough decisions regarding what to keep. Farrington went early and Spurrier delivered its last products in April 2011. For the present, we continue to operate the plant in Glasgow, but we have much more plant space there than we need.

I have to tip my hat to the people who work at Albion. Their attitude and teamwork are extraordinary. They do quality work and have willingly helped us train associates at our operations in Poland and India, knowing full well they were taking their jobs. Thanks to Albion, we now have growing commercial business in the United States, Brazil, India, China, Thailand, and Europe.

Right now, commercial vehicles represent only about 1 percent of AAM's business, but that could go to 10 percent within a few years, up to $500 million in revenues. We are especially excited by our new 16.3 tandem, 40,000-pound axle that is smaller and lighter than the main competition, but just as reliable and more fuel efficient. Working with Carter Logistics, a supply chain management company, and Purdue University, we are conducting extensive road tests of our system that will produce the hard data truck manufacturers demand when considering whether to work with specific suppliers. Carter Logistics burns 60 to 70 million gallons of diesel fuel each year. If we can save them 1–2 percent of their fuel costs—and we believe we can—that's real money for them and a lot of other trucking companies.

Our officer in charge of building the commercial vehicle business, John Sofia, is an incredibly energetic executive with exceptional engineering, manufacturing and quality ability. We thrive because of strong leaders, and John is an excellent example.

BRAZIL

About the same time production began at Guanajuato in 2001, we opened an office in São Paulo, Brazil. Ten years later it is clear that Brazil, along with China and India, is well on its way to becoming one of the world's greatest consumer markets. We got in ahead of the stampede.

Our venture in Brazil offers another example of the many wonderful experiences I have had finding bright people on the AAM staff, just sitting there waiting to be discovered and empowered. Steve Proctor was one of the senior AAM managers who was working for the GM Final Drive and Forge Business Unit (FDFBU) when we bought it. He was responsible for International Sales. We interviewed all of the GM salaried holdovers of course and I saw something in his eye that suggested to me that he was not captive to the old GM culture. On day one, I promoted him to handle our sales to GM, which at the time represented more than 95 percent of our total sales. He performed skillfully and effectively.

After a couple of years, I promoted Proctor again, this time to director of Strategic Planning. I do not believe he had any experience in strategic planning at the time, but he does now. Naturally he was deeply involved in our expansion into Mexico, and performed admirably. He was with the first group to meet with Governor Fox and shortly after I moved Curt Howell from International Sales to manage the Guanajuato operation, I put Proctor in charge of International Sales.

By this time, everyone in AAM management was used to the notion of learning new jobs and responsibilities. I want all of my people to be as versatile and multiskilled as possible, but I recognize this can demand a lot from people. As Rick Rossmann said, "When you work for Dick Dauch, you never know on Friday night what you will be doing Monday morning."

Before long, Proctor, in his role as director of International Sales, won a contract from GM that included a stipulation that we set up shop in Brazil to provide axles for a new line of trucks GM intended to make there. Proctor convinced me it was a good idea to set up shop in Brazil, so I sent him down there to prove it. He had never taken on a multifaceted assignment like that, but before long he and his wife Barbara, who had worked for GM for twenty-two years, and their two little boys were on their way to a foreign adventure.

An adventure it proved to be for all of them, especially Steve. At first we looked around for an established axle company to buy, but our major competitor Dana was the only game in town. So we found a good machining company, and entered into a joint venture with AAM owning 75 percent. The seller soon asked us to buy him out, which we did.

No sooner did Proctor get there than GM announced it would delay the launch of its new product for two years. Soon after that they announced they were going to cancel it entirely. So there we were, all dressed up and ready to dance, when the music stopped.

We are in the business of making components for vehicles, so Proctor went out looking for customers. Soon we were making a variety of products for several customers, increasing revenue and hiring associates. By the time I recalled Proctor to Detroit for a new assignment in 2003, we were generating $50 million in annual revenues and were in the process of moving from a 100,000-square-foot facility to one with 300,000 square feet in the city of Araucaria. Steve did a great job. Thank you, Steve and Barbara.

It did not happen automatically. We always encounter challenges when we invest in a new country. Our first goal is to instill the AAM culture of commitment to integrity, quality, and productivity, without challenging the cultural values of the host country. That was no great hurdle in Mexico where we started from scratch with people who did not have to unlearn anything. But the people in Brazil, especially our managers, came with baggage.

Proctor, who was the only ex-pat on the scene, invested much time and effort trying to persuade his senior Brazilian managers to embrace the AAM culture—especially our focus on developing new talent, bringing people up through the ranks, and giving them increased responsibility. Proctor's younger corps were eager to seize the opportunities that this system offered, but the older guys felt threatened.

"I had to send a message that we would not tolerate resistance to change," Proctor said. "When I made that move, the company started improving immediately. The younger people coming up embraced AAM culture with enthusiasm. Quality got better and production increased." The Brazilian operation quickly became profitable.

In other words, the AAM team in Brazil jelled.

AAM's work in Brazil today is mostly for automobiles, not our usual focus on trucks and SUVs. We have a promising new contract with Volkswagen and, wonder of wonders, GM is finally following through on the plan it had way back when to launch a new small truck in Brazil. We will have that business, but it took ten years of patience and persistence to get it.

We have about 650 people working in Brazil now and expect to be generating about $250 million in annual revenue in the near future. Given the size of the Brazilian market, and its prospects for growth in the years ahead, our operations there could become even bigger in the long term. Make no mistake—we are in for the long haul.

INDIA

One of the ablest people to serve AAM was its third president, my good friend, Yogen Rahangdale. He came here from India many years ago with a few dollars in his pocket and a vague notion that he wanted to do something with his life. He worked with me at VWoA and Chrysler and moved over to AAM about a year after the company got started. He is a master of planning and managing resources. I knew we had to get into India sooner or later, and because of Yogen's background I sent him there several times over a period of years to scout out prospects and build relationships with key people and companies.

Another key figure in our India adventure was Fran Leo, a business consultant from nearby Sri Lanka with extensive contacts and experience in the region. Eventually, when we were getting close to making a commitment in India, Leo arranged a memorable visit to India for Yogen, John Bellanti, and me. We visited the Taj Mahal and rode an elephant on a safari into tiger country. I was charmed by the people I met there, but concerned about the culture we would have to adapt to, and downright alarmed by the primitive infrastructure and environmental conditions. Still, if you're going to be there, you have to handle the entire package. India is a tough, tough challenge.

Yet you cannot ignore India. By 2006, we had decided we needed to manufacture there for an obvious reason—it is a large country that offers almost unlimited opportunity for growth. Indeed, by 2020, India is projected to have a larger population than China. We needed greater name recognition for AAM in the world vehicle market, and more work with commercial vehicles, which are the big opportunity in India. We decided we had to be there. So we began building a plant in Pune, which is 180 kilometers east of Mumbai (Bombay).

We had trouble getting it off the ground. The main problem was finding the right person to manage our business in a country that posed many more challenges than Mexico, Scotland, or Brazil. For a time, we alternated between managers from the United States who could not fathom the Indian culture, and executives from India who could not fathom the AAM culture. Progress was slow, but we were bulldog-determined to make it work.

I finally called on one of my former colleagues who had worked with me at various stops along the way of my career, and had left AAM a few years before to start his own business, Rick Rossmann. Rick had sold his business and was ready for a fresh challenge. I sent him to Pune in 2008 to analyze the situation and report back. He told us one of the senior officers there had inadequate leadership skills and had to go. I said okay, so I had Rick replace him. Rick proved to be the perfect leader for AAM-India, the right guy at the right formative time.

"It is difficult to plan in India," said Leo, who knows whereof he speaks. "The infrastructure is hopeless, people are not accustomed to deadlines, and deliveries are always a problem."

My old reliable workhorse Dave Sibley had more than his share of problems building our AAM facilities in India. "I had built plants in eight countries before, but nothing prepared me for India," he said. "They have the worst quality of workmanship I have ever seen. They have no skilled tradesmen, just unskilled labor. They assign guys to work on high-voltage wires who know nothing about electricity. They do what they are told, but have no idea why."

Rossmann said India has laws and rules for everything, but no one pays any attention to them. Or as Leo said, "Rules are never a problem in India. If you have a horn, you have the right of way."

Rossmann has had a heck of a time getting his Indian staff to grasp the notion of coming to work on time. In India, it seems, you just drift into work whenever it suits you. Of course, the inadequate infrastructure and endless traffic jams compound the problem. To be somewhere on time, you have to leave early, way early.

Rossmann is tough, smart, experienced and resourceful, a force to be reckoned with. He always found ways to solve problems at AAM's plants in the United States and he found ways to solve problems in India. He found highly qualified workers—everyone has an associate degree or better. He gave them responsibility and saw to it that they would handle it. Each associate is responsible for his own equipment, workstation cleanliness, cycle times, gauges, quality checks. Every management person works one shift per month on the factory floor doing basic production work. He insisted that every associate knew what the company makes and be familiar with the processes. He urged every associate to identify ways to produce better products more efficiently.

The results are zero defects, zero injuries, and a profitable, growing business. We are making axles for Tata's three-quarter-ton cargo carrier and another one for their bus. We are launching a forty-ton carrier for Navistar, and expect to get a twenty-five-ton contract from them as well. We have won our first-ever contract from Honda, which I hope will lead to more business in the future. We have opened a second plant in Pantnagar, in the northern part of India, and finished construction of our third plant in Chennai, India, in December 2011. They are producing products for Daimler trucks.

Our Indian operations are becoming profitable and the sky is the limit. AAM is delighted to be a guest in India and looks forward to a long and mutually prosperous experience in that great country.

CHINA

Of course, the biggest opportunities are in China where 1.3 billion people are forging their way into the middle class and the economy is growing by leaps and bounds. In the same years we were launching in Mexico, Brazil, and India, we were building a factory in Changshu, China, a little over an hour north from downtown Shanghai, a "village" of about 1.8 million people very close to where the Yangtze River flows into the South China Sea. The Chinese have set up a twenty-six-square-mile economic zone there with everything you need to operate modern factories. Time was of the essence. We had taken an order for axles from DaimlerChrysler in 2005 and needed to be producing by 2006.

My main man on the ground for the China launch was Bill Smith, who had worked with me at GM and Chrysler. Smith had worked in China before and was familiar with the language and customs.

We had heard some horror stories about doing business in China, but it actually is not so bad if you know your way around, and Smith does. He spent a lot of time schmoozing with Chinese political and government officials, building those all-important relationships that determine success in Asia. We were setting up a wholly owned foreign enterprise (a WOFE), which created additional barriers. It is easier if you have a Chinese partner, but we went it alone on Changshu.

One of our main hurdles was getting labeled a high-tech company, which brings with it all manner of tax breaks and other considerations. The Chinese officials did not think of axles as high-tech products, but ours are. After a seemingly endless parade of dinners and meetings, and more than a few confrontations, we won the designation.

We were forging ahead to get all of the requisite permits and licenses, working with Chinese bureaucrats who did not like to be hurried. We wanted to bring in about $13 million in used manufacturing equipment, which is a big problem for the Chinese, who want everything to be made domestically. That particular issue went down to the wire, but we prevailed in the end. "You have to be careful over there not to offend people," Smith said. "Government officials can let papers sit on their desks indefinitely."

Another issue was a special machine made in Japan that we needed. We had to obtain special approval from Washington, D.C., because someone had determined it could be used for military purposes. Also, Chinese officials reserved the right to ban it after it arrived, which was disconcerting. An agent from the Central Intelligence Agency came by to check it out when it arrived. In the end, though, everyone signed off.

We got past all that and launched on time in 2006 with about 300 associates who earn a standard Chinese rate of 1,400 yuan or $200 a month. I went over there in December for a big celebration to launch the new plant. All the associates and their families were invited. I took a turn serving a traditional American picnic of barbeque ribs with all the usual fixings. The Chinese associates were initially apprehensive to have the big American CEO waiting on them, but they warmed to me quickly. I was told later that this gesture made a lasting impression, and a positive one. At dusk, we had a fireworks display. It was a great moment in the history of AAM.

China is a highly competitive environment. All of our major competitors are there. The average price of a vehicle in China is about $17,000 compared to $29,000 in the United States, so the margins are tight. Our plant there is more labor intensive than some others, but we sacrifice nothing in quality, which remains our major calling card all around the world. Most of what we produce is sold into the China market.

We soon opened another manufacturing facility in Hefei, which is a joint venture with a Chinese company. Our first general manager there was Kim Forshee, who had previously managed our operation in Poland. He did an excellent job. We have recently assigned Colin Huang as our general manager. The business has rapidly and profitably grown. We have all the business we can handle and are on a vigorous growth curve. China looms large in our vision for AAM's future. We are happy to be there. Our China operations are profitable.

THAILAND

We are highly dependent on the pickup truck business both at home and abroad, and Thailand is the world's second largest market for pickup trucks, after the United States. We opened a new manufacturing facility there in Rayong in 2011 and it holds great promise. Our start-up plant manager in Thailand was Joe Tang. He had been with AAM since 1997 and is one of our most resourceful leaders. We recently assigned Greg Bastien to the plant manager position. GM is making its new global market midsize pickup truck there, for which we are providing driveline products.

Thailand has a first-rate infrastructure and aspires to become the automotive hub of Southeast Asia. The government offers excellent incentives for setting up shop there, including no taxes for eight years and the ability to import machinery duty free. The Thai Board of Investment paves the way for us and helps resolve problems. The Thais are seriously concerned about environmental issues, much more so than the Chinese, but AAM is ahead of the curve on that issue and we expect little problem meeting their rules.

We are expecting our Thai business to be from $120 million to $130 million in a few years, but it could be much greater than that. One of the most intriguing possibilities attending our Thailand investment is the Japanese auto companies—Nissan, Honda, Toyota, Suzuki, Mazda—that are assembling vehicles in Thailand but import their axles and other driveline components from Japan. They must pay a stiff duty on those imports because Thailand encourages foreign companies to manufacture all of the components there. The Japanese are well aware of AAM's reputation for quality and engineering and have expressed interest in buying key components from us. If we are successful in acquiring that business, we will be off and running.

The Thai workers are diligent and eager to learn, not afraid of a challenge. They will work late if needed as long as they are paid fairly and receive decent benefits. Absenteeism is negligible. In Thailand, as in China, India, Mexico, and Brazil, we do not have to contend with the entitlement mentality.

EUROPE

We set up a business office in Frankfurt, Germany, in 2006. Europe is a tough market because it has been worked over for decades by some of the biggest names in the automotive industry. Yet it is also filled to overflowing with advanced manufacturing and emerging technologies. We decided we needed to be there to fly the AAM flag, be a part of that scene and look for opportunities to break in. It may seem presumptuous, but the simple fact is that we are the best at what we do. Our quality and technology are second to none and our pricing is market competitive. We are making our presence known, not to mention our capabilities, to Opel, Daimler (Mercedes-Benz), BMW, Volkswagen, Audi—all of the major German automotive names. We are now reaching out to other European OEMs.

We established our European headquarters in Bad Homburg, Germany (a suburb of Frankfurt), but we also needed to establish a competitive manufacturing facility in Europe, and after looking around we decided on Poland. We have a manufacturing facility now in Świdnica. The Polish government helped us find an empty factory with more than ample space for our needs, and helped us get started. I pulled Bill Smith back from China to set it up, and moved Steve Proctor—who had rotated back to the states from Brazil—over to China where he helped establish a regional Asian AAM business.

We had one customer when we set up shop in Świdnica and were about to sign a deal with another when the first customer withdrew at the last minute. It was the time of AAM's troubles—the 2008 UAW strike, the U.S. economic crisis, the bankruptcy of our major customers GM and Chrysler—and this customer had understandable reservations about our future. I believe that was the only business we lost because of the downturn in the United States, but it hurt. You take a hit, get up, dust yourself off, and get back in the game. Life's lessons can be hard.

Today, as in Asia, Brazil, and Mexico, our future in Poland looks bright. We are expanding, winning more contracts, hiring more associates. Our target is to do more than $500 million in Europe within a few years. Our AAM president in Europe, David Culton, is a third-generation automotive executive and totally prepared for the stiff challenge facing him and AAM. His new and highly qualified plant manager in Świdnica, Poland, is Dave Guarisimo, who managed our forge in Guanajuato, Mexico. Dave and his family are adapting to Poland quite well. Dave has moved his operation quickly to profitability.

THE MEXICAN JEWEL IN THE AAM CROWN

The Guanajuato plant's second product, after an 11.5-inch axle, was an 8.6-inch rear axle for the GM plant six miles away. That was the first of many products that today comprise a full array of advanced, high-quality products coming out of the AAM Guanajuato Manufacturing Complex.

Since the initial construction, the Guanajuato facility has seen several major expansions. By 2001, when we had the Guanajuato Forge up and running along with the axle plant, we were producing 1,300 axles a day. By 2010, we were producing more than 6,400 axles and Power Transfer Units (PTUs) a day at that facility. We have more than 110 semi-trucks coming in and going out every day. The plant is getting big at 1.4 million square feet, and employs more than 3,000 people. Guanajuato is a good profit generator for AAM.

The quality at Guanajuato is superb, knocking on zero ppm! The entire facility is a poster child for lean manufacturing. Last year, the Guanajuato Manufacturing Complex was awarded the coveted Shingo Prize, which *BusinessWeek* has called the Nobel Prize of manufacturing. It was a major achievement and one in which everyone at AAM takes great pride. Teamwork is power.

In October 2010, we hosted the AAM board of directors at the Guanajuato plant for its regular fall meeting. Some of the directors had been there before, but even they were dazzled by what they saw. The sprawling facility looks like a bright, shiny new gold piece—like every other AAM facility. Visitors routinely comment that they could eat off the floor, an exaggeration perhaps, but it accurately reflects a place that is modern, clean, safe, efficient and flexible. One of our directors, Sam Bonanno, who worked in the auto industry for forty years, said it was the most awesome manufacturing plant he had ever seen. I second that.

11

Into the New Century

Take calculated risks. That is quite different from being rash.

—Gen. George S. Patton

As we embarked upon the new century, AAM was ready to rock. We had gone through the turmoil of letting about half of our associates "flow back" to GM, and had replaced them with a new, better-educated crew more inclined to embrace AAM values. We had gone through the tough transition from five-cut, wet cut, to two-cut, dry cut that entailed massive investment and wholesale retraining of associates over a period of years. Our investments in research and development were beginning to pay off as a steady stream of innovative new products, technologies and processes were putting us ahead of the curve. And we had obtained freedom to go global. It was time to really spread our wings.

From 1994 to 2004 there were no strikes or disruptions through more than 200 million man-hours of work. Admittedly, we achieved that by always caving to the UAW and yielding to its increasingly unrealistic demands. But GM was riding the gravy train and did not want any disruptions of supply, especially of key components like the axles and drivetrains we made for their hot-selling trucks and SUVs. Every time we tried to stand up to the UAW, GM agreed to pay more for parts to help us cover the increased cost of labor. I knew we were just kicking the can down the road, but there was little I could do about it at the time. I have always said it is a dumb rat that has only one hole. At the time, we were overly dependent on the plants in Detroit, Buffalo, and Three Rivers to produce our products, but we were expanding a new alternative in Mexico* and I knew the day would come when the UAW's stranglehold on us would be lifted.

Early in 2000, we reported 1999 sales revenue of $2,953 billion, an increase of $912.5 million over the year before. Our net income was $115.6 million. In February, we announced record profit-sharing payments to our eligible U.S. employees of $2,692.88. That same month we reached a tentative deal with the UAW averting a possible walkout of our 7,500 UAW associates, which the union ratified in April. No wonder—the agreement provided for a 3 percent wage increase each year for the four years of the contract, an improved cost of living adjustment, and a $1,350 up-front bonus. All told, the deal meant more than $29,900 to a typical UAW associate.

I knew we could not afford that, but the potential long-term impact of the union agreement got lost amid the good economic news of a company doing very well indeed. *Automotive Engineering* magazine reported that in our first year, we had made 9,000 axles a day that were not of the best quality. Six years later volume had doubled and quality, as measured in ppm discrepancies, had improved by 99 percent. More than 95 percent of our products were at zero ppm. Not too shabby. *Automotive Industries* placed us among the "best of the best" automotive suppliers. *Crain's Detroit Business* reported we were tops among the Michigan Superstar 10, finishing first on return on equity and income growth.

For eleven years, AAM's corporate office was on the second floor of Plant #3 at the Detroit facility. I made the decision that the plants should be cleaned up and modernized and associates would get training and skill set advancements before a separate headquarters would be established.

In 2003–4 we fulfilled a longtime goal of mine. AAM committed to build a seven-story headquarters building alongside I-75 adjacent to our Detroit plants, where we are based today. The beautiful modernistic structure looms tall among the Detroit landscape, surrounded by grass, flowers, and trees. My wife Sandy played an active and important leadership role in the design and décor of the building, which is a complicated process that requires a multitude of decisions. She and the rest of the committee did an excellent job as any visitor to our headquarters can attest. It offers a stark contrast to the devas-

---

* In July of 2000, the Associated Press reported that the AAM plant in Mexico was seen as Vicente Fox's "crowning achievement" of his term as governor. Fox by then was President of Mexico.

tated neighborhoods in the surrounding area of the city, dramatic testimony to what Detroit could be if it could only shed the debilitating entitlement mentality that holds it captive.

HELEN'S ROSE GARDEN

My parents raised me with a keen awareness and appreciation for nature. In addition to cows, we maintained beehives. I helped my mother Helen tend the hives, wearing nets and using smoke to discourage the little critters from using their stingers, not always successfully. Bees are crucial to agriculture, providing pollination for a wide variety of crops. They also pollinate flowers, which my mother loved. She was especially fond of roses.

My older brothers teased me unmercifully about my work with bees and flowers, but I do believe my mother was on to something. Flowers are beautiful, they freshen the air, and—most importantly—they make people smile.

I have mentioned earlier the deplorable condition of the facilities when we bought them, but I neglected to mention the smell. In addition to the filth, we had aging coolant systems that had not been cleaned in years. In some parts of the property and on some days, the smell would knock a buzzard off an outhouse. From day one, working with Sandy, we made certain we had flowers in critical areas, especially the reception area where visitors were received.

As we were building our headquarters building, that we dedicated in 2004, I insisted we include plans for landscaped gardens around the building to make it more attractive to our associates and visitors. To honor my mother, I came up with the idea of a rose garden that today is the first thing you will see when you drive up to our building. We have three species of roses, with thirty-three plants of each—a total of ninety-nine plants of different colors. We take good care of those plants year round, and have yet to lose any of them. Every Monday in season, AAM executive assistants are encouraged to cut a few roses and put them in vases on their desks throughout the building, including the front desk in the reception area. We provide tools and instructions because it is easy to incur nicks or worse when cutting roses.

Flowers do not bloom year round in Detroit, of course, but in season those roses brighten up the place, inside and out, and the fragrance is inescapable.

Back in 1964, country singer Lynn Anderson had a big hit with a song "I Never Promised You a Rose Garden," written by Joe South. Well, I did promise my mother a rose garden, which today is known as Helen's Garden. Every time I pass that garden, or see and smell the roses here and there throughout our headquarters, I think of her.

HIGH-WATER MARK

We were reaching our peak size, employing nearly 12,000 associates worldwide building world-class products in more than seven million square feet of manufacturing space in the United States, Brazil, Mexico, Scotland, and England. (We were not yet in China, Thailand, Poland, and India.) On an average day, we were filling nearly three hundred semi-trailers with finished products for shipment by truck and another thirteen boxcars for rail shipment.

We were cashing in on contracts to supply parts for GM's hot-selling light trucks, such as the Chevrolet Silverado pickup truck and GMC Envoy SUV. We were like a teenager growing out of his britches. AAM by then had beaten Wall Street expectations ten times in a row. That does not happen by accident. Our performance on Wall Street was consistently strong as we recorded an 8 percent compound annual growth rate (CAGR) year after year for what would be a ten-year stretch.

"They've got a nice mix of business," Matthew Stover, auto parts analyst for Salomon Smith Barney of New York, said of AAM. "They are on all of GM's large pickups and SUVs, which are selling really well, and GM is really pushing to make as many of them as they can. But it's not like just the chips fell in the right place for Axle. Yes, they're on products like the Yukon and Avalanche, but they're also making quality parts and keeping their costs low."

It wasn't all sweetness and light. The motor vehicle industry is notorious for its ups and downs. By the end of 2000, we could see vehicle sales slowing down. In January 2001, we put 200 of our associates on temporary layoff. Still, the AAM associates got a $2,193 average bonus for 2000. Our sales had grown 4 percent in 2000, and R&D spending had gone up 19 percent to $46.4 million.

In May we announced we would add 225 jobs to our plant in Three Rivers reflecting the great strides the associates there were making. Three Rivers had been a marginal operation when we took over. Three Rivers had gone from producing 7,000 propeller shafts a day in 1994 to 14,000 in 2001. It was becoming an excellent operation!

By the end of July 2000, AAM stock hit $21.06 per share. By October, we reported that profits had increased 5.4 percent despite an overall industry slide. The reason was trucks, trucks, and more trucks. GM's light trucks such as the

Chevrolet Silverado and GMC Envoy SUV were selling like hotcakes and every one of them came equipped with an AAM-made undercarriage. To top it all off, in November we won a $240 million annual contract from DaimlerChrysler to supply axles and drive shafts for a redesigned Dodge Ram heavy-duty truck. Our competitor Dana had held that contract for decades, but we took it away. Thanks to our focus on R&D and the fine work of our Technical Center, our axles ride smoother and quieter, and last longer. From 1994 until 2000, AAM had invested $100 million in associate training and $1.9 billion in capital investments. It was all paying off.

In 1996, AAM had averaged $785 revenue in parts per vehicle. By 2001, we had increased that content to $1,115. That reflected mainly our commitment to R&D. We were constantly adding value to our customers' products.

In January 2002, AAM was named one of five winners of 2001 Shareholder Value Awards jointly presented by *Automotive News* and PricewaterhouseCoopers. The awards recognize the highest total shareholder return for automotive vehicle manufacturers, suppliers and retail distributors. Our stock increase of more than 169 percent for 2001 was ranked eleventh on the New York Stock Exchange. *Forbes* magazine chimed in by including us in the "Platinum 400" as one of the best big companies in North America in terms of outstanding profitability and growth.

The following month, a local magazine, *The Detroiter*, published a feature article about me entitled, "The Quintessential Truck Guy." Trucks had gone from about 10 percent of the consumer vehicle market in 1964 to about 50 percent in 2002.

> *. . . Richard Dauch saw something in the marketplace that few others did . . . .*
>
> *Trucks. And more trucks. And SUVs on truck frames. All using special axles and drivelines developed by—you guessed it—American Axle.*
>
> *If Bob Lutz of GM is a "car guy," then Richard Dauch is the quintessential "truck guy." When Dauch got into American Axle in the early to mid '90s he correctly believed that trucks would continue to grow significantly— at a time when many thought they had peaked out. He predicted that American Axle's truck and four-wheel drive specialties would position it for growth in GM business, while fueling its expansion to other automotives.*

Slowly, the market was coming back. GM boosted its earnings estimates for the year and said it would increase vehicle production by about 20,000 in the first quarter, good news for AAM. Interestingly, auto suppliers as a group reported 170 percent higher losses for last quarter of 2001, and a 185 percent drop for the year. Only four of thirteen companies reported improved results and only three reported profits. AAM was one of the three. We were separating ourselves from the pack.

We won the contract for the GMT900, GM's new generation of full-size trucks and SUVs, to provide front and rear axles, differential and gears and driveshafts. We also got the go-ahead to manage the integration of brakes, springs, shock absorbers and stabilizer bars, sourcing control for the complete driveline. The ten-year deal included one-piece aluminum, one-piece steel, and two-piece steel driveshaft assemblies for GM's full size trucks and SUVs. We projected this contract to bring us about $1.5 billion annually for several years, about half of our total revenues. No one was surprised that we won this business, but it came as a relief, even so. In this business, you just never know when fate is going to throw you a curve ball. The GMT900 contract meant several more years of work for our biggest customer. Unfortunately it did nothing to reduce our dependence on GM, which at that time represented about 87 percent of our business.

INNOVATION AND TECHNOLOGY

We continued our commitment to investing in the future. We announced we would build a multimillion-dollar research and training center near our headquarters to open in stages by 2006. It was designed to enable us to build and test prototype axles, brake components, and gears, and develop new production techniques and provide leadership and safety training for associates in partnership with the UAW.

I was committed to innovation from day one and determined to make it a key part of the AAM's business mentality and action. Also, I realized early on there was an opportunity to carve out a niche as a high-tech provider of axles and other driveline and suspension components. The axle business had long been neglected. For many years, automakers had been pouring money into modern, electronically controlled engines and transmissions, but forgetting about axles—which are the third critical component of a high-tech power train. We saw a golden opportunity.

I was determined to get AAM into the forefront of R&D in electronics. When we bought the assets from GM, we had nothing electrical, no electronic control group. We had to build a brand new electrical laboratory because we knew automotive technology was moving ahead. We wanted to imbed electronics into the product with software and logic. We now have almost fifty electronic engineers on board. AAM has gone from only 5 percent of product with electronic integration in the year 2000 up to more than 80 percent today! Much of this uses sophisticated electronic control units which are basically on-board computers that constantly monitor the operation of the product and control the driving experience. This allows for the intelligent control of torque to each wheel independently to enhance the launch of the vehicle under adverse road conditions as well as providing improved handling under normal highway conditions. AAM has developed the ability to perform computer simulations of the vehicle handling, in order to refine the vehicle control logic and achieve the right balance of performance driving in a nonintrusive manner to the vehicle occupants.

To date, we have 202 patents in our arsenal. One of our latest breakthroughs is the EcoTrac driveline, an innovative combination of technologies that provides the full all-wheel-drive experience with traction control for launch assist and improved road handling while avoiding the fuel economy losses associated with the spinning drag found in most vehicle systems.

This means that all four wheels have driving traction so you can pull out of that snow bank, and it also really improves handling on the road. "You're driving down the street and someone pulls in front of you," said Dr. Glen Steyer, a brilliant applications engineer who leads our creative team in our Rochester Hills Technical Center. "The road may be slippery wet. With a typical vehicle, your tires will lose traction. Rather than power through a turn, you will slide. Handling assist means the vehicle will identify when it needs to send torque to which wheel, will anticipate what you need to do, and activate the right gears to get you there."

BACK TO THREE RIVERS

We made some news in June 2002 when we announced we were moving production of the AAM 11.5-inch axle back from Mexico to our Three Rivers plant. Three Rivers driveshaft production had reached record levels with world class quality and delivery. Through use of "lean" manufacturing, we were able to consolidate all of our driveshaft operations at Three Rivers into one section of the plant. That enabled us to add axle production capability there, and create more jobs. Randy Sherfield, who had followed Bill Webster as the UAW bargaining chairman at Three Rivers, helped immensely on our ability to become market competitive and operationally flexible at Three Rivers. Thank you, Randy.

About the same time, we finally shut down our shared operation in St. Catharines, Ontario. As I have related elsewhere, that facility was something of an anomalous part of AAM's overall production strategy. We did not own the plant itself and the employees were not AAM associates; we just controlled the output and the installed capacity. When the demand evaporated, we were able to step away without expensive obligations to the workforce or impaired asset exposure.

In November, an unnamed analyst was quoted in *The Wall Street Journal* talking about AAM: "I think they took a sow's ear and turned it into a silk purse. Specifically, they have taken a rather mundane business, axles and drive shafts, and turned it into a high value-added area where they truly bring value to vehicle manufacturers."

"To Dauch," wrote Tom Walsh in the March 14, 2003 *Detroit Free Press*, "nothing is sweeter than making fat profits by manufacturing gritty products like axles and gears in an old Detroit factory complex using a UAW workforce."

In 1994, it took AAM approximately eleven hours of labor to generate $1000 in sales. By 2003, that number had dropped to five and a half hours! Overall our sales rose 12 percent in 2002, and we had a productivity increase of 10 percent. Within the space of a year, the rating agencies issued thirty-one downgrades of auto industry debt. AAM got two of three upgrades.

An even more discerning analysis by Jim Gillette was published by *Automotive Design & Production* in January 2003. "In spite of widespread financial distress among their ranks, there are indeed a few examples of suppliers with exceptional financial performance. The superbly managed American Axle & Manufacturing's return on equity of 22.5% and an operating profit margin of 12%, for example, far exceeded the results of Ford and GM."

Of course, a good bit of our success stemmed from the original agreement under which we purchased the GM assets that became AAM. For the first seven years, GM was all but prohibited from buying axles, drive shafts and other critical components used in its pickup trucks and SUVs from any company other than AAM. And the GM employees who had flowed back to GM were singing the blues again when we reported our profit-sharing checks for associates based on 2002's performance—averaging $2,600. That was more than double the profit sharing paid by GM, Ford and Chrysler.

We encountered a brief setback with our associates at Three Rivers, who rejected a six-year contract proposal that would have paid newly hired hourly associates less than the rate paid those already on the payroll. It would have added a third tier to the existing two-tier system. Here again this was part of our continuing struggle to get associate compensation in line with the competition. It would have meant more work for the plant, but it was voted down by 69 percent of the associates. We finally worked out a deal acceptable to them that was ratified in August. It provided for 63¢ an hour to be cut from higher tier associates (about 650 of them) and for starting wages to be $13.50 an hour and go as high as $17. The cuts would average out to about $1,300 per associate.

In August, Michigan governor Jennifer Granholm, who had recently succeeded John Engler in Lansing, came by AAM for a visit. Granholm was increasingly concerned about the loss of manufacturing jobs in Michigan, and the visible decline of Detroit. "The partnership of private business, labor, and state and local government has made the American Axle headquarters project a model for maintaining manufacturing jobs in Michigan," she said at the time. "We are here today to engage in an open discussion about how we can continue to work together to keep these jobs in Michigan and carry the success we see here today forward to retain and grow manufacturing jobs in our state."

Regrettably, Governor Granholm offered no suggestions for persuading her friends at the UAW to curb their excessive compensation demands or defense of nonproductive, restrictive work rules. Granholm is smart and dedicated, but proved unable to rise above the narrow interests of her political base. Her lack of leadership on this issue showed she was part and parcel of the entitlement mentality that has led Detroit, and Michigan, into economic stagnation.

SPEAKING OUT

That same month I took the gavel as chairman of the National Association of Manufacturers (NAM) in Washington, D.C., an opportunity I had really been looking forward to. The NAM is one of the top business voices in the nation's capital. I have never been shy about taking the stage and this was a topic I felt really strongly about. I have an excellent relationship with Jerry Jasinowski,* who was NAM president during my chairmanship, and I looked forward to this opportunity to talk to the American people about what was happening to

---

* Jasinowski retired from the NAM presidency in 2004, and was succeeded by then former Michigan governor John Engler.

manufacturing in our country, and the critical need for pro-manufacturing and business policies. For the next year, I would accept a variety of speaking engagements before business and civic groups throughout the country, talking about the unprecedented challenges posed by intense foreign competition that was steadily wresting much manufacturing—and millions of manufacturing jobs—away from the United States.

Of course, then as now, my primary focus was on the auto industry. But as chairman of NAM, I addressed the full spectrum of manufacturing issues and learned a lot about what is happening to our manufacturing sector—and that despite our adversity, we remain the world's number one manufacturing nation. It is imperative that we sustain that leadership.

That was a busy year for me, as I was primarily engaged in leading AAM through rapid growth. We were doing well and while I always anticipate problems and challenges, the future looked bright as far as I could see.

AAM closed out 2003 on a couple of significant high notes. AAM's debt rating was raised to investment grade for the first time by Standard & Poor's (S&P) reflecting our gradual reduction of dependence on GM. On January 15, 2004, we reported record earnings of $197.1 million for 2003 based on total sales of $3,682 billion. We were buying 250,000 tons of steel a year. We were, in fact, the largest buyer of special bar quality (SBQ) steel in the automotive industry.

Yet every time you get riding high in the automotive industry, reality intervenes to bring you back down to planet earth. The UAW contract was up for renegotiation.

I had been patiently explaining to the UAW leadership for years that its demands were getting way out of line with economic and market reality. In particular, a supplier like AAM could not continue indefinitely to carry wage and benefit packages comparable to those borne by the Big Three. The UAW brass, a changing cast of characters over the years, all assured me they understood this reality and that they would make concessions the next time around. Yet somehow every time negotiations came up again, the new leaders were just as intransigent as previous ones had been. The negotiations in 2004 would be no different.

The UAW was sitting out on a limb and sawing away, heedless of the consequences. From a peak of 1.5 million members in 1979, its membership had dwindled to a little over 600,000 in 2004, but the implications of that trend escaped the new UAW president, Ron Gettelfinger. He pointed out, accurately, that labor-management cooperation had helped AAM to become a top-rated performer. "Not only has American Axle's UAW-represented workforce increased since 1994," he said, "its stock price has more than doubled." He did not explain why that compelled the UAW to demand wages and benefits that were not market competitive.

He was right about our performance—we were doing well. As if to underscore the company's growing success, in February AAM won a $40 million contract to supply axles to Korean SUV maker Ssangyong Motor Company, Korea's fourth-largest automaker with sales of $2.85 billion. It was another one of our innovations, AAM's Power Lite aluminum design that reduced weight and improved gas mileage, that swung the deal. This represented our first real penetration of the Asian market. About the same time, we announced we were investing $28 million to expand our Three Rivers plant.

The UAW dug in its heels, making excessive demands that were clearly unsustainable in the long term. When we balked, the UAW went out on a strike that lasted only one and a half days. It was AAM's first labor interruption, but it would not be the last. Once again, I got the call from GM. GM trucks and SUVs were selling well and the company's management could not bear the thought of a disruption of supply. GM quietly agreed to help cover the increased costs of the UAW contract, and to send us more contracts. *The simple fact is that the UAW had both GM and AAM over a barrel.* Our Mexican plant was expanding, but was not yet strong enough to supply all of our production for GM.

The deal simply postponed the day of reckoning. I stood before a window with colleagues, watching the union demonstrators manning the picket lines below. I told my colleagues not to worry—that the associates would be back at work within hours. But four years from then, when the contract came up for renegotiation in 2008, the shoe would be on the other foot.

In May, I told a reporter from Reuters that the rising costs of operation were impeding the nation's ability to compete in the global marketplace. What is at stake? The absolute survival of Detroit's auto industry as we know it. I pointed out that the Big Three had seen their market share drop from 73 percent in 1997 to under 60 percent in 2003. It was not a cyclical change, but rather a harsh and real structural change that had wiped out thousands of jobs in Michigan and the Midwest.

But when things are going well, it is difficult to make people see looming challenges over the horizon. By summer we were opening our new headquarters building, which makes a powerful impression standing tall over Exit 55 of I-75. We had a big celebration. Our salaried associates were excited about moving into their new surroundings. We had everything we needed to manage our expanding global business right there in one place. The UAW problem was put on a back burner for at least four years. We returned our focus to the commercial enterprise of making quality products and finding new industrial opportunities.

SYSTEMS MIGRATION

When we took over the old GM facilities, we inherited a management information system created and managed by Electronic Data Systems (EDS), which had been a part of GM. After a while, I figured out that EDS was not serving us very well and determined to go it alone. That would prove an arduous journey. In those days, digital communications were evolving and it was hard to find anyone who really understood it.

Fortunately, I knew a fellow named Bob Thomas who had worked with me in earlier years and brought him on board AAM. Thomas began building an IT team and expanding its capabilities year after year, acquiring and mastering new technologies as they came online. Under his leadership, we undertook a program we called Enterprise Resource Planning (ERP) to educate and train associates how to take full advantage of the new, evolving system, and to move from *systems migration*—away from EDS to AAM—into *systems integration*, as we meshed all of our IT capabilities into one coherent, unified system.

It happened gradually, and by midway into the first decade of the new century, we had developed an extraordinary global IT infrastructure that ties all of our thirty-three facilities in thirteen countries together as if they were all in the same block. We have a command center in our headquarters building that provides instantaneous communications throughout the world. On the wall is a global map that clearly depicts all the AAM site locations. If a location is lit in green, we know everything is working smoothly. Other colors reflect problems or potential catastrophes. Whatever happens, we know instantly.

In 2007, Thomas retired and eventually the leadership baton was assumed by Tom Bartol. He is one of AAM's rising stars. Thank you, Bob, for your dedication, determination and inspired and intelligent leadership.

All of our computerized systems—whether for human resources, engineering, customer service, supplier management—are run under a single instance of AAM's Oracle ERP package. How we ship, take inventory, monitor machinery, pay associates is exactly the same throughout the world. "If they had different applications, it would be difficult to keep track of everything," Bartol said. "Our package is multilingual. We do business in U.S. dollars, but we are capable of handling different currencies. We are very big on common processes and common systems. Our buildings look similar and we want our computers to be the same, everywhere around the globe, even down to the wires that run into the walls. In IT, standardization is the key to maintaining a common structure, as well as a low cost operational structure. Our entire system is interconnected."

Every AAM salaried associate has a computer, and about a third of the hourly associates have them as well. Computer technology empowers us to create electronic histories of every part produced by AAM. When we have a problem, we can walk it back to the source and deal with it. An exception would be associates working in the forge. The big machines have computer controls but individual technicians may not be using them.

It is largely a client server environment. The heart of our centralized IT operation—the command center—has row upon row of more than 300 tall, black servers with flickering lights that denote rapid transmission of millions of bytes of information being moved about all over the world 24/7. There is a loud drone of air-conditioning; these monsters generate a lot of heat and constant cooling is required. Without air-conditioning, that room would overheat within twenty minutes, so we really need those redundant backup systems to assure the cold air keeps coming. AAM pays close attention to retaining and securing important data such as e-mail, drawings, and other electronic assets in our corporate data center. We record over one hundred tapes every day that are rotated out to a secure offsite location for safekeeping in case anything could go wrong. A robotic tape backup system schedules day and night.

Of course, IT technology plays a key role in our relentless quest for perfect quality. Computers enable us to put a tracer on every part that comes into and leaves AAM. Our lasers and cameras are constantly catching and filing away that data. Most finished goods are bar coded to show when and where it was made and assures part values are within customer tolerances. It saves us a lot of trouble, especially with regard to warranty claims. Where possible, we make certain our software is in synch with that of our customers, but some customers insist on keeping their software proprietary. Our concern with security is shared by other businesses in whatever line of commerce.

Bartol says that room with the big black servers is the "brain" of AAM. I would prefer to think that senior management is the brain of the AAM, but the truth is we have thousands of active brains that make our company successful.

Our IT system is an awesome creature that empowers us in a variety of ways—and makes us smarter and more efficient. I am delighted we have this extraordinary capability.

If the headquarters building should burn down or be leveled by an earthquake, we have a sister data center exactly like it that will begin to operate at a different location. Within seconds of a disruption, the sister center would kick into action and provide central control for AAM around the world.

A CYCLICAL BUSINESS

To be sure, the cyclical nature of our industry did not change. Our sales revenue dropped 41 percent in the fourth quarter of 2004. Our customers were trimming production and the price of steel, always a major factor for AAM, was going up. Between September 2004 and February 2005, our stock fell 22 percent. As Bloomberg News reported in February 2005: "Any supplier that's dependent on GM and Ford is getting slammed," said Alan Baum, a forecaster for The Planning Edge in Birmingham, Michigan. "If you're an assembler, you can try to mitigate the effects of lower production volume by putting more equipment in your car. If you're a supplier, it's just about volume."

We were getting a little boost from the Hummer 3 launch order, billed as a "kinder, gentler Hummer," a smaller version of its predecessors, but still a Hummer. We were also producing front and rear axles and driveshafts for the H2. We never saw the Hummer as a long-term project, but a contract is a contract.

In May, Daniel Howes wrote in *The Detroit News* that auto suppliers like AAM were facing a brutal shakeout. For some, he wrote, this was "an existential crisis. There are few guarantees—including a union contract—and even fewer loyalties. Bankruptcy, the biggest threat to negotiated wages, pensions and health care benefits, is not so much an abstract legal concept as it is an increasingly useful management tool. Not that it's the tool of choice, but consider the unrelenting vise squeezing most suppliers."

At that point, we had averaged an 8 percent compounded annual growth rate (CAGR) over nine years. The Detroit plant #2 that had produced 1,900 axles a day in 1994 was by then producing 4,600 a day. By June we announced we would invest $80 million in our plants in Detroit and Three Rivers to accommodate GM's next generation of full-size pickup trucks, planning to preserve about 1,600 jobs in Michigan. We were investing $60 million in our Colfor plant in Minerva, Ohio, creating 175 new jobs. That plant had been struggling when we bought it three years before, but we had turned it around and it was producing about $75 million in quality products every year.

By November, one of our major competitors, Delphi, was actually going through bankruptcy, setting itself up for huge wage cuts, putting AAM at an even bigger competitive disadvantage. Meanwhile, our main customer GM was eliminating 30,000 jobs, and closing twelve plants, which CEO Rick Wagoner attributed to foreign competition. Wagoner hoped to get GM operating at 100 percent capacity, up from 85 percent at the time, based on a two-shift schedule. GM said that by 2008, it would have cut production capacity by almost a third to 4.2 million units a year. We were all trying to digest this news, and its implications for AAM. They were not pleasant. D-day for Detroit had arrived.

Wagoner assured everyone that a GM bankruptcy would not be necessary, but people were beginning to think the unthinkable. The price of GM's credit default swaps, the insurance in case the company could not pay its loans, was costing a premium of 12 percentage points of the value of the debt they insured, four times what they had cost the preceding February.

GM's troubles directly affected AAM. Our rating on unsecured debt was lowered to junk status by Moody's Investors Service because of our dependence on GM light truck sales. Our credit rating was cut to Ba2 from Baa3, the lowest investment grade. At that time, we had about $400 million in debt. We were hoping for better things in 2006.

The New Year certainly started out better for me personally. In February, I was awarded the 2006 Donald C. Burnham Manufacturing Management Award by the Society of Mechanical Engineers (SME) for "exceptional success in the integration of the infrastructure and process of manufacturing through innovative use of human, technical and financial resources in founding and leading [AAM]." Phew, that's a mouthful. A day or two later, I was recognized among Michigan's Top 40 Entrepreneurs in the history of the state. A couple of weeks later *Automotive News* reported that AAM ranked thirty-fifth on its list of top global suppliers worldwide. Clearly, we were doing a lot of things right.

But praise and nice words don't count for much when your business is struggling. Our full-year income for 2005 came in at $56 million or $1.10 a share, down from $159.5 million, or $2.98 a share, the year before. We were on a downhill slide.

Then we learned our major competitor Dana was going through bankruptcy. I hated to see that. According to business reporter Robert Sherefkin in

Crain's Detroit Business, AAM was at least partially responsible. During the 1990s, Dana dominated the market for light-vehicle axles and charged GM as much as $1,400 for an axle that cost Dana $800 to build, Sherefkin said. But then things began to change with the rise of AAM. "American Axle put a lot of pressure on our margins," said a former Dana manager, quoted by Sherefkin. Dana was beset by market forces, Sherefkin continued, "but other factors contributed to Dana's collapse, too—like being outmaneuvered and outhustled by an arch competitor."

But the demand for GM vehicles continued to erode. In late March, the *Cleveland Plain Dealer* reported that GM was preparing to offer retirement incentives from $35,000 to $100,000 for nearly all of its 113,000 hourly workers, and to cut 30,000 hourly jobs by 2008. This did not bode well for suppliers. By that time, AAM had about $1,200 content in each GM vehicle. I looked around at the carnage of once mighty auto suppliers now in bankruptcy—Delphi, Dana, Collins & Aikman, Federal Mogul, Meridian, and Oxford. It was like one long business funeral cortege. We were holding meetings with the UAW explaining economic reality and the need to address labor costs, lest AAM be forced to join that dismal band.

I told a reporter from the *Detroit Free Press* we were well leveraged, had excellent liquidity and were looking forward to a positive cash flow in 2006. That claim was reinforced by Jon Rogers, an analyst with Citigroup in New York. "It's the best managed supplier in the world," he said of AAM. "Among the many things that AAM did that was very smart is they used the financial strength of GM's trucks between 2000 and 2003 to shore up their balance sheet which is in very, very good shape."

"Everybody will start coming out of this thing in the second half of 2007," I told the reporter. "I don't see a lot of doom and gloom. I see opportunities."

We soldiered on, keeping faith with our values and belief in the future. We continued to offer our associates training—more than 1,500 classes—and were going ahead with our plans to open a plant in Poland.

It was a new world for auto suppliers. In an address to an automotive conference in Traverse City, Michigan, I said the number of auto suppliers had fallen from 30,000 in 1990 to 10,000 in 2006, and there would be only about 4,000 by the end of the decade. "I hope to see the survivors back here in Traverse City next year," I said. We were in an extreme shakeout period.

By September, we were facing a difficult decision—whether to make axles and drivetrains for GM's new Camaro at our plant in Buffalo, New York, or to shift it to our expanding plant in Mexico. GM had announced its intention to cancel its GMT 360 and 370 platforms, which pulled the rug out from under Buffalo. Without fresh assignments, there would be nothing for that plant and those workers to do.

We were negotiating with the UAW in Buffalo, seeking changes in work rules and more competitive compensation, but could make no headway. We had a quality workforce in Buffalo, but like so many UAW locals they were oblivious to the realities of the marketplace. We had a lot invested there in terms of both worker training and new capital equipment. It was a difficult decision, but I knew early on that Buffalo had to go. They would not compete economically.

We were going into survival mode as so often happens in the auto industry. Shelly Lombard of Gimme Credit LLC said AAM was an "ax-cident waiting to happen." She said we were living on borrowed time, and did not have a sustainable capital structure. "Eventually the cash will run out," she concluded.

No CEO likes to read things like that. Overall, in 2006, we lost $222.5 million. It was our first yearly loss and I did not enjoy it. I was looking for better things ahead, like I always do—but there was more trouble on the horizon.

12

People Power

What you manage in business is people.
—Harold Geneen, chief executive officer, IT&T

In the first week of January 1995, a woman was killed in an accident at one of our Detroit facilities. She was not actually an associate of AAM, but rather worked for a contractor that was doing some work for AAM. She was on the roof for some reason in an area that was clearly marked off limits, she stepped onto a skylight that was clearly designated unsafe to walk on, and she fell fifty feet to her death.

She was one of seven people who lost their lives on the job in the early years of AAM. I do not know much about her, but I assume she had a family and friends who loved her as surely as my family and friends love me. I am sure she was as attached to her life as I am to mine, and that she was looking forward to going home at the end of the workday for a well-earned rest. Regardless of whether she was an AAM associate, and even though the dangers were clearly posted, it is our responsibility to make certain all of the people who work for AAM return home after their shift in good health, and with all of their limbs intact.

I grieved for her and the others. This is not to suggest AAM was culpable in these fatalities, or any of the others. We work hard to provide workplaces free and clear of recognized hazards, and we create and enforce aggressive safety programs.

So why did these tragedies happen? The short answer is that manufacturing tends to be an inherently hazardous activity. We heat steel until it is red hot and employ 5,000-ton presses to shape it. We are constantly grinding steel gears into desired shapes, and putting them through a heat-treat process to make them even harder to withstand rigorous use. The machines that do this work do not stop because someone fails to lock out a safety switch. Our associates must be ever and always alert, and attentive to strict work rules. There is no room on the factory floor for daydreaming.

We took over in March 1994, but as described elsewhere, it took a while to clean up the place and begin changing the culture of the workforce. Those plants were dirty, dark, loud, and dangerous. There were slippery oil spills on the floor. Vision was impaired by oil mist in the air. Safety guards were frequently missing. Indeed, no one thought it strange for people to be killed in one of those plants back then. Debilitating accidents happened and some of them were fatal.

I made it clear to my team from day one that this mentality was not acceptable. We made safety a top priority. It took some time for the new attitude to sink in, among both management and associates, and it took time to identify and eliminate situations that could contribute to accidents, such as oil puddles on the floors, unsafe wiring, missing safety guards, and malfunctioning machinery. We empowered our safety and health people as never before and charged them and all of our associates to make our workplaces safe.

Safety remains our top priority—before products, before productivity, before profits. Our commitment in this regard is reflected in our excellent safety record over the last 10 years. Many of our plants routinely set new records for hours worked without a work related injury. Our fanaticism about safety applies across the board to all of our facilities around the world. When the plant manager at our facility in Araucaria, Brazil, Greg Bastien, shut down that plant for hours to deal with a safety concern, he sent a message to the associates in Brazil that the company's commitment to their safety is sincere and unequivocal, and he received 100 percent backing from senior management in Detroit.

We have color-coded charts posted everywhere in our plants to serve as a report card on how we are doing, and safety is always a prominent feature. It is a measure of our focus on safety that every recordable accident, be it a cut finger or scrape on an elbow, is reported the following week to the Operating Committee of senior staff in Detroit. We don't generally get actively involved in minor injuries, but it is important for our plant managers to know we are looking over their shoulders. Because accidents are unusual events, it is easy to put safety aside to focus on more pressing issues. In fact, one reason we welcome military veterans to AAM is their built-in consciousness of safety, and their understanding that you can never, never let up on it. In the military, a momentary lapse can lead to huge disasters. You have to focus on safety relentlessly, and we encourage military veterans to keep that attitude when they come to work here.

REACHING OUT

Over my many years of management in the auto industry, I developed a strong sense of the importance of human relationships to a company's success. We are all different, but all of us share an innate sense of self-worth and desire for recognition, and after our families, work is the first place we look for that reinforcement. We want to believe that our work is worthwhile and that our supervisors value our contributions. To be a successful manager, you have to grasp this dynamic and respond to it.

Recognition of people must be sincere. Management ranks are filled to overflowing with people who give lip service to this universal imperative, but do not mean it. That fools no one. The people who work for you listen to what you say, but more importantly they watch what you do. A phony is spotted a mile away. It is hard to fake sincerity. On the other hand, I do believe at some level we all truly do care about other people, and effective management is based upon that. A genuine concern for other people, like any other positive quality, can be developed.

In the early days of AAM, we went all out to communicate our values to the associates, to make it clear we valued them and that we were determined to forge a new workplace culture where they could grow and prosper. I and other senior staff appeared before all of our salaried and hourly associates in large plant-wide meetings at all of our facilities to share our vision, answer their questions and ask for their support and cooperation.

To the extent it is humanly possible we established personal one-on-one relationships with all of our salaried and hourly associates. It is part of our people focus that senior management goes to the plant floors frequently and walks about talking to associates, asking them how their work is going, listening to their grievances and, where appropriate, making changes in response to their suggestions. Early on, most of these meetings quickly turned into gripe sessions, but as they got to know us and saw changes taking place, they evolved into more constructive exchanges in which the associates pointed out problems and suggested solutions. Where associate suggestions made sense, we took quick action unless there was some compelling reason not to. For example, we would not replace an expensive machine if we knew we had a different technology in the pipeline that would do the same job more efficiently.

I hasten to add that when doing this kind of outreach to associates, management must be receptive to both suggestions *and* criticism. I have known more than a few senior managers who were not receptive to criticism either from line workers or other senior staff. I understand that aversion but I believe anyone with that problem needs to get over it. If you cannot take criticism in a positive spirit, even if you think it misguided, you are not qualified to manage other people.

I do a lot of this one-on-one outreach personally, but over time, as our workforce grew, I have come to rely more and more on our senior staff to do it. As a general rule, I do not believe management in manufacturing lends itself to sitting at a desk. You have to do some paperwork of course, and God knows there are meetings you must attend and deals you must make, but you need to spend as much time as possible on the factory floor with the people doing the work. It is that personal contact with you, whether you are the CEO or plant manager or supervisor, that confirms an associate's sense of worth and commitment to doing the job well. In the final analysis, the associates are the ones who will determine the company's success or failure.

In sum, I believe developing a personal rapport depends on communication, a willingness to accept criticism and, of course, integrity. The latter—integrity—can never be emphasized enough. If you tell subordinates their comments and criticisms are welcome, you better not go back and put a demerit on their records when they share a gripe. If you promise to look into a problem, you better look into it. If you promise to change something, you better change it. Once a commitment is made, it must be kept. If, as sometimes happens, you agree to a solution and then find out later it will not work, or the company cannot afford it, then you must go back and explain that reality to whoever you made the commitment to. This can become touchy if someone in middle management makes a commitment without checking with senior management to make sure it can be honored. But if you level with your people, they will understand and think no less of you. Remember, your people are not stupid and they want the company to succeed as much as you do. Or they will if you treat them right and make them part of the team. It is first and foremost a matter of keeping them in the loop and showing them respect.

TRAINING

It is a fundamental rule at AAM that if someone is not performing well, the first question we ask is why. We do not automatically assume that person is goofing off or is not committed to the work or lacks ability. We ask what the problem is, what do you need to do the job well, how can we help you do it better? Many times, at least for hourly associates, the problem comes down to training, or the lack thereof.

At AAM we emphasize education, training and skill set expansion in a big way. We do extensive training in the plants and sometimes bring in visiting professors from local universities and community colleges to conduct classes for associates, saving them the inconvenience of having to commute to college campuses, and perhaps the embarrassment of attending classes with youngsters. One scholar of note was Professor Irv Otis of Central Michigan University; I knew him from my Chrysler days. Irv was a frequent visitor to AAM and understood our challenges instinctively. He did some wonderful work with our people and was a true manufacturing professional.

We strive to foster a culture of lifelong learning. The best curricula offer a mix of technical classes for on-the-job skill set development; financial and economic classes for profitability awareness; and collaboration for team building. AAM's training curriculum centers on people, products, process and systems. Because technology is constantly changing, the training curricula must be constantly reviewed and modernized. We offer about 1,500 different classes in any given year, and allocate thirty to fifty hours of training each year for every associate, all at AAM's expense.

One phase of this training, and one that drives our financial people crazy, is my insistence that all salaried associates take product awareness training. I don't care what their job description is, whether they are computer specialists, lawyers, supervisors or clerks. I do not want people working here who do not know what products we make. In product awareness training, they learn all about axles, gears and drivetrains, why they are important to cars and trucks, and why AAM's products are better than those of the competition.

We encourage both salaried and hourly personnel to continue their educations, even if they are pursuing studies not directly related to their work at AAM. We subsidize educational expenses and give them some time off as needed to attend classes.

The money we spend on education and training is money well spent. The world of modern manufacturing has changed dramatically over the last two decades. When we launched AAM in 1994, the average associate had the equivalent of an ninth grade education. Within ten years, the average was a sophomore in college. In fact, many of them have two-year degrees from community colleges. The educational demands for manufacturing are going up everywhere in all industries.

The AAM focus on education, training, and skill sets is not for show. We have these people operating machines that cost more than Ferraris. They are using advanced computers to guide those machines along work processes that were not possible even a few years ago, achieving levels of precision that are unprecedented. You need a high level of education to do the work. You need a strong background in science, math, and communications. The technology is constantly changing and you must change with it. No sooner do you learn a job and get it down right than the technology changes and you are back into a learning curve. The modern industrial workplace is not your father's factory floor. Not by a long shot.

AAM established a program under which industrious seniors from the local Hamtramck High spent Tuesdays working at the Detroit plants as part of a partnership between the public schools and AAM. After they completed sixty-four hours at the plant, they could take a course at Macomb County Community College that prepared them for an apprenticeship exam. Among other things, they learned that if the shift starts at 6:00 A.M., they should be there by 5:45. My philosophy is that if you are on time for work, you are late.

In the first decade of the new century, U.S. manufacturing lost about 8 million jobs. Economists attribute this dramatic shift to foreign competition and changing technology. More accurately, it should be said that U.S. manufacturing accelerated its shift to advanced technologies in response to the challenge of foreign competition. To compete with low cost foreign labor, we must become more efficient and productive, and also focus on more advanced products.

EQUAL OPPORTUNITY

Another serious commitment of mine is equal opportunity. This is one movement from the 1960s that I bought into and am fully in accord with. It is in part a matter of simple justice that people should be treated fairly and judged according to their ability and merit, not their race, gender, national origin, or religious preference.

Equal opportunity is also a matter of economics. To prosper and grow, we need to make full use of all of our human potential. In this age of advanced technologies and unprecedented foreign competition, we need all of our hands on deck, every mind at work. To shut any group out is simply stupid and self-defeating.

A bigger challenge, at least in our industry, has been bringing women into the work force and helping them work up to higher levels of responsibility. At Chrysler, I earned a certain amount of notoriety by appointing women to be plant managers. At AAM, I have made it clear up and down the line that women are to be afforded the same opportunities as anyone else. It used to be assumed that this level of serious industrial work was off limits to women because it can be strenuous and dangerous. The reality, however, is that with modern ergonomics, few jobs in manufacturing today require superior upper body strength. We do not have many women applying for jobs in the forges where red hot steel is being extruded and shaped, but women are well represented in our axle and drive shaft plants. When we took over the GM facilities, women comprised less than seven percent of the overall work force, and many of them had office jobs. Within a few years, we have moved that needle to above 20 percent.

Women associates have significant input in the management of AAM. I believe they bring an important perspective that is missing when women are not participating. In my nearly 20 years at the helm of AAM, I have had two female executive assistants, Karen Conley and Suzanne Lees. They have both been most professional, extremely effective, and confidential.

We sometimes encounter pushback on gender equity in foreign countries where we set up shop. Where the option is open to us, we insist on hiring women and integrating them fully into the AAM workforce. In Mexico, Thailand, and China, for example, there is apparently no bias against women in the workplace, not even the industrial workplace. In Brazil, Poland, Japan, and India, on the other hand, the culture seems to discourage full female participation. In those countries, women are welcome in the office, but not on the plant floor. We strive to move the equity ball forward, but must be careful about offending local cultural sensibilities. We are guests in their countries; we play by their rules and respect their customs. We promote fair play, equal opportunity, and gender equity to the best of our ability wherever AAM is operating.

13

Detroit at the Crossroads

The trick is to make sure you don't die waiting for prosperity to come.

—*Lee Iacocca*

In May 2004, I made a speech to the Detroit Economic Club entitled "Detroit—In The Cross Hairs." It probably should have been titled like this book chapter, "Detroit at the Crossroads." Back then many thought our city had pretty much bottomed out and had no way to go but up. I had become somewhat discouraged by the unfortunate trends in a city that was hemorrhaging jobs even then, but remained optimistic about the future, which is my nature. I remember my wife Sandy said to me, "Cheer up, things could be worse."

So I cheered up and, sure enough, things got worse. A lot worse. And they don't promise to get any better anytime soon. Detroit is caught up in a downward spiral of converging negative forces that beggar description. Other old industrial cities have had their troubles, but most of them are working their way through. Pittsburgh, for example, was devastated when the steel industry went away, but it has since shifted its economic focus from the steel industry to medicine and research. Today, it has a much more diverse economic base and is doing fine, or at least on its way back. But Detroit . . .

I have spent my working lifetime in the auto industry and almost all of it in Detroit. When I led the purchase of the old GM plants that became AAM, I went to great pains to declare my determination to build a profitable, competitive company with union labor *based in Detroit*. We were committed to prove to the world that there was still real life in the Motor City, but more and more, I feel like that fabled little Dutch boy with his finger in the dike trying to hold back the sea.

Between 2000 and 2010, Detroit's population plunged 25 percent to 713,777, down from 951,270 in 2000, reaching the lowest count since 1910. Detroit's loss of people made Michigan the only state of fifty to experience a population loss in that ten-year period. Overall, the state's population fell by about 54,000, a 0.6 percent decline during a time when the nation's overall population grew by 9.7 percent, and it was all because of Detroit.

How did it come to this? Detroit is the cradle of the auto industry that came to dominate the American landscape in the twentieth century. In 1908, Henry Ford built his first automobile assembly plant to make the Model T in Highland Park on the east side of Woodward Avenue, the main drag that divides the city into east and west. In 1910, Ford began paying his workers the unheard of rate of $5 per day. That meant they could not only make cars, they could buy cars. This was surely one of the biggest boosts to a new American middle class that would come into its own in the years after World War II—an era when Detroit ruled supreme.

Over half a century, the east side evolved into the country's premier machine shop. Soon auto plants were sprouting all over like sunflowers after a spring rain—Chrysler, Dodge, Packard, Studebaker, Hudson, Cadillac, Chevrolet, Pontiac. People came from all over the world to work in the "Motor City." Soon skyscrapers were springing up and suburbs were spreading out. The city's population grew from 300,000 to 1.3 million, passing Boston and Baltimore.

Foreigners came to marvel at the scene. "It is the home of mass-production, of very high wages and colossal profits, of lavish spending and reckless installment-buying, of intense work and a large and shifting labor surplus," wrote British historian and MP Ramsay Muir in 1927. "It regards itself as the temple of a new gospel of progress to which I shall venture to give the name 'Detroitism.'"*

In the early years, African Americans in Detroit were subjected to racial discrimination limiting where they could live and socialize, as they were in many places, but the auto companies offered them employment and they came in droves, many of them from the depressed Jim Crow southern states. Poor whites from Appalachia came, too, fleeing the desolate coal towns of West Virginia, Eastern Kentucky, southwestern Virginia, and Tennessee. Detroit was a place where a man with limited education could get an excellent job with benefits. It was, for many, literally the biblical land of milk and honey.

---

* I am grateful to writer Charlie LeDuff, in the November/December 2010 issue of *Mother Jones*, for this quote and some other information related in this section.

Of course, from the earliest days of the auto industry, Detroit was subject to booms and busts. Every time the economy turned sour, consumers stopped buying cars and autoworkers were laid off. And this natural business cycle may have led to Detroit's eventual undoing. When autoworkers were laid off, the city provided free clothing, fuel, rent and $10 a week to adults for food, and another $5 for children. Well ahead of President Lyndon Johnson's Great Society, the city of Detroit began fostering a sense of entitlement. It is today thoroughly entrenched in citizens who believe they are "entitled" to generous government benefits and UAW represented autoworkers who feel the same about lavish pay and benefits. Until the recent elimination of the "jobs bank" they received up to 95 percent of their regular pay even when they were not working. In time, that sense of entitlement took its toll on people who had once been endowed with a strong work ethic.

I assume a lot of immigrants in Detroit wrote home about this wonderful place that must have sounded like a variation of the "Big Rock Candy Mountain," a fantasy hobo song dating back to 1928. The city had reached a population peak of 1.9 million people in the 1950s when it was 83 percent white. In more recent years, that proportion has reversed. With barely 700,000 people, Detroit today is 88 percent minority.

Detroit today is a city in crisis. People who can afford to have moved out to surrounding suburbs or further away. The government cannot afford to supply adequate police protection, ambulance and medical services, road maintenance, social services, all of the basic amenities we expect city governments to provide. The schools are among the nation's worst. Legions of young people are unemployed and essentially unemployable. "Detroit's east side is now the poorest, most violent quarter of America's poorest, most violent big city," Charlie Leduff wrote. "The illiteracy, child poverty and unemployment rates hover around 50 percent." In perhaps the ultimate measure of desperation, many African Americans are moving to the south from where their parents and grandparents fled many years before. They are moving to Georgia, the Carolinas, Alabama, and Arkansas. Many of us who remember what the old South was like find this an astounding development.

In my speech to the Detroit Economic Club, I lamented that I had never before seen the Big Three all losing market share at the same time. The loss of hundreds of thousands of good jobs in the auto industry was the critical factor in Detroit's decline. I cannot resist noting that had not the Big Three created innovative products that launched the craze of minivans, pickups, and SUVs, the job loss tallies would have been even higher. But it clearly was not enough. We were in the midst of a massive and misunderstood decline when I made that speech. And of course I then did not then foresee that within a few years, GM and Chrysler would both go bankrupt.

It is high time we took stock of what is happening to us, and make the tough choices we must make to turn this deplorable situation around, choices we should have made a long time ago.

ECONOMIC TRANSITION

What has happened to Detroit is a reflection of greater trends that have been besetting our nation's industrial base for many years. This is not a cyclical change, but rather a harsh and real structural change that we have been slow to respond to. In the latter part of the twentieth century, a host of foreign nations—most notably Japan and more recently China and Korea—have challenged our leadership in manufacturing, and much of this challenge was focused on the auto industry. Our foreign competitors are striving to build their own industrial powerhouses on the American model. They are succeeding admirably.

Unfortunately, they have built their industries on the same base we used—the American consumer. For many years, we took our consumer base for granted. We became complacent. Detroit fell into bad habits producing low quality products that offered low fuel efficiency for inflated prices. While we were dozing at the wheel, our foreign competitors seized the advantage. Over time, American consumers came to regard foreign automobiles not only as less expensive than the American brand, but also as superior products that lasted longer and were often more stylish. In business, one cannot be complacent.

The Japanese auto companies not only made better products for less money, but they started making them here in the United States, which at least partially reduced whatever reluctance consumers may have had to buy imports. Toyota has had its problems recently, but the fact remains it builds eight models in this country and has created 200,000 jobs here. Of course, Toyota has been careful not to build its vehicles in Detroit or the state of Michigan. There are many perfectly sensible economic reasons, the main ones being the exorbitant compensation and restrictive work rules imposed by the UAW. There is also the lackadaisical work attitudes of the Detroit autoworkers for whom a 20 percent daily absentee rate is considered a God-given right. Toyota's jobs have gone to the Southern states where right-to-work laws provide a more level playing

Laying the first stone. Mexico, April 1998. Governor Vicente Fox and Dick Dauch.

Feeding the troops. China, May 2007. Dick Dauch, Curt Howell, and Bill Smith.

The stealthy AAM Guanajuate Mexico, aerial view, 2009.

October 2010. Members of AAM's Board of Directors on shop floor in Mexico with Alphonso Felix, Plant Manager. Dick Dauch, Lance Reinhard, Forest Farmer, Larry Switzer.

AAM Board of Directors, 2010. Back row: Forest Farmer, Bill Miller, Dick Lappin, Dick Dauch, David Dauch, Larry Switzer, Dr. Henry Yang, Sam Bonanno. Seated: Tom Walker, Beth Chappell.

October 2005, the Taj Mahal. My India travel team and I enjoy a world jewel.

Helping Mayor Bing rebuild Detroit. Dick Dauch, Dave Bing, Sandy Dauch.

June 12, 2007, the GM Heritage Center. At the end of a great evening—shared with two close business friends, Marion Cumo and Allan Rae—where I received the "2007 Quality Leader of the Year Award" from the Automotive Division of the American Society for Quality.

Quality starts at the top—internal training at AAM. American Society for Quality, Certified Quality Engineering Class being recognized, December 2010.

Of all the associates we inherited from GM, perhaps none was as timeless and appreciated as Ben Hogan, seen here with me at AAM's seventeenth birthday party in 2011. Ben worked fifty-five years in the auto industry, finishing his career at AAM. He set a high standard for competence, diligence, and commitment. It was routine for him to stop by the plants on weekends just to make sure everything was all right. Over the years, he and I became good friends. He still stops by to see me from time to time offering wise advice, which I am always thankful for.

AAM Technology Committee Chairman Dr. Henry Yang and Dick Dauch confer on strategy. The technology reviews are voluminous and detailed. Dr. Yang is the Chancellor at the University of California, Santa Barbara, where he also serves as professor of mechanical engineering. Formerly the Dean of Engineering and Neil Armstrong Distinguished Professor in Aerospace Engineering at Purdue University. Dr. Yang's intellect and enthusiasm are contagious.

AAM—UAW negotiations kickoff. Dick Dauch and Ron Gettelfinger, 2007–2008.

Sandy and Dick Dauch at Carnoustie, Scotland, 2003.

Sandy and Dick Dauch enjoy observation of glacier "calving" in Alaska, 1998.

Sandy and Dick Dauch enjoy Maui with Purdue basketball and football teams, 2006.

field for union organization, and workers show up every day eager to earn their pay. Other foreign automakers have likewise avoided Detroit like a leper.

There is some good news. The Big Three have responded to the quality challenge. Today, the U.S. automakers are at, or close to, world parity and leadership on key issues previously considered shortcomings: quality, productivity, design, and advanced technology. Detroit has proven it can compete on those key factors, but the labor factor still leaves us at a profound disadvantage, and its impact is clearly visible in our city today. *Cost structure is the cancer causing noncompetitiveness in Detroit, and its industries.*

To rebuild the auto industry in Detroit, we simply must recognize and take on our number one problem—cost competitiveness. Relentless and often ruthless international competition makes it nearly impossible to raise prices or pass along increased costs. Automakers are demanding from suppliers, like AAM, the lowest price they can get anywhere in the world. They want U.S.-made quality and the pricing of low-labor-cost countries. Manufacturing customers are leveraging global prices as the economic benchmark.

In spite of escalating domestic production costs, the prices of manufactured products have actually been declining in recent years. I know of no other sector that can make such a claim—not insurance, not medicine, not services, not education, not homebuilding, and certainly not government. Only manufacturing has consistently reduced product prices over the years. And while this is viewed as a wonderful thing by consumers, it leaves manufacturers between a rock and a hard place. Because of that intense international competition, we simply cannot raise prices and stay in business for very long.

So where is all that competition coming from? The following are the world's top automotive competitors, listed alphabetically, along with their approximate populations:

- Brazil, with 180 million people
- China, with 1.3 billion people
- France, with more than 60 million people
- Germany, with more than 80 million people
- India, with more than 1 billion people
- Italy, with around 100 million people
- Japan, with nearly 150 million people
- South Korea, with more than 50 million people
- Mexico, with more than 100 million people
- The United States, with more than 300 million people

This represents more than 3.3 billion people. On any given day, these countries and their citizens—every man, woman, and child—are consumers of goods and services from the global marketplace. And on any given day, 45 percent of these populations are at work in the labor force competing for jobs that will feed the voracious appetite of the global marketplace. Our competition is motivated, reliable, educated, youthful, and ready and willing to go to work every day. They are mastering the elements of manufacturing productivity and flexibility.

Our own population recently crested the 310 million mark, with maybe 145 million in the workforce. When you crunch the numbers, the United States represents less than 9 percent of the work force among the nine other major competitors. Clearly, our labor force can no longer dictate economic terms. We must adjust and we must adjust now.

By far, the biggest competition is coming from China, Mexico, Brazil, South Korea, and India.* With populations totaling more than 3 billion people, 87 percent of the supply of labor from our largest competitors comes from those five countries.

In the 1990s, automakers and parts suppliers began a surge of sourcing to those countries to save money and take advantage of local opportunities and reduce their cost structure. Automotive investment in China is especially huge. Assemblers in these low-labor-cost countries know how to continuously add value and lower costs, and consistently turn out higher quality products. They have been discovered by each and every automaker. With today's Internet technology and the application of real-time data, they can be used in effective sourcing patterns from half way around the world.

Not surprisingly, the Big Three have stepped up their investments in these low-cost countries, investing tens of billions in plants that employ tens of thousands of workers—jobs that could be in this country if we had reasonable wage and benefit rates and reliable, skilled workers. Those plants spend billions buying parts and services from local suppliers, even more jobs that could be here in Detroit. AAM has joined the parade of automotive companies investing overseas because that is where the growth and potential profits are.

This trend has been decimating Detroit—and other large swaths of our industrial heartland—for many years, yet our response never rises above head-

---

* I am arbitrarily leaving Japan out because Japan has its own problems, and also has created so many jobs here that it is hard to label Japan strictly as a foreign competitor.

scratching and finger-pointing. We will say and do anything it seems except address the real causes of this phenomenon.

We have to come together with a coherent, tough-minded plan to restore our auto industry, preferably in the Motor City where it all began. Cars and trucks in some form will be one of, if not the largest, industry on the face of this planet for decades to come. We may come up with some remarkable technology breakthrough to replace the gasoline engine, but we will still be producing vehicles. The automotive industry has been the very heartbeat of Detroit and Michigan for a long time, but it is undergoing profound transition. To bring it back to full health will require major surgery.

So we are left with these questions: What must the American auto industry do to restore its global leadership? What can our government in Washington do to help? What does Detroit have to do to restore its reputation as a viable place to do business? *We are truly at a crossroads.* Which way will we turn?

THE CITY OF DETROIT

An effective and honest city government could have done much to mitigate Detroit's decline, to attract new business and work with the UAW to encourage old businesses to stay, but effective and honest are two terms that one never hears in the same sentence with Detroit city government. Detroit has an unfortunate reputation for corruption that goes back a long way.

But there is hope. Our new mayor, Dave Bing, a former star for the Detroit Pistons in the National Basketball Association and a former business executive in his own right, has taken the reins of the city. To be sure, it is a job I would not at this point wish on anyone, much less a person I esteem like Dave Bing, but at least we have an honest broker in the mayor's chair who is trying to clean up the joint and run it efficiently.

Corruption is not unique to Detroit. Lots of mayors in American history have come into office with a mandate to clean up corruption. Quite a few of them have achieved great things and gone on to higher office at the state and national level. But I am not aware of any large-town mayor called upon to do what Mayor Bing must do—downsize a major city to the point it can manage with the resources at its disposal.

The basic problem is that the quarter of the population that departed over the last ten years did not pack up and leave just one part of town. The population was dispersed far and wide across Detroit's 139 square miles. The result is wide swaths of deserted houses and open space interrupted here and there by a few residents still hanging on. This puts intense pressure on the city's limited resources to provide police protection, ambulance services, fire suppression, lighting, garbage collection, and everything else the people expect from an urban government. Mayor Bing is busy demolishing deserted houses and devising great plans to consolidate the population into certain parts of the city that will be much easier to serve. But this means Mayor Bing and the City Council will have to persuade many people to move, even in cases where the people in question may have been in that particular house for generations. This is going to be difficult, very difficult.

Mayor Bing is doing the only thing he can do under the circumstances— manage an orderly transition to a smaller Detroit that can meet the needs of its citizens. There will be weeping, wailing, and gnashing of teeth. He will need a tough hide to ride this bull, and he will need support from everyone— the city council, the courts, the state of Michigan, private citizens, businesses, unions, community organizations, all of us. We have to come together as a team.

MANUFACTURING

In its desperation, Detroit is building gambling casinos. This is not the answer. I can think of nothing more irresponsible and disheartening than for a government at any level to encourage its citizens to indulge in vices. Manufacturing creates wealth and makes it possible for people to prosper; gambling is a zero-sum game that creates nothing but trouble. Money goes in but nothing comes out. Gambling abets poverty and desperation. The last time I looked, Detroit had more than enough of those things. Detroit does not need gambling or handouts from Washington, it needs a culture change that can only begin at home. Detroit needs to relearn the work ethic and focus on innovation and competitiveness. In a word, we need to relearn the magic that made us great in the first place—manufacturing. We must produce things in America.

As I said in my 2004 speech, and I repeat here, Detroit's auto industry needs an action plan for a healthy future. Had they listened to me in 2004, they might have avoided the catastrophe of 2009.* Now GM and Chrysler are getting back

---

* Obviously, Ford Motor Company was doing something right because it alone among the Big Three did avoid bankruptcy.

on their feet, selling vehicles, making profits, paying off government debt and awarding bonuses to employees. All well and good. But if we return to business as usual, we will drive off the cliff again and this time the taxpayers will balk at another bailout.

I have had some success in the auto industry and believe I have enough credibility to make a few suggestions from which the Big Three and other suppliers might benefit. None of this is radical or new, and many of the auto executives I am talking to are ahead of me in at least some of these areas, but they know also that in our business you can never rest or take anything for granted. The quest for quality, productivity, innovation, competitiveness and profitability is brutal and relentless:

- Respect the human resource and realize that our people are our most important asset. We would not be in business without our associates and the positive spirit of our workforces. The people in the executive suites need to go out on the plant floor, get some grease on their shoes and talk to the people who do the work. You will meet some really good people there.

- Where unions are present, you must foster partnerships to maintain sound management and workforce relations. I have much to say about my relationship with the UAW over my 48-year career, both positive and negative. We get along splendidly with the UAW Local at Three Rivers, where we are adding jobs, and are eager to get along well with other locals if they will accept the absolute necessity of competitive compensation and operational flexibility.

- Implement programs for education, training and skill-set development to adequately prepare your workforce for the demands of an increasingly high tech and sophisticated workplace. The massive advance of technology in product, processes and systems requires more advanced worker skills, and diligent dedication to the job.

- Continue to invest in R&D, regardless of the economic climate. At AAM we increase our R&D spending by approximately 10 percent a year, on a dollar basis, even when times are tough and our survival prospects are under a cloud.

- Provide the highest quality products, services and customer response in an efficient, timely manner . . . and at a fair and competitive price.

- "Design in" all the right features in your products, processes and systems to best serve your organization and your customers. *All quality and cost issues start with design.* Provide continuous direction and review of product design from concept to production. All design and process needs to be done simultaneously and concurrently using the latest technical capabilities.

- Negotiate sourcing agreements with organizations maintaining world leadership standards and capability.
- Actively engage your company and human resources in the communities where your associates live and work.
- Work with your governments—local, state, and national—to create a positive operating environment that supports investment, especially in manufacturing and product development.
- Realize that you need good balance among your stakeholders. This includes your associates, the shareholders, unions, suppliers, customers, communities, dealers, and related financial institutions.

PULLING IT ALL TOGETHER

To get our house in order and bring Detroit back from the brink, we must summon the creativity, innovation, and imagination that made U.S. manufacturing the world leader—a position it still holds. We must have the ability to adapt to the ever-changing global marketplace. Winners provide innovations and new technology, the ability to lead change and the ability to provide world class quality, design, technology, and appropriate logistics at competitive pricing.

I am speaking directly to manufacturing because that is the field I know best, and also because I know that other sectors such as services and retail tend to flow in manufacturing's wake. Make no mistake, manufacturing is the bedrock upon which this country was built. It is the driving force and creative catalyst of our continued progress. Yet manufacturing faces severe challenges in America, and auto manufacturing more than most.

Throughout my long career, I have seen the manufacturing industry do great things. I have also seen it make some huge mistakes. Today, the global competition is not coming. It is here. It is real. We must adjust to it. *This is the defining issue of our time in Detroit.* We must all make the decision to commit to the solutions, not add to the problems.

As I write, the Detroit Three, its suppliers and dealers, are selling cars and trucks, making profits and paying off debts—but the long-term structural issues must still be dealt with. If we allow this little spurt of hard-won prosperity to lull us back into complacency, we will be sowing the seeds of our own destruction. To bring our city and our nation back, the domestic auto industry must be healthy and competitive. To be healthy and competitive, *the domestic auto industry must bring labor costs and flexibility* under control. There is no other way. Let's get on with the job.

14

The Entitlement Mentality

The worst crime against working people is a company which fails to operate at a profit.

—Samuel Gompers
Founder, American Federation of Labor

An episode of the original *Star Trek* series that first appeared on television in the 1960s featured an invisible alien aboard the starship *Enterprise* that fed off anxiety, fear, and anger. It arranged to have the *Enterprise* crew save a crew of their nemesis Klingons from a disaster of some kind that led to open conflict on the *Enterprise*. Soon the two factions were at war incessantly, but every time a crewman on either side was killed, he or she somehow sprang back to life and resumed the fight. Eventually, the *Enterprise* crew figured out that there was an alien aboard that drew energy from the raw emotions that spurred the conflict. It took Captain Kirk a while to convince the Klingons about this, but eventually they came around. As soon as the humans and Klingons threw down their weapons, started laughing, and stopped thinking angry thoughts, the alien fled to points unknown.

The UAW is like that alien force. It is a political organization that feeds off distrust and resentment between management and labor. Consequently, the UAW leadership is inclined to encourage that hostility, not work around it, because that is the source of its strength, its reason for being. There are exceptions to this generality, of course. Over the years, I have met and worked with several progressive UAW leaders whose primary concern was keeping their members on the job, not driving their employers out of business. They understood the wisdom of Gompers—the worst enemy of a worker is a company that does not make a profit. But they have been in the minority and rarely seem to have more than transitory impact on UAW policies, and virtually none on the basic mentality of endless confrontation with management.

From the outset, the UAW was a rough and rowdy bunch, and they had to be. The auto companies played rough, hiring goons to fight and intimidate union organizers. It is exceedingly unlikely that the meek and mild would have brought the Big Three to heel. The early years left a legacy of bitterness and distrust between labor and management that survives to this day. It is most difficult to work with an organization that constantly lives in the past. The UAW needs to adopt to modernity and become part of America's solution to adapting to real global competitiveness.

The roughness was not just workers against management, but was also rampant within the ranks of the UAW itself. The UAW also had to suppress the more militant factions within its ranks who were forever instigating "wildcat" strikes over local issues that were not sanctioned by headquarters. The UAW realized it could not hope to negotiate deals with the Big Three if it could not guarantee the workers would honor those deals. That was a continuing battle for many years and even today, wildcat strikes still happen from time to time.

In 1946, Walter Reuther was elected president of the UAW, a post he held until his death in 1970. Under Reuther's leadership the UAW developed a "divide and conquer" strategy in which it would strike one of the Big Three, effectively shutting it down, until it came to terms. If GM was shut down, that meant car buyers went to Ford and Chrysler. Watching its customers go to its rivals, GM would quickly come to terms, and then the union would dictate similar terms to the other two companies. This was the start of the infamous "pattern bargaining" strategy of the UAW. Since all three companies ended up with basically the same wage and benefit packages, none was at a disadvantage, so they made a habit of knuckling under to the UAW. The bill for this largesse, of course, was borne by consumers who, in those days, really had no alternative. The Big Three were virtually the only sources of automobiles and trucks in the years after World War II.

It did not take the UAW long to figure out it had the auto industry by the throat. Over the decades, the UAW earned a reputation as one of the most aggressive and political unions in the country. The union's power was a critical factor in the nation's economy because of the pervasive influence of the auto industry. Huge amounts of money were at stake every time the UAW walked off the job. The nation took notice, and that may also have been a factor in the

UAW's belligerence. Soon the auto companies were accepting responsibility for pensions, medical care, and supplementary unemployment insurance that eventually morphed into the infamous *jobs bank* in which laid-off UAW members received 95 percent of their pay and benefits. In 2005, some 12,000 UAW workers were drawing from this fund! Eventually it reached the point that a typical UAW worker, whether employed by one of the Big Three or a major supplier like AAM, was receiving more than $70 per hour fully loaded, meaning the total cost of wages and benefits prorated across a regular work week. *This is the total antithesis of building value, competitiveness, and lean operations.*

But hindsight is always 20/20. All of this happened over a period of years in which each work action and contract concession was seen as a specific event, not part of the corrosive trend that would eventually bring the domestic auto industry to its knees. My operative point is that the UAW was born in a fiery cauldron that has pretty much defined its attitude and behavior over the years, and still defines its attitude today, despite a conspicuous need for union-management cooperation.

So what began as a worker crusade for justice evolved into a sense of entitlement—a feeling that they are entitled to a job and excellent wages with lavish benefits regardless of how much work they performed or their contribution to productivity or even whether they came to work. Whether the company makes a profit or, for that matter, quality products, was someone else's concern. By the time I came on the scene, this attitude was entrenched. It was reflected in slack work habits, working to the pegs that I have discussed elsewhere, deliberately slowing down the assembly line to guarantee overtime on weekends, occasional acts of industrial sabotage, and an absentee rate that would have been intolerable anywhere else.

Then, later, and now—absentee rates of 20 percent are pretty much the norm in Detroit. This is completely contradictory to a positive and responsible ethic about work and personal accountability. It is difficult to run production efficiently when on any given day one out of five workers simply is not there. GM's Guy Briggs said rampant absenteeism is somehow associated with the I-75 corridor. "There's got to be something in the air starting in Dayton, Ohio, and going all the way to Saginaw, Michigan," he said. "The absentee rate is out of this world compared to any other plants. It was not that the people were not good or did not have good skills, it was just the way they had grown up over the years."

In 1964, that was the world as I found it. I had no mandate to change the culture of the auto industry, I was simply determined to find a place for myself within it. So I set out to do the best I could with the situation as it was. My approach then as now was actively hands-on—to communicate directly and openly with people, make it clear what was expected of them and work closely with them to help them succeed. For most of the hourly staff, my approach was radically different from anything they had experienced before in the auto industry. I was with them on the floor every day, talking to them, pointing out better ways to do things, soliciting their advice and actively listening to them. It took some getting used to and, of course, not everyone bought into what I was doing, but over time most of them did. It was and continues to be a process and basic principle of management.

It was during those first, formative years at GM that I began to build my reputation as a manager who was willing to work with the UAW. Actually, I was working with people but I worked with them within the context of the UAW rules and rituals. I believed then and still believe today that most people really do want to be able to take pride in their work, and will respond to leadership that helps them succeed. I took them seriously and always kept my commitments.

So it was that I got results at GM working with the UAW. I have no doubt that my positive relationship with the UAW and the working man was a key factor in my success, and I took pride in my reputation as a manager who respected the union, and was respected by the rank and file. We earned that relationship by working together.

I took that reputation with me when I joined Volkswagen of America and supervised construction of that company's first assembly plant in Pennsylvania. We brought that plant in ahead of schedule, producing vast numbers of quality Rabbits and pick-up trucks with minimal labor disruptions. Those were boom days for the U.S. auto industry. Back then, you could absorb the inefficiencies related to restrictive work rules and uncompetitive wage scales and pass the costs along to the American consumers.

I took that same reputation with me when I went to work for Lee Iacocca at Chrysler. A major issue before us, back then, was Chrysler's determination to close the old Jefferson Avenue assembly plant in Detroit and build a new plant in the suburbs. A lot of people were upset about that prospect, including Governor James Blanchard and Detroit mayor, Coleman Young. They wanted to keep those jobs in Detroit, but the plant was a real mess. I sent one of my best managers, Leroy Delisle, over there to clean it up as best he could.

Delisle had been with me since 1965, at GM. He was a tough, well-educated, personable, no-nonsense manager who got results. He knew the auto industry and got along with the union. I knew he would not be intimidated, but he would need every ounce of his experience and savvy to right that ship. It was one sick house.

"Dick called me in, said I'm gonna send you to the big house," Delisle said. "He said senior management wants it shut down. It is losing a million dollars a week to base budget. It is in disarray. The previous managers got fired; you're next. You start tomorrow. There were over six thousand workers at Jefferson, with management and labor fighting each other, and fifteen thousand grievances pending! There was drug dealing, prostitution, guns and knives on the shop floor. There were five thousand missing windows, pigeons flying around dropping their stuff on the cars. The roof leaked. I saw operators working their machines with one hand, holding an umbrella with the other. The cafeteria was disgusting. Worst of all was the quality of the products rolling off the assembly line. The audited defect rate was over a hundred demerits when it was supposed to be fifteen. We inherited a mess.

"I knew I had to have a team, I had to have the union on my side. I laid it all on the line for them. I said we're losing our ass here. We have to turn it around or we're going to shut the plant down. I am here to help save your jobs, but I need your personal help. To start, I want those fifteen thousand grievances withdrawn without prejudice. I want to start with a clean slate."

Delisle did not let me down. He got the plant cleaned up and helped forge a positive, can-do attitude on the floor. Within months, the 100 demerit defect rate was down to eighteen! A stunning turnaround was rapidly unfolding.

Meanwhile, Marc Stepp was doing his part persuading the union to get on board with our quality campaign. Mark would tell the workers, "no quality, no sales, no sales, no jobs." Mark would say very directly, "We used it as a theme. If you don't want to contribute to quality, give us your goodwill. If you don't want to give us your goodwill, get the hell out of the way so we can get on with it."

"The union had to make some concessions, not so much in money but in labor operations and classifications. In that plant, there were a hundred and seven job classifications. We reduced that to eleven! Oh there was weeping, wailing and gnashing of teeth about that. Every radical in the union tried to get it voted down. They called me a sellout. Then after all the radical speeches, we put it to a vote. Out of some two thousand people at that meeting, only twenty-five voted against it. It was a big victory."

We were well on our way to preserving a major Detroit asset; there was hope.

I found it most heartening to see Stepp stand in front of all those UAW hourly workers and tell them they had to come to work every day, a radical notion within the culture of the UAW. We saved Chrysler and we saved the Jefferson Avenue plant, too. A few years later, at my instigation, Chrysler spent $1 billion building a new plant directly across the street from the old one. "Dauch is the sole person who gets credit for that new Jefferson North Avenue Plant [JNAP] as far as we are concerned," Stepp said. "That was five thousand jobs. We knew what was going on in the corporate boardroom, and the role Dauch played. He saved the plant."

Perhaps I did, with more than a little help from Stepp. When they tore down the old plant, the workers made two identical plaques featuring the last brick from the old building, cut in half, and the first bolt in the new building. The plaques name me and Marc Stepp as the guys who saved the plant, and the jobs. It is one of my most prized possessions.

It took more than brains—it took dogged determination and extraordinary leadership by many people to accomplish this. "At Chrysler, we had a wonderful working relationship with the union," said Sam Bonanno, who worked for me there, and is now on the AAM board of directors. "We created a quality improvement program and the union signed on. We redesigned work environments for employees. We created our own Chrysler system. We involved the people on the floor and let them influence the redesign of their work areas. They made presentations to management on how to improve operations. We had a great working relationship."

I would like to say that our campaign at Chrysler changed the Detroit mentality about absenteeism, or at least changed it at Chrysler, but whatever changes we saw were short-lived. "The absenteeism went down substantially at Chrysler," Stepp said. "Then it deteriorated over a period of time."

I would have to say that my time with Chrysler was the high point in my relationship with the UAW, or at least with the UAW hourly workers. When Iacocca was preparing for retirement as Chrysler chairman, and it became known that I would not succeed him, a group of UAW members actually planned to conduct a protest carrying signs, "Dauch for Chairman."

"That would have been a first," Stepp said, "but UAW workers campaigning for someone to be Chrysler chairman? I told them they should not do that. Even so, the workers gave their all for Dauch *because they knew he cared*. He respected them and he earned their respect."

ON TO AMERICAN AXLE

While we were negotiating the deal to buy GM's axle plants, I went several times with Bob Mathis to Solidarity House, the UAW headquarters in Detroit, to pitch our plan to union leaders. Bob and I met with UAW president Owen Beiber and vice president Stephen Yokich, suggesting we swap the traditional confrontation for cooperation, creating a win-win situation for both the UAW and AAM.* We agreed to keep the wage scales the UAW had negotiated with GM, but insisted on changes to work rules that impeded flexibility and productivity. We laid it out clearly—if the UAW didn't agree to the changes, the deal would not go through. I told them other Tier One companies would buy the GM facilities and parcel them off until all of the union jobs were gone.

Eventually the UAW leadership bought in, at least in part because they saw me as someone they could work with, but there was no capitulation on their part. They did agree to some changes in work rules. We, in turn, agreed to accept the existing agreement the UAW had with GM, including full wages and benefits as if they were still working for GM. I told them clearly at the time that a supplier could not afford to pay the same wages and benefits as an OEM indefinitely. The UAW leaders assured me they understood that, but that we could make adjustments when the contract came up for renegotiation in 1997 and follow-on contracts. At the time, we were in no position to drive a hard bargain. We needed UAW concurrence to close the deal with GM, and they knew it. Our hands were tied.

"The nature of our purchase was such that the deal would probably never have taken place without the UAW's approval," said Mathis. "The contract carried over for three years. That was all part of the deal. So AAM was not in a position to really take the union on in those first negotiations. The UAW had already made its deal with GM, and that was that."

Of course, we kept working on the UAW. We were persuading our associates to be more flexible in their work habits, and did not want the UAW leadership to think we were running an inside game behind their backs. "We kept going to Solidarity House to tell them what we needed," said Tom Delanoy. "Every morning at five A.M., I took the UAW committeeman on a plant walk through. By the end of six months, I knew all thirty-two-hundred associates by name."

---

* Beiber retired in 1995. Yokich succeeded him and served until 2002, when Ron Gettelfinger became UAW president.

They knew we cared about them and their future. This was all a key feature of our plant tours as we spent time on the shop floors, listened to complaints and concerns, and shared our vision of what AAM could become. "Dick and I went on many plant tours," said Mathis. "We always met first with the union people and then, if appropriate, with management."

We had more than a few strange experiences with associates in those first years. One of my fellow investors, Ray Park, recalled a Saturday he visited the maintenance shop. Of course, everyone working on a Saturday is getting paid time and a half. "This one guy is on the computer looking at his investments," Park said. "I spoke to him; he ignored me. Finally, he looked around and said, 'I shouldn't be doing this, should I?' I said, you're probably right, you should not be doing this at time and a half. He said, 'I am a Christian. I will never do this again.'"

On another occasion, Park visited a plant floor only to see one heavyset guy asleep on a lift truck, with several other associates sitting around doing nothing. It is discouraging to say the least to see people on your payroll sleeping and sitting around. Park said, "Hey, this guy must not have gotten any sleep last night. He woke up, looked at me and told me to go to hell. Actually, what he said was worse than that. That's what we were dealing with in those days."

On the other hand, we got a lot of support and cooperation from both associates and more than a few UAW officials when it became clear what we were doing, such as Jack Kennedy, president of UAW Local 424 in Buffalo. In one interview, Kennedy waxed enthusiastic. "There's a new excitement in the air," he said. "We've gone from a mentality of survival to one of growth. Our plan is one that provides for cost competitiveness and flexibility while maintaining a clean and safe environment for our members." Kennedy and UAW chairman Mike McLeod were longtime leaders of the Buffalo plant.

"With General Motors, we were a noncore business," said Bill Webster, former bargaining chairman of UAW Local 2093 at AAM's prop shaft plant in Three Rivers. "With the new guys, prop shafts, axles and forgings are all we do. Our people can compete. I don't need the security of a corporation that has closed fifty plants [GM] in the last decade." In another interview, Webster said I had made associates at Three Rivers "proud to work there, and believe in their ability to compete."

Even the top UAW brass noticed what was going on at AAM. New UAW president Stephen Yokich told a reporter from *The Washington Post* that AAM was an example of how a unionized company, properly managed, can preserve good jobs and still compete with low-cost suppliers in the auto business. "It's a hell of a success story," he said.

Despite the sweetness and light, the UAW remained as intransigent as ever about compensation and benefits. In 1997, when the contract negotiated with GM expired and it came time to negotiate AAM's first agreement with the UAW as an independent company, it was, at least from their point of view, business as usual. The lead negotiator for the UAW was Vice President Dick Shoemaker.

"They came to the bargaining table with the GM agreement, dropped it on the table, and said that is what we will have," said Mathis. "I told them this company would have to be cost competitive or it would never get new business. When we made the deal with GM, we had agreements built in that guaranteed us further GM business. But we could not compete for non-GM business with that cost structure. I told them we had to factor costs into our bids. They knew this. The UAW's membership had dropped by hundreds of thousands of people, but they do what works for them politically for the members they still have. We went down to the wire with them, but they would not budge on anything significant. It was the GM deal or no deal."

When matters were coming to a head, I got a call from GM urging us to cave. GM was making big money in a time when their bread and butter pickup trucks and SUVs were selling like hotcakes. The company wanted no interruption of supply of axles and drive trains. GM agreed to cover the additional costs that would ensue from the agreement. We were in no position to take on the UAW without GM backing. We gave the UAW what it wanted. This decision simply delayed the day of reckoning.

In 2000, the contract was up for renegotiation again and once again the UAW took a hard line, demanding wage increases and benefits in line with those paid by the OEMs. They were no more interested in our insistence that suppliers could not support that level of compensation than they had been in 1997. This time, the contract negotiations coincided with our schedule to take AAM public. We could hardly expect investors to respond to our offering if we had a strike looming over our heads. It was a most inconvenient time for us to challenge the UAW, but it did not matter much. Once again, GM leaned on us to settle, offering us inducements to cushion the blow. Once again we took the medicine. I knew that time was running out on AAM. We had to get more competitive. Shoemaker, again, was the UAW lead decision maker.

By the time of the next round of negotiations in 2004, the handwriting was on the wall, at least for me. We were struggling mightily to reduce our dependence on GM, but that fat UAW contract made it virtually impossible for us to build up our non-GM portfolio. What non-GM business we were generating was mostly overseas where our new plants were not burdened by UAW contracts. This time I stuck my neck out a bit and told the UAW in no uncertain terms that it was long past time for us to start moving toward a standard automotive supplier's contract, not that of an OEM. We laid it out plain and simple for them, showing what a disadvantage we had in competing with other suppliers like Dana, Delphi, and ArvinMeritor that enjoyed much more advantageous wage and compensation structures.

I must confess I thought the UAW would engage in its customary huffing and puffing, and then, at a minimum, throw us a bone or two. There was no question that the union's intransigence was working to its disadvantage, at least in terms of membership. From a high of 1.5 million members in 1979, it had by that time eroded to about 600,000. That was a dramatic decline for them. Their game plan and strategy simply was not working. Their leadership did not have the political will to work with their represented companies to become more market competitive.

More specific to our situation, some 500,000 people were working for auto suppliers like AAM, and only 20 percent were unionized, down from 50 percent in the 1970s. To us, that meant that we were being severely disadvantaged every time we bid for a non-GM contract in the United States. We knew our competitors were factoring in a much lower labor compensation factor, which was why we were seeing many potentially lucrative contracts snatched away. Many of our Tier One competitors had gone through bankruptcy, which is a tough but effective way of shedding the UAW burden as well as debt. It was vital that we get our labor costs in synch with other U.S. auto suppliers.

Yet that was not the information the UAW was focusing on. Rather, the union saw that we had racked up record earnings for the previous year and seemed to be doing pretty well. The fact that most of those earnings came from our overseas investments was neither here nor there, as far as the UAW was concerned. The new UAW president, Ron Gettelfinger, claimed that it was the union's cooperation that had helped make AAM a top performer, which was partly true. "Not only has American Axle's UAW-represented work force increased since 1994, its stock price has more than doubled," he said. He failed to discuss the lack of profitability at the U.S. plants, and their inability to win new jobs or even replacement business. Gettelfinger and his UAW vice president, Cal Repson, dictated we accept the same terms as the OEMs or there would be a strike.

On February 28, 2004, about 6,500 UAW workers walked off the job. It was the first labor interruption we had since we launched a decade before. We had lost some time due to UAW strikes against GM and Delphi, but this was the first UAW strike against AAM.

The strike lasted about a day and a half. We got the customary call from GM promising us more contracts if we would knuckle under to the UAW. We did win a few concessions from the UAW. New hires were to receive reduced pay and benefits initially, the actual amounts yet to be negotiated. It did not amount to much because we were not hiring anyway. In this instance, the UAW proved to be clever at negotiations, at least in terms of short-term goals.

I was relieved that the crisis had passed, but I knew we had only kicked the can down the road. We were increasing capacity at our Mexican plant as quickly as we could, while preserving our intense focus on quality. Four more years, I thought, and we will have a substantial productive capacity independent of the UAW. That showdown will come. We must be patient, professional and poised and—most important—be ready.

On a more personal level, I felt a sense of futility. I had spent my entire professional life striving to work effectively with the unions to preserve jobs in Detroit and America. In the end I had made little progress against the entitlement mentality and the UAW leadership inflexibility on economic competitiveness. Like those infamous lemmings in Norway, the UAW leadership was leading its members over a cliff and taking our city with them. No amount of logic or persuasion could deter them from their chosen path. It was like a long walk to the gallows. How sad.

15

Passion for Perfection— Quality

No one who produces high-cost, low-quality goods will stay in business long.

—*Richard E. Dauch*

GM did not sell us the Final Drive and Forge Business Unit (FDFBU) within its Saginaw Division because of the dilapidated facilities, obsolete equipment, aging product line, or disgruntled workforce; it sold it because those plants were failing to produce enough axles and drivetrains to meet GM's demand, and because an unacceptably high percentage of its products were of such poor quality that they were generating huge warranty costs or had to be discarded altogether. I have noted that when we took over the old GM operations, the defect rate was 13,441 ppm—an F-minus in my book—but it might mean more to note that in a typical month we had 1,500 axles returned to the company. Every year the Detroit plants were losing millions of dollars in missed production and mismanufactured scrap. That represents a lot of steel, a lot of labor, and a lot of cost. It was bleeding at the gills.

I quickly got a handle on just how bad the return problem was by requiring all returned axles to be sent to a neutral site so we could get an accurate count. Plant managers have a way of making returns disappear to avoid looking bad with senior management. I was myself a plant manager once upon a time and am wise to their ways.

The facilities we acquired were ranked among GM's very worst, and were in fact on GM's "Wall of Shame" for fifty-two consecutive months, which I believe is something of a record. There was no great mystery why GM was eager for someone to take over that operation and get it shaped up. It should be noted that putting this challenge in front of me was equivalent to waving a red flag in front of a bull. I have waged war on sloppy work all of my professional life, and achieved great things in quality at GM, VWoA, and Chrysler. I was ready for AAM.

I made it clear that it was everyone's job—and I would take the lead. One thing I have learned in the auto industry—and I assume it applies to any industry—is that quality begins with the top guy (or gal) and must have a genuine commitment from everyone. You cannot delegate it and hope it will take care of itself. In a situation like the one we inherited, there was no question of delegation. The situation was critical. We had to grab that operation by the throat and change the way it operated from top to bottom. It was very simple—our customers demanded quality and we had to deliver.

We were faced with a double challenge: increasing production *and* making a dramatic improvement in quality at the same time. I put Marion Cumo in charge of a crash program to get the quality situation turned around. Cumo was well-versed in quality management. During my time with Chrysler, he had headed Quality and Product Engineering for all assembly and stamping plants, and had done a brilliant job.

Something was happening in the early 1980s. There was a quality revolution under way. The Big Three were finally realizing they were losing market share to the Japanese because of quality. The Japanese were building better cars, stereos, televisions, motorcycles—and steadily taking away market share from U.S. firms.

Both Ford and GM had hired Dr. W. Edwards Deming, whose pioneering work in quality during the 1950s had made him a legend in Japan. He was so successful with Japanese manufacturers that they created in his honor the top Japanese quality award named after him. His seminars reached thousands of people year after year. His approach was really quite simple: When you improve quality, costs go down because of less rework, fewer mistakes, and better use of machines, time, and materials. Productivity improves as you increase market share with better quality at lower cost. Deming taught workers on production lines that if defects and poor quality get into the hands of the customer, you lose the market and it would cost them their jobs. In the end, you get to stay in business and provide jobs and more jobs.

I sent Cumo, along with Allan Rae, to Washington, D.C., where they met with Deming in his basement, which they described as full of medals, plaques, photographs, and eight certificates of honorary degrees from universities. On the wall in one corner was a replica of the Deming Prize. Rae had participated in Deming's study group and was an expert in the master's statistical approach. Rae had worked with more than 200 companies, and was widely recognized as one of the nation's leading quality experts in his own right. Deming walked them through his full quality philosophy, which is built upon continuous improvements that can be tracked and statistically measured. Cumo and Rae came back inspired to infuse Chrysler top to bottom with Deming's philosophy, and they did. Cumo said meeting Deming was like meeting the Wizard of Oz.

"I said, 'Allan, we're going to do this, we're going to teach the whole company,'" Cumo said. "We had to adapt Deming's approach. We knew we could not treat UAW workers like they were Japanese. We had to make modifications."

We knew we had to get the UAW on board with us, so we went down to Solidarity House on Jefferson Avenue, the UAW headquarters, and met with top UAW officials, including Marc Stepp who understood the need for this quality approach and provided quality leadership. I also had Rae teach Iacocca's senior staff the principles of Deming's quality approach in four-hour seminars addressing every facet of the company—purchasing, engineering, power train, stamping, assembly plants, and supplier quality. Rae ended up helping educate more than 44,000 employees in basic principles of quality and cost.

That experience served us well when we took over the old GM axle and drivetrain plants, especially in Detroit where the conditions were the worst. Our first task was to stop the bleeding—by which I mean preventing defective products from leaving our property. "In the first year, I had to repair many products and got stuck with much too much scrap," said Cumo. "We were losing huge amounts of money in repair and scrap, but it could not be helped. We would not let bad products leave the plant. We inspected each piece one at a time, as long as it took and whatever it cost."

We achieved containment with part-by-part inspection, but it was costing us a fortune to do that and it is not, nor has ever been, an effective way to assure quality. Quality must be integrated throughout the production system. We knew we had to get quality systems in place, and quickly, but we were trying to do an awful lot at once. We were then in the beginning of a great quality migration, when about half of AAM's associates flowed back to GM— maybe 70 percent from the Detroit plants. I have noted earlier that they probably preferred the security of the GM name to that of an upstart like AAM that no one had ever heard of. Another reason might be our sudden focus on quality and cost that demanded a sea change in the way associates performed their tasks. We were definitely disrupting their comfort level, but we were agents of change and that comes with the territory.

I have always said that success in this business requires a laser focus on people, product and process. You need to have the right people working together in a team atmosphere; you have to demand the best quality in our products; and you need to put in place processes that will continue to produce top quality products over and over, year after year—processes that can accommodate new technologies, upgraded product lines, and personnel turnover with no reduction in quality.

PEOPLE

At AAM, the first thing is people. We had to have top quality people on board. There were many such people among the ranks of the associates we inherited, people eager for a chance to do excellent work, but we had to identify them and let them know their knowledge was now highly valued. One of the best ones was a gentleman named Arthur LaRose, who I had met at GM back in the early 1970s. A GM lifer, LaRose had an instinctive talent for ferreting out defects along with a determination to get rid of them. He had retired a few years before, but GM had brought him back on contract to work on quality issues, and I quickly persuaded him to continue working with us.

"Change starts at the top," LaRose said. "Before AAM, an operator just ran his machine and didn't care about the final product. Dick changed that. He made it clear that when you find a defect, you stop it there and then. That's how you change quality. You have to change the culture of the people. That was the biggest problem."

We had to have the right plant managers in place, who agreed with the new AAM philosophy. Good plant managers are a rare and often independent breed. They believe they know what they are doing—that job requires confidence—and sometimes they resist direction. We needed innovative plant managers, we needed associates who were trainable, and we needed the UAW on board. We went to Solidarity House time and again, explaining to the UAW brass what we were doing, why it meant job security to their members, and why it was important for them to cooperate with us. In the early days of AAM, I must say they were receptive and cooperative, at least in terms of work rules. The hourly associates played a major and positive role in the success of AAM.

Training, of course, was a key component of the AAM cultural shift. I have stated elsewhere that we set a target of providing each associate with nearly fifty hours of training each and every year. A major portion of that training was focused on attainment of product quality.

All of this required a great deal of communication and personal attention. I made it clear from the beginning—not that I needed to—that our managers were to be out on the floor talking to associates, seeing the problems first hand and solving problems every day. "We lived on the floor that first year," said Cumo. "The biggest thing Dick taught us was, you do it with people. He walked those facilities and he respected the people."

PRODUCT

As you get good people in place responding to leadership that is on the scene, you focus on producing top quality products. This was no small challenge. A truck axle contains 180–200 parts, mostly metal. Axles have to withstand tremendous pressure and stresses. The critical components are made of top quality steel which, after shaping, is heat treated to make it even harder, as it must be to withstand the tremendous heat and torque it must handle. It is absolutely critical that each part be made according to fine tolerances measured by millimeters, and that it be built correctly. Otherwise, metal will grind against metal, generating noise and excess heat. That can lead to failure on the highway that can result in injury or death. When we speak to quality, it is not just a matter of competing for profit. We want the product to have total integrity.

To ensure that our parts are made precisely to mesh with other parts, we used gauges that are built to measure such things with precision. The amazing thing—at least to me—was that when we took over the old GM plants in Detroit, all of the gauges were put aside in a storage "crib" where they had lain unloved and unused for who knows how long. We brought the gauges out, had them calibrated or replaced as necessary, and put them at key points on the plant floor where they were needed to check the tolerances of the products we were producing. "We were running jobs with nothing and GM management wondered why the result was so bad," said LaRose. "Dick spent a ton of money getting those gauges right and back on the floor. It was enjoyable to watch."

Another happy find was Karen Cairns, who was the resident quality expert at our plant in Three Rivers. "Dick came to the plant and made a speech on quality," Cairns said. "He was the first upper-management person I had ever heard make quality a priority. He brought up ISO 9000 [a worldwide quality standard developed in Europe] and Cpk [a statistical math-based approach to quality taught by Deming]. I was probably the only person in the room who knew what he was talking about. Dick was methodical. He had the gauges calibrated and procedures put in place. He was spending millions every year on training. He had a plan and was implementing a quality system."

Then as now, we have to make the parts precisely and we have to make them efficiently and we have to deliver them in a timely manner. If we do all that, we make a profit and everyone gets to keep working. If we fail, well, failure was never an option.

From my earliest days in the auto industry, I have emphasized over and over that quality begins with design and engineering. At Chrysler, I had for the first time the power to do what I had wanted for years—put process and manufacturing engineers into the design studio. Left to their own, designers produce beautiful concepts with scarcely any attention to the problems of production. Too many times I have seen people on the firing line trying to execute designs that were simply impracticable. The Chrysler minivan was the first totally new vehicle created by designers working with manufacturing engineers up front, which is a major reason for its success. It was near perfect on quality, a gem for manufacturing. It was teamwork in action.

It paid off big time at Chrysler. In 1991, the Chrysler minivan plant in Windsor won the Canada Award for Business Excellence in Quality—Canada's equivalent of the Deming Prize in Japan or the Baldrige Award in the United States—for achieving a dominant position in the minivan market through successful total quality management in all aspects of the organization. The credit for this belongs mainly with the Chrysler employees who built the minivans. Lee Iacocca attended the awards ceremony to provide symbolic support. We learned a lot about quality at Chrysler and brought that quality focus with us to AAM.

At AAM, we recognized it is critically important that our purchasing people know what they are doing, buying materials and parts that are of the highest quality. You cannot make quality axles with poor quality steel and components. One of our first initiatives was to bring more qualified metallurgists on board. We are, in fact, one of the largest users of special bar quality steel; it is imperative that we possess expertise in the field and not have to take it on faith that our suppliers are sending us the best stuff. As President Ronald Reagan famously said, "Trust, but verify." Supplier development and supplier quality assurance are very important.

Also, about 75 percent of the parts that go into our axles and drivetrains are provided by suppliers. Since day one of AAM, we have made our relationship with suppliers a top corporate priority. We have what we call our Production Part Approval Process (PPAP), designed to assure suppliers meet our standards. They must run a series of the parts, perhaps as many as three hundred, and have them measured to establish they are top quality before we accept them from a supplier.

When we buy machinery, the suppliers are expected to pass a rigorous examination. "The supplier has got to set that machine up on his production floor just as if we were running production," said Kevin Smith, AAM vice president for Program Management and Launch. "I'm talking about the machine, fixturing, gauging, material handling, everything. Then the supplier runs a hundred and twenty-five pieces per spindle and we require a Cpk of 2.0 on all parts made before we will accept that machine for shipment. That's step one. Step two is to set that machine on our floor as it was on the supplier's floor. Now the supplier is once again responsible to certify that machine to a 2.0 Cpk in a three-hundred-piece run. Achieving the required process capability on the three-hundred-piece run triggers a *partial* payment to the supplier.

"The third step in the acceptance process requires the vendor to maintain the same statistical capability and quality, and achieve uptime of 92 percent over a twenty-five-day run. Any preventive maintenance, tool changes, any downtime as a result of something the machine supplier is responsible for, all have to be handled within that 92 percent uptime requirement, and they have to do that for twenty-five consecutive days. If there's a problem on day twenty-three, you put in corrective action and start all over for another twenty-five days."

That's a tough regimen, but this is a demanding business. Every year we invite our critical suppliers to our World Headquarters in Detroit for Suppliers' Day, when we give them an honest assessment of the company's prospects, and what we will be expecting from them in the years ahead. Hundreds of them come every year from all over the world. We insist their products meet the most rigorous standards, but we work with them to help them provide what we need. We know how challenging a true quality system is to create and maintain. We help our suppliers achieve superior quality in their products.

We have one other executive who joined AAM from Chrysler, Dr. Bob Karban, executive director of Supplier Quality, who is having a major impact on quality training with us. He took the American Society for Quality (ASQ) certified training classes and began developing ASQ certified quality engineers. That is no small challenge given ASQ's six-hour exam and 54 percent pass rate. Bob's pass rate was 100 percent for his first class, producing fifteen certified quality engineers for AAM. Bob is continuing these classes with associates from all parts of the company. He is also teaching Six Sigma classes concentrated on engineering associates to develop process-driven designs to assure robust manufacturing at our AAM suppliers and AAM manufacturing plants.

Finally, I have never believed in beating suppliers down on price. We all have to be competitive, but we also have to make a profit. We treat our suppliers as our extended business partners.

PROCESS

We find quality people, we focus on quality products, and we develop advanced production systems that produce quality products consistently, year in and year out. A key component of a quality process is technology. I have mentioned earlier our pivotal shift from five-cut, wet cut to two-cut, dry cut. That was a major transition, but it came amid a tidal sweep of new technologies that we embraced steadily from the day we took over. Staying abreast of technology is very expensive, especially in this era of transition, but quality does not come cheap.

"Production was a trip," said George Dellas, who played a key role in our quality campaign. "The production equipment in the plants was old, not maintained, and there was little capital investment. The machines would break down. Some of the people didn't know how to run them right. Nonconforming material was all over the plants, a lot of it wasn't even tagged. The next shift would think it was good stuff, put it back on the line and have it rejected again."

Dellas recalled that when we started out, the plants had quality posters all over the walls. "Even to this day, when I go into a plant and see a bunch of quality posters on the walls, it tells me they don't know what they are doing. A lot of the plants had never had a quality manager give a presentation. They did the talk but not the walk. And the ones who did give quality presentations sounded like they were speaking different languages. None of the plants were measuring quality the way our customers did—in ppm. At every plant review, I insisted that the quality manager give a presentation with a standardized format."

"We had a whole team of associates working with our customers, bringing feedback to the plants, saying we need to do this, we need to do that," said

Cumo. "Dick also toured the plants of every customer plant we had. We all went out there and not just once. We went repeatedly so they knew we were serious about our commitment to quality."

At our Three Rivers plant, Rossmann began with containment. "When we came in, one of the first things we had to do was make sure we were shipping products that would do the job. The next thing was to standardize work, make sure the gauges were calibrated, the workers trained, and that they knew a standard process they could repeat over and over. There was a lot of coaching, shutting lines down, talking to associates about quality, making sure they are doing things the right way, validating the process, taking them to the end of the line to see what they did, clamping down on absenteeism. The containment costs began to go down."

Rossmann points out a basic principle of Deming's, namely that you cannot rely on humans to eliminate all defects. "We've done studies. You give me a hundred washers to inspect, I will miss fifteen defects. We will have to go through six inspections to catch them all. You have to build a standardized process for production, a process that virtually guarantees consistent quality, after which you monitor the process by checking random samples."

I told Cumo also he had three years to attain ISO 9000 status—a comprehensive quality program that touches every aspect of the production process. Actually, the ISO 9000 was a European system embracing twenty elements. The Big Three had improved on that with the QS 9000 that had twenty-three elements. "The quickest way to get there was to systemize it," Cumo said. "We decided to go for it knowing it wouldn't be cheap. We had to get the entire organization engaged, but we did it.

"You have to have a plan that is understandable. We broke it down into a chart and gave everyone clear responsibility. I said we would take this footprint and move on. Some of them thought I was crazy, but I knew as long as we had momentum, we could pull it off and we did. We got there in eighteen months instead of three years, ISO certified in every plant."

I challenged my team to make an all-out assault on that terrible 13,441 ppm problem we inherited. One of my favorite phrases is *degree of excellence*. I told them I wanted that ppm number cut by 50 percent every year. After the first year, we were down to 6,219, well beyond 50 percent. The second year we were down to 2,931 ppm, again well beyond 50 percent. The third year we hit 1,499 ppm, well ahead of schedule, getting much better and before long we were flatlining down around one hundred. At the same time, we were doubling and then redoubling our production to keep up with GM's demand.

"I started every day at seven A.M. with a quality call," said Cumo. "That was for the quality people and the plant managers, too. It let them know quality was not just a slogan, that we took it seriously. That was and remains part of the AAM system. I have retired, but they still start every day at seven with a quality report at every plant. Quality problems go to the Operating Committee. We make sure the problems are solved."

I told GM we would make rapid headway against that massive warranty bill. When we took over, GM's annual warranty costs for products of the final drive and forge business were in the tens of millions of dollars annually. Using hard mathematical data as a benchmark, we took on what GM called the "hardy perennials," the problems that kept reappearing in customer surveys expressing dissatisfaction, the kinds of things that foster disenchantment among consumers and send them to competitors. *Axles always made the top 10 of that warranty list, mainly because of leaks and noise.* We took those issues head-on, led by the resident geniuses at our Technical Center. We got those issues under control pretty quick. Between 1996 and 2010, we reduced GM's warranty costs—for our products—by 85 percent. This saved GM $647 million! Quality pays.

In the early days of AAM, GM met with us regularly and gave us endless grief for the poor quality of our products, making it clear they expected dramatic improvements. We produced those improvements, and within three years the beatings had subsided, evolving into friendly, cooperative meetings where we discussed ways to do even better. We were, and are, strategic business partners.

PHASE TWO

By 1998, we were down to about 100 ppm, which is acceptable to some people, but not to me. I reset the goal to what I called the Five Quality Zeros: zero ppm, zero returned sales, zero problem reports & resolutions, zero controlled shipping (repeated problems with one customer), and zero cost recoveries. Later I added a sixth zero: disruption to a customer's assembly plant. Our eternal quest is for zero defects, zero problems, zero warranty claims.

In 1998, despite extraordinary progress, we still had a long way to go. I took the quality leadership baton from Cumo, who had led us through the critical early years, and passed it to Dellas, who had a more advanced vision of how to move from 100 ppm down to the sub–10 ppm range. We had long since plucked the low-hanging fruit and were producing acceptable products. To realize my quest for AAM to be Six Sigma meant reaching 3.4 ppm consistently, and that requires a much more ambitious agenda and understanding of how true quality is achieved.

"Dellas took what I did to another level," Cumo said. "He built the Quality Engineering Technical Center [QETC] that became our key quality laboratory. I did not have the time to put that together with all the other things I was doing."

"The QETC is our version of CSI [Crime Scene Investigation]," said Cairns. "That is where we analyze problems to find out what went wrong when a warranty claim comes in. Was it the supplier, the dealer, the OEM or AAM? We examine all the evidence to determine where responsibility lies."

A key part of the process is to perform a total tear-down of the product within twenty-four hours of hearing about a customer problem, and lay the components all out on a table. The various parts are measured on the spot by our quality engineers, who are certified by the American Society for Quality (ASQ), to determine where the problem lies. We review our findings with our customers to determine the cause of the quality failure and, where appropriate, do a read across to all of our manufacturing operations.

Our QETC's main impact is to reduce quality problems, prevent recurrence, and reduce costs and inconvenience for our customers. It is a first-class operation where our customers, engineers, quality managers, and often suppliers meet on a weekly basis to focus on quality issues. To underscore its effectiveness, we have reduced warranty costs for GM from $31.39 per vehicle in 1996 to $4.50 in 2010. Warranty costs are a big-ticket item for most manufacturing companies, and the ability to reduce warranty costs can make a big difference in profits and Wall Street valuations.

Allan Rae, who had worked in quality with Cumo at Chrysler, joined AAM in 2005. He began working with our senior quality team to help us reach a higher level. A key facet of Rae's approach is to make certain finance people are directly involved in the cost of quality, because it has a tremendous impact on the bottom line. In earlier years, Rae had actually worked closely with W. Edwards Deming, and is also well versed in the principles expounded by Dr. Joseph Juran, another famed quality expert. At Chrysler, Rae and Cumo went after quality using principles established by both Deming and Juran. In 1988, they put forty-five ASQ certified quality engineers in Chrysler manufacturing plants and found ways to reduce warranty costs based on developing quality case studies using statistical analysis. The average savings per quality engineer was $430,800 per year, not a bad investment. Over five years, hundreds of teams working on the plant floors saved Chrysler $79.6 million on reducing the cost of warranty while improving quality.

In January 2008, I received a call from my old friend Jim McCaslin, then the president of Harley-Davidson, one of our customers. He asked if he could borrow Rae for a day to perform shop floor reviews, look at the cost of quality, and do a lecture at the Harley-Davidson university on how lean manufacturing and quality fit together. McCaslin was interested in improving quality and reducing warranty costs. Harley, of course, had an excellent reputation for quality, but McCaslin wanted to take it to the next level. McCaslin commented that the shop floor reviews by Rae, and the four-hour lecture, were outstanding and had a positive impact on the Harley team. In May of that year, McCaslin called again asking for Rae to make one more visit. I agreed, but reminded him that AAM is not a consulting company. Rae presented his approach to the top five hundred Harley executives. The McCaslin team was so impressed that a few months later they toured one of our plants in Ohio to see our principles in action. Harley was highly impressed with the operation, attention to detail, housekeeping, score boards on the shop floor, and plant turnaround. We took that as high praise from one of our nation's premier companies.

The impact of warranty costs, and the imperative of reducing them, is a story that gets short treatment in the business press, but it deserves headlines. A New York newsletter called *Warranty Week*, published by Eric Arnum, which we have been using for years, spells it out in dramatic fashion. Every year, manufacturing companies must set aside what is called "accruals" to cover the expected costs of warranty claims. However, it is not just a problem for manufacturing companies. In 2011, Caterpillar accrued $1.199 billion in warranty costs, or 2.1 percent of its heavy equipment sales; Boeing accrued $232 million or 0.6 percent of commercial airplane sales; and IBM accrued $435 million or 2.3 percent of its computer hardware sales. That year the total amount of warranty accruals reported by all U.S.-based warranty providers grew nearly 8 percent to $24.7 billion! Arnum said that during the recent recession, most manufactures were forced to reduce costs and improve the efficiency of their warranty process. Now that sales are rebounding, warranty costs are too, but not as fast as sales. The accrual costs for the top 50 warranty providers are listed in the chart below. Warranty is not only an indicator of business cost, it relates to customer satisfaction and repeat sales. Warranty represents customer dissatisfaction. It must be improved continuously.

Here is where the rubber meets the road in the quest for quality. By reducing product defects, and hence warranty claims, companies can save billions. AAM is showing the world how it's done.

$24.7 billion

In 2011 the total amount of warranty accruals reported by all US-based warranty providers grew to $24.7 billion, up nearly 8% from 2010 levels.

The chart below shows some of the top 50 companies and their accrual rates for 2011, and if they have made any improvements from 2010–2011.

Top 50 U.S.-based Warranty Providers
Annual Changes in Warranty Costs
Accrual Rates at Year-End 2011 vs. 2010
(in $ millions and as a percentage of sales)
(ranked by accruals made in 2011)

Company Name	Accrual Made in 2010	Accrual Rate 12/31/10	Accrual Made in 2011	Accrual Rate 12/31/11
General Motors Co.	$3,204	2.4%	$3,062	2.1%
Hewlett-Packard Co.	$2,689	3.2%	$2,657	3.1%
Ford Motor Co.	$1,522	1.3%	$2,215	2.5%
Apple Inc.	$1,151	1.6%	$2,067	1.9%
Caterpillar Inc.	$841	2.1%	$1,199	2.1%
General Electric Co.	$583	0.8%	$935	1.1%
Dell Inc.	$1,146	2.3%	$917	2.0%
Deere & Co.	$568	2.4%	$665	2.3%
Cisco Systems Inc.	$471	1.3%	$497	1.7%
United Technologies Corp.	$440	1.1%	$475	1.2%
IBM Corp.	$407	2.3%	$435	2.3%
Cummins Inc.	$401	3.0%	$428	2.4%
Navistar International Corp.	$269	2.3%	$407	3.0%
Motorola Mobility Holdings Inc.	$323	2.8%	$376	2.9%
Whirlpool Corp.	$349	2.5%	$344	2.4%
Paccar Inc.	$172	0.7%	$304	2.0%
Emerson Electric Co.	$243	1.0%	$240	1.0%
Boeing Co.	$141	0.4%	$232	0.6%
Textron Inc.	$189	1.8%	$223	2.0%
Johnson Controls Inc.	$250	0.7%	$219	0.7%
Ingersoll-Rand plc	$245	1.9%	$210	1.6%
Honeywell International Inc.	$214	0.8%	$197	0.7%
AGCO Corp.	$164	2.4%	$195	2.2%
Seagate Technology plc	$180	1.9%	$182	1.3%
EMC Corp.	$120	1.1%	$175	1.4%
Applied Materials Inc.	$152	1.6%	$170	1.6%
Western Digital Corp.	$184	1.9%	$151	1.2%
Jarden Corp.	$125	2.7%	$146	2.9%
Danaher Corp.	$121	0.9%	$115	0.7%
Eaton Corp.	$99	0.7%	$98	0.6%
Stanley Black & Decker Inc.	$89	1.1%	$97	0.9%
Eastman Kodak Co.	$54	2.0%	$95	3.5%
General Dynamics Corp.	$70	1.3%	$88	1.5%
Lexmark International Inc.	$94	8.8%	$78	7.9%
L-3 Communications Corp.	$62	0.8%	$77	1.0%
Terex Corp.	$75	1.1%	$75	1.2%
Manitowoc Co. Inc.	$51	1.6%	$67	1.8%
Thor Industries Inc.	$59	2.4%	$65	2.5%
A. O. Smith Corp.	$63	4.2%	$65	3.8%
Standard Motor Products Inc.	$53	6.5%	$64	7.3%
Brunswick Corp.	$101	4.0%	$63	2.2%
Agilent Technologies Inc.	$57	1.3%	$61	1.1%
Netgear Inc.	$62	6.9%	$60	5.1%
Harman International Industries Inc.	$58	1.4%	$56	1.3%
Thermo Fisher Scientific Inc.	$41	0.4%	$54	0.5%
Microsoft Corp.	$82	0.5%	$54	0.4%
Exide Technologies	$49	1.7%	$53	1.7%
Juniper Networks Inc.	$50	1.5%	$53	1.5%
Garmin Ltd.	$93	3.5%	$52	0.6%
TRW Automotive Holdings Corp.	$67	0.5%	$52	0.3%

SHAINAN PROBLEM SOLVING

Dellas was a devotee of Dorian Shainin, a quality pioneer who along with Deming, Juran and a few others, provided effective problem solving techniques for quality professionals. As a practical matter, AAM embraced a wide variety of quality tools in our quest for perfection. Shainin applied statistical techniques to manufacturing in a system that he proved to be an effective quality tool. He relied upon an observation of Juran's that "quality defects are unequal in frequency, i.e., when a long list of defects was arranged in the order of frequency, a relative few of the defects accounted for the bulk of the defectiveness."

Accordingly, Shainin recognized that among thousands of variables that could lead to product defects, one cause-relationship had to be stronger than the others. He called this primary cause the "Big Red X" and demonstrated that the cause can exist as an interaction among independent variables. The effect of the Red X is then magnified by the square-root-of-the-sum-of-the-squares law, thereby isolating the root cause.

"Shainin is a problem-solving technique that uses physics and geometry to analyze tough problems," said Dellas. "After working on a few problems, I became an avid fan. It is a powerful, proactive tool. When you have a quality issue, you take factors you think might be the culprit, zero in like with a sniper's scope and get right down to that Red X. Sometimes there is a bit of luck involved. One of our first experiments was with axle noise, one of GM's hardy perennials. We set up a program to test an axle using GM's proving grounds. We had drivers hauling a five-thousand-pound load around the test track at fifty-five miles an hour and intended to keep it up until we burned out an axle, but we never did.

"Then one day the drivers had to leave early to go bowling, so they stepped on the gas to get their routes done faster. When they got out, they smelled burnt axle oil. Next morning when they pulled the axle and opened it up, it was fried. What we learned was that you could never fry an axle at low speed, but if you went faster and the temperature got up to 427 degrees, it would burn out."

Dellas eventually had at least one Shainin expert at every plant. They used the technique to identify a raft of problems. In another example, we had poorly machined ring gears creating all sorts of problems. They were wobbling in the machine process because they had shot peen particles (little bits of metal). So how to get rid of shot peen? We found the dunnage sent from one plant to another was contaminated, so we bought steam cleaners to clean the containers. Yet still the problem would pop back up from time to time. We kept at it, analyzing every aspect of the process. We soon discovered no one was monitoring the wash process. It had to meet a minimum temperature and when it didn't, it would not wash the shot peen off the gears. So now we monitor that at every plant.

Sometimes it really does seem that Murphy's law is valid—if something can go wrong, it will. That is a major reason why quality is such an elusive target.

"Our crowning glory was the Process Failure Mode and Effects Analysis [PFMEA]," said Dellas. "It involves everybody in the process. We get the supervisors and all the associates together and go over each station of the assembly process. You ask, what can I do to avoid a defect at this station? If by chance I make a defect, how do I prevent that defect from going to the next station? By the time you go through this, you have virtually error-proofed the line."

Everyone at AAM got training in the PFMEA, and we had good results from day one. "It got so good," said Dellas, "and we had so few defects after that, that each department was cleaning up its defects after the shift they worked with virtually no defects coming out. When I retired from AAM, we were down to nearly zero ppm."

I put Al Monich, who had served in a variety of senior positions at AAM, in charge of the warranty program. Working closely with Karen Cairns, Monich is steering AAM into a new situation in which we are now contractually responsible for half of any warranty costs our products produce for GM. Money is a great motivator.

"We have been down in single-digit levels for many years now," Monich said, "but how do you keep that going when you are constantly opening up new operations with new people? That is the challenge today. Dick wants bulletproof quality. That starts with perfectly engineered products and quality manufacturing systems in the plants."

Cairns noted that GM, Chrysler, and other OEMs began offering five-year warranties in 2007 that are only now reaching the end of their lifespans. "They don't even know yet what that five-year warranty level will mean," she said.

"Dick's expectation is that we improve warranty 20 percent each year, year after year, a very high hurdle," Monich said. "I don't know another metric we measure ourselves on where the expectation is 20 percent year after year. However, for the most part, we have been able to do it."

A recent example was a problem we encountered with our new electronic torque transfer device on a rear-drive module on a Cadillac SRX. It was an intermittent problem causing a light on the dashboard to flash on and off. We pulled out every stop, seeking the cause of that problem. Using Shainin techniques, we traced it down to a fourth-tier supplier in the mountains of southern Germany who made a little component no bigger than the eraser on a common pencil. It took us a month to figure this out. We even sent an engineer to Germany for two weeks to track it down. It was a component molded into a larger part that we could not really get at. That thing could not have cost more than a quarter and it was compromising a $60,000 vehicle. Producing absolute quality with zero ppm is not a simple challenge.

Today, AAM is, in my humble opinion, the absolute best axle company in the world bar none, and I can produce mounds of data to support that claim. For example, we have five manufacturing plants in a fourteen-month stretch serving our customer Chrysler operating at zero ppm, shipping more than seven million parts. That translates into zero customer complaints. As a company, we have had eight consecutive years with single-digit ppm performance with all of our major customers. That is what I mean by bulletproof quality. Most of the credit for this belongs to AAM's associates, who are to be congratulated for their commitment and world-class performance. Thank you, team members.

Yet our progress has not been an isolated achievement. Across the auto industry landscape, OEMs and suppliers have been making leapfrog gains in quality year after year. Said Dave Sargent, vice president of global automotive for J. D. Power and Associates, one of the top firms measuring consumer satisfaction:

> The Asian and European brands were dominating the new-vehicle quality front in the late 1980s, with only the occasional domestic brand—namely Cadillac and Buick—breaking into the top 10 . . . In the early 1990s, we began to see the Detroit automakers make some inroads in quality improvements, and those improvements were even more dramatic in the 2000s. In 2010, the J. D. Power and Associates Initial Quality Study saw the domestic vehicles catch imports for the first time in the 24-year history of the study. It is important to note that the Detroit Three didn't catch the imports because the Asian and European automakers' quality was declining—they were in fact improving as well—but that the domestic were improving their quality at a greater rate.

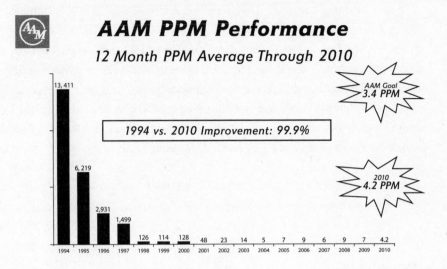

AAM PPM Performance

12 Month PPM Average Through 2010

1994 vs. 2010 Improvement: 99.9%

AAM Goal
3.4 PPM

2010
4.2 PPM

A NEW DEFINITION

Overall, the quest for quality in the auto industry, I learned early in my automotive career, led me to a new definition of quality. It begins with the customer. You have to understand your customers' requirements, both internal and external. Quality starts with the way you hire people, train them and continue developing their skills. It depends on engineering to make certain creative concepts and designs can be manufactured in quantity and quality. It depends on reliability testing to determine how well a product will perform and how long it will last. It depends on suppliers who share your commitment to quality and can deliver quality consistently. It depends on machine builders and tooling companies that are certified by industry quality standards.

Quality depends on top management. *I have to drive and demand quality culture twenty-four hours a day, seven days a week.* Every associate in the company is responsible for quality and every associate on our production lines, as W. Edwards Deming said, must know the score. How is our first-time quality (FTQ)? Are we getting better? They need standardized work and the ability and authority to make changes to continuously improve. Most importantly, do the associates have what they need to do quality work? The right tools? The best maintenance and training? What can senior management do to enable them to raise the bar consistently and perform at ever higher levels? In the final analysis, quality is an endless quest that just gets tougher. If you can't handle that, you're in the wrong business.

I am proud that I was able to lead the quality campaign at AAM. In June 2006, to my surprise, the Automotive Division of The American Society for Quality (ASQ) here in Detroit named me Quality Leader of the Year. The best part of this award was that it was presented to me at the GM Heritage Center. It was a singular honor and I know it does not belong just to me, but rather to the many quality professionals and committed associates who share my commitment to excellence, and accept challenges far beyond the norm. *Quality is ever and always a team effort, and I am proud to be the team leader.*

16

Corporate Responsibility

*We have come tardily to the tremendous task of cleaning up
our environment.*

—Rep. Gerald R. Ford (R-MI)
1970 Earth Day address

Environmental concerns were slow to penetrate Detroit. Maybe it was because the Big Three in those days had a certain smugness that mitigated against accepting new ideas. Even though the auto industry, like any heavy industry, had serious environmental issues, there was no concerted effort to deal with them for many, many years. They just festered.

To be sure, the auto industry was not the only sector that was slow to embrace environmentalism. The movement itself did not really command public attention until the first Earth Day of 1970, when future president Gerald Ford made the speech I quoted from above. That was the year that President Richard Nixon, annoyed by Congressional inaction on the environment, created the Environmental Protection Agency (EPA) with an Executive Order. That was the same year Nixon signed into law the Occupational Safety and Health Act (OSHA) to make worker safety a national priority. Those two agencies—EPA and OSHA—have had a profound and largely positive impact on the way industry operates.

Young people today can have no idea what an environmental nightmare we had on our hands back then. Industries and municipalities all over the country routinely dumped wastes into waterways and thought nothing about it. Vast swaths of the Great Lakes were essentially dead to marine life. In some cities, the level of particulates in the air was so dense experts were afraid it could conduct electricity. On June 22, 1969, the Cuyahoga River in Cleveland, Ohio, actually caught fire. The sight of a burning river got everyone's attention.

Earth Day 1970 is frequently cited as the wakeup call that roused the nation to awareness and action on the environment. In the ensuing decades, we have as a society invested billions of dollars cleaning up our environment. I have no doubt some of that money was wasted, but in any program of that magnitude, there will always be waste. I for one am glad we made this commitment, and believe it has paid rich dividends in terms of human health and quality of life for all of us, not to mention quite a few other species who share our space in the universe.

At Chrysler, I took the lead in the company's environmental program. Up until that time, there had never been a vehicle assembly plant that did not produce tons of greasy sludge that had to be hauled away to a landfill every day. I instructed our technical people and supplier community not to find a better place to put it, or to reduce it by a certain percentage, but rather to find a creative way to *eliminate sludge from the process*. They accepted the challenge and developed some unique processes that essentially eliminated the sludge factor. By 1986, we were running Chrysler's Dodge City truck plant in Warren, Michigan, with zero sludge being transported to landfills. It is truly amazing what creative people can do when they are challenged, motivated, and supported.

When we took over the old GM plants that became the core of AAM, we soon discovered we were producing wastewater containing 1000 ppm of pollutants directly into the Detroit sewer system, and hence the Detroit River. Within sixty days, using conventional methods, we had that down to 25 ppm. It was just a matter of doing it and enforcing an environmental policy of compliance.

That was perhaps our first major environmental initiative, but by no means our last. We're not a social company, but we do have a social conscience. In those years, it was still a basic mentality of the auto industry that waste was the inevitable result of doing business. From the first days of AAM, I have drilled it into our people and into our corporate culture that we are committed to protecting the environment and, as a key aspect of that commitment, to conserving energy. I cannot emphasize this enough—commitment to environment and safety must begin at the top, and the emphasis must be relentless and continuous.

Our first and most conspicuous target was and remains waste. I made it clear to our people from the outset that waste is a misplaced and/or misused resource. Of course, a crusade against waste is a key aspect of our commitment to lean manufacturing, but in that we are focusing primarily on wasted time and to a lesser extent wasted parts that are not made correctly or delivered at the right time.

Waste is also the inefficient use of utilities such as electricity, water, and natural gas, which are traditionally considered unavoidable overheads. AAM realizes that the cost of waste is not only the cost of waste disposal, but also other costs such as:

- Inefficient energy use cost.
- Purchase cost of wasted raw material.
- Production cost for the waste material.
- Management time spent on waste material.
- Lost revenue for what could have been a product instead of waste.
- Potential liabilities due to waste.

I am a firm believer that the key to reducing waste is to tackle the problem at the source in order to prevent pollution, promote cleaner technology, and efficient use of raw materials, electricity, natural gas, and water.

HAZARDOUS WASTE

I have mentioned elsewhere the major shift we made in the early days of AAM from five-cut, wet cut to two-cut, dry cut for shaping steel components. This was a major step forward in our campaign for waste reduction. The new machines eliminated coolant and water usage and avoided water treatment and associated wastes, all while reducing energy consumption. It was a major step forward in quality, efficiency and productivity, and also in energy consumption and reduction of environmental degradation.

That was just the beginning of a continuing process of waste reduction. AAM worked with our commodity manager of chemicals to only supply greases and oils with minimal to no zinc, which led to one of our largest improvements in waste reduction. This eliminated the disposal of waste greases which resulted in significant savings on the disposal (about half the cost of the waste stream) and helped reduce AAM's status as a generator of large quantities of hazardous waste. Reduced zinc also helped the company maintain compliance with the waste water permit discharge, which has a low-zinc limit of 2,610 micrograms per liter. In addition, AAM eliminated all facilities and operations that were oil based in exchange for water based for the same reasons.

Another key to effective waste source reduction is good housekeeping. We install systems to prevent leakage and spillage through preventive maintenance schedules and routine equipment inspection. A computer program is used to track all work orders in order to fine-tune preventive maintenance schedules based on equipment needs. In addition, clearly written working instructions, supervision, awareness, and regular training of associates helped focus attention on good housekeeping. I would stress here that good housekeeping is not an option—it is an integral part of AAM's daily activities.

Some more specifics that we found helpful:

- We recycled steel shot peen that we used in plant #1 in Detroit. We literally had it vacuumed up. The reused steel shot eliminated the need to purchase new shots for several months at a time.
- We introduced bacteria into the waste treatment plant holding tank to help "eat" the sludge buildup and thin out the waste. We estimate a 10 percent reduction in sludge using this chemical free method.
- A tramp oil centrifuge was purchased and used in various plants. The centrifuge collected the bad oil to extend the life of the coolant system. This also extended the life of the machinery cutting tools because tramp oil wears them down faster.
- We set up a cardboard recycling system with a dedicated compactor to reduce the number of times a week the compactor boxes (general trash) were moved off-site to landfills, and to recycle the cardboard.
- We installed water meters at each plant in the Detroit manufacturing site for flow tracking and to monitor and schedule improvements on coolant system dumps and water leaks.
- We rerouted all central coolant systems where excess water/coolant was sent off to waste treatment, and instead recycled it back into the system.
- And we replaced all valves and controls in the central coolant systems to prevent valves being left open. This resulted in improved water/coolant usage and reduce wastewater treatment.

PRODUCING USEFUL BY-PRODUCT

A key aspect of our waste management process is finding opportunities to transform waste material into something else that can be reused or recycled for other applications, either within AAM or for other companies. For example,

AAM began the process of cooking float oil at the waste treatment facility, which increased the amount of recycled oil and reduced the amount of sludge sent to landfills. In addition, AAM was paid for good recycled oil removed from the facility for use by others. (Another item in this general vein—we donate machinery we no longer need for current production to technical schools for training, which serves the twin purposes of reducing scrap sent to landfills and helping train a new generation of manufacturing workers.)

Water is also increasingly recognized as a precious commodity, especially at our plant in Guanajuato, Mexico, which is an arid region. There we recycle wastewater for use in irrigation. At our factory in Supa, India, we collect all runoff rainwater from parking lots and send it to an underground collection tank for reused in irrigation. Even at our World Headquarters in Detroit, rainwater is collected from the upper level parking lot and reused for irrigation of our rather extensive green area surrounding the plants.

In 2001, AAM became ISO 14001 registered. Each year we conduct Environmental Management Programs to make continuous improvement and promote energy efficiency. In 2004, the Detroit facility received the Clean Corporate Citizen designation, and became a member of the Michigan Business Pollution Prevention Partnership (MBP3).

ENERGY CONSERVATION

The primary focus of our environmental program always comes back to energy, if only because we use so much of it. Nationwide manufacturing uses about one-third of the nation's energy because that is the nature of the beast— the transformation of raw materials into final products demands energy, and lots of it. Energy costs have always been a major cost factor for manufacturing, especially in the auto industry.

Consuming energy is not only costly, it increases the release of carbon monoxide into the atmosphere and further depletes the environment. We have all the reason we need and then some to reduce our energy consumption. From day one, AAM has seen energy management as a key component for reducing operating costs, boosting productivity, creating value and, not incidentally, increasing profits.

AAM has established different management practices to guarantee that the company will produce the most with the least amount of energy consumption and waste possible. To that end, we:

- Designated an energy director, a corporate energy team, and energy champions at each facility in the United States and around the world, to underscore the commitment of senior management to energy conservation.
- Published an Energy Policy and Energy Handbook providing guidelines for effective energy management.
- Created an Energy Management Program with the main objective of minimizing energy use, energy cost and CO_2 emissions. The program was introduced to all AAM facilities on April 25, 2007, through an energy champions meeting. Since then, all production and nonproduction facilities have used it to great effect, producing measurable results.

COMMUNICATION

Like safety and quality, energy conservation demands a constant stream of communication with everyone in the organization. The great majority of people even in this day and age are unaware of how their everyday actions and activities at home and at work affect energy consumption and impact the environment. Increasing awareness is vital to encourage support for energy conservation at home and at work. We have created an ongoing energy conservation program at all AAM facilities charged with these goals:

- Providing general energy information and education in attractive formats that invite people to participate.
- Providing associates with home energy savings ideas that they can employ both at home and at work. If we get them thinking in terms of saving their own personal money by reducing energy conservation at home, that consciousness comes with them to the workplace.
- Soliciting energy saving ideas from associates—just as we do in every other aspect of our operations.

I like to think that AAM's aggressive programs for energy conservation and management (reducing emissions) has earned us a reputation for being "environmentally friendly" and eco-conscious members of the community, and it all begins at AAM headquarters. To underscore our commitment, in 2008 we launched an aggressive effort to win the Energy Star label, awarded by the

EPA, for our World Headquarters building in Detroit. Some key elements of this program are:

- Reducing lighting output to actual demand.
- Automatic lighting controls—if no one is using the space, the lights click off.
- Optimized scheduling for heating, ventilating and air-conditioning.
- Cycling of the cooling tower and building pumps.
- Adjusting the hot-water temperature set point.

The AAM headquarters building had a baseline rating of 51 when it was first benchmarked against similar office buildings. The EPA requires a minimum rating of 75 to award the Energy Star Label, so when we first started out that goal seemed remote indeed, but we have never backed down from a challenge. By pursuing the goals itemized above, and making a few other improvements here and there, we reached that goal in 2009 and won the Energy Star label. And we never rest on our laurels; we always push for more. Less than a year later, our Headquarters Building earned an Energy Star rating of 80, putting us among the top 20 percent of best energy performers among office buildings nationwide.

RENEWABLE ENERGY

AAM was among the first to make serious investments in renewable energy. It is fair to ask, as some have, how we could justify that expense when the company was struggling and the payback for investing in renewable energy takes at least ten years. We made the investment in renewable energy for the same reason we kept investing in R&D during the hard times; because we believe in the future. There is no doubt in our minds that short-term investments in renewable energy today will pay rich dividends over the long term.

While we have been investing in renewable energy, others in our industry have focused on alternative fuels. To some extent, this shift has been driven by media reports that are often based more on wishful thinking than economic reality. Wind and solar power are perfectly viable energy sources, but the wind doesn't always blow and the sun doesn't always shine. Today, the combined contribution of wind and solar is about 2 percent of the electrical energy mix, and I frankly don't see that share increasing much in the next twenty to thirty years.

To us it makes more sense to do the easy stuff—beginning with an all-out war on wasted energy. This can be a tough option because you are asking people to change longtime habits. It takes constant communication, repetition and committed management. Yet if you think about it, energy conservation is perfectly clean, remarkably cheap, surprisingly abundant, and immediately available. And it does not depend on the weather. When we determined to become an eco-conscious company, and we embarked on energy conservation, we found a huge amount of low-hanging fruit at AAM, as most companies do when they take on this challenge. At our headquarters we turned over every stone and approached every opportunity that leads to energy savings with little to zero additional cost. More often than not, we actually reduced costs.

I cannot emphasize enough how important energy conservation can be to any company in manufacturing, almost all of which use large amounts of energy. A fraction of a percent shaved from energy costs can run to hundreds of thousands of dollars over a short period of time. Energy management is a responsible and effective use of human intelligence to maximize profits, minimize costs, and strengthen competitiveness. Between 2007 and 2010, AAM reduced its energy consumption by more than 11 percent, and we are still identifying new ways to cut our energy bills. On a monthly basis, our corporate energy team tracks energy performance to:

- Determine the effectiveness of any energy-saving changes that have been made.
- Guard against the reintroduction of waste that has been previously eliminated.
- Check whether or not targets are being met.

As we do in our pursuit of higher quality and other key measures of effectiveness, we employ metrics to keep tabs on our energy conservation efforts, and progress is reported to all AAM executives and associates on a regular basis. The scorecard measures electrical, natural gas, and steam performance for each AAM location. Forecasted usage, based on the previous year, along with production, sales and weather (for some locations) are factored in to assess the overall performance.

It is especially useful to know where energy is being used in the plant so that one can target the largest potential energy savings. We employ continuous energy audits and facility walk-throughs to identify current equipment that wastes energy. Some of our techniques for reducing energy for lighting:

- Reducing load reductions by performing tours of the plants, observing work in progress, and inspecting an area's lighting during production and shutdown periods. For vacant areas we reduce the lighting to a tolerable minimum, turning off lights in areas where equipment is infrequently used.

- We employ lighting upgrades from Metal Halide to high-bay fluorescent. Our Technical Center is a 24/7 facility and lights must necessarily be on at all times in certain areas. The existing Metal Halide fixtures were replaced with high-bay T5, reducing electrical consumption by more than 35 percent and payback in less than one year. We have instituted a program to replace all Metal Halide lights where possible with fluorescent high-bay fixtures in order to reduce energy consumption.

HVAC SYSTEMS

Heating, ventilation and air-conditioning (HVAC) systems are another major energy concern. Building openings can be a significant source of wasted energy. Wind may force cold air into the building where it must be heated, or the building may be positively or negatively pressured based on outside air stillness. Every year beginning in September, all AAM facilities are required to implement a winterization plan that must be completed by October 15. During that period, the plant associates look for openings around truck doors, pipes, or special openings, and are sealed by installing metal flashing, caulking and/or insulation.

With the philosophy that we must start at home to be effective, the World Headquarters building temperature was raised by 2 degrees in the summer months and lowered 2 degrees in the winter months, and the operating schedule was reduced by one hour a day—a half hour in the morning and another half-hour in the evening. The utility bills were reduced by $90,000 per year.

COMPRESSED AIR SYSTEMS

In most plants in our industry, compressed air is critical. As processing equipment is added, the first step is to add more compressed air capacity, thus more capital spending and higher operating costs—or so it seemed. First you need to ask some basic questions. Is new equipment really necessary? Is the existing system really operating at full capacity? Is the existing system optimized?

We answered those questions. When more spending is required, a capital project must be submitted to senior management for approval. All projects related to energy consumption are required to be approved by the Corporate Energy Director. Before purchase of new compressors is approved, the system must be fully analyzed to ensure that all waste (leak and excess pressure) is eliminated. We do this by analyzing pressure profiles, checking for leaks and closing all valves to idle equipment. At our Three Rivers facility, more than fifty pieces of equipment were added, the compressed air system was optimized, and no new compressors were required. We applied the same measures at our plant in Guanajuato, Mexico. More equipment was added and the compressed air was reduced through an aggressive program to reduce pressure, eliminate blow-off by using a low-pressure blower and repairing leaks.

Matching compressed air supply to demand is always analyzed and monitored at all AAM facilities. Power monitoring is installed to track energy consumption and equipment loading and unloading time. Prior to idling most of the Detroit complex facilities after the 2008 strike, compressors were sized to supply more than two million square feet of production area. Due to plant idling, the compressors became oversized, and thus were operating inefficiently at their lowest operating range. We were essentially compressing air and blowing it off into the atmosphere. There is not much percentage in that. We knew something had to be done. We evaluated the cost of shutting down the compressors and installed smaller compressors to match the demand. New rental compressors were installed in October 2009, and they have been running at 90 percent efficiency, generating more than $30,000 a month in energy savings.

STEAM SYSTEMS

AAM uses steam for process and heating at both our Detroit and Three Rivers facilities. The steam at Detroit was purchased from the GM Poletown facility, and the steam at Three Rivers is internally generated. Since 2009, the steam at the Detroit facility was used only for heating and steam consumption was reduced to less than 225,000 MMBTU. In 2010 it was reduced to less than 175,000 MMBTU through regularly monitored energy saving practices such as:

- Steam pressure reduction.
- Elimination of unused portions of steam pipes that are no longer needed for production, eliminating losses.
- Reducing the temperature in the idled plant.
- Conducting steam leak and steam trap surveys regularly, with repair progress updates.

During the summer months, AAM uses about 5,000 MMBTU per month of natural gas to run the boiler in order to generate steam for five washers. Most of the steam generated is wasted in losses through the piping system. We analyzed the conversion of the washers from steam to natural gas, to reduce consumption by half, and expect payback within two years.

In sum, the excess use of energy results in significant air and water pollution, as well as greenhouse gas emissions that contribute to global climate change. We work continuously to improve our energy efficiency programs, and pursue them at all of our facilities around the world. It is in the best interest of all energy consuming facilities to implement these measures. Even for companies committed to alternative fuels, energy conservation still makes sense (and cents). Now more than ever, we must all understand that reducing energy consumption has enormous potential to save money and improve the environment. Wasting energy is equivalent to burning money. At AAM, we are into earning money, not burning it.

17

Trouble Right Here in Motor City

Can anybody remember when the times were not hard and money not scarce?

—*Ralph Waldo Emerson*

A company can make a lot of money in the auto industry provided it can generate sufficient volume to recoup up-front investments in plants, product development, and capital equipment and absorb the prohibitive premium labor costs that characterize the domestic auto industry. Whenever the major auto companies attempt to predict income streams, they can figure out almost to the exact number of vehicles they need to make and sell in order to recover the up-front investment in design, testing, tooling, parts manufacture, assembly, etc. After that, every additional vehicle that rolls off the line is gilded with gold—almost pure profit. Of course, you want to do everything in your power to minimize production costs and increase profits, but the ideal is to get to that all-important break-even point as fast as you can so you can start generating profits for the stockholders.

This basic law of the auto industry—actually it applies to most every highly capitalized manufacturing industry—also applies to suppliers like AAM. We are making key components and systems of vehicles and thus are an extension of the big automakers. Our break-even points are not necessarily the same as those of our customers—we are independent operations after all—but their profitability and ours are tied together. Large volumes spell big profits for all of us; declining volumes spell big trouble for all of us.

In the auto industry, we look at the seasonally adjusted annual rate (SAAR) as the key measure of how cars and trucks are selling. Throughout most of the first decade of this century, sales were strong. The SAAR hit 17.1 million in 2001, and hovered between 16.7 million and 16.9 million through 2005. We can live with that. But in 2006, the SAAR dipped to 16.5 million, which translated into major layoffs by the Big Three and bankruptcies among the ranks of suppliers. AAM's major competitor Dana went into bankruptcy, which really got our attention. Ten years before, Dana was the Big Three's premier supplier of axles and drivetrain products. Dana was joined in Chapter 11 by a murderer's row of suppliers, including Delphi, Visteon, Lear, and Collins & Aikman. These were big companies that had enjoyed sterling reputations. Their bankruptcies portended a long painful shakeout among automotive suppliers, and those suppliers whose main customers were GM, Chrysler, or Ford were most vulnerable. We still depended on GM for the lion's share of our sales.

It has been my observation that troubles usually come in bunches. The impact of this dip in vehicle sales was greatly magnified by the rising labor costs in the auto industry, driven by the insatiable UAW, that had gradually become unsustainable. When the market was strong and vehicles were flying out the door, the burden of excessive labor costs was manageable. But when the market began to erode, it became clear how close to the edge we were operating. The burden of those exorbitant costs had become untenable.

The Big Three reacted to declining sales in the usual way, by laying off employees. GM had, in fact, begun offering to buy out its employees in late March 2006, but it found few takers. GM employees were making big bucks and wanted to keep on making big bucks. GM had hoped to reduce its staff by 30,000 hourly jobs during 2007, but it was slow going.

It was clear to all that big changes were afoot in the auto industry, and the UAW was finally being challenged to pare back its demands. Autoworkers at GM agreed to shoulder more health care costs, saving GM $1 billion a year, but the company still faced shrinking sales and growing pension liabilities. We all assumed we were in the midst of yet another cyclical dip in vehicle sales that would soon turn back upward, yielding to rising sales, as it always had in the past. AAM was preparing for higher volumes linked to GM's full-size trucks and we had invested more than $400 million to support new products associated with GM's new brands. So we were watching GM's financial struggle with intense interest.

We also recognized a need, not just for layoffs, but to reduce our overall staffing level. Our labor costs in the United States had become a major stumbling block for the company. In January 2007, we announced that 1,437 AAM associates had agreed to participate in our special attrition program. "The special attrition program accelerates our ability to realign our hourly workforce with actual and projected production and market conditions," I stated in an AAM press release. "The structural cost benefit to AAM resulting from the special attrition program and other related restructuring actions should exceed $100 million annually. This will enhance our ability to invest in the continuing expansion of AAM's product portfolio, served markets, customer base and global manufacturing footprint."

Brave words, but bravery does not count for much in financial markets. Because of AAM's dependence on GM, the attrition program, and the bankruptcy of many of our competitors, we were under a cloud on Wall Street. Fitch Ratings cut AAM to junk bond status, to BB from BBB-minus, citing our heavy dependence on GM as the reason. That was the lowest investment grade rating. "General Motors' sales are down," said Hilbert College professor Patrick Heraty, January 10, in *Buffalo Business First*. "American Axle is a major supplier to GM and as GM goes, so goes American Axle."

Since day one of AAM, I had campaigned to reduce our reliance on GM, and we had landed many contracts with other companies, but it seemed like every time we added a new customer, GM provided us another contract and our dependence on them remained huge.

On the other hand, we entered the downturn in a strong financial position, at least compared to other major suppliers. We were weathering the storm far better than most, and certainly better than Dana. There was even some speculation, according to *Crain's Detroit Business*, that AAM might buy part of Dana. Standard & Poor's said AAM remained an investment-grade company, at least for the time being.

It was clear to me by early 2007 that there was something going on in the auto industry beyond just another recession. There was no question that foreign competition played a role, but I refused to accept that as an explanation. "Far too many people have characterized globalization as the root of all of our problems," I told Robert Sherefkin of *Automotive News*. "But I do not buy that argument. Whether you like it or not, globalization is here to stay. Manufacturing is how we pay our way in the world. We must create value. We cannot sustain a prosperous economy and the defense of our nation without a viable, vigorous and globally manufacturing sector." I added that it was an era of unprecedented transformation in the U.S. auto industry. "Our business culture has to become increasingly flexible. If we think the restructuring will be over in a year or two, we are kidding ourselves. Real transformation takes time."

As always, we kept working toward a turnaround we believed would come eventually. Even though we lost money in 2006, our first annual loss, we had made progress on our long-term strategic goals by expanding our product portfolio and new business backlog to support the growing all-wheel-drive passenger car and crossover market. We had also launched new products for GM, Chrysler group, Ssangyong Motor, Hino, Jatco, Koyo, and Harley-Davidson, while expanding our served markets and global manufacturing footprint into mainland Europe and Asia.

In fact, I told a reporter that even though the production of light trucks would probably fall in 2007, we expected our sales to increase by $100 million to about $3.3 billion. Even so, I acknowledged it would be a challenging year. "We're in a shakeout right now, make no mistake about it," I said. "You must have the mindset to do twice as much, twice as fast—and if you don't, leave."

By this time, in early 2007, we were seriously embarked upon a process I called Restructure, Resize, and Recover that seemed to be paying off. In April, we reported that we had returned to profitability in the first quarter of 2007. Net income climbed 79 percent to $15.4 million despite a 4 percent decline in sales. That was up from $8.6 million in the same period the year before. We were beginning to make some inroads with Toyota and Honda, which had always relied upon their keiretsu network of Japanese suppliers in the past. They were concerned about political backlash if they did not produce enough product in this country, and were also discovering that some U.S. suppliers, most notably AAM, were making highly engineered quality products for competitive prices.

We won a most promising contract to provide rear-drive modules for a crossover made by Chery Automobile Company, one of the leading vehicle producers in China. The market shift toward all-wheel drive passenger cars and crossover vehicles was playing to AAM's strength in developing advanced engineered, leading edge technology driveline products and systems for the global marketplace. We were building the Chery units in our plant in Changshu, China.

In times like those, one looks for rays of sunshine wherever they can be found. We took some satisfaction in our growing business overseas. And then auto industry writer Mike Weinberg, writing for an industry publication called *Transmission Digest*, came to visit us and filed a report that included this:

> . . . *AAM is a world leader in driveline-systems fabrication and design. AAM employs about 10,000 people in facilities around the world and has yearly sales of about $3.25 billion. It is one of the few Tier One suppliers that are fiscally healthy and not in bankruptcy. AAM's product portfolio includes*

power-transfer units, independent rear-drive axles, torque-transfer devices, transfer cases, TracRite^{TM} electronic locking and limited-slip differentials, multi-piece high-speed passenger-car driveshafts, and complete front and rear chassis/suspension components. What better place could I go to research new ring-and-pinion design?

I have been in auto manufacturing plants around the globe for the past 45 years. The AAM plants are state-of-the-art and very efficient. AAM does everything in house: forging, heat treating, manufacturing, quality control, and research and development. Its return rate on finished goods and warranty is extremely low because of an extreme level of testing and quality control through every step of the manufacturing process.

I spent an entire day with the engineering and manufacturing staff learning about the principles involved in the two-cut process. As you know, high-speed metal cutting usually requires extensive lubrication of the parts during the process. This lubricant is expensive, both in the pumping and recovery process, and in environmental compliance. AAM has developed the two-cut process using full carbide tooling that runs in a dry environment, eliminating the need for lubricant in that part of the process. It was interesting to watch how quickly these machines cut a ring and pinion from a forged blank, throwing dry chips that are conveyed away to be recycled. Every product coming off the line is tested using high-tech, computer-controlled coordinate-measuring machines to assure integrity to all print specifications. . . .

This is not rocket science. All the processes are here for you to increase sales and profits. What is necessary is to start with a quality gear set and to understand the reliably simple setup technique. There is a segment of our industry that is motivated only by price in the parts they buy. They cannot or do not sell their customers on quality and put pressure on the suppliers to provide cheap will-fit product whose durability and proper, quiet operation are a maybe. The best doesn't cost much more and comes with a list of benefits that more than justifies the small differential in price: absolute quality control that is good enough for the vehicle manufacturer to warrant it for 100,000 miles; product that is made to the original design levels and adjusted to improvements in design; technical support; and finished product liability.

Yup. That's AAM, all right.

WardsAuto World also tipped the hat to us: "AAM stands out as a financial stalwart with a long list of major North American suppliers that are either bankrupt or out of business as their major customers—Detroit's Big Three—wallow in red ink and continue to lose market share. Its backlog of new business through 2010 stands at $1.1 billion."

But declining demand for midsized pickup trucks and SUVs put pressure on us to reduce our workforce beyond what we had done so far, and most of the reductions fell on our plant in Buffalo where we made rear axles and gears for the Chevrolet Colorado, the GMC Canyon, the Chevrolet Trailblazer, and GMC Envoy. Sales for all four models had been dropping all year long, especially for the Envoy. GM sold 26,912 units of the midsize SUV through July, 40 percent fewer than in the same period the year before. Consumers were moving away from pickups and SUVs in favor of more fuel efficient cars and crossovers. That may still seem like a lot of vehicles being sold, but as I said before, the loss of volume in this business will kill you. GM had cancelled its GMT 360 and 370 platforms that we made at the Buffalo plant and we had decided not to bring new work there, primarily because of the uncompetitive labor compensation structure.

Our associates in Buffalo were making between $50 and $60 per hour, fully loaded. The market had reached a point that no auto supplier like AAM could afford to pay that level of compensation. We had quality associates at Buffalo, but they were hardwired to the UAW and would not give much on either wages, benefits or work rules. UAW leadership said the union was working to keep the Buffalo plant open, but would not offer concessions. We had had enough of that attitude. Given the continuing obstinacy of the UAW about compensation and work rules, we announced in June 2007 that we would close the Buffalo plant by the end of the year. We began offering buyout and early retirement packages for our 653 associates who still worked there.

We did not do this without intense reflection and discussion. Our Buffalo plant was that city's largest source of factory jobs. Built in the 1920s, it had employed as many as 3,700 people in its heyday. During the early years of AAM, the Buffalo plant was a solid performer for us. But the changing dynamics of the industry were catching up with us—all of us. We kept the plant technically open until the end of the year with a skeleton crew, but production was basically shut down in July.

We have always bent over backward to be fair to our associates in these situations, and Buffalo was a good example. They had a choice of a monthly incentive if they were within four years of retirement, a $50,000 incentive if eligible to retire, a $70,000 buyout if they had less than ten years of service with the company, and a $100,000 buyout if they had ten or more years seniority. We also included an early retirement option for associates with ten or more years of service who were at least fifty years old but less than sixty-five. We anticipated costs up to $85 million for this closure, which would leave us with eight plants in the United States.

There is no evidence that the leadership of the UAW, or the rank and file for that matter, learned anything at all from this experience. In September, 73,000 UAW members at about eighty GM facilities around the country walked off the job. *GM pointed out that its labor costs were about $25 an hour more than its Japanese competitors.* The UAW was unmoved, demanding, among other things, more job security. It was becoming increasingly clear to me by that time, and many other people as well, that the very notion of job security was a pipe dream with no traction in the real world. That strike lasted only a couple of days. But I knew our UAW contract was coming up for renegotiation after the first of the year, and I did not anticipate we would resolve our differences with the union quite so easily.

On the surface, we seemed to be doing pretty well. The reductions in personnel, though they cost a lot initially, quickly showed a benefit on our bottom line. Our income in the second quarter rose to $34 million, up from $20.4 million in the same period the year before. In the second quarter, we reported net income of $13.1 million, quite a bit better than the $62.9 million we lost in that period the year before.

As 2007 drew to a close, we were back in the black, but we were losing money on our U.S. operations. All of our profit margin came from overseas. That underscored the wisdom of our decision years before to go global, but we were still heavily invested in the United States. We were already in preliminary discussions with the UAW about our contract that was up for renegotiation early in 2008. The Big Three had won some significant concessions from the UAW, and we were optimistic we would gain some also. As *Automotive News* reported: ". . . the union fears plant closings and is not in a concessionary mood. The stakes are huge for American Axle—and its customers. A long labor battle could jeopardize production for the company's main customers: General Motors and Chrysler LLC. GM accounts for 76 percent of American Axle's revenues, and Chrysler accounts for about 10 percent."

Our associates were earning $73.48 per hour fully loaded, much more than employees of other suppliers. Most of our competitors had gone through bankruptcy that enabled them to toss their UAW contracts. Dana, for example, expected to shed $100 million in labor costs through bankruptcy protection. Bankruptcy is hard on a company's stockholders, but it does convey certain benefits.

On December 5, our stock fell 4.8 percent, following a decline of 10.7 percent the day before, down below $20 per share for the first time in a long while, as the major domestic auto makers announced continuing declines in sales of vehicles. There was an air of gloom over Detroit as the city's core industry continued to drop.

We were telling the UAW we needed to reduce our total hourly compensation from $73.48 an hour to $27 an hour. We also needed flexibility on job classifications and work rules. And we said also we wanted to end the absurd jobs bank in which laid-off workers sit around on their duffs drawing 95 percent of their pay. At the time that program was providing pay and benefits to about 1,100 laid off AAM workers. We estimated it cost us between $100,000 and $130,000 a year for wages and benefits on each associate in the jobs bank. Overall, U.S. auto companies would spend up to $2 billion in 2006 on jobs bank employees, many of whom have been reporting to the job to read, watch movies and do crossword puzzles for years.

AAM's contract with the UAW would expire February 25, 2008. We had negotiated lower UAW wages in a two-tier package for new production hires in 2004 ($27 an hour in wages and benefits, compared to $73.48 for existing employees). But few new hires were needed, and thus the provision did not help AAM reduce the labor cost gap. *The battle lines were drawn.* At stake was the future market competitiveness of AAM's U.S. operations, which were struggling with overcapacity and lack of profitability, and the UAW's determination to continue winning exorbitant wages and benefits for its declining roster of members.

The most vulnerable of all was AAM's Detroit Gear and Axle Plant—the grande dame of AAM.

18

The Strike

Unions would be a lot better off if their membership was voluntary.

—President Ronald Reagan

On three occasions during the first fourteen years of AAM's history, when we sat down to negotiate a new contract with the UAW leadership, I explained to them the reality of the marketplace—that our ability to operate and make a profit was constrained by market forces—and that we could not, as an automotive supplier, forever continue to provide our associates the same wages and benefits as the major auto companies. On each occasion, the UAW leaders said they understood that fact of life, and that we would deal with that reality in a future contract negotiation.

Not today, of course. Always tomorrow, never today.

The basic flaw in this approach was that every time we sat down to negotiate with the UAW leadership, we found ourselves looking into different faces. The people across the table from us had no recollection of those earlier conversations, or at least claimed not to. They, in fact, *had* been working for the UAW back then, and may even have been in the room and heard what we had to say, but it was not their conversation. That was then, this is now.

As I have stated elsewhere, I knew a showdown was coming with the UAW, but never before had we been in a position to stand tough. Previously, we had been totally dependent on our U.S. plants and our main customer, GM. But slowly over the years we had diversified our installed productive capacity. As I stated earlier, it's a dumb rat that has only one hole. By 2008, we had more than one hole. More specifically, we had a gem of a plant in Guanajuato, Mexico, that could almost by itself supply the needs of our North American customers. The UAW was no longer in a position to dictate to us.

The UAW apparently did not realize that. I would have thought it would be job one of the new UAW leadership, led by recently elected president Ron Gettelfinger, to know what our situation was, and what we were and were not capable of. He and his team should have surely known that the U.S. auto industry at that time was on its heels, struggling to survive, and that inflated wage and benefit packages was a major reason for that.

I had known Gettelfinger for many years, both professionally and personally. We had worked together cooperatively in various charities in the Detroit area. Both AAM and the UAW have always been civic-minded in that regard, and there were many opportunities for the company and the union to work together in worthwhile charitable endeavors, raising money for worthy projects. I have in my office a photo of Gettelfinger and me together at one of those charity functions. It wasn't as if Gettelfinger did not have access to me, or that he had no way of knowing what the situation at AAM was.

We held kickoff negotiations with the UAW beginning December 12, 2007, and continuing into early 2008. Our negotiating team was led by me, AAM president and chief operating officer David C. Dauch, AAM's vice president for Labor Relations John E. Jerge, and our vice president for Finance and chief financial officer Mike Simonte.

We knew it would be a tough session, but we assumed the UAW was aware of the situation and would attempt to meet us at least halfway. It was public knowledge that our major competitors had gone into bankruptcy and emerged with much more favorable compensation scales, giving them a tremendous advantage over AAM. Compensation is factored into every bid for a contract with a major auto maker. If we expected to ever win any *new* or *replacement* business, we had to get our compensation structure in line with our major competitors. It was clear, at least to us, that the UAW would have to make some major, painful concessions.

At that time, we computed our aggregate fully loaded cost for the average AAM associate was $73.48 per hour worked—meaning all wages and benefits combined all-in cost—which was about three times what our domestic competitors were paying to workers who were members of the UAW. That $73.48 figure included base pay, shift premiums, overtime premiums, cost of living allowance, vacation pay, holiday pay, bereavement pay, jury duty pay, performance bonus, FICA tax, joint funds (the things the union and company pay for together like the company picnic), health care costs (the actual amount paid for all health care—not just insurance), group life insurance, federal unemployment insurance, state unemployment insurance, workers compensation costs, sickness and disability costs, extended disability costs, legal services costs, pension costs, and retiree health costs.* From AAM's point of view, a market-competitive labor cost structure in the U.S. automotive supply industry was in the range of $20–$30 per hour. We informed the UAW negotiators that the existing compensation level had to give. We offered various proposals to begin chopping that down to a manageable size. For example, we wanted to shut down the insane jobs bank (paying people not to work) and shift from a defined pension to a 401(k) retirement system for all salaried and hourly staff as the great majority of employers in this country had already done. Most importantly, we had to get the wage scale down to a competitive level. There were no two ways about that. We had evaded that decision for far too long. The day of reckoning was at hand.

To our astonishment, the UAW put on the table a proposal that would have preserved essentially all of their members' benefits as they were, and also hiked the wages in the out years. This was presented to AAM by the UAW vice president for Suppliers, Jimmy Settles. Gettelfinger and his administrative assistant Rich Atwood were also there. "They handed over their book of UAW demands," said Simonte. "A literal interpretation of what was there would have taken us to $106 per hour fully loaded, and cost us more than a billion dollars! To me, it was an irrelevant document, not at all in line with conversations taking place on both sides of the table. It shows how out of touch their approach was with reality. There was no way we were going to increase costs." The UAW had defiantly drawn the long knives of economic warfare.

On February 1, we issued our regular quarterly financial report. We had cut our loss in the fourth quarter of 2007 to $25.5 million, compared with a $188.6 million loss in the same period the year before, when we had taken charges for previous worker buyouts and capacity cuts. All told, we had reduced about 2,500 salaried and hourly associate positions in 2007. For the full year, we had sales of $3.25 billion, and net earnings of $37 million. About 22

---

* To verify the market rate for labor in our industry, AAM hired an independent company to compile the all-in wage and benefit costs, along with work rules for specific manufacturing locations in the U.S. This research included data on union and nonunion locations, some in right-to-work states, that manufacture product lines like AAM's—our competition in the U.S. This study was an essential part of AAM's discussion with the UAW.

percent of our sales were non-GM. So we had made a little money in 2007, but that was all from our foreign operations. In the United States, we lost money, and that was the issue we had with the UAW. Most of our associates and work contracts were still in the United States. We had to get back onto a profit curve at our plants in the United States, or shut them down.

The clock was ticking and there really was not much negotiation taking place. We showed up every day but on many days we simply had no one to talk to. The UAW negotiators declined to deal with us in an earnest manner. I surmised the union was expecting GM to weigh in as it always had in the past, pressuring us to settle, and offering to pay higher prices for AAM products to cushion the blow. The UAW leaders were woefully out of touch with reality. Anyone with access to a newspaper knew that the auto industry was in a free fall, U.S. automakers were struggling, and GM in particular was hanging on by a thread. We were getting no pressure from GM to settle.

It soon became clear to us there would be no early settlement. At one minute past midnight on February 26, 2008, the union members at five UAW locals walked off the job at six AAM locations in Michigan and New York. All told, about 3,650 associates were involved, but most of them—about 2,000—were idled at our flagship axle plant and forge on Holbrook Avenue in Detroit. They immediately erected a picket line in the freezing Detroit winds and snow. Thousands of UAW members were on hand, waving their fists and chanting slogans. "We'll be out here as long as it takes," one associate told a TV reporter.

I was frankly impressed by the turnout. It was impossible to get an accurate count, but it seemed to us that virtually all of the Detroit associates were present and accounted for, at least on the first day of the strike. That would be in stark contrast to a normal work day when, on average, more than 20 percent of the associates would be absent. Our salaried associates continued to come to work, of course, and every day they had to cross the picket line. This experience can be more than a little intimidating—especially when the strikers are members of the UAW. They hurl insults and sometimes more substantive things at autos entering the company parking lot. They employ language that could peel the paint from your fenders and do not defer to women. Many of our female salaried staff had never been exposed to that level of invective, including terms I will not repeat in this book. Even the male salaried staff, at least those who had never been through it before, were taken aback. They felt threatened—they were in fact being threatened—and they endured high anxiety. The police were out in force to prevent violence, but the threat of violence was ever present. To us, this appeared to be part of the UAW game plan—not merely cutting off a company's ability to produce products and pay its bills, but also threats, intimidation and confrontation.

I was to spend a great deal of time in the coming months walking the floors of headquarters, talking to our professional staff, inviting them to share their anxieties and concerns and reassuring them that we were in control of the situation. I spent a good bit of extra time with the female staff because I knew many of them were shocked by the treatment they were receiving every time they came and went from work. Each and every incident of threats and intimidation steeled me in my resolve to stand solid and lead the company through the crisis.

I respect the right of unions to exist and to undertake work actions in defense of what they perceive to be their interests, but to scream vile epithets at women who are merely going to their jobs is, in my mind, cowardly and beneath contempt. I have no respect for people who behave that way toward women—none.

So the great confrontation began and, as always, much of it was fought out in the news media. *The Detroit News* summed up the situation: "At stake is the future competitiveness of American Axle's U.S. operations which have been struggling with over capacity and profitability, and the UAW's ability to secure a solid standard of living for its members during a time of turmoil in the U.S. auto industry."

"The UAW has a proven record of working with companies to improve their competitive position and secure jobs," Gettelfinger told a reporter from the Associated Press, which was news to me. "But cooperation does not mean capitulation. Our members cannot be expected to make the extreme sacrifices American Axle is asking for with nothing in return."

To which I responded with some heat: "All of the changes we have proposed have been accepted by the UAW in agreements with our competitors in the United States. I have no idea why AAM is being singled out for a different set of economic conditions."

I told another reporter that the strike was a result of the UAW's consistent, adversarial and confrontational stance. "They have employed brute force and intimidation for more than 50 years. It is long past time for the UAW to become more pragmatic on competitiveness issues." Not surprisingly, Gettelfinger did not see it that way.

Himanshu Patel, an industry analyst with JP Morgan Securities, Inc., said the UAW's previous agreements made it hard for the union to argue that AAM should have higher wages and benefits. "The UAW's decision to classify all of the hourly workers at Ford's and Chrysler's in-house axle plants as 'noncore' is

AAM'S HISTORICAL UAW FULLY-LOADED LABOR COST (FLLC) (ORIGINAL PLANTS AND CHEEKTOWAGA)

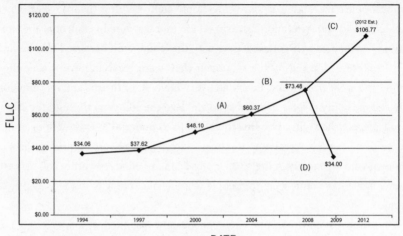

DATE

A = **$60.37** - AAM's average FLLC after the UAW's first strike against AAM (1.5 days)
B = **$73.48** - AAM's average FLLC prior to the UAW's second strike against AAM (87 days)
C = **$106.77** - AAM's estimated average FLLC based on the proposal the UAW presented to AAM on December 12, 2007.
Conservative estimate of the additional cost to AAM of this proposal was $500M per year or $2B over a four-year agreement.
D= **$34.00** - AAM's realized average FLLC after the UAW's 87-day strike was over and the new agreement was ratified. This estimate is
based on the impact of the ratified agreement including the buyouts, buy-downs, early retirement programs, the hiring of new
associates, several plant closures and the relocation of work to more competitive economic locations both in and outside the U.S.

a major precedent indicating that the UAW leadership philosophically agrees that the manufacturing of axles is not a $60-$70 per hour job."

Philosophically perhaps, but not on the operational level. The stance of the UAW was and remains a mystery to us, and to many other people. Of course, when the strike began, none of us knew how it would turn out. Each side expected the other to blink. After all, in the past we had always come to terms with the UAW rather quickly.

Not this time. GM's CEO Rick Wagoner told a reporter GM was not in any way panicked by the AAM strike. "Frankly, our inventories are fairly high," he said, and added that he hoped to see a resolution of the strike soon—which, of course, is an obligatory statement, like wishing for better weather. When the strike began, GM had more than a 150-day supply of pickup trucks sitting on its lots and 100-day supply of SUVs.

"Reality has intruded," I told Tom Walsh of the *Detroit Free Press*, a few days into the strike, citing globalization and the dramatic impact of rising energy costs on truck and SUV sales among key factors that have dramatically altered the industry's competitive math in the previous five years. "We need structural and permanent change in our cost structure. We must eliminate the Detroit entitlement mentality."

I understood clearly that AAM was asking for major sacrifices by its long-term associates. What I did *not* understand was the union's apparent unwillingness to bargain a concessionary deal similar to others already blessed by the UAW for GM, Ford, Chrysler, Dana, Delphi, Visteon, and others. "They have fashioned something to be very supportive to those firms," I told Walsh. "Why are we being focused on, or profiled, not to have a similar pattern to the peer groups we compete with?"

I should note that not all AAM members of the UAW supported the leadership's tough stand. Erv Heidbrink, president of UAW Local 2093 at the AAM plant in Three Rivers, was determined to keep AAM jobs there. The UAW members at Three Rivers were on strike with the rest of the union, but they hedged their bets. They unanimously instructed their local leadership to work to keep the plant open even if that meant sacrifice. As reported by *The Detroit News:* "Even if they cut our pay $10 per hour, even if we don't work here, we need to keep this plant open for this community," said Linda Case, a striker and Three Rivers resident.

There was no shortage of analysts who understood our situation. "Less than a year ago, the UAW found enough common ground with GM, Ford and Chrysler to agree on new labor contracts," wrote Robert Brooks in *Foundry Management & Technology* magazine. "Now those same contracts, and others, have lowered the overall labor costs, making American Axle uncompetitive. Furthermore, American Axle is demonstrating that it can manufacture its products overseas successfully, raising the possibility that high-cost domestic operations may not be essential to its purpose."

"What was once the model (GM) spinoff is now the highest cost supplier in North America," chimed in Sean McAlinden, chief economist at the Center for Automotive Research in Ann Arbor, in *The Grand Rapids Press*. "It's sad to see. It's not a good signal for Michigan once again."

That month the automakers reported sales declines across the board—GM 13 percent, Ford 7 percent, and Chrysler 14 percent. On March 10, *The Wall Street Journal* reported that the strike against AAM had forced GM to either shut down, partially idle, or move to shorter shifts at twenty-nine plants. Wagoner conceded that the strike would have an impact on GM's first quarter earnings, but added, "It is not a huge issue for us."

My friend Dr. David Cole, chairman of the Center for Automotive Research, told a *Buffalo News* reporter in March that Dana's bankruptcy left it with a vastly lower cost structure that put AAM at a disadvantage, but that I was not the sort to just roll over. "You know where [Dick] stands. He's direct. He's not going to shy away from this kind of issue. He's not going to put it off for another year. He's not that way."

No, I'm not. I told Tom Walsh from the *Detroit Free Press* that if the UAW did not get reasonable, we could move our manufacturing out of the United States altogether. "We have the flexibility to source all of our business to other locations around the world, and we have the right to do so," I said. "If we cannot compete for new contracts, there will be no work in the original plants."

"We need structural and permanent change in our cost structure," I told Jewel Gopwani from the *Detroit Free Press*. "We must eliminate the Detroit entitlement mentality." That was what I was determined to do.

Nothing much happened in March. We showed up to negotiate, but the UAW was mostly absent. "There was almost zero negotiations in the first sixty days of the strike," said Jerge. "They had one body in the building every day just to say they were there. We were there every day with top people from the organization ready to negotiate."

Meanwhile, the picketers shivered in the cold and cursed the salaried staff coming and going. On April 1, GM vice chairman Bob Lutz told a reporter the AAM strike was not hurting GM because of its bloated inventory of full-size pickup trucks and SUVs, for which we supplied the axles. "If the market is red hot for pickups and SUVs, and with every day of the strike you are missing production volumes, then it becomes painful," he said. "But when you have lots of retail inventory for the dealers to sell down, then it puts you in a strategically better position to withstand a strike."

Another newspaper reported on that same day that GM's Fort Wayne assembly plant, closed since February 29 because of the strike, was starting to build trucks again. The report said GM declined to discuss where it was getting the axles. The fact was AAM's salaried staff were manning the plants producing axles, driveshafts, and forgings as fast as they could, and our plant in Guanajuato, Mexico, was working overtime producing all the axles and other parts GM requires to make pickups and SUVs. *It is a little known fact, but during the strike AAM never missed a significant delivery to GM.*

For its part, the UAW put the squeeze on GM to make us yield, calling strikes at plants in Michigan, Ohio, and Texas, with a focus on the plants making GM's highly popular Malibu. The Malibu was one of GM's few viable products at the time, and it was one place where the company was vulnerable. The

Detroit Free Press quoted a GM electrician at its Arlington, Texas, facility named Jim Robinson, who said the strike there was to demonstrate support for the UAW in the AAM strike. The battle lines were drawn and every participant was using every means at their disposal.

The standoff took a toll on my reputation as a friend of labor. "Dick Dauch's labor journey: Hero to demon," headlined an article in April's *Automotive News*. "Dauch, 65, has put aside his reflexive empathy for labor to demand wage and benefit concessions he believes are critical for the future of the company, says longtime friend Dave Cole. . . . Dauch's hard-line negotiating stance has destroyed his longtime reputation as a friend of the worker."

I would argue that I was fighting to keep jobs for workers in the United States, and it was the UAW that was driving them out of the country.

There is an old saying that when elephants fight, lots of smaller animals get trampled. One of the unintended victims of the UAW-AAM confrontation was the city of Hamtramck. Our Detroit plant was partially in Hamtramck, and we were one of that city's primary sources of tax revenue. City officials reported they were losing $8,000 to $9,000 per day because of the strike. It put the city in a tough bind, but there wasn't anything we could do about it.

We were, in fact, receiving hundreds of applications from people who were more than willing to work for the wages and benefits we offered. For people in the real world of Detroit where unemployment is at epidemic proportions, those jobs would have been a godsend. But the UAW would have none of it. Its sole aim was to defend to the death the exorbitant wages and benefits it had won over the years, regardless of whether they still made economic sense in the world of 2008. The preservation of jobs was never part of the UAW plan, which is why its membership has declined so precipitously over the years. Rather, the UAW wanted to preserve premium compensation for its Detroit workers.

"The UAW has failed to educate its membership," said Jerge. "They took credit for years for things they could not control. All the costs they drove into the contracts could be passed on to the customer because the Big Three owned the market. They don't own it anymore. The market defines what you can do. Selling concessions is difficult. It's easier for them to just lose membership. They understand this but cannot deal with it. So they have gone from 1.5 million members to about 300,000."

On day fifty-seven of the strike, I received a telephone call from Michigan governor Jennifer Granholm. I had met Governor Granholm on several occasions and always found her concerned and personable, good qualities for a politician.

Unfortunately, she was bound politically to the same entitlement forces that were even then driving Michigan's economy into a ditch. Governor Granholm asked me to call off the strike.

I informed Governor Granholm that she was talking to the wrong guy. I was not on strike. It was her good friend Ron Gettelfinger and the UAW who had called the strike and continued to oppose a reasonable settlement—opting instead to pressure GM (and Governor Granholm) to lean on AAM to settle. That tactic had always worked for the UAW in the past. But that was then, this was now. Governor Granholm told me the UAW-AAM strike was going to bankrupt the state of Michigan, but did not offer to explain that to Gettelfinger.

On April 30, GM reported a $3.3 billion loss, despite strong overseas growth, which it attributed to poor sales and the AAM strike. It said the strike affecting thirty plants had cost $800 million and 100,000 sales. I cannot say how much of this report is verifiable, for as I said, we were supplying GM the products it needed.

On April 24, as our board convened for its regular quarterly meeting, the striking workers turned out in force to jeer them as they entered the building. Many of the picketers brought along their children, enough to form two semicircles around the headquarters building. That was a lot of kids. There were many families struggling to get along on their $200 weekly strike benefit provided by the UAW. One angry striker told Tom Campbell of WJR-AM that I had once been a friend of labor but I had a "black heart." That is tough stuff. I would not recommend this line of work to anyone who does not have a thick skin.

We reported a first-quarter loss of $27 million or 52¢ a share, weak even considering the strike. I told the directors we remained committed to making a deal with the UAW, but we needed as good a deal as the UAW was providing to our main competitors. "The competitors are going around laughing at us," I said, adding that AAM "will be forced to consider additional restructuring and capacity rationalization actions if the International UAW refuses to accept the structural and permanent changes needed to achieve market cost competitiveness at these [U.S.] facilities."

Gettelfinger had asked for a meeting with me and my senior staff, presumably to seek a breakthrough, but nothing in his approach invited compromise. He had already had a one-on-one session with our president and COO David C. Dauch, in which he engaged in the standard UAW profanity-laced tirade. When he paused for breath, David said, "Ron, I am Dick Dauch's son. Do you really think you are going to intimidate me?"

"These original facilities simply are not viable," I told a reporter from

American Metal Market. "These facilities are not profitable. AAM's ability to operate these facilities is not sustainable. Each and every plant must be profitable; there will be no exceptions."

On April 26, 2008, we sat down with the UAW. It was me, David, and John Jerge across the table from Gettelfinger and two of his senior advisors, Jimmy Settles and Rich Atwood. On my instruction, David and John remained mute as Gettelfinger called us everything except honorable family men. When he had finally exhausted his expletives, you could have turned him upside down and not found enough profanity left to disturb your mother with. Then Settles took over, but his tirade was shorter and a bit less colorful. Finally, Atwood continued the party line, but only for a time appropriate for his rank in the pecking order.

I asked if they were finished. I informed them that I was contemplating the closure of AAM's plants in Buffalo, Tonawanda, Cheektowaga, Three Rivers, and the forge plant in Detroit. *The strongest position management can take in a labor negotiation is the closure of a facility.* The closure of plants must have resonated with Settles. He immediately asked if AAM would consider, for Three Rivers, a market competitive labor agreement styled after a deal the UAW had made with the Chinese auto parts company Wangxiang Group Corporation. I responded that AAM would consider this offer for Three Rivers. Finally, after being held hostage for sixty days, one of my plants was being offered a market competitive labor agreement and a chance to compete in the future. Curiously, for the other plants with the threat of closure hanging overhead, the UAW did not suggest the same solution.

In the end, the Three Rivers plant was the only AAM plant to come out of these negotiations with a market competitive all-in labor rate and flexible work rules. The other locations either closed (Detroit Forge, Tonawanda Forge, and Buffalo Gear, Axle, and Linkage) or demanded a premium to the market for all-in wages and benefit levels (Cheektowaga and Detroit Gear and Axle).

On May 1, GM announced it would resume production at its plant in Arlington, Texas, where they made Chevrolet Suburbans, Tahoes, Cadillac Escalades, and GMC Yukons. We were producing and delivering the axles and other components GM needed to make those vehicles. As the company saw demand rising, it resumed production without a hitch.

We were told by a reliable source that the UAW had brought pressure to bear on the union representing AAM associates at our plant in Guanajuato, Mexico, urging them to engage in a work action as a show of solidarity with the UAW members in the United States. The union leaders in Mexico were appalled, or so they told us. They could not understand why they would seek to damage a company that was providing them with thousands of good jobs. Instead, they gladly worked extra hours each week to provide the products we needed to supply our customers, mainly GM.

By then, the UAW had returned to the bargaining table—not to forge an agreement for future work, but rather to cut a deal for us to buy out our associates who were UAW members. By May 3, the strike reached its sixty-eighth day, the eighth-longest in the seventy-three-year history of the UAW. *The Detroit News* noted that the big 1970 UAW strike against GM shut down all of the company's operations, but that AAM's other factories in the United States and Mexico helped us keep GM assembly plants running through this one.

"For the first sixty days of the strike, we would have taken $45 an hour all week long and thought we had the day done," said Simonte. "Had we done it, it would have killed us. We did not know what was coming in 2009. It would have been our best contract ever, it would have been a huge step forward, it would have been moving in the right direction. But we would not have survived 2009 if we had made that deal."

The background noise was filtering in. On May 13, *The Tennessean* reported that GM had resumed production at five plants idled by the strike. The paper said there was no explanation where the parts were coming from, but by then most everyone had figured it out. The next day GM recalled employees to its SUV plant in Morraine, Ohio, a suburb of Dayton. The dam was beginning to break.

Around this time, GM offered to chip in about $200 million—it ended up being $213 million—to help us reach closure with the UAW. It wasn't a matter of the company's access to the axles and drivetrains we made—we were keeping the supply line full—but rather the UAW's work stoppage actions against GM. GM wanted to put this matter to rest, and so did we. By that time, I assume the UAW leadership also wanted relief. It was an intensely stressful time for all concerned.

"GM worked closely with the AAM management team to support the OEM level buyout demanded by the UAW," said Simonte. "The final negotiation of the strike was not between AAM and the UAW, but between the UAW and GM. Basically, GM was passing money through us to the UAW."

Some things never change.

This was the first time a major company in the auto industry had prevailed over the UAW, and only the second time that any company had done so. The first was Caterpillar many years before which, like AAM, had found itself sad-dled with an onerous wage and benefit agreement that it could not sustain.

After eighty-seven days, we had an agreement with the UAW that basically amounted to a massive buyout of associates who chose to leave, and buy-downs for others who were willing to keep working for less compensation. The buy-downs provided partial compensation to soften the blow of shifting to a lower compensation level. We closed our forging plants in Tonawanda and Detroit, idled parts of two other plants, and relocated some business to other AAM fa-cilities in Michigan and Ohio, and also to Mexico. Overall, AAM's total labor costs dropped from $73.48 per hour before the new contract to $30 to $45, de-pending on the factory. The contract included up to $140,000 for buyouts of associates, depending on their status and years of service, and $105,000 for buy-downs over three years to ease transition to lower pay for those who wanted to keep their jobs.

"The strike cost AAM $125 to $130 million in lost profits and $370 million in sales in 2008," said Simonte, "but the company was set to gain $300 million a year with lower labor costs from the new contract."

BRUTE FORCE

James E. Harbour of Harbour & Associates, an expert on manufacturing, writ-ing in *The Detroit News* on June 25, derided the UAW for its lack of strategic thinking, saying it appeared to be sticking to its familiar theme—brute force.

> *Historically, this approach has freed the union from long-term strategic thinking. Brute force pushed forward a drive for instant gratification: More wages; cost-of-living allowances; free health care; huge pensions; more paid vacation and holiday time; supplemental pay for plant shutdowns; guaran-teed wages for plant closings and time not worked; a complex system of plant-level job classifications that dictated more workers doing less work; time and a half pay on Saturdays and double time on Sundays—even if employees didn't work 40 hours on Monday through Friday.*

Harbour wrote that management deserved a share of the blame for permit-ting this to continue year after year, and that is surely true. There were more than a few of us in auto industry management over the years warning we were heading for disaster, but when the money was rolling in, there was never any will in the front office for confrontation.

Harbour continued:

> The UAW used brute force against General Motors Corp. in the 1998 strike in Flint, a walkout that cost GM billions of dollars. Plant after plant was closed, and thousands of workers hit the street. If this was an expression of strategy, it was a disaster. To the extent it was able, GM sent work elsewhere. The city of Flint was devastated, and auto workers watched their futures evaporate.
>
> Then this February, the UAW struck American Axle over pay and benefits for about 3,800 workers. After granting major wage and benefit concessions to bankrupt Delphi Automotive and Dana Corp., the union decided to take on a marginally profitable company that was the sole provider of front- and rear-drive axles for GM trucks and SUVs.
>
> The UAW did not see that the market for these vehicles was disappearing as the economy tanked and gas prices hit $4 a gallon. Ten plants were making these midsize and full size pickup trucks and SUVs. Output was cut by about 330,000 vehicles in the first half of this year.
>
> As the strike's impact filtered through GM's factory system, about 30 plants were closed and thousands of workers got unplanned vacations. GM says it lost $2.6 billion, including supplemental unemployment benefits pay for laidoff workers. Many states were forced to pay unemployment benefits out of already stressed budgets.
>
> Ironically, GM would have booked a similar loss anyway—even without a strike. Given market conditions, the company would have cut production or put another $4,000 or $5,000 on the hoods of these vehicles to move them off dealer lots. _If this was union strategy, it was ill-timed and self-defeating._*
>
> Equally perplexing was the strike at the new GM plant that produces the popular Buick Enclave, GMC Acadia and Saturn Outback crossovers. These are crucial and highly competitive new products—a $1 billion investment that, coincidentally, promised secure jobs for 3,000 union workers.
>
> Then it was time to bring GM to its knees by striking the Fairfax, Kan. assembly plant that produces a key element of GM's future direction—the Chevrolet Malibu. Most analysts said the Malibu, a Car of the Year recipi-

---

* Underscore is mine.

ent, was as good or better than the Toyota Camry and Honda Accord, which have come to define the family sedan.

GM was distressed by the walkouts that disrupted production at a critical introductory period for a billion-dollar car that customers seemed to love. But you can bet Toyota and Honda were happy. What kind of strategy gives encouragement to the main enemy?

It should be no surprise that the majority of foreign-owned auto assembly plants are mainly located in Southern right-to-work states, nor should it be a surprise that these plants are principally nonunion. The Japanese, South Korean and European automakers make no bones about it. They don't want the UAW in their plants and will do whatever is necessary to keep them out.

Once upon a time, brute force was understandable as a union tactic. After all, that's what the companies were using to suppress union membership in the early years of union organizing. But today, it's a prescription for continually declining market share for GM, Ford and Chrysler.

There's only one way that we can make sense of recent developments coming out of the UAW head office. Union leaders may indeed have defined a new strategy: <u>It is to exit the auto business.</u>*

Meanwhile, GM cancelled medical and life insurance benefits for workers striking the Delta Township factory outside Lansing, Michigan, something the company had not done in more than a decade. As Manny Lopez wrote in the May 15 *Detroit News*:

> Call it payback for the myriad walkouts and threats of strikes the UAW has been waging against GM the past month—ostensibly because of local contract issues. In reality, the local walkouts are a poorly disguised attempt at getting American Axle & Manufacturing Holdings Inc., to increase its offer to striking workers there. Or call it appropriate management because the union now will rightly pay those benefits for workers who voluntarily left their jobs, not the company.
>
> Either way, it signals that labor negotiations today are nothing like those of the past.
>
> Rarely would an automaker or supplier go on record insisting it will shut factories as American Axle CEO Richard E. Dauch has done, or take advantage of provisions in national contracts that allow them to take benefits

---

* Underscore is mine.

away. But that's what we've got today, and both GM and American Axle have the advantage in this shoving match.

Lopez pointed out that "the dour economy and diminishing clout that goes with union membership declines" supported our assertion that AAM could not survive "with costs significantly higher than our competitors here and abroad. Throw in the fact that plenty of people are willing, if not begging, to work for $14 an hour and the union's case is made tougher to defend," Lopez wrote. "Perhaps Michigan's automotive entitlement culture finally is taking its last breath. That change isn't easy, but it's necessary, and once it is accepted the game playing can end."

Whether this event denoted the "last breath" of the entitlement culture in Detroit I am not qualified to say, but if it did, I could justly claim it as the crowning achievement of my professional life.

Lopez's observation is profound and troubling. At the end of the strike, we were left with reduced manufacturing operations in Detroit. Today, our manufacturing facilities in our hometown are idle and unused. We could have employed thousands of associates in those plants at excellent wages and benefits in a beleaguered city desperate for jobs, but inability to negotiate competitive labor contracts with the UAW would not permit it. They demanded premium labor rates for Detroit. As of February 26, 2012, we transferred our remaining operations from Detroit to the AAM facility in Three Rivers, Michigan. At Three Rivers, we have an economically competitive contract including wages, benefits, and operating flexibility with the UAW local that represents the associates at that facility. We employ almost 900 associates in Three Rivers, and the number is growing.

AAM survived the storm and is today a competitive world class global company. We have almost 600 associates working at our headquarters in Detroit, and more than 1,400 at other facilities in Michigan, including Three Rivers. We are growing and prospering.

Yet it pains me to look out on the gleaming modern buildings adjacent to our headquarters in Detroit where not so long ago thousands of associates were making top quality automotive components. I think of the countless hours I and my team committed to those plants—all those twenty-four-hour days and seven-day weeks—not to mention more than a billion dollars we invested. But after eighteen years and four ever-growing UAW contracts with premium labor costs, we could no longer meet the UAW's exorbitant demands and expect to attract business to the Detroit facilities.

FULLY LOADED LABOR COSTS (FLLC) PER HOUR

$60.37 = AAM's average FLLC after the first strike against AAM (1.5 days) in 2004

$73.48 = AAM's average FLLC prior to the UAW's second strike against AAM (87 days) in 2008

$106.77 = AAM estimated average FLLC based on the proposal the UAW made to AAM on December 12, 2007. Conservative estimate of the additional cost to AAM of this proposal was $500 million per year or $2 billion over the life span of the four-year agreement!

$34.00 = AAM realized average FLLC after the UAW's eighty-seven-day strike was over and the new agreement was ratified. This estimate is based on the impact of the ratified agreement including the buyouts, buy-downs, early retirement programs, hiring of new associates, several plant closures, and the relocation of work to more competitive economic locations both in and outside the United States.

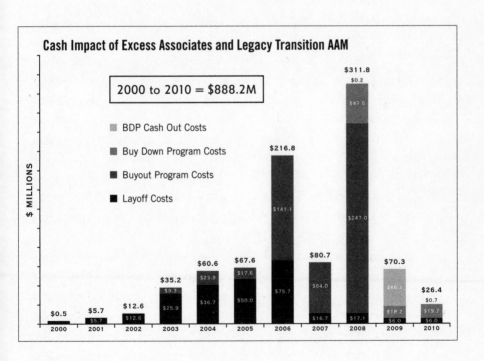

Cash Impact of Excess Associates and Legacy Transition AAM

2000 to 2010 = $888.2M

19

From Bad to Worse

These are the times that try men's souls.
—*Thomas Paine,*
Common Sense

Having struggled through the eighty-seven-day strike, and spent a fortune to shed ourselves of the untenable labor costs that were leading us to ruin, we looked forward to a rebound. We knew—or thought we knew—that once we were free of the excessive labor burden, we would be profitable again and could begin paying down the enormous debts we had acquired in order to pay for the transformation. Jerge calculated that between 2000 and 2008, we paid $888 million to associates to transition them out of the company (or to a lower compensation level). That was just the people costs, not the costs of shuttering factories. That is a lot of money by any standard.

In May 2008 I told Craig Trudell from *Automotive News* that we had a $1.4 billion backlog in new business, and that the new UAW agreement would save us $300 million a year. "American Axle was clear, consistent and direct about the need for a U.S. market competitive agreement that would help us achieve operational flexibility and efficiency," I said. We anticipated that more than half of our production would be outside the United States, and 65–70 percent of it would be shipped back to the United States. About half of our new business would be for rear-wheel drive and all-wheel drive products for cars and crossovers, but we were also excited about getting into electronic products—including transmission differentials and transfer cases.

Our hopes were based on an assumption that the market would rebound and consumers would resume buying pickup trucks and SUVs, as has always happened after recessions. Two days later, though, GM announced it was closing four plants that made trucks and SUVs. In this business, volume is everything. Once you recoup your investments in plants and equipment, you can begin to make money—serious money. But while we were battling the UAW, the country was battling a recession that would prove to be the longest and deepest since the Great Depression of the 1930s. Bad things were happening all around us. The housing crisis was drying up those home equity lines that had once provided money for vehicle purchases. Gas prices soared past $4 a gallon, diverting consumers away from the pickup trucks and SUVs that were our bread and butter.

In 2005, Americans bought 16.9 million light vehicles—a solid number that was strong enough to support a strong industry. But that skidded to 16.5 million in 2006 and 16.1 million in 2007. In 2008, the bottom fell out. Sales fell to 13.2 million. We thought that was horrific, but by the time that number became known, it was clear 2009 would be even worse.

The foreign automakers, which had always had an edge in fuel efficiency, were coming on like gangbusters. In fact, that May—when we finally settled our strike with the UAW—Asian automakers outsold the Big Three for the first time ever in the U.S., capturing 47.8 percent of the U.S. market while the domestic companies held only 45.4 percent. The Honda Civic supplanted the Ford F-Series pickup as the nation's best-selling vehicle. Also, that month 57 percent of all vehicles sold were passenger cars, which the year before had accounted for less than half the market. Overall truck sales nose-dived 23.6 percent in May, continuing a grim trend.

All the remaining auto suppliers were bracing for a summer that promised to cut profits, increase layoffs, and possibly drive more companies into bankruptcy. Suppliers like AAM "are scrambling to realign their work forces and production as U.S. auto makers slash production of sport utility vehicles and pickup trucks because of plunging sales," said *The Wall Street Journal*.

June 27 brought news that GM's stock fell $1.38, or almost 11 percent, to $11.43, its lowest level in thirty-three years. GM's market capitalization slipped to $6.5 billion, the lowest of all companies traded on the Dow Jones Industrial Average. GM had lost 70 percent of its value over the preceding twelve months. A day or two later, Fitch Ratings cut AAM's credit rating one notch, sending us three notches into junk status, with a negative outlook. Fitch said our continuing over-dependence on GM was the reason. "Although [AAM] has shown steady progress in diversifying its products and customers away from GM's North American operations," StreetInsider.com reported, "the concentration in GM's large SUVs and pickups remains very high and will severely affect revenues in the near term." Poor ratings make it difficult and expensive to borrow money for routine purposes.

In July, GM announced it would lay off salaried workers, cut truck production, suspend its dividend, and borrow $2 to $3 billion to weather the downturn in the market. GM's chief operating officer Fritz Henderson said the company would reduce its salaried costs by 20 percent in the United States and Canada. GM was planning to slash truck capacity by 300,000 vehicles by the end of 2009, as oil prices hovered between $130 and $150 a barrel. GM executives were to receive no bonuses in 2008. "Many of the actions we have announced are very difficult, but we take them only after a lot of thought and consideration," said GM chairman and CEO Rick Wagoner. "But we need to take them as part of our plan to keep GM on track so that in the future we will have ample liquidity to fund our ongoing turnaround."

We reported a $644.3 million loss for the second quarter. It worked out to $12.49 per share compared to a profit of $34.6 million or 66 cents a share for the same quarter the year before. The combination of the strike and a weak market cut AAM's revenue by nearly half, free-falling to $490.5 million from $916.5 million in the same quarter of 2007. We were scrambling to keep body and soul together—cutting the cash dividend in the third quarter from 15¢ to 2¢; cancelling the 2008 bonus plan, including bonuses to executives; and considering sale of noncore businesses, such as the stabilizer bar business, as well as excess land and equipment. It all had an air of desperation that I did not like. A restructuring expert named Van Conway said our plan looked comprehensive, but did not mean we would not have to do more. "The market is getting worse by the day," he said.

By the end of July, our stock had fallen to $5.38. Our market capitalization had tanked from $912.6 million at the first of the year to $277.6 million. Key-Banc auto analyst Brett Hoselton downgraded AAM from a buy to a hold rating, despite our turnaround plan. AAM was spiraling down in tandem with GM which reported a $15.5 billion second quarter loss, the third worst in company history. GM's worst problem was falling revenue which was $19.8 billion, or $10 billion less than the same period the year before. Revenue is a strong indicator of an automaker's health because it does not contain any one-time items. "Revenue is a measure of the business going forward," said Dave Cole, chairman emeritus of the Center for Automotive Research in Ann Arbor, Michigan, in an interview for *Automotive News*. "They're in a battle for their life."

AAM was shifting resources overseas as fast as we prudently could. We had plans afoot to spend $73 million on U.S. operations in 2008, but only $30.3 million the following year. But our foreign investments were coming in at $162.3 million in 2008, and we expected that to increase to $189.7 million the following year. We expected international revenues to surpass our domestic revenues by 2010. It was a rational response to a bad situation. Americans simply were not buying trucks and SUVs. "Dick has more capacity here than he needs," said Cole. "He has no choice but to invest where he sees growth opportunities."

Despite the crash of sales of trucks and SUVs, I remained unconvinced they were going the way of the dodo bird. "The New Jersey cowboy, or the fashion buyers in the last five, six years, will pretty well erode out of that pickup buying segment," I told Scott Malone, a Reuters reporter, in September. "But you'll get back then to true functional use of why a pickup was ever created to start with. It basically replaced horses and mules. Nobody's going back to that." But then, there was the question whether we would be able to hang on until consumers started buying trucks and SUVs again.

No matter how tough the situation or intense the pain, you can always count on the UAW to make it worse. It no longer had AAM to pick on, but it still had GM. In 2006, GM lost $10.6 billion. In 2007, it lost $38.7 billion—the largest annual loss in automotive history. Through the third quarter of 2008, GM had lost another $21.2 billion. The company was losing $3.2 billion per month in 2008. In September, GM celebrated its one hundredth birthday, amid open speculation whether the company would reach its hundred and first. The company was bleeding cash and employees. GM by that time had a stock market value of less than $10 billion, one sixteenth that of Toyota. Many believed that would not be enough to keep the auto giant out of bankruptcy.

That same month, the UAW struck GM, shutting down eighty plants. GM was at the time the UAW's largest employer. The company was down for the count. Everyone knew. It was in all the papers. And so . . . the UAW calls a big nationwide strike. There comes a point when human stupidity becomes unwatchable.

The slide continued, and the auto company stocks reflected it. On October 9 AAM hit an historic low of $3.81, and a week later fell even more to $2.99—under $3 a share. The *Detroit Free Press* reported that AAM and Dana were at risk of violating our debt covenants, which could lead to financial penalties or prompt banks to cut back on lending to us. On October 31, 2008, AAM posted a $440.9 million loss for the third quarter compared to $13.5 net income in the same period the year before. The news media was filled with speculation about Tier One auto companies going into Chapter 11, and AAM was usually mentioned. I bought 430,000 shares of AAM stock that week—one of my wisest investments ever.

By November, the Big Three were appealing to Congress for billions in loans to keep them afloat. President Bush's Treasury Secretary Hank Paulson told Congress the administration opposed using funds from the Troubled Asset Relief Program (TARP) to help the automakers, but by December, as the situation grew worse, the administration relented. Around Christmas, President Bush announced his administration would loan the Big Three money. Part of the deal, according to a fact sheet distributed by the White House, was that autoworkers' wages would need to be brought in line with wages earned by U.S. employees of foreign-owned auto companies. I noted that and thought it was coming a bit late for AAM. There was no mention in Washington of whether any of the financial support would go to auto suppliers like AAM. On December 29, our stock closed at $2.18 per share—down 87 percent for the year.

On January 31, 2009, I told a reporter from the *Detroit Free Press* that 2008 was "the year from hell." It was, I said, a turbulent and transformational year. All told, AAM lost about $1 billion in special charges, including paying for associate attrition, and plant closures. We had shed about 3,000 associates through attrition and layoffs. We suspended our quarterly dividend of two cents a share and focused on our Restructure, Resize, and Recover plan (see following chapter). Yet we were looking forward to lower labor costs and $200 million in new business, including new programs for parts with Volkswagen, Audi, Mack Truck, and GM. We cut a deal with FormTech Industries involving an exchange of assets in which we signed over our hub-and-spindle forging business and took over FormTech's differential gear, hypoid pinion and ring gear forging business. FormTech took over our forge in Tonawanda, New York. Through this deal, AAM acquired a new forging process technology that enhanced our ability to expand and diversify. It was a good deal for both companies. We also took over their facility in Ft. Wayne, Indiana.

But our stock continued south—closing at $1.09 the last Friday of January.

By February, AAM was among a group of auto suppliers seeking as much as $10.5 billion in aid from the U.S. Department of the Treasury. One proposal would have given GM and Chrysler access to a $7 billion revolving line of credit from TARP to pay suppliers faster than usual. Another idea was for the government to guarantee payment to suppliers if one of the companies went bankrupt. Under yet another proposal, suppliers would have received about $8 billion directly. About forty suppliers had filed for bankruptcy in 2008; we were one of the few still standing, but we were hanging on by a thread.

The first week of March brought even more bad tidings. The New York Stock Exchange told us we had fallen below the continued listing standard related to total market capitalization and stockholders' equity, which under their rules cannot be under $75 million over a thirty-day period. We promised to submit a plan within forty-five days to demonstrate our ability to meet their standard. *On March 9, AAM stock closed at 29¢ per share.* The next day, *The Detroit News* reported that AAM was "on the bubble." In our annual report filed with the Securities and Exchange Commission, we said we were determined to meet our target of becoming profitable in 2009, but in a letter attached to the report, Deloitte & Touche said uncertainties in the year ahead "raise substantial doubt about the company's ability to continue as a going concern."

Still, we were doing everything right. "We had plenty of room in our financial arrangements," insisted Simonte. "We had truly investment grade credit conditions. We had a lot of leverage to negotiate with our creditors. In late 2008, we concluded a negotiation that would have taken us through 2009."

Then the roof caved in. Some might think that March 9, when our stock closed at 29¢, was our worst day, but we knew the stock would pop back up. Actually April 7 was the worst day for most of us on the firing line. That was the day GM and Chrysler informed us they were going to stop operations in an extended summer shutdown. That call was the straw that truly threatened to break the back of American Axle. Without sales, the company has no money coming in, and GM was still our largest customer by far. Overnight the credit markets dried up. No one would invest in the auto industry because of what was going on with GM and Chrysler.

Several auto suppliers were placed on credit watch, including AAM. "We're going to see a thinning of the herd," said Mike Wall, an analyst at CSM Worldwide. "It'll progress down the chain and we will see Chapter 11 or liquidation at the Tier II and Tier III level."

I told a reporter I was confident that Congress would come through on loans to the Detroit automakers, but that the industry would have to offer realistic ways to change itself to win that aid. "I cannot fathom, in my lifetime, America letting its proud auto industry that put the world on wheels go the way of the horse and buggy," I said. "I have never lost the faith in America or the American auto industry. I'm sending a signal to my people that I have enough confidence, I'm putting my money where my mouth is buying AAM stock."

GM filed for bankruptcy June 1, 2009. Zacks Equity Research analysts warned that AAM might have to follow its primary customer GM into bankruptcy. AAM's lenders agreed to give us relief on certain debts through July 30, but Zacks said our long-term debt was still up 27 percent from the year before, with revenues falling 32 percent over the same period.

"It is AAM's primary objective to complete our restructuring outside of a bankruptcy process," I said. "Bankruptcy is far too extreme and disruptive for AAM and our shareholders."

We had no way of knowing what Congress would do to either save the auto companies or let them fail. Even if Congress did intervene on behalf of the companies, it was by no means clear any support would come to auto suppliers. In the meantime, we did everything we could think of on our own behalf—to Restructure, Resize, and Recover.

20

Restructure, Resize, and Recover

The greater the difficulty, the greater the glory.

—*Cicero*
Roman statesman

I had seen some tough times in the auto business, but I had never faced a confluence of disastrous developments to compare with what befell AAM in the 2005–2009 period. I had seen it coming, or at least I had seen hard times coming, and I warned the AAM board of directors about it, but I had no idea how truly bad it would get.

At no point did I consider bankruptcy a viable option. There are, of course, certain advantages to declaring bankruptcy. Bankruptcy makes it relatively easy to fend off creditors and shed onerous union contracts—the Good Lord knows we had plenty of both weighing us down—but bankruptcy is extremely hard on shareholders who have invested in the company and who stand to lose everything.* To me, resorting to bankruptcy is also a major breach of fiduciary trust and responsibility. I will not go so far as to say that going bankrupt carries a stigma, because I know sometimes it cannot be helped, but I believe that a public corporation carries a serious moral and ethical obligation to avoid bankruptcy if at all possible. We were determined to do everything in our power to avoid it.

---

* I know some will point out that Sandy and I were significant stockholders in AAM, which we were, and still are. I am not motivated by financial gain, but by challenge.

As far back as 2007, after we had recorded our first annual loss in 2006, I launched an initiative we called Restructure, Resize, and Recover. We were already downsizing our workforce, primarily by shutting down our operations in Buffalo and Tonawanda, and we imposed other cost-cutting measures across the board—the standard process for a company entering a downturn. None of what we did back then could be considered draconian, but the confluence of adverse events had greatly exacerbated our situation. I knew we had to take Restructure, Resize, and Recover to a whole new level, and we began making plans accordingly.

I have mentioned earlier that in manufacturing you need to achieve a certain level of production to cover costs for capital, equipment, and labor, after which you can count on substantial profits. Early on in the crisis, I had asked my team what our break-even point was. They told me it was 14,000 axles a day. I told them we had to get that down to 8,000 axles a day. That was a tough challenge, but we were able to do it. Even so, the extremity of the situation was such that we had to go even further. Eventually we got the break-even point down to 6,000 axles a day—a truly incredible achievement—and we were still on the ropes because our primary customer had disappeared.

Having decided to tough it out, I had to make certain I had the backing of AAM's board of directors. Over the years, I had made it a point to work closely with our board, keeping them informed of all developments with the company, good and bad. We had a strong relationship based on trust. We would need it. "Dick brings a unique feature that is very important—he respects and values the input of the board," said Director Bill Miller. "The board is not there as a rubber stamp. He does not just give them information at his discretion, he gives them everything. At board meetings, he frames the entire picture to help us understand his proposed course of action. I don't believe the board members of GM when I worked there were ever as well informed as we are at AAM."

When a company is on the ropes, and the media is filled with reports of pending bankruptcy, corporate directors quite understandably get antsy. No one wants to be on the board of a company that goes bankrupt. It is hard on your reputation, and it can also be hard on your bankbook if lawsuits ensue. In recent years, we have seen several major companies go under, and lawsuits against directors—accused of negligence—have proliferated. The concerns of AAM board members were legitimate.

"The board was pretty cohesive after a short while," said Director Tom

Walker. "Even before GM went bankrupt, we were talking about it. There were some naysayers on the board at first. They came along slowly. Some had been on boards of companies that did not survive. But they stayed with us. Two board members wanted more insurance, which we got. But others of us who had experience with this sort of thing said, all right, let's fight it, let's do what we have to do. We had confidence in Dick, and also AAM's very skilled, young management team."

"The majority of the board never felt like we would not make it," said Director Forest Farmer. "Some of the younger members expressed concerns, but I never for one minute felt like we would not make it. I have seen this kind of thing before. Chrysler was tough, but by 1982 we were okay. This thing with AAM lasted a lot longer. But Dick had been through it before and saw it coming. He pulled back quick, very quick. It got even deeper than I thought it would, but he was on top of it. Dick always says hope for the best, but plan for the worst. He planned for the worst, but it got even worse than he thought."

"You reach a cliff," Miller said. "Once enough pressure is brought to bear, it cascades. The auditor says all who have revenues based on the auto industry are of concern, code for going bankrupt. The stock price gets hammered, debt covenants get looked at, the cost of borrowing goes up, suppliers raise fees. So cost structure goes up at the worst possible time. But Dick never wavered. He never brought his personal equation into the picture either; he was focused on the shareholders. He was very professional, the entire staff was professional. You knew they were hurting, but they didn't wear it on their sleeves."

"The crisis did bring us together," Farmer said.

"The board interacts well together," said Miller. "We have meetings outside the board room. Dick selected board members who have the same ethics, loyalty and passion for the organization that he has. I think that came out at the time. We were all together."

The board did make one significant suggestion that affected the outcome. Though they had the highest respect for our management staff, they believed—correctly—that this was an extraordinary situation that demanded some fresh insights. "The company did not need to be turned around," Walker said, "but it needed to be restructured, and we knew we could use some help on that, especially in terms of handling finances." At the board's behest, I contacted my friends at Blackstone, who sent us a fellow with experience in this kind of situation, Steve Zelin. He proved to be a real quick study who worked closely and effectively with AAM management and the board of directors. His input was invaluable. Thank you, Steve.

LEADERSHIP

I offer a bit of advice for CEOs who have the misfortune to find themselves in my situation—you have to keep your spirits up and exude confidence. As I walked the halls and the plant floors, I made it a point to smile, greet people, and encourage them. Despair is contagious, especially when it begins at the top. I began with my senior staff every day and conveyed it on down through the ranks—our steadily diminishing ranks. Had I not done so, the slow exodus of talent would have become a stampede. As tough as things were, I kept in mind that the heart and soul of AAM is our dedicated salaried staff. While it's true there wasn't a lot of hiring going on in the auto industry in those dark days, our managers were versatile and adaptable. More than a few of them have gone on to successful careers in other industries. We managed to keep the majority of our best people, for which I am most grateful.

"We didn't lose many people," Farmer said. "We had been very successful, coming out of this situation. The people here are highly talented. I was afraid they would be hired away. But they saw what was going on, and they had confidence in the leadership. The confidence and the buy-in by the staff was truly remarkable."

"Plan A was to Restructure, Resize and Recover," said Walker. "We never actually got around to finalizing plan B. There really were few options aside from borrowing money, and we had already run up a lot of debt. We knew Dick and his team were doing everything they could possibly think to do, and we were getting good advice from Blackstone."

In the final analysis, we faced two challenges: to increase revenue and to cut costs. There wasn't much we could do on the revenue side until GM got going again, and that would depend on what happened in Washington, D.C. In the meantime, we steeled ourselves to do the hard work of Restructure, Resize, and Recover. That meant cutting our spending and cutting hard—through the fat, through the muscle, and into the bone. This is not work for the faint of heart because you are dealing with people who have worked hard for years to help you build a company, who deserved to be treated with respect, who deserved better than what was about to happen to them.

We broke RR&R down into 14 categories:

1. Hourly Manpower Reduction

By the time we launched Restructure, Resize, and Recover in earnest, we had already shed a substantial portion of our associates. Overall, we went from about 13,000 associates to about 6,000, and that included our associates and salaried staff at our facilities in Mexico, Brazil, Scotland, Poland, India, Thailand, and China. We did not cut employment overseas very much because those operations were profitable and the people were busy. The impact was in the United States, where inflated wage and benefit scales and restrictive work rules had made it impossible to operate profitably, and where our primary customers had gone bankrupt and ceased production.

2. Salaried Manpower Reduction

We pared down the salaried staff by 355 to about 1,000. We did not resort to last hired, first fired, as is the norm in many places, but carefully distributed the pain evenly among the ranks, taking a toll among some veteran senior managers who had been with AAM from the early days, and who had made great personal sacrifices to help create the company.

The impact of these salaried staff reductions was brought home to me and Sandy the night of June 25, 2009, when we hosted a retirement celebration at World Headquarters for about thirty-five retirees—management people accepting premature retirement at the height of their earning years because the company's survival was at stake. In their own personal ways, many of these people had given as much of themselves to AAM as Sandy and I had. Not only did we know it was going to be a long, hard night, but through a personal scheduling goof I had surgery on my knee the day of the event. I definitely needed the surgery, but I assumed that I would be attending. At the time of the retirement event, I was unfortunately on the couch with my leg elevated, under strict orders—from my doctor, my wife, and my two daughters who are both nurses—not to move.

So I sent a personal delegation to represent me, consisting of my wife Sandy and my son David. Sandy had never held a formal position with AAM, but for the first ten years or so, she was my right arm as we built up the company. She knew these people as well as I did. We had hosted them and their spouses in our home, counseled them when they had troubles, sympathized when they were ill or suffered losses. They were much more than colleagues or subordinates— they were our friends.

"I went to say good-bye to a lot of people," Sandy said. "I was sad, very sad. Dick and I have both put our hearts and souls into this company. For me to have to go to that dinner in his place, to meet with so many good people who had stuck it out with us when they could have left, was very, very tough. So many of them had busted their tails to make the company successful, and we had to let them go."

It was like a roll call of the heroes who built AAM. People who were there told me there were tears all around, not least of all on the faces of David and Sandy. "David cried, too," Sandy said. "I guess he figured if his mother could cry, he could cry, too. My family is very emotional. I could get away with it. A lot of good people who had put in a ton of effort were there. It was very painful to say thanks, but now you have to go. They all seemed to understand, but it was painful to have to do that."

I will refrain from naming everyone there that night, but one name will always stand out for me: Ron Schoenbach, a brilliant and inspired manager who had been with us for many years, would be retiring early. Ron could probably have avoided the axe, but he was sixty-two and eligible for retirement, which many of his colleagues were not. Also, he had a son working for our Three Rivers plant and was thinking about the younger generation. He told me he would make the sacrifice in order to spare someone else. I told him I could call him back when the company got back on its feet, a promise I would keep.

3. Salary, General and Administrative Cost Reduction

We took a hard look at salaries, imposing a wage freeze across the board for everyone and a 10 percent pay cut for senior executives. We slashed general expenses, seeking cuts wherever we could find them. This can quickly get into petty issues like telephone calls, copier supplies and the like, but there is a lot of money involved in administration, and much low hanging fruit available for anyone who will take the time to identify it and deal with it. We went hunting for savings and our hunt was successful. In 2009, in addition to reduced labor costs, we found nonlabor savings of $8.3 million, or a 9.9 percent reduction from the 2008 budget.

4. Eliminate Executive Bonuses

Working with the board of directors, we made a commitment that the pain would be evenly shared among all—from top to bottom. Board members took a 10 percent cut and senior management, in addition to a 10 percent pay cut, agreed to accept no bonuses for two years.

5. Capacity Rationalization

Some industries—particularly service industries—are heavily weighted to labor and must rely almost exclusive on labor efficiency to reduce operating costs. Manufacturing also bears a heavy labor cost, but can have even more resources invested in plants and capital equipment. AAM was no exception to this rule; we set out to reduce our costs associated with physical assets. We had to shed excess capacity—plants and equipment—and realize as much profit from it as we could.

6. Inventory Reduction

A major cost for any manufacturer is inventory, and much of our inventory consisted of expensive high quality steel. We have always operated on just in time deliveries where possible, but raw steel is a heavy deliverable that cannot be adjusted daily. We have long-term contracts with steel companies that must be honored. Even so, when your production is dropping through the floor, you obviously have less need for inventory. So we undertook to reduce our inventory, and realized some real savings—$74 million in direct material and $19 million in indirect material—in a matter of months, for a total saving of $93 million.

7. Capital Expenditures Reduction

Along with capacity rationalization, reducing capital expenditures was an obvious opportunity for cost savings. We were still a live company determined on a future and, as I said, some of our operations were still functioning and producing profits. Where a manufacturer is operating, capital expenditures are as dependable as the seasons—you have to spend money to make money.

We went into the downturn investing an average of 7 percent of sales revenue in capital equipment. We came up with a tough plan to gradually reduce that to 5 percent by 2010 and 2011, going to 4.5 percent in 2012 and 4 percent in 2013, by which time we expected to see a bit of light at the end of the tunnel. We may have had bankruptcy staring us in the face, but we soldiered on in the faith that we would find a way to avoid it. We came up with a plan to spend a total of $802 million, or 4.9 percent of sales, between 2008 and 2013, on capital equipment.

8. Information Technology Spending

Information technology (IT) is a critical element of any manufacturing enterprise, and especially a far-flung one like ours with plants and laboratories all over the world. There is a natural tendency to overspend on IT if only because it is universally recognized as cutting edge, and it takes a certain amount of courage to cut back on it. We set a target of $5 million in savings 2008–2009 and beat it by $2 million. We began with 124 associates working in IT and reduced that to 84, or 33 percent.

We made a serious effort at reducing costs associated with sales, general and administrative expenses. This is often a tough nut to crack because it includes a great many little items dispersed throughout the organization. To get at these costs requires a great deal of attention and relentless pressure on the organization. Often people on the front lines cannot see the point in wringing a few extra dollars out of small items, but they add up. Overall, we came up with $8.3 million, or a saving of 9.9 percent in 2009 compared to the 2008 budget.

We quite naturally went after our customers, more than a few of whom were in arrears on their obligations to us for tooling and other expenses. Normally, you cut your customers some slack on these things—we all have cash flow problems from time to time—but we made it clear to all that we needed the money that was owed to us and we needed it now. We were able to bring in more than $10 million, or about half of what was owed to us, within a few months.

9. Asset Sales

We were already in the process of selling off the assets of shuttered plants. There can be a tendency in these situations to just wash your hands of it and tell your staff to unload that stuff at whatever price they can get. There are enterprises out there that derive all or most of their income from precisely those situations—they buy unwanted properties and equipment at fire sale prices and turn around and re-sell them at a handsome profit. That's okay—that's the free enterprise system at work—but we could not afford to give money away. I knew that a lot of our capital equipment had more than junk steel value; these were expensive, well-designed machines with a lot of life left into them, and there were companies out there doing things I know nothing about who could adapt some of this equipment to their needs fairly easily. The trick was to find those people and get a good price for our surplus property—both buildings and equipment.

We did not have anyone at AAM with expertise in this sort of thing, but I did have one fellow on my staff who had a record of taking on odd assignments and getting good results, though in many instances he had no direct experience to commend him for the specific tasks I had in mind. George Nagher, whom I had known for years through business, first appeared on the scene as a photographer we retained to take photos when we were first launching AAM. I quickly discerned he was also one of those rare "Here am I; send me,"* characters who either do not recognize their limitations or are undeterred by them. Whenever I asked him to do something, he did not explain to me that it was not in his job description; he just went and did it.

I tasked Nagher to take a lead role in the disposal of our excess plants and equipment, and he did not let me down. We sold off the facilities in Buffalo and Tonawanda in a timely manner. We walked away free of any of the legal liabilities that often accompany former industrial properties. Then Nagher found a resourceful auctioneer to handle the capital equipment for us, both at Buffalo and Tonawanda, and in Detroit. When the auctions were held, Nagher had the plants laid out clean and neat, the various equipment stacked neatly and labeled, with comfortable seats, as well as drinks and snacks, for the guests who came to bid. It was all done very professionally, the bidders were very impressed, and we got good results. I had been told by one source that companies in our situation generally can expect to get about 10 cents on the dollar for their excess equipment. We got between 15 and 20 percent. I don't know how much money we have paid Nagher over the years, but I believe he made it all back for us and then some with those auctions. At the time, every penny coming in the door was warmly received, and Nagher brought us quite a few. Thank you George, for that, and for all of your good work over the years.

---

* Isaiah, 6:8

10. Sales Initiatives—Collecting Overdue Bills

In an organization of any size, be it a private company or government agency, there are always a few loose ends here and there that have somehow slipped through the cracks. As we went down the line reviewing every expense large and small, it dawned on us that we had a lot of bills out there for tooling investments we had made on behalf of customers for which we had not been reimbursed—more than $20 million worth, in fact. Some of this missing money was owed by customers that were struggling to survive, but hey, so was AAM. They were skipping payments at least in part because we were not pressing them for payments.

We documented what we were owed and set about collecting it. Within a remarkably short period of time, we had recaptured about $20 million. As the old saying goes, $20 million here, $20 million there, pretty soon you're talking real money.

11. Operating Improvements

The quest for cost savings—like the quest for ever-better quality—is endless. We zeroed in on scrap—which is always an issue for manufacturers, no matter how intensely we work to reduce it. We launched a company-wide campaign to reduce mismanufactured scrap and saved more than $700,000 in one three-month period in late 2008. We instigated a flexible working schedule at our plants in Detroit, Three Rivers, and Cheektowaga, having associates work four ten-hour days instead of five eight-hour days, which reduced consumption of energy and brought a variety of other savings.

We took another shot at our lean manufacturing initiative—reorganizing value stream management, industrial engineering and maintenance under a single reporting structure for future programs. We employed a variety of other lean tools to further improve quality, delivery performance, increase speed of order to delivery, increase capacity, reduce inventory and improve flexibility—while improving profit margins.

12. GPSCM Initiatives

Like all manufacturers, we rely on a complex web of suppliers for a variety of products and services, both here in the U.S. and in the foreign nations where we have operating facilities. We took a hard look at our Global Procurement Supply Chain Management (GPSCM) searching for ways to reduce costs. It is a fact of life that the more suppliers you have, the more waste you have. The continuing challenge with suppliers is to hold their feet to the fire on quality, delivery, technology and price, and the fewer suppliers you have, the easier it is to do that. Where feasible, we localized the extended supply chain for both direct and indirect (capital equipment). We managed to reduce our global supply base—direct and indirect—by 380, or 10 percent in 2008. Closer to home, here in the United States and in Canada, the reduction was closer to 40 percent.

We put all of our payment terms agreements for productive materials contracts under the microscope. Any and all exceptions to AAM's standard payment terms were reviewed and reasons for the exceptions were documented. Suppliers with nonstandard payment terms were reduced from thirty-two to eleven.

We audited all of our external warehousing and identified several opportunities for consolidation and in-sourcing, which we implemented. (It isn't always simple to quantify things like this in terms of dollars saved, but that we were saving was abundantly clear.)

During our annual supplier day on October 23, 2008, we brought in AAM's top 170 suppliers, as we do every year, and laid it on the line with them that our survival depended on reducing costs everywhere, and that suppliers had to step up and do their part. We made it clear we were in for the long haul, and would take careful note of which companies went the extra mile for us. For the most part, our suppliers responded positively to the challenge and their active support would prove a key factor in the drama as it played out.

13. International Operations—Accelerate Growth Opportunities

At our overseas installations, we accelerated our profitable growth initiatives in Poland, China, India, Mexico, Brazil, and Thailand. Basically, those were the only opportunities we had to increase profits while we awaited a turnaround in the United States—and sweated out the future prospects of GM and Chrysler.

14. Pursue Strategic Initiatives

In a time of stress, you always look around for opportunities to raise cash, and we did our best. We attempted to sell a few properties, but except for an asset swap with FormTech Industries, a Detroit area firm that took over part of our Tonawanda plant, we found few takers. The auto and truck business was in the pits—no one was eager to invest in the properties we put on the market.

After all that, we cut and cut and cut, but still faced an uphill climb. As we stumbled into the summer of 2009, GM was still not producing vehicles. On June 1, GM filed for bankruptcy protection. It was a watershed moment in the history of American business. On June 2, *The Wall Street Journal* reported that GM had $82.2 billion in assets and $172 billion in liabilities. The company had 463 subsidiaries and had built 450 million cars and trucks over its 100-year run. It still employed 235,000 people worldwide, including 91,000 in the United States which it paid $476 million each month. It was also paying benefits to 493,000 retirees. It was spending about $50 billion a year for parts and services from vendors in North America—one of which was AAM. At the time, GM owed us at least $300 million for parts delivered, but we were not sure we would ever see that money. Our survival depended on it. On June 8, GM was removed from the Dow Jones Industrial Average, where it had been a bulwark for as long as I could remember.

AAM's CFO Simonte was coming to me regularly to recite the countdown on how long we could survive without an infusion of cash—ninety days, sixty days, thirty days. The clock was ticking, our cash was running out. I was doing all in my power to keep a smile on my face and inspire confidence among my colleagues but there was no denying that things were looking grim. We caught a break when the New York Stock Exchange adjusted its listing requirements threshold from $75 million to $50 million, which meant our stock was still in play.

It was perhaps a measure of our desperation that I took David C. Dauch and Mike Simonte on a trip to New York to call on our friends at the Blackstone Group. They were the ones who had enabled me to buy out Ray Park and helped us go public. They had made a bundle on their investment with us, but under the circumstances they could not help us out of our current fix. Given the state of the auto industry overall, and the dicey prospects for our major customer GM, they could not in good conscience allot their resources to such a risky undertaking, no matter how well we had served them in the past or their respect for me and my team.

So we left New York and went to Washington, D.C. We took up residence at a hotel near the White House and I sent David and Mike to the U.S. Treasury Department to represent us in the continuing negotiations between GM and the

...rating fiftieth wedding anniversary. Rick Dauch, Teri Dauch (Gigot), Sandy Dauch, Dick Dauch, Jane ...a (Harvey), David Dauch.

Dedication of Boys & Girls Club newest campus, 2005.

Afterglow of Detroit's Super Bowl NFL, Youth Education Town.

troit's beautiful Boy Scout Center serving our youth. Dedicated 2002.

umbs up for United Way, $61M for Detroit.

Purdue University's Dauch Alumni Center. Dedicated 2004.

Two loyal Boilermakers! Sandy and Dick Dauch.

The Dick and Sandy Dauch Lecture Hall, with capacity for 140 students, will be the largest room in the addition to the Krannert School of Management Complex, Rawls Hall. Located on the first floor, the room features wireless technology and multimedia capabilities and is video-conferencing enabled.

A S H L A N D   U N I V E R S I T Y

RICHARD E. AND SANDRA J.
DAUCH COLLEGE OF BUSINESS AND ECONOMICS

Richard E. and Sandra J. Dauch College of Business and Economics. Advancing education at Ashland University, New Dauch College of Business and Economics, Ashland, Ohio. Dedicated 2003.

6 Flight Commander and AAM Sales Director, Lt. Colonel Nyquist, 107th Fighter Squadron, Selfridge National Guard Base, MI. Picture taken as squadron promo picture for squadron wall board at air base.

The Dauch family gathers for the dedication of Hospice House built on the donated Dauch farm, 2005.

Federal Government. We figured if the government was going to bail out GM, it would need to include some provision for AAM. Without AAM, GM had no viable source for its axles and drive trains for pickup trucks and SUVs. It was our last hope. Time and money were running out.

Many observers were speculating AAM could be the next to enter Chapter 11, because we would be unable to meet our debt commitments on loans that were coming due in August. Kip Penniman Jr., of KDP Investment Advisors, predicted in *The Wall Street Journal* that AAM would be unable to make the August payment on our 5.25 percent senior notes, and that we were in the midst of negotiating a prepackaged bankruptcy protection filing with its lenders. Actually, we were moving heaven and earth to avoid bankruptcy if at all humanly possible.

"Only three Michigan companies on my nostalgic chart remain unscathed, for now, by bankruptcy or predation: Ford Motor Company, Compuware Corporation and American Axle & Manufacturing, the most likely of the survivors to take its own turn in the ditch depending on the outcome of GM's blast through bankruptcy," wrote Daniel Howes in *The Detroit News*.

J.P. Morgan Funds, quoted in the same *Wall Street Journal* article as Penniman, said AAM appeared to be the next auto supplier headed for bankruptcy. The article cited three caveats—covenant extensions, aid from GM and me—fighting to avoid bankruptcy. We were facing a possible default on $250 million in notes after getting a one-month waiver to avoid breaching terms on bank loans.

On July 11, GM emerged from bankruptcy, but it was unclear what form a new GM would take, or how AAM figured into the picture—if we *did* figure into the picture. We caught a bit of relief when we were able to negotiate an extension on the waiver of our revolving credit facility until August 20, which amounted to a last minute temporary reprieve. On August 7, AAM reported a net loss of $289 million during the second quarter. I kept my feet on the ground and my eyes on the horizon. "We have nearly completed the comprehensive Restructuring, Resizing and Recovery of our business by realigning AAM's global manufacturing capacity and reducing AAM's operating break-even level," I told a reporter from *The Oakland Press*. "As a result of these difficult but necessary restructuring actions, we are achieving permanent and transformational improvements in AAM's cost structure and flexibility. This will position AAM to return to profitability as part of a viable and sustainable future for our company."

All eyes—ours and our lenders—were on Washington, where at long last a deal was beginning to emerge. The Federal Government agreed to put up the money to keep GM in operation. The prospect of GM going under was just too horrific to contemplate in terms of jobs lost and the impact on the overall economy, which would have been disastrous. Under the plan, Uncle Sam was to take 60 percent ownership of GM, the Canadian government would take 12.5 percent, the UAW would get 17.5 percent (of the company its demands had done so much to destroy), and unsecured bondholders would get 10 percent. Stockholders, of course, were wiped out.

In mid-August, we secured a promise from GM to provide us as much as $210 million in loans and payments, out of over $300 million they owed to us. In a filing with the SEC, we said GM had agreed to pay us $110 million to make up for payments lost when GM filed for Chapter 11 in June, and also agreed to loan AAM up to $100 million. The deal would give GM five-year warrants to buy a 7.4 percent stake in AAM. GM also would get warrants on an additional stake of as much as 12.5 percent, depending on how much of the loan AAM took advantage of. And just in case we didn't get the message, GM insisted on a new "access and security" agreement—the nuclear option—like it had when we first bought the old GM assets.

GM's plan was also contingent on AAM arranging new terms for our revolving credit facility after we violated loan covenants. Our lenders, led by JPMorgan Chase Bank and Bank of America, agreed to extend a waiver on those breaches to August 31.

Somewhere along the line, Simonte came into my office to inform me we were down to four days. All those years of blood and sweat equity were on the line. If something didn't break within four days, it would be Chapter 11 for AAM, and all of our shareholders—like the shareholders of GM, Chrysler, and a host of other auto suppliers—would be left holding the bag. An empty bag.

We managed to obtain a third waiver on loan covenants from our lenders that gave us until September 15 to negotiate new terms for our revolving credit facility. Under the revised covenant, AAM was required to maintain at least $75 million in liquidity, down from an earlier requirement of $100 million.

Finally, we reached a deal with our lenders to amend AAM's revolving credit facility, thus clearing the way to receive the desperately needed $110 million liquidity infusion from GM plus a $100 million line of credit, and provisions for accelerated payments to AAM. GM did not make it easy on us. The deal restricted AAM's ability to make acquisitions, pay dividends, buy back stock, or make certain investments. In yet another filing with the SEC, we said we expected to have $300 million of liquidity on September 30, including the GM funds, enough to meet our financial obligations and operate our business.

All of which meant we had survived to fight another day. A few days later, we posted our first quarterly profit in two years, an encouraging sign after deep and painful cost cuts. Our shares jumped more than 9 percent. AAM earned $19.6 million or 35 cents per share compared to a loss of $440.9 million in the third quarter a year before. *We were on our way back.*

While the last-minute payment from GM got us past the crisis, it can fairly be said that had we not undergone our painful Restructure, Resize, and Recover transition, that payment would have been too little, too late. We had stripped AAM down to the bare essentials, eliminating every expense that was not absolutely necessary. The company that emerged was lean, competitive, flexible, profitable, and ready for what the future will bring.

21

Giving Back

We make a living by what we get, but we make a life by what we give.

—Winston Churchill

Paul Allen, the cofounder of Microsoft, has a personal yacht called *Octopus*, 414 feet long, that comes with a crew of sixty, two helicopters, seven boats, and a submarine. He paid about $200 million for it and reportedly spends $384,000 a week to maintain it. It is generally ranked among the top 10 of the world's most lavish yachts, but other billionaires here and there have bigger ones that cost even more.

I do not take issue with the way other people spend their money. Paul Allen is an inspired entrepreneur who, along with Bill Gates, created Microsoft, one of the world's great companies, which has wrought wonderful changes in the world, enabling extraordinary gains in efficiency and productivity that have enhanced the lives of millions of people. He has every right to the money he has earned and is free to spend it any way he pleases. More power to him.

I, too, am a successful entrepreneur who, with a good bit of help from my wife Sandy, friends, and fellow investors, created a prominent company. With that success came financial security. Sandy and I have been most fortunate. We came from humble circumstances and have enjoyed great success, both personally and professionally. Nothing was handed to us.

I put first things first and count my family as my most prized possession. Sandy and I have had a successful union for over half a century. She has been my full partner every step of the way, my personal chief executive officer whose wise counsel and loving support have been my foundation over an adult lifetime.

Our four grown children have inherited our values and work ethic. Somehow we were successful in providing them with everything they needed while growing up without fostering a sense of entitlement. I must credit Sandy with much of this because I was gone a lot of the time. She did a wonderful job. All four of them work hard and are successful in their careers and their personal lives. We have excellent grandchildren and even two great grandchildren! We have encountered some obstacles along the way, but it is in overcoming obstacles that we attain true fulfillment. I always ask my colleagues and subordinates about their families because I believe family should always come first. It does at my house.

I heard a minister say that in this life you should put God first, your spouse second, and your children third, and everything will work out. I believe he was on to something. He did not mention work or patriotism, which are important ingredients to a successful and fulfilling life, but first things first. With a solid home life and strong marriage, I was able to concentrate on work, and the tasks at hand.

Living in the Detroit area, one does not have to look far to see the needs. Over the past two generations, our city has fallen on hard times. Detroit for the last one hundred years has been heavily dependent on the auto industry, and its fortunes have declined in tandem with those of the Big Three. The impact has been felt most heavily in the inner city.

Detroit has all of the pathologies that characterize the inner city, but none in my book are more heartbreaking than the spectacle of tens of thousands of kids living in chaotic circumstances, amid crime and desolation, with little hope of achieving anything better. Our country's future depends on more than one company—it depends on those kids out there who have little to hold on to, scarcity to build upon, little to aspire to, and a lack of positive role models. The poverty rate among children in this country is horrific and getting worse. This bears alarming implications for the future of our country.

I willingly gave my time to chair Detroit's United Way 2006 Torch Campaign because of the importance of the funds raised for the community. Even in tough financial times, we were able to reach the desired goal, which says a lot about the heart of Detroiters and the surrounding communities.

BOY SCOUTS

I have long been a strong believer in the fine work of the Boy Scouts of America, which conveys strong values and useful skills to young people in a variety of creative ways. Nowhere is that work more vitally needed than in Michigan where the loss of so much of our manufacturing base has wrought havoc among many families, and reduced wholesome opportunities for many youth. So I was receptive when John Primrose, chief executive officer of the Detroit Council of the Boy Scouts of America, told me of their critical need for a new home office.

Sandy and I were happy to put up nearly $2 million in seed money that made possible construction of a new central headquarters for the Detroit Council on West Warren Avenue in Detroit. That was my only request, that the headquarters be based in Detroit. It is a beautiful, state-of-the-art 28,000-square-foot building that opened for business in 2002. After a consolidation in 2009, they manage a far-flung scouting empire embracing the three counties of Wayne, Oakland, and Macomb. The new chief executive officer is the highly talented John Reesor. All told, the new Great Lakes Council provides services to 26,500 youth who receive guidance from 10,400 volunteers. In 2010, 482 of those Scouts earned their Eagle badges, and anyone who knows the first thing about scouting knows what a remarkable achievement that is.

These kids are real assets to their communities. In 2010, Boy Scouts in the Great Lakes Council provided more than 71,000 hours of service time to community organizations, and collected 395,725 pounds of food for the needy.

Since Sandy and I made the largest single financial contribution for that headquarters building, they decided to call it the Dauch Scout Center. We are proud of the association. I believe those Scouts will be doing good things for the communities they serve, and for themselves, long after Sandy and I are gone.

BOYS AND GIRLS CLUBS

I cannot personally correct all of the conditions that have contributed to so much tragic poverty among our youth—but I can help. I have long occupied a chair on the board of directors of the Boys & Girls Clubs of Southeastern Michigan. In November 2001, Sandy and I hosted a fund-raiser at Pine Lake Golf Course in Orchard Lake, Michigan, where we helped them raise $170,000 for that fine organization, led by my friend, President and Chief Executive Officer Len Krichko.

A few years later, in 2006, I received an opportunity to make a bigger contribution when I got a call from Krichko and two of his key colleagues, Tom Hoeg and John James. They had an exciting opportunity to discuss with me.

Super Bowl XL (40) was to be played in Detroit that year at Ford Field, and it is customary for the National Football League (NFL) to make a legacy contribution of $1 million to the local community, preferably to fund something positive for young people. This program dated back to the 1990s when it was promoted by Jack Kemp, former secretary of the U.S. Department of Housing and Development, and onetime vice president of NFL charities. Jack, of course, was a star quarterback for the Buffalo Bills for many years. By 2006, Jack was complaining that the program was in disarray, that some of the facilities funded in earlier years were no longer functioning. He recommended the NFL work with the Boys & Girls Clubs, which is how the NFL came to call on Krichko. The NFL told Len it would put up $1 million to help fund a facility for local youth if he could round up a matching sum of $1 million from local sources.

"I told the NFL people that $2 million would not get you very much in Detroit with our union labor," Krichko said. "It would buy maybe a 10,000-square-foot facility. I figured we needed three times that, 25,000 to 35,000 square feet. That would cost at least $6 million."* A smaller building, he said, would be the city of Detroit's and the NFL's worst nightmare. "We will have kids standing around the block waiting to get in so we won't be in violation of fire codes."

Krichko does not indulge small dreams, which is a big reason I admire him. He and his staff were working with some dilapidated facilities that did not begin to serve the need, and with the NFL offer he saw a big opportunity to do something great. He called his people together and laid out a game plan. "I said, here's the deal, we need to raise money, we need to build the right-size facility, and we need to get the NFL to agree to it, and we're going to get the Super Bowl host committee to allow us to do it. We're going to make a presentation and knock their socks off to do what we need to do for the kids of Detroit."

They had one hour to make their presentation, and they did a bang-up job. The NFL agreed to the plan—provided, of course, that Krichko and his organization could raise the additional $5 million. So Krichko called me. Of course, I knew Len and all about the good work he and his team were doing. Sandy and I did not hesitate; we pledged $1.5 million.

That gave Krichko all the leverage he needed to start passing the hat around town. He can be very persuasive. In addition to the $1 million from the NFL

---

* Please note the comment about labor unions was Krichko's, not mine. It isn't just autos and auto parts that are afflicted with Detroit's entitlement mentality. Everything in the city is affected.

and $1.5 million from us, he raked in $1 million from the Super Bowl Host Committee sponsors (GM, Ford, Chrysler and DADA), $2.1 million from the U.S. Department of Housing and Urban Development, $100,000 from NFL Charities, $100,000 from The Ralph Wilson Foundation, $50,000 from the Detroit Lions Charities, and the rest from other donors.

"The immediate Dauch contribution made the difference," Krichko said. "The project came in under budget and on time."

It is a project to love. The beautifully designed 32,000-square-foot facility on a 4.71-acre site within the new Gardenview Estates serves more than 2,500 local youth. It offers a variety of spaces for youth activities including an arts and crafts center, community room, gymnasium, learning center, locker rooms, meeting rooms, outdoor play areas, social and recreational games room, technology center, and multimedia studio and teen center. An athletic field behind the building was provided by Ralph Wilson, a prominent Detroit businessman who owned the Buffalo Bills at one time.

This facility stands out like a jewel in a blighted neighborhood. When school lets out, hundreds of youngsters converge on the place to play, work with computers, socialize, and sometimes just be safe in a neighborhood where safety is hard to come by. I have been told by the staff there that the local gangs leave the youngsters at the center alone—as if in tacit respect that some among them do truly want to find a better life. Certainly, crime has never been a serious problem there at the center. It makes me wonder—how many of those tough guys in the gangs might be doing better if someone had extended a hand to them?

Somehow Len Krichko persuaded the NFL to name that facility the Dick and Sandy Dauch Campus. The NFL normally does not permit the facilities it builds to be named after individuals.

EDUCATION

Helping kids get a good start in life is always a worthy undertaking, and thus the true passion of our philanthropy has always been education. It was education that made it possible for a humble farm boy like me to make something of himself, and it is education that propelled our nation to greatness.

Given who I am and what I do, it stands to reason that my interest in education has focused on preparing bright young people for careers in manufacturing— which is to say I have been focused on a major vacuum in our educational system. Fifty years ago, the public schools devoted considerable resources to vocational training. Somehow that got lost over the years, and today we are paying a steep price for it. Despite all the losses of manufacturing jobs, the biggest single complaint I hear from other manufacturers is about the skills gap—too few people qualified to work in modern manufacturing. Today's industrial environment is not your father's factory floor—it is more like *Star Trek*. The kids coming out of high school today simply cannot handle modern manufacturing jobs. Our American educational system has not adjusted to changing market needs. Our young people are deficient in math, science, and vocational arts.

In particular, I have noted that not one university offers a program to train plant managers in manufacturing. This is surely one of the most challenging and important jobs in the country, and one that offers many rewards, but you must find your own way into it. There is no clearly defined path to that job—at least not in academia.

I took a stab at that challenge way back in 1990 when my employer, Chrysler Corporation, joined with ten other American companies to help establish the Leaders for Manufacturing (LFM) program at the Massachusetts Institute of Technology (MIT). It is a two-year program that produces graduates with degrees in engineering as well as an MBA from the Sloan School of Business. A real world internship at a manufacturing plant is part of the curriculum. My eldest son Rick, a West Point graduate, took advantage of the MIT program and speaks very highly of it. He is a senior manufacturing chief executive officer today and without question that MIT program helped prepare him for his career.

I seized another opportunity to help Ashland University in Ashland, Ohio—a city of about 20,000 in North Central Ohio—establish a first-rate business school on its campus. Neither Sandy nor I attended Ashland University, but we grew up in that community, met each other there, and consider it our home. Ashland University, founded in 1878, offers seventy-three undergraduate majors and nine preprofessional programs to more than six thousand students, about half of them graduate students. The school was offering business courses, but its leadership had a big vision of creating a cohesive business school in one building that would attract entrepreneurial students from around the world. I like educators with big ideas, especially when they are focused on business, economics and operations.

Sandy and I chipped in $5 million to enable Ashland University to build the Richard E. and Sandra J. Dauch College of Business and Economics (COBE) that opened for business in January 2004. The college includes the Burton D. Morgan Center for Entrepreneurial Studies, made possible by a $3.25 million grant from the Burton D. Morgan Foundation. Together these two major donations made possible a 60,000-square-foot state-of-the-art facility, beautifully designed, that houses the latest in instruction technology, a product development lab and an executive training center—in addition to the entrepreneurial center.

One of the most fascinating features of the COBE is the Trading Room where, amid Wall Street–style workstations and wall-mounted displays, students in the Eagle Investment Group perform real-world fund and behavioral analysis, and also invest and manage $1 million of the university's endowment fund. COBE students can choose among ten majors: accounting, business management, economics, entrepreneurship, finance, hospitality management, international business, information systems, marketing and supply chain management.

Ashland University has a great pedigree and offers a remarkable academic range. Anyone who visits that campus cannot help but be impressed. It is a forward-thinking university with a vision. They also have a great athletic program, which always goes a long way with me. They know how to develop the student athlete for the greater good of society. Their president, Dr. Fred Finks, is an extraordinary leader, visionary and academic. We are proud to be associated with Ashland University, and him.

Purdue University

It will come as no surprise to people who know me and Sandy to learn that we have devoted a large portion of our charitable support to my alma mater, Purdue University. I could have gone to other schools based on my football credentials, but I chose Purdue because I knew I would get an excellent education there. They did not let me down and to this day Purdue remains true to its core values. Purdue has a proud sports program, but the first emphasis for all students, including athletes, is academics. "We have gone twenty-six consecutive semesters with our athletes having better grade averages than the student body as a whole," said Purdue athletic director Morgan Burke in 2010, a winning record that is no doubt longer by now. "Of those who exhaust their eligibility here, 90 percent graduate. We have a football player right now, a tight end, who has a 4.0 average at the Krannert School of Management. He's not going to have trouble doing what Dick Dauch did later on."

I have a special interest in the Krannert School. Some years ago, I applied pressure to have the Purdue School of Engineering, the School of Technology, and the Krannert School of Management start working together. It was greeted as a radical concept at the time; as is custom in higher education, the separate departments regarded themselves as independent fiefdoms. But under the leadership of Dr. Henry Yang, dean of the School of Engineering, Dr. Donald K. Gentry, dean of the School of Technology, and Dr. Dennis Weidenaar, dean of the Krannert School, they broke down the barriers between the programs. It has paid off big time in a program that prepares bright young people for careers in industry, including manufacturing. Thank you, Purdue, for your open-minded leadership—and teamwork.

In 2001, Sandy and I donated a $1 million challenge grant to help create the Dauch Center for the Management of Manufacturing Enterprises (CMME). We later gave $6 million more, with $5 million to serve as a kickoff for the Campaign at the Frontier for Krannert. Another $1 million was directed to support Purdue's intercollegiate athletics needs. The new Rawls Hall evolved from this initiative, greatly enhancing Purdue's overall management, physical plant, and educational capacity.

Perhaps Purdue's main claim to academic fame is its connection to the space program. No fewer than twenty-two astronauts, including Neil Armstrong, the first man to walk on the moon, are graduates of Purdue. Armstrong is honored by the Neil Armstrong Hall of Engineering, a breathtaking architectural masterpiece where the engineering and aeronautical pioneers of the future are being trained.

I quite naturally take a keen interest in the athletic program, and do what I can to help boost their success. I work closely with Burke, who I believe is a real asset to the university. Burke got both his undergraduate degree and graduate degree from Krannert, and later attended law school. He worked seventeen years at Inland Steel, now part of Mittal, before he joined Purdue. I am not quite sure how one shifts from the steel industry to college sports, but it seemed a natural move for Burke. He wants to win, of course, but his first concern is the success of the young men and women in his charge—just the way it was when I was a student-athlete. "We're blue collar and not embarrassed about it," Burke said. "We look for kids who are more for the team than themselves. We cannot always control the output, but we always do our best."

Burke has me—and quite a few other alumni—to call on for support, and we are always there. "Every time I have asked Dick Dauch for help, he's helped me," Burke said. "My product at the end of the day is these young kids. It has been a very rewarding experience."

Under President Martin C. Jischke, who served from 2000 through 2007, Purdue embarked on an ambitious building spree that has transformed a rather ordinary campus into a sparkling array of modern facilities that have transformed Purdue into an extraordinary visual feast. When Jischke took the helm at Purdue, they were raising maybe $80–100 million a year in outside funding from alumni and other donors, basically treading water for a large land grant university of almost 75,000 students (40,000 of whom attend the main campus at West Lafayette, Indiana). Jischke announced a bold plan to raise $1.3 billion over six years. Some members of the board said he was off his rocker, but we ended up raising more than $1.7 billion—almost $300 million a year during that stretch. Dr. Jischke was a visionary, an effective and powerful academic leader.

"It was very clear to me that Purdue did not have the size of research capability appropriate to an institution of this size," Jischke said. "We did not have an interdisciplinary approach. For example, we had good people in nanotechnology, but they were limited to theoretical work. They needed a laboratory. That first fall after I got here, I went to see some Purdue graduates who were successful in business. One contributed $30 million and another $15 million. The Lilly Endowment chipped in $25 million. All of a sudden we had $70 million for a nanotechnology center."

The Birck Nanotechnology Center was soon joined by the Hall for Discovery and Learning Research; the Bindley Bioscience Center; the Gerald D. and Edna E. Mann Hall, a center for health care engineering; and the Burton D. Morgan Center for Entrepreneurship. This is a regular murderers' row of advanced academic institutions—comprising Purdue's Discovery Park—that are on the cutting edge of scholarship in a wide range of disciplines. Purdue has catapulted to a leadership role for the nation. Thank you, Dr. Jischke.

My first love, though, is the Krannert School of Management. With my active support and the support of many others, it has become one of the nation's premier business and management schools. It offers a litany of majors in accounting, finance, marketing, operations management, human resources management, quantitative methods, economics, and strategic management. MBA students can enroll in a variety of elective courses that will lead them to an option area certificate in global supply chain management or manufacturing technology management at the Dauch Center for the Management of Manufacturing Enterprises (DCMME). Students also have an excellent opportunity to study business management abroad in internships that prepare them for the modern world of global competition. Purdue has been ranked first, second, or third in operations management for more than fifteen consecutive years.

Jischke knew he could take advantage of me, and he was not the least bit shy of doing so. Not long after he took the helm at Purdue, and figured out who I was, he came to me with a problem. "I knew we needed more money," Jischke said, "therefore we needed a bigger, better fund raising organization. I could not attract top notch people into the facility we had at that time. The alumni organization was scattered all over the place. I said we needed a new building. Dick and Sandy Dauch pledged $2 million to get the project off the ground." Purdue was off and running to get their 440,000 living alumni more involved with the university's future. Purdue has empowered Kirk Cerny to be the president and CEO of the Purdue Alumni Association (PAA). He and his highly capable staff are in residence at the Dauch Alumni Center (DAC).

Today, the Dick and Sandy Dauch Alumni Center is truly one of the more beautiful buildings on a campus teeming with beautiful buildings. It houses both the alumni organization and the fund-raising arm. At special events that draw alumni, such as homecoming, it is always the focal point of a variety of social activities. Having a first class facility like that to work from makes it much easier for Purdue to put the arm on alumni for the benefit of future alumni.

Jischke retired and Dr. France Córdova became the new Purdue president, and she took full advantage of the legacy left to her. "Alumni support is tremendously important to us," she said. "We're a state-funded school and state funding keeps going down. Dick Dauch is a role model for our students. I am a strong believer in bringing business leaders into the classroom to talk about their experiences." Dr. Córdova has recently retired and I look forward to working with Purdue's newly named president, Indiana governor, Mitch Daniels.

I will always be grateful to Purdue for the lessons and experience I gained there as an undergraduate, and am today immensely proud of the job it is doing preparing the next generation of America's leaders—especially in business operations, technology, engineering, and manufacturing.

All told, Sandy and I have given away tens of millions of dollars to various good causes—from the Boy Scouts to Purdue University—and I trust we will give more away in the years to come. Philanthropy can become a challenge when your name is out there as a soft touch. You get hit on a lot, sometimes by people with marginal claims on your time and resources. It is easy to get defensive and evasive. We try to avoid that, and seek to validate claims put before us. As life's problems go, this is a rather pleasant and rewarding one to have. We are concerned about imparting our nation's core values to future generations of Americans—be they youngsters in the inner city or Boy Scouts or graduate business students at Krannert. *Our four main areas of giving through the Dauch Foundation are education, youth development, morality, and health care.* We feel that they are very worthy values and investments in our American way of life.

22

The Future of Manufacturing

The world power that loses its manufacturing base will cease to be a world power.
—*Akio Morita, Founder of Sony Corporation*

There has been a great deal of hand-wringing about the sad state of America's economy in recent years by politicians, economists, and pundits who seem baffled and confused. They offer competing explanations for what is going on. They all agree it's bad, real bad, the weakest economy since the Great Depression of the 1930s, but are at a loss about what to do about it. Our government is sinking in a sea of red ink, that national debt is accumulating at unprecedented speed, unemployment remains stuck at an historically high level, poverty is rising (to 43.6 million—the highest number in the fifty-one years records have been kept), home foreclosures are an epidemic, economic growth is sputtering, and business investment is anemic. Worst of all is a creeping feeling of discontent among our citizens that our system has lost its regenerative power. We have had recessions before, but we always snapped out of it. This time seems different.

It *is* different. This time one factor contributing to the weakness of our economy is the erosion of our manufacturing base. When previous recessions ended in the post–World War II era, millions of manufacturing workers were recalled to their jobs. Not this time. Since 2001, America has suffered 42,400 factories shuttered, of which about 75 percent employed 500 or more workers at one time. Last year more than 1.2 billion cell phones were manufactured around the world, but not one in the United States. In 1959, manufacturing represented 28 percent of U.S. economic output; today it is less than half that. We have lost 8 million manufacturing jobs since they peaked at 19.6 million in 1979, and they were good jobs paying more than those in other sectors. As a result, many of our once great manufacturing cities—like my adopted home towns of Flint and Detroit—have fallen on very hard times.

Starting with policy makers in Washington, D.C., and continuing with the attitudes of Americans, we must become recommitted to making things. Our political leaders spend a lot of time complaining about the aggressive trade policies of our major competitors. They would do well to stop complaining about them and start learning from them.

For example, on February 24, 2011, American Axle & Manufacturing received a high-level delegation of eight senior officials from the state of Guanajuato in central Mexico, led by Governor Juan Manuel Oliva. The following month we received another delegation of five senior government officials from Chongqing in central China. These were by no means the first such visits, because by then we had already built manufacturing plants in Mexico and China. Foreign delegations come to Detroit to see us because they are eager for us to build manufacturing facilities in their countries, or—as with these two groups—to expand what we have already built. They travel long distances—more than twenty hours in the air for the Chinese—to tell us they appreciate our ability to manufacture quality products, and to ask what they can do to assist us. Do we require better transportation? Better training of workers? Resolution of regulatory issues? Subsidized energy? More generous tax incentives? Whatever they can do to help and encourage us to continue investing in their countries, within reason, they will do. They appreciate the importance of manufacturing to their countries. They clearly want our business, and to provide their people with jobs—manufacturing jobs.

As an athlete, I have always understood that when evenly matched teams play, the team that wants victory the most will usually win. The Chinese and Mexicans—among many others—understand how important this competition is and they are determined to win. We are in danger of losing because our leaders, at least at the national level, are not committed to making things—and winning.

THE MIRACLE OF MANUFACTURING

During the Middle Ages, a group of aspiring thinkers known as alchemists invested countless hours trying to invent something called a "philosopher's stone," which they believed would transform base metals into gold. They were unsuccessful.

Modern manufacturing has gone the alchemists one better. Instead of transforming base metals into gold, we transform base metals into cars, trucks, computers, robots, ovens, tractors, advanced medical devices, airplanes, pharmaceuticals, iPods, earth-moving equipment—the host of modern marvels that prolong and enhance the quality of human life. Any legitimate business enterprise benefits mankind, but manufacturing, the transformation of raw materials into useful products, is where real wealth is created. It also drives job creation.

United States manufacturing began to take root in the late nineteenth century, but it truly came into its own during World War II when American manufacturing produced 296,429 aircraft, 102,351 tanks and self-propelled guns, 372,431 artillery pieces, 47 million tons of artillery ammunition, 87,620 warships, and 44 billion rounds of small-arms ammunition. It was reliably reported that when the German dictator Adolf Hitler was informed of this astounding production, he dismissed it as propaganda. He did not believe any country could produce so much war material. *We did; he died.* Much of that material went to the Soviet Union, which bore the brunt of German aggression during the war. At the Tehran Conference in late 1943, Soviet Premier Joseph Stalin proposed a toast "to American production without which this war would have been lost."

When the war ended, economists predicted a major recession would occur when wartime assembly lines were shut down and all those military people were dumped on the unemployment lines. Instead, millions of returning servicemen created a consumer economy like never seen before. War industries switched over to consumer goods—a major line being cars and trucks—and the returning veterans went to work making them. In the 1950s, President Dwight D. Eisenhower launched the Interstate Highway System that gave the car and truck industry an even bigger boost. My adopted home town of Detroit, already the auto capital of the world, prospered mightily. Back then, one out of every seven jobs in this country was related to the auto industry. That was the world I aspired to join when I was a youngster listening to trucks drive by our house at night, a nation on the move.

Yet success breeds complacency. The Detroit Big Three—GM, Ford, and Chrysler—were asleep at the switch when the Japanese and other foreign carmakers began flooding our shores with attractive new products built to high quality standards. By the time Detroit awoke to the challenge, the air was out of the tires. That reality was really brought home in 2009 when GM declared bankruptcy. Such an event, the downfall of our nation's once greatest company, would have been unthinkable even a few years before, but the world has changed. We cannot simply take our industrial leadership for granted anymore. There are no guarantees in life, only challenges and opportunities.

The simple reality is that while we were soaring high, basking in the glow of our postwar supremacy, other nations were rebuilding from the rubble of war and making great strides in launching new manufacturing enterprises. There is no great mystery why they plunged into manufacturing. Other nations aspire to prosperity just as we do, and they learned from us and others that prosperity begins with manufacturing.

This point cannot be emphasized nearly often enough—manufacturing is one of our primary means of creating wealth. It is a core generator of our nation's prosperity and a key contributor to job creation. For more than a decade, we have stood idly by and allowed foreign competitors to hijack major sectors of our manufacturing base. The economic inertia that afflicts our country today is a direct result of this passive inaction and the bloated cost structure that impairs our nation's business sector.

MANUFACTURING'S IMPACT

Manufacturing has substantially increased—and continues to increase—the American consumer's standard of living. Strong productivity gains, rapid advances in innovation, and intense international competition have led to actual deflation of the prices of manufactured goods—in stark contrast to the inflation that has accompanied services. Between 1995 and 2008, manufacturing prices decreased by 3 percent, while the overall price level increased by 33 percent! Falling prices for high quality manufactured goods offer a stark contrast to the soaring costs of health care and education.

The main value that manufacturing provides to consumers is that prices for goods have declined as consumer budgets continue to grow. A good example, and one I know a bit about, is that the producer price index for passenger cars in 2008 was 3.9 percent less than cars in 1995. But the most dramatic deflation has been in electronics. Prices for personal computers and workstations were 98.3 percent less in 2008 than a decade earlier on a quality adjusted basis. In that time, computer prices declined 33 percent a year. Manufacturing is doing more than its share to bring down the cost of living, and improving the quality of human life.

For too long, we have listened to free market economists assuring us that we really don't need manufacturing because we can prosper as a service economy. This is, quite simply, hogwash. Service industries have their place, but no people can maintain prosperity by taking in each other's laundry. Manufacturing made this country great, and if we aspire to maintain our greatness—we must recommit to manufacturing. We must make things.

"Americans have always passed off a more prosperous future to the next generation," said Jay Timmons, president of the National Association of Manufacturers (NAM). "A growing economy will ensure that we can continue this legacy. If our policy makers in Washington choose wisely, manufacturing can be the engine of economic growth for years to come."

There are two basic facts we need to keep in mind. First, we live in a global economy and cannot change that fact of life, and should not want to. Our economic system is built upon the concept of growth, and there are built-in limits to how much we can grow in our own country, given the relative saturation of our market and relatively small population. *A full 95 percent of the world's consumers—more than 7 billion people—live elsewhere, offering us a feast of opportunities for growth.*

Second, economic growth is not a zero-sum game. The fact that one manufacturing nation is doing well does not necessarily mean other nations are losing out. We can all grow together if we can establish fair trading rules and have them enforced.

WE'RE NUMBER ONE

Despite all of our troubles, the United States is still the world's largest manufacturing country in terms of dollar value of manufactured goods. According to Mark Perry, who teaches economics and finance at the University of Michigan at Flint, every year since 2004 U.S. manufacturing output has exceeded $2 trillion in constant 2005 dollars, twice the output produced in America's factories in the 1970s. In 2010, we produced about $100 billion more in manufactured goods than China did. In fact, we produce 21–22 percent of global manufactured products. That share has held steady since 1980. Standing alone, U.S. manufacturing today would rank as the sixth largest economy in the world. On the home front, manufacturing represents about 11.5 percent of our gross domestic product (GDP).

You see those "Made in China" stickers on socks and stuffed toys; sold in Walmart; you don't see the "Made in the USA" sticker on the satellites spinning overhead. Even if China should surge ahead of us one day, as it well could given its population advantage, that can mean more export opportunities for us.

Fears of China are widespread but I see China as a great opportunity. As I write, AAM has two plants in China, both of which are working at a rapid pace to keep up with demand. They are not sending products back here, but are selling into the vigorous Chinese market and elsewhere in Asia. For several years, AAM's profits overseas enabled it to cover mounting losses from our operations in the United States. That could not go on forever, of course, but the ability to turn profits overseas is key to the success of every important U.S. global enterprise.

We need to free ourselves from anxiety about foreign competition and embrace it for what it is—virtually endless opportunity. Our problems can be traced, not to Beijing or Tokyo but right back to our front door. We have lost our competitive edge and our spirit to accept challenge. As the comic strip character Pogo said years ago, "We have met the enemy, and he is us." We need an attitude transformation.

"There is no question that for American manufacturing to flourish, it has to export much more of its production," said Frank Vargo, the National Association of Manufacturers' international vice president for Economic Policy, and one of the smartest people in Washington. "The domestic U.S. market will not increase fast enough to sustain the continued economic growth needed for the profitability, investment and innovation that is imperative for American manufacturing to survive and prosper."

United States manufacturers export about $88 billion worth per month, more than $1 trillion a year and 57 percent of total exports. We are the world's third largest exporter after the European Union and China. Capital goods accounted for about 43 percent of those exports, and consumer goods only 14 percent. As befitting our advanced economy, our top export sectors were advanced technology products such as aerospace equipment, semiconductors, and scientific instruments.

That is impressive but we should export much more than we do. "Much needs to be done to participate more fully in growth markets around the world," said Vargo. "American manufacturing is a weak performer when it comes to exporting. Right now, of the fifteen major manufacturing economies, the United States ranks thirteenth in the proportion of its manufacturing output that is exported."

Much of our economic difficulty in recent years stems from our failure to concentrate on exports. We need a major push to get more small manufacturers into exporting. We also need to overcome the resistance—largely driven by labor unions—to free trade agreements (FTAs). There is simply no question that FTAs bring more business to the United States, and create more jobs. We actually enjoy a trade surplus of more than $20 billion a year with our FTA partners, including those in the North American Free Trade Agreement (NAFTA). Recent approval of FTAs with Panama, Colombia, and South Korea is a step in the right direction.

We do have a worrisome trade deficit, which is another reason why we need to focus on exports. But FTAs are not the problem. Our trade deficit is almost entirely with Asia: China 62 percent and Japan 19 percent while South Korea, Taiwan, and Malaysia account for another 13 percent.

Much of our trade deficit can be attributed to unfair trade practices, in particular the blatant currency manipulation that China uses to make its exports cheaper. Many U.S. manufacturers, especially smaller ones, report that China comes to our country selling products for less than we pay for raw materials. No way can that be legitimate. Workers in China earn less than American workers, but not that much less. We are being had.

Unfortunately, when China buys U.S. currency and debt instruments to keep its own currency undervalued, it provides funding for our huge annual budget deficits which have lately drifted into the stratosphere—more than $1.3 trillion in 2011, the same as the year before, as the federal debt passed $15 trillion! We are essentially borrowing from China to keep our government going and thus are in no position to challenge China's trade practices. This is a devil's bargain if ever I saw one, and it has been going on for years. Like so many of our wounds, this one is also self-inflicted.

I see this one-sided trade imbalance winding down in the not too distant future. As China grows and prospers, its people are demanding a bigger piece of the pie. As Chinese worker compensation and benefits increase, China's competitive advantage will erode. Also, the Chinese people are paying a fearsome price for their disregard of environmental and safety issues. As they move to reduce pollution and workplace hazards, this also will make production there more expensive, as happened here.

In fact, U.S. manufacturers are on the cutting edge of environmental protection technologies. China's growing investment in this area creates even more opportunities for U.S. exports.

OUTSOURCING

We hear a lot about "outsourcing" when U.S. companies are taken to task for investing in foreign countries. I would assume our plant in Mexico is a case in point.

United States labor unions detest that sort of investment because it deprives them of their ability to dictate wage and benefit levels and working conditions to U.S. companies. Their concern is well founded. Without question, our plant in Mexico was a critical factor in our ability to survive the 2008 UAW strike while continuing to supply GM with quality axles and drivetrains, but this was not a question of taking jobs away from the UAW—it was a question of survival. Had we knuckled under to the UAW's demands, an average UAW member's loaded compensation package at AAM would have been on its way north of $106 per hour! A clean Tier One supplier would have ceased to exist long before it got there. The UAW was more worried about their socialist agenda and ideology than representing the workers. The union was trying to pick winners and losers—again to the detriment of those they represent.

Most of our overseas plants—in China, India, Thailand, Brazil, and Poland—were built to serve the markets they are in, markets that in most cases are growing much faster than the U.S. market. Having successful ventures overseas makes U.S. corporations stronger at home, and better able to invest and provide opportunities at home. That is the global marketplace today, and AAM is part of it.

Instead of complaining about outsourcing, we need to promote insourcing—encouraging more foreign companies to invest in the United States. Just as foreign nations send delegations to AAM to encourage us to invest in their countries, we should send delegations to foreign-based corporations to encourage them to invest here.

INNOVATION

United States manufacturing has an impressive record of innovation. In large measure, it is simply a matter of survival. We are competing with nations around the globe where labor is much cheaper than here, and where governments actively support rather than hinder their manufacturing sectors. To compete successfully, we must become ever more productive, and we need to constantly develop new, more advanced products.

There is simply no question that manufacturing is driving the productivity train. Between 1987 and 2008, manufacturing productivity grew by 103 percent, almost double the 56 percent increase in the rest of the business sector. While manufacturing accounted for an average of 15 percent of GDP during that time frame, it was responsible for about 22 percent of productivity growth.

"Modern manufacturing is dynamic, efficient and technology-driven," said NAM's Timmons. "Manufacturing has moved into the twenty-first century, but our country's policies are stuck in the past. We need twenty-first century policies on investment, trade, taxation, the workforce, and innovation to maintain America's global manufacturing leadership."

Our nation's overall commitment to R&D is competitive at 2.6 percent of GDP, modestly above the 2.3 percent average of the thirty nations in the Organization for Economic Cooperation and Development (OECD). Only Japan at 3.4 percent exceeds our commitment, but since our economy is much larger than Japan's, we are investing more than Japan in R&D. Manufacturing accounts for about half of all public and private R&D in the country. Between 20–25 percent of all firms in leading-edge biotech and software development are manufacturers. Further, the industrial sector still dominates materials synthesis development, accounting for 70 percent of all U.S. firms engaged in this area of technological development.

In this critical area, too, we are being challenged. Our foreign competitors are well aware of the advantages we derive from R&D, and are moving aggressively to close the gap with us. Meanwhile, our investment in R&D as a percentage of GDP is declining. Even when AAM's fortunes were at its lowest ebb, we did not sacrifice R&D. We did not save our way into bankruptcy. We kept our faith in the future.

EMPLOYMENT IN MANUFACTURING

As Shakespeare wrote in *Hamlet,* "Aye, there's the rub." In the global marketplace of today, it is simply not feasible to pay people the premium wages and benefits that historically have characterized U.S. manufacturing for performing simple tasks. Times have changed. This evolution has had a devastating impact on millions of people, not to mention the nation's economy. For generations, manufacturing has offered an entry into the middle class for Americans with limited education and skill sets. If you could get through high school, and maybe not even that far, you could land a basic job in a factory. Then you had it made. You could buy a house in the suburbs and send your kids to college.

That door, unfortunately, is no longer open. Millions of people who have been displaced from manufacturing jobs are struggling. They lack the education and skills they need to pursue careers in other fields, or reenter manufacturing. Their fate is often tragic as are the implications for our country. We have some programs for helping displaced workers acquire the skills they need to find new opportunities, but they are scattered around and unfocused. We can and must do more for these people, for their sakes and for ours.

I have seen and participated in this evolution at AAM. When we purchased the original assets from GM, the average associate had about a ninth grade education or the equivalent. Within ten years, that had gone to the equivalent of a sophomore in college! What that means in effect is that a typical associate at AAM has a community college diploma. To work in modern manufacturing today, whether in the auto or any other industry, you need a strong background in mathematics, science, computers and communications. Modern manufacturing is not your father's factory floor; it is exponentially advanced.

For all that, the United States still has almost 12 million employees in manufacturing, and those 12 million jobs, because of the nature of manufacturing, support another 6.6 million jobs in America in other sectors. *Overall, about one in six private sector jobs in this country depend on the manufacturing base.*

The importance of manufacturing jobs cannot be overemphasized. Modern manufacturing is complex, and creates demand for raw materials, energy, construction and services from a broad array of support industries. In addition, many functions previously done within manufacturing companies—from back office and accounting to some kinds of logistics—are now contracted to other service providers, and not formally included as part of the manufacturing workforce. This so-called "backward linkage" measures an industry's impact on the overall economy, and of all the business sectors, manufacturing's backward linkage is the most significant. *Specifically, every dollar in final sales of manufactured goods supports $1.40 in output from other sectors of the economy.* It is this dynamic impact on local economies that motivates states and local governments to offer incentives to attract new manufacturing plants. The politicians in Washington may not understand how important manufacturing is to the country, but many leaders at the state and local level surely do.

Manufacturing jobs are also highly desirable because they pay more, about 9 percent more than the average in other parts of the economy, and usually come with generous benefits, including health insurance. Nearly three-fourths of all manufacturers provide health insurance, and more than eight of ten of their employees participate. All manufacturing companies with more than 1,000 employees provide health insurance, including AAM.

Health insurance does not come cheap. Between 1999 and 2008, the cost of family insurance premiums in manufacturing had risen from $5,788 to $12,181. The 8.6 percent annual increase over nine years was double the rate posted by the Producer Price Index, which reflects the change in prices manufacturers charge for their output. Providing health insurance with its mounting cost is a source of continuing concern. *We have to get medical costs under control in this country.* They are a major factor in making the United States less competitive.

The ultimate irony is that despite the loss of millions of manufacturing jobs over the past decade, one of the biggest problems facing U.S. manufacturers today is finding people with the skills they need to work in modern manufacturing. There is a monstrous gap in our education and training infrastructure. Our public schools are focused on sending bright students to four-year universities, but many of those bright young people should be pursuing careers in our advanced industries. Unfortunately, the public schools are simply out of synch with the needs of the modern workplace.

The Manufacturing Institute, with which I was once affiliated, has a wonderful program called "Dream It! Do It!" that brings public schools, employers, and community colleges together to educate young people about opportunities in industry and help them acquire the skills they need to seize those opportunities. But our country needs a more expansive vision, something bigger and more comprehensive to reach more of our young people.

Our competitors in Japan understand this challenge and have a great program called Kosen that produces about 50,000 graduates each year from a five-year program that prepares them for industrial careers. The students are required to spend time in an actual workplace, integrating abstract subjects such as algebra with the use of cutting edge machinery. Wonder of wonders, local businesses are involved, contributing to the curriculum, which is regularly updated in response to changing technologies and workplace needs. On average, each Kosen graduate can expect at least twenty job offers! If we had that kind of a system today, U.S. manufacturing would be much more competitive, and unemployment would be much less than it is.

"Manufacturing in this country requires an increasingly skilled and educated workforce," said Timmons. "Our challenge is to nurture that talent as our competitors do if we want to continue to lead in the global marketplace."

This is not rocket science. We can do this.

A NATIONAL CHALLENGE

"This country didn't become a world powerhouse by striving to be average," said Timmons. "If we want to maintain our mantle of economic leadership, we must focus on growth and competitiveness, and that means prioritizing manufacturing and ensuring its success."

Largely because of the absence of anything resembling a coherent manufacturing policy in Washington, domestic industry finds itself at a decided disadvantage against foreign competitors whose governments actually promote their interests. Why our government cannot figure this out is anyone's guess, but across the board U.S. manufacturers are operating at a distinct disadvantage against our foreign competitors. For example:

- Taxes: High corporate tax rates are a significant drag on U.S. manufacturing. The combined average federal-state tax rate of 39 percent has held constant for years while our competitors have been aggressively cutting their tax rates. *Our tax rate is 7.6 percent higher on average than those of our nine major trading partners.* Cutting the U.S. corporate tax rate by 5 percentage points would increase manufacturing output by $156 billion over 10 years and create 500,000 jobs. We really need a tax system that deals with this problem.
- Employee benefits: Health care and pensions are a major cost item for manufacturers, virtually all of which provide health insurance to employees. Yet because of the soaring cost of health insurance, a growing number of smaller manufacturers are cutting back on coverage or eliminating it altogether, and the cost of pensions has been so extreme that most companies are moving away from defined benefit plans. Our nation faces a dramatic challenge to rein in soaring health care costs, but the health reform plan enacted by the Obama Administration will serve mainly to drive costs even higher. It is yet another factor encouraging manufacturers to move production offshore.
- Tort litigation: The U.S. tort system is unique in the industrialized world in that each party is responsible for all of its legal costs. This fact, combined with large potential costs for punitive damages and compensatory awards, means that plaintiffs have strong financial incentives to use (or abuse) the tort system for frivolous or unfounded lawsuits. In addition, class-action lawsuits can inflate damages awarded, even if the majority of affected individuals never claim their share. *Many trial attorneys view corporate treasuries the same way bank robbers view bank vaults—that's where the money is.* It has become routine to file unfounded lawsuits against corporations in the expectation that the defendants will settle merely to avoid court costs. In nearly all other countries, plaintiffs

are required to pay for all of the defendant's legal costs if the judgment is in the defendant's favor.

- Pollution abatement: It is a perfectly viable social goal that everyone shares, but too often rules and requirements are imposed without adequate consideration of their economic impact. Many of the activists groups promoting stricter regulation are indifferent to the impact on companies that must divert funds from worker compensation, shareholder returns, and capital investment. United States manufacturers are spending $160 billion a year on pollution abatement.

- There is some good news here in that our pollution abatement costs have been declining in recent years, while those of our main competitors—most obviously China—have been increasing as they come to grips with the environmental degradation caused by their rapid industrialization. Also, U.S. companies have made remarkable advances in pollution control technology which we are now selling to developing countries.

- Energy costs: These have been an increasing concern to U.S. manufacturers who consume about one-third of all of the nation's energy. Wildly fluctuating energy prices in recent years have made life difficult for manufacturers who need stable prices in order to plan future investments. *The lack of a coherent, comprehensive national energy policy in the United States has caused us much unneeded difficulty.*

According to a study performed by the Manufacturing Institute and the Manufacturers Alliance/MAPI, all of *these five issues together put us at a 20 percent cost disadvantage for U.S. manufacturers against our nine major trading partners*—including Germany, Japan, Canada, Mexico, and China. This information has been available for years, but I have yet to see or hear of anyone in our government in Washington attempting to call attention to it or to address it in any meaningful way. In any business, a 20 percent disadvantage is serious if not debilitating. The really amazing thing is that despite that disadvantage, we are doing as well as we are. What a difference it would make if we could only get Washington working for us instead of against us.

A GREAT NEW AGE OF MANUFACTURING

I am optimistic that our political leaders will eventually figure it out and embrace a set of policies—taxes, regulations, trade, legal reforms, education, and training—that will foster a renewed commitment to manufacturing, but it must begin with a fundamental recognition of the importance of manufacturing to our economy and our future. Without such a basic shift in thinking, our best efforts will be hit or miss, one step forward and two steps back, like it has been for many decades.

I am a manufacturing guy, and I freely admit to a pro-manufacturing bias, but I do honestly believe we are on the threshold of a great new age of manufacturing—an age in which the United States will solidify and expand its global leadership. Despite all of our difficulties in recent years, we have managed to preserve our world leadership—and not by accident. We are still the most innovative people in the world, and manufacturing is the seedbed of that creativity, where new ideas are born and translated into reality. Our competitors recognize this is the key to our strength, and they strive to emulate us, but it takes more than money and determination. We operate in a free enterprise system built upon scientific method that both encourages innovation and protects intellectual property. Innovation is very much an outgrowth of cultural values, and nowhere in the world are those core values more cherished and refined than right here in the United States.

It also bears saying that over the past decade, the world has thrown everything at U.S. manufacturing but the kitchen sink. We have taken all the shots—fair and foul—and though we have seemed a bit wobbly at times, our strength remains supreme and our determination undiminished. United States manufacturing today is leaner, meaner and more flexible than ever before. To be sure, we have some formidable challengers out there, but we have taken their best shots and we are still here, achieving new levels of quality, productivity, and creativity, and ever and always on the cutting edge of advanced technology.

As for the future of the U.S. auto industry, and my adopted home town of Detroit, I am a bit less optimistic. We continue to be afflicted by the *same old entitlement mentality* that got us into this fix in the first place. I see scant evidence that the UAW has learned any fundamental lessons or is willing to modify its confrontational mentality in any meaningful way. Already, UAW leaders are sounding the call to regain the ground they lost during the bankruptcy period. They seem to have no understanding that the world has changed, for better or worse, and that they must change with it. For the U.S. auto industry to survive into the future, it simply must bring labor costs and operating flexibility into balance with those of our global competitors. It must embrace lean manufacturing, which means steady elimination of restrictive work rules, and the rank and file must be made to understand that the historic absenteeism disease is no longer acceptable and cannot be tolerated. If the UAW cannot or will not make this transition, the next inevitable downturn in the market will spell the end of the recovery in the domestic auto industry. The American taxpayer will be in no mood for another bailout.

I hope to live long enough to see one or more U.S. auto companies listed again among the Dow Jones 30. But even if I don't, I do believe U.S. manufacturing will continue to grow and prosper, and lead our country back to a solid economic footing. It is already happening. We have only begun to show what we can do. Manufacturers in the U.S.A. have accepted the challenge of world competition and are poised for great things in the years ahead. I am fiercely proud of the creation, success, and sustainability of AAM based in Detroit, Michigan. We are one of America's premier global automotive manufacturers. We have done it against all odds. It has been greatly fulfilling.

EPILOGUE

It had been a dream of mine to become CEO of a Detroit-based automotive company. I will always be grateful that it happened, but how it happened, where it happened, and why it happened were totally different from what I expected. I was too impatient for it to happen at GM. I was too capitalistic for it to happen in the socialistic world of Volkswagen. And I was too product, people, and performance oriented for it to happen amid the bureaucratic and political environment of the Chrysler Corporation.

I studied market forces and real-world consumer needs and found the opportunity I was looking for under my very nose. A vast restructuring of the U.S. auto industry, in response to the pressures of globalization, was under way. GM was re-sourcing many parts, components, and systems outside its traditional business model. It was a new world in the auto industry, bringing with it new opportunities for visionary leadership.

Thus, working with a small investor group, I asserted my independent opportunity to lead a multibillion-dollar, multinational company in the auto industry based in Detroit, Michigan. This twenty-year business odyssey (1993–2012) began with the closing of an asset purchase sale of GM's Final Drive and Forging Business Unit that would become AAM on March 1, 1994. As the man who carried the big risk-taking function as CEO, I knew we would have to move quickly and we did. We cleaned up the mess, changed the culture, adopted modern technologies, modernized the product portfolio, and committed to world-class quality. Within a few years, we became a public company and almost immediately went global. Soon AAM was making tremendous strides in productivity and quality—and earning money!

Yet as we rounded the bend into the new millennium, I knew AAM's Achilles' heel was still our uncompetitive labor costs that stifled earnings and made it difficult for us to acquire new and replacement business. We finally stood up to the UAW in 2008, absorbed the inevitable strike, and by February 25, 2012, we had eliminated the labor legacy contracts and bloated cost structure that was holding us back. After a brief flirtation with disaster during the 2009 economic upheaval, we emerged intact and free of the labor cost ball and chain. Now we are fully engaged in North America, South America, Europe, and Asia, and selling into Australia—all profitably.

At long last, my dream had become a reality. It has been a tough slog, but we have assembled a balanced team of experts in planning, design, engineering, procurement, human resources, manufacturing, quality, finance, sales, and information technology; systemized the organization to minimize the likelihood of a personality driven or politicized bureaucracy taking root; fostered a culture based on integrity of human relationships, products, and financials; and—last but certainly not least—committed to building perfect, "bulletproof" quality into all of our products. For the last ten years, our PPM has been at world-class, single-digit performance levels as measured by our customers. None of this came easy; nothing worthwhile ever does.

AAM has always been about adapting to and meeting the rigors of the ever-changing customer base and marketplace. We set ambitious goals and base them upon real-world data, trends, and facts, not whim or intuition as has often been the case in the U.S. auto industry. We rely upon economic metrics that are essential to business success.

I have taken care to plan for succession and progression so that AAM will continue after I have passed from the scene, preserving the cultural values, strategic principles, and commitment to excellence that we have worked so hard to implant. This is an issue of keen personal interest to me based on Dauch family history. I had an uncle, Jake Dauch, who in the early 1900s was one of the first producers of gasoline tractors and engines in the United States. He had several plants and hundreds of employees. He was a successful industrialist by anyone's definition and business was good, but he had an inadequate succession plan. He was unexpectedly killed in an automobile accident and his company ended up being sold off, piece by piece, because he had not planned sufficiently for the future. I learned from that history and have been careful to lead the plan for AAM's future. I do not know how long I will live—no one does—but if I go tomorrow, this company will continue to grow and prosper. Proper succession planning is essential to the long-term prospects of any business enterprise.

They say failure is an orphan but success has many parents. I am keenly aware that my professional success was made possible by the able support and assistance of many others. I thank my wife, Sandy, who has supported me these many years; my original cofounder J. W. McLernon; and our original investors Ray Park and Mort Harris. I owe a debt of gratitude to the Blackstone Group for their effective and timely partnership in helping AAM go public and expand globally. And special thanks go to all of the AAM associates who helped build the company and made it successful in a wildly demanding global automotive market.

As always, despite adversity and hard times, I continue to believe in the future—for AAM, for U.S. manufacturing, and for our country. We have some mountains to climb, some oceans to navigate, and some valleys to get through, but we will survive and prosper. The American dream is the greatest dream the world has ever known. It will sustain us and future generations for a long time to come. We are now **delivering power** globally. God bless America!

ACKNOWLEDGMENTS

Writing a book is a labor of love—nonetheless, it is hard work. I should know because I authored *Passion for Manufacturing* in 1993. Thus, when I decided to author a second book, I fully knew the time, commitment, and trusting team that would be needed to develop a complete manuscript for this important project.

I made my decision to proceed with my second book in June 2010.

My friend and respected author and writer, Hank H. Cox, would be my choice to help me write my new book. When I early on approached Hank, he responded with his sincere enthusiasm, full-speed-ahead attitude, and a total commitment of purpose to be my collaborator and writer. Thank you, Hank.

My second critical team member would be my long-term friend, fellow Global Automotive executive, world-class authority on quality and the wheres and hows to accomplish it, Allan Rae. Allan would be my personal deputy executive, coordinating, planning, and helping execute the inordinate amount of detail and data needed to prepare a full-scale and balanced approach to develop this book. He has done an incredibly good job in helping to compile all the research and interviews required to bring this compelling story to life. Thank you, Allan.

Allan had to establish an intelligent cadence to developing time well spent by me with him and Hank. From those many and exhaustive sessions came details about my life, my family, my education, my automotive career and the exhausting work of helping to create, lead, preserve, and grow American Axle & Manufacturing. These men helped me with dozens of important editorial suggestions.

Allan arranged, with my coaching, more than sixty critical interviews with talented professionals that had helped me, over decades of work, to create a new and effective business model for the American automotive industry that had struggled since the early 1970s to find methods to compete globally. Allan's calm, disciplined, and intellectual way was most effective and respected by all contributors.

A third important professional is B. G. "Bob" Mathis. I wanted my long-term friend—and confidant—Bob to help me and our team with the important task of editing, checking facts, and utilizing his great command of simplifying the best of the English language. Bob is an absolute wordsmith. Thank you, Bob.

Many people were helpful, in particular, in discussing the early years of AAM. Six specific contributors (alphabetically) were Marion Cumo, Tom Delanoy, George Dellas, Bob Mathis, Rick Rossmann, and Gary Witosky. They were invaluable in providing facts and answering detailed questions. They had the ability to remember and produce factual documents of the critical 150 legal agreements that helped successfully cement the asset purchase sale from GM to create the new stand-alone company, AAM.

At AAM, we had many turbulent years: the beginning (1993–1998), the brutal labor maturation (2004–2008), and the global economic recession and meltdown of the domestic automotive industry (2009). We tried hard to put this all into a proper business perspective as we continued our earnest dedication to our customers and the market.

I felt a selective group of photos would be helpful in this book. A long-trusted and reliable friend, George Nagher, was selected to help our extended team on this assignment. I am grateful to George for his excellent work and personal recommendations in the selection process.

Along the way, with Hank H. Cox's able assistance, I wisely picked Robert Wilson to be my literary agent. He has done an exceptional job on what I assigned him to do. A most critical task was to sort through many qualified publishers for our book. Robert, Hank, Allan, and Bob Mathis guided me toward the highly respected St. Martin's Press. I heeded their advice. They are an excellent firm and executive team to work with.

In October 2011, I first spoke with St. Martin's editor in chief, George Witte. For over twenty-five years George has been a busy editor, publisher, and poet. George has worked at St. Martin's—an imprint of MacMillan Publishers—since 1984. He has edited hundreds of authors. I could tell by our first interview that he liked the story and we would be able to work together.

On November 7, 2011, I took my team—Hank H. Cox, Robert Wilson, and Allan Rae—with me to the landmark Flatiron Building, St. Martin's Press's headquarters in New York City, where Fifth Avenue and Broadway converge.

ACKNOWLEDGMENTS

George Witte was thoughtful enough to convene a large fourteen-person delegation of their staff to meet with me and my team. Included in this meeting was
my first meeting with their extraordinary president, Sally Richardson. We had
a most enjoyable business and social gathering.

I have been blessed in my life with a loving and hardworking family: my
parents, my sister and brothers, most important my wife, Sandy (fifty-two
years), our four "Monuments of Life" children, and eighteen grandchildren and
great-grandchildren. I see this book as an extension of all of them. They are
who I have learned from. I have enjoyed living my life by the five F's:

1. FAITH
2. FAMILY
3. FRIENDS
4. FREEDOM
5. FUTURE

This book has truly been a labor of my love for America's freedom-loving
society—and our continued desire to be competitive and a manufacturing
power in the world's global economy.

WRITER'S NOTE

I first met Dick Dauch in 2003 when he became chairman of the National Association of Manufacturers (NAM), where I was then serving as vice president of Media Relations. Dick has a presence about him that I found compelling. He is the real thing, an entrepreneur willing to take risks and walk through walls to reach his goals, the kind of leader men and women will follow, no matter how tough the challenge. We hit it off from the beginning. Years later, after I retired from the NAM, he asked me to take on this book project for him. I leaped at the chance, knowing this would be a memorable story. I already had two books under my belt, but I knew this one would be in a class of its own.

My chore was greatly facilitated by the able support of two key guys Dick assigned to support me: Allan Rae and George Nagher, both with long histories with AAM and intricate knowledge of the organization, its history, its people, and of Dick himself. Allan and George are also two of the most patient, good-humored people I have ever met. Throughout the almost two years of this project, we never had a cross word among us. I could not have done it without them.

I spent countless hours with Dick, learning his story, picking up his cadence, and absorbing his point of view. In presuming to serve as a writer for a prominent leader, the writer must strive to acquire that leader's voice, and sublimate his own. Dick paid me the highest compliment by saying that in reading my drafts, it was like listening to himself speak. Dick has personally reviewed and edited every sentence several times to make it his own. This is truly Dick Dauch's story told in his own words.

I also interviewed more than sixty other people who have worked with Dick and for Dick over the years, some before he created AAM, others who helped him create AAM, and more than a few who belong on both lists. Some were in senior management and others further down in the organization. All were cooperative and forthcoming, spending many hours with me making recorded interviews, often in more than one session. Throughout the text, I have used their voices to tell the AAM story, supplementing Dick's personal accounts, a technique which I believe makes the narrative flow more smoothly. Dick Dauch will be the first to tell you this is not just his story. He has achieved great things because he has assembled a great cast of characters at AAM and empowered them to do things they did not know they were capable of doing. He makes jobs doable, enjoyable, and productive.

I have toured AAM facilities in the U.S., and joined the board of directors during a meeting at the AAM plant in Guanajuato, Mexico. I spent hours interviewing several members of the board. I toured the facilities Dick and Sandy Dauch helped build for the Boy Scouts and the Boys and Girls Clubs of Southeast Michigan in Detroit, and also visited Purdue University to meet with senior administrators and tour the Dick and Sandy Dauch Alumni Center, one of the most stunning buildings on a campus rich in fine architecture. I went to Ashland University in Ohio, a school I had never heard of, to tour the Dick and Sandy Dauch College of Business and Economics, a marvelous, state-of-the-art facility that is preparing future business leaders of America.

I spent months immersed in dozens of bound volumes of newspaper clippings, speeches, magazine articles, and transcripts from TV and radio news programs that chronicled the rise of AAM from 1994 to the present. I am especially grateful to George Nagher for helping navigate me through this teeming mound of paper.

All in all, this has been for me a voyage of discovery, of meeting fascinating people, and learning the dramatic story of one of our country's great corporate sagas—a saga that continues.

Dick Dauch's story is a story of one man's faith—in himself, in his family, in his God, in his company, in his country, and in the future. He does not just preach solid values—he lives them. There is no contradiction between his talk and his walk. If his competitors and adversaries have underestimated him at times, it may be because they have rarely encountered anyone with such rock solid integrity and gritty determination to succeed. If veteran managers have come out of retirement to work for him time and again over the years, it may be because they are drawn to inspired leadership. And if AAM survived the strike of '08 and the economic crash of '09 without going bankrupt, while most of its competitors went under, it may be because the man in the front office simply refused to buckle. He has the will and determination to lead people to success.

I took on this job because I believed Dick Dauch is one of that rare breed of visionary American entrepreneurs who overcome immense obstacles to build something great. After working my way through this story, I know damn well he is. I will always be grateful to Dick and his CEO, Sandy Dauch, for offering me this opportunity and giving me all the support I needed to get it right.

—Hank H. Cox

INDEX

WHEN MAIDENS MOURN

WHEN MAIDENS MOURN

A Sebastian St. Cyr Mystery

C. S. HARRIS

AN OBSIDIAN MYSTERY

OBSIDIAN
Published by New American Library,
a division of Penguin Group (USA) Inc.,
375 Hudson Street, New York, New York 10014, USA
Penguin Group (Canada), 90 Eglinton Avenue East, Suite 700, Toronto,
Ontario M4P 2Y3, Canada (a division of Pearson Penguin Canada Inc.)
Penguin Books Ltd., 80 Strand, London WC2R 0RL, England
Penguin Ireland, 25 St. Stephen's Green, Dublin 2,
Ireland (a division of Penguin Books Ltd.)
Penguin Group (Australia), 250 Camberwell Road, Camberwell,
Victoria 3124, Australia (a division of Pearson Australia Group Pty. Ltd.)
Penguin Books India Pvt. Ltd., 11 Community Centre,
Panchsheel Park, New Delhi - 110 017, India
Penguin Group (NZ), 67 Apollo Drive, Rosedale, Auckland 0632,
New Zealand (a division of Pearson New Zealand Ltd.)
Penguin Books (South Africa) (Pty.) Ltd., 24 Sturdee Avenue,
Rosebank, Johannesburg 2196, South Africa

Penguin Books Ltd., Registered Offices:
80 Strand, London WC2R 0RL, England

First published by Obsidian, an imprint of New American Library,
a division of Penguin Group (USA) Inc.

First Printing, March 2012
1   3   5   7   9   10   8   6   4   2

Copyright © The Two Talers, LLC, 2012
All rights reserved

OBSIDIAN and logo are trademarks of Penguin Group (USA) Inc.

LIBRARY OF CONGRESS CATALOGING-IN-PUBLICATION DATA:

Harris, C. S.
When maidens mourn: a Sebastian St. Cyr mystery/C. S. Harris.
p. cm.
ISBN 978-0-451-23577-0
1. Saint Cyr, Sebastian (Fictitious character)—Fiction. 2. Private investigators—England—
London—Fiction. 3. London (England)—History—19th century—Fiction. I. Title.
PS3566.R5877W476 2012
813'.54—dc23   2011049244

Set in Weiss
Designed by Elke Sigal

Printed in the United States of America

For my cousin

Kaitlyn Johnston

Out flew the web and floated wide;
The mirror crack'd from side to side;
"The curse is come upon me," cried
The Lady of Shalott.

—*Alfred, Lord Tennyson* (1809–1892),
"The Lady of Shalott"

The place at which he stopped was no more than a mound,
partly surrounded by a ditch, from which it derived the name
of Camlet Moat. A few hewn stones there were, which had
escaped the fate of many others . . . vestiges, just sufficient to
show that "here in former times the hand of man had been."

—*Sir Walter Scott* (1771–1832),
The Fortunes of Nigel

WHEN MAIDENS MOURN

Chapter 1

Camlet Moat, Trent Place, England
Sunday, 2 August 1812

Tessa Sawyer hummed a nervous tune beneath her breath as she pushed through the tangled brush and bracken edging the black waters of the ancient moat. She was very young—just sixteen at her next birthday. And though she tried to tell herself she was brave, she knew she wasn't. She could feel her heart pounding in her narrow chest, and her hands tingled as if she'd been sitting on them. When she'd left the village, the night sky above had been clear and bright with stars. But here, deep in the wood, all was darkness and shadow. From the murky, stagnant water beside her rose an eerie mist, thick and clammy.

It should have wafted cool against her cheek. Instead, she felt as if the heavy dampness were stealing her breath, suffocating her with an unnatural heat and a sick dread of the forbidden. She paused to swipe a shaky hand across her sweaty face and heard a rustling in the distance, the soft plop of something hitting the water.

Choking back a whimper, she spun about, ready to run. But this was Lammas, a time sacred to the ancient goddess. They said that at midnight on this night, if a maiden dipped a cloth into the holy well that lay on the northern edge of the isle of Camlet Moat and then tied her offering to a branch of the rag tree that overhung the well, her prayer would be answered. Not only that, but maybe, just maybe, the White Lady herself would appear, to bless the maid and offer her the wisdom and guidance that a motherless girl such as Tessa yearned for with all her being.

No one knew exactly who the White Lady was. Father Clark insisted that if the lady existed at all—which he doubted—she could only be the Virgin Mary. But local legend said the White Lady was one of the grail maidens of old, a chaste virgin who'd guarded the sacred well since before the time of Arthur and Guinevere and the Knights of the Round Table. And then there were those who whispered that the lady was actually Guinevere, ever young, ever beautiful, ever glorious.

Forcing herself to go on, Tessa clenched her fist around the strip of white cloth she was bringing as an offering. She could see the prow of the small dinghy kept at the moat by Sir Stanley Winthrop, on whose land she trespassed. Its timbers old and cracked, its aged paint worn and faded, it rocked lightly at the water's edge as if touched by an unseen current.

It was not empty.

Tessa drew up short. A lady lay crumpled against the stern, her hair a dark cascade of curls around a pale, motionless face. She was young yet and slim, her gown an elegant flowing confection of gossamer muslin sashed with peach satin. She had her head tipped back, her neck arched; her eyes were open but sightless, her skin waxen.

And from a jagged rent high across her pale breast showed a dried rivulet of darkness where her life's blood had long since drained away.

Chapter 2

*D*riven from his sleep by troublesome dreams, Sebastian St. Cyr, Viscount Devlin, leaned into his outstretched arms, fingers curling around the sill of his wife's open bedroom window. He'd learned long before of the dangers that lurk in those quicksilver moments that come between darkness and the dawn. When the world hovers between night and day, a man could get lost in his own tortured memories of the past if he wasn't careful.

He drew a deep, shuddering breath into his lungs. But the dawn was unusually warm, the air too parched and dusty to bring any real relief. He was aware of a sheen of sweat coating his naked skin; a humming like bees working a hive droned behind his temples. The urge to wrap his hand around a cool glass of brandy was strong.

He resisted it.

Behind him, the woman who just four days before had become his Viscountess stirred in her bed. Their marriage was so recent—and the reasons behind it so complicated—that he sometimes found himself still thinking of her not as Hero Devlin but as "Miss Jarvis," formidable daughter of Charles, Lord Jarvis, the brilliant but ruthless cousin of the King who served as the acknowledged power behind the fragile regency of the Prince of Wales. Once, Jarvis had sworn to destroy Sebastian, however long it might take. Sebastian knew that his marriage to Jarvis's daughter had not changed that.

Looking over his shoulder, he watched now as Hero came slowly awake. She lay motionless for a moment. Then her eyelids fluttered open and she shifted her head against the pillow to stare at him from across a darkened room hung with blue silk and gilded mirrors and scented with lavender.

"Did I wake you?" he asked. "I am sorry."

"Don't be ridiculous."

Sebastian huffed a soft laugh. There was nothing either indulgent or coquettish about Hero.

She slipped from the bed, bringing with her the fine linen sheet to wrap around her nakedness as she crossed to him. In the darkness of the night, she could come to him without inhibition, a willing and passionate lover. But during the day . . .

During the day they remained in many ways essentially strangers to each other, two people who inhabited the same house yet were self-conscious and awkward when they chanced upon each other in the hall or met over breakfast. Only at night could they seem to put aside the wary distrust that had characterized their relationship from the beginning. Only in darkness could they forget the deep, dangerous antagonism that lay between his house and hers and come together as man and woman.

He was aware of the gray light of dawn stealing into the room. She hugged the sheet tighter around her.

"You never sleep," she said.

"I do. Sometimes."

She tipped her head to one side, her normally tidy brown hair tangled by last night's lovemaking. "Have you always had such troublesome dreams, or only since marrying the daughter of your worst enemy?"

Smiling faintly, he reached out to draw her to him.

She came stiffly, her forearms resting on his naked chest, creating some distance between them. She was a tall woman, nearly as tall as Sebastian himself, with her powerful father's aquiline countenance and Lord Jarvis's famous, disconcerting intelligence.

He said, "I'm told it's not uncommon for men to dream of war after they've returned home."

Her shrewd gray eyes narrowed with thoughts he could only guess at. "That's what you dream of? The war?"

He hesitated. "Mainly."

That night, he had indeed been driven from his bed by the echoing *whomph* of cannonballs, by the squeals of injured horses and the despairing groans of dying men. Yet there were times when his dreams were troubled not by the haunting things he'd seen or the even more haunting things he'd done, but by a certain blue-eyed, dusky-haired actress named Kat Boleyn. It was an unintentional but nonetheless real betrayal of the woman he had taken to wife, and it troubled him. Yet the only certain way for a man to control his dreams was to avoid sleep.

The daylight in the room strengthened.

Hero said, "It's difficult for anyone to sleep in this heat."

He reached up to smooth the tangled hair away from her damp forehead. "Why not come with me to Hampshire? It would do us both good to get away from the noise and dirt of London for a few weeks." He'd been intending to pay a visit to his estate all summer, but the events of the past few months had made leaving London impossible. Now it was a responsibility that could be delayed no longer.

He watched her hesitate and knew exactly what she was thinking: that alone together in the country they would be thrown constantly into each other's company. It was, after all, the reason newlywed couples traditionally went away on a honeymoon—so that they might get to know each other better. But there was little that could be termed traditional about their days-old marriage.

He expected her to say no. Then an odd, crooked smile touched her lips and she surprised him by saying, "Why not?"

He let his gaze rove over the smooth planes of her cheeks, the strong line of her jaw, the downward sweep of lashes that now hid her eyes from his sight. She was a mystery to him in so many ways. He knew the formidable strength of her intellect, the power of her sense of justice, the unexpected passion his touch could ignite within her. But he knew little of the life she had lived before their worlds became intertwined, of the girl she had once been or the forces and events that had fashioned her into the kind of woman who could without hesitation or compunction shoot a highwayman in the face.

He said, "We can leave for Hampshire today."

She shook her head. "I'm to meet Gabrielle Tennyson up at Trent Place this morning. She's been consulting with Sir Stanley on the excavations of a site on his property called Camlet Moat, and she's promised to show me what they've discovered."

Sebastian found himself smiling. Hero's driving passion would always be her clearheaded, logical commitment to reforming the numerous unjust and cruel laws that both handicapped and tarnished their society. But lately she'd also developed a keen interest in the need to preserve the rapidly vanishing legacies of England's past.

He said, "They've discovered something of interest?"

"When you consider that 'Camlet' is a recent corruption of 'Camelot,' anything they find is intriguing."

He ran the backs of his fingers along her jawline and smiled when he saw her shiver in the heat. "If I remember my *Morte d'Arthur*, Sir Thomas Malory identified Camelot with what is now Winchester."

She wrapped her hand around his wrist, effectively ending the caress. "Gabrielle thinks Malory was wrong."

From the street below came the scent of fresh bread and the tinkling bell of the baker's boy crying, *"Hot buns."*

Sebastian said, "Tomorrow, then?"

By now, the golden light of morning flooded the room. Hero took a step back out of the circle of Sebastian's arms to hug the sheet tighter around her, as if already regretting her commitment. "All right. Tomorrow."

But it was barely an hour later when a constable from Bow Street arrived at the house on Brook Street with the information that Miss Gabrielle Tennyson had been found dead.

Murdered, at Camlet Moat.

Chapter 3

*A*small, middle-aged man with a balding pate and a serious demeanor stood at the base of the ancient earthen embankment. He had his hands clasped behind his back, his chin sunk into the folds of his modestly tied cravat. A weathered dinghy lay beside him where it had been hauled up onto the moat's bank. It was empty now, but a smear of blood still showed clearly along the edge of the gunwale.

Sir Henry Lovejoy, the newest of Bow Street's three stipendiary magistrates, found himself staring at that telltale streak of blood. He had been called to this murder scene some ten miles north of London by the local magistrate, who was only too eager to hand over his investigation to the Bow Street public office.

Lovejoy blew out a long, troubled sigh. On the streets of London, most murders were straightforward affairs: a drunken navvy choked the life out of his hapless wife; two mates fell out over a dice game or the sale of a horse; a footpad jumped some unwary passerby from the mouth of a fetid alley. But there was nothing ordinary about a murdered young gentlewoman found floating on an abandoned moat in the middle of nowhere.

Miss Gabrielle Tennyson had been just twenty-eight years old. The daughter of a famous scholar, she'd been well on her way to earning a reputation as an antiquary in her own right—a decidedly unusual accomplishment for one of her sex. She lived with her brother, himself a well-known and respected barrister, in a fine house in the Adelphi Buildings overlooking the Thames. Her murder would send an unprecedented ripple of fear through the city, with ladies terrified to leave their homes and angry husbands and fathers demanding that Bow Street *do* something.

The problem was, Lovejoy had absolutely nothing to go on. Nothing at all.

He raised his gaze to where a line of constables moved along the moat's edge, their big boots churning through the murky water with muddy, sucking plops that seemed to echo in the unnatural stillness. He had never considered himself a fanciful man—far from it, in fact. Yet there was no denying that something about this place raised the hairs on the back of his neck. Perhaps it was the eerie way the light filtered down through the leaves of the thick stands of beech and hornbeam trees to bathe the scene in an unnatural green glow. Or perhaps it was a father's inevitable reaction to the sight of a beautiful, dead young woman—a sight that brought back a time of nearly unbearable heartbreak in Lovejoy's own life.

But he closed his mind to that.

He'd heard of this place, Camlet Moat. They said that once it had been the site of a medieval castle whose origins stretched back to the days of the Romans and beyond. But whatever fortified structures once stood here had long since been dismantled, their stones and mighty timbers carted away. All that remained was a deserted, overgrown square isle a few hundred feet across and the stagnant moat that had once protected it.

Now, as Lovejoy watched, one of the constables broke away from the others to come sloshing up to him.

"We've covered the entire bank, sir," said the man. "All the way around."

"And?" asked Lovejoy.

"We've found nothing, sir."

Lovejoy exhaled a long breath. "Then start on the island itself."

"Yes, sir."

A thunder of horses' hooves and the rattle of harness drew their attention to the narrow track that curled through the wood to the moat. A curricle and pair driven by an aristocratic young gentleman in a beaver hat and a caped driving coat drew up at the top of the embankment. The half-grown, scrappy-looking young groom in a striped waistcoat who clung to the rear perch immediately hopped down to race to the chestnuts' heads.

"It's Lord Devlin, sir," said the constable, staring slack-jawed as the Earl of Hendon's notorious son paused to confer with his tiger, then dropped lightly to the ground.

Lovejoy said, "That will be all, Constable."

The constable cast a last, curious glance toward the top of the slope, then ducked his head. "Yes, sir."

Lovejoy waited while the Viscount tossed his driving coat onto the curricle's high seat, then slid down the ancient embankment, the heels of his gleaming Hessian boots digging furrows in the soft leaf litter.

"Sir Henry," said the Viscount. "Good morning."

Lean and dark-haired, he was tall enough to tower over Lovejoy. But it was the man's eyes that tended to draw and hold a stranger's attention. Shading from amber to a feral yellow, they possessed an animallike ability to see great distances and in the dark. His hearing was exceptionally acute too, which could be disconcerting, even to those who knew him well.

The unusual friendship between the two men dated back some eighteen months, to a time when Devlin had been accused of murder and Lovejoy had been determined to bring him in. From those unlikely beginnings had grown respect as well as friendship. In Devlin, Lovejoy had found an ally with a rare passion for justice and a true genius for solving murders. But more important, Devlin also possessed something no Bow Street magistrate would ever have: an easy entrée at the highest levels of society and an innate understanding of the wealthy and wellborn who inevitably came under suspicion in a murder of this nature.

"My lord," said Lovejoy, giving a small, jerky bow. "I must apologize for intruding upon what should be for you and your new wife a time of joy and solitude. But when I learned of the victim's connection to Lady Devlin, I thought you would wish to know."

"You did the right thing," said Devlin. He let his gaze drift around the site, taking in the tangled growth of beech and oak, the green-scummed waters of the abandoned moat. "Where is she?"

Lovejoy cleared his throat uncomfortably. "We sent the remains to London an hour or so ago." Bodies did not keep well in the heat of August.

"To Gibson?"

"Yes, my lord." No one understood human anatomy or could read the secrets a body might have to reveal about its murderer better than Paul Gibson. Lovejoy nodded to the small boat beside them. "She was found in the dinghy—floating just at the edge of the moat here."

"You think this is where she was killed?" asked Devlin, hunkering down to study the blood-smeared gunwale.

"I think it probable she was stabbed in the dinghy, yes. But there were no footprints in the damp earth along this stretch of the bank, which leads me to suspect the boat simply drifted here from elsewhere—perhaps from the land bridge that crosses the moat on the eastern side of the island. We understand that's where it's normally kept moored. Unfortunately, there are so many footprints in that area that it's impossible to identify with any certainty those that might belong to the killer."

Devlin was silent for a moment, his forehead furrowed by a thoughtful frown as he continued to stare at that ugly streak of blood. The Viscount could sometimes be hesitant to commit to an investigation of murder. It was a reluctance Lovejoy understood only too well. More and more, it seemed to him that each death he dealt with, each torn, shattered life with which he came into contact, stole a piece of his own humanity and bled away an irretrievable part of his joy in life.

But surely, Lovejoy reasoned, the connection between this victim and his lordship's own wife would make it impossible for the Viscount to refuse.

Lovejoy said, "A murder such as this—a young woman brutally stabbed in a wood just north of London—will inevitably cause a panic in the city. And unfortunately, the impulse in these situations is all too often to calm public outrage by identifying a culprit quickly—at the cost of true justice."

"Are you asking for my help?"

Lovejoy met that strange, feral yellow stare, and held it. "I am, my lord."

Devlin pushed to his feet, his gaze shifting across the stretch of murky water to where the constables could be seen poking around the piles of fresh earth that edged Sir Stanley's series of exploratory trenches. In the misty, ethereal light of morning, the mounds of raw earth bore an unpleasant resemblance to rows of freshly dug graves. Lovejoy watched Devlin's lips press into a thin line, his nostrils flare on a painfully indrawn breath.

But the Viscount didn't say anything, and Lovejoy knew him well enough to be patient.

And wait for Devlin's reply.

Chapter 4

Sebastian turned to walk along the crest of the ancient rampart that rose beside the stagnant moat. The shade here was deep and heavy, the blue sky above nearly obliterated by the leafy branches of the stands of old-growth timber that met overhead. A tangle of bracken and fern edged the quiet waters of the moat and filled the air with the scent of wet earth and humus and the buzz of insects.

He'd heard that once this wild tract of woodland to the north of London had been known as Enfield Chase, a royal hunting ground that rang with the clatter of noble hoofbeats, the shrill blast of the huntsman's horn, the baying of royal hounds. Through these lands had swept King Henry VIII and Queen Elizabeth and a host of glittering, bejeweled courtiers, their velvet cloaks swirling in the mist, their voices raised in hearty halloos.

But all that had ended long ago. Briars and underbrush had grown up to choke the forest floor, while commoners from the nearby village had carted away the last tumbled stones of whatever grand manor or castle had once stood here. A quiet hush had fallen over the site, unbroken until a beautiful, brilliant, independent-minded young woman with a boundless curiosity about the past had come searching for the origins of a legend—and died here.

He could remember meeting Miss Gabrielle Tennyson only once, a year or so earlier at a lecture on Roman London that he'd attended in the company of the Earl of Hendon. Sebastian recalled her as a striking, self-assured young woman with chestnut hair and an open, friendly smile. He hadn't been surprised to discover that she and Hero were friends. Despite their obvious differences, the two women were much alike. He found it difficult to think of such a strong, vital woman now lying on a surgeon's slab, robbed of her life and all the years of promise that had once stretched before her. Difficult to imagine the terror and despair that must have filled her eyes and congealed her heart when she looked her last on this quiet, secluded site.

He paused to stare again at the small wooded isle where a castle named Camelot had once stood. He was aware of Sir Henry Lovejoy drawing up beside him, his homely features pinched and tight, his hands clasped behind his back.

Sebastian glanced over at him. "You said she'd been stabbed?"

The magistrate nodded. "In the chest. Just once that I could see, although Dr. Gibson will be able to tell us with certainty once he's finished the postmortem."

"And the murder weapon?"

"Has yet to be found."

Sebastian eyed the murky water before them. If Gabrielle's murderer had thrown his knife into the moat, it might never be recovered.

Twisting around, he studied the narrow lane where his tiger, Tom, was walking the chestnuts up and down. "How the devil did she get out here? Any idea?"

Sir Henry shook his head. "We can only assume she must have arrived in the company of her killer."

"No one in the neighborhood saw anything?"

"Nothing they're willing to admit. But then, the nearest village is several miles away, and there are only a few isolated houses in the area. Tessa Sawyer—the village girl who found her—came upon the body quite by chance, shortly before midnight."

"And what was Tessa doing out in the middle of nowhere at night?"

"That is not entirely clear, I'm afraid, given the girl's garbled and rather evasive replies to our questions. However, I understand that yesterday was some sort of ancient pagan holy day—"

"Lammas."

"Yes, that's it," said Sir Henry. "Lammas. I'm told Camlet Moat has a reputation as a place of magic amongst the credulous. In addition to the apparition of a White Lady who is said to haunt the island, there's also the ghost of some unsavory Templar knight who is reputed to appear when provoked."

"I assume you've heard there's also a tradition that this may be the ancient site of King Arthur's Camelot?"

The magistrate sniffed. "A fanciful notion, no doubt. But yes, I understand Sir Stanley Winthrop became intrigued by the possibility after he purchased the estate last year and discovered Miss Tennyson's research on the history of the site."

"You think her murder could in some way be connected to the legends of the island's past?"

Sir Henry blew out a long, agitated breath. "I wish I knew. We're not even certain how long Miss Tennyson's body was lying here before it was discovered. Her brother, Mr. Hildeyard Tennyson, has been out of town for the better part of a fortnight. I've sent a constable to interview her servants, but I fear they may not be able tell us much of anything. Yesterday was Sunday, after all."

"Bloody hell," said Sebastian softly. "What does Sir Stanley Winthrop have to say about all this?"

"He claims he last saw Miss Tennyson when she left the excavations for home on Saturday afternoon."

Something in the magistrate's tone caught Sebastian's attention. "But you don't believe him?"

"I don't know what to believe. He tells us he can't imagine what she might have been doing up here yesterday. They don't work the excavations on Sundays."

Sebastian said, "Perhaps she came up to look around by herself."

Lovejoy frowned. "Yes, I suppose that's possible. She may well have surprised some trespasser, and in a panic, he killed her."

"And then stole her carriage and kidnapped her coachman?"

Lovejoy pulled a face. "There is that."

Sebastian adjusted the tilt of his beaver hat. "Her brother is still out of town?"

Lovejoy nodded. "We've sent word to his estate, but I doubt he'll make it back to London before nightfall at the earliest."

"Then I think I'll start with Sir Stanley Winthrop," said Sebastian, and turned back toward his curricle.

Lovejoy fell into step beside him. "Does this mean you're willing to assist Bow Street with the case?"

"Did you honestly think I would not?"

Sir Henry gave one of his rare half smiles, tucked his chin against his chest, and shook his head.

Chapter 5

"There you are, Jarvis," exclaimed the Prince Regent, his face flushed, his voice rising in a petulant whine as he clenched a sheet of cheap, ink-smeared paper in his fist. "Look at this!" He thumped the offending broadsheet with one plump, beringed hand. "Just look at it."

His Royal Highness George, Prince Regent of Great Britain and Ireland, lay beside the fireplace in his dressing room, his heavy legs draped off the edge of a gilt fainting couch contrived in the shape of a crocodile upholstered in scarlet velvet. Despite the heat of the day, a fire burned brightly on the hearth, for the Prince had a morbid fear of taking chill.

Having been stricken while still in the midst of his toilet, he wore only a pair of exquisitely fitted yellow unmentionables and a shirt ruffled with an extravagant cascade of lace. It was a style of linen that belonged more to the previous century, but the Prince still occasionally indulged his taste for it, perhaps because it reminded him of the golden years of his youth, when he'd been handsome and carefree and beloved by his people. These days, he needed a corset to contain his ever-increasing girth, the people who'd once cheered him now booed him openly in the streets, and shadowy radicals published seditious broadsheets bemoaning the lost days of Camelot and calling for King Arthur to return from the mists of Avalon and save Britain from the benighted rule of the House of Hanover.

So great had been the Prince's distress at the reading of this particular broadsheet that his valet had sent for the Prince's doctor. The doctor, in turn, took one look at the offending verbiage and requested the attendance of the Prince's powerful and infinitely wise cousin, Charles, Lord Jarvis.

"Calm yourself, Your Highness," said Jarvis, catching the eye of the Prince's doctor, who stood nearby. The doctor nodded discreetly and turned away.

"But have you seen this?" wailed the Prince. "They want Arthur to come back and get rid of me!"

Jarvis carefully loosed the broadsheet from the Regent's clutches. "I have seen it, Your Highness." Personally, Jarvis suspected the caricature accompanying the tract—which portrayed George as a grossly fat, drunken, overdressed buffoon with the ears of an ass—offended the Prince more than anything. But it was the implications of the appeal for Arthur's messianic return that concerned Jarvis. "Whoever is responsible for this will be dealt with."

The Prince's valet and doctor exchanged quick, furtive glances, then looked away. There was a reason Jarvis was feared from one end of the Kingdom to the other. His network of spies and informants gave him an eerie omnipotence, while those he "dealt with" were seldom seen again.

The doctor stepped forward with a glass of cloudy liquid on a silver tray. "Here, Your Highness; drink this. You'll feel much better."

"Who gave this broadsheet to the Prince?" Jarvis demanded in a harsh whisper to the Prince's valet as His Highness obediently gulped the doctor's brew.

The valet's plump, sweat-sheened face went pasty white. "I've no notion, my lord. In truth, I do not know!"

Frowning, Jarvis tucked the seditious literature into his coat and bowed himself out of the royal presence.

He was crossing the anteroom of the Prince's chambers when a pimply, half-grown page sidled up to him and bowed low, his mouth opening and closing as he struggled to speak. But all he succeeded in doing was pushing out a series of incoherent squeaks.

"For God's sake, boy, out with it," snapped Jarvis. "As it happens I've already eaten, so you needn't fear I'll have you for breakfast."

The boy's eyes bulged.

Jarvis suppressed a sigh. "Your message; say it."

The boy swallowed and tried again, the words tumbling out in a rush. "It's your daughter, my lord. Miss J—I mean, Lady Devlin. She desired me to tell you that she wishes to speak with you, my lord. She awaits you in your chambers."

No man in England was more powerful than Jarvis. His kinship with the King might be distant, but without Jarvis's ruthless brilliance and steady wisdom, the House of Hanover would have fallen long ago and the Hanovers knew it. Jarvis had dedicated his life to the preservation of the monarchy and the global extension of the might of England. Another man might have insisted on being named prime minister in return for his services. But Jarvis preferred to exercise his power from the shadows, unconstrained by either tradition or law. Prime ministers came and went.

Jarvis remained.

He found his daughter standing at the long window of the chambers reserved for his exclusive use overlooking Pall Mall. Once, Jarvis had possessed a son—an idealistic dreamer named David. But David had been lost years before to a watery grave.

Now there was only Hero: brilliant, strong willed, and nearly as ruthless and enigmatic as Jarvis himself.

She wore a walking dress of dusky blue trimmed with moss green piping, and a jaunty hat with a broad brim turned up on one side and held in place with a silk posy. The sunlight streaming through the paned glass bathed her in a warm golden glow and touched her cheeks with color.

"You're looking good," he said, closing the door behind him. "Marriage seems to agree with you."

She turned to face him. "You're surprised?"

Rather than answer, he crossed the room to where a candlestick stood on a table beside a wing-back chair. The relationship between father and daughter had always been complicated. They were much alike, which meant she understood him as few others did. But that was not to say that she knew everything there was to know about him.

"What brings you here?" he asked, his attention seemingly all for the task of lighting the candle. He was aware of an air of constraint between them, for her recent marriage to Devlin had introduced a new element and subtly shifted the dynamic in a way neither had yet to confront or reveal.

"What makes you think I came for a purpose other than to see you?"

"Because if this were a gesture of familial affection, you wouldn't be at Carlton House. You would have come to Berkeley Square. Your mother is well, by the way—or perhaps I should say she is as well as she ever is. She's quite taken with the new companion you found for her."

Refusing to be distracted, Hero said, "Gabrielle Tennyson was discovered murdered this morning, at Camlet Moat." When he kept silent, she said, "You knew?"

He watched the wick of the candle catch, flare up bright. "There is little that happens in this Kingdom that I do not know about."

"There is also little that happens in this Kingdom that you don't control."

He glanced over at her. She stood with her back to the window, her hands curled so that her palms rested on the sill. Through the glass behind her he could see a heavy traffic of carriages, carts, and horses streaming up and down the Mall. He said, "Are you asking if I had her killed?"

"After what I overheard last Friday night, the thought naturally does occur to me." When Jarvis remained silent, she added impatiently, "Well? Did you?"

"I did not." He drew the broadsheet from his pocket and thrust it into the candle flame. It blackened and smoked for an instant, then caught fire. "Now the question becomes, do you believe me?"

She held herself quite still, her gaze on his face. "I don't know. I've never been able to tell when you're lying."

He tilted the paper as the flames took hold, then dropped it onto the cold, bare stones of the nearby hearth. "I take it Devlin has become involved in the investigation?"

"Lovejoy has asked for his assistance with the case, yes."

"And will you tell your husband that he should add me to his list of suspects, and why?"

She pushed away from the window, her nostrils flaring with a sharp intake of breath. "I am here because Gabrielle was my friend, not as Devlin's agent."

"Perhaps. But that doesn't exactly answer my question."

Their gazes met. They'd both known this day would come, when she'd find herself caught between what she felt she owed her own family and what she owed her new husband. Only, he hadn't expected it to come quite so soon.

She said, "I have no intention of betraying you . . . if you are telling me the truth."

He found himself smiling. "But then, in that case, you wouldn't actually be betraying me, now, would you?" He tipped his head to one side. "And how will your rather headstrong and passionate young Viscount react, I wonder, when he discovers that you have been less than forthcoming with him?"

"I must be true to myself and to what I believe is right. My marriage in no way negates that."

"And if he doesn't understand—or fails to agree?"

She turned toward the door. "Then we will disagree."

She said it evenly, in that way she had. He knew she had analyzed the situation and made her decision calmly and rationally. She was not the kind of woman to waste time agonizing or endlessly analyzing her choices. But that was not to say that the decision had been made lightly or that it would be without emotional consequences. For he had seen the troubled shadows that lurked in the depths of her fine gray eyes. And he knew an upsurge of renewed anger and resentment directed at Devlin, who had put them there.

After she left, he watched the broadsheet on the hearth burn itself out until nothing remained but a blackened ash. Then he went to stand where she had stood, his gaze on the courtyard below. He watched her exit the Palace, watched her climb the steps to her waiting carriage. He watched the carriage bowl away up Pall Mall toward the west, the clatter of her horses' hooves lost in the tumult of drivers' shouts and hawkers' cries and the rattle of iron-rimmed wheels over cobbles.

Turning, he rang for his clerk.

"Send Colonel Urquhart to me," he said curtly when the man appeared. "Now."

Chapter 6

The abandoned isle once known as Camelot lay on the northern edge of Trent Place, a relatively new estate dating only to late in the previous century, when the ancient royal chase had been broken up and sold to help pay for the first round of George III's wars. The properties thus created had proved popular with the newly wealthy merchants and bankers of the city. Sir Stanley, Trent Place's latest owner, was a prosperous banker granted a baronetcy by the King in reward for his assistance in financing the country's long struggle against Napoléon.

"One o' them constables was tellin' me this Sir Stanley already 'as a 'ouse in Golden Square what makes the Queen's Palace look like a cottage," said Sebastian's tiger, Tom, as they turned through massive new gates to a meticulously landscaped park. "So why'd he need to buy this place too, just a few miles from London?"

The boy was thirteen years old now, but still small and gap-toothed and scrappy, for he had been a homeless street urchin when Sebastian first discovered the lad's intense loyalty and sense of honor and natural affinity for horses. In a very real sense, Tom and Sebastian had saved each other. The ties that bound lord to servant and boy to man ran deep and strong.

Sebastian said, "The possession of an estate is the sine qua non for anyone aspiring to be a gentleman."

"The seenkwawhat?"

"Sine qua non. It's Latin for a condition without which something cannot be."

"You sayin' this Sir Stanley ain't always been a gentleman?"

"Something like that," said Sebastian, drawing up before what had once been a graceful Italianate villa but was now in the process of being transformed into something quite different by the addition of two vast wings and a new roofline. The pounding of hammers and the clatter of lumber filled the air; near a half-constructed wall, a tall, elegantly tailored gentleman in his early fifties could be seen conferring with a group of brickmasons.

"Keep your ears open around the stables," Sebastian told Tom as the tiger took the reins. "I'd be interested to hear what the servants are saying."

"Aye, gov'nor."

"Devlin," called Sir Stanley, leaving the bricklayers to stroll toward him.

He was a ruggedly handsome man, his chin square, his cheekbones prominent, his mouth wide and expressive. Despite his years, his body was still strong and powerful, and he had a head of thick, pale blond hair fading gradually to white, so that it formed a startling contrast to his unexpectedly sun-darkened features. The effect was more like what one would expect of a soldier or a nabob just returned from India than a banker.

They said the man had begun his career as a lowly clerk, the son of a poor vicar with sixteen children and no connections. Sebastian had heard that his rise to wealth, power, and influence had been both rapid and brutal and owed its success to his wily intelligence, his driving ambition, and a clear-sighted, unflinching ruthlessness.

"What brings you here?" asked Sir Stanley, pausing beside the curricle.

"I've just come from Camlet Moat," said Sebastian, dropping lightly to the ground.

"Ah. I see." The flesh of the man's face suddenly looked pinched, as if pulled too taut over the bones of his face. "Please," he said, stretching a hand to indicate the broad white marble stairs that led up to the central, original section of the house. "Come in."

"Thank you."

"I was with Squire John when he discovered the body," said Winthrop as they mounted the steps. "He's our local magistrate, you know. Seems some girl from the village showed up at the Grange in the middle of the night, babbling nonsense about white ladies and magic wells and a dead gentlewoman in the moat. The Squire was convinced it was all a hum—actually apologized for coming to me at the crack of dawn—but I said, 'No, no, let's go have a look.'" He paused in the entrance hall, a quiver passing over his tightly held features. "The last thing I expected was to find Gabrielle."

Sebastian let his gaze drift around the vast, marble-floored entrance hall, with its towering, gilt-framed canvases of pastoral landscapes by Constable and Turner, its ornately plastered ceiling picked out in pastel shades evocative of a plate of petit fours. In an age when it was not uncommon for husbands and wives to call each other by their surnames or titles, Winthrop had just referred to Miss Tennyson by her first name.

And Sebastian suspected the man was not even aware of his slip.

"I'd never seen someone who'd been murdered," the banker was saying. "I suppose you've had experience with it, but I haven't. I'm not ashamed to admit it was a shock."

"I'm not convinced anyone gets used to the sight of murder."

Sir Stanley nodded and turned toward the cavernous drawing

room that opened to their left. "It may be frightfully early, but I could use a drink. How about you? May I offer you some wine?"

"Yes, thank you. Sir Henry Lovejoy tells me you don't work on the island's excavations on Sundays," said Sebastian as his host crossed to where a tray with a decanter and glasses waited on a gilded table beside a grouping of silk-covered settees.

Winthrop splashed wine into two glasses. "My wife believes the Sabbath should be a day of rest. On the seventh day, the Lord rested, and so should all of his children."

"Commendable," said Sebastian. Through a long bank of tall windows he could see an angular, bony woman he recognized as Lady Winthrop standing at the edge of an old-fashioned garden of box-edged parterres filled with roses. Despite the heat, she wore a long-sleeved sprigged muslin gown made high at the neck and trimmed with only a meager band of lace. She was younger than Winthrop by some fifteen or twenty years, a second wife as plain as her husband was handsome, her eyes small and protuberant and close set, her chin receding, her head thrust forward in a way that made her look forever inquisitive.

Or aggressive.

She was in the process of giving directions to a cluster of gardeners equipped with wheelbarrows and shovels. As Sebastian watched, she waved her arms in extravagant gestures as she delivered her instructions. Piles of rich dark earth and stacks of brick lay nearby; the Winthrops were obviously expanding their gardens as well as their new house. Watching her, Sebastian wondered if Lady Winthrop also referred to Miss Tennyson as "Gabrielle." Somehow, he doubted it.

Winthrop set aside the decanter to pick up the two glasses. "At first, in her naivety, my wife actually expected the brutes to be grateful. But she soon discovered how mistaken she was. All they do is grumble about being forced to go to church services."

"It's required?"

"Of course." Winthrop held out one of the glasses. "Religion is important to the order of society. It reconciles the lower classes to their lot in life and teaches them to respect their betters."

"So it does," said Sebastian, studying the banker's faintly smiling face as he took the wine handed him. But he was unable to decide whether Winthrop agreed with his wife or quietly mocked her. "So, tell me, do you honestly believe you've found King Arthur's Camelot?" He took a sip of the wine. It was smooth and mellow and undoubtedly French.

"Honestly?" The banker drained his own glass in two long pulls, then shook his head. "I don't know. But the site is intriguing, don't you agree? I mean, here we have a place long associated with the kings of England—a place whose name actually was Camelot. I'm told the word is of Celtic origin. It probably comes from 'Camulus,' the Celtic god of war. Of course, Miss Tennyson says— said," he amended hastily, correcting himself, "that it could also mean 'place of the crooked stream.' Personally, I prefer to think it is named after the god of war." Turning away to pour himself more wine, he raised the decanter in silent question to Sebastian.

Sebastian shook his head. He had taken only the one sip.

"The important thing," said Winthrop, refreshing his own drink, "is that we know the name dates back to well before the time of William the Conqueror. The corruption of 'Camelot' to 'Camlet' is quite recent, within the last hundred years or so."

Sebastian studied the older man's handsome features. His manner could only be described as affable, even likeable. But Sebastian couldn't get past the knowledge that the previous owner of Trent Place had been forced to sell the estate to Winthrop at a steep loss—and then blown his own brains out the next day.

Sebastian took another sip of his wine. "How did you meet Miss Tennyson?"

"By mere chance, actually, at a lecture presented by the Society of Antiquaries. She'd been doing research on the history of Camlet

Moat and approached me when she learned I'd recently purchased the estate. Until then, I'd barely realized the moat existed. But the more I learned about it, the more intrigued I became."

"And you began the excavations—when?"

"A month ago now. We'd hoped to begin earlier, but the wet spring delayed things."

"Find anything interesting?"

"Far more than I'd anticipated, certainly. Foundations of stone walls five feet thick. Remnants of a forty-foot drawbridge. Even an underground dungeon complete with chains still hanging on the walls."

"Dating to when?"

"Judging from the coins and painted tiles we've come across, probably the thirteenth or fourteenth century, for most of it."

"I was under the impression King Arthur was supposed to have lived in the fifth or sixth century, after the Roman withdrawal from Britain—that is, if he lived at all."

"True." Winthrop turned away to reach for something, then held it out. "But look at this."

Sebastian found himself holding a corroded metal blade. "What is it?"

"A Roman dagger." Winthrop set aside his wine and went to open a large flat glass case framed in walnut that stood on its own table near the door. "And look at this." He pointed with one blunt, long finger. "These pottery vessels are third- or fourth-century Roman. So is the glass vial. And see that coin? It's from the time of Claudius."

Sebastian studied the artifacts proudly displayed against a black velvet background. "You found all this at Camlet Moat?"

"We did. The drawbridge and dungeon probably date to the time of the de Mandevilles and their descendants, who held the castle for the Crown in the late Middle Ages. But the site itself is older—much older. There was obviously a fort or villa there in

Roman times, which means that in all probability there was still something there during the days of Arthur, after the Romans pulled out."

Sebastian regarded the other man's flushed face and shining eyes. "Will you continue digging, now that Miss Tennyson is dead?"

All the excitement and animation seemed to drain out of Winthrop, leaving him pensive. "I don't see how we can. She's the one who knew what she was doing—and how to interpret what we were finding."

"You couldn't simply hire an antiquary through the British Museum?"

The banker gave a soft laugh. "Given that they all thought Miss Tennyson mad to be working with me on this, I can't see anyone of stature being willing to risk his reputation by following in her footsteps. And with harvesttime upon us, we were about to quit anyway."

"Any chance she could have come up yesterday to have a quiet look around the site by herself for some reason? Or perhaps to show it to someone?"

Sir Stanley appeared thoughtful. "I suppose it's possible, although she generally devoted her Sundays to activities with the boys."

Sebastian shook his head, not understanding. "What boys?"

"George and Alfred—sons of one of her cousins. I understand the mother's having a difficult confinement and the father isn't well himself, so Miss Tennyson invited the lads to spend the summer with her in London. They generally stayed home with their nurse when she came up to the island, but she liked to spend several days a week showing them around London. The Tower of London and the beasts at the Exchange—that sort of thing."

"So she didn't come every day when you were digging?"

"Not every day, no; she had some other research she was also pursuing. But she generally came three or four times a week, yes."

"How would she get here?"

"Sometimes in her brother's carriage, although she would frequently take the stage to Enfield and get someone at the livery there to drive her out to the moat. In that case, I always insisted she allow me to have one of the men drive her back to London in the afternoon."

It wasn't exactly unheard of for a gentlewoman to take the stage, especially for such a short, local trip. Maintaining a carriage, horses, and groom in London was prodigiously expensive; most families kept only one, if that.

"Her brother begrudged her the use of his carriage?"

"Quite the opposite, actually. It irked him to no end when she insisted on taking the common stage rather than using his carriage—said he was perfectly capable of taking a hackney or walking around London himself."

"But she didn't always listen?"

Winthrop's wide mouth curled into a soft smile that faded away into something sad as he shook his head. "She was like that."

"Like what?"

He went to stand at the long row of windows, his gaze on the scene outside. A few puffy white clouds had appeared on the horizon, but the sun still drenched the beds of roses with a dazzling golden light. The workmen were now bent over their shovels; Lady Winthrop was nowhere to be seen. "She was an unusual woman," he said, watching the distant clouds. "Strong. Opinionated. Unafraid to challenge the conventions and assumptions of her world. And not given to suffering fools lightly."

"In other words," said Sebastian, "the kind of woman who could make enemies."

Winthrop nodded, his gaze still on the scene beyond the glass.

"Anyone you know of in particular?"

The banker drew a deep breath that expanded his chest. "It seems somehow wrong to be mentioning these things now, when the recollection of a few careless words uttered in anger could easily result in a man standing accused of murder."

"Are you saying Miss Tennyson quarreled with someone recently?"

"I don't know if I'd say they 'quarreled,' exactly."

"So what did happen?"

"Well, when I saw her on Saturday . . ."

"Yes?" prompted Sebastian when the man hesitated.

"I knew something was troubling her as soon as she arrived at the site. She seemed . . . strained. Jumpy. At first she tried to pass it off as nothing more than a melancholy mood, but I wasn't fooled."

"Was she given to melancholy moods?"

"She was a Tennyson. They're all melancholy, you know."

"No, I didn't know. Go on."

"She said she didn't want to talk about it. Perhaps I pressed her more than I should have, but in the end she admitted she was troubled by an encounter she'd had the previous day, on Friday. She tried to laugh it off—said it was nothing. But it was obviously considerably more than 'nothing.' I don't believe I'd ever seen her so upset."

The sound of a distant door opening echoed through the house.

"An encounter with whom?" asked Sebastian.

"I couldn't tell you his name. Some antiquary known for his work on the post-Roman period of English history."

"And this fellow disagreed with Miss Tennyson's belief that your Camlet Moat was the site of King Arthur's Camelot?"

Winthrop's jaw tightened in a way that caused the powerful muscles in his cheeks to bunch and flex. For the first time, Sebastian caught a glimpse of the steely ruthlessness that had enabled the banker to amass a fortune in the course of twenty years of war. "I gather he is of the opinion that King Arthur is a figment of the collective British imagination—a product of both our romantic wish for a glorious, heroic past and a yearning for a magical savior who will return to lead us once more to victory and glory."

"And was this disagreement the reason for Friday's 'encounter'?"

"She led me to believe so."

"But you suspect she was being less than open with you?"

"In a word? Yes."

Chapter 7

*Q*uick footsteps sounded in the hall, and Winthrop turned as his wife entered the room. She drew up abruptly at the sight of Sebastian, her expression more one of haughty indignation than welcome. It was obvious she knew exactly why he was there.

"Ah, there you are, my dear," said the banker. "You've met Lord Devlin?"

"I have." She made no move to offer him her hand.

"We met at a dinner at Lord Liverpool's, I believe," said Sebastian, bowing. "Last spring."

"So we did." It was obvious Lady Winthrop had not found the encounter a pleasure. But then, Sebastian did have something of a reputation for dangerous and scandalous living. She said, "You're here because of the death of the Tennyson woman, are you? I told Sir Stanley no good would come of this Camelot nonsense."

Sebastian cast a glance at her husband, but Winthrop's face remained a pleasant mask. If he was embarrassed by his wife's boorish behavior, he gave no sign of it.

"I take it you don't share Sir Stanley's enthusiasm for the investigation of Camlet Moat?" said Sebastian, draining his wine.

"I do not."

Winthrop moved to close the lid on the glass case. "My wife is a God-fearing woman who worries that any interest in the island shown by their betters will merely increase the unfortunate predilection of the locals to fall victim to ancient and dangerous superstitions."

Lady Winthrop threw her husband a quick, veiled look.

"Have you visited the excavations yourself, Lady Winthrop?" Sebastian asked.

"I see no utility in poking about the rubbish of some long-vanished buildings. What's gone is gone. It's the fate of mankind that should concern us, not his past. Everything we need to know is written in the Good Lord's book or in the learned works of theology and morality penned by his inspired servants. It is his intentions that should be the object of our study, not some forgotten piles of stones and broken pots."

Winthrop said, his voice bland, "May I offer you some more wine, Lord Devlin?"

"Thank you, but no." Sebastian set aside his glass. "I must be going."

Neither his host nor his hostess urged him to stay. "I'll send a servant for your carriage," said Lady Winthrop.

"I'm sorry I couldn't have been of more assistance," said Winthrop a few moments later as he walked with Sebastian to the door and out into the blazing sunshine.

Sebastian paused at the top of the broad steps. "Tell me, Sir Stanley: Do you think it possible that Miss Tennyson's death could have something to do with your work at Camlet Moat?"

"I don't see how it could," said Winthrop, his face turned away, his gaze on the gravel sweep where Tom was just drawing up.

"Yet you are familiar with the legend that Arthur is only sleeping on the isle of Avalon, and that in England's gravest hour of need he will arise again to lead us to victory."

The two men walked down the steps. "I find legends endlessly fascinating; tales of noble heroes and beautiful maidens have entranced mankind through the ages. But as an inspiration to murder? I don't see it."

Sebastian leapt up to the curricle's high seat and gathered the reins. "Anything powerful can also be dangerous."

"Only to those who feel threatened by it." Winthrop took a step back. "Good day, my lord."

Sebastian waited until they were bowling away up the drive toward the park's gateway before glancing over at his tiger and saying, "Well? Anything?"

"It's a queer estate, this Trent Place," said Tom, who possessed a knack for inspiring other servants to gossip. "Seems like it changes owners nearly every other year."

"Not quite, but almost," said Sebastian. It was typical of new estates. Ancient manors could stay in the same family for centuries, but the new wealth of merchants and bankers frequently went as easily and quickly as it came. "And what is the servants' general opinion of the current owners?"

"There was some mutterin' and queer looks, but nobody was willin' to come out and say much o' anything. If ye ask me, they're afraid."

"Of Sir Stanley? Or his wife?"

"Maybe both."

"Interesting," said Sebastian. "And what do they think of the excavations at Camlet Moat?"

"That's a bit queer too. Some think it's excitin', but there's others see it as a sacra—sacra—" Tom struggled with the word.

"A sacrilege?"

"Aye, that's it."

"Interesting."

Sebastian guided the chestnuts through the park's massive new gateway, then dropped his hands; the horses leapt forward to eat up the miles back to London. He could see the heat haze roiling up from the hard-packed road, feel the sun blazing down hot on his shoulders. He was intensely aware of the fierce green of the chestnut trees shading a nearby brook, of the clear-noted poignancy of a lark's song floating on the warm breeze. And he found himself unable to stop thinking of the vibrant, intelligent young woman whose pallid corpse awaited him on Paul Gibson's cold granite slab, and to whom all the beauties of that morning—or any other morning—were forever lost.

By the time Sebastian drew up before Paul Gibson's surgery on Tower Hill, the chestnuts' coats were wet and dark with sweat.

"Take 'em home and baby 'em," he said, handing Tom the reins.

"Aye, gov'nor." Tom scrambled into the seat as Sebastian hopped down to the narrow footpath. "You want I should come back with the grays?"

Sebastian shook his head. "I'll send for you if I need you."

He stood for a moment, watching the lad expertly wind his way westward through the press of carts and coal wagons. Near the base of the hill, a ragged boy with a drum tapped a steady beat to attract customers to the street seller who stood beside him hawking fried fish. Nearby, a woman with a cart peddled eel jelly, while a thin man in a buff-colored coat watered a nondescript roan at an old fountain built against the wall of the corner house. Then, realizing he was only delaying the inevitable, Sebastian turned to cut through the noisome, high-walled passage that led to the unkempt yard behind Gibson's surgery.

At the base of the yard lay a small stone outbuilding used by the surgeon both for his official postmortems and for a series of surreptitious dissections performed on cadavers snatched from the city's graveyards under the cover of darkness by stealthy, dangerous men. As Sebastian neared the open door of the building, he could see the remains of a woman lying on the cold, hard granite slab in the center of the single, high-windowed room.

Even in death, Miss Gabrielle Tennyson was a handsome woman, her features gracefully molded, her mouth generous, her upper lip short and gently cleft, her chestnut hair thick and luxuriously wavy. He paused in the doorway, his gaze on her face.

"Ah, there you are," said Gibson, looking up. He set aside his scalpel with a clatter and reached for a rag to wipe his hands. "I thought I might be seeing you."

A slim man of medium height in his early thirties, Paul Gibson had dark hair and green eyes bright with an irrepressible glint of mischief that almost but not quite hid the dull ache of chronic pain lurking in their nuanced depths. Irish by birth, he had honed his craft on the battlefields of Europe, learning the secrets of life and death from an endless parade of bodies slashed open and torn asunder. Then a French cannonball had shattered his own lower left leg, leaving him with a painful stump and a weakness for the sweet relief to be found in an elixir of poppies. He now divided his time between teaching anatomy to the medical students at St. Thomas's Hospital and consulting with patients at his own private surgery here in the shadows of the Tower of London.

"Can you tell me anything yet?" asked Sebastian, looking pointedly away from what Gibson had been doing to the cadaver. Like Gibson, Sebastian had worn the King's colors, fighting for God and country from Italy to the West Indies to the Peninsula. But he had never become inured to the sight or smell of death.

"Not much, I'm afraid, although I'm only just getting started. I might have more for you in a wee bit." Gibson limped from behind the table, his peg leg tap-tapping on the uneven flagged flooring. He pointed to a jagged purple slit that marred the milky flesh of the body's left breast. "You can see where she was stabbed. The blade was perhaps eight or ten inches long and an inch wide. Either her killer knew what he was doing or he got lucky. He hit her heart with just one thrust."

"She died right away?"

"Almost instantly."

Sebastian dropped his gaze to the long, tapered fingers that lay curled beside the body's hips. The nails were carefully manicured and unbroken.

"No sign of a struggle?"

"None that I've found."

"So she may have known her attacker?"

"Perhaps." Gibson tossed the rag aside. "Lovejoy's constable said she was found drifting in a dinghy outside London?"

Sebastian nodded. "On an old moat near Enfield. Any idea how long she's been dead?"

"Roughly twenty-four hours, I'd say, perhaps a few hours more or a little less. But beyond that it's difficult to determine."

Sebastian studied the reddish purple discoloration along the visible portions of the body's flanks and back. He knew from his own experience on the battlefield that blood tended to pool in the lower portions of a cadaver. "Any chance she could have been killed someplace else and then put in that boat?"

"I haven't found anything to suggest it, no. The *livor mortis* is consistent with the position in which I'm told she was found."

Sebastian's gaze shifted to the half boots of peach-colored suede, the delicate stockings, the froth of white muslin neatly folded on a nearby shelf. "These are hers?"

"Yes."

He reached out to finger the dark reddish brown stain that stiffened the delicate lace edging of the bodice. Suddenly the dank, death-tinged air of the place seemed to reach out and wrap itself around him, smothering him. He dropped his hand to his side and went to stand outside in the yard, the buzz of insects loud in the rank grass of the neglected garden as he drew in a deep breath of fresh air.

He was aware of his friend coming to stand beside him. Gibson

said, "Lovejoy tells me Miss Jar—I mean, Lady Devlin was ac-
quainted with the victim."

"They were quite close, yes."

Sebastian stared up at the hot, brittle blue sky overhead. When
the messenger from Bow Street arrived in Brook Street that
morning, Sebastian thought he had never seen Hero more devastated. Yet she hadn't wept, and she had turned down his suggestion
that she drive up to Camlet Moat with him. He did not understand
why. But then, how much did he really know about the woman he
had married?

Hero and this dead woman had shared so much in common—an
enthusiasm for scholarship and research, a willingness to challenge
societal expectations and prejudices, and a rejection of marriage and
motherhood as the only acceptable choice for a woman. He could
understand Hero's grief and anger at the loss of her friend. But he
couldn't shake the uncomfortable sense that something else was
going on with her, something he couldn't even begin to guess at.

Gibson said, "This must be difficult for her. Any leads yet on
the two lads?"

Sebastian glanced over at him, not understanding. "What lads?"

"The two boys Miss Tennyson had spending the summer with
her." Gibson must have read the confusion in Sebastian's face, because he added, "You mean to say you haven't heard?"

Sebastian could feel his heart beating in his ears like a
thrumming of dread. "Heard what?"

"The news has been all over town this past hour or more. The
children have vanished. No one's seen them since yesterday morning."

Chapter 8

The Adelphi Terrace—or Royal Terrace, as it was sometimes called—stretched along the bank of the Thames overlooking the vast Adelphi Wharves. A long block of elegant neoclassical town houses built by the Adams brothers late in the previous century, the address was popular with the city's rising gentry class, particularly with Harley Street physicians and successful barristers such as Gabrielle Tennyson's brother. As Sebastian rounded the corner from Adams Street, he found Sir Henry Lovejoy exiting the Tennysons' front door.

"You've heard about the missing children?" asked Sir Henry, his homely face troubled as he waited for Sebastian to come up to him.

"Just now, from Gibson."

Sir Henry blew out a long, painful breath. "I needn't scruple to tell you this adds a very troubling dimension to the case. A very troubling dimension indeed."

"You've found no trace of them?"

"Nothing. Nothing at all. Right now, we're hoping the children witnessed the murder and ran away to hide in the woods in fright.

The alternative is . . . Well, it's not something I'm looking forward to dealing with."

They turned to walk along the terrace fronting onto the wharves below. The fierce midday sun glinted off the broad surface of the river beside them and the air filled with the rough shouts of bargemen working the river and the rattle of carts on the coal wharf.

"We've had constables knocking on doors up and down the street," said Sir Henry, "in the hopes someone might be able to tell us what time Miss Tennyson and the children left the house, or perhaps even with whom. Unfortunately, the heat has driven most of the residents into the country, and of those who remain, no one recalls having seen anything."

"Any chance the children could have been snatched for ransom?"

"It's a possibility, I suppose, although I must confess I find it unlikely. I'm told the children's father is a simple, impoverished clergyman up in the wilds of Lincolnshire. And while the victim's brother, Mr. Hildeyard Tennyson, is a moderately successful barrister, he is not excessively wealthy." Sir Henry rubbed the bridge of his nose between one thumb and finger. "The elder boy, George, is just nine years old, while the younger, Alfred, is turning three. They were here with Miss Tennyson when the servants left yesterday morning, but as far as we've been able to tell, that's the last time any of them were seen." He hesitated, then added reluctantly, "Alive."

"And the servants never thought to raise the alarm when neither Miss Tennyson nor the children returned home last night?"

"They thought it not their place to presume to know their mistress's intentions."

"Yes, I can see that," said Sebastian. "And now they're so frightened of being blamed for the delay in launching a search that it's difficult to get much of anything out of them?"

"Exactly." Lovejoy sighed. "Although they may prove more willing to open up to you than to Bow Street." The warm breeze blowing off the water brought them the smell of brine and

spawning fish and the freshness of the wide-open seas. His features
pinched, Lovejoy paused to stare out across the barges and wherries
filling the river. "I'm heading back up to Enfield now, to organize
some men to drag the moat."

Sebastian said, "Any possibility the children could have been the
killer's intended targets and Miss Tennyson simply got in the way?"

"Merciful heavens. Why would anyone want to kill two innocent children?" Lovejoy was silent a moment, his gaze still on
the sun-spangled water, a bead of sweat rolling down one cheek.
"But you're right; it is obviously a possibility. Dear God, what is the
world coming to?" He narrowed his eyes against the glare coming
off the water and said it again. "What is the world coming to?"

The Tennysons' housekeeper was a small, plump woman named
Mrs. O'Donnell. She had full cheeks and graying hair worn tucked
neatly beneath a starched white cap, and she struck Sebastian as
the type of woman who in happier times sported rosy cheeks and
bustled about with brisk good cheer and a ready laugh. Now she
sat crumpled beside the empty hearth in the servants' hall, a damp
handkerchief clutched forlornly in one fist, her eyes red and swollen
with tears, her cheeks ashen.

"If only the master had been home," she kept saying over and
over again. "None of this would have happened."

"How long has Mr. Tennyson been gone?" asked Sebastian, settling onto a hard wooden bench opposite her.

"A fortnight, come Tuesday. He wanted Miss Tennyson and the
lads to go into the country with him—get away from all the heat
and dirt of the city. But she wouldn't leave that project of hers."
Mrs. O'Donnell's nose wrinkled when she uttered the word "project,"
as if she spoke of something nasty and improper. It was obvious
that for all her geniality, the housekeeper did not approve of Miss
Tennyson's unorthodox interests.

Sebastian said, "I take it you're referring to the excavations up at Camlet Moat?"

Mrs. O'Donnell nodded and touched her handkerchief to the corner of one eye. "I know it's not my place to say such things, but, well . . . It's not *right*, if you ask me. Women belong in the home. And now look what's come of it! Her dead, and those poor lads gone missing. Such bright little fellows, they were. Quick-tempered and full of mischief, to be sure, but charming and winsome for all of that. Why, just yesterday morning before they left for church, Master George gave me a little poem he wrote all by himself." She pushed up from her seat and went to rummage amongst the litter of recipes and invoices, letters and broadsheets, that covered a nearby table. "It's here somewhere. . . ."

"That's the last time you saw them?" asked Sebastian. "Yesterday morning, when they were on their way to church?"

"It was, yes," she said, distracted by her search.

"Which church do they normally attend?"

"St. Martin's, usually."

"You think that's where they went yesterday?"

"I don't see why not, my lord."

"I'm told Miss Tennyson liked to take the boys on various outings several times a week, particularly on Sunday afternoons."

"Oh, yes. She was enjoying their visit ever so much. It was lovely to see her with them. Her face would light up and she'd laugh like she was a carefree girl again herself." A ghost of a smile animated the housekeeper's features, only to fade away into pinched sorrow. "Course, then there were the times I'd catch her watching them, and she'd go all still and quiet-like, and this look would come over her that was something painful to see."

"What sort of a look?"

"It was like a . . . like a *yearning*, if you know what I mean?"

"You think she regretted not having children of her own?"

"If she did, it was her choice, wasn't it? I mean, it's not like she didn't have plenty of offers. Turned them all down, she did." The housekeeper straightened, a tattered paper clenched in one hand. "Ah, here it is!" She thrust the page toward him.

Sebastian found himself staring at a single stanza of poetry written in a schoolboy's best copperplate. He read aloud:

> *Somewhere the sea, somewhere the sun*
> *Whisper of pain and love untold;*
> *Something that's done and more undone,*
> *Are only the dead so bold?*

He looked up. "George Tennyson wrote this?"

"He did. Oh, it's all great nonsense, to be sure. But it's still fine, wouldn't you say? And he but a boy of nine!"

"Do you mind if I keep it for a day or so? I'll see it's returned to you," he added when she looked hesitant.

"To be sure you may keep it, my lord. Only, I won't deny I would like to have it back."

"I understand." Sebastian tucked the boy's poem into his pocket. "Do you have any idea how Miss Tennyson and the children planned to spend yesterday afternoon?"

She looked thoughtful for a moment, then shook her head. "No, my lord; I don't know as I ever heard her mention it. We always lay out a cold collation for the family in the dining room, you see, before we leave for our half day. They eat when they come home from church, before they go out again. We left a lovely spread, with a side of beef and salmon in aspic and a chilled asparagus soup."

"And did Miss Tennyson and the children eat the meal you left for them on Sunday?"

"Oh, yes, my lord. In fact, the plate with Mrs. Reagan's oatmeal cookies was completely empty except for a few crumbs." She plopped back down in her chair, her hands wringing together so hard the fingers turned white. "Oh, if only Mr. Tennyson had been here!" she cried. "Then we'd have known for certain something was amiss when they didn't come home last night."

"What time did the servants return to the house?"

"The others were back by seven, although I'm afraid I myself wasn't in until nearly eight. I spent the day with my sister in Kent Town, you see; her husband's ever so sick, and Miss Tennyson told me not to worry if I was a bit late. She was that way, you know—so kind and generous. And now—" Her voice cracked and she turned her face away, her throat working silently.

Sebastian said, "Were you concerned when you arrived back and realized Miss Tennyson and the children hadn't returned themselves?"

"Well, of course I was! We all were. Margaret Campbell—she's the boys' nurse, you know—was all for going to the public office at once. She was convinced something must have happened to them. But we had no way of knowing that for certain, and who could ever have imagined that something like *this* had occurred? I mean, what if Miss Tennyson had simply decided to spend the night with some friends and forgot to tell us? Or she could have received bad news from the boys' parents and set off with the children for Lincoln-shire. To tell the truth, I thought she might even have reconsidered staying in London and decided to join her brother in the country after all. I can tell you, she would not have thanked us if we'd raised a ruckus for naught."

Sebastian watched her twist her handkerchief around her fist. "Do you know of anyone who might have wanted to do either Miss Tennyson or the boys harm?"

Her puffy face crumpled. "*No,*" she cried. "None of this makes any sense. Why would anyone want to harm either her or those poor, poor lads? *Why?*"

Sebastian rested his hand on her shoulder. It was a useless, awkward gesture of comfort, but she looked up at him with pleading eyes, her plump, matronly form shuddering with need for a measure of understanding and reassurance he could not give.

Chapter 9

*L*eaving the servants' hall, Sebastian climbed the stairs to the nursery at the top of the Tennyson house.

It was a cheerful place, its walls newly covered in brightly sprigged paper and flooded with light from the rows of long windows overlooking the broad, sun-dappled expanse of the river. The two little boys might have only been visiting for the summer, but it was obvious that Gabrielle Tennyson had prepared for her young cousins' stay with loving care.

Pausing at the entrance to the schoolroom, Sebastian let his gaze drift over the armies of tin soldiers that marched in neat formations across the scrubbed floorboards. Cockhorses and drums and wooden boats littered the room; shelves of books beckoned with promises of endless hours spent vicariously adventuring in faraway lands. On the edge of a big, sturdy table near the door lay a cluster of small, disparate objects—a broken clay pipe bowl, a glowing brown chestnut, a blue and white ceramic bead—as if a boy had hurriedly emptied his pockets of their treasures and then never come back for them.

A woman's voice sounded behind him. "And who might you be, then?"

Turning, Sebastian found himself being regarded with a suspicious scowl by a bony woman with thick, dark red hair, gaunt cheeks, and pale gray eyes. "You must be the boys' nurse, Miss Campbell."

"I am." Her gaze swept him with obvious suspicion, her voice raspy with a thick northern brogue. "And you?"

"Lord Devlin."

She sniffed. "I heard them talking about you in the servants' hall." She pushed past him into the room and swung to face him, her thin frame rigid with hostility and what he suspected was a carefully controlled, intensely private grief. "Seems a queer thing for a lord to do, getting hisself mixed up in murder. But then, London folk is queer."

Sebastian found himself faintly smiling. "You came with the boys from Lincolnshire?"

"I did, yes. Been with Master George since he was born, I have, and little Master Alfred too."

"I understand the boys' father is a rector?"

"Aye." A wary light crept into her eyes.

Seeing it, Sebastian said, "Tell me about him."

"The Reverend Tennyson?" She folded her arms across her stomach, her hands clenched tight around her bony elbows. "What is there to tell? He's a brilliant man—for all he's so big and hulking and clumsy."

"I'm told he's not well. Nothing serious, I hope?"

The fingers gripping her elbows reminded him of claws clinging desperately to a shifting purchase. "He hasna been well for a long time now." She hesitated, then added, "A very long time." Lingering ill health was all too common in their society, frequently caused by consumption, but more often by some unknown debilitating affliction.

Sebastian wandered the room, his attention seemingly all for the scattered toys and books. "And the boys? Are they hale?"

"Ach, you'd be hard put to find two sturdier lads. To be sure, Master George can be a bit wild and hotheaded, but there's no malice in him."

It struck him as a profoundly strange thing for her to say. He paused beside a scattering of books on the window seat overlooking the river. They were the usual assortment of boys' adventure stories. Flipping open one of the covers, he found himself staring at the name *George Tennyson* written in the same round copperplate as the poem given him by the housekeeper.

Looking up, he said, "Do you know where Miss Tennyson planned to take her young cousins yesterday?"

The nursemaid shook her head. "No. She told them it was a surprise."

"Could she perhaps have intended to show them the excavations at Camlet Moat?"

"She could, I suppose. But how would that be a surprise? She'd taken them up there before."

"Perhaps she'd discovered something new she wanted to show them."

"I wouldn't know about that."

Sebastian studied the woman's plain, tensely held face. "What do you think has happened to them, Miss Campbell?"

She pressed her lips into a hard, straight line, her nostrils flaring on a quickly indrawn breath, her forehead creasing with a sudden upwelling of emotion she fought to suppress. It was a moment before she could speak. "I don't know," she said, shaking her head. "I just don't know. I keep thinking about those poor wee bairns out there somewhere, alone and afraid, with no one to care for them. Or—or—" But here her voice broke and she could only shake her head, unwilling to put her worst fears into words.

He said, "Did you ever hear Miss Tennyson mention the name of an antiquary with whom she had quarreled?"

Margaret cleared her throat and touched the back of her knuckles to her nostrils, her formidable composure slamming once more into place. "A what?"

"An antiquary. A scholar of antiquities. You never heard Miss Tennyson speak of any such person?"

"No."

"How about the children? Did they ever mention anyone? Anyone at all they might have met in London?"

She stared back at him, her face pale, her eyes wide.

Sebastian said, "There is someone. Tell me."

"I don't know his name. The lads always called him 'the Lieutenant.'"

"He's a lieutenant?"

"Aye." Her lip curled. "Some Frenchy."

"Where did the children meet this French lieutenant?"

"Miss Tennyson would oftentimes take the lads to the park of an evening. I think they'd see him there."

"They saw him often?"

"Aye. Him and his dog."

"The Lieutenant has a dog?"

"Aye. The lads are mad about dogs, you know."

"When did they first begin mentioning this lieutenant?"

"Ach, it must have been six weeks or more ago—not long after we first arrived in London, I'd say."

"That's all you can tell me about him? That he's a Frenchman and a lieutenant—and that he has a dog?"

"He may've been in the cavalry. I can't be certain, mind you, but it's only since we've come to London that Master George has suddenly been all agog to join the Army. He's forever galloping around the schoolroom slashing a wooden sword through the air and shouting, *Charge!* and, *At 'em, lads!*"

"Any idea where this lieutenant might have seen service?"

"To be honest, I didn't like to pay too much heed to young Master George when he'd start going on about it. Couldn't see any sense in encouraging the lad. The Reverend's already told him he's bound for Eton next year. Besides, it didn't seem right, somehow, him being so friendly with a Frenchy."

Sebastian said, "Many émigrés have fought valiantly against Napoléon."

"Whoever said he was an émigré?" She gave a scornful laugh. "A prisoner on his parole, he is. And only the good Lord knows how many brave Englishmen he sent to their graves before he was took prisoner."

Sebastian went to lean on the terrace railing overlooking the river. The tide was out, a damp, fecund odor rising from the expanse of mudflats exposed along the bank below as the sun began its downward arc toward the west. An aged Gypsy woman in a full purple skirt and yellow kerchief was telling fortunes beside a man with a painted cart selling hot sausages near the steps. Beyond them, a string of constables could be seen poking long probes into the mud, turning over logs and bits of flotsam left stranded by the receding water. At first Sebastian wondered what they were doing. Then he realized they must be searching for the children . . . or what was left of them.

He twisted around to stare back at the imposing row of eighteenth-century town houses that rose above the terrace. The disappearance of the two young children added both an urgency and a troubling new dimension to the murder of Gabrielle Tennyson. Had the boys, too, fallen victim to Gabrielle's killer? For the same reason? Or were the children simply in the wrong place at the wrong time? And if they hadn't suffered the same fate as their cousin, then where were they now?

Sebastian brought his gaze back to the top of the steps, his eyes narrowing as he studied the thin, drab-coated man buying a sausage from the cart.

It was the same man he'd seen earlier, at Tower Hill.

Bloody hell.

Pushing away from the railing, Sebastian strolled toward the sausage seller. Pocketing the drab-coated man's coin, the sausage seller handed the man a paper-wrapped sausage. Without seeming to glance in Sebastian's direction, the man took a bite of his sausage and began to walk away.

He was a tallish man, with thin shoulders and a round hat he wore pulled low on his face. Sebastian quickened his step.

He was still some ten feet away when the man tossed the sausage aside and broke into a run.

Chapter 10

*T*he man sprinted around the edge of the terrace and dropped out of sight.

Sebastian tore after him, down a crowded, steeply cobbled lane lined with taverns and narrow coffeehouses that emptied abruptly onto the sun-splashed waterfront below. A flock of white gulls rose, screeching, to wheel high above the broad, sparkling river.

The genteel houses of the Adelphi Terrace had been constructed over a warren of arch-fronted subterranean vaults built to span the slope between the Strand and the wharves along the river. Sebastian could hear the man's booted feet pounding over the weathered planking as he darted around towering pyramids of wine casks and dodged blue-smocked workmen unloading sacks of coal from a barge. Then the buff-coated man threw one quick look over his shoulder and dove under the nearest archway to disappear into the gloomy world beneath the terrace.

Hell and the devil confound it, thought Sebastian, swerving around a mule cart.

"Hey!" shouted a grizzled man in a cap and leather apron as the mule between the traces of his cart snorted and kicked. "What the bloody 'ell ye doin'?"

Sebastian kept running.

One behind the other, Sebastian and the drab-coated man raced through soaring, catacomblike arches, the bricks furred with soot and mold and perpetual dampness. They sprinted down dark tunnels of warehouses tenanted by wine sellers and coal merchants, and up dimly lit passages off which opened stables that reeked of manure and dirty straw, where cows lowed plaintively from out of the darkness.

"Who the hell are you?" Sebastian shouted as the man veered around a rotten water butt, toward the dark opening of a narrow staircase that wound steeply upward. "*Who?*"

Without faltering, the man clambered up the stairs, Sebastian at his heels. Round and round they went, only to erupt into a steeply sloping corridor paved with worn bricks and lined with milk cans.

Breathing hard and fast, the man careened from side to side, upending first one milk can, then another and another, the cans rattling and clattering as they bounced down the slope like giant bowling pins, filling the air with the hot splash of spilling milk.

"God damn it," swore Sebastian, dodging first one can, then the next. Then his boots hit the slick wet bricks and his feet shot out from under him. He went down hard, slamming his shoulder against a brick pier as he slid back down the slope and the next milk can bounced over his head.

He pushed up, the leather soles of his boots slipping so that he nearly went down again. He could hear the man's running footsteps disappearing around the bend up ahead.

Panting heavily now, Sebastian tore around the corner and out a low archway into the unexpected sunlight of the open air. He threw up one hand to shade his suddenly blinded eyes, his step faltering.

The lane stretched empty and silent before him.

The man was gone.

After leaving Carlton House, Hero spent the next several hours at a bookseller's in Westminster, where she selected several items, one of which proved to be very old and rare. Then, sending her purchases home in the charge of a footman, she directed her coachman to the British Museum.

It was at an exhibition of Roman sarcophagi at the British Museum that Hero had first met Gabrielle Tennyson some six years before. Initially, their interaction had been marked more by politeness than by cordiality. Both might be gently born, well-educated women, but they belonged to vastly different worlds. For while the Jarvises were an ancient noble family with powerful connections, Gabrielle Tennyson came from a long line of barristers and middling churchmen— gentry rather than noble, comfortable rather than wealthy.

But with time had come respect and, eventually, true friendship. Their interests and ambitions had never exactly coincided: Gabrielle's passion had all been for the past, whereas Hero's main focus would always be the economic and social condition of her own age. Yet their shared willingness to challenge their society's narrow gender expectations and their determination never to marry had forged a unique and powerful bond between them.

Now Hero, much to her mingling bemusement and chagrin, had become Lady Devlin. While Gabrielle . . .

Gabrielle was dead.

The bells of the city's church towers were just striking three when Hero's coachman drew up outside the British Museum. She sat with one hand resting casually on the carriage strap, her gaze on the towering portal of the complex across the street as she listened to the great rolling clatter and dong of the bells swelling over the city.

Built of brick in the French style with rustic stone quoins and a slate mansard roof, the sprawling mansion had once served as the home of the Dukes of Montagu, its front courtyard flanked by long colonnaded wings and separated from Great Russell Street by a tall gateway surmounted by an octagonal lantern. She watched a man and a woman pause on the footpath before the entrance, confer for a moment, and go inside. Then two men deep in a heated discussion, neither of whom Hero recognized, exited the gateway and turned east.

One after another the bells of the city tapered off into stillness, until all were silent.

Hero frowned. She had come in search of an antiquary named Bevin Childe. Childe was known both for his formidable scholarship and for his fanatical adherence to a self-imposed schedule. Every Monday, Tuesday, and Thursday between the hours of ten and three he could be found in the Reading Room of the museum. At precisely three o'clock, he left the museum and crossed the street to a public house known as the Pied Piper, where he ate a plate of sliced roast beef and buttered bread washed down by a pint of good, stout ale. This was followed by a short constitutional around nearby Bedford Square, after which he returned to the Reading Room from four until six. But today, Childe was deviating from his prescribed pattern.

The minutes ticked past. "Bother," said Hero softly under her breath.

"My lady?" asked her footman, his hand on the open carriage door.

"Perhaps—" she began, then broke off as a stout man in his early thirties dressed in a slightly crumpled olive coat and a high-crowned beaver came barreling through the museum's gateway, his head down, a brass-headed walking stick tucked under one arm. He had the face of an overgrown cherub, his flesh as pink and white as a baby's, his small mouth pursed as if with annoyance at the realization that he was nearly ten minutes late for his nuncheon.

"Mr. Childe," called Hero, descending from the carriage, her furled parasol in hand. "What a fortunate encounter. There is something I wish to speak with you about. Do let's walk along for a ways."

Childe's head jerked up, his step faltering, a succession of transparent emotions flitting across his cherubic features as his desire to maintain his schedule warred with the need to appear accommodating to a woman whose father was the most powerful man in the Kingdom.

"Actually," he said, "I was just on my way to grab a bite—"

"It won't take but a moment." Hero opened her parasol and inexorably turned his steps toward the nearby square.

He twisted around to gaze longingly back at the Pied Piper, the exaggerated point of his high collar pressing into his full cheek. "But I generally prefer to take my constitutional *after* I eat—"

"I know. I do beg your pardon, but you have heard this morning's news about the death of Miss Tennyson and the disappearance of her young cousins?"

She watched as the pinkness drained from his face, leaving him pale. "How could I not? The news is all over town. Indeed, I can't seem to think of anything else. It was my intention to spend the day reviewing a collection of manor rolls from the twelfth century, but I've found it nearly impossible to focus my attention for more than a minute or two at a stretch."

"How . . . distressing for you," said Hero dryly.

The scholar nodded. "Most distressing."

The man might still be in his early thirties—not much older than Devlin, she realized with some surprise—but he had the demeanor and mannerisms of someone in his forties or fifties. She said, "I remember Miss Tennyson telling me once that you disagreed with her identification of Camlet Moat as the possible site of Camelot."

"I do. But then, you would be sorely pressed to find anyone of repute who does agree with her."

"You're saying her research was faulty?"

"Her research? No, one could hardly argue with the references to the site she discovered in various historical documents and maps. There is no doubt the area was indeed known as 'Camelot' for hundreds of years. Her interpretation of those findings, however, is another matter entirely."

"Was that the basis of your quarrel with her last Friday? Her interpretation?"

He gave a weak, startled laugh. "Quarrel? I had no quarrel with Miss Tennyson. Who could have told you such a thing?"

"Do you really want me to answer that question?"

Her implication was not lost on him. She watched, fascinated, as Childe's mobile features suddenly froze. He cleared his throat. "And your . . . your source did not also tell you the reason for our little . . . disagreement?"

"Not precisely; I was hoping you could explain it further."

His face hardened in a way she had not expected. "So you are here as the emissary of your husband, not your father."

"I am no one's emissary. I am here because Gabrielle Tennyson was my friend, and whoever killed her will have to answer to me for what they've done to her—to her and to her cousins."

If any woman other than Hero had made such a statement, Childe might have smiled. But all of London knew that less than a week before, three men had attempted to kidnap Hero; she had personally stabbed one, shot the next, and nearly decapitated the other.

"Well," he said with sudden, forced heartiness. "It was, as you say, a difference of opinion over the interpretation of the historical evidence. That is all."

"Really?"

He stared back at her, as if daring her to challenge him. "Yes."

They turned to walk along the far side of the square, where a Punch professor competed with a hurdy-gurdy player, and a barefoot, wan-faced girl in a ragged dress sold watercress for a half-penny a bunch from a worn wooden tray suspended by a strap around her neck. A cheap handbill tacked to a nearby lamppost bore a bold headline that read in smudged ink, KING ARTHUR, THE ONCE AND FUTURE KING!

Normally, the square would have been filled with children playing under the watchful eye of their nursemaids, their shouts and laughter carrying on the warm breeze. But today, the sunlit lawns and graveled walks lay silent and empty. Gabrielle's murder and the mysterious disappearance of the two boys had obviously spooked the city. Those mothers who could afford to do so were keeping their children safely indoors under nervous, watchful eyes.

"I was wondering," said Hero, "where exactly were you yesterday?"

If Childe's cheeks had been pale before, they now flared red, his eyes wide with indignation, his pursed mouth held tight. "If you mean to suggest that I could possibly have anything to do with— That—that I—"

Hero returned his angry stare with a calculated look of bland astonishment. "I wasn't suggesting anything, Mr. Childe; I was merely hoping you might have some idea about Miss Tennyson's plans for Sunday."

"Ah. Well . . . I'm afraid not. As it happens, I spend my Fridays, Saturdays, and Sundays at Gough Hall. The late Richard Gough left his books and papers to the Bodleian Library, you see, and I have volunteered to sort through and organize them. It's a prodigious undertaking."

She had heard of Richard Gough, the famous scholar and writer who had been director of the Society of Antiquaries for two decades and who had made the Arthurian legends one of his particular areas of interest. "Gough Hall is near Camlet Moat, is it not?"

"It is."

"I wonder, did you ever take advantage of the opportunity offered by that proximity to visit the excavations on the isle?"

"I wouldn't waste my time," said Childe loftily.

Hero tilted her head to one side, her gaze on his face, a coaxing smile on her lips. "So certain that Miss Tennyson was wrong about the island, are you?"

No answering smile touched the man's dour features. "If a real character known as Arthur ever existed—which is by no means certain—he was in all likelihood a barbaric warrior chieftain from the wilds of Wales whose dimly remembered reality was seized upon by a collection of maudlin French troubadours with no understanding of—or interest in—the world he actually inhabited."

"I take it you're not fond of medieval romances?"

She noticed he was staring, hard, at another handbill tacked up on the wall of the house at the corner. This one simply proclaimed, KING ARTHUR, SAVE US!

Hero said, "Who do you think killed her?"

Childe jerked his head around to look at her again, and for one unexpected moment, all the bombastic self-importance seemed to leach out of the man in a way that left him seeming unexpectedly vulnerable—and considerably more likeable. "Believe me when I say that if I could help you in any way, I would. Miss Tennyson was—" His voice quivered and he broke off, his features pinched with grief. He swallowed and tried again. "She was a most remarkable woman, brilliant and high-spirited and full of boundless energy, even if her enthusiasms did at times lead her astray. But she was also very good at keeping parts of her life—of herself—secret."

His words echoed so closely those of Hero's father that she felt a sudden, unexpected chill. "What sort of secrets are we talking about?"

"If I knew, they wouldn't be secrets, now, would they?" said Childe with a faintly condescending air.

Hero asked again, her voice more tart, "So who do you think killed her?"

Childe shook his head. "I don't know. But if I were intent on unmasking her killer, rather than focus on Miss Tennyson's associates and activities, I would instead ask myself, Who would benefit from the death of her young cousins?"

They had come full circle, so that they now stood on the footpath outside the Pied Piper. The door beside them opened, spilling voices and laughter and the yeasty scent of ale into the street as two gentlemen emerged blinking into the sunlight and crossed the street toward the museum.

"You mean, George and Arthur Tennyson?" said Hero.

She realized Childe was no longer looking at her but at something or someone beyond her. Throwing a quick glance over her shoulder, Hero found herself staring at the watercress girl from the square. The girl must have trailed behind them and now leaned wearily against a nearby lamppost, her wooden tray hanging heavy from its strap, a wilting bunch of greens clutched forlornly in one hand. She couldn't have been more than twelve or thirteen, with golden hair and large blue eyes in an elfin face. Already grown tall and leggy, she was still boy-thin, with only a hint of the breasts beginning to swell beneath the bodice of her ragged dress. And Childe was looking at her with his lips parted and his gray eyes hooded in a way that made Hero feel she was witnessing something unclean and obscene.

As if becoming aware of Hero's scrutiny, he brought his gaze back to her face and cleared his throat. "As I said. And now, Lady Devlin, you really must excuse me." Turning on his heel, he strode into the Pied Piper and shut the door behind him with a snap.

Hero stood for a moment, her gaze on the closed door. Then, digging her purse from her reticule, she walked over to the watercress girl. "How much for all your bunches?"

The girl straightened with a jerk, her mouth agape. "M'lady?"

"You heard me. You've what? A dozen? Tell me, do you always sell your watercress here, by the museum?"

The girl closed her mouth and swallowed. "Here, or at Blooms-bury Square."

Hero pressed three coins into the girl's palm. "There's a shilling for all your watercress and two more besides. But don't let me catch you around here again. Is that understood? From now on, you peddle your bundles only at Bloomsbury."

The girl dropped a frightened, confused curtsy. "Yes, m'lady."

"Go on. Get out of here."

The girl took to her heels and fled, the ragged skirt of her dress swirling around her ankles, her tray thumping against her thin body, her fist clenched about the coins in her hand. She did not look back.

Hero watched until the girl turned the corner and the receding patter of her bare feet was lost in the rumble of the passing carriages and carts, the shouts of the costermongers, the distant wail of the hurdy-gurdy player from the square.

But the uneasiness within her remained.

She was about to turn back toward her carriage when she heard a familiar low-pitched voice behind her say, "I suppose I shouldn't be surprised to find you here, but I must confess that I am."

Chapter 11

Sebastian stood with one shoulder propped against the brick wall of the pub, his arms crossed at his chest, and watched his wife pivot slowly to face him. The hot sun fell full across a face unusually pale but flawlessly composed.

"Devlin," she said, adjusting the tilt of her parasol in a way that threw her features into shadow. "What brings you here?"

He pushed away from the wall. "I was hoping to find someone at the museum who could direct me to a certain unidentified antiquary who quarreled recently with Miss Tennyson. I take it that's the gentleman in question?"

"His name is Bevin Childe." She stood still and let him walk up to her. "Post-Roman England is his specialty."

"Ah, the Arthurian Age."

"Yes. But I wouldn't let Childe hear you call it that. I suspect you'd get an earful."

"Mr. Childe is not a fan of Camelot?"

"He is not."

"How much do you know about him?"

They turned to walk together toward her waiting carriage. "Apart from the fact that he's a pompous ass?" she said with unladylike frankness.

Sebastian gave a startled laugh. "Is he?"

"Decidedly. As for what I know about him, I'm told his father is a Cambridge don. A doctor of divinity."

"I wouldn't have expected such a man to have much to do with Miss Tennyson."

He watched her brows draw together in a frown. "Meaning?" she asked.

"Meaning that however brilliant or accomplished she may have been, Miss Tennyson not only lacked a formal university education, but she was also female. And there's no need to scowl at me; I didn't say I *agreed* with that sort of prejudice, did I?"

"True. I beg your pardon."

"What about Childe himself? Is he a clergyman?"

"I believe he was once rather reluctantly destined for the church. But fortunately for Mr. Childe, a maternal uncle managed to acquire a fortune in India and then died without siring an heir. He left everything to Mr. Childe."

"Fortuitous, indeed—for both Mr. Childe and the church. How do you come to know so much about the gentleman?"

"From Gabrielle. Her brother was up at Cambridge with Childe, and the two men have remained friends ever since—much to Gabrielle's disgust, given that she has heartily detested the man since she was still in the schoolroom."

"Any particular reason why?"

"She said he was arrogant, opinionated, self-absorbed, pedantic, and—strange."

"'Strange'? Did she ever explain exactly what she meant by that?"

"No. I asked her once, but she just shrugged and said he made her uncomfortable."

"Interesting. And precisely how large of a fortune did the arrogant and pedantic Mr. Childe inherit?"

"A comfortable enough independence that he is now able to devote himself entirely to scholarship. I gather he currently divides his time between research here at the museum and a project he has undertaken for the Bodleian Library, which entails cataloging the library and collections of the late Richard Gough."

"That's significant," said Sebastian, studying her face. "Why?"

"Because amongst other things, Mr. Gough made a particular study of the Arthurian legends. And his home, Gough Hall, is near Enfield."

"And Camlet Moat?"

"Precisely."

Sebastian frowned. "So where does Mr. Childe live?"

"I believe he has rooms in St. James's Street."

"He's unmarried?"

"He is, yes. Gabrielle told me several weeks ago that he had become quite vocal in his disparagement of her conclusions about Camlet Moat. And Childe himself says that they quarreled over the issue again just last Friday. But he also made some rather vague references to Gabrielle's 'secrets' that I found disturbing."

"Secrets? What secrets?"

"He declined to elaborate."

They had reached her carriage. Sebastian shook his head at the footman who was about to spring forward; the man stepped back, and Sebastian opened the carriage door himself. "Any chance Childe could have been referring to a certain French prisoner of war with whom Miss Tennyson was apparently friendly?"

Hero turned to face him, her expression one of mingled surprise and puzzlement. "What French prisoner of war?"

"She never talked about him?" Pausing with one elbow resting on the carriage's open window, he gave her a brief summary of what he'd learned from the servants in the Tennyson household. "You're certain she never mentioned such a man to you?"

"Not that I recall, no."

Sebastian let his gaze rove over the shadowed features of her face, the smooth curve of her cheek, the strong, almost masculine angle of her jaw. Once, he would have said she was telling him the truth. But he knew her well enough by now to know that she was keeping something back from him.

He said, "When Bow Street brought word this morning of Gabrielle Tennyson's death, I was surprised that you had no wish to accompany me to Camlet Moat. In my naivety, I assumed it was because you knew Lovejoy would be discomfited by your presence. But you had another reason entirely, didn't you?"

She furled her parasol, her attention seemingly all for the task of securing the strap. Rather than answering him, she said, "We agreed when we married that we would respect each other's independence."

"We did. Yet your purpose in this is the same as mine, is it not? To discover what happened to Gabrielle Tennyson and her young cousins? Or is something else going on here of which I am not aware?"

She looked up at him, the light falling full on her face, and he saw there neither guile nor subterfuge, but only a tense concern. "You've heard the authorities discovered the boys are missing?"

Sebastian nodded silently.

"When I asked Childe who he thought killed Gabrielle, he said that rather than focusing on Gabrielle's associates, I ought to consider who would benefit from the elimination of the children."

Sebastian was silent for a moment, remembering a boy's flowing copperplate and armies of tin soldiers marching silently across a sunlit nursery floor. He refused to accept that the two little boys were dead too. But all he said was, "You've met them?"

"Her cousins? Several times, yes. I'm not one of those women who dote mindlessly on children, but George and Alfred are something special. They're so extraordinarily bright and curious and full of enthusiasm for learning about the world around them that they're a delight to be with. The thought that something might have happened to them too—" She broke off, and he saw the rare glaze of unshed tears in her eyes. Then she cleared her throat and looked away, as if embarrassed to be seen giving way to her emotions.

"'Something that's done and more undone,'" he quoted softly. "'Are only the dead so bold?'"

Hero shook her head, not understanding. "What?"

"It's from a poem George Tennyson wrote." He showed it to her. "Does it mean anything to you?"

She read through the short stanza. "No. But George was always writing disjointed scraps of poetry like that. I doubt it means anything."

"I'm told the boy's father has been ill for a long time. Do you have any idea with what?"

"No. But then, I don't know that much about Miss Tennyson's family. Her parents died before I knew her. Her brother is a pleasant enough chap, although rather typically preoccupied with his legal practice. He has a small estate down in Kent, which is where he is now. It has always been my understanding that he and Gabrielle were comfortably situated, although no more than that. Yet I believe there may be substantial wealth elsewhere in the family. Recent wealth."

"Good God," said Sebastian. "Was Miss Tennyson in some way related to Charles Tennyson d'Eyncourt?"

"I believe they are first cousins. You know him?"

"He was several years behind me at Eton."

His tone betrayed more than he'd intended it to. She smiled. "And you consider him a pretentious, toadying a—" She broke off to cast a rueful glance at the wooden faces of the waiting servants.

"Bore?" he suggested helpfully.

"That too."

For one unexpectedly intimate moment, their gazes met and

they shared a private smile. Then Sebastian felt his smile begin to fade.

For the past fifteen months, d'Eyncourt had served as a member of Parliament from Lincolnshire. A fiercely reactionary Tory, he had quickly managed to ingratiate himself with the block of parliamentarians controlled by Hero's own father, Lord Jarvis.

Sebastian said, "Why do I keep getting the distinct impression there's something you're not telling me?"

She took his offered hand and climbed the step into the waiting carriage. "Would I do that?" she asked.

"Yes."

She gave a throaty chuckle and gracefully disposed the skirts of her dusky blue walking dress around her on the seat. "Will you tell the coachman to take me home, please?"

"Are you going home?"

"Are you?"

Smiling softly, he closed the door and nodded to the driver. He stood for a moment and watched as her carriage rounded the corner onto Tottenham Court. Then he went in search of the pretentious toadying bore who called himself Tennyson d'Eyncourt.

Chapter 12

Charles Tennyson d'Eyncourt was lounging comfortably in one of the leather tub chairs in the reading room of White's when Sebastian walked up to him.

The MP was considerably fairer than his cousin Gabrielle, slim and gracefully formed, with delicate features and high cheekbones and lips so thin as to appear nearly nonexistent. He had a glass of brandy on the table at his elbow and the latest copy of the conservative journal *The Courier* spread open before him. He glanced up, briefly, when Sebastian settled in the seat opposite him, then pointedly returned his attention to his reading.

"My condolences on the death of your cousin, Miss Gabrielle Tennyson," said Sebastian.

"I take it Bow Street has involved you in the investigation of this unfortunate incident, have they?" asked d'Eyncourt without looking up again.

"If by 'unfortunate incident' you mean the murder of Miss Tennyson and the disappearance of the young children in her care, then the answer is yes."

D'Eyncourt reached, deliberately, for his brandy, took a sip, and returned to his journal.

"I'm curious," said Sebastian, signaling a passing waiter for a drink. "How close is the relationship between you and Miss Tennyson?"

"We are—or I suppose I should say were—first cousins."

"So the two missing boys are . . . ?"

"My nephews."

"Your brother's sons?"

"That is correct."

"I must confess that, under the circumstances, I am rather surprised to find you lounging in your club calmly reading a journal."

D'Eyncourt looked up at that, his thin nose quivering. "Indeed? And what would you have me do instead, I wonder? Go charging into the countryside to thrash the underbrush of Enfield Chase like a beater hoping to flush game?"

"You think that's where the children are liable to be found? At Camlet Moat?"

"How the devil would I know?" snapped d'Eyncourt and returned once more to his reading.

Sebastian studied the other man's pinched profile. He couldn't recall many of the younger boys at Eton, but Sebastian remembered d'Eyncourt. As a lad, d'Eyncourt had been one of those ostentatiously earnest scholars who combined shameless toadying with nauseating displays of false enthusiasm to curry favor with the dons. But to his fellow students he was ruthless and vindictive, and quickly acquired a well-deserved reputation as someone who would do anything—and say anything—to get what he wanted.

In those days he'd simply been called "Tennyson," the same as his cousin and missing nephews. But several years ago he had successfully petitioned the Home Secretary to have his name changed to the more aristocratic d'Eyncourt, the extinct patronym of one of his mother's ancestors, to which his claims were, to say the least, dubious. It was well-known that his ambition was to be made Lord d'Eyncourt before he was forty.

"You seem oddly unconcerned about their fates," said Sebastian.

"It is the stuff of tragedy, to be sure. However, none of it alters the fact that my brother and I have never been close. His life is narrowly focused on his benefices in Somersby, whereas I live most of the year in London, where I take my duties at Parliament very seriously indeed. I doubt I would recognize his children if I passed them in the street."

"Is that why they've been staying with Miss Tennyson, their cousin, rather than with you, their uncle?"

D'Eyncourt sniffed. "My wife is not fond of London and chooses to remain in Lincolnshire. I do currently have my sister Mary with me, but I could hardly ask her to undertake the management of two wild, poorly brought-up boys, now, could I?"

"*Are* they wild and poorly bought up?"

"They could hardly be otherwise, given their parentage."

"Really?" Sebastian settled more comfortably in his seat. "Tell me about the boys' father—your brother. I hear he's not well. Nothing serious, I hope?"

A curious hint of color touched the other man's high cheekbones. "I fear my brother's health has never been particularly robust."

"Can you think of anyone who might benefit from the death or disappearance of his sons?"

"Good heavens; what a ridiculous notion! I told you: My brother is a rector. He holds two livings, which together provide him with a respectable income. But he has always been a hopeless spendthrift, and the foolish woman he married is even worse, with the result that my father is forever being forced to tow them out of the river tick."

D'Eyncourt's father was a notorious figure known irreverently as "the Old Man of the Wolds," thanks to his extensive landholdings in the Wolds, an area of hills and wide-open valleys in the northeast of England. His fortune, while of recent origins, was reportedly huge, deriving largely from a series of astute land purchases and the old man's ruthless manipulation of anyone unfortunate enough to drift into his orbit.

Sebastian said, "You are your father's sole heir?"

D'Eyncourt's thin nostrils flared with indignation. "I am. And may I take leave to tell you that I resent the inference inherent in that question? I resent it very much."

"Oh, you have my leave to tell me anything you wish," said Sebastian, stretching to his feet. "Just one more question: Can you think of anyone who might have wished Miss Tennyson harm?"

D'Eyncourt opened his mouth as if to say something, then closed it and shook his head.

"You do know of someone," said Sebastian, watching him closely. "Who is it?"

"Well . . ." D'Eyncourt licked his thin lips. "You are aware, of course, that my cousin fancied herself something of a bluestocking?"

"I would have said she could more accurately be described as a respected antiquary rather than as a bluestocking, but, yes, I am aware of her scholarly activities. Why?"

D'Eyncourt pulled a face. "Most women who indulge in such unsuitable activities have enough regard for the reputations of their families to adopt a male nom de plume and keep their true identities a secret. But not Gabrielle."

"My wife also chooses to publish under her own name," said Sebastian evenly.

D'Eyncourt gave an uncomfortable titter and looked faintly unwell. "So she does. No offense intended, I'm sure."

Sebastian said, "Are you suggesting that Miss Tennyson's investigations into the history of Camlet Moat might have contributed in some way to her death?"

D'Eyncourt gave a dismissive wave of his hand. "I know nothing of this latest start of hers. I was referring to a project she undertook some two or three months ago; something to do with tracing the original line of London's old Roman walls or some such nonsense. Whatever it was, it involved venturing into several of the more un-savory districts of the city. Not at all the proper sort of undertaking for a lady."

"You say this was two or three months ago?"

"Something like that, yes."

"So what makes you think it could have anything to do with her recent death?"

"Last week—Thursday, to be precise—I was on my way to meet with a colleague in the Strand when I happened to see Gabrielle ar-guing with a very rough customer near the York Steps. Thinking her in some sort of difficulty, I naturally approached with the in-tention of intervening. Much to my astonishment, she was not at all appreciative of my attempts on her behalf. Indeed, she was quite curt. Insisted there was no need for me to concern myself—that the individual I had seen her with was someone she had encountered when she discovered that the foundations of his tavern incorpo-rated some extensive vestiges of the city's original Roman walls."

"Did you happen to catch the man's name?"

D'Eyncourt shook his head. "Sorry. But it shouldn't be that dif-ficult to discover. I believe she said the tavern was called the Devil's Head or the Devil's Tower or some such thing. The man was a most unsavory-looking character—tall, with dark hair and sun-darkened skin, and dressed all in black except for his shirt. I thought at the time he reminded me of someone I know, but I couldn't quite place the resemblance."

"What makes you think he was a threat to her?"

"Because of what I heard him say, just before they noticed me walking up to them. He said"—d'Eyncourt roughened his voice in a crude imitation of the man's accent—"'Meddle in this and you'll be sorry. Be a shame to see something happen to a pretty young lady such as yourself.'"

Chapter 13

Sebastian was silent for a moment, trying to fit this incident into everything else he'd been told.

"Of course she tried to deny it," said d'Eyncourt. "Claimed he'd said no such thing. But I know what I heard. And it was obvious she was more than a little discomfited to be seen talking to this individual."

Sebastian studied the other man's narrow, effete features. But d'Eyncourt had spent a lifetime twisting incidents and conversations to serve his own purposes; his face was a bland mask.

Sebastian said, "What do you think it was about?"

D'Eyncourt closed his journal and rose to his feet. "I've no notion. You're the one who dabbles in murder, not I. I have far more important tasks with which to concern myself." He tucked *The Courier* beneath his arm. "And now you must excuse me; I've a meeting scheduled at Carlton House." He gave a short bow nicely calculated to convey just a hint of irony and contempt. Then he strolled languidly away, leaving Sebastian staring after him.

"Your drink, my lord?"

The waiter standing at Sebastian's elbow needed to repeat himself twice before Sebastian turned toward him. "Thank you," he said, taking the brandy from the waiter's silver tray and downing it in one long, burning pull.

It was when he was leaving White's that Sebastian came face-to-face with a familiar barrel-chested, white-haired man in his late sixties. At the sight of Sebastian, the Earl of Hendon paused, his face going slack.

For twenty-nine years Sebastian had called this man father, had struggled to understand Hendon's strangely conflicted love and anger, pride and resentment. But though the world still believed Sebastian to be the Earl's son, Sebastian, at least, now knew the truth.

Sebastian gave a slow, polite bow. "My lord."

"Devlin," said Hendon, his voice gruff with emotion. "You . . . you are well?"

"I am, yes." Sebastian hesitated, then added with painful correctness, "Thank you. And you?"

Hendon's jaw tightened. "As always, yes, thank you."

Hendon had always been a bear of a man. Through all his growing years and well into his twenties, Sebastian had been aware of Hendon towering over him in both height and breadth. But as the moment stretched out and became something painful, Sebastian suddenly realized that with increasing age, Hendon was shrinking. He was now the same height as Sebastian, perhaps even shorter. When had that happened? he wondered. And he felt an unwelcome pang at the realization that this man who had played such a vital role in his life was growing older, more frail, less formidable.

For one long, intense moment, the Earl's fiercely blue St. Cyr eyes met Sebastian's hard yellow gaze. Then the two men passed.

Neither looked back.

※

Sebastian found Hero seated at the table in his library, a pile of books scattered over the surface.

She had changed into a simple gown of figured muslin with a sapphire blue sash and had her head bent over some notes she was making. He paused for a moment in the doorway and watched as she caught her lower lip between her teeth in that way she had when she was concentrating. He'd often come upon her thus, surrounded by books and documents at the heavy old library table in her father's Berkeley Square house. And for some reason he could not have named, seeing her here at work in the library of their Brook Street home made their marriage seem suddenly more real—and more intimate—than the long hours of passion they'd shared in the darkness of the night. He found himself smiling at the thought.

Then she looked up and saw him.

He said, "So you did come home."

She leaned back in her chair, her pen resting idle in her hand. "I did. And did you find Mr. d'Eyncourt?"

"At White's." He went to rest his palms on the surface of the table and lean into them, his gaze on her face. "I need to know the route of London's old Roman walls. Can you trace me a map, with references to existing streets and landmarks?"

"Roughly, yes."

He handed her a fresh sheet of paper. "Roughly will do."

She dipped her pen in the ink. "What is this about?"

As she began to sketch, he told her of his interview with Gabrielle's cousin. "Do you have any idea what d'Eyncourt may have been talking about?"

"I do, actually. Several months ago, Gabrielle undertook to trace the remnants of the old city walls for a volume on the history of London being compiled by Dr. Littleton."

Sebastian frowned. "Isn't that the same volume you've been working on?"

"It is. Although I have been looking into the surviving vestiges of London's monastic houses." She finished her diagram and slid it across to him. "How exactly do you intend to go about finding this tavern owner?"

He stood for a moment, studying her sketch. She'd actually drawn two wall circuits, one older and smaller than the other. The northern stretch of the oldest wall had run roughly along the course of Cornhill and Leadenhall Street, then down along Mark Lane before turning east to Thames Street and Walbrook. The later, larger circuit ran from the Tower to Aldgate and Bishopsgate, before turning westward to St. Giles churchyard and then veering south to Falcon Square. He traced the line to Aldersgate and Giltspur Street, angling over to Ludgate and the Thames, then eastward back toward the Tower again.

"That's a lot of wall," he said, folding the map. "I'll give it to Tom and see what he can find."

"You do realize that Gabrielle could have told her cousin a lie to put him off. I don't think they were exactly close."

"She may have. But I wouldn't be surprised if the part about the tavern and the Roman wall, at least, was true." He nodded to the books scattered across the table's surface. "What is all this?"

"I've been brushing up on my knowledge of King Arthur and Guinevere and the Knights of the Round Table."

He reached for the nearest book, a slim, aged volume covered in faded blue leather, and read the title embossed in gold on the spine. "*La donna di Scalotta.*" He looked up. "What is it?"

"An Italian novella about the Lady of Shalott."

He shook his head. "Never heard of it."

"I wasn't familiar with it, either. But I remembered Gabrielle telling me she was working on a translation."

He leafed through the volume's aged pages and frowned. "I certainly wouldn't want to try to translate it." Sebastian's Italian had come largely from the soldiers, partisans, and bandits he'd encountered during the war and had little in common with the volume's archaic, stylized language. "When was it originally written?"

"The thirteenth century, I believe."

"Do you think it might somehow be related to the excavations at Camlet Moat?"

"I don't believe so, no. Gabrielle was interested in all aspects of the Arthurian legend; this is a relatively unknown part of it." She turned her head as the sound of the front doorbell echoed through the house. "Are you expecting someone?" she asked, just as Sebastian's majordomo, Morey, appeared in the doorway.

"A Mr. Hildeyard Tennyson to see you, my lord. He says he is the brother of Miss Gabrielle Tennyson. I have taken the liberty of showing him to the drawing room."

Chapter 14

*H*ildeyard Tennyson wore the haggard, stunned expression of a man whose world has suddenly collapsed upon him, leaving him shattered and numb.

Dressed in riding breeches and dusty boots that told of a long, hard ride back to town, he stood beside the front windows overlooking the street, his hat in his hands, his back held painfully straight. Of above-average height, with his sister's thick chestnut hair and chiseled features, he looked to be in his early thirties. He turned as Sebastian and Hero entered the room, displaying a pale and grief-ravaged face. "My apologies for coming to you in all my dirt," he said, bowing. "I've just ridden in from Kent."

"Please, sit down, Mr. Tennyson," said Hero gently. "I can't tell you how sorry we are for your loss."

He nodded and swallowed hard, as if temporarily bereft of speech. "Thank you. I can't stay. I'm on my way up to Enfield to hire some men to help extend the search for the children into the woods and surrounding countryside. But I heard from one of the magistrates at Bow Street that you've offered to do what you can to help with the investigation, so I've come to thank you . . . and, I must confess, in the hopes that you might have found something—anything at all—that might make sense of what has happened." He fixed Sebastian with a look of desperation that was painful to see.

Sebastian went to pour brandy into two glasses. "Sit down," he said in the voice that had once commanded soldiers into battle. "It will be getting dark soon. If you'll take my advice, you'll go home, rest, and give some thought as to where and how your energies can be most efficiently exerted in the morning."

Tennyson sank into a chair beside the empty hearth and swiped a shaky hand over his face. "I suppose you're right. It's just—" He paused to blow out a harsh breath. "It feels so damnably wrong—begging your pardon, Lady Devlin—not to be doing *something*. I blame myself. I should have insisted Gabrielle and the boys come with me to Kent."

"From what I know of Gabrielle," said Hero, taking the chair opposite him, "I'm not convinced you would have succeeded even if you had tried to insist."

Gabrielle's brother gave a ghost of a smile. "You may be right. Not even our father could compel Gabrielle to do something she didn't wish to do. She was always far more headstrong than I, despite being four years my junior."

"There were only the two of you?" asked Sebastian.

Tennyson nodded. "We had several younger brothers who died when we were children. Gabrielle was quite close to them and took their deaths hard. I've often wondered if it wasn't one of the reasons she was so eager to have George and Alfred come stay with her this summer."

Sebastian handed him the brandy. "Would you say you and your sister were close?"

"I would have said so, yes."

"You don't sound so certain."

Tennyson stared down at the glass in his hand. "Gabrielle was always a very private person. Lately I've had the sense that our lives were diverging. But I suppose that's inevitable."

Sebastian went to stand beside the cold hearth, one arm resting along the mantel. "Do you know if she had any romantic connections?"

"Gabrielle?" Tennyson shook his head. "No. She's never had any interest in marriage. I remember once when I was up at Cambridge and very full of myself, I warned her that if she didn't get her nose out of books no man would ever want to marry her. She laughed and said that suited her just fine—that a husband would only get in the way of her studies."

"So you wouldn't happen to know the name of a French lieutenant she had befriended?"

"A Frenchman? You mean an émigré?"

"No. I mean a paroled French officer. She never mentioned such a man?"

Tennyson stared at him blankly. "Good heavens. No. Are you suggesting she was somehow involved with this person?"

Sebastian took a slow sip of his own brandy. "I don't know."

"There must be some mistake."

"That's very possible."

Tennyson scrubbed a hand over his eyes and down his face. When he looked up, his features were contorted with agony. "Who could do something like this? To kill a woman and two children . . ."

"Your young cousins may still be alive," said Sebastian. "We don't know yet."

Tennyson nodded, his entire upper body rocking back and forth with the motion. "Yes, yes; I keep trying to cling to that, but . . ." He raised his glass to drink, his hand shaking badly, and Sebastian thought that the man looked stretched to the breaking point.

"Can you think of anyone who might have wished either your sister or the children harm?"

"No. Why would anyone want to hurt a woman like Gabrielle—
or two little boys?"

"Some enemy of the boys' father, perhaps?"

Tennyson considered this, then shook his head. "My cousin is a
simple clergyman in Lincolnshire. I'd be surprised if he knows
anyone in London."

Hero said, "Would you mind if I were to have a look at Gabrielle's research materials, on the off chance there might be some
connection between her death and her work at Camlet Moat? I
could come to the Adelphi myself in the morning."

He frowned, as if the possible relevance of his sister's scholarship to her death escaped him. "Of course; if you wish. I'll be
leaving for Enfield at first light, but I'll direct the servants to provide
you with any assistance you may require. You can box it all up and
simply take it, if that would help."

"It would, yes. Thank you."

Tennyson set aside his glass and rose to his feet with a bow.
"You have both been most kind. Please don't bother ringing; I can
see myself out."

"I'll walk down with you," said Sebastian, aware of Hero's narrowed gaze following them as they left the room.

"It occurs to me there may be something else you felt reluctant
to mention in front of Lady Devlin," Sebastian said as they descended the stairs.

Tennyson looked vaguely confused. "No, nothing."

"Any possibility someone could be seeking to hurt you by
striking at those you love?"

"I can't think of anyone," he said slowly as they reached the
ground hall. "Although in my profession one never—" He broke
off, his eyes widening. "Merciful heavens. Emily."

"Emily?" said Sebastian.

A faint suggestion of color touched the barrister's pale cheeks.
"Miss Emily Goodwin—the daughter of one of my colleagues. She

has recently done me the honor of agreeing to become my wife, although the death of her paternal grandmother has perforce delayed the formal announcement of our betrothal."

"You may count on my discretion."

"Yes, but do you think she could be in danger?"

"I see no reason to alarm her unnecessarily, especially given that the particulars of your betrothal are not known." Sebastian nodded to Morey, who opened the front door. "But it might be a good idea to suggest that she take care."

"I will, yes; thank you."

Sebastian stood in the open doorway and watched the man hurry away into the hot night. Then he went back upstairs to his wife.

"And what precisely was that about?" she asked, one eyebrow raised, as he walked into the room.

Sebastian found himself smiling. "I thought there might be something he was reluctant to discuss in front of such a delicate lady as yourself."

"Really. And was there?"

"No. Only that it seems he's formed an attachment to some Miss Goodwin, the daughter of one of his colleagues, and now he's hysterical with the fear that his sister's killer might strike against her next. I suspect it's a fear shared by virtually every father, husband, and brother out there."

"You think it's possible Gabrielle's death could have something to do with her brother's legal affairs?"

"At this point, almost anything seems possible."

Tom squinted down at Hero's map, his lips pursing as he traced the dotted line of London's old Roman walls, which she had superimposed on her sketch of the city's modern streets.

"Can you follow it?" asked Sebastian, watching him. He knew

that someone at some point had taught Tom to read, before the death of the boy's father had driven the family into desperation.

"Aye. I think maybe I even know the place yer lookin' for. There's a tavern called the Black Devil about 'ere—" He tapped one slightly grubby finger just off Bishopsgate. "It's owned by a fellow named Jamie Knox."

Sebastian looked at his tiger in surprise. "You know him?"

Tom shook his head. "Never seen the fellow meself. But I've 'eard tales o' him. 'E's a weery rum customer. A weery rum customer indeed. They say 'e dresses all in black, like the devil."

"A somewhat dramatic affectation." It wasn't unusual for gentlemen in formal evening dress to wear a black coat and black knee breeches. But the severity of the attire was always leavened by a white waistcoat, white silk stockings, and of course a white cravat.

"Not sure what that means," said Tom, "but I do know folks say 'e musta sold 'is soul to the devil, for 'e's got the devil's own luck. They say 'e 'as the reflexes of a cat. *And* the eyes and ears of—"

"What?" prodded Sebastian when the boy broke off.

Tom swallowed. "They say 'e 'as the eyes and ears of a cat, too. Yellow eyes."

Chapter 15

The Black Devil lay in a narrow cobbled lane just off Bishopsgate.

Sebastian walked down gloomy streets lit haphazardly by an occasional sputtering oil lamp or flaring torch thrust into a sconce high on an ancient wall. The houses here dated back to the time of the Tudors and the Stuarts, for this was a part of London that had escaped the ravages of the Great Fire. Once home to courtiers attached to the court of James I, the area had been in a long downward slide for the past century. The elaborately carved fronts overhanging the paving were sagging and worn; the great twisting chimneys leaned precariously as they poked up into the murky night sky.

By day, this was a district of small tradesmen: leather workers and chandlers, clock makers and tailors. But now the shops were all shuttered for the night, the streets given over to the patrons of the grog shops and taverns that spilled golden rectangles of light and boisterous laughter into the night.

He paused across the street from the Black Devil, in the

shadows cast by the deep doorway of a calico printer's shop. He let his gaze rove over the public house's gable-ended facade and old-fashioned, diamond-paned windows. Suspended from a beam over the door hung a cracked wooden sign painted with the image of a horned black devil, his yellow-eyed head and barbed tail silhou-etted against a roaring orange and red fire. As Sebastian watched, the sign creaked softly on its chains, touched by an unexpected gust of hot wind.

Crossing the narrow lane, he pushed through the door into a noisy, low-ceilinged public room with a sunken stone-flagged floor and oak-paneled walls turned black by centuries of smoke. The air was thick with the smell of tobacco and ale and unwashed, hard-working male bodies. The men crowded up to the bar and clus-tered around the tables glanced over at him, then went back to their pints and their bonesticks and their draughts.

"Help ye, there?" called a young woman from behind the bar, her almond-shaped eyes narrowing with shrewd appraisal. She looked to be somewhere in her early twenties, dark haired and winsome, with a wide red mouth and soft white breasts that swelled voluptuously above the low-cut bodice of her crimson satin gown.

Sebastian pushed his way through the crowd to stand half turned so that he still faced the room. In this gathering of tradesmen and laborers, costermongers and petty thieves, his doeskin breeches, clean white cravat, and exquisitely tailored coat of Bath superfine all marked him as a creature from another world. The other men at the bar shifted subtly, clearing a space around him.

"A go of Cork," he said, then waited until she set the measure of gin on the boards in front of him to add, "I'm looking for Jamie Knox; is he here?"

The woman behind the bar wiped her hands on the apron tied high around her waist, but her gaze never left his face. "And who might ye be, then?"

"Devlin. Viscount Devlin."

She stood for a moment with her hands still wrapped in the cloth of her apron. Then she jerked her head toward the rear. "He's out the back, unloading a delivery. There's an alley runs along the side of the tavern. The court opens off that."

Sebastian laid a coin on the scarred surface of the bar. "Thank you."

The alley was dark and ripe with the stench of rotting offal and fish heads and urine. The ancient walls looming high above him on either side bulged out ominously, so that someone had put in stout timber braces to keep the masonry from collapsing. As he drew nearer, he realized the tavern backed onto the churchyard of St. Helen's Bishopsgate, a relic of a now-vanished priory of Benedictine nuns. He could see the church's ancient wooden tower rising over a swelling burial ground where great elms moaned softly with the growing wind.

He paused just outside the entrance to the tavern yard. The courtyard looked to be even older than the tavern itself, its cobbles undulating and sunken, with one unexpectedly high wall of coursed flint blocks bonded with rows of red tile. Sebastian could understand why a woman with Gabrielle Tennyson's interests would find the site fascinating.

Someone had set a horn lantern atop an old flat stone beside a mule-drawn cart filled with hogsheads. The mules stood with their heads down, feet splayed. At the rear of the tavern the wooden flaps of the cellar had been thrown open to reveal a worn flight of stone steps that disappeared downward. As Sebastian watched, the grizzled head and husky shoulders of a man appeared, his footfalls echoing in the wind-tossed night.

Sebastian leaned against the stone jamb of the gateway. He had one hand in his pocket, where a small double-barreled pistol, primed and loaded, partially spoiled the line of his fashionable coat. A sheath in his boot concealed the dagger he was rarely without. He waited until the man had crossed to the cart, then said, "Mr. Jamie Knox?"

The man froze with his hands grasping a cask, his head turning toward the sound of Sebastian's voice. He appeared wary but not surprised, and it occurred to Sebastian that the comely young woman behind the bar must have run to warn her master to expect a visitor. "Aye. And who might ye be?"

"Devlin. Lord Devlin."

The man sniffed. Somewhere in his mid-thirties, he had a compact, muscular body that belied the heavy sprinkling of gray in this thick, curly head of hair. Far from being dressed all in black, he wore buff-colored trousers and a brown coat that looked in serious need of a good brushing and mending. His face was broad and sun darkened, with a long scar that ran down one cheek. Sebastian had seen scars like that before, left by a saber slash.

The man paused for only an instant. Then he hefted the hogshead and headed back to the stairs. "I'm a busy man. What ye want?"

The accent surprised Sebastian; it was West Country rather than London or Middlesex. He said, "I understand you knew a woman named Miss Tennyson."

The man grunted. "Met her. Came sniffin' around here a while back, she did, prattlin' about Roman walls and pictures made of little colored bits and a bunch of other nonsense. Why ye ask?"

"She's dead."

"Aye. So we heard." The man disappeared down the cellar steps.

Sebastian waited until he reemerged. "When was the last time you saw her?"

"I told ye, 'twere a while back. Two, maybe three months ago."

"That's curious. You see, someone saw you speaking to her just a few days ago. Last Thursday, to be precise. At the York Steps."

The man grasped another hogshead and turned back toward

the cellar. "Who'er told ye that didn't know what he was talkin' about."

"It's possible, I suppose."

The man grunted and started down the steep stairs again. He was breathing heavily by the time he came back up. He paused to lean against the cellar door and swipe his sweaty forehead against the shoulder of his coat.

"You were a soldier?" said Sebastian.

"What makes ye think that?"

"It left you with a rather distinctive face."

The man pushed away from the cellar. "I was here all day Thursday. Ask any o' the lads in the public room; they'll tell ye. Ye gonna call 'em all liars?"

Sebastian said, "I'm told Jamie Knox has yellow eyes. So why are yours brown?"

The man gave a startled laugh. "It's dark. Ye can't see what color a man's eyes are in the dark."

"I can."

"Huh." The tavern owner sniffed. "They only say that about me eyes because of the sign. Ye did see the sign, didn't ye? They also like t'say I only wear black. Next thing ye know, they'll be whisperin' that I've got a tail tucked into me breeches."

Sebastian let his gaze drift around the ancient yard. The massive flint and tile rampart that ran along the side of the court was distinctly different from the wall that separated the yard from the burial ground at its rear. No more than seven feet high and topped by a row of iron spikes designed to discourage body snatchers, that part of the wall lay deep in the heavy shadows cast by the sprawling limbs of the graveyard's leafy elms. And in the fork of one of those trees crouched a lean man dressed all in black except for the white of his shirt. He balanced there easily, the stock of his rifle resting against his thigh.

To anyone else, the rifleman would have been invisible.

Sebastian said, "When he comes down out of his tree, tell Mr. Knox he can either talk to me, or he can talk to Bow Street. I suppose his choice will depend on exactly what's in his cellars."

The stocky man's scarred face split into a nasty grin. "I don't need to tell him. He can hear ye. Has the eyes and ears of a cat, he does."

Sebastian turned toward the gateway. The stocky man put out a hand to stop him.

Sebastian stared pointedly at the grimy fingers clenching his sleeve. The hand was withdrawn.

The man licked his lower lip. "He could've shot out both yer eyes from where he's sittin'. And I'll tell ye somethin' else: He looks enough like ye t'be yer brother. Ye think about that. Ye think about that real hard." He paused a moment, then added mockingly, "*Me lord.*"

Chapter 16

Sebastian walked down Cheapside, his hands thrust deep into the pockets of his coat, the hot wind eddying the flames of the streetlamps to send leaping shadows over the shuttered shop fronts and dusty, rubbish-strewn cobbles.

Once, he had been the youngest of three brothers, the fourth child born to the Earl of Hendon and his beautiful, vivacious countess, Sophie. If there had ever been a time in his parents' marriage that was pleasant, Sebastian couldn't remember it. They had lived essentially separate lives, the Earl devoting himself to affairs of state while the Countess lost herself in a gay whirl of balls and routs and visits to country houses. The few occasions when husband and wife came together had been characterized by stony silences punctuated all too often with stormy bouts of tears and voices raised in anger.

Yet Sebastian's childhood had not been an entirely unhappy one. In his memories, Sophie's touch was always soft and loving, and her laughter—when her husband was not around—came frequently. Her four children had never doubted her love for them.

Though unlike each other in many ways and separated in age, the three brothers had been unusually close. Only Amanda, the eldest child, had held herself aloof. "Sometimes I think Amanda was born angry with the world," Sophie had once said, her thoughtful, worried gaze following her daughter when Amanda stormed off from a game of battledore and shuttlecock.

It would be years before Sebastian understood the true source of Amanda's anger.

He paused to look out over the gray, sunken tombs and rank nettles choking St. Paul's churchyard, his thoughts still lost in the past.

In contrast to his gay, demonstrative wife, the Earl of Hendon had been a stern, demanding father preoccupied with affairs of state. But he'd still found the time to teach his sons to ride and shoot and fence, and he took a gruff pride in their prowess. An intensely private man, he had remained a distant figure, detached and remote—especially from his youngest child, the child so unlike him in looks and temperament and talents.

Then had come a series of tragedies. Sebastian's oldest brother, Richard, was the first to die, caught in a vicious riptide while swimming off the coast of Cornwall near the Earl's principal residence. Then, one dreadful summer when the clouds of war swept across Europe and the fabric of society as they'd always known it seemed forever rent by revolution and violence, Cecil had sickened and died too.

Once the proud father of three healthy sons, Hendon found himself left with only the youngest, Sebastian. Sebastian, the son most unlike his father; the son on whom the Earl's wrath always fell the hardest, the son who had always known himself to be a disappointment in every way to the brusque, barrel-chested man with the piercingly blue St. Cyr eyes that were so noticeably lacking in his new heir.

That same summer, when Sebastian was eleven, Hendon's

countess sailed away for a day's pleasure cruise, never to return. *Lost at sea,* they'd said. Even at the time, Sebastian hadn't believed it. For months he'd climbed the cliffs overlooking the endless choppy waters of the Channel, convinced that if she were in truth dead, he'd somehow know it; he'd feel it.

Odd, he thought now as he pushed away from the churchyard's rusted railing and turned his feet toward the noisy, brightly lit hells off St. James's Street, how he could have been so right about that and so wrong about almost everything else.

Lying alone in her bed, Hero heard the wind begin to pick up just before midnight. Hot gusts billowed the curtains at her open window and filled the bedroom with the smell of dust and all the ripe odors of a city in summer. She listened to the charlie cry one o'clock, then two. And still she lay awake, listening to the wind and endlessly analyzing and reassessing all that she had learned so far of the grinding, inexorable sequence of shadowy, half-understood events and forces that had led to Gabrielle's death and the disappearance of her two little cousins. But as the hours dragged on, it gradually dawned on Hero that her sleeplessness had as much to do with the empty bed beside her as anything else.

It was a realization that both startled and chagrined her. Her motives for entering into this marriage had been complicated and confused and not entirely understood by anyone, least of all herself. She was not a woman much given to introspection or prolonged, agonized examination of her motives. She had always seen this characteristic as something admirable, something to be secretly proud of. Now she found herself wondering if perhaps in that she had erred. For who could be more foolish than a woman who doesn't know her own heart?

A loose shutter banged somewhere in the night for what seemed like the thousandth time. Thrusting aside the covers with a soft exclamation of exasperation, she crossed the room to slam down the sash. Then she paused with one hand on the latch, her gaze on the elegant, solitary figure strolling down the street toward the house.

The night was dark, the wind having blown out most of the streetlights and both oil lamps mounted high on either side of the entrance. But Hero had no difficulty recognizing Devlin's long stride or the lean line of his body as he turned to mount the front steps.

She knew a wash of relief, although she had been unwilling to acknowledge until now the growing concern his long absence had aroused. Then her hand tightened on the drapery beside her.

They were strangers to each other in many ways, their marriage one born of necessity and characterized by wary distrust leavened by a powerful current of passion, a grudging respect, and a playful kind of rivalry. Yet she knew him well enough to recognize the brittle set of his shoulders and the glitteringly dangerous precision of each graceful movement.

Eleven months before, something had happened in Devlin's life, something that had driven him from his longtime mistress Kat Boleyn and created a bitter estrangement between the Viscount and his father, the Earl. She did not know precisely what had occurred; she knew only that whatever it was, it had plunged Devlin into a months-long brandy-soaked spiral of self-destruction from which he had only recently emerged.

But now, as she listened to his footsteps climb the stairs to the second floor and heard the distant click of his bedroom door closing quietly behind him, she knew a deep disquiet . . .

And an unexpected welling of an emotion so fierce that it caught her breath and left her wondrous and shaken and oddly, uncharacteristically frightened.

※

Tuesday, 4 August

"My lord?"

Sebastian opened one eye, saw his valet's cheerful, fine-boned face, then squeezed the eye shut again when the room lurched unpleasantly. "Go away."

Jules Calhoun's voice sounded irritatingly hearty. "Sir Henry Lovejoy is here to see you, my lord."

"Tell him I'm not here. Tell him I'm dead. I don't care what the hell you tell him. Just go away."

There was a moment's pause. Then Calhoun said, "Unfortunately, Lady Devlin went out early this morning, so she is unable to receive the magistrate in your stead."

"Early, you say? Where has she gone?" He opened both eyes and sat up quickly—not a wise thing to do under the circumstances. *"Bloody hell,"* he yelped, bowing his head and pressing one splayed hand to his pounding forehead.

"She did not say. Here, my lord; drink this."

Sebastian felt a hot mug thrust into his free hand. "Not more of your damned milk thistle."

"There is nothing better to cleanse the liver, my lord."

"My liver is just fine," growled Sebastian, and heard the valet laugh.

Calhoun went to jerk back the drapes at the windows. "Shall I have Morey tell Sir Henry you'll join him in fifteen minutes?"

Sebastian swung his legs over the side of the bed and groaned again. "Make it twenty."

Sebastian found the magistrate munching on a tray of cucumber and brown bread and butter sandwiches washed down with tea.

"Sir Henry," said Sebastian, entering the room with a quick step. "My apologies for keeping you waiting."

The magistrate surged to his feet and dabbed at his lips with a napkin. "Your majordomo has most kindly provided me with some much-needed sustenance. I've been up at Camlet Moat since dawn."

"Please, sit down," said Sebastian, going to sprawl in the chair opposite him. "Any sign yet of the missing children?"

"None, I'm afraid. And that's despite the hundreds of men now beating through the wood and surrounding countryside in search of them. Unfortunately, Miss Tennyson's brother has offered a reward for the children—he's even set up an office in the Fleet, staffed by a solicitor, to handle any information that may be received."

"Why do you say 'unfortunately'?"

"Because the result is likely to be chaos. I've seen it happen before. A child is lost; with the best of intentions, the grieving family offers a reward, and suddenly you have scores of wretched children—sometimes even hundreds—being offered to the authorities as the 'lost' child."

"Good God," said Sebastian. "Still, I can understand why he is doing it."

"I suppose so, yes." Lovejoy blew out a harsh breath. "Although I fear it is only a matter of time until their bodies are discovered. If the children had merely been frightened by what they saw and run off to hide, they would have been found by now."

"I suppose you must be right." Sebastian considered pouring himself a cup of tea, then decided against it. What he needed was a tankard of good strong ale. "Still, it's strange that if they are dead, their bodies weren't found beside Miss Tennyson's."

"I fear there is much about this case that is strange. I've spoken to the rector at St. Martin's, who confirms that Miss Tennyson and the two children did indeed attend services this past Sunday, as usual. He even conversed with them for a few moments afterward—although not, unfortunately, about their plans for the afternoon."

"At least it helps to narrow the time of her death."

"Slightly, yes. We've also checked with the stages running between London and Enfield, and with the liveries in Enfield, but so far we've been unable to locate anyone who recalls seeing Miss Tennyson on Sunday."

"In other words, Miss Tennyson and the children must have driven out to Camlet Moat with her killer."

"So it appears. There is one disturbing piece of information that has come to light," said Lovejoy, helping himself to another sandwich triangle. "We've discovered that Miss Tennyson was actually seen up at the moat a week ago on Sunday in the company of the children and an unidentified gentleman."

"A gentleman? Not a driver?"

"Oh, most definitely a gentleman. I'm told he walked with a limp and had an accent that may have been French."

For a gentlewoman to drive in the country in the company of a gentleman hinted at a degree of friendship, of intimacy even, that was quite telling. For their drive to have taken Gabrielle Tennyson and her French friend to Camlet Moat seemed even more ominous. Sebastian said, "I've heard she had befriended a French prisoner of war on his parole."

"Have you? Good heavens; who is he?"

"I don't know. I've yet to find anyone who can give me a name."

Lovejoy swallowed the last of his sandwich and pushed to his feet. "If you should discover his identity, I would be most interested to know it. I've no need to tell you how this latest development is likely to be received. Sales of blunderbusses and pistols have already skyrocketed across the city, with women afraid to walk to market alone or allow their children to play outside. The Prime Minister's office is putting pressure on Bow Street to solve this, quickly. But if people learn a Frenchman was involved! Well, we'll likely have mass hysteria."

Sebastian rose with his friend, aware of a profound sense of unease. He knew from personal experience that whenever Downing Street or the Palace troubled itself with the course of a murder investigation, they tended to be more interested in quieting public hysteria than in seeing justice done. The result, all too often, was the sacrifice of a convenient scapegoat.

Eighteen months before, Sebastian had come perilously close to being such a scapegoat himself. And the man who had pushed for his quick and convenient death was his new father-in-law.

Charles, Lord Jarvis.

Chapter 17

$\mathcal{A}$fter the magistrate's departure, Sebastian poured himself a tankard of ale and went to stand before the empty hearth, one boot resting on the cold fender.

He stood for a long time, running through all he knew about Gabrielle Tennyson's last days, and all he still needed to learn. Then he sent for his valet.

"My lord?" asked Calhoun, bowing gracefully.

To all appearances, Jules Calhoun was the perfect gentleman's gentleman, elegant and urbane and polished. But the truth was that the valet had begun life in one of the most notorious flash houses in London, a background that gave him some interesting skills and a plethora of useful contacts.

"Ever hear of a man named Jamie Knox?" Sebastian asked, drawing on his gloves. "He owns a tavern in Bishopsgate called the Black Devil."

"I have heard of him, my lord. But only by repute. It is my understanding he arrived in London some two or three years ago."

"See what else you can find out about him."

"Yes, my lord."

Sebastian settled his hat at a rakish angle and turned toward the door. Then he paused with one hand on the jamb to glance back and add, "This might be delicate, Calhoun."

The valet bowed again, his dark eyes bright with intelligence, his features flawlessly composed. "I shall be the soul of discretion, my lord."

Hero had begun the morning with a visit to the Adelphi Terrace.

She found Mr. Hildeyard Tennyson already out organizing the search for his missing cousins. But he had left clear instructions with his servants, and with the aid of a footman she spent several hours bundling up Gabrielle's research materials and notes. Having dispatched the boxes to Brook Street, she started to leave. Then she paused to turn and run up the stairs to her friend's bedroom.

She stood for a long moment in the center of the room, her hands clenched before her. She had called Gabrielle friend for six years. But although they had been close in many ways, Hero realized now just how compartmentalized their friendship had been. They had talked of history and art, of philosophy and poetry. Hero knew the pain Gabrielle had suffered at the early loss of her mother and her lingering grief over the brothers who died so young; she knew her friend's fondness for children. But she did not know Gabrielle's reason for turning away from marriage and any possibility of bearing children of her own.

It occurred to Hero that she had simply assumed her friend's reasons mirrored her own. But she knew that assumption was without basis. Gabrielle had challenged the typical role of women in their society by her own enthusiasm for scholarship and her determination to openly pursue her interests. Yet she had never been one to crusade for the kind of changes Hero championed. When Hero spoke of a future when women would be allowed to attend

Oxford or to sit in Parliament, Gabrielle would only smile and faintly shake her head, as if convinced these things would never be—and perhaps never should be.

She had certainly never spoken of her friendship with some mysterious French lieutenant. But then, Hero had never mentioned to Gabrielle her own strange, conflicted attraction to a certain dark-haired, amber-eyed viscount. And Hero found herself wondering now what Gabrielle had thought of her friend's sudden, seemingly inexplicable wedding. They'd never had the opportunity to discuss it.

There were so many things the two friends had needed to discuss—had intended to discuss that morning Hero was to drive up to Camlet Moat. Now Hero was left with only questions and an inescapable measure of guilt.

"What happened to you?" she said softly as she let her gaze drift around her friend's room to linger on the high tester bed and primrose coverlet, the mirrored dressing table and scattering of silver boxes and crystal vials. The chamber was, essentially, as Gabrielle had left it when she went off on Sunday, not knowing she would never return. Yet Hero could feel no lingering presence here, no whispered essence of the woman whose laughter and dreams and fears this place had once witnessed. There was only a profound, yawning stillness that brought a pricking to Hero's eyelids and swelled her throat.

Leaving the house, she directed her coachman to the Park Lane home of a certain member of Parliament from the Wolds of Lincolnshire. Only then, as her carriage rocked through the streets of London, did Hero lean back against the soft velvet squabs, and for the first time since she'd learned of Gabrielle's death, she allowed the tears to fall.

A few carefully worded inquiries at the War Office, the Alien Office, and the Admiralty provided Sebastian with the information that there were literally thousands of paroled French and allied officers in Britain. Most captured enemy officers were scattered across the land in one of fifty so-called parole towns. But some were billeted in London itself.

Prisoners of war from the ranks were typically thrown into what were known as "the hulls." Rotting, demasted ships deemed too unseaworthy to set sail, the hulls were essentially floating prisons. By day, the men were organized into chained gangs and marched off to labor on the docks and in the surrounding area's workshops. At night they were locked fast in the airless, vermin-ridden, pestilence-infested darkness belowdecks. Their death rate was atrocious.

But the officers were traditionally treated differently. Being gentlemen, they were credited with possessing that most gentlemanly of characteristics: honor. Thus, a French officer could be allowed his freedom with only a few restrictions as long as he gave his word of honor as a gentleman—his parole—that he would not escape.

"That's the theory, at least," grumbled the plump, graying functionary with whom Sebastian spoke at the Admiralty. "Problem is, too many of these damned Frog officers are *not* gentlemen. They raise them up from the ranks, you see—which is why we've had over two hundred of the bastards run off just this year alone." He leaned forward as if to underscore his point. "No honor."

"Two hundred?"

"Two hundred and thirty-seven, to be precise. Nearly seven hundred in the past three years. These Frenchies may be officers, but too many of them are still scum. Vermin, swept up out of the gutters of Paris and lifted far above their proper station. That's what happens, you see, when civilization is turned upside down and those who were born to serve start thinking themselves as good as their betters." The very thought of this topsy-turvy world aroused such ire in the functionary's ample breast that he was practically spitting.

"Yet some of the best French officers have come up through the ranks," said Sebastian. "Joachim Murat, for example. And Michel Ney—"

"Pshaw." The functionary waved away these examples of ungentlemanly success with the dismissive flap of one pudgy hand. "It is obvious you know nothing of the Army, sir. Nothing!"

Sebastian laughed and started to turn away.

"You could try checking with Mr. Abel McPherson—he's the agent appointed by the Transport Board of the Admiralty to administer the paroled prisoners in the area."

"And where would I find him?" asked Sebastian, pausing to look back at the clerk.

"I believe he's in Norfolk at the moment. I've no doubt he left someone as his deputy, but I can't rightly tell you who."

"And who might have that information?"

"Sorry. Can't help you. But McPherson should be back in a fortnight."

Hero was received at the Mayflower house of the honorable Charles d'Eyncourt by the MP's married sister, a dour woman in her mid-thirties named Mary Bourne.

Mrs. Bourne had never met Hero and was all aflutter with the honor of a visit from Lord Jarvis's daughter. She received Hero in a stately drawing room hung with blond satin and crammed with an assortment of gilded crocodile-legged tables and colorful Chinese vases that would have delighted the Prince Regent himself. After begging "dear Lady Devlin" to please, pray be seated, she sent her servants flying for tea and cakes served on a silver tray so heavy the poor butler staggered beneath its weight. She then proceeded, seemingly without stopping for breath, to prattle endlessly about everything from her Bible study at the Savoy Chapel to her dear Mr. Bourne's concerns for her remaining in the metropolis with such a ruthless murderer on the loose, and followed that up with an endless description of a recent family wedding at which fandangos and the new waltz had been danced, and the carriages decked out in good white satin. "At a shilling a yard, no less!" she whispered, leaning forward confidingly. "No expense was spared, believe me, my dear Lady Devlin."

Smiling benignly, Hero sipped her tea and encouraged her hostess to prattle on. Mary Bourne bragged (in the most humble way possible, of course) about the morning and evening prayers that all servants in her own household at Dalby near Somersby were required to attend daily. She hinted (broadly) that she was the pseudonymous author of a popular denunciation of the modern interest in Druidism, and from there allowed herself to be led ever so subtly, ever so unsuspectingly, to the subject Hero had come to learn more about: the precise nature of the relationship between Charles d'Eyncourt and his brother, George Tennyson, the father of the two missing little boys.

Charles, Lord Jarvis lounged at his ease in a comfortable chair beside the empty hearth in his chambers in Carlton House. Moving deliberately, he withdrew an enameled gold snuffbox from his pocket and flicked it open with practiced grace. He lifted a delicate pinch between one thumb and forefinger and inhaled, his hard gaze never leaving the sweating pink and white face of the stout man who stood opposite him. "Well?" demanded Jarvis.

"This c-complicates things," stammered Bevin Childe. "You must see that. It's not going to be easy to—"

"How you accomplish your task is not my problem. You already know the consequences if you fail."

The antiquary's soft mouth sagged open, his eyes widening. Then he swallowed hard and gave a jerky, panicky bow. "Yes, my lord," he said, and then jumped when Jarvis's clerk tapped discreetly on the door behind him.

"What is it?" demanded Jarvis.

"Colonel Urquhart to see you, my lord."

"Show him in," said Jarvis. He closed his snuffbox with a snap, his gaze returning to the now-pale antiquary. "Why are you still here? Get out of my sight."

Hat in hand, the antiquary backed out of the room as if exiting from a royal presence. He was still backing when Colonel Jasper Urquhart swept through the door and sketched an elegant bow.

"You wished to see me, my lord?"

The Colonel was a tall man, as were all the former military men in Jarvis's employ, tall and broad-shouldered, with fair hair and pale gray eyes and a ruddy complexion. A former rifleman, he had served Jarvis for two years now. Until today, he hadn't disappointed.

"Yesterday," said Jarvis, pushing to his feet, "I asked you to assign one of your best men to a certain task."

"Yes, my lord. I can explain."

Jarvis sniffed and tucked his snuffbox back into his pocket. "Please don't. I trust the individual in question is no longer in my employ?"

"Correct, my lord."

"You relieve me. See that his replacement does not similarly disappoint."

The Colonel's thin nostrils quivered. "Yes, my lord."

"Good. That will be all."

Sebastian spent three frustrating hours prowling the rooming houses, taverns, and coffeehouses known to be frequented by officers on their parole. But the questions he asked were of necessity vague and the answers he received less than helpful. Without knowing the French lieutenant's name, how the devil was he to find one paroled French officer amongst so many?

He was standing beside the Serpentine and watching a drilling of the troops from the Hyde Park barracks when he noticed a young, painfully thin man limping toward him. A scruffy brown and black mutt with a white nose and chest padded contentedly at his heels, one ear up, the other folded half over as if in a state of perpetual astonishment. The man's coat was threadbare and his breeches mended, but his linen was white and clean, his worn-out boots polished to a careful luster, the set of his shoulders and upright carriage marking him unmistakably as a military man. His pallid complexion contrasted starkly with his brown hair and spoke of months of illness and convalescence.

He paused uncertainly some feet away, the dog drawing up beside him, pink tongue hanging out as it panted happily. *"Monsieur le vicomte?"* he asked.

"Yes." Sebastian turned slowly to face him. "And you, I take it, must be Miss Tennyson's mysterious unnamed French lieutenant?"

The man brought his heels together and swept an elegant bow. This particular French officer was, obviously, not one of those who had been raised through the ranks from the gutters of Paris. "I have a name," he said in very good English. "Lieutenant Philippe Arceneaux, of the Twenty-second Chasseurs à Cheval."

Chapter 18

"We met last May in the Reading Room of the British Museum," said Arceneaux as he and Sebastian walked along the placid waters of the Serpentine. The dog frisked happily ahead, nose to the ground, tail wagging. "She was having difficulty with the archaic Italian of a novella she was attempting to translate, and I offered to help."

"So you're a scholar."

"I was trained to be, yes. But France has little use for scholars these days. Only soldiers." He gazed out across the park's open fields, to where His Majesty's finest were drilling in the fierce sunshine. "One of the consolations of being a prisoner of war has been the opportunity to continue my studies."

"This novella you mentioned; what was it?"

"A now obscure elaboration of a part of the Arthurian legend called *La donna di Scalotta.*"

"*The Lady of Shalott,*" said Sebastian thoughtfully.

The Frenchman brought his gaze back to Sebastian's face. "You know it?" he said in surprise.

"I have heard of it, but that's about it."

"It's a tragic tale, of a beautiful maiden who dies for the love of a handsome knight."

"Sir Lancelot?"

"Yes."

"Convenient, isn't it, the way Camelot, Lancelot, and Shalott all happen to rhyme?"

Arceneaux laughed out loud. "Very convenient."

Sebastian said, "Were you in love with her?"

The laughter died on the Frenchman's lips as he lifted his shoulders in a shrug that could have meant anything, and looked away. It occurred to Sebastian, watching him, that the Lieutenant appeared young because he was—probably no more than twenty-four or -five, which would make him several years younger than Gabrielle.

"Well? Were you?"

They walked along in silence, the sun warm on their backs, the golden light of the afternoon drenching the green of the grass and trees around them. Just when Sebastian had decided the Frenchman wasn't going to answer, he said softly, "Of course I was. At least a little. Who wouldn't be? She was a very beautiful woman, brilliant and courageous and overflowing with a zest for life. While I—" His voice broke and he had to swallow hard before he could continue. "I have been very lonely, here in England."

"Was she in love with you?"

"Oh, no. There was nothing like that between us. We were friends—fellow scholars. Nothing more."

Sebastian studied the Frenchman's lean profile. He had softly curling brown hair and a sprinkling of cinnamon-colored freckles high across his cheeks that gave him something of the look of a schoolboy. At the moment, the freckles were underlaid by a faint, betraying flush.

"When did you last see her?" Sebastian asked.

"Wednesday evening, I believe it was. She used to bring her young cousins here, to the park, to sail their boats on the Serpentine. I would meet them sometimes. The boys liked to play with Chien."

Sebastian glanced over at the brown and black mongrel, now loping methodically from tree to tree in a good-natured effort to mark all of Hyde Park as his own personal territory. "Chien? That's his name?" "*Chien*" was simply the French word for "dog."

"I thought if I gave him a name, I might become too attached to him."

The dog came bounding back to the young lieutenant, tail wagging, brown eyes luminous with adoration, and the Lieutenant hunkered down to ruffle the fur around his neck. The dog licked his wrist and then trotted off again happily.

"Looks as if that's working out well," observed Sebastian.

Arceneaux laughed again and pushed to his feet. "He used to live in the wasteland near that new bridge they're building. I go there sometimes to sit at the end overlooking the river and watch the tide roll in and out. He would come sit beside me. And then one day just before curfew, when I got up to leave, he came too. Unfortunately, he has a sad taste for the low life—particularly Gypsies. And a shocking tendency to steal hams. George used to say I should have called him 'Rom,' because he is a Gypsy at heart."

The Lieutenant watched the dog roll in the grass near the water's edge and his features hardened into grim lines. After a moment, he said, "Do you think George and Alfred are dead too?"

"They may be. Or they could simply have been frightened by what happened to their cousin and run away to hide."

"But the authorities are looking for them, yes? And Gabrielle's brother has offered a reward. If that were true, why have they not been found?"

Sebastian could think of several explanations that made perfect sense, although he wasn't inclined to voice them. Small boys were a valuable commodity in England, frequently sold as climbing boys by the parish workhouses or even by their own impoverished parents. The chimney sweeps were in constant need of new boys, for the work was brutal and dangerous. Even boys who survived eventually outgrew the task. It wasn't unknown for small children to be snatched from their front gardens and sold to sweeps. Very few of those children ever made it home again.

But the chimney sweeps weren't the only ones who preyed on young children; girls and boys both were exploited for sexual purposes the very thought of which made Sebastian's stomach clench. He suspected the trade in children was a contributing factor to Tennyson's decision to ignore the concerns of the magistrates and post a reward for the boys' return. Then he noticed the way the Lieutenant's jaw had tightened, and he knew the Frenchman's thoughts were probably running in the same direction.

Sebastian breathed in the warm, stagnant aroma of the canal, the sunbaked earth, the sweet scent of the lilies blooming near the shadows of the trees. He said, "Did Miss Tennyson seem troubled in any way the last time you saw her?"

"Troubled? No."

"Would you by any chance know how she planned to spend this past Sunday afternoon?"

"Sorry, no."

Sebastian glanced over at him. "She didn't speak of it?"

"Not that I recall, no."

"Yet you did sometimes see her on Sundays, did you not?"

Arceneaux was silent for a moment, obviously considering his answer with care. He decided to go with honesty. "Sometimes, yes."

"Where would you go?"

A muscle worked along the Frenchman's jaw as he stared out over the undulating parkland and shrugged. "Here and there."

"You went up to Camlet Moat a week ago last Sunday, didn't you?"

Arceneaux kept his face half averted, but Sebastian saw his throat work as he swallowed.

One of the conditions of a prisoner's parole was the requirement that he not withdraw beyond certain narrowly prescribed boundaries. By traveling up to Camlet Moat, the Frenchman had violated his parole. Sebastian wondered why he had taken such a risk. But he also understood how frustration could sometimes lead a man to do foolish things.

"I have no intention of reporting you to the Admiralty, if that's what you're worried about," said Sebastian.

"I didn't kill her," said Arceneaux suddenly, his voice rough with emotion. "You must believe me. I had no reason to kill any of them."

Some might consider unrequited love a very common motive for murder. But Sebastian kept that observation to himself. "Who do you think would have a reason to kill them?"

Arceneaux hesitated, the wind ruffling the soft brown curls around his face. He said, "How much do you know about Camlet Moat?"

"I know that Miss Tennyson believed it the lost location of Arthur's Camelot. Do you?"

"I will admit that when I first heard the suggestion, it seemed laughable. But in the end I found her arguments profoundly compelling. The thing is, you see, our image of Camelot has been molded by the writings of the troubadours. We picture it as a fairy-tale place—a grand medieval castle and great city of grace and beauty. But the real Camelot—if it existed at all—would have been far less grand and magnificent. There is no denying that Camlet Moat's name is indeed a recent corruption of Camelot. And it is an ancient site with royal connections that remained important down through the ages."

"One wouldn't think so to look at the island today."

"That's because the medieval castle that once stood there was completely razed by the Earl of Essex in the fifteenth century, its stones and timbers sold to help finance repairs to the Earl's family seat at Hertford."

Sebastian frowned. "I thought the site belonged to the Crown."

"It has, off and on. But it was for several centuries in the possession of the descendants of Sir Geoffrey de Mandeville."

Every schoolboy in England was familiar with Sir Geoffrey de Mandeville, one of the most notorious of the robber barons spawned by the chaos of the twelfth century, when William the Conqueror's grandchildren Matilda and Stephen did their best to turn England into a wasteland in their battle for the throne. Accumulating a band of black knights, de Mandeville pillaged and looted from Cambridge to Ely to the Abby of Ramsey; the treasure he amassed in the course of his bloody career—a king's ransom in gold and coins and precious gems—had reportedly never been found.

"There is a legend," said Arceneaux, "that de Mandeville buried his treasure at Camlet Moat. They say that when he was attained for high treason, he hid on the island in a hollow oak tree overhanging a well. The tree broke beneath his weight, and he fell into the well and drowned. Now his ghost haunts the island, guarding his treasure and reappearing to bring death to anyone who would dare lay hands upon it."

"Don't tell me you believe this nonsense?"

Arceneaux smiled. "No. But that doesn't mean that other people don't."

"Are you suggesting Gabrielle Tennyson might have been killed by a treasure hunter?"

"I know they had difficulty with someone digging at the site during the night and on Sundays too. The workmen would frequently arrive in the morning to find great gaping holes at various points around the island. She was particularly disturbed by some damage she discovered last week. She suspected the man behind it was Winthrop's own foreman—a big, redheaded rogue named Rory Forster. But she had no proof."

"She thought whoever was digging at the site was looking for de Mandeville's treasure?"

The Frenchman nodded. "My fear is that if she and the lads did decide to go up there again last Sunday, they may have chanced upon someone looking for de Mandeville's treasure. Someone who . . ." His voice trailed away, his features pinched tight with the pain of his thoughts.

"When you went with Miss Tennyson to the site, how did you get there?"

"But I didn't—" he began, only to have Sebastian cut him off.

"All right, let's put it this way: If you had visited the site last Sunday, how would you have traveled there?"

The Frenchman gave a wry grin. "In a hired gig. Why?"

"Because it's one of the more puzzling aspects of this murder— Bow Street has yet to discover how Miss Tennyson traveled up to the moat the day she was killed. You have no ideas?"

Arceneaux shook his head. "I assumed she must have gone there in the company of whoever killed her."

As she did with you, Sebastian thought. Aloud, he said, "I'm curious: Why bring this tale to me? Why not take what you know to Bow Street?"

A humorless smile twisted Arceneaux's lips. "Have you seen today's papers? They're suggesting Gabrielle and the boys were killed by a Frenchman. Just this morning, two of my fellow officers were attacked by a mob calling them child murderers. They might well have been killed if a troop of the Third Volunteers hadn't chanced to come along and rescue them."

They drew up at the gate, where Tom was waiting with the curricle. Sebastian said, "What makes you so certain I won't simply turn around and give your name to the authorities?"

"I am told you are a man of honor and justice."

"Who told you that?"

The Frenchman's cheeks hollowed and he looked away.

Sebastian said, "You took a risk, approaching me; why?"

Arceneaux brought his gaze back to Sebastian's face. He no longer looked like a young scholar but like a soldier who had fought and seen men die, and who had doubtless also killed. "Because I want whoever did this dead. It's as simple as that."

The two men's gazes met and held. They had served under different flags, perhaps even unknowingly faced each other on some field of battle. But they had more in common with each other than with those who had never held the bloodied, shattered bodies of their dying comrades in their arms, who had never felt the thrum of bloodlust coursing through their own veins, who had never known the fierce rush of bowel-loosening fear or the calm courage that can come from the simple, unshrugging acceptance of fate.

"The authorities will figure out who you are eventually," said Sebastian.

"Yes. But it won't matter if you catch the man who actually did kill them, first." The Frenchman bowed, one hand going to his hip as if to rest on the hilt of a sword that was no longer there. "My lord."

Sebastian stood beside his curricle and watched the Frenchman limp away toward the river, the scruffy brown and black dog trotting contentedly at his side.

Sebastian's first inclination was to dismiss the man's tale of ghosts, robber barons, and buried treasure as just so much nonsense. But he had a vague memory of Lovejoy saying something about a local legend linking some ancient Templar knight to the moat.

"Was that the Frog ye been lookin' for, gov'nor?" asked Tom.

Sebastian leapt up into the curricle's high seat. "He says he is."

"Ye don't believe 'im?"

"When it comes to murder, I'm not inclined to believe anyone." Sebastian gathered his reins, then paused to look over at his tiger. "Do you believe in ghosts, Tom?"

"Me? Get on wit ye, gov'nor." The boy showed a gap-toothed grin. "Ye sayin' that Frog is a ghost?"

"No. But I'm told some people do believe Camlet Moat is haunted."

"By the lady what got 'erself killed there?"

"By a twelfth-century black knight."

Tom was silent for a moment. Then he said, "Do you believe in ghosts, gov'nor?"

"No." Sebastian turned the chestnuts' heads toward the road north. "But I think it's time we took another look at Camelot."

Chapter 19

Alistair St. Cyr, Earl of Hendon and Chancellor of the Exchequer, slammed his palm down on the pile of crude broadsheets on the table before him. "I don't like this. I don't like it at all. These bloody things are all over town. And I tell you, they're having more of an effect than one could ever have imagined. Why, just this morning I overheard two of my housemaids whispering about King Arthur. Housemaids! We've heard this nonsense before, about how the time has come for the 'once and future king' to return from the mists of bloody Avalon and save England from both Boney and the House of Hanover. But this is different. This is more than just a few yokels fantasizing over their pints down at the local. Someone is behind this, and if you ask me, it's Napoléon's agents."

Jarvis drew his snuffbox from his pocket and calmly flipped it open with one practiced finger. "Of course it's the work of Napoléon's agents."

Hendon looked at him from beneath heavy brows. "Do you know who they are?"

"I believe so." Jarvis lifted a pinch of snuff to one nostril and sniffed. "But at this point, it's more than a matter of simply closing down some basement printing press. The damage has been done; this appeal to a messianic hero from our glorious past has resonated with the people and taken on a life of its own."

"How the bloody hell could something like this have aroused such a popular fervor?"

"I suppose one could with justification blame the success of the pulpit. When people fervently believe the Son of God will return someday to save them, it makes it easier to believe the same of King Arthur."

"That's blasphemy."

"I'm not talking about religion. I'm talking about credulity and habits of thought."

Hendon swung away to go stand beside the window and stare down at the Mall. "I'll confess that at first I found it difficult to credit that there are people alive today who could actually believe that Arthur will return, *literally*. I had supposed these pamphlets were simply tapping into the population's yearning for an Arthur-like figure to appear and save England. But an appalling number of people do seem to genuinely believe Arthur is out there right now on the Isle of Avalon, just waiting for the right moment to come back."

Jarvis raised another pinch of snuff and inhaled with a sniff. "I fear the concept of metaphor is rather above the capacity of the hoi polloi."

Hendon turned to look at him over one shoulder. "So what is to be done?"

Jarvis closed his snuffbox and tucked it away with a bland smile. "We're working on that."

Sebastian had expected to find the moat overrun with parties of searchers eager for the chance to collect the reward posted by Gabrielle Tennyson's brother. Instead, he reined in beneath the thick, leafy canopy at the top of the ancient embankment to look out over an oddly deserted scene, the stagnant water disturbed only by a quick splash and the disappearing ripples left in the wake of some unseen creature. He could hear the searchers, but only faintly, the thickness of the wood muffling the distant baying of hounds and the halloos of the men beating the surrounding countryside. Here, all was quiet in the August heat.

"Gor," whispered Tom. "This place gives me the goosies, it does."

"I thought you didn't believe in ghosts."

"This place could change a body's mind, it could."

Smiling, Sebastian handed his tiger the reins and jumped down. "Walk them."

"Aye, gov'nor."

A distinct scuffing noise, as of a shovel biting dirt, carried on the breeze. Sebastian turned toward the sound. The site was obviously not as deserted as it had first appeared.

The land bridge to the island lay on the eastern side of the moat. He crossed it warily, one hand on the pistol in his pocket. Sir Stanley had run his excavation trenches at right angles on the far side of the bridge, where at one time a drawbridge might have protected the approach to the now vanished castle.

The rushing sound of cascading dirt cut through the stillness, followed again by the scrape of a shovel biting deep into loose earth. Sebastian could see him now, a big, thickly muscled man with golden red hair worn long, so that it framed his face like a lion's mane. He had the sleeves of his smock rolled up to expose bronzed, brawny arms, and rough trousers tucked into boots planted wide as he worked shoveling dirt back into the farthest trench.

He caught sight of Sebastian and paused, his chest rising and falling with his hard breathing. He was a startlingly good-looking man, with even features and two dimples that slashed his cheeks when he squinted into the sun. He swiped the back of one sinewy arm across his sweaty face and his gaze locked with Sebastian's.

"You Rory Forster?" Sebastian asked.

The man slammed his shovel into the dirt pile and wrenched it sideways, sending a slide of dark loam over the edge into the trench. "I am."

"I take it Sir Stanley has decided to end the excavations?"

The man had a head built like a battering ram, with a thick neck and a high forehead, his eyes pale blue and thickly lashed and set wide apart. "'Pears that way, don't it?" he said without looking up again.

Sebastian let his gaze drift around the otherwise deserted site. "Where's the rest of your crew?"

"Sir Stanley told 'em they could go look fer them nippers."

"You're not interested in the reward?"

Rory Forster hawked up a mouthful of phlegm and spat. "'Tain't nobody gonna find them nippers."

"So certain?"

"Ye think they're out there, why ain't ye joinin' the search?"

"I am, in my own fashion."

Forster grunted and kept shoveling.

Sebastian wandered between the trenches, his gaze slowly discerning the uncovered remnants of massively thick foundations of what must once have been mighty walls. Pausing beside a mound of rubble, he found himself staring at a broken red tile decorated with a charging knight picked out in white.

He reached for the tile fragment, aware of Forster's eyes watching him. "Did you come out here this past Sunday?" asked Sebastian, straightening.

Forster went back to filling his trench. "We don't work on Sundays."

"No one stays to guard the site?"

"Why would they?"

"I heard rumors you've had trouble with treasure hunters."

Forster paused with his shovel idle in his hands. "I wouldn't know nothin' 'bout that."

Sebastian kept a wary eye on the man's shovel. "I've also heard you and Miss Tennyson didn't exactly get along."

"Who said that?"

"Does it matter?"

Forster set his jaw and put his back into his digging again, the dirt flying through the air. Sebastian breathed in the scent of damp earth and decay and a foul, dark smell that was like a breath from an old grave. He said, "I can understand how it might get under a man's skin, having to take orders from a woman."

Forster scraped the last of the dirt into the trench with the edge of his shovel, his attention seemingly all for his task. "I'm a good overseer, I am. Sir Stanley wouldn't have kept me on if'n I wasn't."

Sebastian watched Rory Forster move on to the next trench. The man's very name—Forster, a corruption of "forester"—harkened back to the days when this wood had been part of a vast royal hunting park. His ancestors would have been the kings' foresters, charged with husbanding the royal game and protecting them from the encroachments of poachers. But those days were long gone, lost in the misty past.

Sebastian said, "Did Miss Tennyson tell Sir Stanley she suspected you were the one vandalizing the site in search of treasure?"

Forster straightened slowly, the outer corner of one eye twitching as if with a tic, the rough cloth of his smock dark with sweat across his shoulders and chest and under his arms. "Ye ain't gonna pin this murder on me. Ye hear me?" he said, raising one beefy arm to stab a pointed finger at Sebastian. "I was home with me wife all that night. Never left the house, I didn't."

"Possibly," said Sebastian. "However, we don't know precisely when Miss Tennyson was murdered. She may well have met her death in the afternoon."

The twitch beside the man's eye intensified. "What ye want from me?"

"The truth."

"The truth?" Forster gave a harsh laugh. "Ye don't want the truth."

"Try me."

"Huh. Ye think I'm a fool?"

Sebastian studied the man's handsome, dirt-streaked face. "You can say what you have to say to me, in confidence. Or you can tell your tale to Bow Street. The choice is yours."

Forster licked his lower lip, then gave Sebastian a sly, sideways look. "Ye claim it was me what told ye, and I'll deny it."

"Fair enough. Now, tell me."

Forster sniffed. "To my way o' thinkin', them Bow Street magistrates ought to be lookin' into Sir Stanley's lady."

"You mean Lady Winthrop?"

"Aye. Come out here Saturday about noon, she did. In a real pelter."

Sebastian frowned. Lady Winthrop had told him she'd never visited her husband's controversial excavations. "Was Sir Stanley here?"

"Nah. He'd gone off by then. Somethin' about a prize mare what was near her time. But Miss Tennyson was still here. She's the one her ladyship come to see. A right royal row they had, and ye don't haveta take me word for it. Ask any o' the lads workin' the trenches that day; they'll tell ye."

"What was the argument about?"

"I couldn't catch the sense o' most o' it. Her ladyship asked to speak to Miss Tennyson in private and they walked off a ways, just there." Forster nodded toward the northeastern edge of the island, where a faint path could be seen winding through the thicket of bushes and brambles.

"But you did hear something," said Sebastian.

"Aye. Heard enough to know it was Sir Stanley they was fightin' about. And as she was leavin', I heard her ladyship say, 'Cross me, young woman, and ye'll be sorry!'"

Chapter 20

"**Y**ou're certain you heard her right?" asked Sebastian.

The foreman sniffed. "Ye don't believe me, ask some of the lads what was here that day. Or better yet, ask her ladyship herself. But like I said, if ye let on 'twas me what told ye, I'll deny it. I'll deny it to yer face."

"Who are you afraid of?" asked Sebastian. "Sir Stanley? Or his wife?"

Forster huffed a scornful laugh. "Anybody ain't afraid of them two is a fool. Oh, they're grand and respectable, ain't they? Livin' in that big house and hobnobbin' wit' the King hisself. But I hear tell Sir Stanley, he started out as some clerk with little more'n a sixpence to scratch hisself with. How ye think he got all that money? Mmm? And how many bodies ye think he walked over to get it?"

"And Lady Winthrop?"

"She's worse'n him, any day o' the week. Sir Stanley, he'll leave ye alone as long as yer not standin' between him and somethin' he wants. But Lady Winthrop, she'd destroy a man out o' spite, just 'cause she's mean."

Some twenty minutes later, Sebastian's knock at Trent House's massive doors was answered by a stately, ruddy-faced butler of ample proportions who bowed and intoned with sepulchral detachment, "I fear Sir Stanley is not at present at home, my lord."

"Actually, I'm here to see Lady Winthrop. And there's no point in telling me she's not at home either," said Sebastian cheerfully when the butler opened his mouth to do just that, "because I spotted her in the gardens when I drove up. And I'm perfectly willing to do something vulgar like cut around the outside of the house and accost her directly, if you're too timid to announce me."

The butler's nostrils quivered with righteous indignation. Then he bowed again and said, "This way, my lord."

Lady Winthrop stood at the edge of the far terrace, the remnants of last night's wind flapping the figured silks of her high-necked gown. She had been watching over the activities of the band of workmen tearing out the old wall of the terrace. But at Sebastian's approach she turned, one hand coming up to straighten her plain, broad-brimmed hat as she shot the butler a tight-jawed glare that warned of dire future consequences.

"Don't blame him," said Sebastian, intercepting the look. "He denied you with commendable aplomb. But short of bowling me over, there really was no stopping me."

She brought her icy gaze back to Sebastian's face and said evenly to the red-faced butler, "Thank you, Huckabee; that will be all."

The butler gave another of his flawless bows and withdrew.

"My husband is out with the men from the estate searching for the missing Tennyson children," she said, her fingers still gripping the brim of her hat. "He'll be sorry he missed you. And now you really must excuse me—"

"Why don't you show me your gardens, Lady Winthrop?" said

Sebastian when she would have turned away. "No need to allow the interesting details of our conversation to distract these men from their work."

She froze, then forced a stiff laugh. "Of course. Since you are here."

She waited until they were out of earshot before saying evenly, "I resent the implication that I have something to hide from my servants."

"Don't you? You told me yesterday that you never visited the excavations at the moat. Except you did, just last Saturday. In fact, you had what's been described as a 'right royal row' with Miss Tennyson herself."

Lady Winthrop's lips tightened into a disdainful smile. "I fear you misunderstood me, Lord Devlin. I said I did not make it a practice of visiting the site; I did not say I had never done so."

Sebastian studied her proud, faintly contemptuous face, the weak chin pulled back against her neck in a scowl. As the plain but extraordinarily well-dowered only daughter of a wealthy merchant, she had married not once, but twice. Her first, brief marriage to a successful banker ended when her husband broke his neck on the hunting field and left his considerable holdings to her; her second marriage a few years later to Sir Stanley united two vast fortunes. But this second union, like her first, had remained childless, an economic merger without affection or shared interests or any real meeting of the minds.

It must be difficult, Sebastian thought, to be a wealthy but plain, dull woman married to a handsome, virile, charismatic man. And he understood then just how much this woman must have hated Gabrielle Tennyson, who was everything she, Lady Winthrop, was not: not only young and beautiful, but also brilliant and well educated and courageous enough to defy so many of the conventions that normally held her sisters in check.

He said, "And your argument?"

She drew her brows together in a pantomime of confusion. "Did we argue? Frankly, I don't recall it. Have you been speaking to some of the workmen? You know how these yokels exaggerate."

"Doing it a bit too brown, there, Lady Winthrop."

Angry color mottled her cheeks. "I take it that must be one of those vulgar cant expressions gentlemen are so fond of affecting these days. Personally I find the tendency to model one's speech on that of the lower orders beyond reprehensible."

Sebastian let out his breath in a huff of laughter. "So why did you visit Camlet Moat last Saturday?"

"Years before the light of our Lord was shown upon this land, England was given over to a terrible superstition dominated by a caste of evil men bound in an unholy pact with the forces of darkness."

"By which I take it you mean the Druids."

She inclined her head. "I do. Unfortunately, there are those in our age who in their folly have romanticized the benighted days of the past. Rather than seek salvation through our Lord and wisdom in his word, they choose to dabble in the rituals and tarnished traditions of the ignorant."

Sebastian stared off down the hill, to where a doe could be seen grazing beside a stretch of ornamental water. "I've heard that the locals consider the island to be a sacred site."

"They do. Which is why I chose to visit Camlet Moat last Saturday. My concern was that the recent focus of attention on the area might inspire the ignorant to hold some bizarre ritual on the island."

"Because Lammas began Saturday night at sunset?"

Again, the regal inclination of the head. "Precisely."

"So why approach Miss Tennyson? Why not Sir Stanley?"

"I fear I have not made myself clear. I went to the site in search of my husband. But when I found him absent, I thought to mention my concerns to Miss Tennyson." The thin lips pinched into a tight downward curve. "Her response was predictably rude and arrogant."

Those were two words Sebastian had yet to hear applied to Miss Tennyson. But he had been told she didn't suffer fools lightly, and he suspected she might well have perceived Lady Winthrop as a very vain and foolish woman. He said, "She didn't think you had anything to worry about?"

"On the contrary. She said she believed the island was a profoundly spiritual place of ancient significance."

"Is that when you quarreled?"

She fixed him with an icy stare full of all the moral outrage of a woman long practiced in the art of self-deception, who had already comfortably convinced herself that the confrontation with Gabrielle had never occurred. "We did not quarrel," she said evenly.

There were any number of things he could have said. But none of them would have penetrated that shield of righteous indignation, so he simply bowed and took his leave.

He did not believe for a moment that she had overcome her distaste for her husband's excavations in order to drive out to the moat and have a conversation that could just as easily have been held over the breakfast table. Instead, she had deliberately chosen a time when she knew Sir Stanley to be elsewhere.

Jealousy could be a powerful motive for murder. He could imagine Lady Winthrop killing Gabrielle in a rage of jealousy and religious zeal. But he could not imagine her then murdering two children and disposing of their bodies somewhere in the wilds of the chase.

Yet as he drove away, he was aware of her standing at the edge of her garden watching him.

And he wondered why.

Sebastian was standing in the middle of his library and studying the new boxes of books and papers that had appeared since that morning when he heard the peal of the front bell. A moment later, Morey paused in the library's entrance to clear his throat.

"Yes?" prompted Sebastian when the majordomo seemed temporarily at a loss for words.

"A personage to see you, my lord."

"A personage?"

"Yes, my lord. I have taken the liberty of putting him in the drawing room."

Sebastian studied the majordomo's painfully wooden face. Morey normally left "personages" cooling their heels in the hall.

"I'll be right up," he said.

The man who stood before the empty fireplace was dressed all in black: black breeches, black coat, black waistcoat, black cravat. Only his shirt was white. He stood with his dark head tilted back as he stared up at the portrait of the Countess of Hendon that hung over the mantel. With the grace of a dancer or fencer, he pivoted slowly when Sebastian entered the room to pause just inside the doorway.

"So we meet," said Sebastian, and carefully closed the door behind him.

Chapter 21

$\mathcal{T}$he man called Jamie Knox was built tall and lean, taller even than Sebastian, with wavy, almost black hair and the yellow eyes of a wolf or feral cat.

Sebastian had been told once that he had his father's eyes—his *real* father's eyes. But he'd always thought he looked like his mother. Now, as he stared at the face of the man who stood across the room from him, he wondered if it was his imagination that traced a resemblance in the tavern owner's high-boned cheeks and gently curving mouth.

Then he remembered Morey's strange reaction and knew it was not his imagination.

He crossed to where a decanter and glasses rested on a side table. "May I offer you a brandy?"

"Yes, thank you."

The inflections were similar to that of the curly-headed man of the night before. The accent was not that of a gentleman.

"Where are you from?" asked Sebastian, splashing brandy into two glasses.

"Shropshire, by way of a rifle regiment."

"You're a rifleman?"

"I was."

Sebastian held out one of the glasses. After the briefest of hesitations, the man took it.

"I fought beside riflemen in Italy and the Peninsula," said Sebastian. "I've often thought it will be Napoléon's insistence on arming his men with only muskets that will ultimately cause his downfall."

"You may be right. Only, don't go telling the French bugger himself, hmm?" Knox took a deep drink of his brandy, his intense yellow gaze never leaving Sebastian's face. "You don't look much like your da, the Earl, do you?"

"I'm told I resemble my mother."

Jamie Knox jerked his chin toward the portrait over the mantel. "That her?"

"Yes."

He took another sip. "I never knew my father. My mother said he was a cavalry captain. Your father ever in the cavalry?"

"Not to my knowledge."

A faint gleam of amusement lit up the other man's eyes. He drained his brandy with the offhand carelessness of a man well accustomed to hard drinking, then shook his head when Sebastian offered him another.

"You came around asking about my conversation with Gabrielle Tennyson last week."

"So you don't deny the confrontation occurred."

"Why should I? She heard I'd uncovered one of those old picture pavements in my cellars, and she kept pestering me to let her take a look at it."

"You mean, a Roman mosaic?"

"That's it. Picture of a naked fat man holding a bunch of grapes in one hand and riding a dolphin."

"You expect me to believe you threatened a woman over a mosaic?"

Knox's lips curved into a smile, but the glitter in his eyes had become hard and dangerous. He looked to be a few years older than Sebastian, perhaps as much as thirty-three or -four. "I didn't threaten to kill her. I just told her she'd be sorry if she didn't back off. Last thing I need is some bloody bluestocking sniffing around the place. Not good for business."

"Especially if she's sniffing around your cellars."

Knox laughed. "Something like that, yes."

The rifleman let his gaze drift around Sebastian's drawing room, the amusement slowly dying out of his expression. By Mayfair's standards, the Brook Street house was not large; the furnishings were elegant but neither lavish nor opulent. Yet as Sebastian watched Knox's assessing eyes take in the room's satin hangings, the delicate cane chairs near the bow window overlooking the street, the gently faded carpet, the white Carrara marble of the mantelpiece, he had no doubt that the room must appear quite differently to a rifleman from the wilds of Shropshire than it did to Sebastian, who was raised in the sprawling splendor of Hendon House in Grosvenor Square and the halls and manors of the Earl's various estates across Britain.

"Nice place you got here," said Knox, his accent unusually pronounced.

"Thank you."

"I hear you got married just last week."

"I did, yes."

"Married the daughter of Lord Jarvis himself."

"Yes."

The two men's gazes met, and held.

"Congratulations," said Knox. Setting aside his empty glass, he reached for the black hat he had rested on a nearby table and settled it on his head at a rakish angle. Then he gave a faintly mocking bow. "My lord."

Sebastian stood at the bowed front windows of his drawing room and watched Jamie Knox descend the front steps and stroll off down the street. It was like watching a shadowy doppelganger of himself.

Or a brother.

Sebastian was still standing at the window some moments later when a familiar yellow-bodied carriage drew up. He watched Hero descend the coach steps with her usual grace and then enter the house.

She came into the room pulling off a pair of soft yellow kid gloves that she tossed on one of the cane chairs. "Ah, good," she said. "You're finally up."

"I do generally try to make it out of bed before nightfall," he said.

He was rewarded with a soft huff of laughter.

Today she wore an elegant carriage gown of emerald satin trimmed with rows of pintucks down the skirt and a spray of delicate yellow roses embroidered on each sleeve. She yanked at the emerald ribbons that tied her velvet hat beneath her chin and tossed the hat onto the chair with her gloves. "I've just come from an interesting conversation with Mary Bourne."

"Who?"

"Mrs. Bourne. She's sister to both Charles Tennyson d'Eyncourt and the Reverend Tennyson, the father of the two missing boys."

Sebastian frowned. He had a vague recollection of d'Eyncourt mentioning a sister staying with him. "Is she like her brother d'Eyncourt?"

"Oh, no; she's far worse. She's a saint, you know."

Sebastian laughed out loud.

"No, it's true; I mean that quite literally. She's a Calvinist. You can have no notion of the misery it brings her, knowing that she alone can look forward to the joys awaiting her in heaven whilst the vast majority of her family is doomed to suffer the everlasting torments of hell."

"She actually told you that?"

"She did. Personally, I suspect she derives enormous satisfaction from the comfortable conviction that she is one of the chosen elite while everyone around her is doomed to burn. But then, self-perception is not one of her strong suits."

Sebastian leaned back against the windowsill, his arms crossed at his chest, his gaze on his wife's face. Her eyes were sparkling and a faint flush rode high on her cheekbones. He found himself smiling. "So why did you go see her? Or were you looking for d'Eyncourt?"

"No. I knew d'Eyncourt would be at Westminster. I wanted to talk to Mary Bourne alone. You see, I've been puzzled by the arithmetic." Hero sank into one of the chairs beside the empty hearth. "D'Eyncourt told you he is his father's heir, right? Except, d'Eyncourt is only twenty-eight, while little George Tennyson—the elder of the missing boys—is nine years old. That means that if d'Eyncourt's brother were indeed a younger son, he would need to have sired his own son at the tender age of seventeen. Obviously possible, but unlikely, given that he is in holy orders."

"So what did you discover?"

"That the boys' father is actually thirty-four years old."

Sebastian pushed away from the window. "You're certain?"

"Are you suggesting the woman might have mistaken the ages of her own brothers? D'Eyncourt is the baby of the family. He's younger than his brother by a full six years."

The bells of the abbey were tolling seven when d'Eyncourt emerged from Westminster Hall and turned toward Parliament Street. The setting sun soaked the ancient buildings with a rich tea-colored light and cast long shadows across the paving.

Sebastian fell into step beside him.

The MP cast a quick look at Sebastian, then glanced away

without slackening his pace. There was neither surprise nor puzzlement on his smoothly handsome features. "I've just received a note from my sister Mary, telling me she enjoyed a visit from Lady Devlin this afternoon. My sister is an earnest but guileless woman. As such she is frequently slow to see the subterfuge in others. It wasn't until some time after Lady Devlin's departure that my sister began to ponder the direction their conversation had taken."

Sebastian showed his teeth in a smile. "Ah, yes; Lady Devlin is quite practiced in the arts of guile and subterfuge, is she not?"

D'Eyncourt pressed his lips together and kept walking.

Sebastian said, "And once Mrs. Bourne realized the indiscretions of her talkative tongue, she immediately sat down and dashed off a note to her baby brother warning him— What, exactly? That you were about to be caught out in a very telling lie?"

D'Eyncourt drew up at the edge of the Privy Gardens and turned to face him, a slim, elegant man with a smug air of self-assurance. "I never claimed to be my father's firstborn. I simply told you that I am his heir. And that is the truth."

"His only heir?"

"Yes."

"How can that be?"

D'Eyncourt's thin nostrils quivered with indignation. "That is none of your affair."

Sebastian advanced on him, backing the dandified parliamentarian up until his shoulders slammed against the rough stone wall behind him. "Gabrielle Tennyson's death made it my affair, you god damned, pompous, self-congratulatory son of a bitch. A woman is dead and two innocent little boys are missing. If you know anything—*anything*—that can help make sense of what has happened to them—"

"I am not afraid of you," said d'Eyncourt, his Adam's apple bobbing up and down as he swallowed.

"You should be."

"You can't accost me in the streets! What are you imagining? That those two children stand between me and my father's wealth? Well, you are wrong. My father disinherited my older brother and made me his sole heir when I was six years old. Why else do you suppose my brother took holy orders and now serves as a rector? Because that is his future! Everything my father owns—the estates, the investments—all will in due time pass to me."

"I can think of only one reason for a man to disinherit his twelve-year-old son and make his youngest child his sole heir."

Two bright spots of color appeared on d'Eyncourt's cheeks. "If you are suggesting that my brother was disinherited because he is . . . because he is *not* my brother, then let me tell you right now that you are sadly mistaken. My brother was disinherited because by the time he reached the beginnings of puberty it had become obvious to our father that his health and temperament were totally unsuited for the position which would be required of him."

"But not unsuited to his becoming a rector?"

D'Eyncourt stared back at him. "The requirements of the two callings are utterly dissimilar."

"So tell me," said Sebastian, "how has your brother adjusted to having a fortune of some half a million pounds wrested from his grasp?"

"He was, naturally, somewhat aggrieved—"

"Aggrieved?"

"Aggrieved. But he has with time grown more accustomed to his situation."

"As an impoverished rector at Somersby?"

"Just so."

Sebastian took a step back.

D'Eyncourt made a show of adjusting his cravat and straightening the set of his coat. "I can understand how it might be difficult for someone of your background to understand, but you must remember that my family's wealth—while substantial—is only recently acquired. Hence the rules of primogeniture do not apply. My father is free to leave his property as he sees fit."

"True," said Sebastian. "But it occurs to me that if your father could change his will once, he is obviously free to do so again—in favor of his two grandsons, this time."

D'Eyncourt stiffened. "If you mean to suggest—"

"The suggestion is there, whether it is put into words or not," said Sebastian, and turned away.

Sebastian arrived back at Brook Street to be told that Lady Devlin had already departed for a musical evening in the company of her mother, Lady Jarvis.

"However," said Morey, bowing slightly, "I believe Calhoun has been most particular to have a word with you."

"Has he? Then send him up," said Sebastian, heading for the stairs.

"Well?" asked Sebastian when Calhoun slipped into the dressing room a few minutes later. "Find anything?"

"Not as much as I had hoped, my lord," said Calhoun, going to lay out Sebastian's evening dress. "From what I have been able to ascertain, Mr. Knox arrived in London just three years ago. He used to be with the 145th Rifles but was discharged when his unit was reduced after Corunna."

"So he actually was a rifleman."

"He was, my lord. In fact, he's famous for having killed some bigwig Frenchy by shooting the man off his horse at some seven hundred yards. And I'm told he can shoot the head off a running rabbit at more than three hundred yards." Calhoun paused a moment, then added, "In the dark."

Sebastian looked up from unbuttoning his shirt. "How did he end up in possession of the Black Devil?"

"Reports differ. Some say he took to the High Toby for a time before he either won the tavern at the roll of the dice or killed the previous owner." "Taking to the High Toby" was slang for becoming a highwayman. "Or perhaps both."

"He seems very sensitive about his cellars."

"That's not surprising, given the nature of some of his associates."

"Oh? And who might they be?"

"The name that came up most frequently was Yates. Russell Yates."

Chapter 22

Sebastian waited beyond the light cast by the flickering oil lamp at the head of the lane. The theater was still closed for the summer, but rehearsals for the upcoming season were already under way. The dark street rang with the laughter of the departing troupe.

He kept his gaze on the stage door.

The night was warm, the wind a soft caress scented by oranges and a thousand bittersweet memories. He heard the stage door open, watched a woman and two men walk toward the street. The woman paused for a moment beneath the streetlight, caught up in conversation with her fellow players. The dancing flame from the oil lamp glinted on the auburn highlights in her thick, dark hair and flickered seductively over the familiar, beloved planes of her face. She had her head thrown back, lost in laughter at one of her friends' remarks. Then she stilled suddenly, her head turning, her eyes widening in a useless attempt to probe the darkness. And Sebastian knew she had sensed his presence and that the bond between them that had existed all these years, while weakened, had not broken.

Her name was Kat Boleyn, and she was the most celebrated actress of the London stage. Once, she had been the love of Sebastian's life. Once, he had thought to grow old with her at his side, and to hell with the shocked mutterings of society and the outraged opposition of his father—*of the Earl of Hendon*, he reminded himself. Then an ugly tangle of lies and an even uglier truth had intervened. Now Kat was married to a flamboyant ex-privateer named Russell Yates, a man with a secret, forbidden passion for his own gender and shadowy ties to the smugglers and agents who plied the channel between England and Napoléon's France.

Sebastian watched her say good night to her friends and walk up to him. She wore an ivory silk cloak thrown over her shoulders, the hood thrust back in a way that framed her face. He said, "You shouldn't walk alone at night."

"Because of these latest murders, you mean?" She turned to stroll beside him up Hart Street. The pavement was crowded with richly harnessed horses and elegant carriages, their swaying lamps filling the air with the scent of hot oil. "Gibson tells me you have involved yourself in the investigation." He watched her eyebrows pinch together in a worried frown as she said it, for she knew him well. She knew the price he paid with each descent into the dark world of fear and hatred, greed and despair, that inevitably swirled around a murder. Yet even though she knew, intellectually, what drove him to it, she could never quite understand his need to do what he did.

He said, "Don't worry about me."

A smile lit her eyes. "Yet you are free to worry about me?" The smile faded as she paused to turn toward him, her gaze searching. She had deeply set eyes, thickly lashed and of a uniquely intense blue that she had inherited from her natural father, the Earl of Hendon. And every time he looked into them, he knew a searing pain that was like a dagger thrust to the heart.

She said, "You're not here for the sake of auld lang syne, Sebastian; what is it?"

"I'm told Yates has dealings with a tavern owner named Jamie Knox."

She sucked in a quick breath that jerked her chest. It was an unusual betrayal for an actress who could normally control her every look, every tone, her every word and movement.

He said, "Obviously, you know Knox as well. What can you tell me about him?"

"Very little, actually. He is an intensely private person, cold and dangerous. Most people who know him are afraid of him. It's an aura he cultivates."

"You met him through Yates?"

"Yes." She hesitated, then asked, "He is involved in this murder? How?"

"He was seen arguing with Gabrielle Tennyson several days before she was killed. He claims it was over a Roman mosaic."

"You don't believe him?"

"No. But I don't understand how he fits into anything else I've learned, either."

"I'll see what I can find out." The door to a tavern near the corner opened, spilling light and voices and laughter into the street. "Has Knox seen you?"

"Why do you ask?"

Her gaze met his. "You know why."

They had reached the arch where her carriage awaited. Sebastian said, "A few weeks ago, I met a man in Chelsea who told me I reminded him of a highwayman who'd once held up his carriage on Hounslow Heath."

"You believe that was Knox?"

"I'm told he took to the High Toby for a time after he left the Rifles. I wouldn't want to think there are *three* of us walking around."

He said it lightly, but his words drew no answering smile from

her. She said, "I know you've had men on the Continent, searching
for your mother. Have they found her?"

"No."

"You can't simply . . . let it go, Sebastian?"

He searched her pale, beloved face. "All those years when you
didn't know the identity of your father, if you thought you had the
truth within reach, could you have . . . let it go?"

"Yes." She did smile then, a sweet, sad smile. "But then, my
demons are different from yours." Reaching up on tiptoe, she
brushed her lips against his cheek, then turned away. "Good night,
Sebastian. Keep yourself safe."

He walked down increasingly empty streets. The sky above was
dark and starless, the air close; the oil lamps mounted high on the
dark, looming walls of the tightly packed, grimy brick houses and
shops flickered with his passing. At one point he was aware of two
men falling into step behind him. He tightened his grip on the
walking stick he carried tucked beneath one arm. But they melted
away down a noisome side alley, their footfalls echoing softly into
the night.

He walked on, rounding the corner toward Long Street. He
could hear the thin, reedy wail of a babe somewhere in the distance, the jingle of an off-tune piano, the rattle of carriage wheels
passing in the next block. And from the murky shadows of a narrow
passageway up ahead came a soft whisper.

"*C'est lui.*"

He drew up just as the same two men burst from the passage
and fanned out to take up positions, one in front of him, the other
to his rear. Whirling, Sebastian saw the glint of a knife in the hand
of one; the other, a big, fair-haired man in dark trousers and high
leather boots, carried a cudgel he slapped tauntingly against his
left palm.

"Watch!" shouted Sebastian as the man raised the club over his head. "Watch, I say!"

Before the man could bring the club down, Sebastian rushed him, the walking stick whistling through the air toward the assailant's head. The man threw up his left arm, blocking Sebastian's blow at the last instant. The impact shattered the ebony shaft of the walking stick, shearing it off some eight inches from Sebastian's fist. But the shock of the unexpected counterattack was enough to send the man staggering back. He lost his footing and went down.

His companion growled, *"Bâtard!"*

"Watch!" shouted Sebastian again, swinging around just as the second man—smaller, leaner, darker than his companion—lunged, his knife held in an underhanded grip.

Sebastian tried to parry the man's thrust with the broken shaft of the walking stick and felt the blade slip off the wood to slice along his forearm. Then the man on the ground closed his hands around Sebastian's ankle and yanked.

Lurching backward, Sebastian stumbled over the fallen man and went down, bruising his hip on a loose cobblestone as he rolled. Swearing long and hard, he grabbed the cobblestone as he surged up onto his knees.

The man with the cudgel took a swipe. Sebastian ducked, then came up to smash the stone into the side of his attacker's head with a bone crushing *twunk.* The man reeled back, eyes rolling up, the side of his face a sheet of gore. Panting hard, Sebastian reached into his boot and yanked his own dagger from its hidden sheath.

The knife clenched in one hand, the bloody rock still gripped in the other, he rose into a low crouch. "Come on, you bastard," he spat, his gaze locking with that of his remaining assailant.

The man was clean-shaven and relatively young, no more than thirty, his coat worn but clean, his cravat simply but neatly tied. He licked his lower lip, his gaze flicking from Sebastian to the still figure lying between them in a spreading pool of blood.

His nostrils flared on a quickly indrawn breath.

"Well?" said Sebastian.

The man turned and ran.

Sebastian slumped back against the brick wall, his injured arm cradled against his chest, his blood thrumming in his ears, his gaze on the dead man beside him.

Chapter 23

"Ghastly," said Sir Henry Lovejoy, peering down at the gory head of the dead man sprawled on the pavement at their feet. The watch had arrived, panting, only moments after the attack on the Viscount, who sent the man running to Bow Street, just blocks away. Now Sir Henry shifted his glance to Lord Devlin. "Who is he? Do you know?"

"Never saw him before," said Devlin, stripping off his cravat to wind around his bleeding arm.

"And his companion who fled?"

"Was also unfamiliar to me."

Lovejoy forced himself to look more closely at the dead man. "I suppose they could have been common footpads after your pocketbook."

"They could have been."

"But you don't think so. I must confess, he does not exactly have the look of a footpad."

"He's also French."

"French? Oh, dear; I don't like the sound of that. Do you think there could be some connection between this incident and the Tennyson murders?"

"If there is, I'll be damned if I can see it." Devlin looked up from wrapping his arm. "Have you found the children's bodies, then?"

"What? Oh, no. Not yet. But with each passing day, it becomes increasingly difficult to believe that they could still be alive." Lovejoy nodded to the men from the dead house who had arrived with a shell, then stood watching them shift the body. "We've begun to look into the backgrounds of the various men involved in the excavations up at the moat. Some disturbing things are coming to light about this man Rory Forster."

Devlin finished tying off the ends of his makeshift bandage. "Such as?"

"He's said to have quite a temper, for one thing. And he's not above using his fists on women."

"That doesn't surprise me."

"Of course, his wife backs up his claim that he was home with her Sunday afternoon and evening. But I wouldn't put it beyond him to bully her into saying it. The problem is, I don't see how he could possibly be the killer."

Devlin flexed the hand of his injured arm, testing it. "Why's that?"

"Because if he is, how did the Tennysons get up to the moat in the first place? The logical conclusion is they could only have driven up there in the company of their murderer."

"The same could be said of Sir Stanley Winthrop. If he is the killer, then how the devil did the Tennysons get to Enfield?"

Lovejoy cleared his throat. "My colleagues at Bow Street are of the opinion that it is ridiculous even to suggest that Sir Stanley might be involved in any way."

Devlin laughed. "There's no doubt it would negatively impact the nation's war effort, to have one of the King's leading bankers arrested for murder."

Lovejoy studied the blood seeping through the Viscount's makeshift bandage. "Don't you think you should perhaps have that properly attended to, my lord?"

Devlin glanced down and frowned. "I suppose you're right. Although I fear the coat is beyond help."

"You're certain you heard them speaking French?" asked Paul Gibson, his attention all for the row of stitches he was laying along the gash in Sebastian's arm.

"I'm certain." Sebastian sat on a table in the front room of Gibson's surgery. He was stripped to the waist, a basin of bloody water and cloths set nearby.

Gibson tied off his stitches and straightened. "I suppose it could have been a ruse to mislead you."

"Somehow I don't think the intent was to allow me to live long enough to be misled. I suspect my questions are making someone nervous."

Gibson reached for a roll of bandages. "Someone French, obviously."

"Or someone involved with the French."

"There is that."

"Of course," said Sebastian, watching his friend work, "just because my questions are making someone nervous doesn't necessarily mean that particular someone is the killer. He could simply have something to hide."

"Yet it does tell you this 'someone' isn't afraid to kill to keep his secrets."

"Powerful men usually do have a lot of secrets . . . and there are several powerful men whose names seem to keep coming up in this."

Gibson tied off the bandage and frowned. "Who else besides d'Eyncourt and Sir Stanley?"

Lord Jarvis, Sebastian thought, although he didn't say it. He slipped off the table and reached for his shirt. "Isn't that enough?" He pulled the shirt on over his head. "Have you finished the autopsy of Miss Tennyson's body?"

"I have. But I'm afraid there's not much more I can tell you. She was stabbed through the heart sometime Sunday. No other sign of injury. Whoever killed her made no attempt to force himself on her."

"Well, at least the poor woman didn't need to suffer that."

Gibson scratched behind his ear. "There is one thing I noticed that may or may not prove relevant."

Something in his voice caused Sebastian to look up from buttoning his shirt. "Oh? What's that?"

"I said she wasn't forced before her death. But then, neither was she a maiden."

Sebastian expected Hero to have long since retired for the night. Instead, she was sitting cross-legged on the library floor surrounded by a jumbled sea of books and papers. She had her head bent over some manuscript pages; a smudge of ink showed along the edge of her chin, and she was so intent on what she was doing that he suspected she hadn't even heard him come in.

"I thought you had planned a musical evening with your mother," he said, pausing in the doorway.

She looked up, the brace of candles burning on a nearby table throwing a soft golden light over her profile and shoulders. "That finished hours ago. I decided I might as well get started looking at Gabrielle's research materials. I can't help but think that the key to what happened to her and the boys is here somewhere." She looked up, her eyes narrowing at the sight of his arm reposing in a sling. "You're hurt."

"Nothing serious. Two men jumped me in Covent Garden and tried to kill me."

"And you consider that not serious?"

He went to sprawl in a chair beside the empty hearth. "The attempt to kill me was definitely serious. The wound to my arm is not."

"Who were they?"

"I don't know for certain about the one I killed, but the one who got away was swearing at me in French."

She was silent for a moment, lost in thoughts he could only guess at. She was far too good at hiding away bits of herself. Then she pushed up from the floor and went to pour a glass of brandy that she held out to him, her gaze on his face. "There's something else that you're not telling me," she said. "What is it?"

He took the brandy. "Am I so transparent?"

"At times."

She sank into the chair opposite and looked at him expectantly. He was aware of the lateness of the hour, of the quiet darkness of the house around them, and of the absurd hesitation he felt in speaking to his own wife about the sexuality of her dead friend.

"Well?" she prompted.

"Paul Gibson finished the postmortem of Miss Tennyson's body. He says she was not a virgin."

He watched her lips part, her chest rise on a sudden intake of breath. He said, "You didn't know?"

"No. But then, we never discussed such things."

"Yet the knowledge still surprises you."

"It does, yes. She was so determined never to marry."

"She may have been involved in a youthful passion long forgotten."

Hero tipped her head to one side, her gaze on his face. "Are such youthful passions ever forgotten?"

"Perhaps not."

She rose to her feet, and for a moment he thought he caught a glimpse of the soft swelling of her belly beneath the fine muslin of her gown. Then he realized it was probably an illusion, a trick of the light or the drift of his own thoughts. For it was the child growing in her belly—conceived in a moment of fear and weakness when together they had faced what they'd thought was certain death—that had brought them here, to this moment, as husband and wife.

She went to pick up the papers she'd been reading, including a notebook whose pages showed signs of much crossing and reworking. He said, "What is that?"

"Gabrielle's translation of *The Lady of Shalott*."

"Ah. I've discovered the identity of the Frenchman she befriended, by the way. He's a cavalry officer named Philippe Arceneaux."

She looked around at him. "You found him?"

"I'd like to take credit for it, but the truth is, he found me. He says they met in the Reading Room of the British Museum. He was helping her with the translation."

Hero stood very still, the notebook in her hand forgotten. "Do you think he could have been her lover?"

"He says no. But he admits he was at least half in love with her. He seems to have made a practice of timing his walks in the park to coincide with when she took the boys to sail their boats on the Serpentine. And a week ago last Sunday, he drove up to Camlet Moat with her to see the site—although he'll never admit it since it was a flagrant violation of his parole."

She fell silent, her gaze fixed on something far, far away.

"What is it?" he asked, watching her.

She shook her head. "I was just thinking about something Gabrielle told me once, perhaps a month or more ago."

"What's that?"

"She asked if I ever had the sense that I was missing something—something important in life—by choosing to devote myself to research and writing, rather than marrying. She said lately she'd begun to feel as if she were simply watching life, rather than actually living it. She said it was as if she spent her days staring at the pale shadows of other people's lives reflected in a mirror— entertaining at first, perhaps, but ultimately empty and unsatisfying. And then she said . . ."

"Yes?"

"She said, 'Lately, I find I've grown half sick of shadows.'"

Her gaze met his. He was aware, again, of the stillness of the night around them. And he found himself thinking of the exquisite softness of her skin, the silken caress of her heavy dark hair sliding across his belly, the way her eyes widened in wonder and delight when he entered her. He gazed deep into her wide, dark eyes, saw her lips part, and knew her thoughts mirrored his own.

Yet the latent distrust that had always been there between them now loomed infinitely larger, fed by the unknown currents swirling around Gabrielle Tennyson's death and the lingering poisons of Jarvis's unabated malevolence and Sebastian's own tangled, sordid past. They had come to this marriage as two wary strangers united only by the child they had made and the passion they had finally admitted they shared. Now it seemed they were losing even that. Except . . .

Except that wasn't quite right, either. The passion was still there. It was their ability to surrender to it that was slipping away.

He said, his voice oddly husky, "And what did you tell her, when Gabrielle asked if you ever had the sense you were missing something in life?"

A ghost of a smile touched her lips. "I lied. I said no."

He thought for one aching moment that she would come to him. Then she said, "Good night, Devlin," and turned away.

The next morning, a constable from Bow Street arrived to tell Sebastian that one of his Covent Garden attackers had been identified. The dead man's name was Gaston Colbert, and he was a French prisoner of war free on his parole.

Chapter 24

*J*arvis was at his breakfast table when he heard the distant peal of the bell. A moment later, Hero entered the room wearing a shako-styled hat and a walking dress of Prussian blue fashioned à la hussar with epaulettes and double rows of brass buttons up the bodice. She yanked off her gloves as she walked.

"Good morning," Jarvis said, calmly cutting a piece of steak. "You're looking decidedly martial today."

She came to flatten her palms on the table and lean into them, her gaze hard on his face. "Last night, two men tried to kill Devlin. Do you know anything about that?"

He laid his knife along the top edge of his plate. "It is my understanding that the assailant whom Devlin dispatched with his typically lethal efficiency was a French officer on his parole. What makes you think the incident has anything to do with me?"

"Because I know you."

Jarvis took a bite of steak, chewed, and swallowed. "I confess I would not be sorry to see someone remove your husband from the landscape. But am I actively attempting to put a period to his existence? Not at the present moment."

She held herself very still, her gaze still searching his face. "Do you know who is?"

"No. Although I could speculate."

She drew out the nearest chair and sat. "So speculate."

Jarvis carved another slice of meat. "You've noticed the broadsheets that have appeared around town of late, calling for King Arthur to return from Avalon and lead England in its hour of need?"

"Do you know who's behind them?"

"Napoléon's agents, of course."

"And are you suggesting these agents have set someone after Devlin? Why?"

"Those who make it a habit of poking sticks into nests of vipers shouldn't be surprised when one of those vipers strikes back."

"You think that if Devlin finds whoever is behind the broadsheets, he'll find Gabrielle's killer?"

Jarvis reached for his ale and took a deep swallow. "It might be interesting."

"And convenient for you—if Devlin should manage to eliminate them."

He smiled. "There is that."

She collected her gloves and rose to her feet.

Jarvis said, "Have you told Devlin of my interaction with Miss Tennyson last Friday evening?"

Hero paused at the door to look back at him. "No."

Her answer surprised and pleased him, and yet somehow also vaguely troubled him. He let his gaze drift over his daughter's face. There was a bloom of color in her cheeks, an inner glow that told its own story. He said suddenly, "You do realize I know why you married him."

Her lips parted on a sudden intake of breath, but otherwise she remained remarkably calm and cool. "I can't imagine what you mean."

"Your former abigail confessed her observations on your condition before she was killed." When Hero only continued to stare at him, he said, "Is the child Devlin's?"

Her pupils flared with indignation. "It is."

"Did he force himself upon you?"

"He did not."

"I see. Interesting."

She said, "The situation is . . . complicated."

"So it seems." He reached for his snuffbox. "And the child is due—when?"

"February."

Jarvis flipped open the snuffbox, then simply held it, half forgotten. "You will take care of yourself, Hero."

Her eyes danced with quiet amusement. "As much as ever."

He gave her no answering smile. "If anything happens to you, I'll kill him."

"Nothing is going to happen to me," she said. "Good day, Papa."

After she had gone, he sat for a time, lost in thought, the snuffbox still open in his hand. Then he shut it with a snap and closed his fist around the delicate metal hard enough that he heard it crunch.

Lieutenant Philippe Arceneaux was playing chess with a hulking mustachioed hussar in a coffee shop near Wych Street when Sebastian paused beside his table and said, "Walk with me for a moment, Lieutenant?"

The black and brown dog at Arceneaux's feet raised his head and woofed in anticipation.

"*Monsieur!*" protested the mustachioed Frenchman, glaring up at him. "The game! You interrupt!"

The hussar still wore the tight Hungarian riding breeches and heavily decorated but faded dark blue dolman of his regiment. At each temple dangled braided love knots known as *cadenettes*, with another braid behind each ear. The *cadenettes* were kept straight by the weight of a gold coin tied at the end of each braid, for Napoléon's hussars were as known for their meticulous, flamboyant appearance as for their ruthlessness as bandits on horseback.

"It's all right," said Arceneaux in French, raising both hands in rueful surrender as he pushed back his chair and rose to his feet. "I concede. You have thoroughly trounced me already. My situation is beyond hope."

Sebastian was aware of the hussar's scowl following them to the coffee shop's door.

"Who's your friend?" Sebastian asked as they turned to stroll toward the nearby church of St. Clements, the dog trotting happily at their heels.

"Pelletier? Don't mind him. He has a foul disposition and a worse temper, but there's no real harm in him."

"Interesting choice of words," said Sebastian, "given that two of your fellow officers tried to kill me in Covent Garden last night."

Arceneaux's smile slipped. "I had heard of the attack upon you." He nodded to the arm Sebastian held resting in a sling. "You were wounded?"

"Not badly. Yet I now find myself wondering, why would two French officers on their parole want to kill me?"

Arceneaux stared at him, eyes wide. "You think I know?"

"In a word? Yes."

Chien let out a soft whine and Arceneaux paused to hunker down and ruffle the animal's ears. After a moment, he said, "I make a living teaching French to small boys and working as a translator for a Fleet Street publisher. It earns me enough to keep a garret room in a lodging house, just there." He nodded to a nearby lane. "My father is able to send money from time to time. But his life is hard too. He owns a small vineyard near Saint-Malo. His best customers were always the English. War has not been good for business."

"What exactly are you saying?"

Arceneaux pushed to his feet. "Only that men whose profession is war can sometimes find that their most lucrative employment involves using their . . . professional skills."

"For whom?"

The Frenchman shook his head. "That I do not know." They continued walking, the dog frisking ahead. Arceneaux watched him a moment, then said, "There's something I didn't tell you about before—something I think may explain what happened to you last night. When I said I last saw Gabrielle on Wednesday, I was not being exactly truthful. I also saw her Friday evening. She was . . . very distressed."

"Go on."

"She said she had discovered something . . . something that both angered and frightened her."

"What sort of 'thing' are we talking about here?"

"A forgery or deception of some sort. She warned me that it was for my own protection that she not tell me more. All I know is that it was connected to the Arthurian legend in some way."

"A forgery?"

"Yes."

"And why the devil didn't you tell me this before?"

Arceneaux's face had grown so pale as to appear almost white. "She said it was more than a simple forgery. The motive behind it was not monetary."

"Did she say who was involved?"

"There was some antiquary she had quarreled with over it, but I believe he was only a pawn. Someone else was behind the scheme—someone she was afraid of. Which surprised me, because Gabrielle was not the kind of woman to be easily frightened."

"This antiquary—did she tell you his name?"

Arceneaux shook his head.

But it didn't matter. Sebastian knew who it was.

Chapter 25

*I*t took a while, but Sebastian finally traced Bevin Childe to an exhibition of ancient Greek pottery being held at the Middle Temple in a small hall just off Fountain Court.

He was bent over with his plump face pressed close to the glass of a cabinet containing an exquisite redware kylix. Then he looked up to see Sebastian regarding him steadily from a few feet away and his mouth gaped. He jerked upright, his gaze darting right and left as if seeking some avenue of escape.

"No," said Sebastian with a soft, mean smile. "You can't run away from me."

The antiquary gave a weak, sick laugh. Then his jaw hardened. "I have no intention of running. I have heard about you, Lord Devlin. My conversation with your wife was bad enough. I am staying right here. You can't hurt me in a hall full of people."

"True. But do you really want them to hear what I have to say?"

Childe stiffened. "If you expect me to understand what you mean by that rather mystifying pronouncement, I fear you are doomed to disappointment."

Sebastian nodded to the ceremonial cup before them. "Lovely piece, isn't it? It certainly looks authentic. Yet I knew a man with a workshop outside of Naples who could turn out a dozen of these in a week. Forgeries, of course, but—"

Childe hissed. "*Shhh!* Keep your voice down." He cast another quick look around. A fat man with a protuberant mouth and full lips was staring at them over his spectacles. "Perhaps," said Childe, "it would be better after all if we were to continue this conversation outside."

They walked along Middle Temple Lane, toward the broad expanse of the Temple gardens edging the Thames. Once the precinct of the Knights Templar, the Inner and Middle Temples now served as two of the city's Inns of Court, those professional associations to which every barrister in England and Wales belonged. The morning sun soaked the upper reaches of the medieval walls around them with a rich golden light. But here, in the shadows of the closely packed buildings, the air was still cool.

Sebastian said, "I've discovered that your argument with Miss Tennyson last Friday had nothing to do with the location of Camelot. It was over a forgery. And don't even attempt to deny it," he added when Childe shook his head and took a deep breath.

Childe closed his mouth, his fingers playing with the chain that dangled from his watch pocket. His small gray eyes were darting this way and that again, as his frightened brain worked feverishly to analyze what Sebastian knew and how he might have come to know it. With every dart of those frantic eyeballs, Sebastian suspected the man was revising and editing what he was about to say.

"What forgery?" Sebastian asked.

Childe chewed the inside of his cheek.

"God *damn* you; a woman is dead and two little boys missing. What forgery?"

Childe cleared his throat. "Are you familiar with the discovery of the bodies of King Arthur and Guinevere in Glastonbury Abbey in 1191?"

"Not really."

Childe nodded as if to say he had expected this ignorance. "According to the medieval chronicler Gerald of Wales, King Henry the Second learned the location of Arthur's last resting place from a mysterious Welsh bard. The King was old and frail at the time, but before his death, he relayed the bard's information to the monks of Glastonbury Abbey. Following the King's instructions, the monks dug down between two ancient pyramids in their churchyard. Sixteen feet below the surface they came upon a split, hollowed-out log containing the bodies of a man and a woman. Above the coffins lay a stone slab, attached to the bottom of which was an iron cross. The cross bore the Latin inscription 'Here lies buried the renowned King Arthur with Guinevere his second wife, in the Isle of Avalon.'"

"Convenient," said Sebastian. "Almost as if those who buried him looked into the future a few hundred years and knew that someday those monks would be digging up good King Arthur, so they made certain to include in their engraving all the information anyone might need to make the identification complete."

"Just so," said Childe with a slight bow. "Needless to say, the monks collected the newly discovered bones and reburied them, first in the abbey's Lady Chapel, then beneath the high altar in a marble coffin provided by King Edward in 1278."

"Along with the cross?"

"Of course. It was attached to the top of the sepulchre. But when the abbey was destroyed in the suppression of the monasteries under Henry the Eighth, the bones of King Arthur and his Queen disappeared. For a time, the cross was reportedly kept in the parish church of St. John the Baptist. But it, too, eventually disappeared, probably during the time of Cromwell."

"And what precisely does any of this have to do with Miss Tennyson?"

Childe cleared his throat. "As you know, I have been occupied in cataloging the library and collection of the late Richard Gough. Amongst his possessions I discovered an ancient leaden cross inscribed with the words *'Hic Iacet Sepultus Inclitus Rex Arturius in Insula Avalonia.'*"

"Nothing about Guinevere?"

Childe gave another of his little bows. "Just so. Reports on the exact inscription have always varied slightly."

"How large a cross are we talking about here?"

"Approximately one foot in length."

"Where the devil did it come from?"

"That I do not know. As far as I have been able to ascertain, the cross came into Gough's possession—interestingly enough, along with a box of ancient bones—in the last days of his life, when he was unfortunately too ill to give them the attention they deserved. However, Gough apparently believed the cross to be that which the monks discovered in the twelfth century."

"And Gough believed the bones were those of Arthur and Guinevere? You can't be serious."

"I am only reporting on the conclusions reached by Gough himself. There is no more respected name amongst antiquaries."

"I take it Miss Tennyson did not agree with Gough's conclusions?"

Childe sighed. "She did not. Last Friday, she drove out to Gough Hall to view the cross and the bones. The bones are undeniably of great antiquity, but she instantly dismissed the cross as a modern forgery. When I begged to differ with her—"

"You did? I was under the impression you considered Arthur a wishful figment of the collective British imagination."

Childe puffed out his chest. "I may personally doubt the validity of the various tales which have grown up around some obscure figure who may or may not have actually lived. However, I have nothing but respect for the scholarship of Mr. Richard Gough, and I would consider it unprofessional to cavalierly dismiss the relic out of hand, simply because it does not conform to my preconceived notions."

"So what happened with Miss Tennyson?"

"We argued. Heatedly, I'm afraid. Miss Tennyson became so incensed that she seized the cross from my hands and hurled it into the lake."

"You were walking beside a lake? Carrying a foot-long iron cross?"

Childe stared at him owlishly. "We were, yes. You could hardly expect Miss Tennyson to enter the house to view the artifact. I may have known her since she was in pigtails, but it still would not have been at all proper. So we chose instead to walk in the park. Gough Hall has a lovely—and unfortunately very deep—ornamental lake."

"Unfortunate, indeed."

"Needless to say, her intemperance in positively flinging the cross into the lake enraged me. I fear I flew into quite a passion myself. Heated words were exchanged, and she departed in high dudgeon. I never saw her again."

Sebastian studied the stout man's flushed, self-satisfied face. He was obviously quite pleased with the tale he had concocted. But where the actual truth lay was impossible for Sebastian to guess. He said, "I assume the servants at Gough Hall can corroborate your story?"

"There is only an elderly caretaker and his wife in residence at the moment, but I have no doubt they will vouch for me, yes. Old Bentley even helped me drag a grappling hook along the edges of the lake. But we gave it up after an hour or so. I fear the cross is lost—this time forever."

"You believe it was genuine?"

"I believe it was the cross presented to the world by the monks of Glastonbury in 1191, yes."

Which was not, Sebastian noted, precisely the same thing.

He watched a cluster of legal students hurry across the gardens, their black robes flapping in the hot wind. "You say Miss Tennyson was angry?"

"She was, yes. It's a very choleric family, you know."

"And melancholy."

"Melancholy, yes."

From here they could see the broad expanse of the sun-dazzled river, the massive bulk of the bridge, and the warehouses and wharves of the opposite bank. Sebastian said, "There's just one thing I don't understand."

"Oh?"

"What in the incident you describe could possibly have made her afraid?"

Childe's smug smile slipped. "Afraid?"

"Afraid."

Childe shook his head. "I never said anything about her being afraid."

"That's because you left out the part about the dangerous forces with a nonmonetary motive."

A sudden gust of hot wind stirred the branches of the beeches overhead, letting through a shaft of golden sunlight that cut across Childe's face when he turned to stare blankly at Sebastian. "I'm sorry; I don't have the slightest idea what you're talking about."

"You don't?"

"No." Childe cleared his throat and nodded to the arm Sebastian still had resting in a sling. "You injured yourself?"

"Actually, someone tried to kill me last night; do you have any ideas about that?"

Childe's jaw went slack. "*Kill you?*"

"Mmm. Someone who doesn't like the questions I'm asking.

Which tells me that Gabrielle Tennyson had good reason to be afraid. Whatever is going on here is dangerous. Very dangerous. It's not over yet, and it looks to me as if you're right in the middle of it. You might want to consider that, next time you're tempted to lie to me."

The antiquary had turned a sickly shade of yellow.

Sebastian touched his good hand to his hat and smiled. "Good day, Mr. Childe. Enjoy the rest of your pottery exhibition."

Chapter 26

Twenty minutes later, Sebastian turned his curricle into Bow Street to find the lane ahead clogged by a raucous, tattered mob that spilled out of the public office to overflow the footpath and completely block the narrow carriageway. Ragged men and gaunt-cheeked women clutching an assortment of howling, filthy, mal-nourished children jostled and shoved one another in a frantic melee swirling around a small, bespectacled magistrate endeavoring to push his way through the motley crowd.

"Lord Devlin!" called Sir Henry Lovejoy, determinedly turning his steps toward the curricle.

"What the devil is all this?" asked Sebastian as Tom jumped down to run to the frightened chestnuts' tossing heads.

Lovejoy staggered against the side of the carriage, buffeted by the surging crowd. "It's been like this since yesterday. We've been positively besieged by parents offering up their children for Mr. Tennyson's reward—everything from babes in arms to sturdy lads of twelve and fourteen. Even girls. And this is only the overflow. Tennyson has hired a solicitor with chambers near Fleet Street to whom anyone with information is supposed to apply."

"My God," said Sebastian, his gaze traveling over the desperate, starving mass. "No indication yet of what actually happened to the Tennyson children?"

Lovejoy blew out a long, tired breath and shook his head. "It's as if they simply vanished off the face of the earth."

The magistrate gave a lurch and almost fell as a wild-eyed, pock-scarred woman clutching what looked like a dead child careened into him. He righted himself with difficulty. The crowd was becoming dangerous. "Have you discovered anything of interest?"

"Not yet," said Sebastian. As much as he trusted Sir Henry, when it came to murder investigations, Sebastian had learned to play his cards close to his chest. "I was wondering if you could provide me with the direction of the girl who found Miss Tennyson's body."

"You mean, Tessa Sawyer? She lives with her father a few miles to the southwest of the moat in a village called Cockfosters. I believe the mother is dead, while the father is something of a layabout. Why do you ask?"

"I have some questions I thought she might be able to answer."

Sebastian was aware of the magistrate giving him a long, steady look. But Lovejoy only nodded and took a step back into the shouting, jostling crowd.

Cockfosters proved to be a tiny village consisting largely of a church, an aged inn, and a few villas and scattered cottages lying to the west of Camlet Moat.

Following directions given by the curate at the village church, Sebastian drove up a rutted track to a tumbledown thatched cottage of whitewashed, rough-coursed stone that lay on the far edge of the hamlet. A young girl of some fifteen or sixteen years of age was in the dusty, sunbaked yard pegging up clothes on a line stretched between a corner of the house and a half-dead mulberry tree. A slim, tiny thing with baby-fine brown hair and eyes that looked too big for her face, she hummed a fey, haunting tune as she worked, so lost in her own world that she seemed oblivious to the elegant curricle drawing up outside her gate.

Sebastian jumped down into the dusty lane and felt a shooting jolt of pain in his arm, for he had dispensed with the sling on the drive out to Enfield. He paused a brief moment to catch his breath, then said, "Excuse me, miss; are you Tessa Sawyer?"

"*Oh!*" The girl jerked, her hands clenching the wet shirt she held to her chest, her nostrils flaring in alarm. "Ye startled me, ye did."

"I beg your pardon." Sebastian paused with one hand on the gate's rusty latch. "May I come in?"

The girl dropped a nervous curtsy, her eyes widening as she glanced from Sebastian to the carriage waiting in the sun-soaked lane, its high-bred chestnuts flicking their tails at the flies. "Oh, yes, sir. But if yer lookin' fer me da, he's not here. He's out helpin' search for the bodies of them dead boys, he is."

Sebastian had to whack his hip against the gate to get it to open. "Actually, you're the one I wished to speak to. What makes you think the boys are dead, Tessa?"

Tessa shook her head in some confusion. "It's what everyone's sayin', isn't it? I mean, it stands to reason, don't it?"

Sebastian let his gaze drift around the yard. A few scrawny chickens pecked halfheartedly at the bare earth, while a brown goat with a bell around its neck nuzzled a pile of rubbish beside the remnants of an old stone shed. If there had ever been any glass in the cottage's windows, it was long gone, the unpainted shutters hanging at drunken angles. From the looks of the worn, moldy thatch, Sebastian had no doubt the roof leaked when it rained.

He said, "Did you see any sign of the children when you were at the moat Sunday night?"

Tessa shook her head. "No, sir. I didn't see nor hear nothin' 'cept a little splash. And I can't rightly say what that was. It coulda been a water rat, or maybe a frog."

"Had you ever seen the lady in the boat before?"

Tessa swallowed, her face becoming pinched. "Just once."

"Really? When was that?"

"Last week, sometime. I think maybe it was Sunday."

"You mean, this past Sunday?"

"No. The Sunday before."

"You saw her at the island?"

"Oh, no, sir. She came here, she did—to Cockfosters."

Sebastian knew a flicker of surprise. "Do you know why?"

Tessa sucked her lower lip between her teeth and bit down on it, her gaze drifting away.

"Tell me," said Sebastian.

She drew in a quick breath. "She come here lookin' fer Rory Forster. Lit into him somethin' fierce, she did, just outside the smithy's."

"Forster lives in the village?"

"On a farm, to the east of here. Didn't ye know?" Sebastian's ignorance obviously shocked her. "Most o' the men doin' the diggin' at the moat come from Trent Place. But Sir Stanley hired Rory on account of how he once worked for some famous gentleman down in Salisbury."

"You mean, Sir Richard Colt Hoare? At Stonehenge?"

The girl looked at him blankly. "I wouldn't know about that."

"And what precisely was Miss Tennyson's interest in Forster?"

Tessa turned away and began pegging up the shirt. "I weren't there for most of it."

"But you did hear about it afterward, didn't you? Didn't you?" Sebastian prodded when the girl remained mute.

Tessa smoothed her hands down over the worn cloth. "Folks say she was mad at Forster for tearin' out the linin' of the island's well. They say somebody turned it into a muddy mess."

"A well?"

She nodded, her face hardening. "He shouldn't have done that. It's a special place."

"Special in what way?"

She threw him a quick, sideways glance. "You know what it's like when you sit in a really old church and you're all alone, and it's quiet and the sun's streamin' through the stained-glass windows and you just feel this . . . this kind of peace and joy settle over you? That's what it's like at the White Lady's well."

"What White Lady?"

"The White Lady. I've never seen her meself, but others have. She guards the well. She always has."

Sebastian studied the girl's fine-boned face, the wistful look in her big hazel eyes, and resisted the urge to point out that the White Lady of Camlet Moat had obviously failed to guard her well from some treasure hunter's shovel. He'd heard of the well maidens, ancient nature spirits said to guard the sacred wells and springs of Britain and Ireland. Although belief in the well maidens predated Christianity, it had never completely disappeared, and small shrines to the well maidens could still be found scattered across the countryside. Somehow, it seemed all of a piece with everything else he'd learned about the island that it should have a sacred well too. He realized Miss Tennyson must have come upon the destruction when she visited the island in the company of Arceneaux and the children.

He said, "Did she drive to the village in a gig? With a man and two children?"

"Yes, sir."

"Where would I find Forster?"

Tessa sniffed and jerked her head back toward the crossroads. "He married the Widow Clark just last year. Her farm's on the edge of the old chase."

Sebastian touched his hat and swept the girl an elegant bow. "Thank you, Miss Sawyer. Good day."

Turning away, he was reaching for the gate's latch when Tessa said suddenly, "You know, I did hear the last part of what Miss Tennyson said to Rory."

Sebastian swung to face her. "Oh? And what was that?"

"She told him she was going to ask Sir Stanley to fire him."

"And did you hear Rory's response?"

"Aye. He said that weren't a good idea. And when she asked him if he was a-threatenin' her, he said—" Tessa broke off, all color leaching from her cheeks.

"What did he say?"

The girl swallowed. "He said yes."

Chapter 27

*S*ebastian found Rory Forster clearing rocks from a grassy field edged by a small stream.

Reining in beneath the shade cast by a spreading elm, Sebastian paused to watch as the man heaved a watermelon-sized stone up onto the pile in the bed of the low cart beside him. The cart's brown mule stood placidly in the afternoon heat, ears twitching as Sebastian left the curricle in Tom's care and climbed over the stile.

"Good afternoon," Sebastian called.

Straightening with another large gray stone clutched in both hands, Forster threw a quizzing glance at Sebastian, then dropped the rock into the cart. "Wot ye doin' here? Didn't ye hear? The diggin' at Camlet Moat is finished. I don't work fer Sir Stanley no more and I got nothin' else to say to ye."

Sebastian brushed away a fly buzzing about his face. "When we spoke the other day, you forgot to mention your confrontation with Miss Tennyson a week ago last Sunday. Here, in Cockfosters. Outside the smithy's."

"Me brother's the smithy—like our da was before him."

"Which I suppose explains how Miss Tennyson knew where to find you."

Forster turned away to stoop down and grasp another rock.

Sebastian said, "The incident was witnessed by half the village."

Forster grunted. "Aye. She were a feisty thing, that woman. She could squawk all she wanted, but I knew that in the end she wasna gonna go to Sir Stanley. She'd no proof of anything."

"Maybe she recently discovered something. Maybe that's why you killed her."

Forster heaved another rock up and over the side of the cart. "I told ye and the magistrate both: I was home with me wife Sunday."

Sebastian stared off to where the field sloped gently toward a line of chestnuts growing along a small watershed to the west. The air was hot, the pasture a bright emerald green and scattered with small daisies. The scene was deceptively peaceful, with an air of bucolic innocence that seemed to have no place for passion and greed. Or murder.

He said, "Do you believe Sir Geoffrey de Mandeville hid his treasure on the island?"

Forster glanced over at him and smiled, the dimplelike slashes appearing in his tanned cheeks. "De Mandeville? Nah. But did ye never hear of Dick Turpin?"

"Dick Turpin? You mean, the highwayman?"

"Aye. Him as once worked Finchley Common. Used to hide out at the island, he did. His uncle Nott owned the Rose and Crown by the Brook, across the chase at Clay Hill. Seems to me, if there's treasure on that island, it's more likely Dick Turpin's than some old knight what's been dead and gone for who knows how many hundreds of years."

"Is that what you were looking for? A highwayman's gold?"

Forster reached for his mule's reins. "Never claimed it were me. All I'm sayin' is, Turpin's story is well-known about here. Coulda been anyone lookin' for what he mighta hid."

"So why did Miss Tennyson accuse you?"

Forster urged the mule forward a few feet, then stopped to reach for another stone. "She didn't like me much. Never did."

"And you didn't like her," said Sebastian, keeping his eyes on the hefty rock in Forster's hands.

"I won't deny that. She threatened to tell Sir Stanley I was the one who tore apart the well. But she had no proof and she knew it."

"So why did you threaten her?"

"I didn't. Anyone who tells you different is either makin' stuff up or jist repeatin' crazy talk he heard." Forster slammed the rock down on the growing pile, then paused with his fists propped on his lean hips, his breath coming hard, his handsome, sun-browned face and neck glistening with perspiration. "I been doin' me some thinkin'. And it occurs to me that meybe Sir Stanley has more to do with what happened to the lady than I first suspicioned."

"Odd, given that yesterday you seemed more intent on casting suspicion on Sir Stanley's wife, Lady Winthrop, than on Sir Stanley himself."

"I told ye, I been doing me some thinkin'. It occurs to me this might all have somethin' to do with the way Sir Stanley likes to fancy himself one of them ancient Druids."

"A Druid," said Sebastian.

"That's right. Dresses up in white robes and holds heathen rituals out at the island. I know for a fact Miss Tennyson seen him doin' it just the other day. He coulda been afraid she'd give away his secret."

"Couldn't have been much of a secret if you knew about it."

Forster's eyes narrowed with unexpected amusement. He laid a finger beside his nose and winked, then turned away to stoop for another stone.

Sebastian said, "And how precisely do you know that Miss Tennyson saw Sir Stanley enacting these rituals?"

Forster hawked up a mouthful of phlegm and spit it into the

grass. "Because I was there meself. Last Saturday evening, it was, long after we'd finished work for the day. Sir Stanley was at the island in his robes when Miss Tennyson comes back—"

"How?" interjected Sebastian.

"What do ye mean, 'how'?"

"You said Miss Tennyson came back. So was she walking? In a gig? Who was driving her?"

"She come in a gig, drivin' herself."

It was the first Sebastian had heard of Gabrielle Tennyson driving herself. It was not unusual for a woman to drive in the country without a groom. But Gabrielle would have driven out from London, which was something else entirely. He said, "Did she do that often? Drive herself, I mean."

"Sometimes."

"So you're saying she arrived at the island and found Sir Stanley about to engage in some sort of ancient ritual?"

"That's right. Just before sunset, it was."

"Did either of them know you were there?"

"Nah. I was hid behind some bushes."

"And what precisely were you doing at the island?"

"I'd forgot me pipe."

"Your pipe."

Forster stared at Sebastian owlishly, as if daring Sebastian to doubt him. "That's right. Went back for it, I did. Only then I seen Sir Stanley in his strange getup, so I hid in the bushes to see what was goin' on."

"And you were still hiding in the bushes when you saw Miss Tennyson drive up?"

"I was, yes." Forster turned away to reach down for a big, jagged rock. "I couldn't hear what they was sayin'. But there's no doubt in me mind she seen him and that rig he was wearin'."

"And then what happened?"

"I don't know. I left."

"So you're suggesting—what, precisely? That Sir Stanley was so chagrined by Miss Tennyson's discovery of his rather unorthodox behavior and belief system that he lured her back to the island on Sunday and killed her?"

"I ain't suggestin' nothing. Just tellin' ye what happened, that's all."

"I see. And have you told anyone else about this encounter?"

"No. Why would I?"

"Why, indeed?" Sebastian started to turn away, then paused as a thought occurred to him. "One more question: Did you discover anything unusual or interesting in the course of the excavations at the island last Saturday?"

Forster frowned. "No. Why?"

"I'm just wondering why Miss Tennyson would return to the island, first on Saturday evening, then again on Sunday."

"That I couldn't say."

"You've no idea at all?"

"No." Forster reached for his mule's reins.

"What precisely did you discover Saturday?"

"Just an area of old cobblestones—like a courtyard or somethin'."

"That's all?"

"Ain't nothin' to kill a body over, is it? Well, is it?"

"I wouldn't have thought so," said Sebastian. "Except for one thing."

Forster wrapped the reins around his fists. "What's that?"

"Miss Tennyson is dead."

"And them two nippers," said Forster.

"Are they dead?" Sebastian asked, his gaze hard on the countryman's beard-shadowed face.

"They ain't been found, have they?"

"No," said Sebastian. "No, they have not."

※

"Ye think 'e's tellin' the truth?" Tom asked as Sebastian leapt up into the curricle's high seat.

Sebastian glanced back at his tiger. "How much did you hear?"

"Most o' it."

Sebastian gathered his reins. "To be frank, I'm not convinced Forster has the imagination required to invent such a tale entirely out of whole cloth. But do I believe him? Hardly. I suspect he went out to the island that night on a treasure-hunting expedition. But he may indeed have seen something." He turned the horses' heads toward Enfield Chase. "I think I'd like to take a look at this sacred well."

The island lay deserted, the afternoon sun filtering down through the leafy canopy of old-growth elms and beech to dapple the dark waters of the moat with rare glints of light.

"Ain't nobody 'ere," whispered Tom as Sebastian drew up at the top of Camlet Moat's ancient embankment. "I thought they was still lookin' for them two boys."

"They are. But I suspect they've given up hope of finding any trace of them around here," said Sebastian, his voice also low. Like Tom, he knew a reluctance to disturb the solemn peace of the site.

Without the scuffing sounds from Forster's shovel or the distant shouts of the searchers they'd heard the day before, the silence of the place was as complete as if they had strayed deep into a forgotten, enchanted forest. Sebastian handed his reins to the tiger and jumped lightly to the ground, his boots sinking into the soft leaf mold beside the track. One of the chestnuts nickered, and he reached out to caress the horse's soft muzzle. "Walk 'em a bit. I shouldn't be long."

"Aye, gov'nor."

He crossed to the island by way of the narrow land bridge. The trenches dug by Sir Stanley's workmen had all been filled in, leaving long, narrow rows of mounded dark earth that struck Sebastian as bearing an unpleasant resemblance to the poor holes of church-yards. But he knew that in a year or so, the grass and brush of the island would cover them again, and it would be as if no one had ever disturbed the site.

Sebastian paused for a moment, his gaze drifting around the abandoned clearing. One of the more troublesome aspects of this murder had always been the question of how Gabrielle Tennyson—and presumably her cousins—had traveled up to the moat that fateful Sunday. The discovery that Gabrielle sometimes drove herself here in a gig opened up a host of new possibilities.

It was an unorthodox thing for a young woman to do, to drive herself into the countryside from London. Perhaps she thought that at the age of twenty-eight she was beyond those restrictions. Or perhaps she considered the presence of her nine-year-old cousin and his brother a sufficient sop to the proprieties. But if the Tennysons had driven themselves here that fatal day, the question then became, What the bloody hell happened to the horse and gig? And why had no liveryman come forward to say he had hired the equipment to them?

Sebastian turned to follow the path he'd noticed before, a faint trail that snaked through the brambles and brush to the north-eastern corner of the island. It was there, in a small clearing not far from the moat's edge, that he found what was left of the old well.

Once neatly lined with dressed sandstone blocks, the well now looked like a dirty, sunken wound. Ripped from the earth, the old lining stones lay jumbled together with wet clay and shattered tiles in a heap at the base of a gnarled hawthorn that spread its bleached branches over the muddy hole. From the tree's branches fluttered dozens of strips of tattered cloth.

Sebastian drew up in surprise. They called them rag trees or, sometimes, clootie trees. Relics of an ancient belief whose origins were lost in the mists of time, the trees could be found at sacred places to which suppliants with a problem—be it an illness, grief, hardship, or unrequited love—came to whisper a prayer and leave a strip of cloth as a token offering that they tied to the branches of the tree. As the cloths rotted in the wind and sun and rain, the suppliants' believed their prayers would be answered, their illnesses cured, their problems solved. Rag trees were typically found beside sacred wells or springs, for dipping the cloth in holy water was said to increase the power of the charm.

He understood now why Tessa had ventured out to Camlet Moat by moonlight.

He watched as a hot breeze gusted up, flapping the worn, weathered strips of cloth. And he found himself wondering how many other villagers came here to visit the island's sacred well.

Quite a few, from the look of things.

He went to hunker down beside the pile of muddy stones. The desecration of the well had obviously occurred quite recently. But it was impossible to tell if the man—or men—who'd done this had found what they were looking for.

A faint sound drew Sebastian's head around as his acute hearing distinguished the distant clatter of approaching hooves, coming fast. He listened as the unseen horse and rider drew nearer, then checked. A man's low voice, asking a question, drifted across the water, followed by Tom's high-pitched reply.

Sebastian stayed where he was and let the current owner of Camelot come to him.

Chapter 28

Dressed in the supple doeskin breeches and well-cut riding coat of a prosperous country gentleman, Sir Stanley Winthrop paused at the edge of the clearing, his riding crop dangling from one hand. "Lord Devlin. What brings you here?"

Sebastian pushed to his feet. "You didn't tell me the island was the site of a rag tree."

"I suppose I didn't consider it relevant. Surely you don't think it could have something to do with Gabrielle's death?"

Sebastian turned to let his gaze rove over the ancient hawthorn with its tattered, weathered offerings. "It's an interesting superstition."

"You consider it a superstition?"

Sebastian brought his gaze back to the banker's face. "You don't?"

"I think there are many things on this earth we don't understand, and the power of the human will is one of them."

Sebastian nodded to the pile of muddy stones at his feet. "When did this happen?

"Gabrielle found it this way when she came up here a week ago. There's an old legend that Geoffrey de Mandeville buried his treasure beneath the well."

"Any idea who's responsible?"

"Some ignorant fool, I'm afraid. Obviously searching for gold."

"De Mandeville's gold? Or Dick Turpin's?"

"Ah, you've heard the stories about Turpin as well, have you?" Winthrop stared down at the muddy mess, and Sebastian caught a flash of the steely rage he'd glimpsed briefly once before. "Unfortunately, both have become associated with the island."

"Did Miss Tennyson tell you who she thought had done it?"

"She told me that she had her suspicions. But when I pressed her to elaborate, she said she had no real proof and was therefore hesitant to actually accuse anyone."

"She never said she suspected your foreman, Rory Forster?"

"She suspected Rory? No, she didn't tell me. How very disturbing."

Sebastian studied the other man's face. But Winthrop once more had his emotions carefully under control; the even features gave nothing away. Sebastian said, "Why didn't you tell me Miss Tennyson returned to the island the evening before she died? Or that you were here that evening too?"

Winthrop was silent for a moment, as if tempted to deny it. Then he pursed his lips and shrugged. "If you know we were here, am I to take it you also know why?"

"I'm told you have an interest in Druidism. That you came here last Saturday dressed in white robes to enact a pagan ritual in observance of Lammas. Is that true?"

A faint glimmer of amusement shone in the other man's eyes. "What precisely are you imagining, Lord Devlin? That Gabrielle came upon me by chance and I was so horrified to be discovered that I murdered her to keep her quiet?"

"It has been suggested."

"Really? By whom?"

"You know I can't answer that."

"No, I suppose you can't."

"*Are* you interested in Druidism?"

"Does it shock you that I should have an interest in the religions of the past?"

"No."

Winthrop raised an eyebrow in surprise. "In that you are unusual. Believe me."

Sebastian said, "And did Miss Tennyson share your interest in the religion of our ancestors?"

"She shared my interest, yes. I can't, however, say she shared my belief."

"Do you believe?"

Again that faint gleam of amusement flickered in the banker's light gray eyes. "I believe there are many paths to wisdom and understanding. Most people are content to find the answers to life's questions in the formal dogmas and hierarchies of organized religion. They find comfort in being told what to believe and how to worship."

"And you?"

"Me? I find my peace and sense of meaning in ancient places such as this"—Winthrop spread his arms wide, his palms lifted to the sky—"with the trees and the water and the air. The exact beliefs of our ancestors may be lost, but the essence of their wisdom is still here—if you listen to the whispers on the wind and open your heart to our kinship with the earth and all her creatures."

"Is Lady Winthrop aware of your beliefs?"

Winthrop's hands dropped back to his sides. "She is aware of my interest."

Which was not, as Winthrop himself had pointed out, the same thing at all. Sebastian said, "I gather Lady Winthrop's own religious beliefs are rather . . . orthodox." *And rigid,* he thought, although he didn't say it.

"We must each follow our own individual paths."

Sebastian studied the older man's craggy face, the chiseled line of his strong jaw, the fashionably cut flaxen hair mixing gracefully with white. He found it difficult if not impossible to reconcile this talk of spiritualism and harmony with what he knew of the hard-driven banker who had amassed a fortune by financing war and ruthlessly crushing anyone who stood in his way.

As if sensing Sebastian's doubt, Winthrop said, "You're skeptical, of course."

"Do you blame me?"

"Not really. It's no secret that my life has been spent in the pursuit of money and power. But men can change."

"They can. Although it's rare."

Winthrop went to stand beside the dark waters of the moat, his back to Sebastian, the tip of his riding crop tapping against his thigh as he stared across at the opposite bank. "I once had five children; did you know? Three girls and two boys, born to me by my first wife. They were beautiful children, with their mother's blue eyes and blond curls and winsome ways. And then, one by one, they died. We lost Peter first, to a fever. Then Mary and Jane, to measles. I sometimes think it was grief that killed my wife. It was as if she just faded away. She died less than a month after Jane."

"I'm sorry," said Sebastian softly.

Winthrop nodded, his lips pressed together tightly. "I married again, of course—a most brilliant alliance to the widow of a late colleague. I knew she was likely to prove barren since she'd never given my colleague children, but what did it matter? I still had two children. When I bought Trent Place last year, I believed I'd finally achieved everything I'd ever wanted. Then my last two children died within weeks of each other. Elizabeth caught a putrid sore throat; then James fell and broke his neck jumping his hack over a ditch. There are just too many ways children can die. And when I buried James . . ." Winthrop's voice cracked. He paused and shook his head. "When I buried James, I realized I'd dedicated my life to amassing a fortune, and for what? So that I could build my family the most elaborate monument in the churchyard?"

Sebastian remained silent.

After a moment, Winthrop gave a ragged laugh. "The current Lady Winthrop is of the opinion that my grief over the loss of my children has affected the balance of my mind. Perhaps she is right. All I know is that I find neither peace nor comfort in the righteous dogmas of her church, whereas in a place like this—" He blew out a long, painful breath. "In a place like this, I find, if not peace, then at least a path to understanding and a way to come to grips with what once seemed unbearable."

"And Miss Tennyson? Did she come to Camlet Moat at sunset last Saturday to participate in . . . whatever it was you were here to do?"

"Participate?" Winthrop shook his head. "No. But she was interested in observing. I may feel no compulsion to advertise my spiritual beliefs, but neither am I ashamed of them. So you see, if you are imagining that I killed Miss Tennyson because she discovered my interest in Druidism, you are wrong."

Sebastian said, "Were you romantically involved with her?"

Winthrop looked genuinely startled by the suggestion. "Good God, no! I'm practically old enough to have been her father."

Sebastian shrugged. "It happens."

"Not in this instance. There was nothing of that nature between us. We were friends; I respected her intelligence and knowledge and the strength of her will. If my own daughters had lived, I like to think they would have grown up to be like her. But that is how I thought of her—as a daughter."

From what Sebastian had learned of Miss Tennyson, she was the kind of woman who tended to intimidate and alarm most men, rather than inspire them to admiration. But there were always exceptions.

He said, "I'm told Miss Tennyson sometimes drove herself out here in a gig. Is that true?"

"Sometimes, yes. She didn't do it often, though." Winthrop gave a soft smile that faded rapidly. "When her brother complained about her habit of taking the stage, she said she always threatened to take to driving herself instead."

"But she did drive herself out here Saturday evening?"

"She did, yes."

"Do you think it is possible she drove herself out here Sunday, as well?"

"I suppose it's possible."

The wind gusted up again, fluttering the weathered strips of cloth on the rag tree. Sebastian said, "What else can you tell me about Sir Geoffrey de Mandeville?"

Winthrop frowned. "Mandeville?" The sudden shift in topic seemed to confuse him.

"I understand he's said to haunt the island."

"He is, yes. Although the local legend that claims he drowned in this well is nonsense. He was killed by an arrow to the head at the siege of Burwell Castle—miles from here."

"Where is he buried?"

"At the Temple, in London."

Sebastian knew a flicker of surprise. "So he was a Knight Templar."

"The association is murky, I'm afraid. They say that the Knights Templar came to him when he lay dying and flung their mantle over him, so that he might die with the red cross on his breast."

"Why?"

"That is not recorded. All we know is that the Templars put de Mandeville's body in a lead casket and carried him off to London, where his coffin hung in an apple tree near the Temple for something like twenty years."

"A lead coffin? In a tree?"

"That's the tale. He'd been excommunicated, which meant the Templars couldn't bury him in their churchyard. Those were dark times, but there's no denying de Mandeville was an exceptionally nasty piece of work."

"'Those were the days when men said openly that Christ slept and his saints wept,'" said Sebastian softly, quoting the old chroniclers.

Winthrop nodded. "In the end, the Pope relented. The edict of excommunication was lifted and the Knights Templar were allowed to bury him. You can still see his effigy on the floor of the Temple today, you know."

"Unusual," said Sebastian, "if he wasn't actually a Templar."

"It is, yes."

"And the belief that his treasure lay at the bottom of this well?"

Winthrop was silent for a moment, his gaze on the muddy hole the well had now become. "Tales of great treasure often become associated with sacred sites," he said. "The memory of a place's importance can linger long after the true nature of its value has been forgotten. Then those who come later, in their ignorance and greed, imagine the place as a repository of earthly treasures."

"You think that's what happened here?"

"Unfortunately, there's no way of knowing, is there? But the association of Camelot, the Templars, and the tales of lost treasure is definitely intriguing."

"Intriguing?" said Sebastian. "Or deadly?"

Sir Stanley looked troubled. "Perhaps both."

Hero spent the rest of the morning sorting through the stacks of Gabrielle Tennyson's books and papers, looking for something— anything—that might explain her friend's death.

She couldn't shake the conviction that the key to Gabrielle's murder lay here, in the piles of notes and translations the woman had been working on. But Gabrielle's interests had been so wide-ranging, reaching from the little-known centuries before the Celts through the time of the Romans to the dark ages that befell Britain following the collapse of the Empire, that wading through her research was a formidable undertaking.

It was when Hero was studying Gabrielle's notes on *The Lady of Shalott* that a loose sheet of paper fluttered to the floor. Reaching down to pick it up, she found herself staring at a handwritten poem.

> *Bid me to weep, and I will weep*
> *While I have eyes to see:*
> *And having none, yet I will keep*
> *A heart to weep for thee.*
>
> *Bid me despair and I'll despair,*
> *Under that cypress tree:*
> *Or bid me die, and I will dare*
> *E'en Death, to die for thee.*
>
> *Thou art my life, my love, my heart*
> *The very eyes of me,*
> *And hast command of every part,*
> *To live and die for thee.*

Hero leaned back in her seat, her hand tightening on the paper, the breath leaving her lungs in a rush as a new and totally unexpected possibility occurred to her.

Chapter 29

Hero was curled up with a book in an armchair beside the library's empty hearth, a volume of seventeenth-century poetry open in her lap, when Devlin came to stand in the doorway. He brought with him the scent of sunshine and fresh air and the open countryside.

"What happened to your sling?" she asked, looking up at him.

"It was in my way."

"Now, there's a good reason to stop wearing it."

He huffed a soft laugh and went to pour himself a glass of wine. "Did Gabrielle ever mention an interest in Druidism to you?"

"Druidism? Good heavens, no. Why on earth do you ask?"

He came to stand with his back to the empty fireplace. "Because it turns out that she went back out to Camlet Moat at sunset the night before she died, to watch Sir Stanley enact some pagan ritual at an ancient sacred well on the island. *Drove herself* there, in fact, in a gig."

"You can't be serious."

"I wish I wasn't. But Rory Forster saw her there, and Sir Stanley himself admits as much."

"What was Forster doing at the island at sunset?"

"According to Rory? Retrieving a forgotten pipe—and hiding in the bushes. Although I suspect it far more likely that he went there with the intent of digging for buried treasure and was perplexed to discover he wasn't going to have the island to himself that night."

"Treasure?"

"Mmm. Buried by either Dick Turpin or a Knight Templar, depending upon which version one believes. Exactly a week before she was killed, Miss Tennyson stormed into Cockfosters and publicly accused Rory of ripping out the lining of the island's sacred well."

"In search of this treasure?"

Devlin nodded. "According to the legend, Sir Geoffrey de Mandeville hid his ill-gotten gains beneath the bottom of the well, and his spirit is supposed to appear to frighten away anyone who attempts to remove it. But his ghost must have been asleep on the job, because I checked, and someone recently made a right sorry mess of the thing."

"You say she confronted Rory a week ago Sunday?"

He drained his wine. "The timing is interesting, isn't it? That's the day she was out there with Arceneaux. Then, just a few days later, she drove out to Gough Hall and had a stormy argument with Bevin Childe. She was a very confrontational and contentious young woman, your friend."

Hero smoothed a hand down over her skirt. "So you spoke to Bevin Childe?"

"I did. He claims to have discovered something called the Glastonbury Cross amongst Richard Gough's collections. I'm told it's the cross that was said to have marked the graves of King Arthur and Guinevere at the abbey. Have you ever heard of it?"

"Yes."

"Well, it seems Miss Tennyson was convinced the cross was a modern forgery, and in the midst of a rather violent argument with Childe, she seized the cross and threw it in a lake."

She was aware of him watching her intently. "What a . . . strange thing to do," she said, keeping her voice level with effort.

He frowned and came to take the seat opposite her. "Are you all right, Hero?"

"Yes, of course; just tired."

"Perhaps, under the circumstances, you're doing too much." He said it awkwardly; the coming babe, despite being the reason for their marriage, was something they never discussed.

She made an inelegant sound of derision. "If by 'the circumstances' you are referring to the fact that I am with child, let me remind you that gestation is a natural occurrence, not a dread debilitating disease."

"True. Yet I do take special care of my mares when they are with foal."

At that, she laughed out loud. "I don't know if I should be flattered or insulted by the comparison."

The corners of his eyes crinkled with amusement. "Oh, flattered, definitely."

Their gazes met, and the moment stretched out and became something intimate and unexpected.

She felt her cheeks grow warm, and looked away. "How did you come to learn of Gabrielle's confrontation with Childe over the cross?"

"Lieutenant Arceneaux told me."

"Arceneaux? Now, that's interesting." She picked up the sheet of parchment she'd discovered and held it out to him. "I found this with Gabrielle's papers."

"'Bid me to weep, and I will weep,'" he read, "'while I have eyes to see.'" He looked up at her. "You know the poem?"

"No. But it does sound familiar, doesn't it? I believe it may be from one of the Cavalier poets." She closed the poetry book and set it aside. "But so far I haven't been able to find it."

"It's the last three stanzas from Robert Herrick's 'To Anthea, Who May Command Him Anything.'"

Her eyes widened. "You know it?"

He smiled. "That surprises you, does it? Did you imagine I spent all my time riding to hounds and drinking brandy and trying to pop a hit over Gentleman Jackson's guard?"

She felt an answering smile tug at her lips. "Something like that."

"Huh." He pushed up and went to compare the bold hand of the poem to the flowing copperplate that filled Gabrielle Tennyson's notebooks. "This doesn't look like her writing," he said after a moment.

"It's not."

He glanced over at her. "You know whose it is?"

She came to extract one of the notebooks from the pile. "Here. Look at the translation of *The Lady of Shalott* Gabrielle was working on; you'll see the handwriting of the poem matches that of the alterations and notations someone else made in the margins of her work. I think the poem was given to her by Philippe Arceneaux."

Devlin studied the notations, his lips pressing into a tight line.

Hero said, "Do you think the Lieutenant was more in love with her than he led you to believe?"

"'Thou art my life, my heart, my love,'" he quoted, setting the translation aside. "It rather sounds that way, does it not? Not only that, but I'd say Miss Tennyson was in love with him too."

Hero shook her head. "How can you be so certain?"

He looked down at the creased sheet he still held in his hand. "Because she kept this."

Lieutenant Philippe Arceneaux and his scruffy little dog were watching a cricket match at Marylebone Park Fields on the northern outskirts of the city when Sebastian came to stand beside him.

A warm sun washed the grass of the nearby hills with a golden green. They could hear the lowing of cows, see a hawk circling lazily above the stand of oaks edging the field. The batsman scored a run and a murmur of approval rippled through the crowd of spectators.

Sebastian said, "You've acquired a fondness for cricket, have you? You must be one of the few Frenchmen ever to do so."

Arceneaux huffed a low laugh. "Most of my fellow officers consider it incomprehensible, but yes, I have."

"I gather you've also acquired a fondness for our Cavalier poets."

"Pardon?"

"'A heart as soft, a heart as kind, / A heart as sound and free / As in the whole world thou canst find / That heart I'll give to thee,'" quoted Sebastian softly as the bowler delivered the ball toward the batsman.

"A lovely piece of poetry," said Arceneaux, his attention seemingly all for the bowler. "Should I recognize it?"

"It's from a poem by Robert Herrick."

"No ball," called the umpire.

The relentless August sun beat down on the open field, filling the air with the scent of dust and hot grass. Arceneaux held himself very still, his features wooden, his gaze on the fielders.

Sebastian said, "The same poem you copied out and gave to Miss Tennyson."

The Frenchman's throat worked as he swallowed. A sheen of perspiration covered his newly sun-reddened face. "You found it, did you?"

"Lady Devlin did."

"How did you guess it was from me?"

"The handwriting matches the notations you made on Miss Tennyson's translation of *The Lady of Shalott.*"

"Ah. Of course."

They turned to walk away from the crowd and take the lane that curled toward the rolling countryside stretching away to the north. The dog trotted on ahead, tongue lolling happily, tail wagging. Sebastian said, "I hope you don't intend to insult my intelligence by attempting to continue denying the truth."

Arceneaux shook his head, his gaze on the herd of cows grazing placidly in the grassy, sunbaked pasture beside them. At the top of the slope, a stand of chestnuts drooped in the airless heat, their motionless leaves a vivid green swath against an achingly clear, forget-me-not blue sky. "You want the truth, my lord? The truth is, I fell in love with Gabrielle the first time I saw her. I was in the Reading Room at the museum going over some old manuscripts, and I just happened to look up and . . . there she was. She was standing beneath the high windows of the Reading Room, waiting for an attendant to hand her the book she wanted, and . . . I was lost."

"She returned your affections?"

He gave an odd smile. "She didn't fall in love with me at first sight, if that's what you're asking. But we quickly became good friends. We'd go for walks around the gardens of the museum and argue passionately about the competing visions of love in the two sections of the *Roman de la rose* or the reliability of the various medieval chroniclers. She was several years older than I, you know. She used to tease me about it, call me a little boy. I suspect that if I'd been her own age or older, she would never have allowed our friendship to progress the way it did. But as it was, she felt . . . safe with me. She told me later she'd fallen in love with me before she'd even realized what was happening."

"Did you ask her to marry you?"

"How could I? Situated as I am, a prisoner of war?" He pointed to the mile marker in the grass beside the road. "See that boundary? Under the terms of my parole, I am allowed to go no farther."

"Yet you did venture beyond it, the day you and Gabrielle went up to Camlet Moat."

Sebastian expected the man to deny it again. Instead, he gave a halfhearted shrug and said, "Sometimes . . . sometimes men succumb to mad impulses, I suppose, of frustration and despair and a foolish kind of bravado. But . . . how could I ask her to be my wife? How could I ask any woman to share such a circumscribed life, perhaps forever?"

"Yet some paroled French officers do marry here."

"They do. But they don't marry women like Gabrielle Tennyson. I loved her too much to ask her to live in a garret with me."

"She had no independence of her own?"

The Frenchman swung to face him. "Good God. Even if she had, what do you take me for?"

"You would hardly be the first man to live on his wife's income."

"I am not a fortune hunter!"

"I never said you were." Sebastian studied the other man's boyish, tightly held face and asked again, "Did you ask her to marry you?"

"I did not."

Arceneaux turned away, his gaze following the dog, who now had his nose to the ground, tail flying high as he tracked some fascinating scent to the prickly edge of the hedgerow, then sat down and let out a woof of disappointment and frustration.

Sebastian said, "I think you're still lying to me, Lieutenant."

Arceneaux gave a ragged laugh. "Oh? And would you blame me if I were?" He flung his arm in an expansive arc that took in the vast urban sprawl stretching away to the south. "You know the mood of hysteria that has swept over the city. Tell all those people Gabrielle Tennyson had a French lover and see what sort of conclusions they leap to. They'd hang me before nightfall."

"Were you lovers? And I mean that in every sense of the word."

"*Monsieur!*" Arceneaux held his head high, his nostrils flaring with indignation, his hands curling into fists at his sides.

"I should tell you that a postmortem has been performed on Miss Tennyson's remains." Sebastian hesitated. "We know she was no maid."

"Why, you—"

Sebastian flung up a forearm to block the punch Arceneaux threw at his jaw.

"Bâtard!" spat Arceneaux when Sebastian grabbed his wrist and held it.

Sebastian tightened his grip, his lips peeling away from his teeth as he leaned in close, enunciating his words with careful precision. "God damn it. Cut line, Lieutenant. Whose honor do you imagine I've insulted? Yours?" To suggest that a gentleman had seduced a woman he was unable or unwilling to marry was indeed a grave insult. "Because this isn't about you, Lieutenant—"

"If you think I care about that—"

"And it isn't about Gabrielle Tennyson's honor, either," Sebastian continued, ignoring the interruption. "It's about finding the man—or woman—who killed her, and who probably killed those two little boys with her. So tell me, what do you know of Miss Tennyson's interactions with Sir Stanley?"

"For the love of God, what are you suggesting now?" Arceneaux jerked back hard against Sebastian's hold.

Sebastian let him go. "Take a damper, would you? I'm asking because when an attractive young woman and an older but still virile man are thrown often into each other's company, people talk."

"Who?" Arceneaux's fists clenched again. "Who is suggesting there was anything between them?"

"Lady Winthrop, for one. The woman was obviously more than a little jealous of the time Miss Tennyson spent with her husband."

The Frenchman spat in distain. "Lady Winthrop is a fool."

"Is she?"

"She lost her husband long ago, only not to Gabrielle. She lost him to his grief over his dead children, and to his passion for the past, and to the whispered wisdom of the Druids."

"So Miss Tennyson knew about Sir Stanley's interest in the Druids, did she?"

"She did. I told you, they were friends—good friends. But nothing more."

Sebastian studied the French officer's fine-boned, scholarly face. "And you had no concerns about the woman you loved spending so much time in another man's company?"

"I did not. Does that surprise you? Was it not your William Shakespeare who wrote of the 'marriage of true minds'?"

"'If this be error and upon me proved,'" quoted Sebastian, "'I never writ . . .'"

"'Nor no man ever loved.'" Arceneaux straightened his cravat and smoothed the front of his worn coat with painful dignity. "I loved Gabrielle, and I knew she loved me. I never doubted her. Not for a moment."

"And you know of no other man in her life?"

"No!"

"Do you know anything about her previous suitors?"

Arceneaux frowned as he watched Chien prance contentedly toward them, ears cocked. "I know there was one man—a suitor who pressed her repeatedly to marry him. Nothing she said seemed to dissuade the man. It was very odd."

"Who was this?"

"She didn't tell me his name, although I gathered he was a friend of the family."

"So her brother would likely know him?"

"I should think so, yes. The man was quite open in his pursuit of her. She told me he'd been dangling after her for years—even used to send her sweets and collections of love poems when she was still in the schoolroom."

"That sounds rather . . . distasteful."

"She found it so, yes."

Chien ran one happy, panting circle around them, then dashed off again after a sparrow chirping on the branch of a nearby rambling rose.

Sebastian said, "Did Miss Tennyson ever tell you why she was so determined never to wed?"

Arceneaux watched the sparrow take flight, chattering in annoyance. Chien paused with his tail up, ears on the prick. "It is not so unusual, is it, amongst women who have decided to devote themselves to scholarship?"

Chien came trotting back to stick his cold wet nose under Sebastian's hand. Sebastian let his hand drift down the dog's back. There had been a time when Hero, too, had sworn never to wed. She had only agreed to become his wife because she'd discovered she carried his child—and even then he'd had the devil's own time convincing her. He thought he could understand Miss Tennyson sticking resolutely to her choice.

Yet the sense that the Frenchman was lying remained with him.

Chapter 30

*J*arvis stood at the edge of the terrace, a glass of champagne balanced in one hand as he let his gaze drift over the sweating men in tails and snowy cravats who chatted in desultory tones with gaily laughing ladies wearing filmy muslins and wide-brimmed hats. The sun was devilishly hot, the champagne warm. Normally Jarvis avoided such affairs. But this particular al fresco party was being hosted by Lady Elcott, the Prince's latest flirt, and Jarvis was here in attendance on the Prince.

A faint apprehensive fluttering amongst the crowd drew Jarvis's attention to a tall, familiar figure working her way across the terrace toward him. She wore a striking gown of cream silk trimmed in black and a black velvet hat with a cockade with black and cream feathers. She was not in any sense the most beautiful woman present, but she still managed to draw every eye.

"And here I thought you'd given up the frivolous amusements of society in order to join your husband in his sordid passion for murder investigations," said Jarvis as Hero paused beside him.

"I told you my involvement in this has nothing to do with

Devlin. Gabrielle Tennyson was my friend, and whoever killed her will have to answer to me." She let her gaze, like his, slide over the ladies and gentlemen scattered across the lawn below. "Apart from which, I see no reason to view the two pursuits as mutually exclusive."

"Society and murder, you mean? You have a point. If truth were told, I suspect you'd probably find that Lady Elcott numbers more murderers amongst her guests than you'd be likely to find down at the corner pub . . . although I doubt any of these worthies will ever find themselves in the dock for their crimes."

She brought her gaze back to his face. "You do realize I now know about the Glastonbury Cross."

"Do you?" He took a slow sip of his champagne. "And what, precisely, do you 'know' of it?"

His response was obviously not what she had hoped for. Her eyes narrowed, but she covered her disappointment by taking a sip of her lemonade.

He smiled. "You learned this game from me, remember? And I'm still better at it than you. Shall I tell you precisely what you know? You know that amongst the late Richard Gough's collections, Bevin Childe found a box of ancient bones and a graven artifact he identified as the Glastonbury Cross. You also know that Miss Tennyson, when she heard of Childe's discovery, dismissed the cross as a modern forgery and—in a rather alarming fit of unbridled choler—threw the item in question into the lake."

Hero returned his smile with one of her own. "Actually, I've figured out a bit more than that. I've been looking into those broadsheets you were telling me about—the ones expressing a longing for the 'once and future king' to return and lead the English to victory by ridding us of the unsatisfactory usurpers currently on the throne." She glanced over to where the Prince Regent, red-faced and sweating, his coat of Bath superfine straining across his back, had his face and shoulders hunched over a mounded plate of buttered crab. "I can see how the expression of such sentiments might be causing distress in certain circles, even if, as you intimated, the broadsheets were originally the work of French agents. These things can sometimes take on a life of their own. And while we like to think our own age too sophisticated to give heed to such legends, the truth is that far too many people out there are still both ignorant and woefully credulous—and all too ready to believe in a miraculous savior."

"How true."

A warm wind gusted up, shifting the spreading branches of an elm overhead and casting dancing patterns of light and shadow across the strong features of her face. She said, "Some six hundred years ago, Henry the Second was also troubled by restless subjects who yearned for Arthur to return from the dead and save them. Fortunately for him, the monks of Glastonbury Abbey stepped into the breach with their well-timed discovery of what they claimed were King Arthur and Guinevere's bones."

"Most fortuitous, was it not?" said Jarvis with a smile.

"Mmm. And how injudicious of good old King Henry the Eighth to lose such a valuable national treasure in his scramble to take over the wealth of the church, thus allowing all those nasty rumors to start up again."

"Shockingly careless of him," agreed Jarvis, consigning his champagne glass to a passing waiter.

"Yet history does sometimes have a way of repeating itself . . . or should I say, rather, that it can be made to repeat itself? Particularly if a certain courageous young woman who threatens to get in the way is removed."

Jarvis drew a figured gold snuffbox from his pocket and flipped it open with one finger.

Hero watched him, her gaze on his face. "Gabrielle was not the type of woman to frighten easily. Yet before she died, she was afraid of someone. Someone powerful. I think she was afraid of you."

He raised a pinch of snuff to one nostril and sniffed. "She had a unique way of showing it, wouldn't you say?"

Hero leaned into him, the polite society smile still curving her lips, her voice low. "I think Gabrielle was right: That cross is a forgery. I think you somehow coerced Childe into claiming he had discovered the fake cross amongst Gough's collections, in the hopes that news of its recovery would help dampen these dangerous murmurs calling for King Arthur's return. After all, if it worked for the Plantagenets a few hundred years ago, why shouldn't it work now?"

"Why not, indeed?"

"The one thing I haven't figured out yet is how you convinced Childe to cooperate."

"Really, Hero; perhaps you should consider giving up this budding interest in murder investigations and turn your hand instead to writing lurid romances." He saw something he couldn't quite read flicker in her eyes, and closed his snuffbox with a snap. "I told you, I did not kill your troublesome friend."

When she remained silent, he gave a soft laugh. "You don't believe me, do you?"

"Almost. But not entirely." She tilted her head to one side. "If you considered it necessary, would you have killed her—even knowing she was my friend?"

"Without hesitation."

"And would you tell me?"

"Before, yes. Now . . . I'm not so certain."

"Because of Devlin, you mean?"

"Yes." He let his gaze drift once more across the assembly of hot aristocrats. "And are you regretting it? Your decision to be less than forthcoming with your new husband, I mean."

"No."

He brought his gaze back to her face. "So sure, Hero?" he asked, and saw her color deepen.

She said, "I don't believe you deliberately had Gabrielle killed. But can you be so certain you are not indirectly responsible?"

Father's and daughter's gazes locked, and held.

"*Darling!*"

Hero turned as Lady Elcott fluttered up to them trailing a cloud of filmy lime organza and yards of cream satin ribbon. She rested the tips of her exquisitely manicured fingers on Hero's arm and arched her overplucked brows. "You came! What a delight! Did you bring that wicked husband of yours with you?"

"Not this time," said Hero.

"Excuse me," said Jarvis with a bow, moving adroitly to the Prince's side in time to prevent him from starting on a second plate of crab.

When he looked back toward the edge of the terrace, Hero had managed to escape their hostess's clutches and disappear.

Sebastian found Paul Gibson leaning over the stone platform in the center of the outbuilding behind his surgery. He whistled softly as he worked, his arms plunged up to the elbows in the gory distended abdomen of a cadaver so bloated and discolored and ripe that it made Sebastian gag.

"Good God," he said, his eyes watering as the full force of the foul stench engulfed him. "Where the devil did they find that one?"

"Pulled him out of Fleet Ditch, at West Street. Caught up under the bridge, he was, and from the look of things, he was there a good long while."

"And no one smelled him?"

"There's an abattoir at the corner. I suppose the odors just sort of . . . mingled." The surgeon grinned and reached for a rag to wipe his hands and arms. "So what can I do for you, then? And please don't tell me you're sending me another corpse, because I've already got two more to deal with when I'm through with this one."

"No more corpses." Retreating to the sun-blasted yard, Sebastian stood hunched over with his hands braced on his thighs as he sucked fresh air into his lungs. "Just a question, about Gabrielle Tennyson. You said she was no longer a maid. Any chance she could have been with child?"

"No trace of it that I saw."

"Would you be able to tell for certain? I mean, even if she wasn't very far along?"

"Let's put it this way: If she was far enough along to know it, I'd know it."

Sebastian straightened, then swallowed quickly as another whiff of the cadaver hit him. "Bloody hell. I don't know how you stand it."

Gibson gave a soft chuckle. "After a while, you don't notice the smell." He thought about it a moment, then added, "Usually."

"I wasn't talking about just the smell."

"Ah." The Irishman's gaze met Sebastian's, the merriment now gone from his face. "The thing of it is, you see, by the time I get them, they're just so much tissue and bone, and that's what I focus on—that's the mystery I need to unravel. I don't need to dwell on the fear and pain they must have experienced during whatever happened that landed them on my table. I don't need to pry into whatever betrayal and hurt, or anger and despair was in their lives. That's what you do. And to tell you the truth, Devlin, I don't know how *you* do it."

When Sebastian remained silent, Gibson rested a hand on his shoulder, then turned back toward the stone outbuilding and its bloated, decaying occupant.

"Was he murdered?" Sebastian called after him. "The man on your table in there, I mean."

Gibson paused in the open doorway to look back at him. "Not this one. Tumbled into the water drunk and drowned, most likely. I doubt he even knew what hit him—which is probably not a bad way to go, if you've got to go."

"I suppose it does beat some of the alternatives."

Gibson grunted. "You think Gabrielle Tennyson and her young cousins were killed by a man who was afraid he'd planted a babe in her belly?"

Sebastian started to remind him that no one knew for certain yet that either Alfred or George Tennyson was dead. Then he let it go. Surely it was only a matter of time before one of the search parties or some farmer out walking with his dog came upon the children's small bodies half submerged in a ditch or hidden beneath the leaf mold in a hollow left by a downed tree?

He shook his head. "I don't know. At this point, anything's possible."

"Poor girl," said Gibson with a sigh. "Poor, poor girl."

The setting sun was painting purple and orange streaks low on the western horizon by the time Sebastian reached the Adelphi Buildings overlooking the Thames. He was mounting the steps to the Tennyson town house when he heard his name called.

"Lord Devlin."

Turning, he saw Gabrielle's brother striding across the street toward him. "Have you some news?" asked Hildeyard Tennyson, his strained features suffused with an agonized hope.

"I'm sorry; no."

Tennyson's lips parted with the pain of disappointment. He'd obviously been out again looking for the children; dust layered his coat and top boots, and his face was slick with sweat and tinged red by too many hours spent beneath a hot sun.

"You're still searching the chase?" asked Sebastian as they turned to walk along the terrace overlooking the Thames.

"The woodland and the surrounding farms and fields, yes. But so far, we've found nothing. Not a trace. It's as if the children vanished into the mist." The barrister blew out a long, ragged breath. "Simply . . . vanished."

Sebastian stared off over the river, where the sinking sun spilled a wash of gold across the water. Barges loaded with coal rode low and dark in the water; a wherryman rowing his fare across to Lambeth plied his oars. The splash of his wooden panels threw up arcs of droplets that glistened like diamonds in the dying light.

Tennyson followed Sebastian's gaze, the circles beneath his eyes dark as he watched the wherryman's progress across the river. "I know everyone, from the magistrates and constables to the farmers and workmen I've hired, thinks the boys must be dead. I hear them speaking amongst themselves. They all think they're looking for a shallow grave. But they don't let on to me."

Sebastian kept his gaze on the water.

After a moment, Tennyson said, "My cousin—the boys' father—is on his way down from Lincolnshire. He's not well, you know. I just hope to God the journey doesn't kill him." He hesitated, then added, "Or the inevitable grief."

Sebastian found it difficult to meet the other man's strained, desperate eyes. "You told me the other day your sister had no interest in marriage."

"She didn't, no," said the barrister slowly, obviously struggling to follow Sebastian's train of thought. "She quite fixed her mind against it at an early age. Our father blamed her attitude on the influence of the likes of the Misses Berry and Catherine Talbot. But the truth is, Gabrielle was far more interested in Roman ruins and the inscriptions on medieval tombstones than in bride clothes or layettes."

"Nevertheless, she must have attracted some suitors over the years."

"Some, yes. But without encouragement, few stayed around for long."

"Do you remember any who were more persistent than the others?"

Tennyson thought about it a moment. "Well, I suppose Childe

held out longer than most. But— Good God; no one could suspect him of such a deed."

"Childe? You mean, Bevin Childe?"

"Yes. You know him? Frankly, I would have thought if anyone had a chance with Gabrielle, it would be Childe. I mean, the man has both a comfortable independence and a passion for antiquities that matched her own. She'd known him since she was still in the schoolroom—indeed, he claims he first fell in love with her when she was little more than a child in pigtails and a torn flounce. But she would have none of him."

"How did he take her rejection of his suit?"

A touch of amusement lit up the barrister's haggard features. "Frankly? With incredulity. No one could ever accuse Childe of having a low opinion of himself. At first he was convinced she was merely displaying what he called 'a becoming degree of maidenly modesty.' Then, when he was finally brought to understand that she was not so much shy as merely disinterested, he credited her lack of enthusiasm to an imperfect understanding of his worth. I'd never before realized what an insufferable bore the man could be. I'm afraid he made quite a cake of himself."

"When did he finally get the hint?"

"That his suit was hopeless? I'm not certain he ever did. She was complaining about him shortly before I left for Kent."

"Complaining about his disparagement of her theories about Camlet Moat, you mean?"

"No. About his continued refusal to accept her rejection of his suit as final."

Chapter 31

$\mathcal{B}$evin Childe was feeling his way down the unlit stairs from his rooms in St. James's Street when Sebastian stepped out of the shadows of the landing to grab the scholar by the back of his coat with both fists and swing him around to slam him face-first against the wall.

"Merciful heavens," bleated the antiquary as his protuberant belly *thwumped* into the paneling. "Oh dear, oh dear, oh dear. My purse is in the inner pocket of my coat. You're welcome to it, sir, although I must warn you that you will find there scant reward for this brutish act of violence upon my person."

"I am not interested in your bloody purse," growled Sebastian.

"Devlin?" The antiquary went limp with relief. "Is that you?" He attempted to twist around but found himself frustrated when Sebastian tightened his grip. "Good God; I imagined you a cutpurse." He stiffened with gathering outrage. "What is the meaning of this?"

Sebastian kept his voice low and deadly calm. "I should perhaps have warned you that when it comes to murder, I am not a patient man. And you, Mr. Childe, are sorely trying my patience."

"There are laws in this country, you know. You can't simply go around accosting gentlemen in their lodgings. It's not legal. It's not right. It's not—not the done thing!"

Sebastian resisted the urge to laugh out loud. Instead, he leaned into the antiquary until the man's plump face was squished sideways against the elegantly paneled wainscoting. "You didn't tell me you were a suitor for Miss Tennyson's hand. A disgruntled and annoyingly persistent suitor."

"Well, it's not the sort of thing a gentleman does go around talking about, now, is it? I mean, a man has his pride, don't you know?"

"So you're saying your pride was offended by Miss Tennyson's rejection of your suit?"

Childe quivered, as if suddenly becoming aware of the pit yawning at his feet. "I don't know if I'd say that, exactly."

"Then what would you say? *Exactly?*"

"Women such as Miss Tennyson must be delicately wooed. But I'm a persistent man. I've no doubt my suit would eventually have prospered."

"You've no doubt."

"None." Childe's voice had grown in confidence to the point of sounding smug.

"So you would have me believe you didn't know she'd recently fallen in love with a dashing young cavalry officer she met at the British Museum?"

"What?" Childe tried again to twist around, but Sebastian held him fast. "I don't believe it! Who? Who is this man? This is nonsense. You're making that up. It's impossible."

"You'd better hope I don't discover that you did know."

Childe blanched. "What does that mean?"

"It means," said Sebastian, shifting his grip, "that there is a certain kind of man who doesn't take kindly to the realization that the woman he's decided to honor by making her his wife has scorned his courtship not because she was shy and needed to be 'delicately wooed,' but because she quite frankly preferred another man to him. What does it take to drive a man like you to violence, Childe? Hmm? A threat to your scholarly reputation? Or an affront to your manhood? How would you react, I wonder, if the very same woman who'd humiliated you as a suitor then threatened to destroy your credibility as an antiquary? Would that be enough to compel you to murder?"

Perspiration glistened on the man's forehead and clustered in droplets on the end of his nose. A foul odor of sweat and fear rose from his person, and his voice, when he spoke, was a high-pitched crack. "This is madness. Miss Tennyson and I disagreed about the authenticity of the cross in Gough's collection; that is all. My credibility as an antiquary was never threatened in any way."

"Then why—"

Sebastian broke off at the sound of the street door opening below. Men's voices, slurred by drink, echoed up the stairwell. He loosed his hold on the antiquary and took a step back.

"I'm not through with you. When I find out more, I'll be back. And if I discover you've been lying to me, I can guarantee you're going to regret it."

Sebastian returned to Brook Street to find Hero perusing an improving pamphlet written by one Ezekiel Smyth and entitled *Satan, Druidism, and the Path to Everlasting Damnation*.

"Good God," he said. "What are you reading?"

She laughed and cast it aside. "Believe it or not, this piece of sanctimonious drivel was written by George and Alfred Tennyson's aunt, Mary Bourne."

"You can't be serious."

"Oh, but I am. She also attends a weekly Bible study class with one Reverend Samuel at the Savoy Chapel. Another member of the study group is none other than Lady Winthrop."

He reached for the pamphlet and flipped through it. "Now, that's interesting."

"It is, isn't it?" She looked over at him, her eyes narrowing. "You've split the shoulder seam of your coat; what have you been doing?"

He glanced down at his coat. "Ah. I hadn't noticed. It could have been when Lieutenant Arceneaux tried to draw my cork for insulting the honor of the woman he loved—"

"How did you do that?"

"By asking if he lay with her. He says he did not, incidentally."

"Do you believe him?"

"No. He did, however, provide me with one bit of information which proved to be valuable: It seems Mr. Bevin Childe was a suitor for Miss Tennyson's hand—an annoying suitor who refused to take no for an answer. According to Hildeyard, the man has been in love with Gabrielle since she was a child."

Hero stared at him. "Did you say, since she was a child?"

"Yes; why?"

But she simply shook her head and refused to be drawn any further.

Thursday, 6 August

By 9:50 the next morning, Hero was seated in her carriage outside the British Museum, a sketch pad open on her lap and her pencils sharpened and at the ready.

She had no illusions about her artistic abilities. She was able to draw a fairly credible, easily recognizable likeness of an individual. But her sketches were competent, nothing more. If she were a true artist, she could have sketched Bevin Childe from memory. As it was, that was beyond her.

And so she waited in the cool morning shade cast by the tall fronts of the town houses lining Great Russell Street. At exactly

9:58, a hackney pulled up outside the Pied Piper. His movements slow and ponderous in that stately way of his, Mr. Bevin Childe descended from the carriage, then stood on the flagway to pay his fare.

He cast one disinterested glance at the yellow-bodied carriage waiting near the museum, then strode across the street, his brass-handled walking stick tucked up under one arm.

Within the shadows of her carriage, Hero's pencil scratched furiously, capturing in bold strokes the essence of his likeness.

As if somehow aware of her intense scrutiny, he paused for a moment outside the museum's gatehouse, the high points of his shirt collar digging into his plump cheeks as he turned his head to glance around. Then he disappeared from her view.

She spent the next ten minutes refining her sketch, adding details and nuances. Then she ordered her coachman to drive to Covent Garden.

The man's jaw sagged. "I beg your pardon, m'lady, but did you say 'Covent Garden'?"

"I did."

He bowed. "Yes, m'lady."

Chapter 32

$\mathcal{S}$ebastian was alone at his breakfast table reading the latest reports on the Americans' invasion of Canada when a knock sounded at the entrance. He heard his majordomo, Morey, cross to open the front door; then a dog's enthusiastic barking echoed in the hall.

Sebastian raised his head.

"*Chien! No!*" someone shouted. "Come back!"

Morey hissed. "Sir! I really must insist that you control your— Oh, merciful heavens."

A scrambling clatter of nails sounded on the marble floor in the hall, and a familiar black and brown mongrel burst into the room, tail wagging and tongue lolling in confident expectation of an enthusiastic reception.

"So you're proud of yourself, are you?" said Sebastian, setting aside his paper.

"*Chien!*" Lieutenant Philippe Arceneaux appeared in the doorway. "I do most profusely beg your pardon, my lord. *Chien*, heel!"

"It's all right," Sebastian told the anxious majordomo hovering behind the French officer. "The Lieutenant and his ill-mannered hound are both known to me. And no, you are not to take that as an invitation to further liberties," he warned as the dog pawed at his gleaming Hessians. "Mar the shine on my boots, and Calhoun will nail your hide to the stable door. And if you think that an idle threat, you have obviously not yet made the acquaintance of my valet."

"He might be more inclined to believe you," observed Arceneaux with a smile, "if you were not pulling his ears."

"Perhaps. Do come in and sit down, Lieutenant. May I offer you some breakfast? And no, that question was not addressed to you, you hell-born hound, so you can cease eyeing my ham with such soulful intent."

"Thank you, my lord, but I have already eaten—we have *both* eaten," he added, frowning at the dog. "Shame on you, Chien; you have the manners of a tatterdemalion. Come away from there."

The dog settled on his hindquarters beside Sebastian's chair and whined.

"Obedient too, I see," observed Sebastian, draining his tankard.

"He likes you."

"He likes my ham."

Arceneaux laughed. Then his smile faded. "I have brought him with me because I have a request to make of you."

Sebastian looked up from scratching behind the dog's ears. "Oh?"

"It seems to me that if I could take Chien up to Camlet Moat, there's a good possibility he might pick up some trace of Alfred and George, something to tell us where they've gone or what has happened to them. Something the authorities have missed. He was very fond of the children."

Sebastian was silent for a moment, considering the implications of the request. "Sounds like a reasonable idea. But why come to me?"

"Because I am not allowed to journey more than a mile beyond the boundaries of the city. But if you were to square it with the authorities and go with us . . ."

Sebastian studied Arceneaux's fine-boned, earnest face, with its boyish scattering of freckles and wide, sky blue eyes. "Why not? It's worth a try." He pushed to his feet. "See what you can do to keep your faithful hound out of the ham while I order my curricle brought round."

A bored clerk at the Admiralty, the government department in charge of all prisoners of war, grudgingly granted permission for Arceneaux to leave London in Sebastian's custody. As they left the crowded streets of the city behind, Sebastian let his hands drop; the chestnuts leapt forward, and Chien scrambled upright on the seat between the two men, his nose lifted and eyes half closed in blissful appreciation of the rushing wind.

Sebastian eyed the mongrel with a healthy dose of skepticism. "Personally, I wouldn't have said he numbered any bloodhounds amongst his diverse and doubtless disreputable ancestry."

Arceneaux looped an arm over the happy animal's shoulders. "Perhaps not. But the boys used to play hide-and-seek with him, and he was always very good at finding them."

Sebastian steadied his horses. "When you drove Miss Tennyson and the lads out to the moat last week, did you take Chien with you?"

"I never said I—"

"Just answer the bloody question."

Arceneaux let out a huff of resignation. "We did, yes." A faint smile of remembrance lightened his features. "Chien leapt into the moat after a duck and then rolled around in the loose dirt beside the trenches. Gabrielle told him he was not welcome up there ever again."

The Frenchman fell silent, his grip on the dog tightening as he stared off across the sun-drenched fields, his own thoughts doubtless lost in the past. It wasn't until they had reached the overgrown woods of the chase that he said, "I've been thinking and thinking, trying to come up with some reason for her to have taken the boys there again this past Sunday." He shook his head. "But I can't."

"Did you know that Bevin Childe had in his possession a lead cross that was said to have come from the graves of King Arthur and Guinevere?"

"*Mon dieu.* You can't mean the Glastonbury Cross?"

"That's it. Childe claims to have found it along with a box of old bones amongst the collections he's been cataloging at Gough Hall. But Miss Tennyson was convinced it was a recent forgery."

"Is that what she was talking about? But . . . if that's all it was, why wouldn't she have told me?"

"I was hoping perhaps you could help explain that. I gather the controversy surrounding the discovery of Arthur's grave in the twelfth century is considerable?"

Arceneaux nodded. "The problem is, it all seems just a shade too tidy. At the time, the Anglo-Norman kings were facing considerable opposition to their attempts to conquer Wales, and much of that resistance used Arthur as a rallying cry. The country people still believed in the old legends—that Arthur had never really died and would one day return from the mystical Isle of Avalon to expel the forces of evil."

"With the Normans and the Plantagenet kings being identified as the forces of evil?"

"Basically, yes. The thing of it was, you see, there was no grave anyone could point to and say, 'Here lies King Arthur, dead and buried.' That made it easy for people to believe that he hadn't actually died—and could therefore someday return. So the grave's discovery was a true boon to the Plantagenets. They could then say, 'See, Arthur is dead. Here is his grave. He's not coming back. We are his rightful heirs.'"

"Why Glastonbury Abbey?"

"Well, at one time the site of Glastonbury actually was a misty island surrounded by marshland, which helps give some credibility to the association with Avalon. But what makes the monks' discovery particularly suspect is that at the time they claimed to have found Arthur's grave, the abbey church had just burned down and their chief patron and benefactor—Henry the Second himself— had died. They needed money, and what better way to increase their pilgrim traffic than with the discovery of the burial site of King Arthur and his queen?"

"In other words, it was all a hoax."

"It's tempting to see it that way. The problem is, if it was simply a scheme to increase the abbey's revenue, then the monks didn't do a very good job of advertising their find. And the way the burial was described—sixteen feet down, in a hollowed-out log—sounds oddly appropriate to a sixth-century burial. One would have thought that if they were manufacturing a hoax, the monks in their ignorance would have come up with something a bit more . . ." He hesitated, searching for the right word.

"Regal?" suggested Sebastian, guiding his horses onto the narrow track that led to the moat.

"Yes."

"I'm told the cross disappeared during the Commonwealth."

"It did, although it was reportedly seen early in the last century."

"In other words, Bevin Childe could conceivably have found the Glastonbury Cross amongst the collection he's been cataloging— leaving aside the question of whether it was actually manufactured in the twelfth century or the sixth."

"Theoretically, I suppose he could have."

"So why was Miss Tennyson convinced it was a recent forgery?"

Arceneaux looked out over the shady glade surrounding the moat. "I don't know. I gather Childe believes the cross to be genuine—at least to the twelfth century?"

"So he claims."

"Where is it? Would it be possible for me to see it?"

Sebastian drew up near the land bridge to the island, the horses snorting and sidling nervously. Tom jumped down and ran to their heads.

"Unfortunately, no. Childe claims Miss Tennyson threw it into Gough Hall's ornamental lake the Friday before she died."

"She did what?"

Sebastian dropped to the ground, his boots sinking into the soft earth. "I gather she had something of a temper?"

"She did, yes." Arceneaux climbed down more carefully, the dog bounding after him. "But it still seems a strange thing to have done."

Sebastian started to say, "Maybe she—" Then he broke off, his gaze caught by a dark, motionless shape floating at the edge of the moat's stagnant green waters. The dog stopped in his tracks, the fur on his back rising as his lips pulled away from his teeth and a deep, throaty growl rumbled in his chest.

Arceneaux rested a hand on Chien's head, his own voice a whisper. "What is it?"

"Stay here," said Sebastian, sliding down the embankment to the water's edge.

The man's body floated facedown in the algae-scummed water, arms flung stiffly to its sides. Splashing into the murky shallows, Sebastian fisted his hand around the collar of the brown corduroy coat and hauled the body up onto the bank, the bracken and ferns crushing beneath his boot heels and the dead man's sodden, squelching weight.

"Is he dead?" Arceneaux asked, holding the dog at the top of the ancient earthen works. "Who is it?"

Sebastian hesitated a moment, his breath coming uncomfortably hard. The man's clothes were rough, his boots worn, his golden red hair worn a bit too long. Hunkering down beside the body, Sebastian slowly rolled it over.

The man flopped onto his back with a sodden plop, arms flailing outward, to reveal a pale, dripping face and blankly staring eyes. A water-blurred stain discolored the torn, charred front of his leather jerkin and smock.

Sebastian sank back on his heels, one hand coming up to adjust his hat lower over his eyes as he blew out a long breath. "It's Rory Forster."

Chapter 33

$\mathcal{T}$he local magistrate proved to be a foul-tempered, heavy-featured squire named John Richards.

Well into middle age and running comfortably to fat, Squire John was far more interested in his hounds and the joint his cook was preparing for his dinner than in all the sordid, tedious require-ments of a murder investigation. When Tom—upon discovering that Sir Stanley and his lady had removed to London for a few days—carried Sebastian's message to the Squire, the tiger had a hard time convincing the man to leave his cow pasture.

The Squire now stood on the shady bank of the moat, one beefy hand sliding over his ruddy, sagging jowls as he stared down at the waterlogged body at his feet. "Well, hell," he muttered, his brows beetling into a fierce scowl. "Truth be told, I was more than half convinced your tiger was making up the whole tale when he came to me. I mean, two bodies found floating in Camlet Moat in one week? Impossible, I'd have said. But here's another one, all right."

"At least this one's local," observed Sebastian.

The Squire drew a handkerchief from his pocket and wiped his bulbous nose. "But that's the worst part of it, you see. Can't imagine Bow Street interesting themselves in the murder of some black-smith's son from Cockfosters." A hopeful gleam crept into his watery gray eyes. "Unless, of course, you think this might have something to do with that young gentlewoman we found here last Sunday?"

"I wouldn't be surprised but what it does."

The Squire brightened. "I'll send one of the lads off to London right away." A flicker of movement drew his attention across the moat, to where Philippe Arceneaux was methodically crisscrossing the island with Chien bounding enthusiastically at his side. The Squire wiped his nose again, his eyes narrowing with suspicion. "Who did you say that fellow was?"

"My dog handler."

"That's your dog?"

"It is."

"Huh. Fellow's got a Frenchy look about him, if you ask me. They're saying it was a Frenchman who killed that gentlewoman, you know. What is this fellow doing with that dog, exactly?"

"I was hoping the dog might pick up some trace of the missing Tennyson children."

When the Squire still looked doubtful, Sebastian added, "It's a . . . a Strand hound. They're famous for their ability to track missing persons. This one is particularly well trained and talented."

"Well trained, you say?" asked the Squire, just as Chien flushed up a rabbit and tore off after it through the underbrush.

Behind him, Arceneaux shouted, "Chien! *À moi. Imbécile.*"

"He is sometimes distracted by the local fauna," Sebastian admitted.

The Squire sniffed. "Best keep him away from Forster here. Don't reckon Bow Street would fancy dog prints all over the place."

Sebastian hunkered down again to study the dead man's charred clothing and gaping raw wound. The flies were already busy, and he brushed them away with his hand. He didn't need Gibson to tell him that the man had been shot—and at close quarters. But whatever other secrets the dead man had to reveal would need to wait for the anatomist's examination. After a moment, Sebastian said, "I'm told Forster married a local widow this past year."

"That's right. Rachel Clark, of Hollyhock Farm. I sent one of the lads over there to warn her, just in case what your tiger was telling me turned out to be true." The Squire sniffed again. "She could've done a sight better, if you ask me. Very prosperous property, Hollyhock Farm. But then, there's no denying Forster was a handsome man. And when it comes to good-looking men, it's a rare woman who doesn't make a fool of herself." The Squire's lips pursed as he shifted his brooding gaze to Sebastian. "Course, it's even worse when they deck themselves out like a Bond Street beau and drive a fancy sporting carriage."

Sebastian cleared his throat and pushed to his feet. "Yes, well . . . I'd best remove my Strand hound and his handler before they contaminate the scene." He motioned to Arceneaux, who dragged Chien from where he was now intently following the hopping progress of a toad and hauled the reluctant canine off toward the curricle.

For one moment, Sebastian considered as a courtesy telling the Squire of his intention to visit the twice-widowed Rachel of Hollyhock Farm. Then the Squire added darkly, "And a title, of course. Just let a man have looks and a title, and when it comes to the ladies, it doesn't matter what sort of a dastardly reputation the sot might have."

Sebastian touched his hat and bowed. "Squire John."

As they drove away, he was aware of the Squire still standing at the water's edge, the shade of the ancient grove pooling heavily around him, one meaty hand swiping the air before his face as he batted at the thickening cloud of flies.

"I would like to apologize," said Arceneaux stiffly, one hand resting around the damp, happy dog as they drove toward Hollyhock Farm. "I put you through all this, and for what? Chien found no trace of the boys. Nothing."

Sebastian glanced over at him. "It was worth a try."

The Frenchman stared straight ahead, his face troubled. "None of this makes any sense. What could have happened to them? How could they have simply disappeared like this? And why?"

But it was a question Sebastian could not begin to answer.

Hero found the area around Covent Garden's vast square crowded with a swarm of fruit and vegetable sellers. Vendors' cries of "Ripe cher-ries, sixpence a pound" and "Buy my primroses, two bunches a penny" echoed through the narrow streets; the scent of freshly cut flowers and damp earth and unwashed, closely packed bodies hung heavily in the air. As they pushed their way closer to the market, the coachman was forced to check his horses to a crawl.

She kept her gaze focused straight ahead, ignoring the pleading cries of the urchins who leapt up to press their faces against her carriage windows and the roar of laughter from the ragged crowd gathered around a Punch and Judy show on the church steps. By day, the classical piazza laid out before St. Paul's by Inigo Jones was the site of London's largest produce market. But later, when the shadows of evening stretched across the cobblestones and the square's motley collection of stalls and lean-tos closed for the night, willing ladies in tawdry satins with plunging necklines and husky crooning voices would emerge to loiter beneath the colonnades and soaring porticos and hiss their lewd invitations to passersby.

Slowly inching through the throng, the carriage finally swung onto King Street and then drew up before a once grand mansion now divided into lodgings. Hero lowered her hat's veil and waited while her footman knocked on the house's warped, cracked door. It wasn't until the door was opened and the large, familiar form of Molly O'Keefe, the house's mistress, filled the entrance that the footman came to let down the carriage steps.

The two women had come to know each other months earlier, when Hero was researching a theory on the economic causes of the recent explosion in the number of prostitutes in the city. Clucking at the sight of her, Molly whisked Hero into a dilapidated hall with stained, once grand paneling and a broken chandelier that dangled precariously overhead, then slammed the door in the faces of her gawking neighbors. "Yer ladyship! Sakes alive, I ne'er thought to be seeing ye again."

"Molly, I need your help," said Hero, and drew the portrait of Bevin Childe from her sketch pad.

$\mathcal{T}$rue to its name, Hollyhock Farm proved to be a rambling brick cottage with a low slate roof and white-painted windows surrounded by a riot of hollyhocks and lavender and fat pink cabbage roses as big as Sebastian's fist. At the edge of the garden curled a lazy stream spanned by an old, honeysuckle-draped wooden bridge. A flock of white geese waddling along the stream's banks looked up, the warm wind ruffling their feathers, their necks arching in alarm as Chien stood up on the curricle's seat and let out a woof in their direction.

"Do try to keep that hell-born hound out of the geese, will you?" said Sebastian, dropping lightly to the gravel verge outside the garden.

"Chien," whispered Arceneaux, pulling the dog's head around. "Behave."

Sebastian had expected to find the widow of Hollyhock Farm surrounded in her grief by family and neighbors. But she was alone in her garden, her arms wrapped across her chest, the skirts of her simple muslin gown brushing the trailing plantings of lady's mantle and alyssum as she paced the cottage's flagstone paths. She was obviously past the first blush of youth, perhaps even a year or two older than her dead husband, but still slim and attractive, with softly waving golden hair and a sweet, heart-shaped face.

"Mrs. Forster," said Sebastian, drawing up a few feet away from her. "If I might have a word with you?"

The face she turned to him was dry-eyed, a pale mask of shock and grief and something else—something that looked suspiciously like relief, as if she were slowly wakening from a seductive nightmare. She nodded and swallowed hard, her throat cording with the effort. "They're saying Rory might be dead. That his body was found by some London lord out at Camlet Moat. Is it true, then?"

"It is, yes. I'm sorry. Please allow me to offer my condolences on the loss of your husband."

She sucked in a deep breath that shuddered her chest. But otherwise she struck him as remarkably composed. "Thank you."

"I know the timing is awkward, but would you mind if I asked a few questions?"

She shook her head and drew in another of those shaky breaths. "No. Although I don't know what I can tell you that would be of any use to you. I didn't even know Rory was going out to the moat this morning. He said he was planning to work on the roof of the cow shed. Lord knows it's needed mending these past six weeks or more."

"I would imagine things have been rather neglected around the farm, with your husband working for Sir Stanley at Camlet Moat."

She turned to walk along the path, Sebastian beside her. "I told him he was going to need to give up that nonsense for the harvest. But . . ."

"He was reluctant to quit?"

"He said he could hire Jack Williams to take his place around here for half what he was making with Sir Stanley. But a farm needs more than hired men. It's one of the reasons I—" She broke off and bit her lip.

It's one of the reasons I married him. The unsaid words hung in the air.

Pausing beside a rose-covered arch, she let her gaze drift to the slowly sliding waters of the stream. She was obviously better bred than her husband, her farm prosperous. She would have been quite a catch for a blacksmith's younger son.

Sebastian drew up beside her. "Sir Stanley has given up the excavations and filled in the trenches," he said. "So why would your husband go out to the moat this morning?"

She threw him a quick glance. Then her gaze skittered away, but not before he saw the leap of fear in her eyes.

"Did he go out to the moat last Sunday?" asked Sebastian.

"Rory? Oh, no. He was here with me, all night."

"He told you to say that, didn't he?"

She shook her head, her face pinched.

"You can't do your husband any harm by admitting the truth now. He's dead. But the more we know, the better chance we'll have of finding who killed him." Sebastian hesitated, then said again, "He went to the moat Sunday, didn't he?"

Her voice was a painful whisper. "He warned me not to tell anyone. Made me swear to keep his secret."

And probably threatened to beat her if she let the truth slip, Sebastian thought. Aloud, he said, "What time did he leave the farm last Sunday?"

She pressed a tight fist against her lips. "Not long before sunset. Even though it was Sunday and there wasn't likely to be anyone about, he still thought it best to wait till late."

"Do you know why he went?"

Her lip curled. "On account of the treasure, of course. He was mad for it. Much rather dig useless holes in the dirt out there than dig the new well we needed here."

"What time did he come home?"

"About midnight, I suppose. All wet, he was. Said he'd lost his footing and slipped into the moat. I was that put out with him. But he told me to shut up. Said we were going to be rich—that I was going to have fine silks and satins, and my own carriage, just like Squire John's lady."

"Do you think he actually found something?"

"If he did, he didn't come home with any of it; I can tell you that much." A faint hint of color touched her cheeks. "I checked his pockets, you see, after he fell asleep. Of course, he could've hid it someplace again, before he came in." She paused, then added, almost bitterly, "And now he's gone and got himself killed."

"Had you noticed him behaving in any way out of the ordinary these last few days?"

She thought about it a moment, then shook her head. "Not unless you count going into London yesterday."

"Did he often go to London?"

"Never knew him to do it before."

A shout drew Sebastian's attention to the stream, where Chien could be seen advancing on the geese in a low crouch, his tail tucked between his legs, his eyes fixed and focused.

Sebastian said, "Did he tell you why he went?"

"No. Although he was in a rare good mood when he came home. I hadn't seem him in such high spirits since the days when he was courting me." At the memory, a softness came over her features, then faded.

Arceneaux's voice drifted up from the banks of the stream. "Chien."

Sebastian asked quickly, "Is there anything else you can tell me that might help?"

She shook her head just as Arceneaux shouted, "Chien! *Mon dieu.* No!"

The message from Molly O'Keefe reached Hero late that afternoon.

She returned to Covent Garden just as the slanting, golden light of early evening was beginning to flood the mean, narrow streets. The residents of Molly's lodging house were already stirring.

"What have you found?" Hero asked Molly as a raucous trill of laughter floated from somewhere on the first floor above and two blowsy women pushed past them toward the lodging house door. The lodging house was not a brothel, although there was no denying that many of its occupants were Cyprians. But these women took their customers elsewhere, to establishments known as "accommodation houses."

One of the Cyprians, a black-haired woman in feathers and a diaphanous silver-spangled gown, smacked her lips and cocked one hip provocatively at Hero. "Shopping for a bit o' muslin to raise yer old sod's flag, are ye, me lady? Bet I can do the trick. Do you like to watch?"

"Thank you, but no," said Hero.

"Lizzy, ye foulmouthed trollop," hissed Molly, flapping her apron at the woman. "Ye mind yer bloody manners and get out o' here."

Lizzy laughed and disappeared into the night with a jaunty backward wave of one white hand.

"I've a girl by the name of Charlotte Roach waiting for ye in me sitting room," said Molly, drawing Hero toward the rear of the house. "Although if truth be told, I'm not certain a gently bred lady such as yerself should be hearing wot she's got to say."

"Nonsense," said Hero. "You should know by now that I am not so easily shocked."

Molly paused outside the closed door, her broad, homely face troubled. "Ye ain't heard wot she's got to say yet."

Charlotte Roach couldn't have been more than fourteen or fifteen years old. She had a thin, sharp-boned face and straw-colored hair and pale, shrewd eyes rimmed by short, sparse blond lashes. Her tattered gown of pink and white striped satin had obviously been made for someone both older and larger, and then cut down, its neckline plunging to expose most of the girl's small, high breasts. She sat in an unladylike sprawl on a worn settee beside Molly's empty hearth, a glass of what looked like gin in one hand, her lips crimped into a tight, hard line that didn't soften when Hero walked into the room. She looked Hero up and down in frank appraisal, then glanced over at Molly. "This the gentry mort ye was tellin' me about?"

"I am," said Hero.

Charlotte brought her gaze back to Hero's face, one grubby finger reaching out to tap the sketch of Childe lying on the settee beside her. "'E yer Jerry sneak?"

"If by that you mean to ask if the man in that sketch is my husband, then the answer is no." With slow deliberation, Hero drew five guineas from her reticule and laid them in a row across the surface of the table before her. "This is for you . . . *if* you tell me what I want to know. But don't even think of trying to sell me Grub Street news, for I'll know a lie if I hear it."

A flash of amusement shone in the girl's pale, hard eyes. "What ye want to know, then?"

"When was the last time you saw this gentleman?"

The girl took a long swallow of her gin. "That'd be goin' on two years ago, now. I ain't seen 'im since I was at the Lambs' Pen, in Chalon Lane."

Hero cast a quick glance at Molly. She had heard of the Lambs' Pen, a discreet establishment near Portland Square that catered to men who liked their whores young—very young. Two years earlier, Charlotte Roach couldn't have been more than thirteen. Even though the girl was only confirming what Hero had already suspected, she felt her flesh crawl. With effort she said, "Go on."

"'E used t'come into the Lambs' Pen the first Monday o' the month. Always the first Monday, and at nine o'clock exactly. Ye coulda set yer watch by 'im. A real rum duke, 'e was." Charlotte sucked her lower lip between her teeth, her gaze drifting back to

the shiny guineas laid in a row across the top of the table. "Anythin'
else ye want t' 'ear?"

Swallowing the urge to simply give the girl the money and
leave, Hero went to sink into the broken-down chair opposite her.
"I want to hear everything you know about him."

Chapter 35

Hero paused at the entrance to the Reading Room of the British Museum, her gaze sweeping the rows of clerics, physicians, barristers, and antiquaries hunched over their books and manuscripts. The room was dark, with rush matting on the floor and a dusty collection of stuffed birds that seemed to peer down at her from above.

Bevin Childe was not there.

"Miss. I say, *miss*." A bantam-sized, plumpish attendant in a rusty black coat and yellowing cravat bore down on her, his hands raised in horror, his voice hushed to a hissing whisper. "This room is not part of the museum tour. Only registered readers are allowed in the library. You must leave. Leave at once."

Hero let her gaze sweep over the little man with a look that not only stopped him in his tracks, but also caused him to stagger back a step. "I am Lady Devlin," she said calmly. "Lord Jarvis's daughter."

"Lord J—" The man broke off, swallowed, and gave a shallow titter. "Oh . . . Lady Devlin, of course!" He bowed so low his bulbous nose practically touched his knees. "How—how may we assist you?"

"I require a word with Mr. Bevin Childe."

"I'm afraid Mr. Childe is in one of our private research rooms."

"Then if you would be so kind as to direct me to him?"

"I'm afraid Mr. Childe does not like to be disturbed when— I mean, of course, Lady Devlin. This way, please."

He led her down a cramped corridor and around a dogleg to pause before a closed, peeling door. "Mr. Childe is here, my lady," he whispered, his somewhat prominent front teeth digging into his lower lip. "Shall I announce you?"

"Thank you, but I'll announce myself. You may leave us."

A wave of relief wafted across his lumpy features. "Yes, my lady. If you should require anything—*anything*—please do not hesitate to call."

Hero waited until he had bowed himself back down the corridor. Then she turned the door's handle and quietly pushed it open.

The room was small, lit only by a high dusty window, and hemmed in by piles of crates and overflowing shelves. Seated in a straight-backed chair, Bevin Childe had his head bent over the tattered pages of a manuscript held open on the table before him by a velvet-covered, sausage-shaped weight. He had a pen in one hand and was running the index finger of the other down a row of figures. Without even looking up, he said tartly, "You are disturbing my concentration. As you can see, this room is already engaged. Kindly remove yourself at once."

Hero shut the door behind her and leaned against it.

Childe continued frowning down at the figures, apparently secure in the assumption that he was once more alone. She walked across the room and drew out the chair opposite him.

"Did you not hear what I said?" His head jerked up. His myopic gaze focused on Hero and he dropped his pen, the loaded nib

splattering a blot of ink across the pages of his notes. "Good heavens. Not you again."

Smiling, she settled herself in the chair and leaned forward, her elbows on the table, her chin propped on her hands. "What a nice, private place for a comfortable little chat. How fortuitous."

He half rose to his feet.

"Sit down," said Hero.

He sank back into his seat, hands splayed flat on the surface of the table before him, lips puckering out in a scowl that clenched his eyebrows together. "When will you and your husband simply leave me alone?"

"As soon as you stop lying to us."

Childe stiffened. "I'll have you know that I am a respected scholar. A very respected scholar! Nothing I have told you is false. Nothing!"

"Really? You told me your argument with Miss Tennyson last Friday was a scholarly disagreement over her identification of Camlet Moat as Camelot. That certainly wasn't true. The quarrel was over the Glastonbury Cross."

His face reddened. "Miss Tennyson was a very contrary woman. After a point it becomes difficult to correctly separate these choleric episodes in one's mind."

"I might believe you if she hadn't ended that particular confrontation by hurling the cross into the lake. That strikes me as a comparatively memorable moment."

Childe pressed his lips into a tight, straight line and glared at her from across the table.

Hero settled more comfortably in her chair, her hands shifting to the reticule in her lap. "I can understand why you were selected to play the starring role in this little charade. Your skepticism toward all things Arthurian is well-known, which means that for you to be the one to step forward and present the Glastonbury Cross and a box of crumbling bones—particularly with the added

fiction that they were found amongst Richard Gough's collection—
would obviously help to make the discovery more believable."

"This is an outrage!" blustered Childe. "Why, if you were a man
I would—"

"You would—what, exactly? Challenge me to a duel? I'm a very
good shot, you know."

"To the best of my knowledge," said Childe through clenched
teeth, "the cross I discovered in Mr. Gough's collection is the very
same artifact presented to the world by the monks of Glastonbury
in 1191. As it happens, the scholarly community will soon have the
opportunity to judge for itself. The cross has been recovered from
the lake and will be made available for inspection next week."

"Having a new one made, are you?"

Childe leaned back in his chair and folded his arms over his
chest. "I see no reason to dignify that statement with a response."

Hero smiled. "But there's another reason you were selected for
this charade; is that not so, Mr. Childe? You see, I kept thinking,
Why would a respected scholar possessed of a comfortable independence lend himself to such a scheme? And then it came to me:
because you have a deep, dirty little secret that makes you vulnerable to blackmail."

Childe shifted uncomfortably, his jaw set.

"That's why you killed Gabrielle, isn't it? Not because she
somehow discovered the true origins of your so-called Glastonbury
Cross, or because she spurned your suit, but because she found out
about your taste for little girls."

He jerked, then sat very still. "I don't have the slightest idea
what you're talking about."

"I'm talking about the Lambs' Pen. And don't even think about
trying to deny it. They keep very good records, you know. And—"

Childe came up out of his seat, his face purple and twisted with
rage, one meaty hand flashing toward her. *"Why you bloody little—"*

Hero drew a small brass-mounted flintlock muff pistol from her reticule, pulled back the hammer, and pointed the muzzle at his chest. "Touch me and you're dead."

He froze, his eyes flaring wide, his big, sweaty body suspended over the table, his chest heaving with his agitated breathing.

"If you will recall," she said calmly, "I did mention that I am a very good shot. True, a weapon of this size is not particularly accurate, but then at this distance it doesn't need to be. *Now, sit down.*"

He sank slowly, carefully back into his chair.

"You, Mr. Childe, are a fool. Did you seriously think that I would closet myself in private with a man I believe could be a murderer and not come armed?"

Having been red before, his face was now pasty white. "I did not murder Miss Tennyson."

"You certainly had a motive—several, actually. You have just displayed a shocking propensity for violence toward women. And last Sunday, you were at Gough Hall in the afternoon and in your rooms in St. James's Street that night. You could easily have killed Gabrielle and her young cousins while traveling between the two."

"I wouldn't do that! I would never do that!"

"And why, precisely, should I believe you?"

Childe swallowed.

Hero rose, the gun still in her hand. "Stand up, turn around, and put your hands on the boxes in front of you."

"What are you going to do?" he asked, throwing a quick glance at her over his shoulder as he moved to comply.

"Keep your eyes on the wall."

"But what are you going to *do?*"

Hero opened the door behind her. "That depends largely on you, does it not?"

"What does that mean?"

She heard him repeat the question again when she was halfway down the hall.

"*What are you going to do?*"

❉

By the time Sebastian made it back to London, the setting sun was casting long shadows through the streets.

He found Hero seated at the bench before her dressing table. She wore an elegant, high-waisted evening gown of ivory silk with tiny slashed puff sleeves and an inset of rose silk laced with a criss-cross of ivory down the front, and she had her head bowed as she threaded a slender ribbon of dusty rose through her crimped hair. He leaned against the doorframe of her dressing chamber and watched as the flickering candlelight played over her bare shoulders and the exposed nape of her neck. And he knew it again, that baffling swirl of admiration and desire combined with a troubling sense that he was losing something he'd never really had. Something that was more than passion and far, far different from obligation or honor or duty.

She finished fastening the ribbon in place and looked up, her gaze meeting his in the mirror. Whatever she saw there caused her to nod to the young abigail waiting to assist her. "That will be all, Jane; thank you."

"Yes, miss," said the woman, dropping a curtsy.

Sebastian waited until Jane left; then he came into the room and closed the door. "Rory Forster is dead. I found him floating in Camlet Moat."

"Good heavens." Hero swung around to stare at him. "What happened to him?"

"He was shot point-blank in the chest. Sometime this morning, I'd say. Gibson should have the body by now, although I'd be surprised if he's able to tell us much more."

"But . . . why was he killed?"

"I had an interesting conversation with Rory's widow, who owns a prosperous farm to the east of the old chase. She married the man just last year, and if you ask me, she was well on her way to regretting the bargain. Forster might have been a handsome devil, but he seems to have been far more interested in searching for buried treasure than in taking care of things around the farm. I suspect he also wasn't above using his fists on his wife when she angered him . . . and his kind anger easily and often."

"Maybe she's the one who shot him."

Sebastian huffed a surprised laugh. "I confess that thought hadn't occurred to me. But I think it more likely Rory was trying to blackmail someone and ended up getting his payment in the form of a bullet."

"You think he knew who killed Gabrielle? But . . . how?"

"According to the Widow Forster, Rory took his shovel out to Camlet Moat at sunset on Sunday and came back later that night soaking wet and full of big talk about buying her silks and satins and a carriage to rival the Squire's lady. At the time she seems to have thought he must have found some of the island's famous treasure."

"When in fact he'd witnessed the brutal murder of a woman and two children?"

"I suspect so. The first time I spoke to him, he laughed at the men out looking for the Tennyson boys. He said no one was going to find 'them nippers.'"

"Because he knew they were already dead," said Hero softly. "Dear God."

"His wife says he made a trip into London yesterday, which may have been when he confronted the killer and offered his silence in exchange for gold."

"With the payment to be made this morning at Camlet Moat." Hero pushed up from her dressing table. "Interesting choice of locales—and telling, perhaps?"

"It might be more telling if it weren't for the fact that Sir Stanley and his wife both happen to be in London at the moment."

"I know." She went to select a pair of long ivory gloves from her glove box. "My father has invited them to a dinner party tonight at Berkeley Square."

"Ah. So that's where you're going."

She looked over at him. "You are invited as well, if you'd like."

He let his gaze rove over her face. She looked as calm and self-possessed as ever. Yet he was coming to know her better, and he was uncomfortably conscious of a sense of artifice, of concealment about her. And it occurred to him that in her own way she was as gifted an actress as Kat Boleyn.

As if aware of the intensity of his scrutiny, she gave a sudden laugh and said, "What? Why are you looking at me like that?"

"There's something you're not telling me."

She tipped her head to one side, a strange smile lighting her eyes. "And would you have me believe that you have been entirely open with me?"

He started to tell her that he had. Then he remembered the folded paper that lay in his pocket, a note he had received just moments earlier that read, *I have some information you might find interesting. Come to the theater before tonight's rehearsal. K.*

The words of assurance died on his lips.

He watched her eyes narrow. She had her father's eyes: a pale silvery gray at the outer rim with a starlike burst of sooty charcoal around the pupil and a gleam of intelligence almost frightening in its intensity. She said, "I don't imagine there are many couples who find themselves thrown into a murder investigation within days of their marriage."

"No. Although I suppose it's appropriate, given how we met."

She turned away. "Am I to take it that you're declining my father's dinner invitation?"

"I have an appointment with someone who may be able to provide me with information about Jamie Knox."

She waited for him to tell her more, and when he didn't, he saw the flare of some emotion her eyes, although whether it was hurt or suspicion or a gleam of malicious satisfaction, he couldn't have said.

Chapter 36

*W*ar was very much the topic of conversation that evening in the reception rooms of Lord Jarvis's Berkeley Square residence. War in Europe, war on the high seas, war in America.

Hero discussed Wellington's successes in Spain with Castlereagh, the depredations of those damnable upstart Americans on British shipping with Bathurst, and Napoléon's newest rampage against Russia with Liverpool. Most of the members of Liverpool's government were in attendance, along with the city's premier bankers, for war was very much a financial enterprise.

She found the night almost unbearably hot and close, the air in the crowded rooms unusually stifling. The hundreds of candles burning in the chandeliers overhead only added to the heat, and she could feel her cheeks start to burn. Ignoring the discomfort, she was working her way through her father's guests to where she could see Sir Stanley Winthrop in conversation with her mother, Lady Jarvis, when the Earl of Hendon stopped her.

"I'd hoped I might find my son here with you tonight," said Devlin's father, his intensely blue St. Cyr eyes narrowed with a combination of anxiety and hurt. She did not understand the obvious estrangement that had grown between father and son, yet at the same time she didn't feel quite right inquiring into it.

"I fear it will take more than a mere wedding to affect a rapprochement between Devlin and my father," she said lightly.

"But he is well?"

"Devlin, you mean? He is, yes."

"I heard he was set upon the other night in Covent Garden."

"A minor wound. Nothing serious."

Hendon sighed. "I'll never understand why he continues to involve himself in these murder investigations. Is it boredom? Some quixotic delusion that he can somehow make all right with the world?"

"I don't think Devlin suffers from any such delusions." She tipped her head to one side. "Who told you of the attack on Devlin in Covent Garden?"

An uncharacteristic softness stole over his features. "A mutual friend," he said, then bowed and moved on, leaving her staring thoughtfully after him.

She was brought out of her preoccupation by a woman's voice saying, "My dear Lady Devlin, please allow me to offer my felicitations on your recent marriage."

Hero turned to find herself being regarded by Sir Stanley Winthrop's wife, who was looking hot and vaguely sweaty in a gown of pink tulle and satin made high at the neck and with long sleeves.

It was the knowledge that Lady Winthrop would be at tonight's dinner that had inspired Hero to attend.

"Why, thank you," said Hero, smiling as she drew the banker's wife a little to one side. "I'm so glad you were able to come tonight; I've been wanting to talk to you about Gabrielle Tennyson."

Lady Winthrop's own somewhat ingratiating smile vanished, her gaze darting anxiously from left to right as if she were embarrassed by the thought that someone might have overheard Hero's remark. "But . . . do you think this is quite the proper place to discuss—"

"Did you know her well?" Hero asked, ignoring the woman's discomfiture.

Lady Winthrop cleared her throat and swallowed. "Not well, no."

"But you are an intimate of Miss Tennyson's cousin, Mary Bourne, I believe."

"I don't know if I would describe myself as an *intimate*, precisely—"

"No? I thought someone told me you frequently study the Bible together with the Reverend Samuel at Savoy Chapel."

"We do, yes. God's chosen ones may be saved by his irresistible grace, but with God's grace comes an imperative to examine and consider the wisdom and beauty of his teachings. *Particularly* in these dangerous times, when so many are tempted by the blandishments of Satan and the lure of those ancient pagan beliefs so hostile to God."

"Ah, yes; I'd heard Mrs. Bourne is the author of a pamphlet warning of the dangers of Druidism—written under a pseudonym, of course. Is she familiar, I wonder, with the legends associating Camlet Moat with the ancient Celts?" Hero let her gaze drift, significantly, to where Sir Stanley, looking splendid in silk knee breeches and tails, stood in conversation with Liverpool.

Lady Winthrop followed her gaze, her jaw hardening; something very like hatred flashed in her eyes as she stared across the room at her tall, handsome husband. "I'm not certain I understand precisely what you mean to imply, Lady Devlin," she said, her voice low.

"Only that it's fascinating, don't you think, the subtle linkages that can connect one person to the next?"

"We are all joined together in sin."

"Some more so than others, I suppose," said Hero wryly.

Lady Winthrop's nostrils flared on a quickly indrawn breath.

"Gabrielle Tennyson was a woman separated from God. St. Paul tells us that it is a woman's place to receive instruction with utter submission. The Lord does not allow women to teach or exercise authority over men, but enjoins them to remain quiet. Eve was created after Adam, and it was she who was deceived and fell into transgression. That is why a godly woman does not seek to go forth into the world and challenge men, but submits herself to a husband and devotes herself to the care of her household. I sometimes find myself wondering, if she had lived, what Miss Tennyson would have done, once her brother married. I don't imagine his recent betrothal sat well with her."

"What recent betrothal?"

A slow, unpleasant smile slid across the other woman's features. "Oh, dear; have I betrayed a confidence? I knew the betrothal was being kept quiet due to the death of Miss Goodwin's maternal grandmother, but I had assumed that as an intimate of Miss Tennyson's, you would have known. Did she not tell you?"

"No," said Hero. "She did not. How came you to know of it?"

"Emily Goodwin's mother is a dear friend of mine."

Kat Boleyn was wiggling a heavy costume of purple velvet trimmed with gold braid over her head when Sebastian slipped into her cramped dressing room at Covent Garden Theater and closed the door behind him.

"I was beginning to wonder if you were going to make it before rehearsal," she said, turning her back to him and lifting the heavy fall of auburn hair from her neck. "Here. Make yourself useful."

It was a natural request, for she was pressed for time and they were old friends. As his fingertips brushed against her warm body, he tried to think of her as an old friend—as a sister, although he knew only too well that she was not.

"You've learned something?" he asked, his voice strained.

She busied herself clasping a bracelet around her wrist. "You were right about Jamie Fox. He is indeed involved with a group of smugglers plying the Channel. They work out of a small village near Dover, running mainly French wine and brandy." She hesitated a moment, then added, "But there's something more going on . . . something I can't tell you about."

He swung her around to face him, his narrowed gaze studying the gentle curve of her cheek, the childlike upturned nose, the full, sensuous lips. "I thought you knew you could trust me—that nothing I learn from you will ever go any further, no matter what it is."

"This confidence is not mine to betray." Her familiar blue eyes narrowed with some emotion he could not name. "The only thing I can tell you is that what's going on here is dangerous—very dangerous. Jamie Knox is dangerous. He's loyal to no one except himself—and perhaps to his friend, a fellow rifleman named Jack Simpson."

"I've met him."

She touched his arm lightly. "I heard you were set upon the other night and hurt. Are you all right?"

"Where did you hear that?"

She gave him a jaunty smile. "Gibson told me."

"Gibson has a big mouth. It's just a scratch."

"Uh-huh."

A warning bell sounded in the distance. He hesitated a moment, then took her hand in his and kissed her fingers. "Thank you," he said, and turned toward the door.

"Sebastian—"

He paused to look back at her.

"They say Jamie Knox's hearing, eyesight, and reflexes rival yours. And we both know he looks enough like you to be your brother—or at least your half brother. What's going on here?"

All the noise of a theatrical troupe about to begin a dress rehearsal echoed around them—quickly stifled giggles, a hoarse shout for some missing prop, the thump of hurrying feet on bare floorboards. Sebastian said, "I don't know. He claims his father was a cavalry captain."

"But you don't believe him?"

"I don't know what to believe. Amanda told me once that my father was probably a groom."

Kat's lip curled. "That sounds like something Amanda would say, just to be hurtful." Sebastian's sister, Amanda, had hated him from birth—for being male, for being eligible to inherit their father's title and riches, and, as Sebastian had learned recently, for being living evidence of their mother's endless, indiscriminate infidelities.

He said, "That doesn't mean it couldn't be true."

Sebastian was standing before the empty hearth in his library, a booted foot on the cold grate, a glass of brandy in his hand, when he heard a carriage draw up before the house and Hero's quick steps mount to the front door. A single brace of candles burned on the mantel; the rest of the room lay in shadow. He listened to her low-voiced consultation with Morey. Then she appeared at the entrance to the library, one gloved hand raised to release the throat catch of her evening cloak.

"You're home early," he said, straightening as he turned toward her.

"I'm glad I found you," she said, advancing into the room. "I've just learned the most astonishing information."

In spite of himself, Sebastian found himself smiling. "Really? What?"

She swung off her cloak and draped it over the back of a nearby chair. "Hildeyard Tennyson isn't just courting this Miss Goodwin; they're betrothed!"

"I know."

Hero stared at him, dawning indignation chasing incredulity across her features. "You knew!"

"Tennyson mentioned it when he first arrived back in London. He said the betrothal was arranged shortly before he left for Kent, but was never formally announced due to the sudden death of Miss Goodwin's grandmother in the midst of the settlement negotiations."

"But if you knew, why didn't you tell me?"

"I thought I did."

"No. You told me he'd formed an attachment to the daughter of one of his colleagues; you said nothing of a betrothal."

"I beg your pardon. I suppose I didn't consider it significant. You obviously disagree; why?"

"Think about it. Gabrielle was still in the schoolroom when she took over the management of her father's household after her mother died. She was mistress of the Tennyson town house in the Adelphi and their small estate in Kent for something like thirteen years. Can you imagine a woman like Gabrielle meekly turning over to her brother's new eighteen-year-old bride the reins to two houses she'd considered hers for years, and then continuing to live there in any kind of comfort?"

Sebastian took a slow sip of his brandy. "To be honest, I never gave a thought to the effect his marriage would inevitably have on his domestic arrangements."

The look on Hero's face said so clearly, *Men,* that he almost laughed out loud.

He said, "So tell me exactly what all I've missed by being so, well, male about this."

She jerked off her long gloves and tossed them on the chair beside her cloak. "The thing is, you see, if Gabrielle were penniless, she would have had no option but to continue living at the Adelphi with her brother and his new bride. But Gabrielle wasn't penniless;

her father had left her an independent income. It might not have been excessive, but it was enough to enable her to live on her own, or—"

"Or with the man she loved," said Sebastian. "And under the circumstances, I can't see his qualms about being seen as a fortune hunter stopping him." The inclination to laugh was gone.

Hero walked to where she had left the book of English Cavalier poets lying on the table beside the chair. "I was thinking about that poem Arceneaux gave Gabrielle, the one by Robert Herrick. He copied out the last three stanzas to give to her. But it's the first three that I think may be important." She flipped through the book. "Here it is; listen:

> *Bid me to live, and I will live*
> *Thy Protestant to be:*
> *Or bid me love, and I will give*
> *A loving heart to thee.*
>
> *A heart as soft, a heart as kind,*
> *A heart as sound and free*
> *As in the whole world thou canst find,*
> *That heart I'll give to thee.*
>
> *Bid that heart stay, and it will stay,*
> *To honor thy decree—*

Sebastian recited the poem from memory along with her, his gaze locked with hers, their voices blending together, tenor and contralto. "'Or bid it languish quite away, / And't shall do so for thee.'"

"Bloody hell," he said, and drained his brandy to set the glass aside with a snap.

Chapter 37

Arceneaux's lodgings lay in a dark, narrow lane not far from the church of St. Clements. While not exactly a slum, the once genteel area had long ago begun the slow slide into poverty. As Sebastian paused on the footpath, his gaze scanning the old house's dusty windows and crumbling facade, a bedraggled woman well past her youth, her face gaunt and haunting, separated herself from the shadows of a nearby archway to hiss at him invitingly.

He shook his head and pushed open the street door.

The atmosphere inside the house was hot and close and filled with the smells of cooked cabbage and dry rot and the faint but inescapable odor of uncollected night soil. He climbed the worn, darkened stairs to the attic, trying to imagine Gabrielle's gentle, scholarly French lieutenant in this place. From behind one door came a man's hoarse, angry shouts and a woman's soft weeping; from the next, the wail of a babe went on and on. Someone somewhere was coaxing a sad melody from a violin, the bittersweet notes mingling bizarrely with the yowl of mating cats in the back alley.

There were only two doors at the very top of the stairs. Neither showed any trace of light through their cracks, but Sebastian knocked on both anyway and stood listening for some hint of movement.

Nothing.

Under the terms of his parole, Arceneaux should have been in his lodgings by now. Sebastian turned back toward the stairs, hesitating a moment with one hand on the battered newel post. Then he headed for the Angel on Wych Street.

He found the coffeehouse nearly empty in the heat. Tobacco smoke and the smell of freshly roasted coffee hung heavy in the pale flickering light. As he closed the door quietly behind him, the barman looked up questioningly. Sebastian shook his head, his gaze drifting slowly over the desultory groups of men hunched sullenly around their tables, their conversations low voiced.

Arceneaux was not amongst them. But in a corner near the empty hearth, the big blond hussar captain, Pelletier, was playing chess with a gaunt infantry officer in a tattered blue coat. At Sebastian's approach, the hussar lifted his head, the gold coins at the ends of his love knots winking in the candlelight, the fingers of one hand smoothing his luxurious mustache as he watched Sebastian cross the room toward him.

"Come to ruin another of my games, have you?" he said when Sebastian paused beside the table.

"Has Arceneaux been here tonight?"

The hussar pursed his lips and raised one shoulder in a shrug.

"Does that mean you haven't seen him? Or that you don't know where he is?"

"It means he is not here now."

"Do you know where I might find him?"

The man's lips parted in an insolent smile. "*Non.*"

"I thought under the terms of your parole you were confined to your lodgings after eight p.m."

"Our lodgings are here," said the infantry officer when the hussar remained silent. "We've rooms upstairs."

Sebastian glanced down at the chessboard. "Interesting. Whose move?"

"Mine," said the infantry officer, plucking at his lower lip with one thumb and forefinger, his brow knit in a puzzled, hopeless frown.

"Try queen to F-seven," said Sebastian, turning away.

"*Casse-toi*," hissed the hussar with an angry growl, half rising from his seat.

"Not a wise idea," said Sebastian, turning back with one hand on the flintlock in his pocket.

For a moment, the hussar's fiery eyes met his. Then the Frenchman sank back into his seat, his jaw set hard, his chest rising and falling with his rapid breathing.

Sebastian was aware of the man's angry gaze following him to the door.

Outside, the night had taken on a strange, breathless quality, the air hot and heavy and oppressive. He stood on the flagway, aware of a rising sense of frustration. Where the *hell* was Arceneaux? For a paroled officer to be found outside his lodgings after curfew meant the revocation of his parole and consignment to the same hell holes as men from the ranks.

Sebastian felt the faintest suggestion of a breeze wafting through the streets, carrying with it a coolness and the promise of a change. He smelled the river and the inrushing tide and a touch of brine that hinted at faraway lands.

And he knew where the French lieutenant had gone.

Only ten months into its building, the new Strand Bridge rose from the bank of the river at the site of what had once been the Savoy, the grandest palace on the Thames. But the Savoy had long since degenerated from its days of glory, first into an almshouse, then a prison and barracks. Now it was only a shattered, half-demolished ruin that stretched between the Strand and the riverbank below, a wasteland scattered with rubble and piles of dressed stone and brick and timber that extended out onto the rising bridge itself. As Sebastian worked his way down the darkened slope, he could see the curving stone foundations of a small medieval guard tower and a long brick wall pierced by empty mullioned arches. Beyond the ruins, the jagged, looming bulk of the new bridgehead stood out pale against the blackness of the sky.

The first four of the bridge's vast arches were already complete, although the wooden forms at their centers were still in place and a rope-suspended walkway and scaffolding ran beneath the beginnings of what would eventually be an entablature, cornice, and balustrade above. When finished, the bridge's carriageway would rise even with the level of the Strand. But now it lay some feet below it, a rough, unpaved grade that stretched out toward the opposite bank only to end abruptly over the rushing water.

As he walked out onto the bridge, Sebastian could hear the tide splashing against the cofferdams at the base of the piers, feel the unexpected coolness of the breeze wafting against his sweat-sheened face. He kept his gaze focused on the solitary figure of a man that showed against the sliding expanse of the Thames beyond. The man sat at the jagged end of the bridge, his legs dangling over the water hundreds of feet below, one hand resting companionably on the brown and black dog at his side.

"How did you know where to find me?" Arceneaux asked when Sebastian paused some ten feet away from him.

"I remembered what you told me, about liking to come here."

The Frenchman tilted back his head, the wind off the water ruffling the hair around his face. "Are you going to turn me in?"

"No."

Arceneaux took a long breath, eyes closing, nostrils flaring, lips pressed into a tight smile as he drew the air deep within him. "Do you smell it? It's the sea. The same sea that at this very moment is swelling the estuary of the Rance and battering the stone ramparts of Saint-Malo."

Sebastian stood very still, the growing wind tugging at the tails of his coat.

"Sometimes I wonder if I'll ever see any of it again," said Arceneaux. "We have the illusion of being free here, but we're not really. Whatever happened to all the prisoners of the Hundred Years' War? Do you know? What happens to the prisoners of a war that never ends? Is this my destiny, I wonder? To live out my life alone in a dusty, dark garret, scrabbling for a few shillings here and there, teaching bored little boys to speak French and—" His voice cracked and he shook his head.

Sebastian said, "Two weeks ago, Mr. Hildeyard Tennyson asked the daughter of one of his associates for her hand in marriage. Word of the betrothal was kept private due to the intended bride's recent bereavement. But I can't believe Miss Tennyson didn't tell you, her dear, beloved friend."

For a moment, Arceneaux sat motionless. Then Chien nuzzled his head against his friend's side. The Frenchman ran one hand down the dog's back, his attention seemingly focused on his companion. "She told me, yes."

"I'll admit the significance of Tennyson's betrothal escaped me at first. But as my wife—far more acute in such matters than I—pointed out, a woman of Miss Tennyson's temperament and independent ways would never have continued living as a mere sister-in-law and hanger-on in the houses where she herself had been mistress for more than a decade."

Arceneaux continued to stare silently out over the river, his hand running up and down the dog's back.

Sebastian said, "She must have been upset and in need of comfort. You had already declared your love for her. Yet you would have me believe that you still didn't ask her to marry you? That you didn't press her to marry you?"

"No." The world was a soft, halfhearted lie nearly lost in the wind.

Sebastian quoted,

> Bid that heart stay, and it will stay,
> To honor thy decree
> Or bid it languish quite away,
> And't shall do so for thee.

He paused, then said, "Were you thinking about violating your parole and going back to France?"

"No!"

"I think you were. I think you changed your mind because Gabrielle Tennyson finally agreed to marry you." Sebastian suspected that was probably when the two lovers had first lain together, but he wasn't going to say it.

Arceneaux scrambled to his feet and took a hasty step forward, only to draw up short. "All right, damn you! It's true. I thought about escaping. Do you imagine there is a prisoner of war anywhere who doesn't sometimes dream of breaking his parole and escaping? Who isn't tempted?"

Sebastian stared at the young French lieutenant. In the fitful moonlight his face was pale, his eyes like sunken bruises in a pain-ravaged face. The wind ruffled the fine brown hair around his head, flapped the tails of his coat. Sebastian had the impression the man was holding himself together by a sheer act of will. But he was coming dangerously close to shattering.

"Did she agree to marry you?"

Rather than answer, the Frenchman simply nodded, his gaze turning to stare out over the wind-whipped waters of the river.

I'm half sick of shadows, thought Sebastian, watching him. He said, "There's something you're still not telling me. God damn it, Lieutenant; the woman you loved is dead. Who do you think killed her?"

Arceneaux swung to face him again. "You think if I knew who killed her, I wouldn't make them pay?"

"You may not be quite certain who is to blame. But you have some suspicions, and those suspicions are weighing heavily on you. It's why you're here now, risking your parole. Isn't it?"

The wind gusted up, stronger now, scurrying the tumbling dark clouds overhead and obscuring the hazy sickle of the moon.

"Who do you think killed her?" Sebastian demanded again.

"*I don't know!*" The Frenchman's features contorted as if the words were being torn from him. "I lie awake every night, wondering if I might somehow be responsible for the death of the woman I loved."

"Why?" pressed Sebastian. "What makes you think you might be responsible?"

Chien rose to his feet, his gaze fixed on the rubble-strewn bank, ears at half cock as he trotted a few steps toward the bridgehead and then stopped.

Arceneaux went to rest a hand on the dog's neck. "What is it, boy? Hmm?"

Sebastian was aware of an inexplicable but inescapable intimation of danger that quickened his breath and brought a burning tingle to the surface of his skin. He scanned the ruins of the ancient palace, his eyes narrowing as he studied the piles of stone and timber, the long line of broken wall with its empty windows a dark and melancholy tracery against the stormy sky.

"Arceneaux," he said warningly, just as a belching tongue of flame erupted from the foundations of the old guard tower and the crack of a rifle shot echoed across the water.

Chapter 38

"Get down!" Sebastian shouted as he dove for cover behind the half-built cornice.

Looking back, he saw Arceneaux stagger, a bloom of shiny dark wetness spreading high across the center of his waistcoat.

"*Arceneaux!*"

The Frenchman's knees buckled slowly, his head tilting back, his face lifted as if he were looking at the sky.

Sebastian scrambled into the open to grab the man as he fell and dragged him into the protective lee of the stonework. "Bloody hell," swore Sebastian, clutching the shuddering man to him.

Chien crouched beside them, his harsh barks splitting the night.

The entire front of the Frenchman's waistcoat was wet with blood, his mouth open and gasping in great sucking wheezes that blew little bubbles in the wet sheen on his chest.

Sebastian knew only too well what that meant.

He ripped off his cravat anyway and rolled it around his fist to form a thick pad.

"No . . . point . . ." Arceneaux whispered as Sebastian pressed the cloth against the gaping, oozing wound in his chest. Then he choked and blood poured from his mouth and nose.

"You're going to be all right," Sebastian lied, hauling the wounded man up so that his back lay against Sebastian's own chest in a desperate attempt to keep Arceneaux from drowning in his own blood.

Arceneaux shook his head, his eyes rolling back in his head. "Gabrielle . . ."

"Talk to me, Philippe," shouted Sebastian, the Frenchman's warm blood pouring over his hand as he desperately pressed the padded cloth to Arceneaux's shattered, jerking chest. "Who would want to kill you?"

The jerking stopped.

"Philippe? *Philippe!*"

Beside him, the dog whined, his nose thrusting against the Frenchman's limp hand.

"*Damn,*" said Sebastian on a hard expulsion of pent-up breath.

Despite the coolness of the rising wind, he was sweating, his breath coming in quick pants. Shifting carefully, he eased the Frenchman's weight off his own body. He could smell the acrid pinch of burnt powder, see the drift of gun smoke as he slewed around to peer cautiously over the edge of the stone wall.

Nothing.

He focused his gaze on the remnants of the old medieval tower that lay to the right and just below the broken stretch of palace wall. Most of the tower's superstructure was long gone, leaving only a curving section of stone foundation perhaps four feet high. Studying it, Sebastian estimated that the shooter's position lay some two hundred yards from where he crouched, possibly three. It would have been a difficult shot to make in good light on a calm day. At night, with clouds obscuring the moon and a wind kicking up, most men would have said it was impossible.

But not a trained rifleman who could bring down a running rabbit at three hundred yards in the dark.

Sebastian swiped the back of his hand across his forehead. The problem was, why would Jamie Knox want to kill Gabrielle Tennyson's French lieutenant? It made no sense. . . .

If the shooter was indeed Jamie Knox, and if his intended target was actually Arceneaux and not Sebastian himself.

A faint flicker of movement showed above the jagged top of the tower wall, then stilled. The shooter was still there.

Sebastian considered his options. He was essentially pinned down. He had a flintlock in his own pocket, but the pistol was small, its range limited. Against a rifle over any distance, it was useless.

Right now, he was protected by the solid length of the half-constructed cornice that ran along the edge of the bridge. But if the shooter was to shift—or if he had a confederate who could come in from the west—Sebastian would be as exposed at the end of that long, open bridge as a target in a shooting gallery.

He needed to move.

Shifting his gaze, he assessed the distance from where he lay to a stack of dressed stone that stood perhaps a third of the way back toward the bridgehead. Sebastian had heard enough Baker rifles in his day to know exactly what was shooting at him. The Baker was a single-shot weapon. But a good rifleman could reload and fire four times in a minute.

An exceptional rifleman could make it to five.

Sebastian had no doubt that the man shooting at him was an exceptional rifleman.

That meant that if Sebastian could lure the rifleman into firing, he would have at most twelve seconds to make it to the safety of that pile of stones before the shooter finished reloading and was able to fire again.

He was trying to figure out how he could trick the rifleman into firing—without actually getting shot—when Chien, who had been lying stretched out whining beside Arceneaux's still body, suddenly stood up.

"Down, boy," whispered Sebastian.

The dog hunkered into a lowered stance, eyes alert and fixed as it stared at the near bank.

"Chien," cautioned Sebastian. Then he shouted, "Chien! No!" as the dog tore into the night, a black and brown streak against the pale stone length of the bridge.

He watched, helpless, as the dog raced up the slope. Chien was nearly to the guard tower when the rifle cracked again, spitting fire into the night.

The dog yelped, then fell silent.

"Bloody son of a bitch," swore Sebastian, and took off running.

He could feel the wind off the water whipping at his coattails, the rubble of the roadway shifting dangerously beneath the soles of his boots as he mentally counted off the seconds since the last shot.

. . . six, seven . . .

He swerved around a pile of broken stone—*eight, nine*—and leapt a small chasm—*ten, eleven*—to dive behind the looming stones just as the next rifle shot reverberated across the open waterfront.

A cascade of pulverized grit exploded beside his face.

"Hell and the devil confound it," he swore, wiping his sleeve across his bloody cheek. Then he was up and running again, this time for the pile of timbers he could see near the bridgehead.

. . . seven, eight . . .

He could hear the inrushing tide slapping against the cofferdam at the base of the first pier, the rumble of what sounded like distant thunder.

. . . ten, eleven . . .

The timbers were farther than he'd realized. He skittered the last ten feet flat out on his stomach, the rubble of roadway tearing at his clothes as he braced himself for the next shot.

It never came.

Clever bastard.

Sebastian lay stretched out prone behind the pile of timbers, his heart pounding, the blood rushing in his ears. The rifleman had obviously figured out exactly what Sebastian was doing. Rather than wasting his shot, the man now had a loaded weapon; all he needed to do was wait for Sebastian to fully show himself again, and then calmly squeeze the trigger.

He can shoot the head off a running rabbit at three hundred yards in the dark.

The wind gusted up, bringing with it the smells of the river and the creaking of the suspended walkways that ran along both sides of the partially built bridge, just above the summit of the arches. Sebastian hesitated for a moment, his gaze fixed on the darkened ruins, his ears straining to catch the least sound.

Nothing.

Rolling quickly to the far side of the bridge, he lowered himself carefully over the edge until he hung suspended, his fingers digging into a gap in the stonework, feet dangling in space above the narrow suspended walkway, the river rushing far below.

Then he let go.

He landed lightly on the boards of the walkway, the suspension ropes swaying dizzily as the structure took his weight. Then, with the massive stone bulk of the bridge now between him and the shooter, Sebastian sprinted for the riverbank, the walkway dancing and swaying beneath him.

The last arch of the bridge soared high above the tidal mudflats of the riverbed to butt into the rubble-strewn bank. He reached solid ground and paused for a moment, his senses straining to catch any movement, any sound. He scanned the dry, rutted slope of the bank, the matted half-dead weeds, the looming wreck of the ancient palace. He found himself remembering other nights in what seemed like a different lifetime, when death waited in each dark shadow and around every corner, when the rumble in the distance was artillery, not thunder, and the broken walls were Spanish villages blackened by the stains of fires not yet grown cold.

He drew a deep breath, suddenly aware of a powerful, raging

thirst. He swallowed hard, his throat aching. Then, hunkering low, he darted across the open ground and ducked behind the broken fragment of the old palace wall.

Once, this section of the palace had overlooked the river, an elegant facade pierced by high, pointed windows and supported by massive buttresses. Now only the one wall remained, stretching eastward to end abruptly just above the small round tower where the shooter waited. Moving as quietly as possible, Sebastian crept through the ruins, painfully aware of the rustle of the long, dry weeds, of each broken stone that shifted beneath the soles of his boots. He passed the yawning opening of what had once been a massive medieval fireplace, an empty doorway, a spiral of steps going nowhere. Through the gaping windows he could see the massive works of the new bridge, the dark, sliding shimmer of the river, the low curve of the old guard tower's stone foundations.

Pausing at the jagged end of the wall, he slipped his flintlock pistol from his pocket and quietly eased back the hammers on both barrels. He could hear the distant clatter of the carriages on the Strand up above, feel the powerful thrumming of his own blood in the veins of his neck. He took a deep breath. Then he burst around the end of the broken wall, his pistol pointing down into the foundations of the guard tower, his finger already tightening on the first trigger.

But the tower was empty, the weeds within it matted and scattered with debris. The shooter had vanished into the night, leaving only the Baker rifle leaning mockingly against the worn, ancient stones.

Chapter 39

$\mathcal{S}$ir Henry Lovejoy was not fond of heights.

He stood well back from the jagged edge of the bridge's last, half-constructed arch, his legs splayed wide against the powerful buffeting of the growing wind. He could see the river far below, the dark waters churning and frothing against the rough temporary coffer dams. The air was thick with the smell of the inrushing tide and the damp mudflats of the nearby bank and the coppery tang of freshly spilled blood.

"What did you say his name was?" Lovejoy asked, his gaze on the dead man sprawled in the lee of the bridge's half-built cornice.

Devlin stood beside him, his evening clothes torn and dusty and soaked dark with the dead man's blood. In one hand he gripped a Baker rifle, his fingers showing pale against the dark forestock. "Arceneaux. Lieutenant Philippe Arceneaux, of the Twenty-second Chasseurs à Cheval."

Grunting, Lovejoy hunkered down to study the French officer's fine-boned features, the sensitively molded lips and lean cheeks. In death, he looked shockingly young. But then, Lovejoy thought, by the time a man reaches his mid-fifties, twenty-four or -five can seem very young indeed.

Pushing to his feet, he nodded briskly to two of the men he'd brought with him. Between them, they heaved the Frenchman's body up and swung it onto the deadhouse shell they would use to transport the corpse through the city streets.

"You've no idea of the identity of the shooter?" Lovejoy asked Devlin.

"I never got a good look at him. He was firing from the ruins of the old guard tower. There, to the right."

"Want I should go have a look?" asked Constable Leeper, a tall beanpole of a man with an abnormally long neck and a badly sunburnt face.

Lovejoy nodded. "Might as well. We'll see better in the daylight, but we ought to at least do a preliminary search now."

As the constable turned to go, Devlin stopped him, saying, "The Lieutenant had a medium-sized brown and black dog that the rifleman shot. I've searched the riverbank for him myself without success. But if you should happen to come upon him—and if he should still be alive—I would like him taken to someone capable of caring for his wounds."

"Aye, yer lordship," said the Constable, his torch filling the air with the scent of hot pitch as he headed back down the bridge.

Lovejoy squinted into the murky distance. From here, the near bank was only a confused jumble of dark shapes and indistinct shadows. "Merciful heavens. The ruins of that tower must be three hundred yards away."

Devlin's face remained impassive. "Very nearly, yes."

"If I hadn't seen the results myself, I would have said that's impossible. In the daylight it would be phenomenal; how could anyone even *see* a target over such a distance at night, let alone hit it?"

"If he had good eyesight, good night vision, and a steady finger, he could do it. I've known sharpshooters who could hit a man at seven hundred yards, if the man is standing still and it's a sunny day."

Something in the Viscount's voice drew Lovejoy's gaze to him. He stood with his back held oddly rigid, his face stained with blood and dust and sweat.

Lovejoy said, "Are you certain Arceneaux was the shooter's intended target? He did continue firing at you, after all."

"He did. But that was only to keep me pinned down long enough for him to get away. I think he killed the man he came here to get."

With a succession of grunts, the two men from the parish lifted the shell to their shoulders and headed back toward the riverbank. Lovejoy picked up the lantern and fell into step behind them, the rubble of the half-constructed bridge crunching beneath his feet. "Am I to take it this Lieutenant Arceneaux is the young Frenchman who befriended Miss Gabrielle Tennyson?"

"He is," said Devlin. "Only, I gather they were considerably more than friends."

"Tragic."

"It is, yes."

"And you have no notion at all who could have done this, or why?"

Devlin paused beside the ruins of the ancient palace, his strange yellow eyes glinting in the fitful light from Lovejoy's lantern as he stared into the darkness.

"My lord?"

Devlin glanced over at him, as if only suddenly reminded of Lovejoy's presence. "Excuse me, Sir Henry," he said with a quick bow and turned away.

"My lord?"

But Devlin was already gone, his long legs carrying him easily up the dark, rubble-strewn bank, the rifle in his hand casting a slim, lethal shadow across the night.

Sebastian strode into the Black Devil with the Baker rifle still gripped in his fist. His shirt front and waistcoat were drenched dark red with Arceneaux's blood; his cravat was gone. His once elegant evening coat hung in dusty tatters. He'd lost his hat, and a trickle of blood ran down one side of his dirty, sweat-streaked face.

"Jesus, Mary, Joseph, and all the saints," whispered the buxom, dark-haired barmaid as Sebastian drew up just inside the door, the Baker propped at an angle on his hip, his eyes narrowing as he scanned the smoky, low-ceilinged room.

"Where's Knox?" he demanded, his words carrying clearly over the skittering of chairs and benches, the thumps of heavy boots as the tavern's patrons scrambled to get out of his way.

The girl froze wide-eyed behind the bar, her lips parted, the half-exposed white mounds of her breasts jerking and quivering with her agitated breathing.

"Where the bloody hell is he?" Sebastian said again.

"You do favor the dramatic entrance, don't you?" said a sardonic voice from a doorway that opened off the back of the room.

Sebastian turned. His gaze met Knox's across the now empty expanse of the public room, twin pairs of yellow eyes that shared an ability to see great distances and at night with an accuracy that struck most normal men as inhuman.

Or evil.

Sebastian laid the Baker on the scarred surface of the bar with a clatter. "I'm returning your rifle."

A faint smile curled the other man's lips. "Sorry. Not mine. Did someone lose it?"

"Where were you an hour ago?"

Jamie Knox advanced into the room, still faintly smiling. He wore his usual black coat and black waistcoat and black cravat, his face a dark, handsome mask. "Here, of course. Why do you ask?"

"Ever meet a Frenchman named Philippe Arceneaux?"

"Arceneaux?" Knox frowned as if with the effort of concentration. "Perhaps. It's rather difficult to say. I own a tavern; many men come here."

"Lieutenant Philippe Arceneaux."

"Does he say I know him?"

"He's dead. Someone shot him through the heart tonight from a distance of some three hundred yards. Know anyone who could make a shot like that?"

"It's a rare talent. But not unheard of."

"Your friend tells me you can shoot the head off a running rabbit at more than three hundred yards. In the dark."

Knox glanced over to where the wide-eyed girl still stood behind the bar. "Leave us."

She let herself out the front door, pausing on the threshold to throw him a last, questioning glance that he ignored. The public room was now empty except for the two men.

Knox sauntered behind the bar and reached below the counter for a bottle of brandy. "You've obviously been talking to my old mate, Jack Simpson." He eased the stopper from the brandy. "He'll also tell you that I can catch a will-o'-the-wisp out of the air and hear the whispers of the dead. But just between you and me, I wouldn't be believing everything he says."

Sebastian wandered the room, his gaze drifting over the low-beamed rafters, the massive old stone fireplace, and broad hearth. "I've heard it said you won this place at the roll of the dice—or that you killed a man for it. Which was it?"

Knox set the bottle and two glasses on the counter beside the Baker. "Like I said, you don't want to be believing everything you hear about me."

"I also hear you were at Corunna. Lieutenant Arceneaux was at Corunna, as well. Is that where you met him?"

"I never met your Lieutenant Arceneaux, God rest his soul." Knox poured brandy into the two glasses and tucked the bottle away. "Here. Have a drink."

"Thank you, but no."

Knox laughed. "What do you think, then? That I'm trying to

do away with you?" He pushed both glasses across the bar. "There. You choose one; I'll drink the other. Will that allay your superstitions?"

Moving deliberately, Sebastian came to select one of the glasses of amber liquid.

His yellow eyes gleaming, Knox lifted the other to his lips and drank deeply. "There. Now, shall we wait to see if I drop to the floor and start thrashing about in my death throes?" He took another sip, this time letting the brandy roll around on his tongue. "It's good stuff, this. Comes from a château just outside Angoulême."

"And how did it make its way into your cellars?"

Knox smiled. "Would you have me believe you've no French brandy in your cellars, then?"

"Arceneaux hailed from Saint-Malo, another wine region. He told me once his father owned a vineyard. Perhaps that's how you met him."

Knox was no longer smiling. "I told you. I never met him."

"I'll figure it out eventually, you know."

"When you do, come back. But as it is, you've nothing against me but conjecture."

"So sure?"

"If you had anything you thought might begin to pass as proof, I'd be down at Bow Street right now, talking to the magistrates. Not to you."

"Thanks for the brandy." Sebastian set his glass on the bar and turned toward the street.

"You're forgetting your rifle," Knox called after him.

"Keep it. You might need it again."

The tavern owner laughed, his voice ringing out loud and clear. "You remember how I told you my father was a cavalry officer?"

Sebastian paused with one hand on the doorjamb to look back at him.

Knox still stood behind the bar. "Well, I lied. My mother never knew for certain which of the three bastards she lay with had planted me in her belly. She was a young barmaid named Nellie, you see, at the Crown and Thorn, in Ludlow. According to the woman who raised me, Nellie said her baby's da could've been either an English lord, a Welsh captain, or a Gypsy stableboy. If she'd lived long enough, she might have recognized my actual sire in me as I grew. But she died when I was still only a wee babe."

Sebastian's skin felt hot; the abrasions on his face stung. And yet he knew the strangest sensation, as if he were somehow apart from himself, a disinterested observer of what was being said.

Knox said, "I saw the Earl of Hendon in Grosvenor Square the other day. He looks nothing like me. But then, it occurs to me, he don't look anything like you, either. Now, does he?"

Sebastian opened the door and walked out into the warm, wind-tossed night.

Chapter 40

*T*he storm broke shortly before dawn, with great sheets of rain hurled through the streets by a howling wind and thunder that rattled the glass in the windowpanes with all the savage power of an artillery barrage.

Sebastian stood on the terrace at the rear of his Brook Street house, his outstretched arms braced against the stone balustrade overlooking the garden. He had his eyes closed, his head tipped back as he let the rain wash over him.

When he was a very little boy, his mother used to take him for walks in the rain. Sometimes in the summer, if it was warm, she'd let him out without his cap. The rain would plaster his hair to his head and run off the tip of his nose. He'd try to catch the drops with his tongue, and she wouldn't scold him, not even when he waded and splashed through every puddle he could find, squealing as the water shot out from beneath his stomping feet.

But his favorite walks were those they took in the rain in Cornwall, when the fierce winds of a storm would lash the coast and she'd bundle him up and take him with her out to the cliffs.

Together they would stand side by side, mesmerized by the power of the wind and the fury of the waves battering the rocks with an awe-inspiring roar. She'd shout, *Oh, Sebastian, feel that! Isn't it glorious?* And the wind would slam into her, rocking her back a step, and she'd laugh and fling wide her arms and close her eyes, surrendering to the sheer exhilaration of the moment.

So lost was he in the past that he failed to mark the opening of the door behind him. It was some other sense entirely that brought him the sudden certainty that he was no longer alone.

"Devlin?"

He turned to find Hero standing in the doorway. She still wore the ivory gown with the dusky pink ribbons, and he wondered if she had awakened and dressed to come in search of him, or if she had not yet made it to her bed.

He had stripped off his torn, blood-soaked coat and waistcoat, but he still wore his ruined shirt, his collar askew. "My God," she said, her eyes widening when she saw him. "You're covered in blood."

"It's not mine. Philippe Arceneaux is dead."

"Did you kill him?"

"Why would I kill him? I liked him."

She walked out into the rain, the big drops making dark splotches on the fine silk of her dress as she reached up to touch his cheek. "You're hurt."

"Just scratched."

"What happened?"

"Whoever killed Arceneaux shot him from a distance of three hundred yards. In the dark."

"Who can shoot accurately at such a distance?"

"A Bishopsgate tavern owner and ex-rifleman named Jamie Knox, for one."

"Why would a tavern owner want to kill Arceneaux?"

"I don't know." He stared out over the wind-tossed garden, a jagged flash of lightning splitting the sky. The rain poured about them. "There's too much I don't know. And because of it, people keep dying."

"It's not your fault. You're doing everything you can."

He looked at her again. "It's not enough."

She shook her head, an odd smile hovering about her lips. In the darkness, her eyes had a strange, almost luminous quality. The rain ran down her cheeks, dripped off the ends of her wet hair, soaked the bodice of her gown so that her high, round breasts showed clearly through the thin silk of her gown.

His voice hoarse, he said, "You're ruining your dress. You need to go inside."

"So do you."

Neither of them moved.

Slowly, she slipped her hand behind his neck, her thumb flicking across his throat in a soft caress, her gaze tangling with his. Then, her eyes wide-open, she tilted her head and touched her lips to his.

He opened his mouth to her, drank deeply of her kiss, swept his hands up her back. He felt her tremble. But before he could pull her to him, she slipped away from him.

She paused at the door to look back. He saw a succession of raw, naked emotions flash across her face—guilt and regret and a fierce, hopeless kind of longing. She said, "When this is all over, we need to . . . begin again."

The rain pounded down on him, the wind billowing his wet, bloodstained shirt and plastering his hair to his head. He was aware of the lateness of the hour, the fullness of her lips, the unexpected raw wanting that surged through him for this woman who was his wife, the mother of his unborn child . . . and his enemy's daughter.

He said harshly, "And what if it's never over?"

But she had no answer, and long after she had gone, the question remained.

Friday, 7 August

The next morning, the rain was still falling out of a gunmetal gray sky when Sebastian climbed the steps of the elegant Mayfair town house of his sister, Amanda, Lady Wilcox.

The door was opened by Lady Wilcox's well-trained and normally stoic butler, who took a step back and said, "My lord Devlin!" in a voice pregnant with consternation and a touch of fear.

"Good morning," said Sebastian, handing his hat, gloves, and walking stick to the butler before heading for the stairs. "I assume my sister is still in the breakfast room?"

"Yes, but . . . My lord—"

Sebastian took the steps two at a time. "Don't worry; I'll announce myself."

He found his sister seated at a small table overlooking the rain-washed rear gardens, an empty plate before her. She'd been reading the *Morning Post* but looked up at his entrance, a delicate pink floral teacup arrested halfway to her puckered lips.

"Good morning, Amanda," he said cheerfully.

She set the cup down with enough force to send its contents sloshing over the rim. "Good God. You."

The first child born to the Earl of Hendon and his beautiful, errant countess, Amanda had never been a particularly attractive woman. She had inherited her mother's slim, elegant carriage and striking golden hair. But there was a bluntness to her features that she owed to Hendon, and at forty-two she had reached an age at which her disposition showed quite clearly on her face.

She wore a simple morning gown of dove gray made high at the waist and edged along the neckline with a dainty ruffle of lace, for she had been widowed just eighteen months and was not yet completely out of mourning. The role Sebastian had played in the death of her husband was a subject brother and sister did not discuss.

She reached for her tea again, her lips turning down at the corners as she took a sip. "What do you want?"

Without waiting for an invitation he suspected would not be forthcoming, Sebastian drew out the chair opposite her and sat. "And I'm delighted to see you too, dear sister."

She gave a delicate sniff. "I've heard you're doing it again—that you've involved yourself in yet another murder investigation, this time of some mere barrister's sister, of all things. One might have hoped that your recent nuptials would put an end to this plebeian nonsense. But obviously such is not the case."

"Obviously not," said Sebastian dryly.

She sniffed again but said nothing.

He let his gaze drift over the familiar features of her face, the tightly held lips, the broad, slightly bulbous nose that was so much like her father's, the piercing blue St. Cyr eyes that had come to her, too, from her father. He was her brother—or at least, her half brother, her only surviving acknowledged sibling. And yet she hated him with a passion so raw and visceral that it could at times steal his breath.

As Hendon's firstborn child, she would have inherited every-thing—land, wealth, title—had she been a boy. But because she was a girl, she had been married off with only a dowry—a handsome one, to be sure, but still a mere pittance compared to all that would someday pass to Sebastian. Her two children, Bayard, the new Lord Wilcox, and Stephanie, his eighteen-year-old sister, were Wilcoxes; by the laws of male primogeniture, they had no claims on the St. Cyr estates.

It was the norm in their society. And yet for some reason, Amanda had always felt cheated of what she still somehow stub-bornly believed in her heart of hearts should by rights have been hers. Even Richard and Cecil, Hendon's first- and second-born sons, had earned her resentment. But her true hatred had always been reserved for Sebastian. For she had known—or at least suspected—from the very beginning that this last son born to the Countess of Hendon had not in truth been begotten by the Earl.

She set her teacup down again. "Whatever it is you are here for, say it and go away so that I can read my paper in peace."

"I'm curious about the December before I was born; how well do you remember it?"

She twitched one shoulder. "Well enough. I was eleven. Why do you ask?"

"Where did Mother spend that Christmas?"

She thought about it for a moment. "Lumley Castle, near Durham. Why?"

Sebastian remembered Lady Lumley quite well, for she'd been one of his mother's particular friends, nearly as gay and beautiful— and faithless—as the Countess herself.

He saw Amanda's eyes widen, saw the faintly contemptuous smile that deepened the grooves bracketing her mouth, and knew that she understood only too well his reason for asking. "I can do sums, Sebastian. You're trying to figure out who her lover was that winter. Well, aren't you?"

Pushing up, he went to stand at the window overlooking the garden, his back to her. In the rain, the daylight was flat and dim, the shrubbery a sodden green, the slate flagstones of the terrace dark and shiny wet. When he didn't respond, she gave a sharp laugh. "An understandable exercise, given the circumstances, but unfortunately predicated upon the assumption that she took only one lover at a time. She could be quite shameless, you know."

Her scornful words sent a surge of raw fury through him. It startled him to realize that no matter how much Sophie had lied to him, no matter how cruel and destructive her betrayal and aban- donment, the protective urge he'd felt for her as a boy still flared in him.

"And that Christmas?" he asked, keeping his voice level with difficulty, his gaze still fixed on the scene outside the window.

"I actually can't recall."

He watched the long canes of the arbor's climbing roses bend in the wind, watched the raindrops chase each other down the window glass.

Amanda rose to her feet. "You really want to know who begat our mother's precious little bastard? Well, I'll tell you. It was her groom. A lowly, stinking *groom*."

Turning, he looked into her familiar, pinched face and didn't believe her. Refused to believe her.

She must have read the rejection of everything she'd said in his eyes, because she gave a harsh, ringing laugh. "You don't believe me, do you? Well, I *saw* them. That autumn, on the cliffs over-looking the sea, in Cornwall. He was lying on his back and she was riding him. It was the most disgusting thing I've ever witnessed. Jeb, I believe his name was. Or perhaps Jed, or something equally vulgar."

He stared into his sister's hate-filled blue eyes and knew a re-vulsion so intense as to be physical. "I don't believe you," he said out loud.

"Believe it," she sneered. "I see him every time I look at you. Oh, his hair might have been darker than yours, and he might not have been as tall. But there has never been any doubt in my mind."

A sudden gust of wind blew rain against the window with a startlingly loud clatter.

He wanted to say, *Was the groom a Gypsy?* But he couldn't so betray himself to this cold, angry woman who hated him more than she'd ever hated anyone in her life. So instead he asked, "What happened to him?"

"I neither knew nor cared. He went away. That was all that mattered to me."

Sebastian walked to the door, then paused to look back to where she still stood, her hands clenched at her sides, her face red and twisted with hatred and some other emotion.

It took him a moment to recognize it, but then he knew.

It was triumph.

Sir Henry Lovejoy hesitated at the entrance to the Bow Street public office, his face screwing into a grimace as he stared out at the ceaseless torrent driven sideways by the force of the wind. Water sluiced in sheets from the eaves, swelled in the gutters, pinged off the glass of the building's tall windows. Sighing, he was about to unfurl his umbrella and step out into the deluge when he became aware of a gentleman crossing the street from the Brown Bear toward him.

A tall, military-looking gentleman, he seemed oblivious to the elements, the numerous shoulder capes on his coat swirling about him as he leapt the rushing gutter. "Ah, Sir Henry, is it not?" he said, drawing up on the flagway. "I am Colonel Urquhart."

Swallowing hard, Lovejoy gave a jerky bow. The Colonel was well-known as Jarvis's man. "Colonel. How may I help you?"

"I'm told you are heading up the search for the killer of the Tennyson family."

"I am, yes. In fact, I was just about to—"

Urquhart tucked his hand through Lovejoy's elbow and drew him back into the public office. "Let's find someplace dry and private where we can have a little chat, shall we?"

Chapter 41

*I*t had become Kat Boleyn's habit of late to frequent the flower market on Castle Street, not far from Cavendish Square. She'd discovered there was a rare, elusive peace to be found amidst the gaily colored rows of roses and lavender and cheerful nosegays. Sometimes the beauty of a vibrant petal or the faintest hint of a familiar scent was so heady it could take her far back in time to another place, another life.

The morning's rain had only just eased off, leaving the air cool and clean and smelling sweetly of damp stone. She wandered the stalls for a time, the handle of her basket looped casually over one arm. It wasn't until she paused beside a man selling small potted orange trees that she became aware of being watched.

Looking up, she found herself staring at a tall gentlewoman in an exquisitely fashioned walking gown of green sarcenet trimmed in velvet. She had her father's aquiline nose and shrewd gray eyes and a surprisingly sensuous mouth that was all her own.

"Do you know who I am?" asked Devlin's new Viscountess in a husky voice that could have earned her a fortune on the stage, had she been born to a less elevated position in society.

"I know."

By silent consent, the two women turned to walk toward Oxford Market, pushing past a Negro band and shouting costermongers hawking everything from apples to fried eels. After a moment, Kat said, "I assume you have sought me out for a reason."

"I wonder if you know someone nearly killed Devlin last night."

Kat felt a quick stab of fear that left her chest aching, her breath tight. "Is he all right?"

"He is. But the man who was standing beside him is dead, shot through the heart from a distance of some three hundred yards."

Kat knew of only one man with the ability to make such a shot. Two, if she counted Devlin. But she kept that knowledge to herself.

The Viscountess said, "I believe you are familiar with a tavern owner named Jamie Knox."

"I have heard of him," Kat said warily.

The Viscountess glanced over at her. "I should tell you that I know quite a bit about Russell Yates and his various . . . activities." She paused, then added, "My information does not come from Devlin."

Kat understood only too well what that meant. Kat's own encounters with this woman's father, Lord Jarvis, had been brutal, terrifying, and nearly fatal. He had promised her torture and a heinous death, and while that threat had abated, it had not disappeared. Kat knew he was simply waiting for the right opportunity to strike. She had to call upon all of her years of theatrical training to keep her voice sounding calm. "And?"

"I gather this Knox is one of your husband's . . . shall we call them 'associates'?"

Kat drew up abruptly and swung to face her. "Exactly what are you trying to say?"

The Viscountess met her gaze. "I think Knox is a danger to Devlin. I also think you know more about the man than you are willing to let on—even to Devlin."

Kat was aware of the darkening clouds pressing down on them, promising more rain. She could feel the dampness in the breeze, smell the earthy scent of the vegetables in the market stalls.

When she remained silent, the Viscountess said, "I can understand the problems that are created by divided loyalties."

Kat gave a startled laugh and turned to continue walking. "Well, I suppose that's one more thing you and I have in common, is it not?"

"My father at least is not trying to kill Devlin."

Kat glanced over at her. "Can you be so certain?"

Something flared in the other woman's eyes, quickly hidden. They continued along the side of the square for a moment; then the Viscountess said, "I don't know exactly what happened to cause the estrangement between you and Devlin last winter. But I believe you still care for him—at least enough not to want to see him hurt. Or dead."

"I think you underestimate your husband."

"He's mortal."

Kat stopped again. The wind was flapping the draping on the market stalls, scuttling handbills across the wet cobbles. She said, "Why did you come here?"

A gleam of unexpected amusement shone in the woman's eyes. "I should have thought that was rather obvious."

"My God," whispered Kat as understanding suddenly dawned. "You love him."

Rather than respond, the Viscountess simply tilted her head and turned away.

"Why are you so afraid to admit it?" Kat called after her. "You don't want to acknowledge it even to yourself, do you?"

She thought the woman would keep walking. Instead, the Viscountess paused to look back at her. "I would have expected you to understand that better than anyone."

"He is no longer my lover," said Kat, knowing exactly what the other woman meant. "He hasn't been, for nearly a year."

"No. But that doesn't mean he isn't still in love with you . . . as you are with him."

"Devlin will always love me," said Kat. "No matter who else he comes to love. He doesn't love easily, but once he lets someone into his heart, they are there forever. It's simply the way he is. It's the same reason he will always love Hendon, however much he might wish it were otherwise."

Kat saw the puzzlement in the other woman's eyes, and she thought, *Oh, Sebastian; you haven't told her. Why haven't you told her?*

Aloud, Kat said, "Have you ever seen Jamie Knox?"

"No; why?"

Because if you were to see him, thought Kat, *you would know.* But all she said was, "You're right; he is dangerous. For your sake as well as Devlin's, you would do well to stay away from him."

With any other woman, the warning might have worked. But this woman was Jarvis's daughter. Kat watched a thoughtful gleam light the Viscountess's eyes.

And knew she'd just made a terrible mistake.

Sebastian left his sister Amanda's house and drove through the slackening rain to the Strand.

He paused at a butcher shop near Villers Street to buy a side of ham, then continued on to the half-cleared stretch of land that fell away steeply from the street to the site of the new bridgehead. The river was running swollen and sullen with the rain, a pockmarked expanse of muddy water that frothed and boiled around the new piers. Against the dull gray sky, the soaring arches of the bridge itself stood out pale and stark.

Reining in, he let his gaze drift over the work site. Far to the left rose the massive neoclassical elevation of the new Somerset House, bustling now with its usual assortment of functionaries; to the right lay the Savoy Chapel and its burial ground, the sole surviving relics of the vast medieval palace that had once stood here. In the dreary light of day, the rain-washed expanse of churned mud, sodden weeds, and broken walls looked forlorn and empty.

The night before, in the hour or more that had elapsed between when he sent word of Arceneaux's shooting to Bow Street and the arrival of Sir Henry, Sebastian had scoured these ruins in an increasingly wide but ultimately futile search for a certain scruffy black and brown dog with a white blaze down his nose and a weakness for ham. He wasn't entirely certain what he thought he could do today that he hadn't done the previous night, but he felt compelled to try.

"If you were an injured dog," he said to Tom, "where would you go?"

The tiger screwed up his face with the labor of thought, his gaze, like Sebastian's, studying the rain-drenched riverbank. After a moment, he said, "Ain't we just downriver from the Adelphi?"

"We are."

"Well, if that Frenchy lieutenant used to 'ang around Miss Tennyson and them two boys, then I reckon maybe 'is little dog'd go there—if 'e could make it that far. Plenty o' places to 'ide in them vaults under the terrace."

Sebastian reached for the ham. "Tom, you are a genius."

Chapter 42

*I*gnoring the curious stares and ribald comments that followed him, Sebastian plunged deep into the dank, shadowy subterranean world of the Adelphi.

"Chien," he called, unwrapping the ham. "À *moi*, Chien. Chien?"

He tromped through the warehouses of the wine merchants, their owners' angry shouts and threats following him; he scrambled over dusty coal piles and penetrated deep into the dank recesses of the wharf's vast stables.

"Chien?"

He stood with one hand on his hip, watched the dust motes drift lazily in the gloom, breathed in the odor of manure and moldy hay. "Chien!" he bellowed, his voice echoing through the cavernous, high-vaulted space.

Blowing out a long, frustrated breath, he turned to leave . . .

And heard a faint, plaintive whimper.

"Can you help him?" Sebastian asked.

Paul Gibson stared down at the dog that lay stretched out and panting on the table in the front room of his surgery. "Well, I don't suppose dogs are *that* much different from people, when it comes right down to it." He probed the bloody wound in the dog's shoulder with gentle fingers and frowned. "Leave him with me. I'll see what I can do."

"Thank you," said Sebastian, turning toward the door.

"But if word of this ever reaches my esteemed colleagues at St. Thomas's," Gibson called after him, "I'll never forgive you."

The ancient, soot-stained church of St. Helen's Bishopsgate squatted like a ragged wet hen in the midst of its swollen graveyard.

Wearing a plain cloak with the hood drawn up against the drizzle, Hero wandered amongst the overgrown churchyard's gray, lichen-covered headstones and broken tombs, her gaze narrowing as she studied the yard of the gable-ended public house that backed onto the ancient priory grounds. The sky had taken on the color of old lead, the leafy boughs of the elms overhead hanging heavy with the weight of the day's rain. She could easily trace the line of the Roman wall that Gabrielle had once come here to examine; it ran from the rear of the churchyard along the inn's court to disappear between the Black Devil and the decrepit structure beside it.

So absorbed was she in her study of the ancient masonry that it was a moment before she became aware of a tall gentleman dressed all in black walking toward her. He wore black trousers tucked into high black boots, a black coat, and a black waistcoat. Only his shirt was white, the high points of his collar standing out stark against the darkness of his cravat. He had the lean, loose-limbed carriage of a soldier and the grace of a born athlete. His hair was dark, darker even than Devlin's, although he had Devlin's high cheekbones and fine facial structure. But it was his eyes that instantly drew and held her attention. And she knew then why Kat Boleyn had warned her away from this man—understood exactly what the actress had been trying to keep her from seeing—and guessing.

"I know who you are," he said, pausing some half a dozen feet before her.

"Then you have the advantage of me."

He swept her a bow tinged with just a hint of mockery. "I beg your pardon. Please allow me to introduce myself. Mr. Jamie Knox, at your service."

His accent was not that of a gentleman.

"Ah," she said noncommittally.

He straightened, his gently molded mouth curving into a smile that did not touch those strange yellow eyes. "Why are you here?"

"What makes you assume I am here for any reason other than to study the architecture and monuments of St. Helen's? Did you know it was once the parish church of William Shakespeare?"

"No. But I don't think you're here because of some long-dead scribbler. Are you spying on us, then?"

"And if I were to do so, would I see anything interesting?"

His smile broadened unexpectedly, a genuine if somewhat sardonic smile, and for a moment he looked so much like Devlin that the resemblance nearly took her breath. He said, "I see you left your carriage up the lane. That was not wise."

She raised one eyebrow in a deliberately haughty expression. "Are you threatening me?"

He laughed. "Me? Ach, no. But the neighborhood's not the best. You never know what might happen to a young gentlewoman such as yourself, all alone on a wet, gloomy day such as this."

She slipped her right hand into the reticule that hung heavily against her. "I am better able to defend myself than you may perhaps realize."

A gust of wind swelled the canopy of the trees overhead, loosing a cascade of raindrops that pattered on the aged tombstones and rank grass around them.

"That's good to know," he said, his gaze locked with hers. He took a step back and tipped his head. "Do tell your husband I said hello."

And he walked away, leaving her staring after him and wondering how he had known who she was when she herself had never seen him before that day.

Sebastian was stripping off his bloody, coal-stained shirt in his dressing room when he heard the distant pounding of the front knocker. Reaching for the pitcher, he splashed hot water into the washbasin.

An angry shout drifted up from the entry hall below, followed by a scuffle and the thump of quick feet on the stairs.

"Sir!" came Morey's outraged cry. "If you will simply wait in the drawing room, I will ascertain if his lordship— *Sir!*"

Sebastian paused, his head turning just as Charles Tennyson d'Eyncourt, the honorable member from Lincolnshire, came barreling through the dressing room door.

"You bloody interfering bastard," d'Eyncourt shouted, drawing up abruptly in the center of the room. His face was red from his run up the stairs, his hands curled into fists at his sides, his cravat askew. "This is all your fault. You've ruined me! Do you hear me? You have positively *ruined* my hopes of having any significant future in government."

Sebastian nodded to the majordomo hovering in the open doorway. "It's all right, Morey; I can handle this."

The majordomo bowed and withdrew.

Sebastian reached for a towel. "Tell me how, precisely, am I supposed to have injured you?" he said to d'Eyncourt.

Gabrielle's cousin stared at him, his nostrils flaring, his chest lifting with his agitated breathing. "It's all over town!"

Sebastian dried his face and ran the towel down over his wet chest. "What is all over town?"

"About Gabrielle and her French lover. This is your fault—you and your damnable insistence on pushing your nose into other people's private affairs. I've been afraid this would come out."

Sebastian paused for a moment, his head coming up. "You knew about Lieutenant Philippe Arceneaux?"

Suddenly tight-lipped and silent, d'Eyncourt stared back at him.

Sebastian tossed the towel aside. "How? How did you know?"

D'Eyncourt adjusted the set of his lapels. "I saw them together. Indeed, it was my intention to alert Hildeyard to what was happening as soon as he returned to town. Not that anyone ever had much success in curbing Gabrielle's wild starts, but still. What else was one to do?"

"When did you see them together? Where?"

"I fail to comprehend how this is any of your—"

Sebastian advanced on him, the pompous, arrogant, self-satisfied mushroom backing away until his shoulders and rump smacked against the cupboard behind him. "I'm going to ask you one last time: when and where?"

D'Eyncourt swallowed convulsively, his eyes going wide. "I first came upon them quite by chance in the park, last—last week sometime. They were so nauseatingly absorbed in each other that they didn't even see me. I thus had the opportunity to observe them without being perceived myself. It was quite obvious what direction the wind was in with them."

Sebastian frowned. "You said that was the first time you saw them. When else?"

D'Eyncourt's tongue slipped out to moisten his lower lip. "Thursday. He was there, you know—when she had that confrontation with the tavern owner I was telling you about, at the York Steps. The two men nearly came to blows."

"Arceneaux was with her when Gabrielle quarreled with Knox?"

"If Knox is the rogue's name, then, yes."

"And when you told me about the incident, you left Arceneaux's presence out—why?"

"I should think my reasons would be self-evident. My first cousin—my *female* cousin—involved in a sordid affair with one of Napoléon's officers— Do you have any idea what this is going to do to my political career?"

Sebastian was aware of a bead of water from his wet hair running down one cheek. "A man is dead because of you, and you stand there and bleat about your bloody political career?"

D'Eyncourt put up a hand to straighten his cravat, his chin lifting and turning to one side as if to ease a kink in his neck. "What man are you suggesting is dead because of me?"

"Arceneaux!"

D'Eyncourt looked dumbfounded. "I don't know how you think you can hang his death on me, but who cares if he is dead? The man killed Gabrielle and my nephews. Or hadn't you heard?"

Sebastian swiped the back of his arm across his wet cheek. "What the devil are you talking about?"

A condescending smirk spread over d'Eyncourt's self-satisfied face. "Seems that the night before he died, Arceneaux confided to one of his fellow French officers that he killed Gabrielle and the boys." D'Eyncourt's tight smile widened. "What's the matter? Did Bow Street forget to tell you?"

Chapter 43

$\int$ir Henry Lovejoy paused beneath the protective arches of the long arcade overlooking the market square of Covent Garden. The rain had started up again, sweeping in great windblown sheets over the shuttered stalls and lean-tos in the square. He was not a man prone to profanity, but at the moment the urge to give vent to his anger against Charles Tennyson d'Eyncourt was undeniably powerful.

He swallowed hard and said to the man who stood beside him, "I would like to apologize, my lord. I had not intended for you to learn of this development in such a manner."

"Never mind that," said Devlin. "How did this come about?"

"A gentleman approached us this morning with word that Arceneaux's death had inspired one of his fellow French officers to come forward with the information."

"What's this officer's name?"

"Alain Lefevre—an infantry captain, I believe, taken at Badajos. He says Arceneaux confessed whilst in his cups to having stabbed Miss Tennyson in the midst of a lover's quarrel."

"And the two boys, Alfred and George?"

"He says Arceneaux claimed at first to have been overcome with remorse for what he'd done, so that he set out to drive the boys back to London. Only, he panicked and decided to kill the boys too, in an attempt to cover up his guilt. The children's bodies are hidden in a ditch or gully somewhere. We've set men out searching the routes between the moat and the city, but at this point it's becoming doubtful the poor lads' bodies will ever be found."

Devlin kept his gaze focused on the square, where loose cabbage leaves fluttered in the wind. "I'd be interested to speak with this Lefevre."

"Unfortunately, the man is already on his way back to France."

Devlin swung his head to stare at him. "He what?"

"As a reward for his cooperation. I understand they thought it best to get him out of the country quickly, for his own protection."

An eddy of wind blew a fine mist in their faces. Lovejoy removed his spectacles and wiped them with his handkerchief before carefully fitting them back on his face. "His information does fit the facts as we know them."

"Only if one were unacquainted with Philippe Arceneaux."

When Lovejoy remained silent, the Viscount said, "What was the basis of Arceneaux's quarrel with Miss Tennyson supposed to have been?"

"Lefevre did not know. But there are some recent developments that may shed light on the subject. Earlier today, four paroled French officers were captured attempting to escape to France. One of the men retaken—a hussar captain named Pelletier—was reputedly one of Arceneaux's intimates."

Devlin frowned. "Is this Pelletier a big bear of a man with blond lovelocks and a long mustache?"

"That sounds like him, yes. Do you know him?"

"I've seen him. When did the escaping men leave London?"

"Sometime before dawn this morning, we believe. They were

found hidden in the back of a calico printer's cart that had been fitted out with benches on the inside. The speculation is that there were originally to have been six men involved in the escape attempt, with Arceneaux being one of the missing men, and the other being the French officer you killed when he attacked you in Covent Garden the other night. There appears to have been some sort of falling out amongst the conspirators, which is doubtless why Arceneaux was killed—for fear that he meant to betray them."

"Does this hussar captain, Pelletier, confirm that?"

"All of the fugitives taken up are refusing to speak to anyone about anything. One of the constables attempting to retake the men was shot and killed, which means they'll all now hang for murder." Lovejoy shook his head. "Shocking, is it not? For officers to go back on their sworn word . . . It displays such an utter want of all the feelings and instincts of a gentleman."

Lovejoy expected Devlin, as a former military man himself, to be particularly harsh in his condemnation of any officer who so dishonored himself. The Viscount was silent for a moment, his eyes narrowing as he stared out at the rain. But when he finally spoke, his voice was oddly tight. "I suppose they were homesick and despaired of ever seeing France again. Sometimes it does seem as if this war will never end."

"I suppose so, but—"

Devlin turned toward him suddenly, an arrested expression on his face. "Did you say a *calico printer's* cart?"

Lovejoy blinked. "Yes. Although I fear we may never determine precisely which calico printer is involved—if indeed one is. You find that significant for some reason, my lord?"

"It just may be."

Jamie Knox was supervising the loading of a dray in the rain-washed courtyard of Calvert's Brewery in Upper Thames Street when Sebastian came to stand under the arch. Propping one shoulder against the rough bricks, he crossed his arms at his chest and watched the tavern owner at work.

The air was heavy with the yeasty smell of fermenting hops, the tang of wet stone and brick, the odor of fish rising off the nearby rain-churned river. Knox threw him one swift glance but continued barking orders to the men lashing barrels to his wagon's high bed. He conferred for a moment with his driver. Then he walked over to stand in front of Sebastian, rainwater running down his cheeks, his yellow eyes hooded.

"You're obviously here for a reason; what is it, then?"

Sebastian stared into the lean, fine-boned face that was so much like his own. "I know why you killed Philippe Arceneaux."

Knox let out a bark of laughter. "That's rich. So tell me, then; what reason would I have for killing this young French—ah, lieutenant, was he not?"

"He was." Sebastian stood back as a cart piled with sacks of hops and drawn by a bay shire horse turned in under the arch, steam rising from the animal's wet hide, hooves clattering over the cobbles. "I noticed there's a calico printer's shop across the lane from your tavern."

"So there is. But there must be several dozen or more calico printers scattered across London. So if you're thinking there's any connection between the calico printer's cart I hear those four escaping French officers were taken up in and my tavern, then let me tell you right now, you're fair and far out."

"I might have believed you if I hadn't discovered that Philippe Arceneaux was present at that little set-to you had with Miss Tennyson last Thursday at the York Steps. I'm thinking there's a reason you left that detail out, and this is it."

Knox stood with his hands on his slim hips, his cheeks slightly hollowed, a faint smile dancing around his mouth as if he were amused.

Sebastian said, "You see, I'm thinking there were originally supposed to be six Frenchmen in that cart, with Arceneaux being one
of them. Only, somehow the woman he loved—that would be
Miss Tennyson, by the way—found out he was planning to escape
and begged him to stay. So he backed out."

"An interesting theory, to be sure. Although I fail to see what
the hell any of this has to do with me."

Sebastian watched the team of heavy dapple grays hitched to
Knox's beer wagon lean into their collars. "I'm told that six hundred
and ninety-two paroled French officers have escaped—or attempted
to escape—from England in the past three years. That's an extraordinary number of men. Is that how you pay for the French wine
and brandy you smuggle in? With escaped prisoners of war?"

The rain drummed around them, pounding on the puddles in
the courtyard and sluicing off the brewery's high roof. Knox stared
back at him, silent, watchful.

Sebastian said, "It's a clever, lucrative rig you're running, but it's
also dangerous. Did Gabrielle Tennyson discover what you were
doing? Is that why you were quarreling with her by the York Steps
last Thursday? Because there's some men who might consider that
kind of threat a good motive for murder, if they thought a woman
was going to give their game away. Did Arceneaux accuse you of
killing her, I wonder? Did you decide to kill him before he could
cause you any trouble?"

A cold, dangerous light glittered in the depths of the rifleman's
eyes. "And the two lads? Am I to have killed them too, just for the
sport of it?"

"In my experience there's a certain kind of man who can turn
decidedly lethal when he's feeling cornered. Maybe you saw an opportunity to strike against her and you didn't let the fact that the
boys were there, too, stop you."

"And what was I doing out at that moat with Miss Tennyson
and the two brats? Mmm? You tell me that. You think she drove out

there with me? Her in love with Arceneaux and thinking me a smuggler and all-around degenerate character?"

It was the one inescapable flaw in Sebastian's theory, and he'd known it when he decided to approach the rifleman. "I don't know why she went out there with you. Maybe you followed her. Maybe she wasn't even killed at the moat. Maybe that's why the two lads' bodies have never been found, because you killed and buried them someplace else."

The tight smile was back around Knox's lips. "Someplace such as St. Helen's churchyard, perhaps? Now, there's a clever place to hide a couple of bodies, don't you think? In a graveyard full of moldering corpses?"

"Perhaps," said Sebastian. "Then again, it's always possible you didn't kill Miss Tennyson at all—that someone else killed her for a different reason entirely. But Arceneaux would have no way of knowing that, would he? Something he said to me the other day suggested he was afraid he might be responsible for what had happened to her. So maybe he accused you of killing her, even when you hadn't. Maybe he threatened to expose you once his friends escaped. The timing of his death is curious, wouldn't you agree?"

All trace of amusement had drained from the rifleman's face, leaving it hard and tight. "I've killed many men in my day; what soldier hasn't? But I've never killed a woman or a child, and I've never murdered a man in cold blood."

The two men stared at each other. The rain poured around them, loud in Sebastian's ears. He settled his hat lower on his forehead. "If I find out you shot Philippe Arceneaux, I'll see you hang for it."

Brother or no brother, he thought. But he didn't say it.

Chapter 44

$\mathcal{S}$ ebastian stood at the top of the Cole Harbour Steps, the storm-churned waters of the Thames slapping the ancient masonry at his feet. Behind him loomed the soot-covered brick walls of the brewery and the steelyard beyond that. Dark clouds pressed down on the city, heavy with the promise of rain.

More and more, he was beginning to think there was something in Gabrielle Tennyson's life that he was missing, something that would explain the puzzle that was her death and the mysterious disappearance of her two young cousins. He had pieced together much of it—her love for the scholarly young French lieutenant, the conflicts swirling around her work on the legends of King Arthur and Camelot, the ill-fated escape attempt by Arceneaux's fellow officers. But something still eluded him. And he couldn't shake the growing conviction that the missing children were the key.

Had Gabrielle and the two boys driven up to Camlet Moat in the company of their killer? Or was her body simply planted there for reasons Sebastian could only guess at? Why would the killer leave Gabrielle at the moat and then take her young cousins else-where to kill or bury them? *Had* the cousins been killed, or were they even now out there, somewhere, alive?

Sebastian turned, his gaze narrowing as he stared up the river. From here he could look beyond the soot-blackened expanse of Blackfriars Bridge to the distant bend marked by the rising arches of the new Strand Bridge. Farther beyond that, lost in the mist, lay the imposing facade of the Adelphi. An idea was forming in his mind, a scenario that made more sense as the different possibilities he was looking at spiraled narrower and narrower.

Swinging away from the river, he darted through the rain to Upper Thames Street, where he flagged down a hackney and di-rected the driver to Tower Hill.

"Come to collect your dog, have you?" asked Gibson, limping ahead of Sebastian down his narrow hall.

Sebastian swung off his wet cloak and swiped his sleeve across his dripping face. "Is he going to be all right, then?"

Gibson led the way into his tattered, cluttered parlor, where the little black and brown dog raised his head, his tail thumping against the worn rug in welcome. But Chien made no effort to get up, and Sebastian could see blood still seeping through the thick bandage at his shoulder.

"It might be better if you left him with me a wee bit longer, just so I can keep an eye on him." Gibson rasped a hand across his chin, which from the looks of things he hadn't bothered to shave that morning. "Although there's no denying he's a sore trial."

"What have you been doing, Chien? Hmm?" Sebastian went to hunker down beside the dog. "Stealing the ham Mrs. Federico had intended for our good surgeon's dinner?"

"As a matter of fact, he tried. But that's not the worst of it. I let him out in the yard to answer nature's call, and what does he do but bring me back a bone. Thankfully, he wasn't chewing on it—just presented it to me like he'd found something precious and expected a reward."

"Did Mrs. Federico see it?" Gibson's housekeeper, Mrs. Federico, was both extraordinarily squeamish about her employer's activities and blissfully ignorant of what lay buried in his yard.

"Fortunately, no. But if he starts digging holes out there, I'm going to be in trouble." Gibson eyed Sebastian darkly. "Go on, then, laugh if you want. But if you're not here for the dog, then why are you here?"

"Do you still have the clothes Gabrielle Tennyson was wearing when she was murdered?"

"I do, yes. Why?"

"Something's been bothering me."

Sebastian found Hero sipping a hot cup of tea in the drawing room. She wore a sarcenet walking dress and her hair was damp, as if she had just come in out of the rain. He set a brown paper–wrapped bundle on the table beside her and said, "I'm beginning to think it's more and more likely that Gabrielle Tennyson was actually murdered in London and then taken up to Camlet Moat."

Hero looked at him over the rim of her cup. "I thought Gibson said there was no evidence that she'd been moved after death."

"He did. But just because he found no evidence of it doesn't mean it didn't happen." He untied the string holding the bundle together. "This is what Gabrielle was wearing when she was killed. Is it the sort of thing she would be likely to put on to go up to Enfield?"

She reached out to touch one of the gown's short puffed sleeves, a quiver passing over her features as she studied the blood-stained tear in the bodice. "The material is delicate, but it is a walking dress, just the sort of thing a woman might wear for a stroll in the country, yes." She turned over the froth of petticoats to look at the peach half boots. Then she frowned.

"What is it?" asked Sebastian, watching her.

"Is this everything?"

"Yes. Why?"

"She had a pretty peach spencer with ruched facings and a stand-up collar I would have expected her to be wearing with this. Only, it isn't here."

"Sunday was quite hot. She might have left the spencer in the carriage. The shade in the wood is certainly dense enough that she wouldn't have needed to worry about protecting her arms from the sun."

"True. But I wouldn't have expected her to take off her bonnet, as well. She had a lovely peach silk and velvet bonnet she would have worn to pick up the color of the sash and these half boots. And it's not here, either."

"Would you recognize the spencer and bonnet if you found them in her dressing chamber?"

Hero met his gaze. Then she set aside her tea and rose to her feet. "I'll get my cloak."

"Hildeyard could have already directed Gabrielle's abigail to dispose of her clothes," said Hero as they drove through the rain, toward the river.

"I doubt it. His energy has been focused on the search for the missing children. And even if he did, the woman will surely remember what was there."

Hero was silent for a moment, her gaze on the wet streets. "If you're right, and Gabrielle was killed here in London, then what do you think happened to the children?"

"I'd like to think they're in the city someplace, hiding—that they ran away in fear after witnessing the murder. But if that were true, I think they'd have been found by now."

She turned to look at him. "You think it's d'Eyncourt, don't you? You think he killed George and Alfred over the inheritance and hid their bodies someplace they'll never be found. And then he drove Gabrielle up to Camlet Moat to make it look as if her death were somehow connected to the excavations or her work on the Arthurian legends."

Sebastian nodded. "I keep going back to the way he was just sitting there, calmly reading *The Courier* in White's. What kind of man wouldn't be out doing everything he could to search for his own brother's children? He's either more despicable than I thought, or—"

"Or he knew they were already dead," said Hero, finishing the thought for him.

They arrived at the Adelphi to find Hildeyard Tennyson still up at Enfield.

Rather than attempt to explain their mission to the servants, Hero claimed to have forgotten something during her previous visit and ran up the stairs to Gabrielle's room, while Sebastian asked to see the housekeeper and returned George Tennyson's poem to her.

"Oh, your lordship, I'm ever so grateful for this," said Mrs. O'Donnell, tearfully clasping the paper to her ample bosom. "I thought sure you must've forgotten it, but I didn't feel right asking you for it."

"My apologies for keeping it so long," said Sebastian with a bow.

Looking up, he saw Hero descending the stairs. Their gazes met. He bowed to Mrs. O'Donnell again and said, "Ma'am."

He waited until he and Hero were back out on the pavement before saying, "Well?"

Hero was looking oddly flushed. "All her things are still there; Hildeyard obviously hasn't had the will to touch any of it yet. I found the spencer and bonnet immediately. In fact, it looked as if Gabrielle had worn them to church that morning and hadn't put them away properly because she was planning to wear them again."

The mist swirled around them, thickening so fast he could barely see the purple skirt and yellow kerchief of the old Gypsy fortune-teller at the end of the terrace. Sebastian said, "Well, we can eliminate Sir Stanley from the list of suspects; he would never have taken Gabrielle's body to the one place certain to cast suspicion on him. And while I wouldn't put it beyond Lady Winthrop to cheerfully watch her husband hang for a murder she herself committed, the logistics—" He broke off.

"What?" asked Hero, her gaze following his.

Today the Gypsy had a couple of ragged, barefoot children playing around her skirts: a girl of perhaps five and a boy a few years older. "That Gypsy woman. I noticed her here on Monday. If she was here last Sunday as well, she might have seen something."

"The constables questioned everyone on the street," said Hero as Sebastian turned their steps toward the Gypsies. "Surely they would have spoken to her already."

"I've no doubt they did. But you can ask a Rom the same question ten times and get ten different answers."

The Gypsy children came running up to them, bare feet pattering on the wet pavement, hands outstretched, eyes wide and pleading. "Please, sir, lady; can you spare a sixpence? Only a sixpence! Please, please."

"Go away," said Hero.

The boy fixed Hero with a fierce scowl as his wheedling turned belligerent and demanding. "You must give us a sixpence. Give us a sixpence or I will put a curse on you."

"Don't give it to them," said Sebastian. "They'll despise you for it."

"I have no intention of giving them anything." Hero tightened her grip on her reticule. "Nor do I see why we are bothering with this Gypsy woman. If she lied to the constables, what makes you think she will tell you the truth?"

"The Rom have a saying: *Tshatshimo Romano.*"

Hero threw him a puzzled look. "What does that mean?"

"It means, 'The truth is expressed in Romany.'"

Chapter 45

"*Sarishan ryor*," Sebastian said, walking up to the fortune-teller.

The Gypsy leaned against the terrace's iron railing, her purple skirt and loose blouse ragged and tattered, her erect carriage belied by the dark, weathered skin of a face etched deep with lines. Her lips pursed, her eyes narrowing as her gaze traveled over him, silent and assessing.

"*O boro duvel atch pa leste*," he said, trying again.

She snorted and responded to him in the same tongue. "Where did you learn your Romany?"

"Iberia."

"I should have known." She turned her head and spat. "The Gitanos. They have forgotten the true language of the ancients." She eyed him thoughtfully, noting his dark hair. "You could be Rom. You have something of the look about you. Except for the eyes. You have the eyes of a wolf. Or a *jettatore*." She touched the blue and white charm tied around her neck by a leather strap. It was a *nazar*, a talisman worn to ward off the evil eye.

Sebastian was aware of Hero watching them, her face carefully wiped free of all expression. The entire conversation was taking place in Romany.

He said to the Gypsy, "I want to ask you about the lady who used to live in the second house from the corner. A tall young woman, with hair the color of chestnuts."

"You mean the one who is no more."

Sebastian nodded. "Did you see her leave the house last Sunday?"

"One day is like the next to the Rom."

"But you know which day I mean, because the next day the *shanglo* came and asked you questions, and you told them you had seen nothing."

She smiled, displaying tobacco-stained teeth. "And what makes you think I will tell you anything different? Hmm?"

"Because I am not a *shanglo*."

No one was hated by the Rom more than the *shanglo*—the Romany word for police constable.

"Did you see the woman and the two boys leave the house that day?" Sebastian asked.

The light had taken on an eerie, gauzelike quality, the mist eddying around them, wet and clammy and deadening all sound. He could hear the disembodied slap of oars somewhere unseen out on the water and the drip, drip of moisture nearer at hand. Just when he thought the Gypsy wasn't going to answer him, she said, "I saw them leave, yes. But they came back."

He realized she must have seen Gabrielle Tennyson and the two children leaving for church that morning. He said, "And after that? Did someone come to visit them? Or did they go out again?"

"Who knows? I left soon after." The Gypsy's dark gaze traveled from Sebastian to Hero. "But I saw her."

Sebastian felt his mouth go dry and a strange tingling dance across his scalp.

The old woman's lips stretched into a smile that accentuated the high, stark bones of her face. "You didn't want to hear that, did you? But it's true. She came here not that day, but the day before, in a yellow carriage pulled by four black horses. Only, there was no one home and so she went away again."

As if aware that she had suddenly become the topic of conversation, Hero glanced from him to the Gypsy, then back again. "What? What is she saying?"

Sebastian met the old woman's dark, unblinking eyes. "I want to know the truth, whatever it might be."

The old woman snorted. "You just heard it. Now the question becomes, what will you make of it?"

They walked along the edge of the terrace, the sound of their footsteps echoing hollowly in the white void. Sebastian could feel the mist damp against his face. The opposite bank, the wherries on the river, even the tops of the tall brick houses beside them had all disappeared behind the thick white blur of fog.

It was Hero who broke the silence, saying, "Where did you learn to speak Romany?"

"I traveled with a band of Gypsies for a time, in the Peninsula."

She stared at him, her gaze solemn. "And are you going to tell me what the woman said?"

"She says you came to see Gabrielle on Saturday. And don't even think about denying it because she described your carriage and horses. Did you not notice her? Or did you simply assume she wouldn't recognize you?"

He watched as her lips parted on a suddenly indrawn breath. Then she said, "Ah," and turned her head away to gaze out at the fog-choked river.

He studied her tense profile, the smooth curve of her cheek, the faint betraying line of color that rode high along the bone. "There's only one reason I can come up with that would explain why you've kept this from me, and that's because Jarvis is somehow involved. Am I right?"

"He says he didn't kill her."

"And you believe him?"

She hesitated a moment too long. "Yes."

He gave a sharp bark of laughter. "You don't exactly sound convinced."

The figure of a man materialized out of the mist and walked toward them, a workman in rough clothes with what looked like a seaman's bag slung over one shoulder.

Sebastian saw the flush along her cheekbones darken now with anger. He said, "Tell me what's going on."

"You know I can't."

He gave a ringing laugh. "Well, I suppose that answers the question about where your loyalties lie."

"Does it?" She brought her gaze back to his face. "You think I should betray my father to you? So tell me, would you expect me to betray you to him?" She laid her hand on the soft swell of her belly. "And twenty years from now, if this child is a girl, would you think it right that she betray *you* to whatever man she marries?"

When he remained silent, she said, "Have you been so honest with me, Devlin? Will you tell me why you can't even bear to be in the same room with your father? And will you tell me about Jamie Knox? Will you tell me why a common ex-rifleman and tavern owner looks enough like my husband to be his brother? Neither one of us has been exactly open with the other, have we?"

"No," said Sebastian, just as the man passing them pivoted quickly, his bag slumping to the pavement as he raised a cudgel and brought it down hard across Sebastian's back.

The breath left his body in a huff, the pain of the blow dropping him to his knees.

Sebastian fumbled for the dagger in his boot, fought to draw air back into his lungs. He saw the man raise his club to strike again, was aware of Hero beside him, her hands at her reticule.

Then she drew a small walnut-handled pistol from her reticule, pulled back the hammer, and fired point-blank into the assailant's chest.

"*Jesus Christ,*" yelped Sebastian as the man staggered back and went down, hard. He gave a jerking kick with one leg, the worn heel of his boot skittering over the wet paving.

Then he lay still.

"Is he dead?" Hero asked.

His dagger held at the ready in his hand, Sebastian went to crouch beside the man.

He looked to be somewhere in his thirties or early forties, his body thick and hard, his face darkened by the weather, his hair a light brown, badly cut. A thin trickle of blood ran from the corner of his mouth; his eyes were already glazing over. Sebastian dropped his gaze to the pulverized mess that was the man's chest.

"He's dead."

"Are you all right?"

He twisted around to look at her over his shoulder. She stood straight and tall, her face pale but composed. But he could see her nostrils flaring with her rapid breathing, and her lips were parted, as if she were fighting down an upsurge of nausea. "Are you?"

She swallowed, hard. "Yes."

His gaze dropped to the pistol in her hand. It was a beautiful if deadly little piece, a small muff flintlock with a burnished walnut stock and engraved gilt mounts. "Where did you get that?"

"My father gave it to me."

"And taught you to use it?"

"What would be the point in my having it otherwise?"

Sebastian nodded to the dead man. "Is he one of your father's men?"

"Good heavens, no. I've never seen him before."

Sebastian drew in an experimental deep breath that sent a white flash of pain shooting across his back and around his side, so that he had to pause with one arm propped on his bent knee and pant for a minute.

She watched him, a frown drawing her brows together. "Are you certain you're all right? Shall I get one of the footmen to help you up?"

"Just give me a moment." He tried breathing again, more cautiously this time. "Are you going to tell me about the connection between Childe and your father?" he asked when he was able. "That is how Jarvis comes into this, isn't it?"

She met his gaze. "You know I can't do that. But I see no reason why you can't ask him about it yourself."

Sebastian grunted and reached out to grasp one of the dead man's arms and haul the lifeless body up over his shoulder.

She watched him. "Is that wise, considering you are hurt?"

He pushed to his feet with another grunt, staggering slightly under the dead man's weight.

"What are you doing?" she asked.

"Taking your father a present."

He thought she might object.

But she didn't.

Chapter 46

 $\mathscr{J}$ ebastian's knock at the house on Berkeley Square was answered
by Jarvis's butler, who took one look at the bloody corpse slung over
Sebastian's shoulders and staggered back with a faint mew of horror.

"Good afternoon, Grisham," said Sebastian, pushing past him
into the elegant entrance hall.

"Good gracious, Lord Devlin; is that . . . is that man *dead*?"

"Decidedly. Is his lordship home?"

Grisham stared in awful fascination at the dead man's flopping
arms and blue-tinged hands. Then he seemed to recollect himself,
swallowed hard, and cleared his throat. "I fear Lord Jarvis is not at
present—"

A burst of male laughter filtered down from the floor above.

"In the drawing room, is he?" Sebastian headed for the delicately curving staircase that wound toward the upper floors, then
paused on the first step to look back at Grisham. "I trust there are
no ladies present?"

"No, my lord. But—but— My lord! You can't mean to take
that—that corpse into his lordship's drawing room?"

"Don't worry; I suspect Bow Street will want to come collect it.

Perhaps you could dispatch someone to advise them of the need to do so?"

Grisham gave a dignified bow. "I will send someone right away, my lord."

Charles, Lord Jarvis stood with his back to the empty hearth, a glass of sherry in one hand. "The Americans have shown themselves to be an abomination," he was telling the gentlemen assembled before him. "What they have done will go down in history as an insult not only to civilization but to God himself. To attack Britain at a time when all our resources are directed to the critical defense against the spread of atheism and republican fervor—"

He broke off as Viscount Devlin strode into the room with a man's bloody body slung over his shoulders.

Every head in the room turned toward the door. A stunned silence fell over the company.

"What the devil?" demanded Jarvis.

Devlin leaned forward and shrugged his shoulder to send the slack-jawed, vacant-eyed corpse sprawling across Jarvis's exquisite Turkey carpet. "We need to talk."

Jarvis felt a rare surge of raw, primitive rage, brought quickly under control. "Is this your version of a brace of partridges?"

"The kill isn't mine. He was shot by an elegant little muff pistol with a burnished walnut handle and engraved brass fittings. I believe you're familiar with it?"

Jarvis met Devlin's glittering gaze for one intense moment. Then he turned to his gawking guests. "My apologies, gentlemen, for the disturbance. If you will please excuse us?"

The assemblage of men—which Sebastian now noticed included the Prime Minister, the First Lord of the Admiralty, and three other cabinet members—exchanged veiled glances, and then, murmuring amongst themselves, filed from the room.

Sebastian found himself oddly relieved to notice that Hendon was not one of them.

Jarvis went to close the door behind them with a snap. "I trust you have a damned good explanation for this?"

"Actually, that's what I'm here to ask you. I want to know why the hell my wife and I were attacked by—"

"*Hero?* Is she all right? My God. If my daughter has been harmed in any way—"

"She has not—with no thanks to you."

"I fail to understand why you assume this has anything to do with me. The world must be full of people only too eager to put paid to your existence."

"He's not one of your men?"

"He is not."

Devlin's gaze narrowed as he studied Jarvis's face. "And would you have me believe you didn't set someone to follow me earlier this week?"

Jarvis took another sip of his sherry. "The incompetent bumbling idiot you chased through the Adelphi was indeed in my employ—although he is no longer. But I had nothing to do with"—he gestured with his glass toward the dead man on the carpet—"this. Who is he?"

"If I knew, I wouldn't be here."

Jarvis went to peer down at the dead man. "Something of a ruffian, I'd say, from the looks of him." He shifted his gaze to the dead man's torn, bloody shirt. "Hero did this?"

"She did."

Jarvis looked up, his jaw tightening. "Believe it or not, until my daughter had the misfortune of becoming involved with you, she had never killed anyone. And now—"

"Don't," said Devlin, one hand raised as if in warning. "Don't even think of laying the blame for this on me. If Hero was in any danger this afternoon, it was because of you, not me."

"Me?"

"Two days before she died, Gabrielle Tennyson stumbled upon a forgery that involved someone so ruthless and powerful that she feared for her life. I think the man she feared was you."

Jarvis drained his wineglass, then stood regarding it thoughtfully for a moment before walking over to remove a crumpled broadsheet from a nearby bureau and hold it out. "Have you seen these?"

Devlin glanced down at the broadsheet without making any move to take it. "I have. They seem to keep going up around town faster than the authorities can tear them down."

"They do indeed, thanks to certain agents in the employ of the French. The aim is to appeal to—and promote—disaffection with the House of Hanover. I suspect they've succeeded far better than Napoléon ever dreamt."

"Actually, I'd have said Prinny does a bang-up job of doing that all by himself."

Jarvis pressed his lips into a flat line and tossed the broadsheet aside. "Dislike of a monarch is one thing. The suggestion that he sits on his throne as a usurper is something else again. The Plantagenets faced similar nonsense back in the twelfth century. You might think people today wouldn't be as credulous as their ancestors of six hundred years ago, but the idea of a messianic return has proved surprisingly appealing."

"It's a familiar concept."

"There is that," said Jarvis.

"I take it that like the Plantagenets before you, you've decided to deal with the situation by convincing the credulous that King Arthur is not, in fact, the 'once and future king,' but just another pile of moldering old bones?"

"Something like that, yes."

"So you—what? Approached a scholar well-known for his skepticism with regards to the Arthurian legend—Bevin Childe, to be precise—and somehow convinced him to come forward with the astonishing claim of having found the Glastonbury Cross and a box of ancient bones amongst Richard Gough's collections? I suppose a competent craftsman could simply manufacture a copy of the cross from Camden's illustrations, while the bones could be acquired from any old churchyard. Of course, history tells us the cross was separated from the relevant bones long ago, but why allow details to interfere with legend?"

"Why, indeed?"

"There's just one thing I'm curious about: How did Miss Tennyson realize that it was a forgery?"

Jarvis reached into his pocket for his snuffbox. "I'm not certain that's relevant."

"But she did quarrel with Childe and throw the forgery into the lake."

"Yes. A most choleric, impetuous woman, Miss Tennyson."

"And determined too, I gather. Which means that as long as she was alive, your plan to convince the credulous that you had King Arthur's bones was not going to succeed."

Jarvis opened his snuffbox with the flick of one finger. "I am not generally in the habit of murdering innocent gentlewomen and their young cousins—however troublesome they may make themselves."

"But you would do it, if you thought it necessary."

"There is little I would not do to preserve the future of the monarchy and the stability of the realm. But in the general scheme of things, this really wasn't all that important. There would have been other ways of dealing with the situation besides murdering my daughter's troublesome friend."

"Such as?"

Jarvis lifted a small pinch of snuff to one nostril and sniffed. "You don't seriously expect me to answer that, do you?"

Devlin's lips flattened into a thin, hard line. "Last night, someone shot and killed a paroled French officer named Philippe Arceneaux. Then, this morning, one of Arceneaux's fellow officers supposedly stepped forward with the information that before his death, Arceneaux had confessed to the killings. As a reward, our conveniently community-minded French officer was immediately spirited out of the country. The only person I can think of with the power—and the motive—to release a French prisoner that quickly is you."

Jarvis closed his snuffbox. "Of course it was I."

"And you had Philippe Arceneaux shot?"

"I won't deny I took advantage of his death to shut down the inconvenient investigation into the Tennysons' murders. But did I order him killed? No."

"The *inconvenient investigation*? Bloody hell. Inconvenient for whom?"

"The Crown, obviously."

"Not to mention you and this bloody Glastonbury Cross scheme of yours."

When Jarvis remained silent, Devlin said, "How the devil did you convince Childe to lend his credibility to such a trick?"

"Mr. Childe has certain somewhat aberrant tastes that he would prefer others not know about."

"How aberrant?"

Jarvis tucked his snuffbox back into his pocket. "Nothing he can't indulge at the Lambs' Pen."

"And did Gabrielle Tennyson know about Childe's aberrations?"

"Possibly."

"So how do you know Childe didn't kill the Tennysons?"

"I don't. Hence the decision to shut down the investigation. It wouldn't do to have this murder be seen as linked in any way to the Palace." Jarvis straightened his cuffs. "It's over, Devlin; a murderer has been identified and punished with his own death."

Devlin nodded to the dead man before them. "Doesn't exactly look over to me."

"You don't know this attack was in any way related to the Tennyson case. The authorities are satisfied. The populace has already breathed a collective sigh of relief. Let it rest."

Devlin's lip curled. "And allow the real murderer to go free? Let those boys' parents up in Lincolnshire live the rest of their lives without ever knowing what happened to their children? Let Arceneaux's grieving parents in Saint-Malo believe their son a child killer?"

"Life is seldom tidy."

"This isn't untidy. This is an abomination." He swung toward the door.

Jarvis said, "You're forgetting your body."

"Someone from Bow Street should be here for it soon." Devlin paused to look back at him. "I'm curious. What exactly made Hero think you killed Gabrielle Tennyson?"

Jarvis gave the Viscount a slow, nasty smile. "Ask her."

Chapter 47

Rather than return directly to Brook Street, Sebastian first went in search of Mr. Bevin Childe.

The Cheese, in a small cul-de-sac known as Wine Office Court, off Fleet Street, was a venerable old eating establishment popular with antiquaries and barristers from the nearby Temple. A low-voiced conversation with a stout waiter sent Sebastian up a narrow set of stairs to a smoky room with a low, planked ceiling, where he found Childe eating a Rotherham steak in solitary splendor at a table near the bank of heavy-timbered windows.

The antiquary had a slice of beef halfway to his open mouth when he looked up, saw Sebastian coming toward him, and dropped his fork with a clatter.

"Good evening," said Sebastian, slipping into the opposite high-backed settee. "I was surprised when your man told me I might find you here. It's my understanding you typically spend Fridays at Gough Hall."

The antiquary closed his mouth. "My schedule this week has been . . . upset."

"How distressing for you."

"It is, yes. You've no notion." Very slowly, the antiquary retrieved his fork, took a bite of steak, and swallowed, hard. "I . . ."
He choked, cleared his throat, and tried again. "I had hoped I'd explained everything to your wife's satisfaction yesterday at the
museum."

Sebastian kept his face quietly composed, although in truth he
didn't know what the bloody hell the man was talking about.
"You're quite certain you left nothing out?"

"No, no; nothing."

Sebastian signaled the waiter for a tankard of bitter. "Tell me
again how Miss Tennyson discovered the cross was a forgery."

Childe threw a quick, nervous glance around, then leaned
forward, his voice dropping. "It was the merest chance, actually.
She had made arrangements to drive out to Gough Hall on Friday
to see the cross. I'd been expecting her early in the day, but as time
wore on and she never arrived, I'd quite given up looking for her.
Then the craftsman who'd manufactured the cross showed up."
Childe's plump face flushed with indignation. "The scoundrel had
the unmitigated gall to come offering to make *other* artifacts. I was
in the stables telling him precisely what I thought of his suggestion
when I turned and saw her standing there. She . . . I'm afraid she
heard quite enough to grasp the truth of the situation."

"How did she know Jarvis was involved?"

Childe's tongue flicked out nervously to wet his lips. "I told her.
She was threatening to expose the entire scheme, you see. So I
warned her that she had no idea who or what she was dealing
with."

"The knowledge didn't intimidate her?"

"Unfortunately, no. If anything, it only enraged her all the
more."

Sebastian let his gaze drift over the stout man's sweat-sheened
face. "Who do you think killed her?"

Childe tittered.

"You find the question amusing?"

Childe cut another bite of his steak. "Under the circumstances? Yes."

"It's a sincere question."

He paused in his cutting to hunch forward and lower his voice. "In truth?"

"Yes."

The antiquary threw another of his quick looks around. "Jarvis. I think Lord Jarvis killed her—or rather, had her killed."

"That's interesting. Because you see, he rather thinks you might have done it."

Childe's eyes bulged. "You can't be serious. I could never have killed her. I loved her! I've loved her from the moment I first saw her. Good God, I was willing to marry her despite knowing only too well about the family's fits."

Sebastian stared at him. "About the what?"

Childe pressed his napkin to his lips. "It's not something they like to talk about, I know. And while it's true I've never seen any indication that either Hildeyard or Gabrielle suffered from the affliction, there's no doubt it's rife in the rest of the family. Their great-grandfather had it, you know. And I understand the little boys' father—that Reverend up in Lincolnshire—suffers from it dreadfully."

Sebastian stared at the man across the table from him. "What the devil are you talking about? What kind of fits?"

Childe blinked at him owlishly. "Why, the falling sickness, of course. It's why Miss Tennyson always insisted she would never marry. Even though she showed no sign of it herself, she feared that she could somehow pass it on to any children she might have. She called it the family 'curse.' It quite enraged d'Eyncourt, I can tell you."

"D'Eyncourt? Why?"

"Because while he'll deny it until he's blue in the face, the truth is that he suffers from it himself—although nothing to the extent of his brother. When we were up at Cambridge, he half killed some sizar who said he had it." Childe paused, then said it again, as if the implications had only just occurred to him. "He half killed him."

Chapter 48

Sebastian found Hero at the library table, one of Gabrielle Tennyson's notebooks spread open before her.

The pose appeared relaxed. But he could practically see the tension thrumming in every line of her being. She looked up when he paused in the doorway, a faint flush touching her cheeks. He was aware of a new sense of constraint between them, a wariness that hadn't been there before. But he couldn't think of anything to say to ease the tension between them.

She said it for him. "We haven't handled this situation well, have we? Or perhaps I should say, I have not."

He came to pull out the chair opposite her and sit down. The raw anger he'd felt, before, along the Thames, had leached out of him, leaving him unexpectedly drained and weighed down by a heaviness he recognized now as sadness.

He let his gaze drift over the tightly held lines of her face. "I'd go with 'we.'"

She said stiffly, "I might regret the situation, but I can't regret my decision."

"I suppose that makes sense. I can admire you for your loyalty to your father, even if I don't exactly agree with it."

He was surprised to see a faint quiver pass over her features. But she still had herself under rigid control. Only once had he seen her self-control break, in the subterranean chambers of Somerset House when they faced death together—and created the child she now carried within her.

He said, "I spoke to Jarvis. He said to ask you how you came to know of his involvement with Gabrielle. Did she tell you?"

"Not exactly. I was visiting my mother Friday evening when I heard angry voices below. I couldn't catch what they were saying—" A hint of a smile lightened her features. "We aren't all blessed with your hearing. But I thought I recognized Gabrielle's voice. So I went downstairs. I'd just reached the entrance hall when she came out of my father's library. I heard her say, 'I told Childe if he attempts to go ahead with this, I'll expose him—and you too.' Then she turned and saw me. She just . . . stared at me from across the hall, and then ran out of the house." Hero was silent for a moment, her face tight with grief. "I never saw her again."

"Did you ask your father what it was about?"

"I did. He said Gabrielle was an overly emotional and obviously imbalanced woman. That she'd had some sort of argument that day with Childe but that it was nothing that need concern me."

"He doesn't know you well, does he?"

She met his gaze; the smile was back in her eyes. "Not as well as he likes to think." She closed the notebook she'd been reading and pushed it aside. He realized now that it was Gabrielle's translation of *The Lady of Shalott*. She said, "I went to the Adelphi the next day to try to talk to her. Unfortunately, she was still out at the moat."

"What time was that?"

"I don't know, precisely. Midafternoon sometime. I left her a message. Later that evening, I received this from her." She withdrew a folded note from the back cover of Gabrielle's book and pushed it across the table to him.

He flipped open the paper and read,

Hero,
Believe me, I would be the last person to blame anyone else for
the actions of their family. Please do come up to see the excavations
at Camlet Moat on Monday, as we'd planned. We can discuss
all this then.
           Your friend,
           Gabrielle

Sebastian fingered the note thoughtfully, then looked up at her. "Did Gabrielle ever tell you why she was so determined never to marry?"

His question seemed to take Hero by surprise. She looked puzzled for a moment, then shook her head. "We never discussed it. I always assumed she'd decided marriage wasn't compatible with a life devoted to scholarship."

"Bevin Childe claims it was because there is epilepsy in her family and she feared passing it on to her own children."

Hero's lips parted, her nostrils flaring as she drew in a quick breath. "Epilepsy? That's the falling sickness, isn't it? Do you think Childe knows what he's talking about?"

"I'm not certain. I went by the Adelphi to try to ask Hildeyard, but he's still out searching for his cousins. There's no denying it makes sense of a number of things—all the strange statements made about the Reverend Tennyson's health, d'Eyncourt being made his father's heir, even some of the things said about the two boys."

"You think the children could suffer from it?"

"I don't know. You never saw any sign of it?"

"No. But the truth is, I know almost nothing about the affliction. Do you?"

"No." Sebastian pushed to his feet. "But I know someone who does."

"The falling sickness?"

Paul Gibson looked from Sebastian to Hero and back again. They were seated on the torn chairs of the Irishman's cluttered, low-ceilinged parlor, the black and brown dog stretched out asleep on the hearth rug beside them.

Sebastian said, "It's the more common name for epilepsy, isn't it?"

Gibson blew out a long breath. "It is, yes. But . . . I'm not sure how much I can tell you about it. I'm a surgeon, not a physician."

"You can't know less about it than we do."

"Well . . ." Gibson scrubbed one hand down over his beard-shadowed face. "It's my understanding no one knows exactly what causes it. There are all sorts of theories, of course—one wilder than the next. But there does seem to be a definite hereditary component to it, at least most of the time. I suspect there may actually be several different disorders involved, brought on by slightly different causes. Some affect mainly children; others don't seem to start until around the age of ten or twelve."

"The age at which the Old Man of the Wolds disinherited his firstborn son and changed his will to leave everything to d'Eyncourt," said Sebastian.

Hero looked at Gibson. "There's no treatment?"

"None, I'm afraid. The usual advice to sufferers is to take lots of long walks. And water."

"Water?"

"Yes. Both drinking water and taking soaking baths or going for swims is said to help. Sufferers are also—" Gibson looked at Hero and closed his mouth.

"What?" she said.

The Irishman shifted uncomfortably and threw Sebastian a pleading look. "Perhaps you could come with me into the kitchen for a wee moment?"

"You may as well say it; I'll just turn around and tell her."

Gibson shifted again and cleared his throat. "Yes, well . . . There are indications . . . That is to say, many believe that the attacks can be brought on by certain kinds of activities."

"What kind of activities?"

Gibson flushed crimson.

Hero said, "I gather you're referring to activities of a sexual nature?"

The Irishman nodded, his cheeks now darkened to a shade more like carmine.

Sebastian said, "I suspect that belief is a large part of why there is such a stigma attached to the affliction."

"It is, yes. Smoking and excessive drinking have also been identified as bringing on seizures. The interesting thing is, when we think of epilepsy, we tend to think of full seizures. But the malady can also manifest in a milder form. Sometimes sufferers will simply become unresponsive for a few minutes. They appear conscious, but it's as if they aren't there. And then they come back and they're totally unaware that anything untoward has occurred."

Sebastian noticed Hero leaning forward, her lips parted. "What?" he asked, watching her.

"Gabrielle used to do that. Not often, but I saw it happen twice. It was as if she'd just . . . go away for a minute or so. And then suddenly she would be all right."

Gibson nodded. "Sometimes the malady progresses no further. But occasionally a moment of great stress or excitement or something else we don't even understand can trigger a full seizure."

Hero glanced over at Sebastian. "If you think this is the key to Gabrielle's murder, I still don't understand it."

"I keep thinking about something Childe said to me, that Charles d'Eyncourt half killed one of the poor scholars at Cambridge who suggested he suffered from it. Most people see epilepsy as something shameful, a family secret to be kept hidden at all costs, like madness."

"And no one is more ruthless and ambitious than d'Eyncourt," said Hero. "So what are you suggesting? That young George started showing signs of epilepsy? And that when Gabrielle refused to bundle the child back up to Lincolnshire, d'Eyncourt killed her? Her and the boys, both?"

Chien lifted his head and whimpered.

"It wasn't George and d'Eyncourt I was thinking about," said Sebastian, going to hunker down beside the dog. "There's no doubt the man is an arrogant, unprincipled liar, but he's also a coward. I'm not convinced he has what it takes to haul his cousin's dead body ten miles north of London to some deserted moat he's probably never heard of and surely never seen. And I suspect if someone like Rory Forster tried to blackmail him, he'd pay the bastard off—he wouldn't arrange to meet him in a dark wood and shoot him in the chest."

Hero watched him pull the dog's ears, her eyes widening. "Good lord. You can't think *Hildeyard*— Because of Gabrielle?" She shook her head. "But that's impossible. He was in Kent."

"He was. But his estate is only four hours' hard ride from London. He could conceivably have left Kent early Sunday morning, ridden up to London, killed Gabrielle, driven her body up to Camlet Moat, and then ridden back to Kent late that night. We know he was there when the messenger arrived from Bow Street on Monday with word of Gabrielle's death, but I seriously doubt the man inquired into Mr. Tennyson's movements the previous day."

A flicker of lightning showed outside the room's narrow window, illuminating Hero's face with a flash of white that was there and then gone. "But why? Why would he do such a thing?"

"I think Gabrielle had a seizure—one much worse than anything she'd ever had before. It was probably provoked by the emotional turmoil of learning the man she loved was thinking about escaping to France, or perhaps by their lovemaking, or maybe even by the fear and anger she experienced when she discovered the truth about Childe's deception. I think she wrote her brother about it and told him he needed to warn his betrothed that there was epilepsy in the family. And that's when he rode up to London."

Thunder rumbled in the distance. "To kill her? I don't believe it."

"I don't think he came here with the intention of killing her. I think he came here to argue with her. Then he lost his temper and stabbed her in a rage."

"And murdered the children too?" Hero shook her head. "No. He's not that . . . evil."

"I seriously doubt he sees himself as evil. In fact, I suspect he even blames Gabrielle for driving him to do it. In my experience, people kill when their emotions overwhelm them—be it fear, or greed, or anger. Some are so stricken afterward with remorse that they end up destroying their own lives too. But most are selfish enough to be able to rationalize what they've done as necessary or even justified."

"The problem is," said Gibson, "you've no proof of any of this. Even if you discover Tennyson did leave his estate on Sunday, that would only prove that he could have done it, not that he did. D'Eyncourt could have done it too. Or Childe. Or Arceneaux."

"What I don't understand," said Hero, "is if you're right—and I'm not conceding that you are—then why would Hildeyard hide the children's bodies someplace else? D'Eyncourt would have a clear reason—to shift the investigation away from the children's deaths onto Gabrielle. But not Hildeyard. He's been up at Enfield every day, looking for them."

Sebastian let his hand rest on his thigh. "Has he? We know he went up there on Tuesday and made a big show of organizing a search for his cousins. But do we know for certain he's actually been there all day, every day, since then?"

She thought about it, then shook her head. "No."

"For all we know, he could have been spending the bulk of his time scouring London in the hopes of finding the children—and silencing them."

"But if they're not dead, then where are they?"

Chien nudged Sebastian's still hand, and he moved again to stroke the brown and black dog's silken coat. He was thinking about a nine-year-old boy telling Philippe he should have called his dog "Rom." Not Gypsy, but "Rom." He had a sudden image of a blue and white *nazar* worn on a leather thong around the neck of an old Gypsy woman, and an identical talisman lying on a nursery table beside a broken clay pipe bowl and a horse chestnut.

"What?" said Hero, watching him.

He pushed to his feet. "I think I know where the children are."

"You mean, you know where they're buried?"

"No. I don't think they're dead. I think they've gone with the raggle-taggle-Gypsies-oh."

Chapter 49

They drove first to the Adelphi Terrace in hopes the Gypsy woman might still be there. But the angry clouds roiling overhead had already blotted out much of the light from the setting sun. The windows in the surrounding houses gleamed golden with lamplight, and the terrace lay wet and deserted beneath a darkening sky.

"Now what do we do?" asked Hero, shouting to be heard over the din of the wind and driving rain.

Sebastian stared out over the rain-swollen river. Lightning flashed again, illuminating the underbellies of the clouds and reflecting off the choppy water. A charlie on his rounds came staggering around the corner, headed for his box. He wore an old-fashioned greatcoat and held one hand up to hold his hat against the wind; his other hand clutched a shuttered lantern.

"Sure, then, 'tis a foul night we're in for," he said when he saw them.

"It is that," agreed Sebastian. "We were looking for the Gypsy woman who's usually here reading palms. Do you know where we might find her?"

"Has she stolen something from you, sir? Nasty thieving varmints, the lot of 'em."

"No, she hasn't stolen anything. But my wife"—Sebastian nodded to Hero, who did her best to look credulous and eager—"my wife here was desirous of having her palm read."

The charlie blinked. But he was obviously inured to the strange ways of quality, because he said, "I think she belongs to that band what camps up around Nine Elms this time of year. I seen her leaving once or twice by wherry." The hamlet of Nine Elms lay on the south side of the river, beyond Lambeth and Vauxhall in a low, marshy area known for its windmills and osier stands and meadows of rue and nettle.

"Thank you," said Sebastian, turning to shout directions to his coachman and help Hero climb into the carriage.

"Funny you should be asking about them," said the charlie.

Sebastian paused on the carriage steps to look back at him. "Why's that?"

"Mr. Tennyson asked me the same thing," said the charlie, "not more'n a couple of hours ago."

They found the Gypsy camp in a low meadow near a willow-lined brook, where some half a dozen high-wheeled caravans were drawn up in a semicircle facing away from the road. Wet cook fires burnt sluggishly in the gloaming of the day, their blue smoke drifting up into the mist, the penetrating smell of burning wood and garlic and onions carrying on the wind. At the edge of the encampment, a herd of tethered horses sidled nervously, their heads tossing, their neighs mingling with the thunder that rolled across the darkening sky.

As Sebastian signaled to his coachman to pull up, a motley pack of lean yellow dogs rushed barking from beneath the wagons. A tall man wearing a broad-brimmed black hat and a white shirt came to stand beside the nearest caravan, his gaze focused on them. He made no move to approach, just stood with one hand cupped around the bowl of his clay pipe, his eyes hidden by the brim of his hat as he watched the dogs surround them.

"Now what do we do?" asked Hero as the pack leapt snapping and snarling around the carriage.

"Stay here." Throwing open the door, Sebastian jumped to the ground to scoop up a rock and hurl it into the pack. They all immediately drew back, ears flattened, tails low.

"Impressive. Did you learn that in Spain too?" Hero dropped down behind him. But he noticed she kept one hand in her reticule.

"Even if you don't have a rock, all you need to do is reach down and pretend to throw one, and the effect is the same."

"I'll try to remember that."

They crossed the waterlogged meadow toward the camp, the tall, wet grass brushing against their clothes. They could see more men, and women in full, gaily colored skirts, crouched around the fires, pretending not to notice their approach. But the children hung back in the shadows, still and quiet as they watched with dark, sullen eyes.

"*O boro duvel atch pa leste,*" called Sebastian to the lone man standing beside the nearest caravan.

The man grunted, his teeth clenching down on the stem of his pipe, his eyes fierce. He had weathered, sun-darkened skin and a bushy iron gray mustache and curly dark hair heavily laced with gray. A pale scar cut through his thick left eyebrow.

"The woman who tells fortunes near the Adelphi and the York Steps," said Sebastian, still in Romany. "We would like to speak to her."

The Gypsy stared at Sebastian, not a line in his face moving.

"I know you have two Gadje children here with you," said Sebastian, although the truth was, he didn't know it; he was still only working on a hunch. "A boy of nine and a younger child of three."

The Gypsy shifted his pipe stem with his tongue. "What do you think?" he said in English. "That we Rom are incapable of producing our own children? That we need to steal yours?"

"I'm not accusing you of stealing these children. I think you've offered them protection from the man who killed their cousin." When the Gypsy simply continued to stare at him, Sebastian said, "We mean the children no harm. But we have reason to think that the man who murdered their cousin now knows where they are."

Hero touched Sebastian's arm. "Devlin."

He turned his head. The old woman from the York Steps had appeared at the front doorway of the nearest caravan. She held by the hand a small child, his dark brown hair falling around his dirty face in soft curls like a girl's. But rather than a frock he wore a blue short-sleeved skeleton suit. The high-waisted trousers buttoned to a tight coat were ripped at one knee, the white, ruffle-collared shirt beneath it grimy. He stared at them with wide, solemn eyes.

"Hello, Alfred," said Hero, holding out her arms. "Remember me, darling?"

The Gypsy woman let go of his hand, and after a moment's hesitation, he went to Hero. She scooped him off the platform into her arms and held him tight, her eyes squeezing shut for one betraying moment.

Sebastian said, "And the older child? George?"

It was the woman who answered. "He went down the river with some of our boys to catch hedgehogs. They were coming back to camp along the road when a man in a gig drove up behind them and grabbed the lad."

"How long ago?" said Sebastian sharply.

"An hour. Maybe more."

Hero met his gaze. "Dear God," she whispered.

Fishing his engraved gold watch from his pocket, Sebastian turned back to the mustachioed Gypsy. "I'll give you four hundred pounds for your fastest horse and a saddle, with this standing as security until I can deliver the funds. And to make damned certain you give me your best horse, I'll pay you another hundred pounds if I catch up with that gig in time."

"But we don't know where they've gone," said Hero.

"No. But I can guess. I think Hildeyard is taking him to Camlet Moat."

Chapter 50

The Gypsies sold him a half-wild bay stallion that danced away, ears flat, when Sebastian eased the saddle over its back.

"I don't like the looks of that horse," said Hero. She had the little boy balanced on her hip, his head on her shoulder, his eyelids drooping.

"He's fast. That's what matters at this point." He tightened the cinch. "Lovejoy should still be at Bow Street. Tell him whatever you need to, but get him to send men out to the moat, fast."

"What if you're wrong? What if Hildeyard isn't taking George to Camlet Moat?"

"If you can think of anyplace else, tell Lovejoy." Sebastian settled into the saddle, the stallion bucking and kicking beneath him.

"Devlin—"

He wheeled the prancing horse to look back at her.

For one intense moment their gazes met and held. Then she said, "Take care. Please."

The wind billowed her skirts, fluttered a stray lock of dark hair against her pale face. He said, "Don't worry; I have a good reason to be careful."

"You mean, your son."

He smiled. "Actually, I'm counting on a girl—a daughter every bit as brilliant and strong and fiercely loyal to her sire as her mother."

She gave a startled, shaky laugh, and he nudged the horse closer so that he could reach down and cup her cheek with his hand. He wanted to tell her she was also a part of why he intended to be careful, that he'd realized how important she was to him even as he'd felt himself losing her without ever having actually made her his. He wanted to tell her that he'd learned a man could come to love again without betraying his first love.

But she laid her hand over his, holding his palm to her face as she turned her head to press a kiss against his flesh, and the moment slipped away.

"Now, go," she said, taking a step back. "Quickly."

Sebastian caught the horse ferry at the Lambeth Palace gate. The Gypsy stallion snorted and plunged with fright as the ferry rocked and pitched, the wind off the river drenching them both with spray picked up off the tops of the waves. Landing at Westminster, he worked his way around the outskirts of the city until the houses and traffic of London faded away. Finally, the road lay empty before them, and he spurred the bay into a headlong gallop.

His world narrowed down to the drumbeat of thundering hooves, the tumbling, lightning-riven clouds overhead, the sodden hills glistening with the day's rain and shadowed by tree branches shuddering in the wind. He was driven by a relentless sense of urgency and chafed by the knowledge that his assumption—that Hildeyard was taking his young cousin to Camlet Moat to kill him—could so easily be wrong. The boy might already be dead.

Or Hildeyard might be taking the lad someplace else entirely, someplace Sebastian knew nothing about, rather than bothering to bury him on or near the island in the hopes that when he was eventually found the authorities would assume he'd been there all along.

A blinding sheet of lightning spilled through the storm-churned clouds, limning the winding, tree-shadowed road with a quick flash of white. He had reached the overgrown remnant of the old royal chase. The rain had started up again, a soft patter that beat on the leaves of the spreading oaks overhead and trickled down the back of his collar.

The Gypsy stallion was tiring. Sebastian could smell the animal's hot, sweaty hide, hear its labored breathing as he turned off onto the track that wound down toward the moat. He drew the horse into a walk, his gaze raking the wind-tossed, shadowy wood ahead. In the stillness, the humus-muffled plops of the horse's hooves and the creak of the saddle leather sounded dangerously loud. He rode another hundred feet and then reined in.

Sliding off the stallion, he wrapped the reins around a low branch and continued on foot. He could feel the temperature dropping, see the beginnings of a wispy fog hugging the ground. As he drew closer to the moat he was intensely aware of his own breathing, the pounding of his heart.

The barrister's gig stood empty at the top of the embankment, the gray between the shafts grazing unconcernedly in the grass beside the track. On the far side of the land bridge, a lantern cast a pool of light over the site of Sir Stanley's recent excavations. Hildeyard Tennyson sat on a downed log beside the lantern, his elbows resting on his spread knees, a small flintlock pistol in one hand. Some eight or ten feet away, a tall boy, barefoot like a Gypsy and wearing only torn trousers and a grimy shirt, worked digging the fill out of one of the old trenches. Sebastian could hear the scrape of George Tennyson's shovel cutting into the loose earth.

The barrister had set the boy to digging his own grave.

Sebastian eased down on one knee in the thick, wet humus behind the sturdy trunk of an ancient oak. If he'd been armed with a rifle, he could have taken out the barrister from here. But the small flintlock in his pocket was accurate only at short range. Sebastian listened to the rain slapping into the brackish water of the moat, let his gaze drift around the ancient site of Camelot. With Hildeyard seated at the head of the land bridge, there was no way Sebastian could approach the island from that direction without being seen. His only option was to cut around the moat until he was out of the barrister's sight, and then wade across the water.

Sebastian pushed to his feet, the flintlock in his hand, his palm sweaty on the stock. He could hear the soft purr of a shovelful of earth sliding down the side of George's growing dirt pile. The fill was loose, the digging easy; the boy was already up to his knees in the rapidly deepening trench.

Moving quietly but quickly, Sebastian threaded his way between thick trunks of oak and elm and beech, the rain filtering down through the heavy canopy to splash around him. The undergrowth of brush and ferns was thick and wet, the ground sloppy beneath his feet. He went just far enough to be out of sight of both boy and man, then slithered down the embankment to the moat's edge. Shoving the pistol into the waistband of his breeches, he jerked off his tall Hessians and his coat. He retrieved his dagger from the sheath in his boot and held it in his hand as he eased into the stagnant water.

Beneath his stocking feet, the muddy bottom felt squishy and slick. A ripe odor of decay rose around him. He felt the water lap at his thighs, then his groin. The moat was deeper than he'd expected it to be. He yanked the pistol from his waistband and held it high. But the water continued rising, to his chest, to his neck. There was nothing for it but to thrust the pistol back into his breeches and swim.

Just a few strokes carried him across the deepest stretch of water. But the damage was already done; his powder was wet, the pistol now useless as anything more than a prop.

Streaming water, he rose out of the shallows, his shirt and breeches smeared with green algae and slime. He pushed through the thick bracken and fern of the island, his wet clothes heavy and cumbersome, the small stones and broken sticks and thistles that littered the thicket floor sharp beneath his stocking feet. Drawing up behind a stand of hazel just beyond the circle of lamplight, he palmed the knife in his right hand and drew the waterlogged pistol from his waistband to hold in his left hand. Then he crept forward until he could see George Tennyson, up to his waist now in the trench.

He heard Hildeyard say to the boy, "That's enough."

The boy swung around, the shovel still gripped in his hands. His face was pale and pinched and streaked with sweat and dirt and rain. "What are you going to do, Cousin Hildeyard?" he asked, his voice high-pitched but strong. "The Gypsies know what you did to Gabrielle. I told them. What do you think you can do? Shoot all of them too?"

Hildeyard pushed up from the log, the pistol in his hand. "I don't think anyone is going to listen to a band of filthy, thieving Gypsies." He raised the flintlock and pulled back the hammer with an audible click. "I'm sorry I have to do this, son, but—"

"*Drop the gun.*" Sebastian stepped into the circle of light, his own useless pistol leveled at the barrister's chest. "Now!"

Rather than swinging the pistol on Sebastian, Tennyson lunged at the boy, wrapping one arm around his thin chest and hauling his small body about to hold him like a shield, the muzzle pressed to the child's temple. "No. You put your gun down. Do it, or I'll shoot the boy," he added, his voice rising almost hysterically when Sebastian was slow to comply. "You know I will. At this point, I've nothing to lose."

His knife still palmed out of sight in his right hand, Sebastian bent to lay the useless pistol in the wet grass at his feet. He straightened slowly, his now empty left hand held out to his side.

Hildeyard said, "Step closer to the light so I can see you better."

Sebastian took two steps, three.

"That's close enough."

Sebastian paused, although he still wasn't as close as he needed to be. "Give it up, Tennyson. My wife is even as we speak laying information before Bow Street."

The barrister shook his head. "No." His face was pale, his features twisted with panic. He was a proud, self-absorbed man driven by his own selfishness and a moment's fury into deeds far beyond anything he'd ever attempted before. "I don't believe you."

"Believe it. We know you left Kent at dawn on Sunday morning and didn't return to your estate until long past midnight." It was only a guess, of course, but Tennyson had no way of knowing that. Sebastian took another step, narrowing the distance between them. "She wrote you a letter, didn't she?" Sebastian took another step forward, then another. "A letter telling you she'd had an epileptic seizure."

"No. It's not in our side of the family. It's not! Do you hear me?"

"Did she think you owed it to your betrothed, Miss Goodwin, to warn her that you might also share the family affliction? Is that why you rode into town to talk to her? And when you told her you wanted her to shut up and keep it a secret, did she threaten to tell Miss Goodwin herself?" Sebastian took another step. "Is that when you killed her?"

"I'm warning you, stay back!" Hildeyard cried, the gun shaking in his hand as he swung the barrel away from the boy, toward Sebastian. "She was going to destroy my life! My marriage, my career, everything! Don't you see? I had to kill her."

For one fleeting moment, Sebastian caught George Tennyson's frightened gaze. "And the boys?"

"I forgot they were there." Hildeyard gave a ragged laugh, his emotions stretched to a thin breaking point. "I forgot they were even there."

Sebastian was watching the man's eyes and hands. He saw the gun barrel jerk, saw Hildeyard's eyes narrow.

Unable to throw his knife for fear of hitting the boy, Sebastian dove to one side just as Hildeyard squeezed the trigger.

The pistol belched fire, the shot going wide as Sebastian slammed into the raw, muddy earth. He lost the knife, his ears ringing from the shot, the air thick with the stench of burnt powder. He was still rolling to his feet when Hildeyard threw aside the empty gun and ran, crashing into the thick underbrush.

"Take the gig and get out of here!" Sebastian shouted at the boy, and plunged into the thicket after Hildeyard.

Sebastian was hampered by his heavy wet clothes and stocking feet. But he had the eyes and ears of an animal of prey, while Hildeyard was obviously blind in the darkness, blundering into saplings and tripping over roots and fallen logs. Sebastian caught up with him halfway across the small clearing of the sacred well and tackled him.

The two men went down together. Hildeyard scrabbled around, kicked at Sebastian's head with his boot heel, tried to gouge his eyes. Then he grabbed a broken stone from the well's lining and smashed it down toward Sebastian's head. Sebastian tried to jerk out of the way, but the ragged masonry scraped the side of his face and slammed, hard, into his shoulder.

Pain exploded through his body, his grip on the man loosening just long enough for Hildeyard to half scramble up. Then Sebastian saw George Tennyson's pale face looming above them, his jaw set hard with determination, the blade of his shovel heavy with caked mud as he swung it at his cousin's head.

The flat of the blade slammed into the man's temple with an ugly *twunk*. Tennyson went down and stayed down.

Sebastian sat up, his breath coming heavy. "Thank you," he said to the boy. He swiped a grimy wet sleeve across his bloody cheek. "Are you all right?"

The boy nodded, his gaze on his cousin's still, prostrate body, his nostrils flaring as he sucked in a quick breath of air. "Did I kill him?"

Sebastian shifted to rest his fingertips against the steady pulse in Hildeyard's neck. "No."

Stripping off his cravat, Sebastian tied the man's hands together, then used Hildeyard's own cravat to bind his ankles, too. He wasn't taking any chances. Only then did he push to his feet. His shoulder was aching, the side of his face on fire.

George Tennyson said, "I still don't understand why he killed her. She was his sister."

Sebastian looked down into the boy's wide, hurting eyes. He was aware of the wind rustling through the leaves of the ancient grove, the raindrops slapping into the still waters of Camelot's moat. How did you explain to a nine-year-old child the extent to which even seemingly normal people could be blindly obsessed with fulfilling their own personal needs and wants? Or that there were those who had such a profound disregard for others—even their closest family members—that they were willing to kill to preserve their own interests?

Then he realized that was a lesson George had already learned, at first hand; what he didn't understand was how someone he knew and loved could be that way. And with that, Sebastian couldn't help him.

He looped an arm over the boy's shoulders and drew him close. "It's over. You're safe, and your brother's safe." Inadequate words, he knew.

But they were all he had.

Chapter 51

Saturday, 8 August

$\mathcal{G}$ustav Pelletier sat on the edge of his hard bunk, his laced fingers tapping against his mustache.

"You're going to hang anyway," said Sebastian, standing with one shoulder propped against the prison cell's stone wall. "So why not tell the truth about Arceneaux?"

The tapping stopped. "You would like that, yes? So that you can make all tidy?" The hussar's lips curled. *"Casse-toi."* Then he turned his face away and refused to be drawn again into conversation.

Lovejoy was waiting for Sebastian in the corridor outside. "Anything?" he asked as the turnkey slammed the heavy, ironbound door closed behind him.

Sebastian shook his head.

They walked down the gloomy passageway, their footsteps echoing in the dank stillness. "If he did shoot Philippe Arceneaux," said Sebastian, "he's going to take the truth of it to the grave."

Sebastian had already identified one of the recaptured French officers, a Lyonnais by the name of François LeBlanc, as the second of the two men who had jumped him that night in Covent Garden. The man confessed that he and his fellow officer had attacked Sebastian out of fear the Viscount's persistent probing might uncover their escape plan. But the Frenchman swore he knew nothing about Arceneaux's death.

Lovejoy sighed. "You think Arceneaux abandoned his plans to escape with his comrades for the sake of Miss Tennyson?"

"I think so, yes."

"But then, why, once she was dead, didn't he reconsider?"

"Perhaps he'd come to regret the decision to break his parole. Although I think it more likely because he suspected his comrades of killing the woman he loved. He said as much to me right before he was shot, only at the time I didn't know enough to understand what he was saying."

They walked out the prison gates into the brilliant morning sunlight. The rain had cleared the dust and filth from the city streets to leave the air blessedly clean and fresh. Lovejoy said, "I'm told the children's father, the Reverend Tennyson, has arrived from Lincolnshire. Fortunately, Hildeyard provided us with a full confession, so young George shouldn't need to testify against him."

"Thank God for that," said Sebastian. The previous night, while they were waiting for Bow Street to reach Camlet Moat, Sebastian and the boy had sat side by side in the golden light of the lantern, the rain falling softly around them. In hushed tones, George had told Sebastian of how they'd been playing hide-and-seek that morning after church. Gabrielle was "it" and the two boys were hiding behind the heavy velvet drapes at the dining room windows when Hildeyard came barging into the house. Much of the argument between brother and sister had gone over George's head. But the confrontation had ended in the dining room, with Hildeyard grabbing the carving knife from the table in a fit of rage to stab Gabrielle.

The boys had remained hidden, silent and afraid, until Hildeyard stormed from the house—probably to fetch a gig. Then George grabbed Alfred's hand and ran to his friends the Gypsies.

Lovejoy said, "To think the man went out every day looking for his young cousins—even posted a reward! I was most impressed with him. He seemed such an admirable contrast to the boys' uncle."

"Well, unlike d'Eyncourt, Hildeyard sincerely wanted to find the boys—and silence them. He might have made a great show of hiring men to comb the countryside around the moat, but he advertised the reward he was offering here in London—and set up a solicitor in an office in Fleet Street to screen any information that might come in."

Lovejoy nodded. "The solicitor has proved most anxious to cooperate with us, for obvious reasons. Seems he received a tip yesterday from a wherryman who'd seen the two lads with the Gypsies. Of course, he claims he was utterly ignorant of Tennyson's real reason for wanting to find the boys."

"I suspect that he's telling the truth."

"One would hope so. He also admits to having put Tennyson in contact with the ruffian who attacked you beside the Thames yesterday—once again claiming no knowledge of Tennyson's purpose in hiring such an unsavory individual."

"A most incurious gentleman, if he's to be believed."

"He claims it's an occupational hazard."

"I assume he'll hang?"

"Tennyson, you mean? I should think so." Lovejoy paused to look back at the prison's grim facade. "Unfortunately, he insists he knows nothing about the death of the French lieutenant. I'd like to believe Pelletier or one of the other escaping officers was responsible. But I don't know. I just don't know. . . ."

He glanced over at Sebastian, the magistrate's brows drawing together in a frown as if he knew there was something Sebastian was keeping from him.

But Sebastian only shook his head and said, "I wonder if the boys would be interested in a dog."

He came to Hero in the quiet of the afternoon, when the sun streamed golden through the open windows of her bedchamber and the breeze wafted clean and sweet.

She was watching a small boy and girl roll a hoop along the pavement, their joyous shouts and laughter carrying on the warm breeze. She didn't realize she was crying until he touched his fingers to her wet cheeks and turned her to him.

"Hero," he said softly. "Why now?"

The night before, she had insisted on driving out to Camlet Moat with Lovejoy and his men. The magistrate hadn't wanted her to come, but she had overridden his objections, impatient with every delay and tense but silent until they arrived at the old chase. Then, for one intensely joyous moment, her gaze had met Devlin's across the misty dark waters of the moat. But she had turned away almost at once to focus all her attention on the comfort and care of her dead friend's nine-year-old cousin.

And she hadn't shed a tear.

Now she laid her head against his shoulder, marveling at the simple comfort to be found in the strength of his arms around her and the slow beat of his heart so close to hers. She said, "I was thinking about Gabrielle. About how she felt as if she were missing out on all the joys and wonders that make life worth living. And so she gave in to her love for Lieutenant Arceneaux. And then she died because of it."

"She didn't die because she loved. She died because she was noble and honest and wanted to do the right thing, whereas her brother wanted only his own pleasure. Her choice didn't need to end in tragedy."

"Yet it did."

"It did, yes."

A silence fell between them. And she learned that the silence of a shared sorrow could also bring its own kind of comfort.

His hand shifted in a soft caress. She sucked in a shaky breath, then another, and raised her head to meet his gaze. His lips were parted, the sunlight glazing the high bones of his cheeks.

"Did you close the door behind you?" she asked, her voice husky with undisguised want.

"Yes."

Her gaze still locked with his, she brushed her lips against his. "Good."

She saw the flare of surprise in his eyes, felt his fingers tug impatiently at the laces that held her gown. He said, "It's not dark yet."

She gave him a wide, saucy smile. "I know."

Later—much later—Sebastian lay beside her in a shaft of moonlight spilling through the open window. She raised herself on one bent arm, her fingertips skimming down over his naked chest and belly. He drew in his breath with a quiet hiss, and she smiled.

"Is the offer of a honeymoon still open?" she asked.

He crooked his elbow about her neck. "I think we deserve one, don't you?"

She shifted so that her forearms rested on his chest, her hair falling forward to curtain her face, her eyes suddenly serious. "We can do better than this, Sebastian."

He drew her closer, one hand drifting to the small of her back. "In the end I'd say we worked quite well together." He brought up his free hand to catch her hair away from her face. "But I think we can do better, yes."

And he raised his head to meet her kiss.

Author's Note

This story was inspired by Alfred, Lord Tennyson's haunting poem "The Lady of Shalott," first published in 1833, then revised and republished in 1842. Tennyson himself was inspired by a thirteenth-century Italian novella, *La donna di Scalotta*.

Gabrielle and Hildeyard Tennyson are fictional characters of my own invention, but the family of Alfred Tennyson was indeed plagued by epilepsy, alcoholism, and insanity. The poet's own father, a brilliant but troubled reverend from Somersby, Lincolnshire, was severely afflicted with epilepsy, and two of Alfred's brothers spent most of their lives in mental institutions. Alfred feared the family affliction his entire life, although to my knowledge I am the only one to suggest that this is the "curse" referenced in his poem. Alfred did indeed have an older brother named George, although he was born in 1806 and died in infancy.

Alfred's uncle, Charles Tennyson d'Eyncourt, is much as depicted here; however, while he attended Cambridge and sent his sons to Eton, there is no actual record of him having attended Eton. Six years younger than Alfred's father, he was nevertheless named the heir of the "Old Man of the Wolds" when his elder brother began exhibiting signs of severe epilepsy at puberty. The animosity between the two households was intense, with the wealthy Charles ironically coming to look down upon his older brother's family as "poor relations." Although he always denied it, Charles, too, suffered from a milder form of epilepsy. He did serve many years as a member of Parliament, although not until after the end of the Napoleonic Wars, and he did indeed change his name to d'Eyncourt, although his repeated attempts to do so were frustrated until 1835. I have moved the date of that name change up to avoid the confusion of too many Tennysons in the story. Later in life, d'Eyncourt bitterly resented his nephew's literary fame and was especially incensed when Alfred was made a lord (d'Eyncourt did finally achieve that honor himself, but much later in life). Charles's sister, Mary Bourne, is also a real figure, a dour, unhappy woman who found singular solace in the conviction that she would go to heaven while the rest of her family—particularly the Somersby Tennyson branch— suffered the everlasting torments of hell. I am indebted to Robert Bernard Martin for his groundbreaking study of the Tennyson family in *Tennyson: The Unquiet Heart*.

Epilepsy, once also known as "the falling sickness," was little understood in the nineteenth century and considered something shameful, to be kept hidden.

In 1812, archaeology was still in its infancy, although some of the first excavations at Stonehenge were undertaken as early as the seventeenth century. Further work was carried out there in 1798 and 1810 by William Cunnington and Richard Colt Hoare.

The legend that Arthur is not actually dead but will someday return to save England in her hour of need is real, hence his sobriquet "the once and *future* king." For obvious reasons, this legend was the bane of unpopular British monarchs, who were repeatedly driven to try to convince their subjects that Arthur really was dead. The lack of a grave site complicated this effort, which may have led to the "discovery" of Arthur's burial site at Glastonbury Abbey in the twelfth century.

Camlet Moat, once called Camelot, is a real place whose history is much as described here. It is now part of Trent Park, a country park open to the public, although the original eighteenth-century estate was named Trent Place. Over the years Trent Place went through many owners, several of whom instituted extensive remodeling projects. The amateur excavations on the island described here were actually carried out by two later owners, the Bevans during the 1880s and Sir Philip Sassoon in the early twentieth century. Curiously, the findings of those excavations are not reflected on the local council's information board currently in place at the site.

The island has long been reputed to have an association with the grail maidens of old, and yes, Sir Geoffrey de Mandeville's ties to the site also are real, as are his strange relationship with the Templars and the tales of his treasure. The story that he drowned in the well on the island and still haunts it, protecting his treasure, is indeed a local legend, although he actually died from an arrow in the head. Even the tales tying the highwayman Dick Turpin to the site are real; he frequently hid out at Camlet Moat during the course of his brief, ill-fated career. The numerous legends associated with the island can be found in various nineteenth-century works on the environs of London, including Jerrold's *Highways and Byways in Middlesex*, Thorne's *Handbook to the Environs of London*, and Lysons's *The Environs of London*. For a modern, more fanciful interpretation of the site, see Street's *London's Camelot and the Secrets of the Holy Grail*.

The antiquarian Richard Gough was a real figure who did indeed live at Gough Hall near Camlet Moat. He left his library to Oxford, but not his collections, which were sold.

In the 1990s, a local man named Derek Mahoney claimed to have found the leaden cross from Arthur's Glastonbury grave amongst mud dredged from an ornamental lake near Gough Hall. The local council claimed the find; Mahoney went to jail rather than surrender it, and then committed suicide. The cross, seen only briefly by the British Museum, again disappeared. It is assumed but has never proven to be a modern forgery.

The system of billeting paroled French and allied officers around England is as described, albeit slightly more complicated. Although the concept of a gentleman's "word of honor" might seem strange to many today, paroled officers—as gentlemen—were given a startling amount of freedom. Many began businesses, married British women, and had children. The British government even allocated them a half-guinea-a-week allowance. Their restrictions were few: a curfew, a circumscribed location within which movement was allowed, an injunction to obey the laws of the land and to communicate with France only through the agent appointed by the Admiralty. From 1809 to 1812, nearly 700 paroled officers tried to escape, of whom some 242 were recaptured. The calico printer's cart described here (basically a closed cart of a type typically used by tradesmen who printed designs on cloth) was one of the ruses used in an escape attempt in the summer of 1812.

Although the waltz was not allowed at Almack's in London in 1812, it was danced elsewhere in England well before that date. The family wedding Mary Bourne prattles about to Hero in chapter 17 actually took place in 1806; her letters about the event mention the waltz.

Although we tend to think of neo-Druidism as a modern phenomenon, it was actually quite popular in the eighteenth and nineteenth centuries as part of the Romantic movement, which identified the Druids as national heroes. An Ancient Order of Druids was formed as early as 1781. Among the writers associated with the movement were William Stukely (who incorrectly believed Stonehenge was built by the Druids) and Iolo Morganwg (born Edward Williams), a Welsh nationalist with a deep admiration for the French Revolution. A form of spiritualism that stressed harmony with nature and respect for all beings, eighteenth- and

nineteenth-century Druidism also drew on the teachings of the En-
lightenment. Lacking any written texts, a rigid dogma, or a central
authority, neo-Druidism was basically a philosophy of living that
located the divinity within all living creatures.

The foundation stone for what was then known as the Strand
Bridge was laid in October of 1811, at the site of the old Savoy
Palace. By the time the bridge opened nearly six years later, it had
been renamed the Waterloo Bridge.

Although women were not a common sight in the British Museum's Reading Room, they were allowed to become registered
readers. According to the museum's records, three were listed as
registered readers for the years 1770 to 1810, and five were listed
in 1820 alone. The museum closed in August and September, but
for the sake of my story I have allowed it to remain open a few
extra days.